T0230176

Lecture Notes in Computer S

Commenced Publication in 1973
Founding and Former Series Editors:
Gerhard Goos, Juris Hartmanis, and Jan van Leeuwen

Editorial Board

Paul De Bra   Wolfgang Nejdl (Eds.)

Adaptive Hypermedia and Adaptive Web-Based Systems

Third International Conference, AH 2004
Eindhoven, The Netherlands, August 23-26, 2004
Proceedings

 Springer

Volume Editors

Paul De Bra
Eindhoven University of Technology, Department of Computing Science
5600 MB Eindhoven, The Netherlands
E-mail: debra@win.tue.nl

Wolfgang Nejdl
University of Hannover, Institut für Informationssysteme
Appelstr. 4, 30167 Hannover, Germany
E-mail: nejdl@kbs.uni-hannover.de

Library of Congress Control Number: Applied for

CR Subject Classification (1998): H.5.4, H.4, H.5, H.3

ISSN 0302-9743
ISBN 3-540-22895-0 Springer Berlin Heidelberg New York

Springer is a part of Springer Science+Business Media

springeronline.com

© Springer-Verlag Berlin Heidelberg 2004
Printed in Germany

Typesetting: Camera-ready by author, data conversion by Olgun Computergrafik
Printed on acid-free paper   SPIN: 11307587   06/3142   5 4 3 2 1 0

Preface

On behalf of the AH 2004 Program Committee, we were pleased to welcome attendees to Eindhoven for the 3rd International Conference on Adaptive Hypermedia and Adaptive Web-Based Systems.

Similar to previous years, the number of research groups involved in research and innovative applications of personalization and adaptation functionalities has continued to grow, resulting in a further increase of 33% in the number of papers submitted to the conference, compared to the previous conference. From the 138 submissions we received, the program committee, in a rigorous review process, accepted 27 submissions (i.e., 20%) as full papers and 18 (i.e., 13%) as short papers. The large number of papers submitted generated a tremendous amount of work for the program committee members and the external reviewers, and we are immensely greatful for the effort they put into the process of selecting the very best papers.

Together with three invited talks (by Emile Aarts, Philips Research, Candy Sidner, Mitsubishi Research, and Eric Horvitz, Microsoft Research), the AH 2004 papers provide an excellent view on the successful approaches for innovative personalization and adaptation functionalities in a variety of areas, including eLearning, eCommerce, mobile tourist guides and many more. They also show the integration of personalization functionalities being employed in Web environments, in ambient intelligence and intelligent agent contexts, and building upon adaptive hypermedia and Semantic Web technologies, Web search, Web services, social and peer-to-peer networks, and recommender systems, among others.

In addition, we were able to include four doctoral consortium papers in the proceedings, accompanying two doctoral consortium sessions at the conference, where young Ph.D. students presented promising initial work and got additional feedback on their presentations and ideas for their future research careers. Seventeen additional projects were presented during the AH 2004 poster reception, providing insights into new projects, many of which we expect to yield interesting results in several new innovative application areas in the future.

Many people contributed to the success of the program. First and foremost, we would like to thank all the authors for providing such an excellent set of papers for AH 2004, and the AH 2004 program committee members and external reviewers for their dedication in the review process. The three main professional organizations most related to the field of adaptive hypermedia all endorsed the AH 2004 conference: the International World-Wide Web Conference Committee (IW3C2), the Association for Computing Machinery (ACM), and in particular SIGART, SIGCHI, SIGecom, SIGIR and SIGWEB, and User Modeling, Inc. AH 2004 was actively sponsored by the Eindhoven University of Technology, the School for Information and Knowledge Systems, and the PROLEARN Network of Excellence in Professional Learning.

Last, but not least, the AH 2004 conference was run by a team of enthusiastic organizers, from the Eindhoven University of Technology and the University of Hannover. We wish to mention Ad Aerts, Lora Aroyo, Alexandra Cristea, Nicola Henze, Geert-Jan

Houben, Pim Lemmens and Reinier Post who dealt with submissions, workshops, tutorials, the industrial track, proceedings, registrations, the website and all local arrangements. A special word of thanks goes to Riet van Buul who did all the local coordination and administration.

August 2004   Wolfgang Nejdl
                                                                              Paul De Bra

Organization

AH 2004 was organized by the Eindhoven University of Technology, Eindhoven, The Netherlands.

General Chair

Paul De Bra (Eindhoven University of Technology)

Program Chair

Wolfgang Nejdl (University of Hannover and L3S)

Doctoral Consortium Chairs

José-Luís Pérez de la Cruz (Universidad de Málaga, Spain)
Peter Brusilovsky (University of Pittsburgh, USA)

Workshops/Tutorials Chairs

Lora Aroyo (Eindhoven University of Technology, The Netherlands)
Carlo Tasso (University of Udine, Italy)

Industry Chairs

Mehmet Göker (Kaidara Software, USA)
Geert-Jan Houben (Eindhoven University of Technology, The Netherlands)

Program Committee

Elisabeth André, DFKI GmbH, Germany
Liliana Ardissono, Università degli Studi di Torino, Italy
Helen Ashman, University of Nottingham, UK
Peter Brusilovsky, University of Pittsburgh, USA
Ricardo Conejo, University of Malagà, Spain
Alexandra Cristea, Eindhoven University of Technology, The Netherlands
Serge Garlatti, ENST Bretagne, France
Franca Garzotto, Politecnico di Milano, Italy
Wendy Hall, University of Southampton, UK
Lynda Hardman, CWI, Amsterdam, The Netherlands
Nicola Henze, University of Hannover, Germany
Charalampos Karagiannidis, Informatics and Telematics Institute, Greece
Judy Kay, University of Sydney, Australia

Table of Contents

Keynote Speakers (Abstracts)

Ambient Intelligence.. 1
Emile Aarts

Collaborative Agents for 2D Interfaces and 3D Robots 2
Candace L. Sidner

A Curse of Riches or a Blessing?
Information Access and Awareness Under Scarce Cognitive Resources 3
Eric Horvitz

Full Papers

Supporting Metadata Creation with an Ontology Built
from an Extensible Dictionary 4
Trent Apted, Judy Kay, and Andrew Lum

Interaction with Web Services in the Adaptive Web........................ 14
Liliana Ardissono, Anna Goy, Giovanna Petrone, and Marino Segnan

Social Adaptive Navigation Support
for Open Corpus Electronic Textbooks.................................... 24
Peter Brusilovsky, Girish Chavan, and Rosta Farzan

PROS: A Personalized Ranking Platform for Web Search 34
Paul-Alexandru Chirita, Daniel Olmedilla, and Wolfgang Nejdl

A P2P Distributed Adaptive Directory 44
Gennaro Cordasco, Vittorio Scarano, and Cristiano Vitolo

Developing Active Learning Experiences for Adaptive Personalised eLearning ... 55
Declan Dagger, Vincent P. Wade, and Owen Conlan

Adaptive User Modeling for Personalization of Web Contents 65
Alberto Díaz and Pablo Gervás

Invoking Web Applications from Portals: Customisation Implications 75
Oscar Díaz and Iñaki Paz

The Personal Reader: Personalizing and Enriching Learning Resources
Using Semantic Web Technologies.. 85
Peter Dolog, Nicola Henze, Wolfgang Nejdl, and Michael Sintek

An Experiment in Social Search   95
    Jill Freyne and Barry Smyth

Recent Soft Computing Approaches to User Modeling in Adaptive Hypermedia . . 104
    Enrique Frías-Martínez, George Magoulas, Sherry Chen,
    and Robert Macredie

A Flexible Composition Engine for Adaptive Web Sites 115
    Serge Garlatti and Sébastien Iksal

Intelligent Support to the Retrieval of Information About Hydric Resources 126
    Cristina Gena and Liliana Ardissono

CUMAPH: Cognitive User Modeling for Adaptive Presentation
of Hyper-documents. An Experimental Study. 136
    Halima Habieb-Mammar and Franck Tarpin-Bernard

Personalized Web Advertising Method. 146
    Przemysław Kazienko and Michał Adamski

Flexible Navigation Support in the WINDS Learning Environment
for Architecture and Design 156
    Milos Kravcik and Marcus Specht

Evaluation of WINDS Authoring Environment 166
    Milos Kravcik, Marcus Specht, and Reinhard Oppermann

On the Dynamic Generation of Compound Critiques
in Conversational Recommender Systems 176
    Kevin McCarthy, James Reilly, Lorraine McGinty, and Barry Smyth

Evaluating Adaptive Problem Selection 185
    Antonija Mitrovic and Brent Martin

Adaptive Presentation and Navigation for Geospatial Imagery Tasks 195
    Dympna O'Sullivan, Eoin McLoughlin, Michela Bertolotto,
    and David C. Wilson

Myriad: An Architecture for Contextualized Information Retrieval and Delivery . . 205
    Cécile Paris, Mingfang Wu, Keith Vander Linden, Matthew Post,
    and Shijian Lu

Cross-Media and Elastic Time Adaptive Presentations:
The Integration of a Talking Head Tool into a Hypermedia Formatter 215
    Rogério Ferreira Rodrigues, Paula Salgado Lucena Rodrigues, Bruno Feijó,
    Luiz Velho, and Luiz Fernando Gomes Soares

Assessing Cognitive Load in Adaptive Hypermedia Systems:
Physiological and Behavioral Methods 225
    Holger Schultheis and Anthony Jameson

Context-Aware Recommendations
in the Mobile Tourist Application COMPASS 235
Mark van Setten, Stanislav Pokraev, and Johan Koolwaaij

Utilizing Artificial Learners to Help Overcome the Cold-Start Problem
in a Pedagogically-Oriented Paper Recommendation System 245
Tiffany Tang and Gordon McCalla

Unison-CF: A Multiple-Component, Adaptive Collaborative Filtering System ... 255
Manolis Vozalis and Konstantinos G. Margaritis

Using SiteRank for Decentralized Computation of Web Document Ranking 265
Jie Wu and Karl Aberer

Short Papers

Web Information Retrieval Based on User Profile 275
Rachid Arezki, Pascal Poncelet, Gérard Dray, and David W. Pearson

Adaptive Support for Collaborative and Individual Learning (ASCIL):
Integrating AHA! and CLAROLINE 279
Carlos Arteaga, Ramon Fabregat, Jorge Eyzaguirre, and David Mérida

Specification of Adaptive Behavior Using a General-Purpose Design
Methodology for Dynamic Web Applications 283
Peter Barna, Geert-Jan Houben, and Flavius Frasincar

Using the X3D Language for Adaptive Manipulation of 3D Web Content 287
Luca Chittaro and Roberto Ranon

Evaluation of APeLS – An Adaptive eLearning Service
Based on the Multi-model, Metadata-Driven Approach 291
Owen Conlan and Vincent P. Wade

SearchGuide: Beyond the Results Page 296
Maurice Coyle and Barry Smyth

Modeling Learners as Individuals and as Groups 300
Roland Hübscher and Sadhana Puntambekar

Adaptive Help for Webbased Applications 304
Dorothea Iglezakis

Empirical Evaluation of an Adaptive Multiple Intelligence
Based Tutoring System 308
Declan Kelly and Brendan Tangney

Evaluating Information Filtering Techniques
in an Adaptive Recommender System 312
John O'Donovan and John Dunnion

Adaptive Educational Hypermedia Proposal
Based on Learning Styles and Quality Evaluation 316
 Marcela Prieto Ferraro, Helmut Leighton Álvarez,
 and Francisco García Peñalvo

Adaptive Course Player for Individual Learning Styles 320
 Katja Reinhardt, Stefan Apelt, and Marcus Specht

Rhetorical Patterns for Adaptive Video Documentaries 324
 Cesare Rocchi and Massimo Zancanaro

Location-Aware Adaptive Interfaces for Information Access
with Handheld Computers 328
 Golha Sharifi, Ralph Deters, Julita Vassileva, Susan Bull, and Harald Röbig

PSO: A Language for Web Information Extraction and Web Page Clipping 332
 Tetsuya Suzuki and Takehiro Tokuda

Swarm-Based Adaptation: Wayfinding Support for Lifelong Learners 336
 Colin Tattersall, Bert van den Berg, René van Es, José Janssen,
 Jocelyn Manderveld, and Rob Koper

Giving More Adaptation Flexibility to Authors of Adaptive Assessments 340
 Aimilia Tzanavari, Symeon Retalis, and Panikos Pastellis

A Generic Adaptivity Model in Adaptive Hypermedia 344
 Paul de Vrieze, Patrick van Bommel, and Theo van der Weide

Doctoral Consortium

Extreme Adaptivity 348
 Mário Amado Alves, Alípio Jorge, and José Paulo Leal

A Learner Model in a Distributed Environment 353
 Cristina Carmona and Ricardo Conejo

A Semantic Meta-model for Adaptive Hypermedia Systems 360
 Patricia Seefelder de Assis and Daniel Schwabe

Adaptive Navigation for Self-assessment Quizzes 366
 Sergey Sosnovsky

Posters

Towards Adaptive Learning Designs 372
 Adriana Berlanga and Francisco J. García

Time-Based Extensions to Adaptation Techniques 376
 Mária Bieliková and Rastislav Habala

On the Use of Collaborative Filtering Techniques for the Prediction
of Web Search Result Rank 380
  Peter Briggs and Barry Smyth

A Thematic Guided Tour Model for Contextualized Concept Presentations 384
  Benjamin Buffereau and Philippe Picouet

A Fuzzy Set Based Tutoring System for Adaptive Learning 389
  Sook-young Choi and Hyung-jung Yang

Offering Collaborative-Like Recommendations When Data Is Sparse:
The Case of Attraction-Weighted Information Filtering..................... 393
  Arnaud De Bruyn, C. Lee Giles, and David M. Pennock

Using Concept Maps for Enhancing Adaptation Processes
in Declarative Knowledge Learning 397
  Fabien Delorme, Nicolas Delestre, and Jean-Pierre Pécuchet

An Adaptive Tutoring System Based on Hierarchical Graphs 401
  Sergio Gutiérrez, Abelardo Pardo, and Carlos Delgado Kloos

A Brief Introduction to the New Architecture of SIETTE 405
  Eduardo Guzmán and Ricardo Conejo

A Reinforcement Learning Approach to Achieve Unobtrusive
and Interactive Recommendation Systems for Web-Based Communities 409
  Felix Hernandez, Elena Gaudioso, and Jesús G. Boticario

GEAHS: A Generic Educational Adaptive Hypermedia System
Based on Situation Calculus 413
  Cédric Jacquiot, Yolaine Bourda, and Fabrice Popineau

Problem Solving with Adaptive Feedback 417
  Rainer Lütticke

Machine Learning Methods for One-Session Ahead Prediction
of Accesses to Page Categories 421
  *José D. Martín-Guerrero, Emili Balaguer-Ballester,
  Gustavo Camps-Valls, Alberto Palomares, Antonio J. Serrano-López,
  Juan Gómez-Sanchís, and Emilio Soria-Olivas*

Gender-Biased Adaptations in Educational Adaptive Hypermedia 425
  Erica Melis and Carsten Ullrich

An Overview of aLFanet: An Adaptive iLMS Based on Standards 429
  Olga C. Santos, Carmen Barrera, and Jesús G. Boticario

A General Meta-model for Adaptive Hypermedia Systems 433
  Patricia Seefelder de Assis and Daniel Schwabe

Adaptive Services for Customised Knowledge Delivery 437
  *Alexander Smirnov, Mikhail Pashkin, Nikolai Chilov, Tatiana Levashova,
  and Andrew Krizhanovsky*

Author Index 441

Ambient Intelligence

Emile Aarts[1,2]

[1] Philips Research
Eindhoven, The Netherlands
emile.aarts@philips.com
[2] Eindhoven University of Technology
Eindhoven, The Netherlands

Abstract. In the near future our homes will have a distributed network of intelligent devices that provides us with information, communication, and entertainment. Furthermore, these systems will adapt themselves to the user and even anticipate on user needs. These consumer systems will differ substantially from contemporary equipment through their appearance in peoples' environments, and through the way users interact with them. Ambient Intelligence is the term that is used to denote this new paradigm for in-home computing and entertainment. Salient features of this new concept are ubiquitous computing, and natural interaction. Recent developments in technology, the Internet, the consumer electronics market, and social developments indicate that this dream might become reality soon. First prototypes of ambient intelligent home systems have been developed, but the realization of true ambient intelligence calls for much additional research of multidisciplinary teams consisting of technologists, designers, and human behavior scientists.
The presentation will elaborate on some of these aspects and show where we are in the development of ambient intelligence.

W. Nejdl and P. De Bra (Eds.): AH 2004, LNCS 3137, p. 1, 2004.
© Springer-Verlag Berlin Heidelberg 2004

Collaborative Agents for 2D Interfaces and 3D Robots

Candace L. Sidner

Misubishi Electric Research Labs
Cambridge, MA, USA
sidner@merl.com

Abstract. In this talk I will discuss our several years experience in systems for collaborative interface agents. I will discuss the tool called COLLAGEN(tm) for COLLaborative AGENts. COLLAGEN(tm) is a Java middleware system, that makes it possible to build an agent with a rich model of conversation and collaboration for a set of tasks with a user for an application, provided by the developer using Collagen. I will demo two of the many systems built in our lab and elsewhere, which rely on COLLAGEN(tm): one with speech for a desktop application, and one for a 3D robot (via videclips). I will discuss the way Collagen was developed from theories of conversation and collaboration, how plan recognition plays a role in COLLAGEN(tm), and I will point out new directions of our work, especially given the nonverbal gestural abilities of our humanoid robot.

W. Nejdl and P. De Bra (Eds.): AH 2004, LNCS 3137, p. 2, 2004.

A Curse of Riches or a Blessing?
Information Access and Awareness
Under Scarce Cognitive Resources

Eric Horvitz

Microsoft Research
Redmond, WA, USA
horvitz@microsoft.com

Abstract. The informational landscape of the world has been changing quickly. The fast-paced drop in the cost of storage and bandwidth over the last decade, coupled with the rapid expansion in the number of content sources, has made unprecedented quantities of information available to people. Beyond external sources of content, typical personal stores now rival the size of the entire Web just a short time ago. But we face a challenging bottleneck: In stark contrast to the explosive growth in public and private content, stands our limited time- and unchanging abilities. For increasing numbers of people in the world, the primary informational bottleneck is our scarce attentional and memory resources. I will present research on addressing such informational bottlenecks with tools for searching, browsing, remembering, and staying aware. I will review challenges and opportunities of employing automated learning and reasoning methods, including efforts to construct and leverage models of attention and memory. Finally, I will touch on the promise of developing new designs for interaction and display informed by psychological findings on visual attention and spatial memory.

W. Nejdl and P. De Bra (Eds.): AH 2004, LNCS 3137, p. 3, 2004.
© Springer-Verlag Berlin Heidelberg 2004

Supporting Metadata Creation with an Ontology Built from an Extensible Dictionary

Trent Apted, Judy Kay, and Andrew Lum

School of Information Technologies,
University of Sydney, NSW 2006
Australia
{tapted,judy,alum}@it.usyd.edu.au

Abstract. This paper describes Metasaur, which supports creation of metadata about the content of learning objects. The core of Metasaur is a visualisation for an ontology of the domain. We describe how we build lightweight ontologies for Metasaur automatically from existing dictionaries and how a user can enhance the ontology with additional terms. We report our use of Metasaur to mark up a set of audio lecture learning objects for use in a course.

1 Introduction

Metadata tagging is a problem, especially in systems with many existing documents and a large metadata term vocabulary [1]. This task is challenging and non-trivial because it is hard to be thorough and consistent, and the task is both demanding and boring. The task becomes even harder when the documents might be multimedia objects such as an audio clip.

A reflection of the importance and difficulty of metadata markup is the growing number of tools which are exploring ways to support the task. For example, one such tool, Annotea [2] builds on Resource Description Format (RDF) technologies, providing a framework to allow users to add and retreive a set of annotations for a web object from an "annotation server".

Since it is such a tedious task to add the metadata by hand, there is considerable appeal in finding ways to automate part of the process. Even in this case, there is likely to be a need for human checking and enhancing of the metadata. We need interfaces that can support both the checking of metadata, which was created automatically, as well as hand-crafting of metadata. We call this the *metadata-interface problem*.

We believe that ontologies will provide an important tool in allowing people to create metadata by providing a common vocabulary of terms and relationships for a domain. It makes sense to exploit the technologies and standards developed as part of the Semantic Web initiative [3] for this task, for example using the Ontology Web Language (OWL) [4]. Ontologies can provide a common vocabulary to describe a particular domain.

However, there are also problems in exploiting ontologies. One is that ontologies are often time consuming to construct [5]. It is, therefore, appealing to find ways to

W. Nejdl and P. De Bra (Eds.): AH 2004, LNCS 3137, pp. 4–13, 2004.

create ontologies automatically. OntoExtract [6] is an example of one system. One problem with such approaches to automated ontology construction is that they may not include all the concepts needed for metadata markup. We call this the *restricted-ontology problem*.

Another challenge in exploiting ontologies relates to issues of interfaces. If we are to exploit ontologies as an aid in the metadata markup, we need to provide intuitive and effective interfaces to the ontology. These are critical in supporting users in navigating the ontology, to find the terms they want and to easily see the closely related ones that may also deserve consideration as potential metadata candidate terms. The importance of the *ontology-interface problem* is reflected in the range of novel ontology visualisations tools such as Ontorama [7], Bubbleworld [8] and the graph drawing system by Golbeck and Mutton [9].

This paper describes a new and novel interface, Metasaur, which tackles the *metadata-interface problem*. It builds on the SIV interface [10], which we have created as an exploration of solutions to the *ontology-interface problem*. In this paper, we describe new approaches to address the *restricted-ontology problem* by supporting users in adding new dictionary entries to an existing dictionary, which is then automatically analysed and incorporated into the ontology.

Sect. 2 provides an overview of user interface to Metasaur, and Sect. 3 describes the back-end architecture of the system. Sect. 4 discusses our approach to the restricted ontology problem. We conclude with a discussion of related work, our evaluations and plans for future work.

2 Interface Overview

The driving application domain for Metasaur is the need to markup metadata on learning objects in an online course. The User Interface Design and Programming course is taught in the February semester at this university. The course is taught through a combination of online material and face-to-face tutorials. It consists of 20 online lectures that students are expected to *attend* at times they can choose, but partly dictated by the assignment deadlines. There are recommended deadlines for attending each lecture. Each lecture has around 20 slides, and each slide has associated audio. Generally this audio provides the bulk of the information, with the usual slide providing a framework and some elements of the lecture. This parallels the way many lecturers use overhead slides for live lectures. A user profile keeps track of student marks and lecture progress.

Fig. 1 gives an example of the Metasaur interface. There are two main parts. The left contains a visualisation called the Scrutable Inference Viewer (SIV) that allows users to easily navigate through the ontology structure. The concepts in the ontology are displayed in a vertical listing. Perspective distortion is used to enable users to navigate the ontology. At any point in time, the concept with the largest font is the one currently selected. Users can navigate through the ontology by clicking on concept to select it. The display changes so that the newly selected concept becomes the focus.

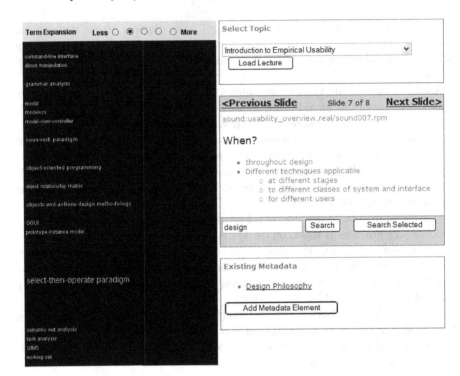

Fig. 1. The Metasaur interface showing the SIV interface on the left, and the slide with associated metadata on the right. The SIV interface currently has the term *select-then-operate paradigm* in focus with related terms such as *noun-verb paradigm* and *objects-and-actions design methodology* are shown as a secondary focus. Note: this image and subsequent ones have been rendered in black and white for publication clarity. A demonstration version of Metasaur is available online[1].

A subgraph is created encompassing this term and those related. Concepts connected directly to the selected concept are put into a secondary focus, appearing in a larger font size, spacing and brightness than those further away in the ontology. Similarly, concepts at lower levels in the tree are shown in progressively smaller fonts, less spacing and lower brightness. Concepts that are not relevant are bunched together in a small dimmed font. In Fig. 1, the main focus is *select-then-operate* paradigm. Some secondary terms are *noun-verb paradigm* and *objects-and-actions design methodology*.

The *Term Expansion* radio buttons above the visualisation allows users to limit the spanning tree algorithm to the selected depth. This effectively changes the number of visible terms. This is described in further detail in Sect. 3.

The learning object contents and visualisation control widgets are on the right. The top right pane allows the user to select a particular online lecture to view. In Fig. 1, the current topic is *Introduction to Empirical Usability*.

---

[1] http://www.it.usyd.edu.au/~alum/demos/metasaur_hci/

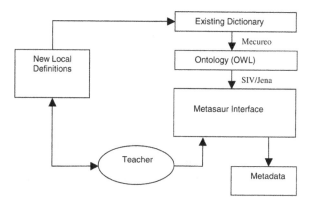

Fig. 2. Overview of the Metasaur architecture. The teacher can interact with the interface in two ways. Firstly they can find terms in the ontology display in the interface (see Fig. 1). Alternatively, if the teacher wants to add terms, they write a New Local Definition as shown at left. This is added to the dictionary, processed into OWL and made available to the interface.

The middle right pane then displays one slide of the lecture at a time. The content of each lecture slide currently consists of the slide itself, an audio object associated with the slide, and questions related to the concepts. This pane also contains a text input for searching out terms in the ontology, The *Search Selected* button enables users to select a portion of text from the slide to use as input to the search. This allows for very rapid searching of the ontology through mouse actions rather than typing in the search strings manually.

The bottom right pane contains the metadata terms associated with the current lecture slide in the middle pane. In Fig. 1, the slide has the term *Design Philosophy* associated with it. The *Add Metadata Element* button adds the currently focused concept in the visualisation to the metadata for the slide.

3 Architecture Overview

There are existing systems that allow instructors to add metadata to learning objects [11] as well as standards for metadata about Learning Objects [12]. These systems employ an extensive description of the domain that is usually defined by the course instructors. In contrast, Metasaur use a lightweight ontology [13] that is automatically constructed from an existing data source.

We want to base our ontology on such a dictionary because we want to build *scrutable* systems. With a dictionary which was written expressly for the prurpose of explaining terms to people, we can always explain any ontological reasoning and relationships by showing the user the relevant dictionary entries. Fig. 2 shows the main architectural elements of Metasaur. Of note are the Existing Dictionary as input to Mecureo [14], and OWL format. This is then processed by the SIV/Jena tools to create the input needed to drive the left pane of the Metasaur interface (as, for example in Fig. 1). The teacher interacts with this to create metadata terms as explained in the last section. We now explain the elements of the *restricted ontology problem*.

The process taken by Mecureo to generate a directed graph of the terms in the dictionary involves making each term a node. It then scans through each of the definitions for terms that are also nodes and generates a weighted link between them. The graph is gradually built up as more definitions are parsed until there are no more to do. In the usability glossary [15] there are 1127 defined terms. This includes category definitions.

This means that there will be many words that appear in the definitions that will not be in the final graph because they are not a term in the dictionary. As an example, the word *novice* appears many times in the Usability Glossary (such as in the definition for *hunt and peck*) but it is not a term because it is not in the glossary.

If a word like *novice* would be a suitable metadata term, we would like to be able to enhance the core Mecureo ontology to include it. Fig. 2 illustrates how we augment the existing dictionary by allowing the user to create new glossary definitions. We call these user defined definitions *local* definitions. These local definitions are merged with the existing dictionary and processed into the ontology graph by OWL. These local definitions need to be no more than just a declaration of the word as a term, and do not require a full definition of their own since Mecureo will form links to and from the local definition to existing terms through their definitions.

4   Overcoming the Restricted Ontology Problem

Through our own experience and evaluations, we have discovered that the unaugmented Usability Glossary has only a very small overlap with the terms used in the learning objects of the User Interface Design and Programming course. The course used less than 10% of the terms defined in the dictionary. This poor term coverage is attributed to two facets.

Firstly, there are cases where we use slightly different terminology. For example, the term *cognitive modeling* in the glossary is used in a similar sense to the term *predictive usability* which is used in the course and associated textbooks.

The second problem is that there are some concepts that are considered important in the course and which are part of several definitions in the Usability First dictionary but are not included as actual dictionary entries. This is the case for terms such as *novice*. We wanted this term as metadata on learning objects which describe usability techniques such as *cognitive walkthough*. It is this problem that the current extensions to Mecureo particularly address.

We have run a series of evaluations of our approach. One that was intended to assess the usability of the Metasaur interface [16] indicated that users could use it effectively to search the SIV interface for terms that appeared in the text of an online lecture slide. This also gave some insight into the ways that SIV might address the problem of slightly different terminology.

The participants were asked to select terms that seemed most appropriate to describe a particular slide of the online lecture. The participants were a mix of domain experts and non-experts. Participants were frustrated when words on the slides did not appear in the ontology. Domain experts navigated the ontology to find close terms to those words. Non-experts chose to continue onto the next slide.

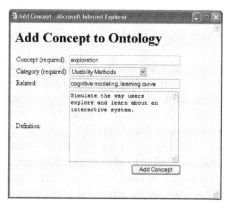

Fig. 3. The interface for a user defining a new definition, The Concept name and category are required. Related concepts and the definition are optional. Here the user has filled in a new local definition of the word *exploration*.

The current version of Metasaur addresses this problem by allowing users to define their own terms. It would clearly be far preferable to tackle this in a more systematic and disciplined way so that when a new term is added to the metadata set for a learning object, it is also integrated well into the set of terms available for future learning objects. Our most recent work has explored simple ways to enhance the ontology with terms used in the course and relate them to the existing terms in the Usability Glossary. In this way, metadata added by a user who chooses only to add terms that appear on the slides of the online lecture will still be extremely useful, as similar terms can be inferred from the ontology.

Our implementation involves adding an additional screen to Metasaur that allows users to define a new term (and explicitly) state the category, definition and related words if they wish. This can be seen in Fig. 2 where the teacher can create local definitions (described in further detail in Sect. 3).

Table 1. Added Term Linkage.

Term	Term name only	Term and Definition	Term, Definition and Related
novice users	2	3	5
discretionary users	0	1	3
casual users	0	1	3
Exploration	9	10	12
usability technique	0	1	1
testing process	1	2	4

Ideally, we would like to make the ontology enhancement process as lightweight as possible. The simplest approach would be to nominate a term, such as novice, to become treated as a new, additional term in the dictionary so that Mecureo will then link this term within existing dictionary definitions to other parts of the ontology. It would be very good if this alone were sufficient. The first column in Table 1 shows the results of this very lightweight approach for the terms that we wanted to include as metadata for the collection learning object slides in the lecture on *cognitive walkthrough*.

Each column represents a separate resulting graph after Mecureo processed a dictionary with the user defined terms added. They were created with the same parameters. Minimum peerage was set to 0 and the link weight distance was set to 100. This means that all nodes in the graph are included in the OWL output file. More information on Mecureo parameters can be found in [17].

Term name only shows the linkage to the new terms when we only had the term name and category in the user-defined list of terms. With no bootstrapping of definitions or related terms, words such as *novice user* and *exploration* result in a number of relationships in the ontology simply by appearing in the definitions of existing terms. Other words such as *discretionary user* do not occur in any of the definitions, resulting in a node not connected to any other node in the graph. This is due to differences in terminology between the authors of this dictionary and the authors of the materials used in our course.

Term and Definition shows the linkage to the new terms when we used the contents of the online lecture slide that taught this concept as the definition. This meant that links to other existing terms could be inferred from the words appearing in the definition.

The *Term, Definition and Related* column shows the linkage to the new terms when we use two keywords, in addition to the definition as just described. Essentially this allowed us to 'force' a relationship between our new term and one or more existing terms in the dictionary.

Bootstrapping the parsing process by giving the local definitions some existing related terms and a short definition minimizes this effect and gives more favourable results. For the longer local definitions, the lower number of links occurs because of the text matching level in the parser (which controls things such as case-sensitivity and substring matching). There is an obvious bias towards shorter words. Processing the dictionary with the *Term name only* local definitions and same parameters with *novice users* replaced with the word *novice*, results in *novice* having 8 directly connected terms.

5 Related Work

There has been considerable interest in tools for ontology construction and metadata editing. This section briefly discusses some existing tools and constrast them to our own research.

In [18], Jannink describes the conversion of the Webster's dictionary into a graph. This gives a much more general ontology. It is not clear whether approaches that are suited to basic generic concepts should be particularly suited to our more specialised concept sets. AeroDAML [19] is a tool that automatically marks up documents in the DAML+OIL ontology language. The SemTag [20] application does semantic annotation of documents, designed for large corpora (for example, existing documents on the Web).

Another very important element of the current work is that text available of the learning objects is just a small part of the learning object. The bulk of the content of most slides is in the audio *lecture* attached to the text of each slide. If we were to aim for automated extraction of metadata, that would requires analysis of this audio stream, a task that is currently extremely challenging with current speech understanding technology. But even beyond this, the accurate markup of the metadata is challenging even for humans as we found in our earlier evaluations [16] where less expert users made poor choices of metadata compared with relatively more expert users, who had recently completed this course satisfactorily. This later group defined metadata that was a much better match to that created by the lecturer. Indeed, this is one reason that we believe an interesting avenue to pursue is to enhance the interaction with the learning objects by asking students to create their own metadata after listening to each of the learning objects. Checking this against the lecturer's defined metadata should help identify whether the student appreciated the main issues in that learning object.

The novel aspect of our work is the emphasis on the support for the user to scrutinise parts of the ontology. Users can always refer to the original dictionary source that the ontology was constructed from since all the relationships are inferred from the text. Because the dictionary source is online, it is easily available to the users, and changes to the ontology can be made either through the addition of new terms, or regenerating the ontology with a different set of parameters for Mecureo.

6 Discussion and Conclusions

We have performed a number of evaluations on SIV and Metasaur. Results show that users were able to navigate the graph and use it as an aid to discover new concepts when adding metadata. The evaluation of Metasaur described in [16] was on an earlier version of the system that did not allow users to define their own terms. A larger evaluation is currently being planned that will incorporate the ability to add new concepts to the ontology.

The Metasaur enhancements that enable users to add additional concepts, with their own definitions, is important for the teacher or author creating metadata for the learning objects they create and use. An interesting situation arises when users have different definitions for terms – they will be able to merge their definitions with the core glossary definitions at runtime, resulting in a different ontology for each user. Users could potentially share their own dictionary or use parts from other user's dictionaries to create their own ontologies.

There are still some issues with the current design. The differences between UK and US spellings are not picked up by the parser, though we have been experimenting with different stemmers to address this problem. There is also the likely possibility of users adding words that do not appear in any of the definitions.

We believe that Metasaur is a valuable tool for aiding users mark-up data. For teaching, it will not only be useful to instructors wishing to add metadata to learning objects, but also to students who will be able to annotate their own versions of the slides, providing potential to better model their knowledge for adaptation. The local definitions enrich the base ontology resulting in better inferences about the concepts. In our teaching context this means the metadata will be a higher quality representation of the learning objects allowing for better user models and adaptation of the material for users.

We are creating user models from web usage logs and assessment marks of students doing the User Interface Design and Programming course. The current version of Metasaur provides an easy way to navigate the domain ontology and to create metadata. The same terms as are used as metadata are used as the basic components in the user model. In addition, the user model will, optionally, include the ontologically related terms with the possibility of inferring that the user's knowledge of the basic terms might be used to infer their knowledge of closely related terms that are not used in the metadata. The enhancements made to allow users to add terms to the ontology results in a higher quality representation of the concepts taught by the course.

Acknowledgements

We thank Hewlett-Packard for supporting the work on Metasaur and SIV.

References

1. Thornely, J. *The How of Metadata: Metadata Creation and Standards.* In: *13th National Cataloguing Conference*, (1999)
2. Kahan, J., et al. *Annotea: An Open RDF Infrastructure for Shared Web Annotations.* In: *WWW10 International Conference*, (2001)
3. Berners-Lee, T., Hendler, J., and Lassila, O., *The Semantic Web.* In Scientific America. (2001)
4. *OWL Web Ontology Language Overview*, Available at http://www.w3.org/TR/owl-features/. (2003)
5. Fensel, D., *Ontologies: A Silver Bullet for Knowledge Management and Electronic Commerce*: Springer (2001)
6. Reimer, U., et al., *Ontology-based Knowledge Management at Work: The Swiss Life Case Studies*, in J. Davis, D. Fensel, and F.v. Harmelen, Editors, *Towards the Semantic Web: Ontology-driven Knowledge Management.* 2003, John Wiley & Sons: West Sussex, England. p. 197-218.
7. Ecklund, P. *Visual Displays for Browsing RDF Documents.* In: J. Thom and J. Kay, Editors. *Australian Document Computing Symposium*, (2002) 101-104
8. Berendonck, C.V. and Jacobs, T. *Bubbleworld : A New Visual Information Retrieval Technique.* In: T. Pattison and B. Thomas, Editors. *Australian Symposium on Information Visualisation.* Australian Computer Society, (2003) 47-56
9. Mutton, P. and Golbeck, J. *Visualisation of Semantic Metadata and Ontologies.* In: E. Banissi, et al., Editors. *Seventh International Conference on Information Visualisation.* IEEE Computer Society, (2003) 306-311
10. Lum, A. *Scrutable User Models in Decentralised Adaptive Systems.* In: P. Brusilovsky, A. Corbett, and F.d. Rosis, Editors. *9th International Conference on User Modelling.* Springer, (2003) 426-428

11. Murray, T., *Authoring Knowledge Based Tutors: Tools for Content, Instructional Strategy, Student Model and Interface Design.* In Journal of Learning Sciences. Vol. 7(1) (1998) 5--64

12. Merceron, A. and Yacef, K. *A Web-based Tutoring Tool with Mining Facilities to Improve Learning and Teaching.* In: U. Hoppe, F. Verdejo, and J. Kay, Editors. *Artificial Intelligence in Education.* IOS Press, (2003) 201-208

13. Mizoguchi, R. *Ontology-based systemization of functional knowledge.* In: *TMCE2002: Tools and methods of competitive engineering,* (2002) 45-64

14. Apted, T. and Kay, J. *Automatic Construction of Learning Ontologies.* In: L. Aroyo and D. Dicheva, Editors. *International Conference on Computers in Education.* Technische Universiteit Eindhoven, (2002) 55-62

15. *Usability Glossary,* Available at http://www.usabilityfirst.com/glossary/main.cgi. (2002)

16. Kay, J. and Lum, A., *An ontologically enhanced metadata editor,* TR 541, University of Sydney (2003)

17. Apted, T. and Kay, J. *Generating and Comparing Models within an Ontology.* In: J. Thom and J. Kay, Editors. *Australian Document Computing Symposium.* School of Information Technologies, University of Sydney, (2002) 63-68

18. Jannink, J. and Wiederhold, G. *Thesaurus Entry Extraction from an On-line Dictionary.* In: *Fusion '99,* (1999)

19. Kogut, P. and Holms, W. *AeroDAML: Applying Information Extraction to Generate DAML Annotations from Web Pages.* In: *First International Conference on Knowledge Capture (K-CAP 2001) Workshop on Knowledge Markup and Semantic Annotation,* (2001)

20. Dill, S., et al. *SemTag and Seeker: Bootstrapping the Semantic Web via Automated Semantic Annotation.* In: *Twelfth International World Wide Web Conference,* (2003)

Interaction with Web Services in the Adaptive Web

Liliana Ardissono, Anna Goy, Giovanna Petrone, and Marino Segnan

Dipartimento di Informatica, Università di Torino
Corso Svizzera 185, Torino, Italy
{liliana,goy,giovanna,marino}@di.unito.it

Abstract. The provision of personalized services based on the orchestration of simpler Web Services is often viewed as an activity that can be performed in an automated way, without involving the end-user. This paper addresses the need to involve the user in the loop and discusses the communication challenges imposed by this viewpoint. The paper also presents a conversation model for the management of the communication between Web Service consumers and providers aimed at addressing those challenges.

1   Introduction

The composition of Web Services is the focus of the Service Oriented Computing paradigm (SOC), which "utilizes services as fundamental elements for developing applications" [17]. According to [17], several ingredients are needed to enable applications to operate in a SOC environment. For instance:

- A machine-readable service specification language for the description of the services.
- A service discovery protocol for directory services enabling consumers to locate Web Services and to discover their details.
- An open communication protocol enabling consumers to invoke Web Services and to capture the results of the requested operations.
- Quality of Service support, in terms of transactional integrity, security and authentication, and privacy protection.

Moreover, as discussed by Curbera et al. in [9], coordination protocols are needed to orchestrate the invocation of services in complex business logics and to handle failure and recovery during the service execution.

Up to now, the main factor pushing the research on Web Services has been the management of business interactions in electronic commerce, where standard flow languages, such as BPEL4WS [9], have been defined integrate legacy software in open, distributed systems. As the main priority of this research is the composition of suppliers in a possibly complex workflow, major efforts have been devoted to orchestrate the invocations of the suppliers. However, the individual service provider has been modeled as a functional unit providing an atomic service that may be requested by means of synchronous, one-shot interactions.

W. Nejdl and P. De Bra (Eds.): AH 2004, LNCS 3137, pp. 14–23, 2004.

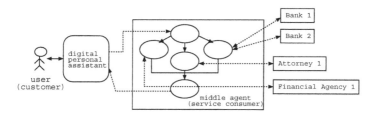

Fig. 1. Interaction between end-user, middle agent and Web Services.

The exploitation of Web Services in the Adaptive Web may be seen as an evolution of the SOC paradigm where the consumer application and/or the integrated Web Services customize the services they offer to the individual end-user. We foresee two main directions (see Fig. 1):

- *Making a personalized service, such as a recommender system, available as a Web Service.* For instance, a movie recommender could be extended with a public interface that enables some digital personal assistants to invoke it on behalf of their users. Moreover, a bank might offer a loan customization service that can be exploited by distributed commercial applications to negotiate financial support for their customers. Furthermore, an information service might tailor the type of content it delivers to the end-user's device by choosing different electronic formats depending on bandwidth and device capability constraints.
- *Composing Web Services in a consumer application offering a personalized service to the end-user.* For instance, middle agents, such as real estate agents and car sellers, could develop Web-based applications supporting a completely automated interaction with the customer (or with her digital personal assistant), from the selection of the good to be purchased to the contract definition. Similar to the traditional scenario, populated by human operators, the middle agent will manage a complex workflow, invoking and orchestrating services such as attorneys, banks and/or financial agencies, in order to offer the customer a personalized solution. Moreover, the middle agent could select, out of the pool of alternative Web Services offering the same service, those best satisfying the customer's preferences [3, 4].

The exploitation of adaptive systems as Web Services, as well as the personalized composition and selection of Web Services in a complex consumer application, deeply challenge the Web Service management and composition technologies developed so far. To provide a few examples:

- Rich (but scalable) communication protocols and infrastructures should enable consumers and providers to interact with each other. For example, the composition of a set of Web Services in a workflow may require the management of long-lasting interactions, to be suspended and resumed, depending on the availability of the invoked service providers. Moreover, highly interactive Web Services might need to manage several interaction turns with the consumers, including repairs to possible service failures, before the services are fulfilled.

- The provided communication protocols and infrastructure have to support a flexible type of interaction with the customer. Some personalized services, such as those supporting the booking of hotel rooms and flights, could in principle interact with a digital personal assistant operating on behalf of the customer. However, other interactive services, such as those supporting the configuration of complex products (e. g., a bicycle, or a loan) and services (e. g., an IP/VPN, or a video conference service) need to explicitly involve the end-user during the decision making, in order to guarantee that the configuration result fulfills her requirements. If this is not the case, they should start a new configuration process. In fact, configuration choices have advantages and disadvantages that, for trust and transparency reasons, should be handled by explicitly involving the user, and possibly repaired by means of a negotiation phase that can hardly be carried out by an automated assistant.

In a scenario similar to the one depicted in Fig. 1, the middle agent needs rich communication capabilities to suitably compose and orchestrate the various Web Services into a personalized interactive service for the end-user (customer). Specifically, the middle agent has to manage flexible interactions with the invoked Web Services, as well as to bridge the communication between the end-user and the service providers. Unfortunately, the current standards for the Web Services composition neglect this communication aspect and reduce the invocation of service providers to simple *request-reply* interactions, where the consumer application requests the execution of an operation on the provider and collects the results (the current Web Service communication standards are however evolving to the management of asynchronous communication; e. g., see WSDL 2.0 [21]). Similarly, the recent proposals concerning user-centered Web Services (e. g., [4]), base the retrieval of personalized service results on the iteration of one-shot invocations on the Web Services; in these invocations, the consumer application employs personalization and relaxation strategies to retrieve a bunch of alternative proposals to be presented to the end-user. In contrast, few efforts have been devoted to the enhancement of the interaction between all the parties of the Business to Business relationship, including the customer. In order to address this issue, we have proposed a conversation model for Web Services, aimed at supporting complex interactions, where several messages have to be exchanged before the service is completed. Our framework, described in detail in [2, 1], takes inspiration from the traditional dialog-management approaches developed in the Computational Linguistics research [7]. However, we have simplified the conversation model to take the emerging Web Services standards into account and to make the development of an effective conversation framework feasible.

Before presenting our framework, it is worth noting that we assume that the service discovery phase has been performed and we focus on the service execution phase. The identification of the service provider is a separate activity, to be performed either directly, as suggested in the SOC research (e. g., see [14]), or by exploiting mediation agents, as investigated in the Semantic Web community [19, 12]. Moreover, after a provider is identified, the consumer should carry an explicit binding activity out in order to match its own ontology with that exploited by the service provider.

In the rest of this paper, we sketch our conversation model and the communication infrastructure we are developing. In particular, we explain in which way the communication features provided by our conversation model support the management of highly interactive Web Services, which need to put the end-user in the loop during the service execution. Specifically, Sect. 2 describes the framework we are developing; Sect. 3 presents the related work and Sect. 4 concludes the paper.

2   A Conversation Model Supporting Web Service Interaction

Our model focuses on two main requirements: first, the model should be compatible with the current standards for the service publication and invocation. Second, the management should be easy for the consumer, in order to make the interaction with multiple providers as seamless and possible. We thus designed a model charging the service provider with the control of the conversation and explicitly guiding the consumer application in the service invocation. specifically:

- The service provider describes the offered service by listing the operations to be invoked.
- The service provider may also publish the interaction flow specification, although this is not necessary for the run time management of the interaction with the consumers.
- As the service provider is in charge of controlling the interaction with the consumers, it has to maintain a local interaction context, for each active conversation.
- At each step, the provider enriches the messages it sends with contextual and turn management information in order to make the consumer aware about the eligible turns it may perform.

2.1   Conversation Flow Language

We adopted a Finite State Automaton representation to specify the conversation flow at the conceptual level, as FSA are a simple formalism and they are well understood; see also [5] and [6]. As far as the conversation turns are concerned, we have clearly separated the representation of the turn-taking activity (for instance, which party can send messages at each conversation step) from the arguments of the messages that the peers exchange. Each conversation turn is aimed at invoking an operation on the receiver: the sender asks the recipient to perform the operation occurring as an argument. For instance, the sender may invoke the execution of a domain-level operation, it may notify the partner about the results of an operation it has just performed (success, failure), or it may suspend/resume the interaction.

The conversation turns are represented by means of send message (*SendM*) activities described as WSDL (Web Services Description Language, [20]) operations and having the following arguments:

- The message sender, which may be either the consumer C, or the service provider S.
- The recipient of the message (similar).
- The object-level operation to be executed by the message recipient.
- The list of the possible continuations of the conversation (*nextOps*). As the service provider is in control of the interaction, this argument is only present in the messages directed to the consumer. The argument includes the set of alternative operations offered by the provider which the consumer may invoke in the next conversation step.

Our *SendM* activities are requests that the message sender performs to make the receiver execute the object-level operations. This is different from the normal usage of WSDL statements, which directly refer to object-level operations, without wrapping them in conversation turns.

2.2   Conversation Flow of a Product Configuration Service

In order to guide the development of our conversation model we selected a use case concerning the customization of loans. This use case imposes interesting requirements on the interaction between the (human) customer, the middle agent and the Web Services providing basic services; moreover, the use case provides a realistic example where the customer has to be explicitly engaged in the negotiation of the overall service.

The scenario of the loan customization use case is depicted in Fig. 1: the customer exploits a personal assistant to contact a middle agent providing personalized loans. The middle agent offers a complex service accessible via a standard Web Service interface. The middle agent exploits and orchestrates "simpler" Web Services (banks, financial agencies, attorneys, etc.) to build the overall service; moreover, it retrieves the customer's requirements from the personal agent. In turn, the personal agent can get the requested information (e. g., her age) from the customer's user model. However, when the needed information is not available, the personal agent asks the customer and forwards her response to the middle agent, which sends the information to the requesting Web Service.

The interaction between personal agent and middle agent may be rather complex and involve different phases; e. g., acquisition of some information about the customer, needed to select the most convenient service providers to be contacted[1], the management of the interaction with the providers, the signature of the contract. However, in this description, we focus on the loan configuration process, assuming that the middle agent has selected a specific bank to negotiate the loan for the customer. In this case, the loan definition is guided by the bank, which runs the configuration engine for the generation of loan proposals and retrieves the customer information necessary to propose a solution from the middle agent. The key point is that simple customer data, such as her age, might be directly provided by the personal agent, but the agent might not be able to make critical decisions and is expected to ask the user about them. For instance, the customer should be in charge of choosing between different combinations of the loan duration and its maximum rate. The information items requested by the bank have to be provided *during* the configuration process to generate a suitable configuration solution. Moreover, the user can be involved again at the end of the process, in order to choose between alternative solutions; e. g., she may inspect the details of the proposed solution and accept it, or refuse it and start the configuration of a different one.

This use case is also interesting from the viewpoint of the interaction between the middle agent and the orchestrated Web Services (e. g., the bank) because the interaction flow has to be decided during the service execution, depending on the business logics of the invoked Web Service. Therefore, depending on the type of Web Service invoked by

---

[1] For example, banks adopt stricter policies than financial agencies to decide whether a customer is eligible for funding.

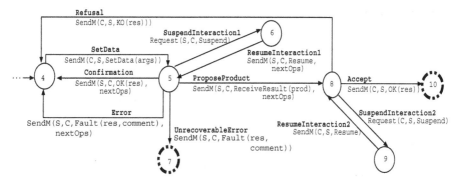

Fig. 2. Portion of the representation of the conversation flow of the loan customization service. Notice that we have labeled the arcs with a boldface identifier (e. g., "Refusal") to simplify the identification of the conversation turns.

the middle agent, different contract features could be set. Furthermore, both the invoked Web Services and the middle agent may need to suspend the conversation and resume it later on, in order to carry out a nested interaction with other parties involved in the business relationship. For instance, the bank might need to invoke some remote services to complete the controls on the good to be funded. Moreover, the middle agent might need to suspend the interaction waiting for the customer to provide the requested data, or to decide whether accepting or rejecting the proposed solution.

Fig. 2 shows a portion of the conversation flow specification for the loan customization service. The automaton, held by the bank Web Service, describes the data acquisition and the product proposal phases. The states of the automaton represent the dialog states: the plain circles denote the conversation states and the thick dotted ones (7, 10) are final dialog states. The labels of the arcs represent the conversation turns. The states having more than one output arc are alternative conversation turns.

In the data acquisition phase, the consumer sends the customer data and the requirements on the loan to the Web Service. When the consumer sets data, e. g., the preferred monthly rate (*SetData(args)* operation), the service provider may react in different ways. For instance, it may confirm the correct acquisition of the data ($Confirmation$ arc) and enable another invocation of the $SetData$ operation to let the consumer set other product features. Or, the Web Service may notify the consumer that there was a failure in the product customization process ($Failure$) and enable the selection of other values for the conflicting features. The failure management supports the search for a compromise between customer requirements and domain-specific constraints.

The data acquisition phase can end in two ways. Either an unrecoverable error (e. g., the customer's requirements are incompatible with one another and thus they cannot be jointly satisfied), or the customization process succeeds and the service continues the interaction by proposing the product (*ProposeProduct*). The consumer application may accept the proposal (*Accept*) or reject it (*Refusal*), in which case a different loan can be configured; the acceptance/rejection depends on the customer's decisions. Notice that both parties may suspend the interaction and resume it later on, in order to handle delays due to the invocation of sub-suppliers, or the customer's responses.

2.3   Architecture of Our Conversation Framework

The previously described conceptual conversation flow specification has to be translated to a standard, executable format, so that service consumers can easily understand it and it can be run by a flow engine within the service provider. Indeed, the *SendM* activity is a normal WSDL operation, with the only difference that some of its arguments are complex XML objects describing the object-level operation to be invoked on the other participant. The executable specification of the automaton can be derived from the conceptual one by translating states and transitions to a suitable process language, such as, for instance, BPEL4WS, which can be executed by existing flow engines.

Although the WSDL representation of the *SendM* operations makes our conversation model compatible with the emerging standards for the Web Service publication and management, it proposes a peculiar exploitation of the constructs offered by such language. Therefore, specific software is needed to manage the interpretation of the incoming WSDL messages (i. e., to extract the information about the next operations and the invoked object-level operation at the recipient side) and to generate the responses. In order to manage the conversation at both sides, the two peers should therefore run, respectively, a *Conversation Manager* and a *Conversation Client* modules. The former is employed by the provider to manage the interaction with the consumers, which would only rely on the light Conversation Client to parse the incoming messages and return the responses.

The Conversation Client has three main responsibilities:

- *Facilitating the reception and interpretation of messages at the consumer side,* especially as far as the interpretation of the eligible continuations of the interaction is concerned (*nextOps* argument of *SendM* messages).
- *Supporting the correct invocation of the operations on the provider,* by performing type and consistency checks to guarantee that the parameter values set by the consumer application satisfy the constraints on the arguments of the operations to be invoked.
- *Facilitating the management of the outbound messages to the provider,* by generating and sending the *SendM* messages that specify the invocation of operations on the provider.

Before binding the invocation of operations to its own business logic, the consumer should download from the Web Service site the Conversation Client to be run during the service invocation. Moreover, the service provider should exploit the Conversation Manager and run it on its own flow specification (executable version of the conversation automaton). It should be noted that the XML representation of the *SendM* messages supports the interoperability between service consumers and providers, but the Conversation Client we implemented can only be run in a Java-based environment. The idea is therefore that other versions of the Client should be implemented to provide advanced conversation capabilities in different environments such as, for instance, .Net. Details can be found in [1].

3   Related Work

The main difference between our work and other recent approaches to the management of personalized Web Services is that we aim at providing a framework that can be exploited to enhance the interaction with current Web Services, while most of the related work is focused on Semantic Web Services. For instance, Balke and Wagner propose to base the personalization of services for the end-user on the availability of an intelligent system that reasons about Semantic Web Services descriptions and applies logical inference engines to support the run-time invocation of operations [3,4]. In contrast, our proposal bases the management of personalized services on the possibility of managing long-lasting, flexible communication between the end-user, the middle agent taking care of the Web Service invocation, and the Web Services; moreover, our proposal relies on the emerging Web Service standards and has thus more changes to be employed in the immediate future.

As discussed in [8] and [3,4], the personalization features offered by Adaptive Hypermedia techniques could also be applied to support the composition of Web Services. All these authors suggest that automated problem solvers could be employed to suggest suitable compositions of Web Services in order to build complex services, i. e., to satisfy the goals to be fulfilled by the complex service under definition. As a matter of fact, the automated generation of flow specifications for Web Service composition is a major goal to be achieved and is attracting a lot of attention in the Semantic Web Services research; e. g., see [16]. However, no techniques have been developed that can easily be applied to carry this activity out in large Business-to-Business application domains, without human intervention. In fact, Web Services are usually described in standard formalisms such as WSDL, that do not specify their semantics. Noticeably, other approaches have been proposed that support the customization of a complex service without requiring semantic information about the services to be composed. For instance, Han et al. [11] explain that a business level composition language should be defined, as an abstraction of the low-level flow specifications typically provided by flow languages such as BPEL4WS, in order to support the service administrator in the customization of the overall service; e. g., the administrator might activate certain subservices only at night, or during certain week days. In this perspective, the technical details concerning the Web Service composition, and the related bindings to services, are resolved by a software engineer, who prepares the environment to be customized by possibly non-expert service administrators.

A different example is provided in more restricted environments, such as the educational one, where the knowledge representation and reasoning frameworks typical of the Semantic Web are attracting a lot of attention. For instance, an interesting approach to bring adaptivity into the Semantic Web is proposed by Dolog et al., who focus on providing personalized access to distributed resources in an open environment; see [10]. Within the perspective of the Semantic Web, where heterogeneous resources (information and services) are described by means of standardized metadata, user requirements should also be represented in a formal and standard language, in order to apply reasoning mechanisms able to personalize the access to such resources.

4 Conclusions

The provision of personalized services based on the orchestration of simpler Web Services is often viewed as an activity to be performed in an automated way, without involving the end-user in the service negotiation. In this paper, we introduced a different viewpoint, which includes the user in the loop, and we discussed the communication challenges imposed by this viewpoint. We also presented a conversation model for the management of the communication between Web Service consumers and providers aimed at addressing those challenges. Our model enables the management of flexible interactions between:

- The end-user who interacts with services by exploiting her own digital assistant;
- The middle agents offering complex services by orchestrating other simpler Web Services;
- The composed Web Services themselves.

The communication features offered by our model support the provision of highly interactive Web Services, such as those carrying out problem solving activities (e. g., the configuration of complex products and services), but can be applied to simpler Web Services, as well.

We believe that our proposal addresses important open issues in the provision of personalized services based on the exploitation of Web Services. However, we recognize that our approach is rather conservative as far as the knowledge-sharing aspects underlying the Web Services cooperation are concerned. For instance, the management of a personalized Web Service might rely on the availability of a user model (either directly accessible, or provided by a User Modeling Server [13]) describing the individual user's preferences; see [18, 15, 10]. Unfortunately, until the Semantic Web becomes a reality, we believe that this scenario will be hardly applicable in wide Business to Business domains.

References

1. L. Ardissono, D. Cardinio, G. Petrone, and M. Segnan. A framework for the server-side management of conversations with Web Services. In *Proc. of the 13th Int. World Wide Web Conference*, pages 124–133, New York, 2004.
2. L. Ardissono, G. Petrone, and M. Segnan. A conversational approach to the interaction with Web Services. *Computational Intelligence*, 20(4), 2004.
3. W.T. Balke and M. Wagner. Towards personalized selection of Web Services. In *Proc. of 12th International World Wide Web Conference (WWW'2003)*, Budapest, 2003.
4. W.T. Balke and M. Wagner. Through different eyes - assessing multiple conceptual views for querying Web Services. In *Proc. of 13th International World Wide Web Conference (WWW'2004)*, New York, 2004.
5. B. Benatallah, F. Casati, F. Toumani, and R. Hamadi. Conceptual modeling of Web Service conversations. In *Proc. Advanced Information Systems Engineering, 15th International Conference, CAiSE 2003*, Klagenfurt, Austria, 2003.
6. D. Berardi, F. De Rosa, L. De Santis, and M. Mecella. Finite state automata as a conceptual model of e-services. In *Proc. Integrated Design and Process Technology (IDPT 2003)*, Austin, Texas, 2003.
7. P.R. Cohen and H.J. Levesque. Rational interaction as the basis for communication. In P.R. Cohen, J. Morgan, and M.E. Pollack, editors, *Intentions in communication*, pages 221–255. MIT Press, 1990.
8. O. Conlan, D. Lewis, S. Higel, D. O'Sullivan, and V. Wade. Applying Adaptive Hypermedia techniques to Semantic Web Service composition. In *Proc. International Workshop on Adaptive Hypermedia and Adaptive web-based Systems (AH 2003)*, pages 53–62, Johnstown, PA, 2003.

9. F. Curbera, R. Khalaf, N. Mukhi, S. Tai, and S. Weerawarana. The next step in Web Services. *Communications of the ACM, Special Issue on Service-Oriented Computing*, 46(10), 2003.

10. P. Dolog, N. Henze, W. Nejdl, and M. Sintek. Towards the Adaptive Semantic Web. In *Proc. 1st Workshop on Principles and Practice of Semantic Web Reasoning (PPSWR'03)*, Mumbai, India, 2003.

11. Y. Han, H. Geng, H. Li, J. Xiong, G. Li, B. Holtkamp, R. Gartmann, R. Wagner, and N. Weissenberg. VINCA - a visual and personalized business-level composition language for chaining Web-based Services. In *Proc. International Conference on Service-Oriented computing (ICSOC 2003)*, pages 165–177, Trento, Italy, 2003.

12. T. Kamamura, J. DeBlasio, T. Hasegawa, M. Paolucci, and K. Sycara. Preliminary report of public experiment of semantic service matchmaker with UDDI business registry. In *Proc. International Conference on Service-Oriented computing (ICSOC 2003)*, pages 208–224, Trento, Italy, 2003.

13. A. Kobsa. Generic user modeling systems. *User Modeling and User-Adapted Interaction, Ten Year Anniversary Issue*, 2000.

14. F. Leymann and K. Güntzel. The business grid: providing transactional business processes via grid services. In *Proc. International Conference on Service-Oriented computing (ICSOC 2003)*, pages 256–270, Trento, Italy, 2003.

15. M. Maybury and P. Brusilovsky, editors. *The adaptive Web*, volume 45. Communications of the ACM, 2002.

16. M. Paolucci, K. Sycara, and T. Kamamura. Delivering Semantic Web Services. In *Proc. of 12th International World Wide Web Conference (WWW'2003)*, Budapest, 2003.

17. M.P. Papazoglou and D. Georgakopoulos. Service-oriented computing. *Communications of the ACM*, 46(10), 2003.

18. D. Riecken, editor. *Special Issue on Personalization*, volume 43. Communications of the ACM, 2000.

19. DAML Services Coalition (A. Ankolekar, M. Burstein, J. Hobbs, O. Lassila, D. Martin, S. McIlraith, S. Narayanan, M. Paolucci, T. Payne, K. Sycara, and H. Zeng). DAML-S: Web Service description for the Semantic Web. In *Proc. International Semantic Web Conference*, pages 348–363, Chia Laguna, Italy, 2002.

20. W3C. Web Services Definition Language. http://www.w3.org/TR/wsdl, 2002.

21. W3C. Web Services Definition Language Version 2.0. http://www.w3.org/TR/wsdl20/, 2004.

Social Adaptive Navigation Support
for Open Corpus Electronic Textbooks

Peter Brusilovsky[1,2], Girish Chavan[1], and Rosta Farzan[2]

[1] School of Information Sciences
gchavan@mail.sis.pitt.edu
[2] Intelligent Systems Program
University of Pittsburgh, Pittsburgh PA 15260, USA
peterb@pitt.edu, rosta@cs.pitt.edu

Abstract. Closed corpus AH systems demonstrate what is possible to achieve with adaptive hypermedia technologies; however they are impractical for dealing with the large volume of open corpus resources. Our system, Knowledge Sea II, presented in this paper explores *social adaptive navigation support,* an approach for providing personalized guidance in the open corpus context. Following the ideas of *social navigation,* we have attempted to organize a personalized navigation support that is based on past learners' interaction with the system. The social adaptive navigation support implemented in our system was considered quite useful by students participating in the classroom study of Knowledge Sea II. At the same time, some user comments indicated the need to provide more powerful navigation support.

1 Introduction

The electronic textbook is an emerging form for delivering structured educational resources over the Web [10]. Web-based electronic textbooks successfully attempt to resemble classic textbooks, a proven form for expressing and communicating knowledge. Web-based electronic textbooks are attractive for both providers (publishers, teachers) and consumers (students). Teachers use online textbooks to deliver structured content to their students with minimal efforts. Publishers explore the use of Web-based textbooks to deliver the content faster while decreasing the costs for maintaining the rapidly changing information. Students embrace the online form since it can be accessed "anytime, anywhere". They also appreciate that the Web can bring more information to their fingertips than traditional paper-based sources can. It's quite typical nowadays for one to find a selection of electronic textbooks on the Web, in a number of popular subjects – ranging from a simple, hierarchically-structured set of HTML pages prepared by individual teachers to professionally-produced electronic copies of popular, printed textbooks.

Wider choice is beneficial – potentially it gives more opportunities for everyone to locate their most-personally-relevant learning objects. Unfortunately the benefits of online access come with its price – an information overload. As we have found in the course of our earlier research [7], it is very hard for regular students to select relevant reading fragments on a specific topic from multiple online textbooks. It is known that users with weak knowledge of the subject (that is usually the case for students) have navigation problems in educational hypermedia even when dealing with a single hyperdocument [3]. The problems can be resolved to some extent by *navigation support*

W. Nejdl and P. De Bra (Eds.): AH 2004, LNCS 3137, pp. 24–33, 2004.

that is aimed to help students in locating the most relevant fragments of educational content. In a traditional educational context this navigation support is provided by a teacher who assigns relevant readings for every lecture or topic of the course being taught. An even higher level of navigation support can be provided by adaptive educational hypermedia systems [2]. These systems rely on individual student models and expert knowledge about educational material to guide the students to the most relevant fragments.

The problem addressed in this paper is that traditional, expert-based approaches can only provide guidance within a relatively limited set of resources (so-called Closed Corpus) and can't cope with the increasing volume of online information (known as Open Corpus). No teacher can recommend the most relevant reading from dozens of relevant online sources. Adaptive educational hypermedia systems can potentially deal with large volumes of information but detailed content knowledge is required. While in some application areas such as aircraft maintenance [5] it is feasible to have a team of experts to encode the complete content knowledge about thousands and thousands of available content fragments, the educational economies of most fields preclude this investment of time and money.

Our system, Knowledge Sea II presented in this paper, explores an alternative approach for providing personalized guidance to students. Following the idea of *social navigation* [15] we have attempted to organize a personalized navigation support that is based on past learners' interaction with the system. We call this *social adaptive navigation support* (SANS). Unlike traditional adaptive navigation support that relies on expert-provided knowledge about each resource, *social* adaptive navigation support relies on the *collective knowledge* of a large community of learners gathered through different forms of feedback. This paper discusses the idea of SANS and presents the Knowledge Sea II system that implements some simple form of SANS. In addition, we report the results of our classroom study of the system and discuss these results in the context of our future work.

2   Navigating Multiple Educational Resources in Closed Corpus and Open Corpus Hypermedia

As we have pointed out in the introduction, adaptive hypermedia systems can provide a high level of navigation support by helping users of educational hypermedia find educational material that is most relevant in the context of their current knowledge and goals. While early adaptive hypermedia systems developed for the E-Learning context [9, 12] have focused on providing adaptive navigation support in a single hyperdocument, more recent systems have demonstrated an ability to deal with multiple independent sources. Such systems as InterBook [6], KBS-Hyperbook [17], and SIGUE [11] have explored several ways to integrate the content of several electronic textbooks or Web sites.

For example, InterBook suggested the metaphor of a bookshelf - a collection of independently developed electronic textbooks on the same subject. To allow students to navigate seamlessly between different textbooks, InterBook introduced *concept-based navigation* though the glossary [8]. Each concept used for indexing bookshelf content in InterBook can be visualized as a *glossary* page. The glossary page for a specific concept shows some authored definition of the concept and automatically generates links to all pages in all textbooks on that shelf that are related to this concept. Glossary pages support goal-based access to educational material by providing the student with one-click access to all resources on that shelf that either present each specific concept or require knowledge about the concept. It also provides an additional level of knowledge-based navigation support by indicating pages that present no new information to the student, pages that are ready to be learned, and pages beyond the student's current learning ability.

Unfortunately, the InterBook's adaptive navigation support power is available only within a relatively small set of documents that were structured and indexed with concepts at design time. Modern AH systems are predominantly *closed corpus* adaptive hypermedia since the *document space* of these adaptive systems is a closed set of information items manually indexed by domain experts. KBS-Hyperbook [18], and SIGUE [11] are two of only a few systems that have attempted to deal with an *open corpus* such as the Web. However, even in KBS-Hyperbook and SIGUE the ability to handle open corpus resources comes for a price: each Web page added to these systems has to be manually indexed with domain model concepts.

To support students in navigating open corpus educational resources, we have to use methods that do not require manual indexing of content. One of the fields that can provide relevant methods is information retrieval. Information retrieval approaches are mostly based on automatic content indexing on the level of keywords. Information retrieval methods are far from reaching the precision of classic adaptive hypermedia in determining the most relevant pages, yet they are able to operate with huge amounts of "open Web" content [1].

In our earlier Knowledge Sea project [7] we explored the possibility of automatically structuring a reasonable amount of the open corpus Web resources. Knowledge Sea provides structured access to several online textbooks on C programming language in the context of an introductory programming course. Knowledge Sea used a keyword-level automatic page analysis and self-organized maps (SOM) to allocate pages of several hierarchically-structured Web textbooks (open corpus) and lecture handouts (closed corpus) on an 8 by 8 grid. We have relied on the remarkable ability of SOM to group similar pages in the same cells as well as to place reasonably similar groups of pages in neighboring cells. SOM allowed us to provide what we called *map-based* navigation for multiple educational resources. It resembles InterBook's concept-based navigation to some extent, but does not require manual indexing or structuring. Cell keywords (identified by SOM) and lecture landmarks were placed on the map to help students finding cells that are close to their current goal. Each cell can be "opened" in a separate window that will show the content of the cell - a list of links to pages from multiple tutorials. This allowed the students to navigate "horizontally" between tutorials in addition to hierarchical navigation supported by each tutorial.

The system was called Knowledge Sea because the cells on the map were colored using several shades of blue to express the amount of resources under the cell. Similar to real Ocean maps, deeper color saturation indicated that the Information Sea under the cells was "deeper" - i.e., more resources were available. The system was evaluated in several classroom studies. The students praised highly the ability of Knowledge Sea to group similar resources together and to help them find relevant pages. Least appreciated feature of the system was the interface. A number of students have been confused by our attempt to use color saturation to indicate the depth of the Information Sea. In addition, a number of students have noted that Knowledge Sea provided no help in locating relevant resources within a cell. Since pages in a cell are grouped on the basis of keyword level similarity, very good pages can be located next to difficult-to-comprehend pages or pages that contain no useful information.

The goal of our more recent Knowledge Sea II system was to extend the power of Knowledge Sea by providing navigation support within a cell. Knowledge Sea II uses adaptive annotation technology that had already been used in InterBook in a very similar context. Our challenge was to replace the InterBook adaptation engine (based on closed corpus indexing) with an engine that could work with open corpus resources. In Knowledge Sea II we explored the possibility of building an adaptation engine based on the concepts of social navigation theory.

3   Social Adaptive Navigation Support
for Open Corpus Hypermedia

Social navigation [15] is a new stream of research that explores methods for organizing users' explicit and implicit feedback, in order to support information navigation in a meaningful way. The field of social navigation began with a few now classic projects [14, 21] that attempted to support a known social phenomenon: people tend to follow the "footprints" of other people. Another important feature of all social navigation systems is *self-organization*. Social navigation systems are able to work with little or no involvement of human administrators or experts. They are powered by a community of users. Properly organized community-powered systems such as Web auctions (www.ebay.com) or Weblogs (www.lifejournal.com) are known to be among the most successful Web applications. Self-organization is critical to the goals of our project. In an online educational context, self-organization means the ability to guide students to the most useful resources without the need for continuous involvement of human content experts to index resources. The feasibility of social navigation in the context of E-Learning has been explored in a few pioneer projects [16, 19, 20]. These projects provided an inspiration for our work. We have attempted however, to move one step further by developing a social adaptive navigation support technology that can navigate within much larger volumes of educational content.

The first version of Knowledge Sea II combines the concepts of group user modeling with the original "footprint" approach [21]. It uses the simplest implicit feedback: group traffic. For each tutorial page it counts how many times the users of the same group accessed it. Summing up group traffic for individual pages belonging to the same map cell, the system can also calculate group traffic for each cell. To keep the original ocean map metaphor, we have decided to visualize the cell traffic using multiple shades of blue. The more saturated the color is the more times the pages belonging to the cell were accessed. As a group of users navigates though pages of multiple electronic textbooks, the knowledge map becomes gradually darker. As we had expected, during the classroom study of Knowledge Sea II, we observed that cells with the most useful content become darker much faster. At the end of the course (Fig. 1), from the teacher's point of view, the colors of the cells have remarkably well captured the usefulness of the map cells in the context of the given course. The darkest color indicated "treasure" cells with a good number of pages presenting important course topics. The cells that focus on topics not covered by the course have remained nearly white.

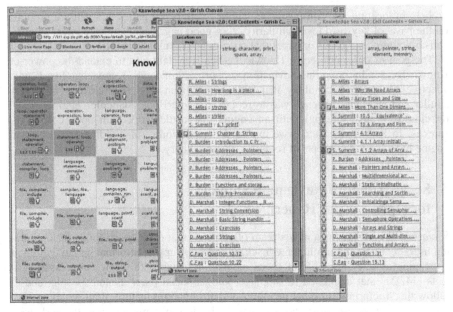

Fig. 1. The map view and two cell views in Knowledge Sea II

In addition to expressing the amount of group traffic through color saturation, each cell on the map shows four other cues. The list of top three cell keywords (identified by SOM) helps the students in finding cells by content. Lecture numbers play the role of landmarks allowing users to locate open corpus documents that are similar to well-known closed corpus documents. The icon shaped as a stack of papers indicates the relative number of documents in the cell and serves as an anchor for accessing the cell. A small yellow note on this icon hints about the presence of user notes on some cell pages. The human-shaped icon indicates the number of user's own visits to the documents of the cells using the same metaphor – darker shades for more visits. This technique provides an extended form of history-based navigation support explored in some early educational adaptive hypermedia [13]. The user can see which pages are well explored and which are not. In addition, the colors of the background and the icon are generated to ensure their matching. As a result, if the user has visited the cell more than the average user of her group, the icon is darker than the background. If she has visited it less than average, the icon is lighter than the background. It allows the users to instantly distinguish potentially useful cells that they have underexplored as well as possibly over-explored cells.

The same traffic-based approach is used to annotate links within the map cell (Fig. 1) and individual tutorial pages (Fig. 2). Each link is annotated with a human-shaped blue icon on a blue background (right on Fig. 1). The color of the icon shows user's own navigation history. The color of the background shows the cumulative navigation history of the whole class. In addition, a note-shaped icon indicates the presence of user notes on a page. The annotations in the cell window are generated by Knowledge Sea II. The annotations on tutorial pages are added by the AnnotatED service which processes all tutorial pages, adding annotations to visited and commented pages.

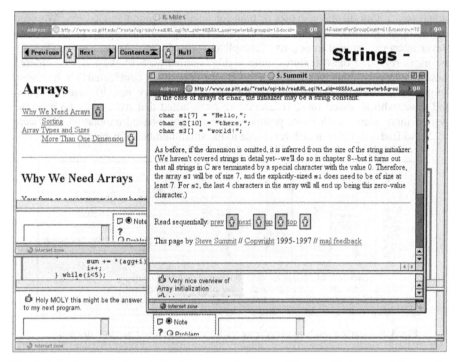

Fig. 2. Adaptive annotations indicating user and group traffic are added to tutorial pages by AnnotatED service.

4   A Classroom Study of Social Adaptive Navigation Support

We performed the first classroom study of Knowledge Sea II in a regular introductory programming course at the University of Pittsburgh. To compare two versions of the system we used the original Knowledge Sea system for the first 1/3 of the course and switched to Knowledge Sea II for the rest of the course. The teacher has briefly demonstrated the system during several lectures and invited students to use it in addition to the printed textbook used in class. Access to the Knowledge Sea map was provided through our KnowledgeTree course portal and tracked by the user model server [4]. In addition, links to several tutorial pages that the teacher considered useful were provided directly as an additional reading for some lectures. Out of 28 students in class 16 used the system. These students have made between 2 and 201 page hits. The average number of hits was 54.

At the end of the class [or semester?], we asked the students who tried the system to fill out a non-mandatory questionnaire. The students were offered extra credit for participation. The questionnaire included 22 questions aimed to collect user feedback about various aspects of the system. Out of 16 eligible students 13 filled in the questionnaire. Due to lack of space, we present here only the results that are directly related to the topic of this paper – history-based social navigation support. Two groups of questions are relevant here. One group of four questions asked students to evaluate separately the idea of indicating individual and group traffic on the map and on individual pages with different shades of blue for icon/background annotations. We used a 4-point asymmetric scale where the answers ranged from highly positive (very clever interface feature) to negative (completely wrong idea). As we can see (Fig. 3), the users regarded these features quite highly – about 80% of the users considered these features as either good or very good and none have considered it a bad idea. Splitting the users in two groups – those who accessed less than 30 pages (7 users) and those who accessed more (6 users), we have noted that the users who used the system more were much more positive about the color-based annotation. We were unable to find a significant difference due to the small number of subjects.

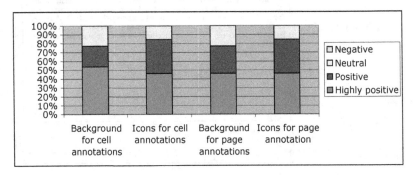

Fig. 3. Student's attitude to visualizing traffic with shades of blue, in four contexts

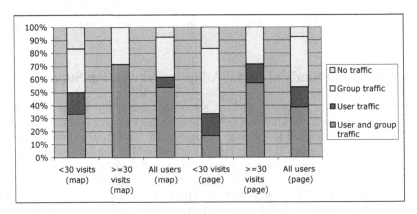

Fig. 4. User preferences about traffic visualization, split by user experience

Another group of two questions was designed to assess what kind of traffic-based annotations the students prefer to have in general. For each of two contexts (map navigation and page navigation) we asked the users what kind of traffic they would like to see visualized in both map and page context. The answer options were: Only group traffic, Only user traffic, Both, or None. The answer analysis (Fig. 4) allows making two interesting observations. First, students in general consider visualization of group traffic more useful than visualization of user traffic. While most users want to see either group traffic or both, merely one or two want to see only user traffic. Second, users who have reasonable experience working with the system (more than

30 hits) appreciate traffic visualization more than less experienced users. Moreover, most experienced users prefer to see both kinds of traffic visualized in both contexts.

Despite a very positive attitude toward traffic visualization in general and a specific preference for using icons and backgrounds colored in various shades of blue, some students indicated in their free form comment field that the traffic-based SANS is not sufficient for making informed navigation decisions. Two students noted that group traffic is not a reliable way to indicate page relevance. They wanted to see "good pages" that were considered useful for other group members. One student wanted to see what course lecture is relevant to each page listed.

In addition, we have compared the student attitude to the overall system's interface in the original Knowledge Sea system (as evaluated in several earlier studies) and the newer Knowledge Sea II. We were pleased to see that the student attitude toward the interface in the new system was quite a bit more positive than it was in our Knowledge Sea studies. Without any prompting, several students noted in their free form comment field that the new system is better and easier to use than the original Knowledge Sea. Since traffic-based adaptive annotations were the only significant change in the new system, we think that SANS has contributed to the increase of the user satisfaction with the new system.

5 Conclusions and Future Work

In this paper we have discussed problems encountered when providing adaptive navigation support for open corpus electronic textbooks. We have presented the Knowledge Sea II system that provides social adaptive navigation support – an open corpus adaptive navigation support based on the ideas of social navigation. While traffic-based SANS implemented in our system is relatively simple, it was considered quite useful by students participating in the classroom study of the system. At the same time, some user comments indicated the need to provide more powerful navigational support such as a method for the user to rate useful pages. We address these and other problems in the new version of Knowledge Sea II that is being evaluated in class this semester.

The main new idea that we are exploring in the new version is harvesting the feedback that the users provide through notes and comments that can be added to any open corpus page using AnnotatED service. In the version of the system described in this paper, notes were untyped and private (i.e., each student was able to see his or her notes only). In the newest version of the system we introduced typed notes and provided an option to make a note public. We hope that the analysis of students' extended commenting in the new version will give us some ideas on using the collective wisdom encapsulated in the comments for more precise SANS.

References

1. Brin, S. and Page, L.: The anatomy of a large-scale hypertextual (Web) search engine. Computer Networks and ISDN Systems. **30**, 1-7 (1998) 107-117
2. Brusilovsky, P.: Adaptive hypermedia. User Modeling and User Adapted Interaction **11**, 1/2 (2001) 87-110, available online at http://www.wkap.nl/oasis.htm/270983

3. Brusilovsky, P.: Adaptive navigation support in educational hypermedia: the role of student knowledge level and the case for meta-adaptation. British Journal of Educational Technology **34**, 4 (2003) 487-497

4. Brusilovsky, P.: KnowledgeTree: A Distributed Architecture for Adaptive E-Learning. In: Proc. of The Thirteenth International World Wide Web Conference, WWW 2004 (Alternate track papers and posters), New York, NY, ACM Press (2004) 104-113

5. Brusilovsky, P. and Cooper, D. W.: Domain, Task, and User Models for an Adaptive Hypermedia Performance Support System. In: Gil, Y. and Leake, D. B. (eds.) Proc. of 2002 International Conference on Intelligent User Interfaces, San Francisco, CA, (2002) 23-30, available online at http://www2.sis.pitt.edu/~peterb/papers/IUI02.pdf

6. Brusilovsky, P., Eklund, J., and Schwarz, E.: Web-based education for all: A tool for developing adaptive courseware. Computer Networks and ISDN Systems. **30**, 1-7 (1998) 291-300

7. Brusilovsky, P. and Rizzo, R.: Using maps and landmarks for navigation between closed and open corpus hyperspace in Web-based education. The New Review of Hypermedia and Multimedia **9** (2002) 59-82

8. Brusilovsky, P. and Schwarz, E.: Concept-based navigation in educational hypermedia and its implementation on WWW. In: Müldner, T. and Reeves, T. C. (eds.) Proc. of ED-MEDIA/ED-TELECOM'97 - World Conference on Educational Multimedia/Hypermedia and World Conference on Educational Telecommunications, Calgary, Canada, AACE (1997) 112-117

9. Brusilovsky, P., Schwarz, E., and Weber, G.: ELM-ART: An intelligent tutoring system on World Wide Web. In: Frasson, C., Gauthier, G. and Lesgold, A. (eds.) Intelligent Tutoring Systems. Lecture Notes in Computer Science, Vol. 1086. Springer Verlag, Berlin (1996) 261-269

10. Brusilovsky, P., Schwarz, E., and Weber, G.: Electronic textbooks on WWW: from static hypertext to interactivity and adaptivity. In: Khan, B. H. (ed.) Web Based Instruction. Educational Technology Publications, Englewood Cliffs, New Jersey (1997) 255-261

11. Carmona, C., Bueno, D., Guzman, E., and Conejo, R.: SIGUE: Making Web Courses Adaptive. In: De Bra, P., Brusilovsky, P. and Conejo, R. (eds.) Proc. of Second International Conference on Adaptive Hypermedia and Adaptive Web-Based Systems (AH'2002) Proceedings, Málaga, Spain (2002) 376-379

12. De Bra, P. M. E.: Teaching Hypertext and Hypermedia through the Web. Journal of Universal Computer Science **2**, 12 (1996) 797-804, available online at http://www.iicm.edu/jucs_2_12/teaching_hypertext_and_hypermedia

13. de La Passardiere, B. and Dufresne, A.: Adaptive navigational tools for educational hypermedia. In: Tomek, I. (ed.) Computer Assisted Learning. Springer-Verlag, Berlin (1992) 555-567

14. Dieberger, A.: Supporting social navigation on the World Wide Web. International Journal of Human-Computer Interaction **46** (1997) 805-825

15. Dieberger, A., Dourish, P., Höök, K., Resnick, P., and Wexelblat, A.: Social Navigation: Techniques for Building More Usable Systems. interactions **7**, 6 (2000) 36-45

16. Dron, J., Boyne, C., and Mitchell, R.: Footpaths in the Stuff Swamp. In: Fowler, W. and Hasebrook, J. (eds.) Proc. of WebNet'2001, World Conference of the WWW and Internet, Orlando, FL, AACE (2001) 323-328

17. Henze, N. and Nejdl, W.: Extendible adaptive hypermedia courseware: Integrating different courses and Web material. In: Brusilovsky, P., Stock, O. and Strapparava, C. (eds.) Adaptive Hypermedia and Adaptive Web-Based Systems. Lecture Notes in Computer Science, Springer-Verlag, Berlin (2000) 109-120

18. Henze, N. and Nejdl, W.: Adaptation in open corpus hypermedia. International Journal of Artificial Intelligence in Education **12**, 4 (2001) 325-350, available online at http://cbl.leeds.ac.uk/ijaied/abstracts/Vol_12/henze.html

19. Kurhila, J., Miettinen, M., Nokelainen, P., and Tirri, H.: EDUCO - A collaborative learning environment based on social navigation. In: De Bra, P., Brusilovsky, P. and Conejo, R. (eds.) Proc. of Second International Conference on Adaptive Hypermedia and Adaptive Web-Based Systems (AH'2002), Málaga, Spain (2002) 242-252

20. Mitsuhara, H., Ochi, Y., and Yano, Y.: Open-Ended Adaptive System for Facilitating Knowledge Construction in Web-Based Exploratory Learning. In: De Bra, P., Brusilovsky, P. and Conejo, R. (eds.) Proc. of Second International Conference on Adaptive Hypermedia and Adaptive Web-Based Systems (AH'2002), Málaga, Spain (2002) 547-550

21. Wexelblat, A. and Mayes, P.: Footprints: History-rich tools for information foraging. In: Proc. of ACM Conference on Human-Computer Interaction (CHI'99), Pittsburgh, PA (1999) 270-277

PROS: A Personalized Ranking Platform
for Web Search

Paul-Alexandru Chirita, Daniel Olmedilla, and Wolfgang Nejdl

L3S and University of Hannover
Deutscher Pavillon Expo Plaza 1
30539 Hannover, Germany
{chirita,olmedilla,nejdl}@learninglab.de

Abstract. Current search engines rely on centralized page ranking algorithms which compute page rank values as single (global) values for each Web page. Recent work on topic-sensitive PageRank [6] and personalized PageRank [8] has explored how to extend PageRank values with personalization aspects. To achieve personalization, these algorithms need specific input: [8] for example needs a set of personalized hub pages with high PageRank to drive the computation. In this paper we show how to automate this hub selection process and build upon the latter algorithm to implement a platform for personalized ranking. We start from the set of bookmarks collected by a user and extend it to contain a set of hubs with high PageRank *related* to them. To get additional input about the user, we implemented a proxy server which tracks and analyzes user's surfing behavior and outputs a set of pages preferred by the user. This set is then enriched using our HubFinder algorithm, which finds related pages, and used as extended input for the [8] algorithm. All algorithms are integrated into a prototype of a personalized Web search system, for which we present a first evaluation.

1 Introduction

Using the link structure of the World Wide Web to rank pages in search engines has been investigated heavily in recent years. The success of the Google Search Engine [5, 3] has inspired much of this work, but has lead also to the realization that further improvements are needed. The amount and diversity of Web pages (Google now indicates about 4.3 billion pages) lead researchers to explore faster and more personalized page ranking algorithms, in order to address the fact that some topics are covered by only a few thousand pages and some are covered by millions. For many topics, the existing PageRank algorithm is not sufficient to filter the results of a search engine query. Take for example the well-known query with the word "Java" which should return top results for either the programming language or the island in the Pacific: Google definitively prefers the programming language because there are many more important pages on it than on the island. Moreover, most of the existing search engines focus only on answering user queries, although personalization will be more and more important as the amount of information available in the Web increases. Recently, several approaches to solve such problems have been investigated, building upon content analysis or on algorithms which build page ranks personalized for users or classes of users. The most ambitious investigation so far for personalized ranking has been [8], which we have used as starting point for our work.

W. Nejdl and P. De Bra (Eds.): AH 2004, LNCS 3137, pp. 34–43, 2004.

This paper describes the design and implementation of *PROS*, a personalized ranking platform which uses the algorithm presented in [8] (called the *"PPR algorithm"* – Personalized PageRank – hereafter) plus new algorithms for automated input generation to drive and optimize this algorithm. Our platform is based on HubFinder, an algorithm we developed to find related pages (or hubs, depending on the user) and on a proxy server meant to (temporarily) capture user's surfing behavior. Hubs in this context are Web pages pointing to many other important pages (i. e. with a high rank). Their counterpart are authorities, which are high quality pages pointed by many hubs.

In the original [8] paper, PPR user profiles, used as input for building personalized ranks, are gained by presenting users a set of pages/hubs with high PageRank (as computed using [14]) from which they can choose a set of preferred pages. The disadvantage of this procedure is that this operation takes time and might often be superfluous as most Internet users have some bookmarks of their own already, which could be used to derive their user profile. We therefore wanted to build such a preference set *automatically*, using user's bookmarks and/or most surfed pages (i. e. pages read for a longer period of time, or voted for by a user). This resulting set can then be extended using an algorithm which finds high quality related pages.

The contributions of this paper are: (1) a platform which automates the computation of personalized ranks by generating more comprehensive input data with less user effort, and which consists of two modules: one based on user's bookmarks and the other based on the output of a specialized proxy server which computes the pages most likely to be considered interesting by the user; (2) both modules use HubFinder – a fast and flexible algorithm for finding related pages using the link structure of the World Wide Web, and HubRank – a modified PageRank algorithm which combines the authority value with the hub value of Web pages, in order to further extend these sets of Web pages into the input data needed by the PPR algorithm; and (3) first experimental results from integrating PROS into a personalized Web search system.

We will start by covering the algorithms related to or directly used as background of our research in section 2. Section 3 discusses our PROS platform, which automates the computation of personalized ranks. First experimental results are presented in section 4. Finally, section 5 describes other related Web search systems, and section 6 concludes with discussion of further work.

2 Background

2.1 Web Graph

In the paper we will use a notation similar to [8]. $G = (V, E)$ represents the *Web graph*, where V is the set of all Web pages and E is the set of directed edges $< p, q >$. E contains an edge $< p, q >$ iff a page p links to page q. $I(p)$ denotes the set of in-neighbors (pages pointing to p) and $O(p)$ the set of out-neighbors (pages pointed to by p). For each in-neighbor we use $I_i(p)$ $(1 \leq i \leq |I(p|)$, the same applies to each out-neighbor. We refer $v(p)$ to denote the *p-th* component of **v**. We will typeset vectors in boldface and scalars (e. g., $v(p)$) in normal font.

Let A be the adjacency matrix corresponding to the Web graph G with $A_{ij} = \frac{1}{|O(j)|}$ if page j links to page i and $A_{ij} = 0$ otherwise.

2.2   PageRank

PageRank is an algorithm for computing a Web page score based on the graph inferred from the link structure of the Web. The motivating idea for PageRank is that pages with many backlinks are more important than pages with only a few backlinks. As this simple definition would allow a malicious user to easily increase the "importance" of his page simply by creating lots of pages pointing to it, the PageRank algorithm uses the following recursive description: "a page has high rank if the sum of the ranks of its backlinks is high". Stated another way, the vector **PR** of page ranks is the eigenvector of A corresponding to its dominant eigenvalue.

Given a Web page p, the PageRank formula is:

$$PR(p) = (1 - c) \sum_{q \in O_p} \frac{PR(q)}{\|O(q)\|} + cE(p) \tag{1}$$

The dumping factor $c < 1$ (usually 0.15) is necessary to guarantee convergence (A is not irreducible, i. e. G is not strongly connected) and to limit the effect of rank sinks [2]. Intuitively, a random surfer will follow an outgoing link from the current page with probability $(1 - c)$ and will get bored and select a different page with probability c.

2.3   Personalized Page Ranking

PageRank. Initial steps towards personalized page ranking are already described by [14] who proposed a slight modification of the PageRank algorithm to redirect the random surfer towards preferred pages using the **E** vector. Several distributions for this vector have been proposed since.

Topic-Sensitive PageRank. [6] builds a topic-oriented PageRank, starting by computing off-line a set of 16 PageRank vectors based on the 16 main topics of the Open Directory Project [13]. Then, the similarity between a user query and each of these topics is computed, and the 16 vectors are combined using appropriate weights.

Personalized PageRank. *Description.* As the most recent investigation, [8] uses a new approach: it focuses on user profiles. One Personalized PageRank Vector (PPV) is computed for each user. The personalization aspect of this algorithm stems from a *set of hubs* (H), each user having to select her *preferred pages* from it. PPVs can be expressed as a linear combination of basis vectors (PPVs for preference vectors with a single non-zero entry corresponding to each of the pages from P, the preference set), which could be selected from the precomputed basis hub vectors, one for each page from H, the hub set. To avoid the massive storage resources the basis hub vectors would use, they are decomposed into partial vectors (which encode the part unique to each page, computed at run-time) and the hub skeleton (which captures the interrelationships among hub vectors, stored off-line).

Algorithm. In the first part of the paper, the authors present three different algorithms for computing basis vectors: "Basic Dynamic Programming", "Selective Expansion" and "Repeated Squaring". In the second part, specializations of these algorithms are combined into a general algorithm for computing PPVs, as depicted below:

1. Compute one partial vector for each page in H using a specialization of the Selective Expansion algorithm.
2. Compute the hubs skeleton using a specialization of the Repeated Squaring algorithm and taking the intermediate results from step 1 as input.
3. Compute the PPV using the computed partial vectors and hubs skeleton, and the preference vector.

For an in-depth view of this process, we refer the reader to [8].

3   PROS: A Personalized Ranking Platform

Introduction. As explained before, personalized rankings can improve current Web search systems by adapting results to user preferences. The algorithm presented in [8] is the most recent step in this direction. An issue left open in [8] is how a set of highly rated hubs, needed as input for the adaptation process, is selected by the user. The personalization (and therefore success) relies on the user's ability to choose such high quality hubs which match her preferences.

In this section, we describe how to exploit information collected from the user to derive the highly rated hubs that represent the user profile. The computation is performed automatically based on the following *input*:

- *Most surfed pages.* Pages visited by the user are tracked using a specialized proxy we implemented. The proxy records information about the duration the user looked at a page and how frequently she returned to it.
- *User's bookmarks.* Additionally, we use the user's bookmarks as an indication for user preferences. Currently, bookmarks are directly provided by the user, but this interaction could also be automated (e. g. using a browser plugin).

Architecture. The PROS platform consists of two main modules, which use the two input sets described above. They use HubFinder and HubRank, two algorithms we developed for finding related pages using the Web link structure and for ranking Web pages, respectively (presented briefly later in this section and in more detail in [4]).

The first module consists of applying the following operations:
1. Get bookmarks from the user.
2. Add bookmarks to the *preference set*.
3. Apply HubFinder, using user's bookmarks as input and HubRank scores as trimming criterion. HubRank is the best criterion in this situation, because the PPR algorithm needs hubs with high PageRank as input and HubRank has been designed as a biasing of PageRank towards hubs, as discussed later in this section.
4. Add the preference set and the output from the previous step to the *hub set*.

The second module is based on using a proxy server for a limited period of time in order to capture user's "surfing behavior". Its modus operandi is described below:
1. The user surfs the Web using a given proxy. The proxy will output the pages examined by the user for a certain period of time (there must be both a lower threshold and an upper one to avoid the situation when the user leaves the browser open for a long period of time without using it), as well as those most frequently revisited. The more time it is used, the better ranking accuracy will be aquired.

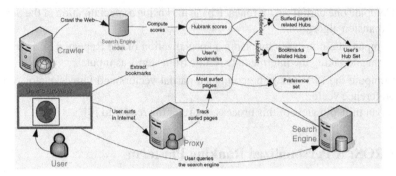

Fig. 1. Personalized Ranking Platform

2. Add the user's most surfed pages (as recorded by the proxy) to the *preference set*.
3. Apply HubFinder with HubRank as criterion and a small radius and number of output pages. We want the pages related to user's bookmarks to be more important than the pages related to his/her most surfed ones and using a smaller radius is a way to achieve this.
4. Add user's most surfed pages, as well as the pages related to them to the *hub set*.

Finally, the PPR algorithm is executed using the newly computed preference and hub sets. The complete process is depicted in Fig. 1.

HubFinder is an algorithm for finding hubs, related to an initial base set of Web pages. We define *related* similarly to [7], i. e. using only link information as input. Two pages are related if one is accessible from the other via the link structure of the Web graph (following either in-going or out-going links). We should also add that the distance (the number of links followed) between such two pages is usually less than 6 (according to our experiments, in cases where the distance is bigger the link information becomes insufficient to say that pages are similar in context with a high enough probability), and thus the related hubs are in the vicinity of the starting page. The maximum distance (noted σ and also called radius) is a parameter for HubFinder.

In order to get a good set of related pages we took into account the following aspects: the set has to be small, rich in relevant pages and it should contain many of the strongest authorities. [10] extracts the top results of a query sent to a search engine and builds a focused sub-graph of the WWW around them. It then extends this base set by adding all pages pointed to and at most d pages pointing to each page from it. This operation is called *Kleinberg extension*. The author extends the initial set only once, but he focused on computing Hub and Authority scores, whereas we were focusing on finding related pages or hubs. Therefore we iteratively apply the Kleinberg extension several times on the resulting set of each previous iteration in order to obtain more pages and thus more representative results. As this scenario leads to very big output sets (up to 500,000 pages), trimming is necessary after each intermediate step. The pseudo-code of the resulted HubFinder algorithm is as follows:

Let Γ be the Base Set of pages whose related hubs we are looking for
$\Gamma \leftarrow$ Apply the Kleinberg Extension on Γ once

$\Gamma' \leftarrow \Gamma$
For $i = 1$ to σ do:
    $\Gamma'' \leftarrow$ Apply the Kleinberg Extension on Γ' once
    Trim Γ'' to contain only *interesting* pages, *not* contained in Γ
    $\Gamma \leftarrow \Gamma + \Gamma''$
    $\Gamma' \leftarrow \Gamma''$
End For
Trim Γ to contain as many interesting pages as desired
Return Γ

Two aspects have to be considered: how many pages should we keep after each iteration and which are the *interesting pages*? Regarding the former one, we keep one percent of the current set size, whereas the best criterion tackling the latter issue are global rank scores (e. g. as computed with PageRank or a similar algorithm). [4] contains an in-depth discussion of the algorithm, a formula on the exact number of pages to keep, as well as a proposed extension based on text analysis.

HubRank. We started from the idea that a page pointing to a good hub is a candidate for having a high hub rank as well. Often we encounter pages (perhaps good authorities) with only a few out-going links, but towards very important hubs. We consider such pages more important than the hubs themselves, because while a hub can cover lots of topics, such a page will usually contain information about the content addressed by the hubs it is pointing to, about the value of their content (e. g. author opinions), etc.

To compute these hub scores, we modified the PageRank personalization vector to consider the out-degree of the pages. Intuitively, the random surfer prefers pages with a big out-degree when it gets bored. This way, the global importance of the pages will play an important role in defining general scores, as the random surfer will follow the out-going links with a higher probability than the random ones, and on the other hand, the out-degree of pages will always be considered. In PageRank, the vector $\mathbf{E}$ is a uniform distribution with $\frac{1}{NP}$ in each entry (where NP is the total number of pages). We set the value of each entry i of $\mathbf{E}$ to $E_i = |O(i)| \frac{NP}{|O|}$ where $|O|$ is the summation of the out-going links over the whole Web graph. As PageRank focuses on authorities in the first part of the formula, we focused on hubs in the second part.

Prototype. Current Web search systems apply only basic personalization techniques (e. g. presenting a user interface in Spanish if the access is from a Spanish IP address). However, this refers only to how the search engine interacts with the user, but it uses the same ranking process no matter who submits the query. To exemplify this problem, let us imagine that a user searches using the keyword "architecture". Output topics may vary from computer architecture to building architecture or even something else. By extracting user's interests from her bookmarks (if she likes building architecture she would have some bookmarks on it) and from her most visited pages (she would check buiding architecture pages often), we can create a personalized view of the global ranks, and thus provide tailored output for each user. A screenshot of our prototype can be seen in Fig. 2. As a comparison, we present the results obtained when ranking URLs with the PageRank algorithm [14] on the left side, and with PROS on the right. Our tester was interested in building architecture. While with PageRank only two output URLs were relevant, all five generated by PROS were worth checking.

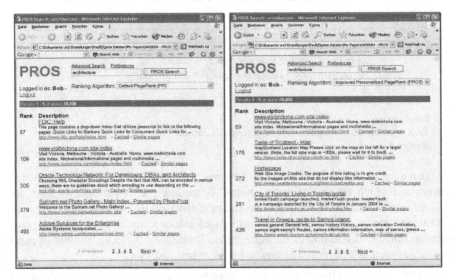

Fig. 2. Prototype of the PROS Web Search System

4   Experiments and Results

Input Data. We performed tests on several small Web crawls (3 to 40 thousand pages) and on two bigger ones, one with one million and one with three million Web pages. The results presented in this paper use the largest set. Furthermore, we ran PPR and PROS using several data sets as input and several users, but selected only the most representative experiments here because of space constraints.

Table 1. Input Data for the PPR algorithm experiments

Algorithm	Preference Set	Hub Set
PPR	30 user defined bookmarks.	User's bookmarks (30) plus top ranked PageRank pages. Totally about 1200 pages.
PROS	30 user defined bookmarks plus 78 pages selected tracking user's surfing behavior (108 pages in total).	The preference set plus its related pages plus top ranked PageRank pages. Totally about 1700 pages.

Our first experiment follows all guidelines of the original paper. It has 30 user bookmarks as preference set and a hub set mixing user's bookmarks with top PageRank documents. The second experiment uses the input we obtained with our ranking platform. A tester surfed the Web for about two weeks using our proxy and we selected 78 pages as her "fingerprint". These were merged with her 30 bookmarks (same as in the first experiment) into the *preference set*. Then, we applied HubFinder with HubRank as criterion on both the set of bookmarks and the set of most surfed pages, obtaining about 900 pages from the former one and about 400 from the latter one (we used a radius of 5 for the bookmarks and a radius of 2 for the most surfed pages). To these 1300 pages some top PageRank pages were added and the resulting set was used as *hub set*. A description of the input data used can be found in table 1. Our tester was an architect, having traveling and software as other hobbies, and sports as a secondary interest. Her bookmarks were distributed accordingly: 15 on architecture, 7 on traveling, 6 on software and 2 on sports.

Results. To analyze the resulting ranks, we selected some general keywords (see table 2) and performed Web searches, exactly as in a search engine. Results were sorted with respect to their ranks, without considering term frequency of keywords in output documents. The ranking algorithms used were PageRank, PPR, and PROS. Although the first one does not involve any personalization, we decided to implement it too, as it is the most popular algorithm and useful as background for our evaluation.

Table 2. Relevancy value for different search keywords and different algorithms

Query Keywords	PageRank			PPR			PROS		
	Rel.	Par. Rel.	Irrel.	Rel.	Par. Rel.	Irrel.	Rel.	Par. Rel.	Irrel.
architecture	5	3	2	3	7	0	8	2	0
building	3	2	5	2	3	5	4	1	5
Paris	6	0	4	2	3	5	6	2	2
park	6	0	4	8	0	2	10	0	0
surf	3	0	7	4	2	4	7	2	1
Total	23	5	22	19	15	16	35	7	8

The top 10 URLs obtained by ranking the search results with each algorithm were classified into the following categories: (a) Relevant (denoted by "Rel." in table 2) if the URL was on one of the four topics of interest of our tester; (b) Partially Relevant (noted as "Par.Rel.") if it was on a topic related to one of the above-mentioned four ones (e. g. an URL on hardware architectures was considered partially related to computer software); or (c) Irrelevant ("Irrel." in table 2) if it was not in any of the previous categories. A detailed list with all the output URLs can be found in [15].

Discussion. The most important issue is that, as expected, the original PageRank algorithm provides top results on several topics, even though the searcher is almost always interested in only a specific one. This behavior is understandable, as the algorithm cannot disambiguate results based on user preferences.

The PPR algorithm performs only slightly better in this experiment (the total number of possibly relevant URLs is 34, whereas for PageRank it is 28), mostly because the input sets were too sparse and qualitatively not very good. This might be improved by adding additional top PageRank pages to the preference set, but we did not use this approach, as it would have definitely damaged the personalization aspect (remember that top PageRank pages can be on any topic).

Finally, we see significant improvements when using PROS. The number of relevant pages is much higher than for the other two algorithms. However, we still got some bad output URLs (e. g. for the search keyword "building"). We think this happened because of the general profile of our tester. Other tests performed with more focused testers (i. e. with a profile on exclusively one topic, such as "architecture") provided even better results, but we consider the experiment presented in this paper to be the closest to a real-life situation.

As we know from [8], pages from the preference set may have different importance. In our tests, all pages had the same weight, that is $\frac{1}{|PS|}$, where PS is the preference set. Let us denote by B the set of bookmarks and S the set of user's most surfed pages. In this case, we can give for example $\frac{2}{3*|B|}$ importance to bookmarks and $\frac{1}{3*|S|}$ to user's most surfed pages. We think this approach (or a more complex one which automatically gives an importance value to each of the most surfed pages, depending on the amount of surfing time or revisits) would provide even more accurate ranks. Further experiments are needed to define the correct biasing of these pages.

Generally, our experiments allow us to conclude that PROS increases the ranks of pages similar to user's bookmarks, as well as those that are most likely to be considered interesting by the user (and thus the granularity of relevant results when performing a Web search). If the tester uses the proxy server for longer periods, the accuracy of the latter set is proportionately bigger (i. e. the size of the "most surfed pages" set is bigger, and therefore the rankings are more accurate).

5   Other Web Search Systems

Research on Web searching usually focused on algorithms, as they comprise the most important part of such an engine. However, these algorithms are not always straightforward to integrate into a search engine and attention must also be paid to the user - search engine interaction. [12] for example aims at satisfying all types of users (either experienced, or novice) by translating the search goal into good query keywords. Although search goals must be manually disambigued (e. g. solve a problem, find people who, etc.), the system allows users to type queries in natural language and produces the search keywords automatically using an inference engine.

[11] is somehow similar to PROS in the sense that user profiles are built automatically and Web pages are recommended to users based on personalization approaches. However, its contributions are orthogonal to ours: surfers are guided towards relevant pages while they are browsing judging on the pages they have previously visited, whereas we focus on integrating such personalization into page ranks used by a search engine. [16] presents a new system for computing Web page ranks in a distributed fashion, which could be nicely extended by our PROS approach.

Another interesting approach is described in [1], which adds personalization to the JobFinder [9] search engine. It uses profile jobs and Information Retrieval operators to classify retrieved jobs as relevant or irrelevant.

6   Conclusions and Further Work

We presented the design and implementation of a personal ranking platform (PROS), providing personalized ranking of Web pages based on user preferencees, while automating the input generation process for the PPR algorithm [8]. To achieve this, we use user bookmarks as well as a record about the user's surfing behavior (gained with a proxy), which are then extended using our new HubFinder algorithm with HubRank scores as trimming criterion. HubRank score is based on PageRank but additionally takes hub quality of pages into account.

We are currently extending our tests towards more users and different environments in order to get in depth evaluations of our platform. Furthermore, we are investigating the additional inclusion of collaborative filtering algorithms to PROS, which would allow us to also use personalize ranking based on groups of similar users instead of single users, to further increase the input set available for the personalization algorithm.

References

1. K. Bradley, R. Rafter, and B. Smyth. Case-based user profiling for content personalization. In *Proceedings of the International Conference on Adaptive Hypermedia and Adaptive Web-Based Systems*, pages 133–143. Springer-Verlag, 2000.
2. Sergey Brin, Rajeev Motwani, Lawrence Page, and Terry Winograd. What can you do with a web in your pocket? *Data Engineering Bulletin*, 21(2):37–47, 1998.
3. Sergey Brin and Lawrence Page. The anatomy of a large-scale hypertextual Web search engine. *Computer Networks and ISDN Systems*, 30(1–7):107–117, 1998.
4. Paul-Alexandru Chirita, Daniel Olmedilla, and Wolfgang Nejdl. Pros: A personalized ranking platform for web search. Technical report, L3S and University of Hannover, Feb 2004.
5. Google search engine. http://www.google.com.
6. T. Haveliwala. Topic-sensitive pagerank. In *In Proceedings of the Eleventh International World Wide Web Conference, Honolulu, Hawaii*, May 2002.
7. G. Jeh and J. Widom. Simrank: A measure of structural-context similarity. In *Proceedings of the 8th ACM International Conference on Knowledge Discovery and Data Mining*, 2002.
8. G. Jeh and J. Widom. Scaling personalized web search. In *Proceedings of the 12th International World Wide Web Conference*, 2003.
9. Jobfinder search engine. http://www.jobfinder.ie.
10. Jon M. Kleinberg. Authoritative sources in a hyperlinked environment. *Journal of the ACM*, 46(5):604–632, 1999.
11. Nicholas Kushmerick, James McKee, and Fergus Toolan. Towards zero-input personalization: Referrer-based page prediction. In *Proceedings of the International Conference on Adaptive Hypermedia and Adaptive Web-Based Systems*, pages 133–143, 2000.
12. Hugo Liu, Henry Lieberman, and Ted Selker. Goose: A goal-oriented search engine with commonsense. In *Proceedings of the Second International Conference on Adaptive Hypermedia and Adaptive Web-Based Systems*, pages 253–263. Springer-Verlag, 2002.
13. Open directory project. http://dmoz.org/.
14. Lawrence Page, Sergey Brin, Rajeev Motwani, and Terry Winograd. The pagerank citation ranking: Bringing order to the web. Technical report, Stanford University, 1998.
15. Pros project home page. http://www.learninglab.de/~chirita/pros/pros.html.
16. Jie Wu. Towards a decentralized search architecture for the web and p2p systems. In *Proceedings of the Adaptive Hypermedia and Adaptive Web-Based Systems Workshop held at the HyperText03 Conference*, 2003.

A P2P Distributed Adaptive Directory

Gennaro Cordasco, Vittorio Scarano, and Cristiano Vitolo

ISISlab–Dipartimento di Informatica ed Applicazioni "R.M. Capocelli"
Università di Salerno, 84081 Baronissi (SA), Italy
{cordasco,vitsca}@dia.unisa.it cvitolo@n3xt.it

Abstract. We describe a P2P system that offers a distributed, cooperative and adaptive environment for bookmark sharing. DAD offers an adaptive environment since it provides suggestions about the navigation based on (*a*) the bookmarks, (*b*) the feedback implicitly provided by users and (*c*) the structure of the Web. Our system is fully scalable because of its peer-to-peer architecture and provides, also, an infrastructure to build easily P2P overlay networks.

1 Introduction

The navigation within the World Wide Web is usually performed in isolation and, in a certain way, it is surprising that the World Wide Web is successful despite the fact that it does not fully resemble everyday life and activity. In fact, our daily actions are continuously dictated and influenced by others as well as, of course, our actions influence others' choices. Our society relies on such background activities with continuous feedback that induce a sense of community that makes everybody conscious of everybody's behavior.

This dimension is hard to find on the World Wide Web. The popularity of Blogs as well as the decades-old success of newsgroups strengthen the feeling that the WWW is missing an important part of our standard interaction patterns, i. e., cooperation.

Given the copiousness of resources on the Web, information-finding would greatly benefit by the collaboration since others can draw our attention to unexplored (or partially explored) parts of the gigantic amount of resources available. As well as people usually rely on the experiences and behavior of others to help make choices and find desired information. Just watching customers moving in a store, or observing how the visitors of a museum gather together suggest which item/piece is more popular and deserves a visit.

Bookmarks are, nowadays, an important aid to navigation since they represent an easy way to reduce the cognitive load of managing and typing URLs. All the browsers have always provided, since the very beginning of the WWW, friendly ways of managing bookmarks. In this paper we deal with the problem of enriching this supportive framework for bookmarks (as provided by the browsers) by adding collaboration and (group) adaptation with a P2P system.

In this paper we present DAD, a distributed adaptive directory for cooperative bookmarks management. DAD provides a Peer to Peer environment that allows to share bookmarks with all the users connected. Based on the bookmarks, the system can evaluate suggestions to be recommended and inserted into the system. Users can provide

W. Nejdl and P. De Bra (Eds.): AH 2004, LNCS 3137, pp. 44–54, 2004.

feedback to the system so that interesting bookmarks rank higher as well as bookmarks suggested by users whose bookmarks are well appraised by the group (i. e., that got a high score).

DAD offers users the same environment they are accustomed to, since our system can be used only to share bookmarks with others and the navigation occurs with user preferred browser. Nevertheless, our system offers a good degree of interoperability with Microsoft Internet Explorer bookmarks, in spite of being an external applications developed in 100% pure Java. DAD lets users organize the shared bookmarks in a limited-size version of an ontology that is distributed by Open Directory Project (http://www.dmoz.org/).

DAD is a Peer to Peer system (P2P), i. e., a distributed system where each node plays the same role and shares the same responsibility and all the communication is potentially symmetric. P2P characteristics, such as scalability and fault tolerance, make it a popular architecture for Internet applications (see, for example, Napster, Gnutella and Kazaa).

In the next section we refer to some related work; then, in Sect. 3 we describe the architecture of our system and briefly sketch the P2P infrastructure. Then we show the main characteristics of DAD. We describe some evaluation tests that were recently conducted in Sect. 4 and conclude the paper with Sect. 5 where we give some final remarks and the description of further work.

2   Related Work

Since our investigations lie at the crossing of two different areas, we describe here some of the related work in each of the following topics: Bookmarks sharing and Cooperative systems on the Web.

Bookmark sharing systems. Opencola (http://wwww.opencola.com/) is a commercial system that allows to share bookmarks between any web user. The architecture is based on a client component (on user machine) and on a server (that offers communication among clients and additional services). Each client offers to the user the possibility to search bookmarks by keyword, forwarding the search both to other clients and to a meta search engine (based on several other popular search engines).

Opencola main feature certainly consists in the way each user can provide feedback on the search results. In fact, each user can mark as interesting some of the bookmarks that are returned by the system. In this way, returned bookmarks are rearranged based on the similarity with the marked bookmarks. Sharing bookmarks can be configured by the user but Opencola does not use a single ontology for all the clients (which makes difficult for the categorization once the bookmark is found). Nevertheless, it allows to view the classification chosen by the "owners" of the bookmark so that a certain amount of suggestion on the categorization is provided.

WideSource (http://widesource.com/) is a freeware system. Unlike Opencola, Widesource uses a base ontology (i. e., common for all the clients) where to categorize bookmarks. Users can add folders to the lower levels of the tree (initially set to 2). WideSource places a certain overhead on the users since it forces the users to place all the bookmarks to be shared in a single folder (loosing information on personal categorization) and, successively, into the system ontology. Then, the bookmarks are available for public searches. The same overhead on re-categorization is necessary when importing the bookmark.

Other systems are BISAgent [8], CoWing (Collaborative Web IndexiNG) [9], Baboo (http://www.baboo.com/), Siteseer [17] and WebTagger [10].

Recommendation systems. Recommendation systems are a branch of social navigation systems [6, 14, 16]. A recommendation system suggests resources to users based on their preferences, similarities, and consumer and product attributes (e. g., user skills preferences, titles, authors, brands). The classical application of recommendation system is in on-line stores.

Social navigation in information space uses information about other people's behavior and suggestions to decide what to suggest to users in similar situations. The goal is to take advantage of the navigation of others who have similar tastes or interests.

Among the most popular systems, we name GroupLens [12], Fab [2] and Plastic (http://www.plastic.com/).

Group Adaptive System (GAS) [3] is a collaborative and adaptive environment for web users. It provides information that adapts to web users based on their navigation and their interests. GAS enables people in a group to perform asynchronous collaborative navigation on the web: in particular, people can interact and communicate with each other, be aware of group activity using footprints left on the pages, judge and comment viewed pages. The systems puts together pages discovered by group members and suggestions by CLEVER-based model [4] in order to provide participants with recommendations (new resources) based on group interest.

WebMemex [13] provides recommended information based on the captured history of navigation from a list of people well-known to the users. It uses Latent Semantic Indexing to identify similarities between HTML pages in order to suggests links.

In [7] the authors use a RDF-based P2P infrastructure called Edutella [15] (based on JXTA(http://www.jxta.org)) to share educational material (data and metadata) with the goal of implementing personalized access to distributed learning materials.

3   Adaptivity and Cooperation in DAD

Our system is structured on three separated layers (see Fig. 1 Left): on the bottom we have an overlay network named CHILD (CHord with Identification and Lonely Discovery). We would like to emphasize that the infrastructure (in Java) provided by CHILD[1] can be used as a base to develop a distributed hash table(DHT) for any pure P2P system.

The middle layer, named DAD (Distributed Adaptive Directory), exploits the bottom level to obtain information about bookmarks and users, providing a collaborative and adaptive system to manage bookmarks. Finally the top layer, named MOM (Multipurpose Ontology Manager), realizes the graphical user interface that represents a

---

[1] The Java package is freely available under the GNU public license at the project home page
http://isis.dia.unisa.it/projects/DAD.

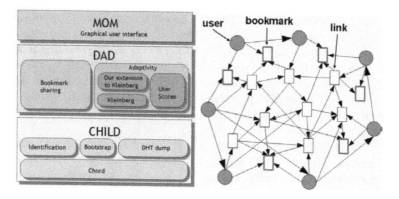

Fig. 1. (Left) The diagram of the architecture of our system. (Right) The graph used as starting set in our modified version of Kleinberg algorithm. Here pages are rectangles while users are circles.

typical DAD-peer and allow to use all the functionalities of our system. It also provides a smooth interaction with the top most used browser (MS Internet Explorer) but can be used with any other browser.

We describe the functionalities and the structure of the middle and top layer of our architecture. The architecture of the bottom layer is described in [5]. As pictorially described by the architecture of the system in Fig. 1 (Left), the functionalities of the middle layer are divided in two parts: the component that is in charge of sharing the bookmarks and the component that offers the adaptation by suggesting bookmarks and collecting feedback and scores for bookmarks and users.

3.1 Bookmarks Sharing

Bookmarks represent an important aid to navigation since they provide a way to place landmarks on the huge information space composed of the Web. As mentioned in the introduction, it is extremely helpful to share information about the navigation in order to support and guide the navigation of users. This component is in charge of providing the sharing and organization of bookmarks.

Several different kind of representation are used for sharing bookmarks. One of the main differences of the bookmark sharing systems described in Sect. 2 is whether the system archives the bookmarks in a fixed ontology (such as Widesource) or asks users to build their own classification (such as Opencola).

Our architecture uses an intermediate approach: while we recognize the importance of providing a fixed infrastructure for the shared bookmarks we also let the users organize their own bookmarks as they prefer.

Bookmarks organization is typically a crucial key to efficiently place landmarks on the information space. Since research shows that a high percentage of users usually does not organize at all the bookmarks (or organize them poorly) [1] we believe that leaving the users create their own ontology for sharing bookmarks can be confusing. The compromise proposed here allows users to create their own organization (even none, if that is the choice) for local (*private*) bookmarks but share them (or importing them) with a fixed ontology (*public* bookmarks).

As base ontology we choose a shortened version (i. e., only the first four levels) ontology of the Open Directory Project DMOZ (http://www.dmoz.org/) stored by using XML Bookmark Exchange Language (XBEL) [18]. The limitation in size of the original version of the ontology provided by DMOZ is due to the size: since it is distributed with the application, the complete version was too large (almost 300 Mbytes) to ensure easy downloading of our software.

Of course, specialized versions of the ontology can be used for specialized groups: one can think to distribute DAD for Java programmers, DAD for movie fans, etc. with the appropriate (and more detailed) ontology. In fact, some indications in this directions come from the results of preliminary tests: homogeneous communities feel disoriented by an ontology that is perceived as uselessly large. As a consequence, we report experiments with an additional specific community-oriented category and the comments are much better in terms of cooperation and versatility.

Bookmarks are stored in the DHT that is acting like a distributed filesystem. When a user places a bookmark in the ontology (i. e., makes it shared with the system) his/her peer is in charge of storing the bookmark for the whole system. When a user needs to look into a category in the ontology (an operation called *expansion*) his/her peer needs to know all the peers that are storing bookmarks for the category (called *interest group*).

When an expansion of a folder is asked, the peer has to contact all the peers that contain at least a bookmark in the folder. This set of peers is called the *interest group* for the category. The DHT (offered by the bottom layer CHILD) stores information about each interest group. Each category of the ontology is associated with an ID, the peer interested in the bookmarks of a category, first, accesses the DHT to get the members of the associated interest group and, successively, asks each member the bookmarks that it contributed to the category. Of course, the DHT holds information about all the members, whether present or not; the bookmarks that are effectively retrieved by the successive operation depend on the members of the interest group that are currently in the system. This means that, in general, one cannot be sure that an interesting bookmark that is found once will be there later on, since the member that holds it may not be logged anymore. As a consequence, when something interesting is found, a user should copy it among his/her own private bookmarks. This characteristic of the system is used to measure relative similarity among users (see next subsection).

Joining/leaving an interest group is totally transparent to the user and is managed by the operations of insertion/deletion of bookmarks into the ontology.

3.2 Adaptivity

Our system is adaptive since utilizes user bookmarks as well as user feedback and the underlying structure of the web to suggest and improve the navigation on the Web of all the users. DAD is also adaptable since the user has an explicit control on the rating of the bookmarks and the way they are presented/suggested. When a user places a bookmark in the ontology, the system extracts the links contained in the corresponding page and store the bookmark and the links together in the DHT.

In order to add adaptivity to our system we extended Kleinberg algorithm [11], used in systems like CLEVER [4]. The original algorithm allows to discover authoritative sources of information (authorities and hubs) and is based on the links structure of the Web. Next, we briefly sketch Kleinberg algorithm and motivations and, successively, we show our extensions.

Kleinberg Algorithm. The goal of the algorithm is to assign a score to nodes of a graph (i.e., HTML pages) based on the edges among them (i.e., links among HTML pages). Of course, pages with high scores are signaled as significant. Two related scores are evaluated for each node: *authority* weight and *hub* weight. Initial authority and hub weights are set to 1 for each node. The algorithm requires a starting set S of pages, build a graph $G = (V, E)$ where $V = S \cup \{$pages linked from $S)\}$ and E represent the set of link between the pages on V. Then an iterative algorithm is run on the graph, alternatively evaluating authority and hub weights depending on neighbors' weights.

The algorithm is shown to converge in identifying *good authorities* (nodes recognized as good sources of information) and good *hubs* (nodes recognized as containing good pointers to useful information). The motivating idea is that a link $X \Rightarrow Y$ is meant as "inferring authority from X on Y" and is explicitly chosen (suggested) by X's author that knows both resources.

Our Extension to Kleinberg Model. In our setting, the starting set S consists of the bookmarks that are present (at a given time) in a category of our ontology. Our extension to Kleinberg algorithm consists in adding users to the set of nodes (i.e., bookmarks) therefore modelling the interactions between users and bookmarks. In this way, we add a new type of nodes (i.e. users) and new links (from a user to a page or from a user to another user) on the graph G (see Fig. 1 (Right)).

In fact, the original motivation in Kleinberg work was that a link $X \Rightarrow Y$ on the Web is meant as "inferring authority from X on Y" and is explicitly chosen (suggested) by X's author that knows both resources. We noticed that, if user U_1 and user U_2 access page P_1 and page P_2, (authored, respectively, by A_1 and A_2) and both pages point to a page P_3 (which was not actually visited by either user) the algorithm can "discover" P_3 and propose it as a possibly useful resource to U_1 and U_2 (or to any other similar user). Since this suggestion derives, in a certain way, both from U_1 and U_2 accesses and from A_1 and A_2 choices, it is widely supported by an authoritative chain that begins at users, passes through page authors and identifies a useful resource.

The new kinds of links in graph G have the following meaning:

- *from user U to a page P*: when U is the owner of page P, i.e., U placed P as shared bookmark into the category of the ontology.
- *from user U_1 to user U_2*: when U_1 is showing interest in a bookmark that was inserted in the system by U_2, i.e., when U_1 copies the bookmark inserted by U_2 locally among his/her own private bookmarks.

It should be noticed that there can be multiple owners of a bookmark if different users spontaneously inserted a bookmark in the system. In this case, however, the bookmark is presented only once to users of the system, keeping track, however, of the multiple ownership.

The reader should remember that the design of our system contemplates that a bookmark is available only if its owner is logged. Therefore, if user U finds interesting a bookmark and expects to use it afterward, then U must "copy" it into his/her own bookmarks, to be sure it will be accessible anytime. This action is referred to as "*marking a bookmark*" and makes a bookmark local on the peer. Marking is somewhat "forced" by our architecture so that we can use it to measure the approval and interest of other users' suggestions.

User Score. We define a user score for each category in the ontology, initially set to 0. When user U_1 shows interest in bookmark B (in category C) owned by U_2, then the score of U_2 is increased. Which action is considered to "show interest" in a bookmark? We decided that when user U_1 marks B (i. e. copy it locally) he/she is showing explicit interest in B since he/she wants it to be available even if U_2 is not logged on.

User scores are stored in the DHT as fields of the interest group[2]. For each category, the information about the interest group consist of the list of members, each with his/her score in the category.

For each interest group, we store information about all the members (and their score) as well for each user we store all the scores in the interest groups he/she is a member of. In this way, we efficiently support both the following queries: (*a*) given a category list all the members with their score, (*b*) given a user list all the interest groups he/she belongs to and the relative score. When a user looks into a category, the system can locally obtain the bookmarks (exploiting the DHT) and compute the bookmarks scores.

Adaptability. Each bookmark currently in our system has four scores:

- *authority* and *hub weight*: provided by Kleinberg algorithm;
- *owners' scores*: the scores of the user(s) that inserted the bookmark;
- *occurrences*: the number of users that keeps locally the bookmarks stored.

Notice that the occurrence of a bookmarks represents an additional evaluation of popularity among users (see Fig. 2). Notice also that the number of occurrences can be (and usually is) larger than the number of owners: each time a user marks a bookmark, the number of occurrence increases.

The problem is how to combine all these scores in such a way that the user is presented with a "global" ranking of bookmarks. We believe that the way scores are combined is not only dependent on the nature of topics treated (e. g., professional categories vs. entertainment categories) but is also strongly influenced by personal characteristics, attitude and tastes.

Given the subjectivity of the choice, our system provides an *adaptability* mechanism that allows each user to choose the relevance of each of the scores shown above. By using a control panel user can tune the relative weights of each score to compute a global score for each bookmark in a [1, 10] range.

---

[2] There is a single DHT that, for each ID, stores information on a peer (user), information on a folder (interest group) or both.

3.3   The User Interface

Bookmark Visualization. We show in Fig. 2 the main window of our application. On the left-hand side, the button "System" offers the bookmark sharing. We can insert a bookmark in each folder of the unique ontology either by button "New bookmark" or by the (native) cut-and-paste facilities. By using the button "Internet Explorer" one can import all the bookmarks (Favorites) in IE by specifying the pathname of the directory that stores the Favorites. Folders in the ontology that contain at least a bookmark are presented in boldface.

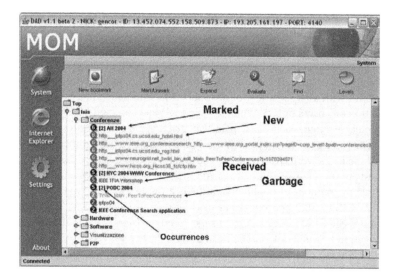

Fig. 2. The user interface (MOM).

A user can browse the hierarchy by asking to *expand* a folder which generates a request to the DHT to get all the bookmarks in the corresponding category. Of course, user can simply navigate by clicking on the bookmark name (user preferred browser can be configured).

When a folder of the hierarchy is shown, bookmarks are shown with different colors (see Fig. 2) in order to help the user in recognizing the status. Moreover, each bookmark is also shown with the number of occurrences (i. e. number of users that copied it locally). The bookmarks can be of four species:

Marked (Black): present locally to the user and that is shared with the users. Without an expansion of the folder only marked bookmarks are shown.

Received (Blue): found on the system (i. e. shared by another user).

New (Red): not inserted by any user but suggested by the system, applying the extended version of Kleinberg algorithm to all the bookmarks in the folder.

Garbage (Gray): ready to be disposed: it was originally marked and has now been unmarked (by using the "Mark/Unmark" button). The bookmark will not be visible anymore after the user logs out. Finally, it is possible (in the configuration) to set a limit to the number of bookmarks that are suggested by the system.

Some Utilities. DAD allows each user to know the owner(s) of every bookmark, about their IDs, nicknames and his/her score. Moreover, our system is particularly well integrated with MS Internet Explorer: DAD keeps synchronized a category in the IE Favorites, with the non-empty folders of the ontology. Synchronization happens both ways: user can place bookmarks in DAD by placing in the category of the IE favorites and viceversa.

4   Preliminary Evaluation

Two rounds of tests were conducted, the first with 12 participants and the second with 21, where 9 participants were in both tests. Both rounds took place for approximately 2 weeks (each), with a large variety of browsers (MS Internet Explorer, Mozilla, Opera, Safari) with many users on MS Windows 2000/XP, and some on Mac OS and Linux.

Before each round, each participant was given a pre-test questionnaire to inquiry on the way of using bookmarks and a brief personalized briefing on configuration and usage. All the users were left free to use the system at work as they preferred.

Pre-test questionnaire results show a wide variety of ways of organizing bookmarks: for example the number of bookmarks in their browser[3] was I: Avg. 188, Std. 350,8; II: Avg. 73.4, Std. 56.7 and the depth of the hierarchy was I: Avg. 2.17, Std. 0.98; II: Avg. 2.18, Std. 0.91). Anyway, the users were consistently using the bookmarks in their navigation habits: bookmarks inserted in the last week was I: Avg. 4.9, Std. 3.4; II: Avg. 5.8, Std. 3.9. Each day they visited bookmarks I: Avg. 6.5, Std. 5; II: Avg. 5.37, Std. 4.74.

The qualitative analysis was performed by a post-test questionnaire was given to ask about how much they found interesting the bookmarks provided by the other users, how much were interesting the bookmarks provided by the system and some questions on the user interface and the integration. The users were asked to indicate the agreement with statements from 1 (completely disagree) to 5 (completely agree). Finally, the subjects were asked for comments.

In the first round the users were given the base ontology (almost 65000 on 4 levels (DMOZ). After the first round, all the users (even the ones that used bookmarks less often) gained new interest in bookmarking resources. While, in general, users did not found particularly interesting the bookmarks of other users (62% 1-2, 30% 3, 8% 4-5), they appreciated much more the bookmarks suggested by the system (15% 1-2, 50% 3, 35% 4-5). Among the comments, the users found that the size of the ontology used was too large and that it took too much to browse the hierarchy and demanded for smaller size and more focused ontology.

Given the suggestions by the user, in the second round of tests we *added* an ad-hoc category that contained a small number of subcategories (10) that were directly related to the activity of the group. Participants were anyway left free to place bookmarks

---

[3] We indicate the I/II round and the value average (Avg) and the Standard deviation (Std).

anyway on the base ontology. The result was that, while the activity decreased but not substantially (the total number of bookmarks was I: 238 (12 users); II: 241 (21 users)), the participants appreciated the bookmarks inserted by other participants (20% 1-2, 45% 3, 35% 4-5) as well as the bookmarks suggested by the system (15% 1-2, 50% 3, 35% 4-5). The maximum score of a user was 8 (compared to 3 in the first round). Some bookmarks were very popular: one of them was copied by 5 users, considering that the most active participants in II round was 10/11. Moreover, in the second round the participants were able to recognize (and liked) the utility of the adaptability mechanism (bookmarks ranking) given the ability to focus the activity on a subset of categories.

Almost 70% of the users that were browsing with MS Internet Explorer considered useful DAD's integration with the browser. Furthermore, 70% of users judged positively the opportunity of choosing the relative weights of bookmark scores by using the control panel.

5   Conclusions and Future Work

Our system is a pure P2P application (therefore inherently scalable) for managing communities of users that want to share the resources that they found, being supported by an adaptive mechanism and by a highly tunable ranking mechanism. We believe that efficiency (i. e. scalability and fault-tolerance) in providing adaptive services is an important factor and should be addressed, because of the growing interest in these services by a larger and larger audience. Our system is one of the first P2P systems to provide access to adaptive support to the navigation on the Web. In fact, as far as we know, in this field only the system in [7] exhibits a similar P2P architecture (taken by Edutella) but with a different purpose.

As future developments of this project, we plan to investigate the necessary modifications to our system in order to support bookmarks placed simultaneously in multiple folders. Several advantages can be obtained by this extensions as, for example, enrich the hierarchical structure of the ontology with cross-links among categories which several bookmarks contemporaneously belong to.

Another possible avenue of research is to use the Kleinberg model (as modified by us) in determining subgroups and similarities among users. From the architectural point of view, we are planning to add backup capabilities by adding a certain degree of redundancy therefore improving the reliability of the whole application.

References

1. D.Abrams, R.Baecker, M.Chignell, *"Information Archiving with Bookmarks: Personal Web space Construction and Organization"*. In Proc. of Human Factors in Computing Systems (CHI 98) ACM Press, pp 41-48.
2. M. Balabanovic, Y. Shoham, *"Fab: Content-Based, Collaborative Recommendation"*. In Communications of the ACM. Vol. 40, N. 3. March 1997.
3. M. Barra, P. Maglio, A. Negro and V.Scarano, *"GAS: Group Adaptive Systems"*. In Proc. of 2th Inter. Conf. on Adaptive Hypermedia and Adaptive Web-based Systems (AH2002). May 29-31, 2002. Malaga, Spain.

4. S. Chakrabarti, B. Dom, D.Gibson, J. Keinberg, P. Raghavan and S. Rajagopalan, *"Automatic Resource list Compilation by Analyzing Hyperlink Structure and Associated Text"*. Proc. of the 7th Inter. World Wide Web Conference, 1998.
5. G. Cordasco, V. Scarano, C. Vitolo, *"Architecture of a P2P Distributed Adaptive Directroy"*. In Proc. of 13th Int. World Wide Web Conf. (WWW04) (Poster) New York May 17-22, 2004.
6. A. Dieberger , K. Hook, "Applying principles of social navigation to the design of shared virtual spaces' ", presented at WebNet'99, Honolulu, Hawaii, 1999.
7. P. Dolog, R. Gavriloaie, W. Nejdl, J. Brase, "Integrating Adaptive Hypermedia Techniques and Open RDF-based Environments". In Proc. of 12th Inter. World Wide Web Conf. (WWW03) Budapest (Hungary) May, 2003.
8. J.Jung, J. Yoon, G. Jo, *"BISAgent: collaborative Web browsing through sharing of bookmark information"*, 16th World Computer Cong. 2000. Proc. of Conf. on Intelligent Inf. Processing.
9. R.Kanawati, M. Malek, *"A multi-agent system for collaborative bookmarking"*, Proc. of the first Inter. joint Conf. on Autonomous Agents and multiagents Syst. (AAMAS 2002), Bologna, Italy, July 15-19, 2002.
10. R.M. Keller, S.R. Wolfe, J.R. Chen, J.L. Rabinowitz, N. Mathe, *"A bookmarking service for organizing and sharing URLs"*. In Proc. for the Sixth Inter. World Wide Web Conf. (Santa Clara, Calif., Apr 1997).
11. J. Kleinberg, *"Authoritative sources in a hyperlinked environment"*. In Proc. of the ACM-SIAM Symp. on Discr. Alg., 1998.
12. J. A. Konstan, B. N. Miller, D. Maltz, J.L. Herlocker , L. R. Gordon, J. Riedl, *"GroupLens: Applying Collaborative Filtering to Usenet News"*. In Commun. of the ACM. Mar 1997.
13. A. A. Macedo, K. N. Truong, J. A. Camacho-Guerrero, M. Pimentel, "Automatically Sharing Web Experiences through a Hyperdocument Recommender System". In Proc. of ACM Hypertext 2003, Nottingham, UK.
14. A. J. Murno, K. Hook, D. Benyon, *"Computer Supported Cooperative Work. Social Navigation of Information Space"*. Springer-Verlag. G. Britain 1999.
15. W. Nejdl, B. Wolf, C. Qu, S. Decker, M.Sintek, A. Naeve, M. Nilsson, M. Palmer, T. Risch, "Edutella: A P2P Networking Infrastructure Based on RDF". 11th International World Wide Web Conference (WWW2002), Hawaii, USA, May 2002.
16. P. Resnick , H.R. Varian, *"Recommender Systems"*. In Commun. of the ACM,40,3. Mar 1997.
17. J. Rucker, M.J. Polanco, *"Siteseer: Personalized navigation for the web"*. Communication of ACM, vol: 40 no: 3, pp. 73-75, 1997.
18. http://pyxml.sourceforge.net/topics/xbel/docs/html/xbel.html

Developing Active Learning Experiences
for Adaptive Personalised eLearning

Declan Dagger, Vincent P. Wade, and Owen Conlan

Knowledge and Data Engineering Group, Department of Computer Science,
Trinity College Dublin, Ireland
{Declan.Dagger,Vincent.Wade,Owen.Conlan}@cs.tcd.ie
http://kdeg.cs.tcd.ie

Abstract. Developing adaptive, rich-media, eLearning courses tends to be a complex, highly-expensive and time-consuming task. A typical adaptive eLearning course will involve a multi-skilled development team of technologists, instructional developers, subject matter experts and integrators. Even where the adaptive course attempts to reuse existing digital resources, considerable effort is still required in the integration of the adaptive techniques and curriculum. This paper tackles the fundamental challenges of extending adaptivity across not only content (based on prior knowledge, goals, learning styles, connectivity etc.) but also across adaptive pedagogic approaches, communication tools and a range of e-activity types which are required for effective, deeper learning. This paper identifies key activities and requirements for adaptive course construction and presents the design of a tool to allow the rapid construction of such courses. The paper outlines the usage of this tool in the form of a case study and presents its research findings.

1 Introduction

Adaptivity in eLearning has become one of the key areas in which adaptive hypermedia (AH) is being applied and extended [1]. However, such adaptivity has tended to focus on adaptive content retrieval and (simple) content sequencing based on domain models, or more recently ontologies [2]. From an educational (learning) perspective, this adaptive content retrieval typically supports lower cognitive aspects of learning (recall & understanding) [3]. To provide support for higher cognitive skills in areas, such as analysis, synthesis and evaluation, the adaptivity needs to be intimately integrated with sound pedagogic approaches and models [4, 6].

A second problem with current adaptive web based systems is the difficulty of authoring adaptive experiences. Because of cost and difficulty (complexities) in authoring it is not scalable within learning institutions, typically schools, higher education and further education. The complexity, cost and effort required to develop adaptive eLearning experiences is very high in traditional adaptive systems (or intelligent tutoring systems) [7-9].

This paper tackles the fundamental challenges of extending the axes of adaptivity across not only content (based on prior knowledge, goals, learning styles, connectivity

W. Nejdl and P. De Bra (Eds.): AH 2004, LNCS 3137, pp. 55–64, 2004.

etc.) but also across adaptive pedagogic models, communication and e-activities which are required for effective, deeper learning. The paper argues that for successful adaptive authoring, a single tutor/teacher needs to be empowered to rapidly develop adaptive experiences by constructing and controlling adaptive narratives (based on sound pedagogic models), adaptive content composition, adaptive e-activities, adaptive layout (presentation) and adaptive connectivity as well as prescribing adaptive learner controls to empower greater learner control over the experience. The paper also presents the research and development of an Adaptive Course Construction Toolkit (ACCT) which supports an adaptive eLearning activity management approach to eLearning. The paper presents a process to illustrate the multiple axes of adaptivity which can be specified in such an environment, and describes the empowerment such systems offer both the tutor and learner

2 Adaptive/Non-adaptive Course Composition for Personalized eLearning

Personalized eLearning employs an active learning strategy which empowers the learner to be in control of the context, pace and scope of their learning experience [10]. It supports the learner by providing tools and mechanisms through which they can personalize their learning experience. This learner empowerment and shift in learning responsibility can help to improve learner satisfaction with the received learning experience.

Two of the predominant difficulties with authoring and building adaptive personalised eLearning systems are complexity and lack of course developer support. The restraining complexity of the course construction process can be somewhat alleviated by providing the course developer with a support-oriented environment in which they can create, test and publish adaptive courses. Some systems, for example LAMS, actively support the creation of activity based learning experiences [11]. Theses systems however do not support the description and application of adaptivity to the created course models in order to produce an adaptive personalized eLearning experience.

A direct requirement from teachers is the ability to choose passages of a lesson which are group adaptive, to fit with a curriculumized classroom scenario, so that the information domain appears the same to all members of the "class". This type of functionality requirement can be realised by the construction of adaptive personalized eLearning experiences.

To support the construction of adaptive and non-adaptive courses this research has extended the multi-model metadata-driven approach [12] to define requirements for constructs such as pedagogical modelling and adaptivity modelling. The modelling of pedagogy and adaptivity has formed the basis for Narrative Structures, Narrative Concepts and Narrative Attributes. This extension of the multi-model metadata-driven approach has led to the creation of the Adaptive Course Construction Toolkit (ACCT) which provides a course developer-oriented support framework.

2.1 Multiple Models

The Architecture for multi-Model Metadata-driven Adaptivity [12] created at Trinity College Dublin attempts to rectify these flexibility and reusability issues by adopting a separation of concerns. Current approaches to AHS development combine the content with the intelligence that describes the adaptive delivery of the content. The multi-Model Metadata-driven approach is to separate the content from the rules that govern its adaptive delivery. This separation of concerns increases the potential for reuse, not only of the content but also the intelligence (pedagogy and narrative structure) behind how to adaptively deliver such content.

2.1.1 Concept Space/Domain Ontology

One of the key challenges of the adaptive course construction process is to identify the abstract domain of information within which the adaptive course will exist. To describe the concepts from which a course is to be constructed, a subject matter expert specifies and describes the course concepts in a content independent way. This creates a flexible abstract overview of the concepts of the adaptive course. Learning resources can be abstractly referenced by the concepts of the ConceptSpace model.

2.1.2 Narrative

The Narrative Model captures the semantics of the pedagogical strategy employed by a course. It describes the logic behind the selection and delivery of learning activities/concepts within the scope of a course. Using the narrative, the adaptive course can be personalized towards the goals and objectives of the learner, the preferred learning style of the learner, the prior knowledge and learning history of the learner and the context in which they are learning [12].

The Narrative Model is the mechanism through which the separation of intelligence (adaptivity) and content is realized. This separation increases the potential for the reuse of the learning resources involved, i.e. the content, the intelligence and the teaching strategies. It does not reference physical learning resources, instead it references Candidate Content Groups (CCG) [9]. CCG are used to group pedagogically and semantically similar learning resources into virtual groups from which the Narrative Model, during execution, can reference and use.

The Narrative is used during the reconciliation of the multiple models used by the Architecture for multi-Model Metadata-driven Approach. For example, the learner model can be used to make candidate selection decisions based on the characteristics and learning preferences of the learner. The tutor model is reconciled by the Narrative to specify scoping boundaries on the subject matter concept space/domain ontology. This notion of bounding course scope gives the tutor the flexibility to use the same narrative across different classes or different groups within a single class, while concurrently producing differently scoped courses. The candidate content groups are used by the narrative during the candidate selection process, whereby the narrative chooses the most appropriate candidate(s) to deliver to the learner.

2.1.2.1 Narrative Concepts

Narrative Concepts are used to create conceptual containers for elements of narrative structures. They are organized to provide a detailed description of a narrative domain in terms of learning activities. Narrative Concepts are concepts that are utilized within the narrative description process. An example of a Narrative Concept (learning activity) might be "Observation and Discussion". This activity may use resources and tools that are simulation-based and collaboration-based. While the simulation-based resources may be adapted based on learning style preferences for example, visual and kinesthetic, the collaboration-based resources may be adapted based on the learners' environmental characteristics for example, device type, network type and latency and context. This flexibility allows the course developer to rapidly build adaptive courses which contain both simple and complex storylines (plots).

2.1.2.2 Narrative Attributes

Narrative Attributes consists of adaptive axes, adaptive techniques, associated descriptions and usage guidelines. Adaptive Axes are high-level descriptions of learner and learning environment characteristics to which narrative concepts can be adapted. For example, an Adaptive Axes may describe adaptation based on a learner's prior knowledge of the subject matter, learner's goals and objectives, learner's communication needs or learner's learning style preferences. Adaptive Techniques are the low-level mechanisms which adaptive axes can employ to fulfill an adaptive task. For example, through the adaptive axes "prior knowledge", I would like to use a learning object inclusion/exclusion technique or a link hiding technique depending on the level of granularity that exists with the content-space, i.e. whether the content is "pages" or "pagelet" [12] size.

Narrative Concepts are used to create the custom teaching structure for a non-adaptive online course. To make an online course adaptive, the course developer must choose which sections, concepts or learning activities they would like to be adapted to the learner. Narrative Attributes can be used to describe the behavior of a Narrative Concept. A narrative attribute may, for example, be used to describe some adaptive context in which the Narrative Concept will exist. The course developer can associate narrative attributes with narrative concepts indicating their desire for these concepts to be adaptively delivered. Such association may infer that concepts be rendered in a particular fashion, for example; adapt this concept to the visual preferences of the learner, while at the same time insuring that a set curriculum is adhered to and that the overall course is delivered based on a learner's prior knowledge.

Narrative Attributes can be used, for example, to apply adaptive effects to concepts based on learner characteristics, tutor characteristics, learning context and device specifications. Narrative Attributes are key elements in the conversion of a non-adaptive online course to a personalized adaptive online course.

2.1.2.3 Narrative Structures

Instructional Design Principles, Pedagogical and Andragogical theory formalize and describe learning and teaching strategies. Narrative Structures are a model-based representation of theses descriptions. The models can be used as templates when constructing an online course and the descriptions can be presented as usage guidelines for the strategy. The combination of guideline and model can be used during reconciliation and validation of the online course.

Narrative Structures are used to provide the course developer with a solid foundation, based on sound pedagogical and instructional design principles, from which to build their online course. These models are interpreted to produce real-time support for the course developer. This support forms a framework for the online course based on the selected narrative structure(s). The use of Narrative Structures allows the course developer to produce online learning based on single or multiple instructional design principles. For example, the course developer could be assembling a course on "How to teach online". The general course structure may follow a didactic approach. Within the scope of this course however their may be lesson activities that are best taught using a case-based or a web-quest approach.

One key challenge of online learning is to facilitate the reuse of all learning resources within a knowledge domain. Narrative Structures are formalized metadata models outlining the general narrative concepts and the flow of narrative concepts outlined by a particular instructional design strategy. They can be used in whole or as part of a customized teaching strategy. They offer guideline support to the course developer by offering usability information. Narrative structures can then be used by course developers to share their particular teaching strategy for a domain of information.

2.1.3 Actors

During the process of specifying and creating an adaptive/non-adaptive course there are two major roles to be considered, the learner and the tutor. The desired effects from each are quite different yet both are equally important to the produced course. The role of the learner is fundamental to the active learning pedagogy which specifies a learner-centric learning environment. The role of the tutor is fundamental in directing the scope of the learning environment.

2.1.3.1 Learner

Constructivism implies that the learner become active and interactive within their own learning experiences to develop their own understanding of the knowledge domain. One key goal of the multi-model approach taken in TCD involves the empowerment of the learner. The learner should be in control of their learning experience and should have the capability to modify and abstract their personal learning path. Through learner empowerment [13] the reach and effectiveness of adaptive personalized eLearning can be extended [10].

The Learner Model (LM) is defined as a schema representing the layout and the elements that must be present. The schema will define the structuring of the LM to provide a mechanism for cross-session interoperability and consistency. The ACCT will produce this LM schema which can be used when testing and publishing the course. The ACCT will update the LM schema automatically with regard to the changing characteristics of the Concept Space (Both Subject Matter and Narrative).

Since the LM is only consulted during the decision making phase of the candidate selection process, the main influence of the attributes of the LM will be the narrative concept space since it is here that the adaptive axes are applied to the narrative concepts.

2.1.3.2 Tutor

The Tutor model can be used to scope the course towards a group of learners or the curriculum of the domain ontology. It allows the course developer to specify semantic boundaries around the information space. The tutor model will also influence the learner modelling instrument. Based on recommendations made by the Tutor, the pre-course questionnaire can be dynamically generated in line with the tutor restrictions. The Tutor model will also feed into the candidate selection process, i.e. if the tutor decides that a specific concept must always be taught, adaptively taught, or never taught. The learner model would then reflect the curriculumized decisions of the tutor.

2.2 Adaptive Course Construction Toolkit (ACCT)

Due to the complex and dynamic process of authoring Adaptive Hypermedia, the need for author support in creating pedagogically sound adaptive personalized eLearning is evident [2], [14], [9]. From current work in adaptive hypermedia and personalized eLearning it is evident that there are two areas of research which need future development, the design of pedagogically sound courses and the support offered to the course developer during the construction of pedagogically sound courses.

This need for a pedagogical and course developer support framework has lead to the development of the Adaptive Course Construction Toolkit (ACCT). The ACCT is a design-time tool which allows the course developer to create adaptive and non-adaptive activity-oriented course narratives based on sound pedagogical strategies in a developer-supported environment. The ACCT provides the course developer with such tools as concept space/domain ontology editor, custom narrative builder, content package assembler, learning resource repository interactivity and a real-time course test and evaluation environment. The architecture of the ACCT is built upon a reusability-focused, developer-supported and service-oriented architecture. For example, the ACCT allows the course developer to interact with the learning resource repository, searching for candidates based on keywords and contextual prior use, through a web-service interface.

The abstraction mechanisms employed by the ACCT allow the course developer to define their teaching strategies and subject matter domains in a reusable and collaboratively supported way. This active promotion of reusability not only at the asset level but also the pedagogical, instructional design, concept and activity level will aid in the rapid construction of pedagogically sound online adaptive learning experiences.

Pedagogical and instructional design principles were studied and modelled to form reusable and scaleable design guidelines for writing narratives supported by the selected principles. The guidelines will identify and describe the abstract logic and reasoning behind the conceptual layout of the course. The guidelines are also represented in model form whereby the course developer can see and interact with the model structure during the creation of their customized course narrative. The developed model guidelines, or schema, will be translated into the model support framework for the adaptive hypermedia authoring architecture of the ACCT.

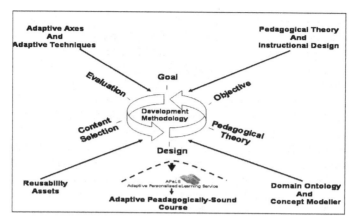

Fig. 1. Sample Methodology for Constructing Pedagogically-sound Adaptive Courses.

The sample methodology in fig. 1 outlines an adaptive course construction process whereby the course goals and objectives are initially identified, a pedagogical strategy(s) for the course is chosen, the subject matter domain is modelled and applied to the chosen pedagogy(s), the learning resources are selected, the adaptivity is applied to the pedagogically-based course structure and the course semantics are tested. This rapid course prototyping approach can be achieved with the ACCT.

2.2.1 Subject Matter Concept Space Creation

The Subject Matter Concept Space (SMCS) is a light-weight ontology describing the relationships and interrelationships that exist within a subject matter domain. The ACCT actively supports the course developer during the creation of the SMCS through facilitating addition, deletion and modification of subject matter concepts.

The ACCT allows the course developer to describe the relationships between the concepts of the SMCS. The relationships are provided as a set of guidelines that the course developer can utilize to created relationship definitions. These relationships however can be customized. The ACCT allows the course developer to create and define new customized relationships, hence offering more control to the course developer during the course construction process.

2.2.2 Customized Narrative Model Creation

The custom narrative model editor is used by the course developer to describe the course structure in pedagogically-supported narrative terms. The course developer is supported with a drag and drop interface providing tools built from sample pedagogical models, pedagogical narrative concepts, narrative attributes, previously defined subject matter concept space model, learning activities and collaboration paradigms. A learning resource repository interaction service is provided allowing the course developer to search for learning resources.

A Narrative Structure consists of a collection of Narrative Concepts. The Narrative Concepts allow the course developer to apply aspects of pedagogical strategies to certain parts of the adaptive course. For example, the sample pedagogical model for a case-based approach might contain narrative concepts to represent learning-activities such as "The Case-study introduction", "The Context of the case-study", "The Problem to be addressed", "A collection of Resources", "A mixture of activities", "A Collection of case tools", "An Epilogue" and "Some case evaluation".

The ACCT pedagogically supports and guides the course developer during the design of the custom course narrative by providing a palette of fully customizable sample pedagogical models. The sample models provided are used to from the basis for the customized course narrative. Narrative Structures have been created to represent pedagogical strategies such as case-based, didactic and web-quest teaching. This approach implies that the course developer has the flexibility to apply a blend of pedagogical strategies. For example, a course on "How to Program" may follow the general didactic pedagogical strategy but certain sections within that course may better lend themselves to be taught through a case-based pedagogical strategy. This flexibility empowers the course developer with a tool that is capable of creating complex, and realistic, pedagogically-sound adaptive course offerings.

The course developer will be offered guidance on how to best use such Narrative concepts within the scope of the sample pedagogical model. Based on course developer preference, all or part of the supplied sample pedagogical model can be used. There is also a "blank" Narrative Concept which will allow the course developer to customize and expand the supplied sample pedagogical models.

The Narrative Structures allow the course developer to build a non-adaptive narrative model based on sound pedagogical strategies. To make the narrative model adaptive the course developer must selected Narrative Attributes from the available palette. The course developer will associate the Narrative Attribute with the Narrative Concept to which they want the adaptivity to be applied. Narrative Attributes are defined to facilitate adaptivity on axes such as prior knowledge and learning objectives, learning context, preferred learning modalities and delivery device. By "tagging" the Narrative Concept with the Narrative Attribute the course developer is saying that he/she would like to have this Narrative Concept delivered in an adaptive way based on the adaptive axes that has been applied. The course developer is supported during this process through guideline information and sample implementation domains. The course developer can view examples and best practice information based on the current selected Narrative Attribute.

The ACCT has a plug-in service that allows the course developer to search across multiple remote learning resource repositories to identify and select appropriate learning resources based on keywords and prior usage information. The ACCT actively promotes the reuse of learning resources by empowering the course developer to select learning resources from a shared repository. The course developer can then associate learning resources with the concepts of their narrative model. Multiple resources can be associated with multiple concepts. It is the role of the candidate selector to choose the appropriate candidates during the execution of the customized Narrative Model. Note that the learning resources do not necessarily have to exist. One of the features of the ACCT is to act as a content specification tool whereby the course developer can describe the concepts of the course and their context in a content-independent way. This implies that the content need not exist during the building of the ACCT courses.

2.2.3 Course Verification

One of the key challenges of authoring adaptive and non-adaptive courses is the ability to test the output of the course. The ACCT offers the course developer a mechanism to test, evaluate and re-develop their course through a multi-Model Metadata-driven Adaptive Engine service that can interact with and interpret the course and models produced by the ACCT.

The ACCT allows the course developer to publish their course in the form of a content package. The content package contains such information as the course manifest, subject matter concept space and relationship definitions, the custom narrative model, narrative/pedagogical structures and the narrative attributes/adaptive axes. The content package is then used during the runtime execution/reconciliation of the course allowing the course developer to test the pedagogical coherence of their adaptive course.

2.3 Initial Evaluation

The initial evaluation of the ACCT, ending 05/06, concerned its user-friendliness, the user's ability to create short adaptive courses and the user's understanding of the models used by the ACCT. The evaluation process involved initial presentations of the functionality of the ACCT, a demo of how it can be used, followed by a description of the content and concept space (SQL) in a workshop environment. The testers where provided with a pre defined SMCS and asked to develop custom narratives based on the supplied SMCS. The users where satisfied with the interface provided and the ability to create and describe the subject matter area. They felt empowered by the ability to describe pedagogically-based course narratives in a graphical manner. By allowing real-time course verification the testers felt it would increase the potential stability of the end course. However, users felt the view of the SMCS was confusing at times, the narrative creation process could be made easier by using examples and certain look and feel characteristics were inconsistent.

The second phase of evaluation will be carried out in both the Centre for Learning Technologies in Trinity College Dublin and the IT Innovation Centre at Intel Ireland, the latter being the sponsor of this research. The results and feedback from both evaluation phases will influence the future development of the ACCT.

3 Conclusion

The paper introduced research in the area of authoring and developing adaptive personalized eLearning which resulted in the development of the Adaptive Course Construction Toolkit (ACCT). The paper described a framework for supporting the course developer during the process of creating adaptive and non-adaptive learning experiences. The paper identified and described the core models required for building adaptive personalized pedagogically-sound courses. The paper introduced an adaptive course construction methodology for building adaptive courses based on sound pedagogical strategies in a content-independent way. The paper concludes by outlining the initial ACCT evaluation results.

References

1. Brusilovsky, P. Maximizing educational opportunity for every type of learner: adaptive hypermedia for Web-based education Towards and Information Society for All. Vol. 3 (2001) 68-72.
2. De Bra, P., Aerts, A., Berden, B., De Lange, B., Escape from the Tyranny of the Textbook: Adaptive Object Inclusion in AHA!. Proceedings of the AACE ELearn 2003 Conference, Phoenix, Arizona, (2003), 65-71
3. Bloom, B.S. (Ed.) Taxonomy of educational objectives: The classification of educational goals: Handbook I, cognitive domain. New York (1956)
4. Johannesson, P. Action Workflow Loops for Distance Education - Design Principles for Integrating CAL and CMC, 7th International Conference on Human-Computer Interaction, San Francisco, August, (1997)
5. Bonwell, C. C., & Eison, J. A. Active learning: Creating excitement in the classroom. Washington, DC: ASHE-ERIC Higher Education Report No. 1. (1991)
6. Brusilovsky, P., Eklund, J., and Schwarz, E. Web-based education for all: A tool for developing adaptive courseware. Proceedings of Seventh International World Wide Web Conference, (1998), 291-300
7. De Bra, P., Aerts, A., Houben, G.J., Wu, H Making General-Purpose Adaptive Hypermedia Work. Proceedings of the WebNet Conference, pp. 117-123, (2000)
8. Dagger, D.; Conlan, O.; Wade, V. An Architecture for Candidacy in Adaptive eLearning Systems to Facilitate the Reuse of Learning Resources. E-Learn 2003, World Conference on E-Learning in Corporate, Government, Healthcare and Higher Education, Phoenix (2003) 49-56
9. Conlan, O., Wade, V. Evaluating the Multi-model, Metadata-driven Approach to producing Adaptive eLearning Services, Submitted to AH2004. (2004)
10. Dalziel, J. Implementing Learning Design: The Learning Activity Management System (LAMS), ASCILITE (2003)
11. Conlan, O.; Wade, V.; Bruen, C.; Gargan, M. Multi-Model, Metadata Driven Approach to Adaptive Hypermedia Services for Personalized eLearning. Second International Conference on Adaptive Hypermedia and Adaptive Web-Based Systems, Spain, May (2002)
12. Bajraktarevic, N., Hall, W., Fullick, P. Incorporating learning styles in hypermedia environment: Empirical evaluation, Workshop on Adaptive Hypermedia and Adaptive Web-Based Systems, (2003) 41-53
13. Brusilovsky, P. and Nijhawan, H. A Framework for Adaptive E-Learning Based on Distributed Re-usable Learning Activities. AACE Proceedings of World Conference on E-Learning, E-Learn 2002, Montreal, Canada, (2002) 154-161

Adaptive User Modeling for Personalization of Web Contents*

Alberto Díaz[1] and Pablo Gervás[2]

[1] CES Felipe II – Universidad Complutense de Madrid
c/ Capitán 39, 28300 Aranjuez, Madrid
adiaz@cesfelipesegundo.com
[2] Departamento de Sistemas Informáticos y Programación
Facultad de Informática – Universidad Complutense de Madrid
c/ Juan del Rosal, 8, Madrid 28040
pgervas@sip.ucm.es

Abstract. This paper presents a system for personalization of web contents based on a user model that stores long term and short term interests. Long term interests are modeled through the selection of specific and general categories, and keywords for which the user needs information. However, user needs change over time as a result of his interaction with received information. For this reason, the user model must be capable of adapting to those shifts in interest. In our case, this adaptation of the user model is performed by a short term model obtained from user provided feedback. The evaluation performed with 100 users during 15 days has determined that the combined use of long and short term models performs best when specific and general categories and keywords are used together for the long term model.

1 Introduction

Web content appears in many forms over different domains of application, but in most cases the form of presentation is the same for all users. The contents are static in the sense that they are not adapted to each user. Content personalization is a technique that tries to avoid information overload through the adaptation of web contents to each type of user.

A personalization system is based on 3 main functionalities: content selection, user model adaptation, and content generation. For these functionalities to be carried out in a personalized manner, they must be based on information related to the user that must be reflected in his user profile or user model [8].

Content selection refers to the choice of the particular subset of all available documents that will be more relevant for a given user, as represented in his user profile or model. In order to effect this choice one must have a representation of the documents, a representation of the user profile, and a similarity function that computes the level of adequacy of one to the other.

---

* This research has been partially funded by the Spanish Ministerio de Ciencia y Tecnología (TIC2002-01961).

W. Nejdl and P. De Bra (Eds.): AH 2004, LNCS 3137, pp. 65–74, 2004.

User model adaptation is necessary because user needs change over time as a result of his interaction with information [2]. For this reason the user model must be capable of adapting to those interest changes, it must be dynamic. This adaptation is built upon the interaction of the user with the system, which provides the feedback information used to evolve the profile.

In our case, content generation involves generating a new result web document that contains, for each selected document, its title, its relevance as computed by the system, a summary, and a link to the full document.

In this paper we focus on user model adaptation and the various possible combinations of modeling alternatives for this process. The aim is to identify which is the best way of carrying out the user model adaptation process to improve content selection.

2   Available Methods and Techniques

Existing literature provides different techniques for defining user interests: keywords, stereotypes, semantic networks, neural networks, etc. A particular set of proposals [2; 11] model users by combining long term and short term interests: the short term model represents the most recent user preferences and the long term model represents those expressed over a longer period of time.

Various classification algorithms are available for carrying out content selection depending on the particular representation chosen for user models and documents: cosine formula, rules associated to stereotypes, neural networks, nearest neighbour classifier, naive Bayes classifier, etc.

The feedback techniques needed to achieve a dynamic modeling of the user are based on feedback given by the user with respect to the information elements selected according to his profile. The information obtained in this way can be used to update accordingly the user models in representation had been chosen: term weights, semantic networks, rules associated to stereotypes, etc.

The representation of the text content of the documents by means of techniques based on term weight vectors [9] allows a number of classification algorithms and feedback techniques and constitutes a good option in which to test and compare the relative efficiency of different approaches. The vector associated with a document can be obtained by eliminating the words contained in a stop list and extracting the stems of the remaining words by means of a stemmer. Weights are usually calculated by means of the tf · idf formula, based on frequency of occurrence of terms [9].

Text categorization, the assignment of subject labels to text items, is one of the most prominent text analysis and access task nowadays [10]. In particular, some authors have used Yahoo! categories to semantically characterize the content of documents [6]. They suggest that the best result occurs when using the very brief descriptions of the Yahoo! categories entries.

3   Our Proposal

We propose a browsable user model or user profile that represents user interests from three different points of view [1]. The user model stores three types of information:

personal information, information concerning the format in which information is to be received, and specific information about user interests according to various reference systems that are used to carry out the personalization.

The proposal is similar to [4] but adding more information to the long term model. This additional information comes from the use of the first level categories of Yahoo! Spain as an extra reference framework for describing information needs, that allows users a richer language in which to define their user model.

Long term user interests are modelled with respect to two reference frameworks: the first one based on a domain specific system of classification, and the second one based on the content of the documents.

A basic reference system is the classification system specific to the particular domain under consideration - for instance, in a digital newspaper, this system will be based on the set of sections used by the newspaper -. This system is composed of a set of first level categories that represent different types of information - for instance, examples of sections of digital newspapers would be: national, international, sport, etc. Each web document belongs to a category of that classification system. Information concerning these specific categories is stored as a matrix where rows correspond to specific categories and columns correspond to users (C_{cu}). Users may assign a weight to each specific category to indicate their interest in them.

The reference system based on the content of documents is subdivided in two reference systems, a fine grain model based in keywords and a coarse grain model based on domain independent general categories.

The user can enter a number of keywords to characterise his fine grain model. The appearance of these keywords in the documents will be taken to indicate that the document may be interesting to the user. For each keyword the user introduces a weight that indicates its importance to him. These keywords are stored, for each user u, as a term weight vector (k_u).

To define the coarse grain model the user must choose the general categories in which he is interested. Information concerning these general categories is stored as a matrix where rows correspond to general categories and columns correspond to users (G_{gu}). Users may assign a weight to each general category to indicate their interest in them. The general categories are the first level of categories of Yahoo! Spain and they are represented as term weight vectors (g) obtained from the very brief descriptions of the first level of Yahoo! categories entries.

Short term interests are represented by means of feedback terms. These terms are obtained from user provided feedback over the documents he receives. That is, the user provides positive or negative feedback over the documents he receives, and a set of representative terms is extracted from them. This information is handled by the user model adaptation process, which returns a term weight vector (t_u) for each user. This term weight vector is taken to represent the current short term interests of that user. Short terms interests tend to correspond to temporary information needs whose interest to the user wanes after a short period of time. Therefore their weight must be progressively decreased over time.

Documents are downloaded from the web as HTML documents. For each document, title, category, URL and text are extracted and stored for subsequent processing. Term weight vector representations (d_d) are obtained by application of stop lists, stemmer, and the tf · idf formula for computing actual weights [9].

The only restrictions that must be fulfilled by a domain for the proposed model to be applicable are that there exist textual information associated with web documents and that a domain specific classification exists to classify the documents.

4 Content Selection

Content selection refers to the choice of those among the available documents that are particularly relevant for a user, according to his profile. Once particular representations have been fixed for documents and user model, it becomes feasible to establish which documents are more adequate for each user.

Since we have different reference frameworks in the user model we will indicate how content selection is performed with respect to each one of them, and later we will explore different possible combinations of the resulting selections. Combinations will be based on the relevance obtained for each document within each particular reference framework, and the relative weight used for each reference framework in a particular combination. For all combinations, the final result is a ranking of the set of documents according to the computed overall relevance.

4.1 Selection with Respect to the Long Term Model

As each web document has a preassigned specific category, selection with respect to this reference framework is immediate. Each document is assigned the weight associated with the corresponding specific category in the particular user model. The relevance between a document d, belonging to a specific category c, and a user model u is directly the value assigned to the specific category c by user u:

$$r_{du}^c = C_{cu} . \tag{1}$$

The relevance between a document d and a general category g is computed using the cosine formula for similarity within the vector space model [9]:

$$r_{dg} = sim(d_d, g) \tag{2}$$

The relevance between a document d and the general categories of a user model is computed using the next formula:

$$r_{du}^g = \frac{\sum_{i=1}^{14} G_{iu} r_{dg_i}}{\sum_{i=1}^{14} G_{iu}} \tag{3}$$

The relevance between a document d and the keywords of a user model is computed using the cosine formula for similarity within the vector space model [9]:

$$r_{du}^k = sim(d_d, k_u).$$

(4)

When all documents have been ordered with respect to the various reference frameworks, the results are integrated using a particular combination of reference frameworks. Therefore, the total relevance between a document d and a user model u is computed with the following formula:

$$r_{du}^l = \frac{\alpha r_{du}^c + \beta r_{du}^g + \chi r_{du}^k}{\alpha + \beta + \chi}.$$

(5)

where Greek letters α, β and χ represent the importance assigned to each reference framework (α, for specific categories, β, for general categories and, χ, for keywords). These are parameters to allow easy configuration of the modes of operation of the system. For this combination to be significant, relevance obtained for each framework must be normalised with respect to the best results for the document collection under consideration.

5   User Model Adaptation

Adaptation of the user model involves obtaining / updating a short term model of the user from the feedback information provided by the user. This model can be used to improve the process of selection in the personalization system.

5.1   Obtaining the Short Term Model

The short term model is obtained as a result of the process of adaptation of the user model. The user receives a web document that contains an automatically generated summary [5] for each of the 10 web documents that the system has found more relevant according to his user profile. With respect to this information the user may interact with the system by giving positive or negative feedback - refraining from providing feedback is interpreted as a contribution as well, taken to imply indifference - for each of the information elements that he has received. The feedback terms of the short term model are obtained from the news items for which either positive or negative feedback has been provided.

Because these terms represent an interest of the user over a short period of time, an algorithm is used to decrement their value over time: each day the starting value of the new weights is obtained by subtracting 0.1 from the previous day's value. Terms that reach a weight less or equal to 0 are eliminated from the model.

To select / update the new feedback terms all documents are preprocessed in the same way as was done for the selection process: stop list and stemmer are applied. The starting point for the adaptation process are the terms of the representation of the documents, with their associated frequency (tf).

The algorithm in [4] is then applied to obtain the feedback terms. The final result of this process is a set of terms ordered according to their new interest value. A subset of them is selected - the 20 most relevant ones - to obtain / update the feedback terms of the short term model.

5.2 Selection with Respect to the Short Term Model

Relevance between a document d and a short term user model u is computed in the same way used for the keywords of the long term model, but using the term weight vector obtained in the process of adaptation of the user model:

$$r_{du}^s = r_{du}^t = sim(d_d, t_u)$$ (6)

5.3 Selection with Respect to the Combined Long Term – Short Term Model

When all documents have been ordered with respect to the different sources of relevance, the results are integrated using a particular combination of reference frameworks. Therefore, the total relevance between a document d and a user model u is computed with the following formula:

$$r_{du} = \frac{\delta r_{du}^c + \varepsilon r_{du}^g + \phi r_{du}^k + \gamma r_{du}^t}{\delta + \varepsilon + \phi + \gamma}$$ (7)

where Greek letters δ, ε, ϕ, and γ represent the importance assigned to each of the reference frameworks -δ, for specific categories, ε, for general categories, ϕ, for keywords, γ, for feedback terms. Again, for this combination to be significant, the relevance obtained from each reference framework must be normalised with respect to the best results over the document collection being used.

6 Evaluation

As an example of web documents for experimentation we have chosen the web pages of the digital edition of a Spanish newspaper[1]. Experiments are evaluated over data collected for 106 users and the news items corresponding to three weeks – the 14 working days - of the digital edition of the ABC Spanish newspaper. These days correspond to the period 1st-19th Dec 2003. The average of news items per day is 78.5.

To carry out the evaluation, judgements from the user are required as to which news items are relevant or not for each of the days of the experiment. To obtain these judgements users were requested to check the complete set of news items for each day, stating for each one whether it was considered interesting (positive feedback), not interesting (negative feedback) or indifferent (no feedback). Users were explicitly asked not to confine their judgements on interest to relevance with respect to the initial user profiles they had constructed on first accessing the system, but rather to include any news items that they found interesting on discovery, regardless of their similarity with respect to their initial description of their interest. It is hoped that enough information to cover these rogue items will be captured automatically and progressively by the system through the feedback adaptation process.

The three possibilities in each judgment are used to the adaptation process to obtain / update the short term model, but also are used as the relevance judgment of the inter-

---

[1] This provides a consistent format, which simplifies systematic processing.

est for the user for a news item. However, we consider only two possibilities: interesting, for positive feedback, and not interesting, for negative or no feedback.

Because the evaluation is based on these judgments, significant results can only be obtained for those users that have provided feedback over and above a minimum threshold in terms of number of judgements per day. As the evaluation process involved an effort for the users, only 37.4 users per day actually provided judgments. Additionally, some users only perform feedback for less than 10 news items per day. These users have been eliminated for the evaluation in order to obtain more significant results. This restriction does not constitute a limitation in as much as it is not a particular system that is being evaluated, but rather the relative efficiency of various combinations of methods for specifying information needs. The final collection employed for evaluation presented, on average, 28.6 user per day.

6.1 Metrics

Since our experimental set up combines a binary relevance judgement from the users and a ranking of news items provided by the system, it was decided to use normalised precision [7; 9] as our evaluation metric. In addition, with respect to equal relevance values for consecutive positions of the ranking, the average ranking of the whole set of conflicting positions has been taken as ranking for each and all of them. This adjustment avoids the problem of ordering items at random within the ranking when they have equal relevance.

6.2 Statistical Significance

Data are considered statistically significant if they pass the *sign-test*, with paired samples, at a level of significance of 5% ($p \leq 0.05$). This decision is based on the fact that no specific assumption is made concerning the distribution of data, and that due to the different normalisation processes carried out, it is more convenient to consider relative values instead of absolute values [9].

6.3 Experiment 1

The following experiments have been carried out to check the validity of the proposed model. Each experiment combines different possibilities for long term modeling - only specific categories, L(C), only general categories, L(G), specific and general categories, L(CG), specific categories and keywords, L(CK), general categories and keywords, L(GK), specific and general categories and keywords, L(CGK) - either acting on their own or in combination with the short term model, S. This implies giving different values to the parameters δ, ε, ϕ and γ of formula (7).

For example, L(CG)S is the combination of long and short term model when the long term model includes specific and general categories ($\delta=1$, $\varepsilon=1$, $\phi=0$, $\gamma=1$).

The results in Table 1 can be interpreted as follows. The first line shows the comparison for alternatives in which the long term model uses only specific categories, L(C). The first two columns indicate that the combination is 16.6 % better than the long term model on its own; the middle columns indicate that the combination is 20.9 % better than the short term model; and the last two columns show that the long term model is 5.2 % better than the short term model. Other lines present results for different configurations of the long term model as described above.

Table 1. Relative increments (% Pr) in normalised precision between different combinations of long term model and short term model

combination > long	% Pr	combination > short	% Pr	long > short	% Pr
L(C)S > L(C)	16.6	L(C)S > S	20.9	L(C) > S	5.2
L(G)S > L(G)	4.4	L(G)S > S	18.4	L(G) > S	14.7
L(K)S > L(K)	26.9	L(K)S > S	11.4	S > L(K)	21.2
L(CG)S > L(CG)	1.7	L(CG)S > S	27.8	L(CG) > S	26.5
L(CK)S > L(CK)	11.8	L(CK)S > S	25.7	L(CK) > S	15.8
L(GK)S > L(GK)	5.6	L(GK)S > S	22.2	L(GK) > S	17.5
L(CGK)S > L(CGK)	2.9	L(CGK)S > S	29.8	L(CGK) > S	27.7

All the results in Table 1 are statistically significant. This leads to the conclusion that the combination of the long term model with the short term model is always better than using each model separately. Also the long term model alone is better than the short term model alone except if the long term model is only constituted for the keywords, in this case, is better the short term model. This means that the worst characterization for the long term model are clearly the keywords.

6.4 Experiment 2

This experiment compares the best performing combinations of previous experiments - long and short term models used together - when the long term model is built using: only specific categories L(C)S ($\delta=1$, $\varepsilon=0$, $\phi=0$, $\gamma=1$), only general categories L(G)S ($\delta=0$, $\varepsilon=1$, $\phi=0$, $\gamma=1$), only keywords L(K)S ($\delta=0$, $\varepsilon=0$, $\phi=1$, $\gamma=1$), specific and general categories L(CG)S ($\delta=1$, $\varepsilon=1$, $\phi=0$, $\gamma=1$), specific categories and keywords L(CK)S ($\delta=1$, $\varepsilon=0$, $\phi=1$, $\gamma=1$), general categories and keywords L(GK)S ($\delta=0$, $\varepsilon=1$, $\phi=1$, $\gamma=1$) and all of the possibilities L(CGK)S ($\delta=1$, $\varepsilon=1$, $\phi=1$, $\gamma=1$).

Table 2. Relative increments (% Pr) in normalised precision (Pr) between the use of all the reference systems and combinations of L and S together

	L(CGK)S	L(CG)S	L(CK)S	L(GK)S	L(G)S	L(C)S	L(K)S	S
% Pr		2.8	5.5	9.9	11.2	14.0	20.8	29.8
Pr	0.606	0.589	0.572	0.546	0.538	0.521	0.480	0.425

All results are statistically significant (Table 2). This means that the long term / short term combination that uses specific and general categories, and keywords in the long term model, is better than whatever combination of each of them for the long term model.

The second best combination is specific and general categories, and the third is specific categories and keywords, moreover significantly. It can also be observed that the specific categories, when combined, offer the best selection method for the users.

Between L(GK)S, L(G)S y L(C)S there are no significant differences, therefore they performed in a similar way. Finally, the worst result is for the short model alone followed by the combination with the keywords.

6.5 Comparison with Previous Work

The results reported here can be compared with existing evaluations of combinations of methods over similar data. With respect to [3], the set of possible combinations has been extended with the inclusion of short term modeling via relevance feedback. Additionally, normalised precision is used as a metric instead of precision and recall to better take into account the kind of relevance judgements being considered. With respect to [4], the set of possible combinations has been extended with the inclusion of general categories. Also, a new set of data has been collected, with a much higher number of users and evaluation days than in any of the previous collections, to ensure significance of the data.

7 Conclusions

This paper presents the improvement in personalisation achieved by the inclusion of a process of user model adaptation, due to the fact that the selection that is obtained by combining the long term and short term profiles performs better than the one obtained by using the long term model on its own.

The results show that using a combination of a long term model based on specific and general categories and keywords, together with a short term model, improves the adaptation to the user because values of normalised precision increase. These results are obtained for a set of experiments covering various combinations of interest specification methods, and tested over a collection of data for over a hundred users during 14 days. Over this set of data, the conclusion is proved to be statistically significant.

References

1. Amato, G. & Straccia, U., 1999. "User Profile Modeling and Applications to Digital Libraries". Third European Conference on Research and Advanced Technology for Digital Libraries (ECDL'99), LNCS 1696, pp. 184-197.
2. Billsus, D. & Pazzani. M.J., 2000. "User Modeling for Adaptive News Access", User Modeling and User-Adapted Interaction Journal 10(2-3), pp. 147-180.
3. Díaz, A., Gervás, P., García, A., 2001. "Sections, Categories and Keywords as Interest Specification Tools for Personalised News Services". Online Information Review, Volume 25 No 3 (2001), MCB University Press

4. Díaz, A. & Gervás, P., 2004. "Dynamic user modeling in a system for personalization of web contents". Proceedings of CAEPIA 2003, LNAI 3040.
5. Díaz, A. & Gervás, P., 2004. "Item Summarization in Personalisation of News Delivery Systems". Proceedings of TSD 2004, LNAI. In press.
6. Labrou, Y. & Finin, T., 2000. "Yahoo! As an Ontology: Using Yahoo! Categories to Describe Documents". Proceedings of the 8th International Conference on Information and Knowledge Management (CIKM-99), pp. 180-187, ACM Press, November 2-6 2000.
7. Mizzaro, S., 2001. "A New Measure Of Retrieval Effectiveness (or: What's Wrong With Precision And Recall)". International Workshop on Information Retrieval (IR'2001), Infotech Oulu, pp. 43-52.
8. Mizarro, S. & Tasso, C., 2002. "Ephemeral and Persistent Personalization in Adaptive Information Access to Scholarly Publications on the Web". 2nd International Conference on Adaptive Hypermedia and Adaptive Web Based Systems, Málaga, España, 2002.
9. Salton, G., 1989. Automatic Text Processing: The Transformation, Analysis and Retrieval of Information by Computer, Addison-Wesley Publishing, Reading, Massachussets, 1989.
10. Sebastiani, 2002. "Machine learning in automated text categorization". ACM Computing Surveys (CSUR), 34(1), pp. 1-47, ACM Press, 2002.
11. Widyantoro, D.H., Ioerger, T.R., Yen, J., 2001. "Learning User Interest Dynamics with a Three-Descriptor Representation". Journal of the American Society for Information Science and Technology 52(3), pp. 212-225.

Invoking Web Applications from Portals: Customisation Implications

Oscar Díaz and Iñaki Paz

ONEKIN Research Group
University of the Basque Country*
Department of Computer Languages and Systems
PO Box: 649, 20080 San Sebastián, Spain
{oscar,jibparei}@si.ehu.es

Abstract. Customisation sits at the core of current portal technology. So does content syndication as well as the most recent, application syndication whereby external applications can be integrated into the portal realm through the use of Portlet technology. However, these applications do not always exhibit the sophisticated customisation mechanisms available within a portal. This leads to a discontinuity in the user experience when accessing an external application being syndicated within a portal. This work introduces the notion of *bridge Portlet* as a proxy to an external Web application. This Portlet is responsible for customising the external application to the portal environment, supplementing it with commodities such as single sign on, profiles and the like. The paper illustrates how to improve the adaptation of the external application through a bookmarking module enhancement. Now, portal users can enjoy bookmarking facilities not only for portal-oriented applications but also for external Web applications.

1 Introduction

Portals integrate the access to information sources in a Web-friendly environment. The provision of a seamless, consistent, and personalized experience anywhere and anytime, along with the integration of different media assets, represents the current battleground for the leading portals [4]. Customisation sits at the core of current portal technology.

Moreover, the significance of portal applications stems not only from being a handy way to access data but also from being the means of facilitating the integration with third-party applications (e. g. ERP, CRM, Web applications). Over the last few years, organizations have invested in web-enabling some of their existing systems. Also, the Web itself is now a rich source of information and applications. Both aspects vindicate the effort of being able to tap into these resources, making them available from the portal.

Invoking a Web application from a portal poses no problem. An *<href>* tag can do the job. However, **integrating** a Web application into a portal is a different matter.

* This work was partially supported by the Spanish Science and Technology Ministry (MCYT) and European Social Funds (FEDER) under contract TIC2002-01442. It also benefits of funding from la "Consejería de Ciencia y Tecnología" de la Junta de la Comunidad de Castilla La Mancha (PCB-02-001).

W. Nejdl and P. De Bra (Eds.): AH 2004, LNCS 3137, pp. 75–84, 2004.

Integration entails a stronger weaving with the functionality offered from the portal framework so that the End-user enjoys the commodities offered by the portal when working with the Web application.

This integration can be shallow or deep. A shallow integration makes the "home page" of the Web application accessible from the Portal. This is also known as "web clipping", and tools are currently available in main Portal IDE providers such as Oracle Portal or IBM's WebSphere [12, 10]. This mechanism allows to obtain a doorway to the Web application from the portal. As an example, consider a Web application such as *www.easyjet.com*. A shallow integration implies to be able to display the home page of *easyjet* from the portal rather than rendering this page in a separated browser agent. This permits the profiles stored at the portal framework to be applied to the *easyjet* home page (e. g. a default value for the *departure airport* parameter), and in so doing, improves the user experience. However, once this doorway is crossed, the customer moves to the Web application, and a new browser agent is open. Now, you are no longer within the Portal realm.

By contrast, a deep integration makes the entire application -not just the home page- available from the portal framework. If the *easyjet* site is deeply integrated into the portal framework then, all interactions with *easyjet* are achieved without leaving the portal. Even more, the *easyjet* functionality should be supplemented with the customisation or identification commodities offered by the portal framework. Implementation wise, this implies to wrap the Web application as a **Portlet**.

A Portlet is a multi-step, user-facing application to be delivered through a third party Web application. Portals as application-integration platforms have rapidly embraced this technology, and they are currently the most notable Portlet consumers[1]. A main step forward towards Portlet interoperability between IDE vendors has been the recent delivery of the *Web Services for Remote Portlets* (WSRP) specification (April, 2003) [8] by OASIS and the *Java Portlet Specification* (JSR168) [11] (October, 2003) by JCP. The goal is to define a component model that would enable Portlets to be easily plugged into standards-compliant portals. This work is JSR168 compliant.

Besides all the technicalities that go to make an *external Web application* behave as a Portlet, this work focuses on customisation issues. To this end, the term **bridge Portlet** is coined to refer to a Portlet that permits to wrap a Web application as a Portlet. That is, the Portlet, which follows the bridge pattern [3], handles the Application as a black box, and accesses it only using URL requests, while the Application treats the Portlet as any other Web client. Hereafter, the term *Application* (with capital *A*) is used to denote the external Web application.

The essence is not about using semantic wrappers [7] and regenerating the presentation, but reusing everything possible from the original web application (e. g. *easyJet*). The advantage of this approach is that an existing application can be integrated into a portal without impacting the application in any way. This means that you can integrate both local intranet applications and remote Internet applications into your portal.

The rest of the paper is structured as follows. Sect. 2 introduces the main customisation implications. Sect. 3 outlines an architecture for the bridge Portlet that faces these implications. Finally, conclusions are given in Sect. 4.

---

[1] Portlets are endorsed and supported by IBM, BEA, Oracle, Sybase, Viador, Verify, PeopleSoft, Plumtree and Vignette. Portlets are also referred by some vendors as *Web parts* or *gadgets*.

2   Customisation Implications

Customisation has been defined as *"the adaptation of an application's services towards its context"* [5]. Kappel et al. introduce an evaluation framework where customisation approaches are arranged along two orthogonal dimensions: context and adaptation. Next subsections place this work according to these dimensions.

2.1   Context

Context refers to the environment of the application (e. g. location, time, device, user, etc) whose diversity should be faced by ubiquitous applications. When a Web application is syndicated within a portal, an additional environmental property should be considered: the characteristics of the portal where this external application is being framed. These characteristics include profile data, window states, Portlet modes, Single sing-on, and Cascade StyleSheets.

Profile Data. In a traditional Web application, user data [6] is normally collected from the End-user. However, when this Web application is accessed from a portal, the portal itself can become a source of user data. Indeed, one of the benefits of Portlet-ising a Web application is that the profile mechanism comes for free. When an organization includes the *easyjet* Portlet into its portal, the employee profiles can be used to personalize the *easyjet* parameters, i. e. each employee can have some parameter set based on her preferences or her profile (e. g. CEOs always go in business class).WSRP standardizes the structure of this user information which has been derived from P3P User Data [8].

Window States. Web applications are designed for being rendered in a full page. A page is the unit of delivery. By contrast, Portlets tend to be rendered together with other Portlets. The Portlet markup (known as *fragments*) is delivered together with other Portlets in the same *portal* page. Besides the prohibition of using some HTML tags in the Portlet markup, this mainly implies that the space available for Portlet rendering is limited. As a result, Portlet designers should be thrifty when deciding what to include in a the Portlet.

The space left for Portlet rendering is indicated through the so-called *Window state*. Options contemplated by WSRP include: *normal,* indicates the Portlet is likely sharing the aggregated page with other Portlets; *minimized,* instructs the Portlet not to render visible markup, but lets it free to include non-visible data such as JavaScript or hidden forms; *maximized,* specifies that the Portlet is likely the only Portlet being rendered in the aggregated page, or that the Portlet has more space compared to other Portlets in the aggregated page; and *solo,* denotes the Portlet is the only Portlet being rendered in the aggregated page. This property is set by the Portlet consumer among the values supported by the Portlet.

Portlet Modes. A mode is a way of functioning. Web applications normally have a single way of behaving. However, WSRP distinguishes more modes for Portlets. Both the content and the activities offered by a Portlet depends on its current mode. WSRP introduces the three modes: *view, edit,* and *help*. The bridge Portlet needs to ascertain which Application pages correspond to which Portlet mode.

Single Sign-On (SSO). By the time the End-user accesses a Portlet, it is most likely he has already been identified by the Portal. The SSO facility avoids the End-user going

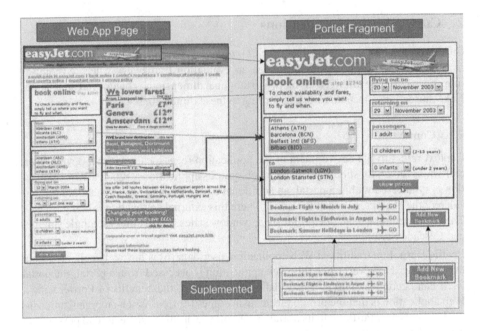

Fig. 1. Turning a Web page into a Portlet fragment: page is filtered while the fragment is supplemented with some bookmarking markup.

through the identification process each time a portal application is accessed. To this end, the bridge Portlet should transparently log the current End-user by automatically issuing the appropriate *http* requests.

CSS. The portal environment can include look-n-feel guidelines. All Portlets' rendering should share some aesthetic guidelines to preserve the identity of the portal. To this end, the Portlet markup should use Cascade StyleSheets (CSSs) [13]. WSRP standardizes the CSS classes that Portlets should use. Thus, the bridge Portlet should attempt to translate look-n-feel guidelines from the Application to those CSS class being standardised by WSRP.

Adaptable Customisation. According to [9], systems supporting fully automatic adaptation are called *adaptive*, whereas *adaptable* systems require some user involvement in terms of semi-automatic adaptation. Customisation is a key enabler to personalise the offerings of a portal. So portals normally exhibit both adaptive (e. g. profiling) and adaptable mechanisms. Indeed, the *"edit"* mode of a Portlet permits the End-user to customise the Portlet along some pre-set parameters (e. g. default values for leaving airport or bookmarks). This option is not a must for Web applications.

2.2 Adaptation

Kappel et al. characterise adaption in terms of the kind of adaptation (i. e. what changes have to be done), the subject of adaptation (i. e. what to change), and the process of adaptation (i. e., how adaptation is performed). Next paragraphs address these questions for the current work.

The Kind of Adaptation. Broadly speaking, a Web application is an aggregate of *pages*, whereas a Portlet is an aggregate of *fragments*. A main difference is that a fragment should normally share the page space with other Portlets. Hence the content of a page can not be framed within the region available at the portal end. The mediator can resort to filter out some of the content/images of the Application output which are not strictly necessary to proceed with the Application flow. For the *easyjet* example, this implies that the Portlet markup should focus on the elements that pursue the goal of buying a ticket, while removing banners, navigation bars, etc. Another alternative is for the returned page to be fragmented and gradually presented. In this case, a Portlet interaction (i. e. an End-user click on the Portlet fragment) does not necessarily lead to a new *http* request to the remote application. This option implies the Portlet to cache the HTML page, split it into different fragments, and render a fragment at a time.

Besides removing some markup, the content of the Application might need to be supplemented with additional markup that support the extra functionality required for the Application when syndicated within the portal. Bookmarking[2] is a case in point. Fig. 1 illustrates this situation for the first fragment of our sample Portlet. The Application page is "customised" to become a fragment by either selecting user interface components (*UIComponents*), and by so filtering unwanted markups from the Application page (e. g. advertisement), or supplementing the fragment with some *UIComponents* (e. g. the bookmarks). These *UIComponents* are referred to as *DerivedMarkupGenerators* and *SupplementMarkupGenerators,* respectively. Moreover, additional functionality may require bright new fragments.

The Subject of Adaptation. This is characterised by looking at the level of the web application which is effected by the adaptation (i. e. content, navigation or presentation) as well as at the concrete elements (e. g. pages, links, input fields, etc).

Turning pages into fragments can affect all the content (e. g. addition/removal of markup chunks), navigation (e. g. a page is split into distinct fragments) and presentation (e. g. CSS mapping with the portal guidelines is needed).

The Process of Adaptation. This work strives to support automatic adaptation (i. e. no user involvement), and deferred dynamic adaptation (i. e. the adaptation is done not before the user requests the page which is subject to adaptation).

3   The Bridge Portlet Architecture

A proxy-based architecture is followed where the Application is completely unaware of (portal-related) customisation, and additional external customisation [2] issues are handled by the proxy. That is, the Portlet should handle the external application as a black box, and accesses it only using URL requests, while the Application treats the Portlet as any other Web client. Motivations that vindicate this approach, include

---

[2] By bookmarking in a Portlet context, we mean generating a bookmark for a previously visited Portlet fragment, independently of the portal context. Further reading in the intricacies of bookmarking can be found at [1].

- tight-time developing constraints. A company can be interested in speeding the channeling of its Web-enabled services through third-party portals by capitalising on its Web site. Portlet-ising the existing Web site can be an effective solution.
- the complexity of the presentation layer. Web sites with every appearance of elegance and sophistication on the outside, may on the inside be a disorganized mess of "spaghetti code" that is cheaper to throw away and rebuild from scratch than trying to decipher. The cost of internal maintenance can be high, and outweighs its benefits. Out approach allows to disregard such complexity, just extracting those elements needed to realise the Portlet interface.
- third-party ownership. Applications to be integrated include remote Internet applications whose owners can be reluctant to do the Portlet-isation themselves. Portlet-isation accounts for a detach approach where you can leverage the remote application without touching it, provided appropriate agreements have been reached with the owners.

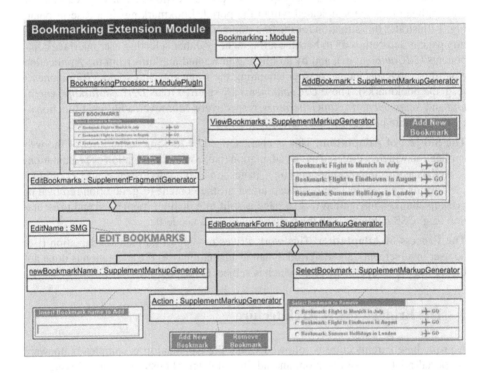

Fig. 2. The *bookmarking* module. Each *markupGenerator* is associated with a markup sample for easy identification.

Previous section identifies distinct customizations (e. g. bookmarking. default parameters) and characteristics of the portal environment (e. g. Single Sign-On, distinct windowStates, or CSS guidelines). We propose an architecture where each of these concerns are separately addressed by a **supplement module**. Each module includes:

- *SupplementMarkupGenerator*s, which can be inlayed in somewhere else fragments,
- *SupplementFragmentGenerators,* which obtains fragments whose only purpose is supporting the module's functionality
- a *plug-in* routine that obtains profile information or any other state information that impacts the functionality of the module, and acts as a controller for the rendering markups either components or fragments,
- local repositories, where to store ad-hoc data required for the module. This way, the module could provide some aggregate information about previous enactments of the user (e. g. total amount spent on flight tickets) without the requirement for the remote application to provide this information

This architecture is illustrated for the *bookmarking* module (see Fig. 2). Bookmarking affects at least two fragments:

- the *derivedFragment* which prompts the End-user for flight booking data. This fragment, shown in Fig. refcap:Portlet-Fragment-realization, incorporates *derived-Markup* from the Application page as well as a *supplementMarkup* that conveys the bookmarking functionality. As shown in Fig. refcap:Portlet-Fragment-realization, this includes the rendering of a link, labelled *flightToEindhovenConference,* which leads to a markup fragment that facilitates the purchase of a ticket to visit *Eindhoven* (i. e. a bookmark).
- a *supplementFragment, editBookmarks*. This fragment is totally foreign to the external Application. It has to be built from scratch and lets the user edit the bookmarks.

To obtain these two fragments, the *bookmarking* modules includes (see Fig. 2):

- distinct *supplementMarkupGenerators,* one for each *derivedMarkup* (e.g. *addBookmarks* that renders the namesake button, *viewBookmarks* that renders a set of links to the bookmarking pages)
- a *supplementFragmentGenerator* (i. e. *editBookmarks*) which comprises several *supplementMarkupGenerators* (e. g. *action* that renders two buttons for adding/removing bookmarks)
- a plug-in, which reads and stores which URLs are being invoked so as to re-create this scenario whenever the user adds a bookmark. All the invocation sequence from the initial page to the bookmarked page will be stored in user's profile in order to re-generate the state of the Portlet whenever the user clicks on a bookmark.

3.1   The Interaction Diagrams

Portlets follow a two-phase protocol (see [11, 8] for a detailed account). First, the End-user interacts with the markup of a Portlet; this interaction is routed to this Portlet; the Portlet changes its state; each state is associated with a, probably, different markup. This is achieved through the *processAction()* method. Second, *all* the Portlets are required to

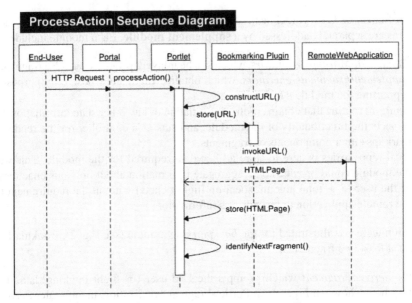

Fig. 3. Simplified *processAction()* sequence diagram.

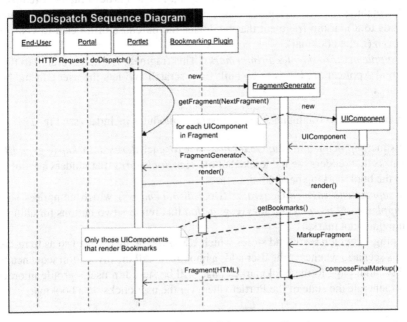

Fig. 4. Simplified *doDispatch()* sequence diagram.

render their current state, better said, the fragment associated with their current state. The *doDispatch()* method retrieves this markup. This subsection addresses how these two methods are realised to support the idiosyncrasies of the bridge Portlet.

The *processAction()* **method.** Fig. 3 shows a simplified view of the interaction diagram for this method. On reception, the Portlet builds the URL of the Web application from the parameters of *processAction()*. Next, this URL is stored and sent to any module that requires it for longer storage. Finally, the Portlet invokes that URL and identifies the name of the next fragment to be rendered back (e. g. *entryFragment, searchResultFragment*, etc). Hence, a page is requested to the external application at the time the bridge Portlet needs it to construct the fragment being required by the portal.

The *doDispatch()* **method.** Fig. 4 depicts the interaction diagram for this method. The Portlet begins by retrieving the name of the next fragment to be shown. First the Web page is requested, and the *DerivedMarkupGenerators* extracted through XPath [14] expressions[3]. Next, these *DerivedMarkupGenerators* further process the extracted markup for the embedded URLs to be made WSRP compliant[4]. Additionally, if the fragment includes *SupplementMarkups* then, calls are made to the corresponding generators. Once all the *UIComponents* have been created, the *render()* method retrieves the whole set of markups by redirecting *render()* to each of the components.

4   Conclusions

The recent release of the WSRP and JSR168 standards is encouraging the process of moving from content syndication to Portlet syndication. Portlets facilitate external applications to be included within a portal. This leads some organisations to consider portals as potential corporate-wide desktop replacements. In this case, the ability to turn existing Web Applications into Portlets will become a must of future Portlet IDEs. This paper addresses customisation concerns.

The notion of the bridge Portlet is introduced as a proxy to an external Application. This Portlet is responsible for customising this external application to the portal environment. Special attention has been paid to support the bridge Portlet using an extensible architecture. To this end, each feature is addressed by a separate module of the architecture. This permits to extend or specialise the number of modules to cater for the peculiarities of the remote Web application.

A case is made for leveraging a Web application with a bookmarking supplement. The bridge Portlet is responsible for enhancing the external Application with this additional functionality when the Application is syndicated in the portal. In this way, the commodities of the portal framework are also brought to syndicated, external Web applications.

We are currently implementing similar modules to leverage existing Web applications to address concerns such as single sign-on and Portlet modes.

Acknowledgements

Our gratitude to Salvador Trujillo and Juan Jose Rodríguez for their valuable comments while preparing this manuscript.

---

[3] Page needs to be previously converted to XHTML. JTidy [15] is used for this purpose.

[4] The actual context implies that the URLs that appear in Portlet markup must be replaced for specific ones to the portal, which will redirect the request to the Portlet [11, 8]. By contrast, URLs that appear in a web page are direct links to the web application. Thus a URL re-writing process should be in place.

References

1. V. Anupam, J. Freire, B. Kumar, and D. Lieuwen. Automating web navigation with the WebVCR. In *Proceedings of the 9th international World Wide Web conference on Computer networks: the international journal of computer and telecommunications networking*, pages 503–517. North-Holland Publishing Co., 2000.
2. B. Badrinath, A. Fox, L. Kleinrock, G. Popek, P. Reiher, and M. Satyanarayanan. A conceptual framework for network and client adaptation. *IEEE Mobile Networks and Applications (MONET)*, 5(4):221–231, 2000.
3. E. Gamma, R. Helm, R. Johnson, and J. Vlissides. *Design Patterns: Elements of Reusable Object-Oriented Software*. Addison-Wesley, 1994.
4. José Cláudio Terra and Cindy Gordon. *Realizing the Promise of Corporate Portals: Leveraging Knowledge for Business Success*. Butterworth-Heinemann, 2003. ISBN: 0-7506-7593-4.
5. G. Kappel, B. Pröll, W. Retschitzegger, and W. Schwinger. Customisation for Ubiquitous Web Applications: A Comparison of Approaches. *International Journal of Web Engineering and Technology (IJWET)*, 1(1):79–111, 2003.
6. A. Kobsa and J. Koenemann. Personalised Hypermedia Presentation Techniques for Improving Online Customer Relationship. *The Knowledge Engineering Review*, 16(2):111–155, 2001.
7. N. Kushmerick. *Wrapper Induction for Information Extraction*. PhD thesis, University of Washington, 1997.
8. OASIS. Web Service for Remote Portlets Specification Version 1.0, 2003. http://www.oasis-open.org/commitees/tc_home.php?wg_abbrev=wsrp.
9. R. Oppermann and M. Specht. A Nomadic Information System for Adaptive Exhibition Guidance. In David Bearman and Jennifer Trant, editors, *Proceedings of the International Conference on Hypermedia and Interactivity in Museums (ICHIM99)*, pages 103–109, Washington, September 1999.
10. Oracle. Oracle9iAS Portal Web Clipping Portlet, October 2003. at http://portalcenter.oracle.com/.
11. Java Community Process. JSR 168 Portlet Specification Version 1.0, September 2003. at http://www.jcp.org/en/jsr/detail?id=168.
12. I. Smith. Doing Web Clippings in under ten minutes. Technical report, Intranet Journal, March 2001. at http://www.intranetjournal.com/articles/200103/ pic_03_28_01a.html.
13. W3C. Cascading Style Sheet (CSS), 1998. at http://wwww.w3c.org/Style/CSS/.
14. W3C. XML Path Language (XPath) Version 1.0, 1999. http://www.w3.org/TR/xpath.html.
15. W3C/Tidy. Clean up your Web pages with HTML TIDY, 2002. at http://www.w3.org/People/Raggett/tidy/.

The Personal Reader:
Personalizing and Enriching Learning Resources Using Semantic Web Technologies*

Peter Dolog[1], Nicola Henze[2], Wolfgang Nejdl[1,2], and Michael Sintek[3]

[1] L3S Research Center,
Expo Plaza 1, D-30539 Hannover, Germany
{dolog,nejdl}@learninglab.de
[2] ISI – Knowledge-Based Systems, University of Hannover,
Appelstr. 4, D-30167 Hannover, Germany
{henze,nejdl}@kbs.uni-hannover.de
[3] DFKI GmbH, Knowledge Management Department,
Postfach 2080, D-67608 Kaiserslautern, Germany
Michael.Sintek@dfki.de

Abstract. Traditional adaptive hypermedia systems have focused on providing adaptation functionality on a closed corpus, while Web search interfaces have delivered non-personalized information to users. In this paper, we show how we integrate closed corpus adaptation and global context provision in a Personal Reader environment. The local context consists of individually optimized recommendations to learning materials within the given corpus; the global context provides individually optimized recommendations to resources found on the Web, e. g., FAQs, student exercises, simulations, etc. The adaptive local context of a learning resource is generated by applying methods from adaptive educational hypermedia in a semantic web setting. The adaptive global context is generated by constructing appropriate queries, enrich them based on available user profile information, and, if necessary, relax them during the querying process according to available metadata.

Keywords: adaptive hypermedia, personalization, adaptive web, semantic web, reasoning rules, querying the semantic web.

1 Introduction

Over the last years, adaptive hypermedia techniques have been used to enhance and personalize learning experiences in e-Learning scenarios. In this paper, we show how personalized e-Learning can be realized in the Semantic Web. The personalization functionalities which we present in this paper aim at showing the context of learning resources, e. g., personal recommendations for general topics, more detailed aspects, linking to quizzes, similar courses, tutorials, FAQs, etc. We can distinguish two general cases: In the first case, we generate a personally optimized context of the learning

---

* This work was partially supported by EU/IST project ELENA (www.elena-project.org) and Network of Excellence REWERSE (www.rewerse.net).

W. Nejdl and P. De Bra (Eds.): AH 2004, LNCS 3137, pp. 85–94, 2004.

resource with respect to the course this resource belongs to – *local context*. The second case – *global context* – extends personalization towards the outside world; i. e., references to related learning resources from other repositories are retrieved and personalized.

The majority of existing adaptive hypermedia systems has in the past focused on *closed corpus adaptation*. The corpus of documents / learning resources the system can adapt to is already known at design time. For our *adaptive local context* we show how closed corpus adaptive functionality can be realized using semantic web technologies and (standard) metadata descriptions of resources. Providing an *adaptive global context* extends the corpus of documents to the open world, thus providing adaptation in an *open corpus*. Like local context, global context is generated by using (standard) metadata descriptions and semantic web technologies. However, for computing the global context we cannot assume the resources to be as richly annotated as our course materials in the local context setting.

The Personal Reader embeds learning resources in a personalized context, providing a local context within a course or corpus, as well as a global context with references to external resources. An overview on the functionality of the Personal Reader is given in Sect. 2. Required metadata annotations of learning materials, most of them referring to standardized metadata descriptions, are presented in Sect. 3. Sect. 4 shows how adaptation is realized both for local and global context. The paper ends with a discussion of related work as well as current and future work.

2   Overview of the Personal Reader

Let us start with a specific scenario, involving a user, Alice, interested in learning Java programming. Alice is currently learning about variables in Java by accessing some learning resource in an online tutorial. During her studies she realizes that she needs some clarifications on naming variables. The Personal Reader shows where detailed information on variables can be found in this online tutorial, and also points out recommended references for deeper understanding. For ensuring that Alice understands the use of variables, the Personal Reader provides several quizzes. When practicing, Alice does some of the recommended exercises. For the chosen exercises, the Personal Reader provides Alice with appropriate links to the Java API, and some already solved exercises. A further source of information are the JAVA FAQ references pointed out to Alice by the Personal Reader.

The primary goal of the Personal Reader is to support the learner in her learning in two ways:

- *Local context provision:* Provides the learner with references to summaries, more general information, more detailed information, examples, and quizzes within a course which might help her to clarify open questions raised during visiting the currently visited learning resource.
- *Global context provision:* Provides the learner with references to additional resources from the educational semantic web which are related to the currently visited learning resource which might further help to improve his background on the topic of learning.

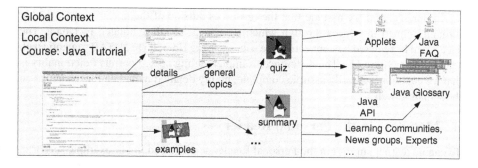

Fig. 1. Functionality of the Personal Reader

The learner profile is taken into account to personalize the presentation of the local context and the global context. Fig. 1 summarizes the functionality of the Personal Reader.

Local Context Functionality. The local context takes resources included with the current course materials into account. In our scenario, Alice would retrieve further details on Java variables as well as a summary about variables. In addition, she gets advice which details are recommended for her depending on what she has learned already.

This *adaptive context generation* comprises several subtasks: *searching for additional resources* within a course corpus, and *generating recommendation information*. In our example, the Personal Reader searches for *generalizations, further details, summaries*, and *quizzes* and will generate links to them based on the metadata information. Generated *recommendation information* annotates those links based on the learner profile.

Besides those functionalities, others can be considered as well as depicted in Fig. 1: Further Java examples associated with the lecture can help to understand implementation details, further comparisons with other programming languages can clarify benefits and shortcomings of specific Java constructs.

Global Context Functionality. The global context considers resources outside of the corpus, available on the semantic web. In our scenario Alice takes advantage of context sensitive references to the Java API while practicing the use of variables. She benefits from solutions for similar exercises recommended by the Personal Reader and as well as from appropriate Java FAQ entries. As the resources reside outside the closed corpus we refer to this functionality as *global context functionality*. In addition, global context references are enriched with personal recommendations based on the learner profile.

Similarly to the closed corpus, we provide two kinds of functionalities: *searching for additional resources*, and *generating recommendation information*. Alice's Personal Reader will *generate links* to resources about relevant *Java applets*, relevant pages describing the *Java API* for current exercises, and related answers from the *Java FAQ*. In addition, definitions from the *Java Glossary* related to the terms currently used in the presented resource are provided.

In our scenario we assume that the resources outside of the corpus are accessible through defined interfaces through which we can get RDF annotated metadata. The access can be realized by connecting the sources using Edutella [12], TAP semantic web search [9], or Lixto [1]. The difference to implementing closed corpus functionality is that we cannot necessarily assume complete, highly detailed metadata for resources on the semantic web.

3   Metadata in the Personal Reader

To enable learner support in the Personal Reader as described in our example scenario, components realizing the adaptation services require meta-information about courses, learning resources, and about learners. The Personal Reader makes use of RDF descriptions based on several well-defined RDF schemas and learning specific standards to support interoperability, as discussed in the following paragraphs.

Describing Learning Resources and Courses. For structuring and describing learning resources, there are the Dublin Core standard[1] and the Learning Objects Metadata (LOM) standard[2] with their RDF bindings.

For example, part of an RDF-based metadata annotation for a learning resource on the Java programming language is:

```
1 <rdf:Description
       rdf:about="http://java.sun.com/.../tutorial/index.html">
2  <rdf:type
       rdf:resource="http://ltsc.ieee..../lom-educational#lecture"/>
3  <dc:title>The Java Tutorial (SUN)</dc:title>
4  <dc:description>A practical guide for programmers with hundreds
       of complete working examples and dozens of trails.
           </dc:description>
5  <dc:subject
       rdf:resource="http://hoersaal.kbs.uni-hannover.de/rdf
                /java_ontology.rdf#Java_Programming_Language"/>
6  <dcterms:hasPart>
7  <rdf:Seq>
       <rdf:li
       rdf:resource="http://java.sun.com/.../java/index.html"/>
       ....
   </rdf:Seq>
   </dcterms:hasPart>
  </rdf:Description>
```

The most important information commonly used in adaptive systems are *type*, *structure*, *prerequisites*, and *subject* of a resource.

In the Personal Reader, a type designates a resource as a web page, a learning resource, an online tutorial, or a lecture. The subject of a resource indicates concepts which are exposed by the content of the resource, e.g., as in line 5 dc:subject to a concept from the the Java programming language ontology[3]. Prerequisites and structure are specified by the *hasPart* property from Dublin Core, as in lines 6 and 7. In

---

[1] http://dublincore.org/

[2] http://ltsc.ieee.org/

[3] A domain ontology for the Java Programming language, consisting of ˜ 500 concepts, is available at http://www.personal-reader.de

this relation, a reference to concepts from a domain ontology is used. In the same manner, further information like title (line 3), description (line 4), authors, copyright, target audience and authoring date can be provided.

Describing Learners. Information about learners is needed to recommend appropriate learning resources relevant to user interests, learner performance in different courses within one domain or different domains, user goals and preferences. The learner profile schema provides slots for information about a learner. In the Personal Reader (for both local and global contexts), the learner's *performance* maintains (besides other records) a *reference to a resource* (e. g., on Java variables from our scenario) as a learning experience identifier, a *reference to the entry from the Java ontology* as a learning competency identifier, and a certificate of the issuing institution, which in this case is Sun as a content provider. A *portfolio* record points, for example, to the solved exercises (e. g., on Java variables from our scenario), with subject, type, and creator attributes, which are used in the global and local context functionalities. A *preference* record usually points to the language which the learner prefers.

4   Functionality of the Personal Reader

The personal reader integrates several functions to fulfill the requirements for *local context* and *global context* provision. Context generation in both cases follows a sequence of activities: *identifying metadata for the currently visited resource, ontology mapping, constructing a query for additional resources, query rewriting based on user preferences, query relaxation, generating recommendations.*

In this section we discuss how to implement the most important functionalities for both contexts. The examples use TRIPLE[4], a rule-based query language for the semantic web; the implementation is based on TRIPLE as well as Edutella and its RDF-QEL language.

4.1   Closed Corpus Adaptation

The personal reader enables the learner to work with learning resources in an embedding context. In the local context, more details related to the topics of the learning resource, the general topics the learner is currently studying, examples, summaries, quizzes, etc. are generated and enriched with personal recommendations according to the learner's current learning state, as shown in Fig. 2.

We assume that the closed corpus uses just one subject ontology (the Java ontology) and one common metadata schema. Ontology mapping functionality is not required. Query rewriting based on language preferences is usually useful in big corpora with several languages. In our corpus we consider just one language, so query rewriting based on language preferences is not needed. We also assume high quality metadata in our closed corpus, no query relaxation is needed.

---

[4] http://triple.semanticweb.org

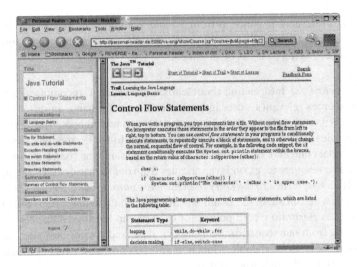

Fig. 2. Screenshot of the Personal Reader, showing the adaptive context of a learning resource in a course. The Personal Reader is available at www.personal-reader.de

Searching for Resources. Generating links to more detailed learning resources is one functionality mentioned in Sect. 2. A *query/rule is constructed* taking the isa/subclassOf hierarchy of the Java ontology into account. More details for the currently used learning resource is determined by `detail_learningobject(LO, LO_DETAIL)` where LO and LO_Detail are learning resources, and where LO_DETAIL covers more specialized learning concepts which are determined with help of the domain ontology described in Sect. 3. The rule does not require that LO_DETAIL covers all specialized learning concepts, nor that it exclusively covers specialized learning concepts. Further refinements are of course possible and should, in a future version of the Personal Reader, be available as tuning parameters under control of the learner.

```
FORALL LO, LO_DETAIL detail_learningobject(LO, LO_DETAIL) <-
    learning_resource(LO) AND learning_resource(LO_DETAIL) AND
    EXISTS C, C_DETAIL (detail_concepts(C,C_DETAIL)
                    AND concepts_of_LO(LO,C)
                    AND concepts_of_LO(LO_DETAIL, C_DETAIL)).
```

Another example of a *constructed query/rule* for generating embedding context is the recommendation of quiz-pages. A learning resource Q is recommended as a quiz for a currently learned learning resource LO if it is a quiz (the rule for determining this is not displayed) and if it provides questions to at least some of the concepts learned on LO.

```
FORALL LO, Q quiz(LO, Q) <-
    EXISTS C (concepts_of_LO(LO,C) AND concepts_of_Quiz(Q,C)).
```

Generating Recommendations. Recommendations are personalized according to the current learning progress of the user within this course. The following rule depicts a learning resource LO in the local context as recommended if the learner studied at least one more general learning resource (UpperLevelLO):

```
FORALL LO, U learning_state(LO, U, recommended) <-
   EXISTS UpperLevelLO ( upperlevel(LO, UpperLevelLO) AND
                         p_obs(UpperLevelLO, U, Learned) ).
```

Additional rules derive stronger recommendations (e. g., if the user has studied *all* general learning resources), less strong recommendations (e. g., if one or two of these haven't been studied so far), etc.

4.2   Global Context Provision

While providing locally available information with high-quality annotations, we also use external semantic web resources to provide a broader range of information, although these annotations will be, in general, of lower quality.

We assume that external resources are semantically annotated with current semantic web technology (embedded or external RDF(S) annotations). The generation of these annotations is outside the scope of our system; standard approaches, apart from manual techniques, include statistical and linguistic techniques for analyzing text and html documents, and esp. ontology-focused crawling of web documents [7]. It is obvious that such techniques can successfully be applied to structured document collections like Java APIs, FAQs, news, glossaries, Wikis, etc.

Starting from the user's initial query and the already identified sections from the closed corpus that match the user's query, we construct queries sent to external repositories like the Edutella network (for query construction, see [6]). To do this, we need three functionalities: ontology mapping, query relaxation, and result filtering.

Ontology Mapping. Even in the case of already annotated resources, these will, in general, not use the same ontologies/schemas that are used locally. We therefore need strategies to match queries and user preferences with these external annotations. As was described in detail in [11], TRIPLE views can be used to solve the problem of mapping resources formulated according to one ontology to resources formulated in a different one.

Query Relaxation. Since externally annotated web resources will often be annotated in a less precise way (simpler ontologies, missing metadata, and even inconsistent metadata), we also need heuristics to construct queries that cope with these difficulties. If the exact query returns no (or too few) results, the query is relaxed by replacing some restrictions with semantically similar (usually, more general) ones, or by dropping some restrictions entirely. For this, we also need a strategy to decide which attributes to relax first (e. g., first relax dc:subject, then relax type, . . .). The following TRIPLE predicate similar_concept(C, CS, D) shows how to enumerate, for a given concept C, similar concepts CS by traversing the underlying ontology and extracting superconcepts, subconcepts, and siblings with a given maximum distance D from C in the ontology. We assume here that the predicate direct_super connects concepts with their direct superconcepts.

```
FORALL C,CS similar_concept(C,CS,1) <- // direct super/subconcept
    direct_super(C, CS) OR direct_super(CS, C).
FORALL C, CS, D, D1 similar_concept(C, CS, D) <- // recurse
    D > 1 AND D1 is D - 1 AND similar_concept(C, CS1, D1) AND
    (direct_super(CS, CS1) OR direct_super(CS1, CS))
                            AND not unify(C,CS).
```

This predicate is used iteratively to relax the query: first, get all similar concepts with $D = 1$, relax the query (by query rewriting), and send it to the remote repositories. If the returned result set is empty (or too small), increment D and reiterate. The maximum number of iterations should be significantly smaller than the "height" of the ontology to avoid completely meaningless results.

Result Filtering. In the case that these relaxations produce too general queries and therefore too many results are returned, additional heuristics have to be applied. For example, similarity measures defined on text strings can be applied to resource titles (dc:title), textual representations of subjects (dc:subject), descriptions (dc:description), names (dc:creator), etc. Such heuristics can use simple statistical methods, like counting the number of overlapping n-grams. For attributes with non-textual ranges (dates, numbers, etc.), other straightforward heuristics can be applied.

Generating Recommendations. As external resources are not annotated as parts of specific courses, we cannot assume the recommendations based on part/whole relation as in Sect. 4.1. On the other hand, we can derive prerequisites from the subject and required background for the resource [6]. Similarly to result filtering, additional similarity measures can be employed, for example, to dc:title to get the subject of the resource and to compare it with entries in a subject ontology and learner performance.

5   Related Work

Related work includes recent content presentation personalization systems [8, 4] as well as personalized learning portals [3]. Theoretical foundations on adaptive hypermedia which led to our approach can be found in [10].

[8] focuses on content adaptation, or more precisely on personalizing the presentation of hypermedia content to the user. Both adaptability and adaptivity are realized via slices: Adaptability is provided by certain adaptability conditions in the slices, e. g., the ability of a device to display images. Adaptivity is based on the AHAM idea [2] of event-conditions for resources: A slice is desirable if its appearance condition evaluates to true.

Personalized learning portals are investigated in [3]. The learning portals provide views on learning activities which are provided by so-called *activity servers*. The activity servers store both learning content and the learning activities possible with this special content. A central student model server collects the data about student performance from each activity server the student is working on, as well as from every portal the student is registered to.

Similar to our approach, [5] builds on separating learning resources from sequencing logic and additional models for adaptivity: Adaptivity blocks in the metadata of learning objects as well as in the narrative model, candidate groups and components define which kind of adaptivity can be realized on the current learning content. A rule engine selects the best candidates for each user in a given context. Adaptivity requirements are considered only in the adaptivity blocks, however, while our approach relies on standard metadata descriptions.

TAP [9] considers contextual information generated from semantic web based annotations enriching, e. g., Google results. Our approach combines context generation with personalization. This and the specificity of the technology supported learning domain required additional techniques not considered in TAP like query relaxation and rewriting, ontology mapping, and more close ties between the generated contexts and visited learning resource.

6   Conclusion

This paper describes the Personal Reader, an experimental environment supporting personalized learning based on semantic web technologies. The prototype implements several methods needed for personalization suitable for an environment based on a fixed set of documents (a closed corpus) plus personalized context sensitive information from the semantic web. On the closed corpus, semantic web technologies allow us to experiment with and realize existing adaptation methods and techniques in a more rigorous and formalized way. In the global context, they provide compatibility with metadata on the semantic web. Our prototype is appropriate for an e-learning context, providing, annotating and recommending learning material suitable for specific courses. To implement the retrieval of appropriate learning resources from the semantic web, we have proposed several heuristics and query rewriting rules which allow us to reformulate queries to provide personalized information even when metadata quality is low.

Future work will focus on further experiments with different combinations of the functionalities discussed in this paper, further contextualization possibilities for the semantic web, and an evaluation of the proposed approach with respect to learning support (are the personalization services value-adding services, what kind of personalization services is required by students and teachers, etc.), and to "open corpus" learning (effects of the personalized context provision / additional learning resources on learning progress).

References

1. R. Baumgartner, S. Flesca, and G. Gottlob. Declarative information extraction, web crawling, and recursive wrapping with lixto. In *6th International Conference on Logic Programming and Nonmonotonic Reasoning*, Vienna, Austria, 2001.
2. P. D. Bra, G.-J. Houben, and H. Wu. AHAM: A dexter-based reference model for adaptive hypermedia. In *ACM Conference on Hypertext and Hypermedia*, pages 147–156, Darmstadt, Germany, 1999.
3. P. Brusilovsky and H. Nijhawan. A framework for adaptive e-learning based on distributed re-usable learning activities. In *In Proceedings of World Conference on E-Learning, E-Learn 2002*, Montreal, Canada, 2002.

4. O. Conlan, D. Lewis, S. Higel, D. O'Sullivan, and V. Wade. Applying adaptive hypermedia techniques to semantic web service composition. In *International Workshop on Adaptive Hypermedia and Adaptive Web-based Systems (AH 2003)*, Budapest, Hungary, 2003.

5. D. Dagger, V. Wade, and O. Conlan. Towards "anytime, anywhere" learning: The role and realization of dynamic terminal personalization in adaptive elearning. In *Ed-Media 2003, World Conference on Educational Multimedia, Hypermedia and Telecommunications*, Hawaii, 2003.

6. P. Dolog, N. Henze, W. Nejdl, and M. Sintek. Personalization in distributed e-learning environments. In *Proc. of WWW2004 — The Thirteenth International World Wide Web Conference*, May 2004.

7. M. Ehrig and A. Maedche. Ontology-focused crawling of Web documents. In *Proc. of the 2003 ACM symposium on Applied computing*, Melbourne, Florida, 2003.

8. F. Frasincar and G. Houben. Hypermedia presentation adaptation on the semantic web. In *Proccedings of the 2nd International Conference on Adaptive Hypermedia and Adaptive Web-Based Systems (AH 2002)*, Malaga, Spain, 2002.

9. R. Guha, R. McCool, and E. Miller. Semantic search. In *WWW2003 — Proc. of the 12th international conference on World Wide Web*, pages 700–709. ACM Press, 2003.

10. N. Henze and W. Nejdl. Logically characterizing adaptive educational hypermedia systems. In *International Workshop on Adaptive Hypermedia and Adaptive Web-based Systems (AH 2003)*, Budapest, Hungary, 2003.

11. Z. Miklos, G. Neumann, U. Zdun, and M. Sintek. Querying semantic web resources using triple views. In *Proc. of the 2nd International Semantic Web Conference (ISWC)*, Sundial Resort, Sanibel Island, Florida, USA, October 2003.

12. W. Nejdl, B. Wolf, C. Qu, S. Decker, M. Sintek, A. Naeve, M. Nilsson, M. Palmér, and T. Risch. EDUTELLA: a P2P Networking Infrastructure based on RDF. In *In Proc. of 11th World Wide Web Conference*, Hawaii, USA, May 2002.

An Experiment in Social Search*

Jill Freyne and Barry Smyth

Smart Media Institute, Department of Computer Science,
University College Dublin, Belfield, Dublin 4, Ireland
{Jill.Freyne,Barry.Smyth}@ucd.ie

Abstract. Social search is an approach to Web search that attempts to offer communities of like-minded individuals more targeted search services, based on the search behaviour of their peers, bringing together ideas from Web search, social networking and personalization. In this paper we describe the I-SPY architecture for social search and present the results of a recent live-user evaluation that highlight the potential benefits of our approach in a realistic search setting.

1   Introduction

The brief history of Web search to date is characterised by a variety of significant technological developments that have seen Web search engines evolve beyond their information retrieval (IR) origins. For example, Meta-search [1, 2] was an early attempt to combine the capabilities of many underlying search engines in order to improve overall coverage and relevance ranking. More recently, search engines such as Google [3] have argued for the need to consider factors such as link-connectivity information (in addition to the more traditional IR term-based factors) as a way to guide search towards more informative documents; see also [4]. Currently most of the main Web search engines adopt a "one size fits all" approach to search – two users with the same query receive the same result-list, regardless of their preferences or context – and while there is broad agreement that this is far from optimal, real developments towards *practical* personalization techniques, that are both capable of coping with Internet-scale search tasks, and that are likely to be acceptable to today's privacy conscious users, have been slow to emerge. Although, that said, a number of researchers have looked at the issue of context-sensitive search, where the search engine draws additional information context from the searcher [5].

One area of research that may have the potential to offer the right mix of personalization, while at the same time protecting user privacy, comes from recent work that has focused on the intersection between social networking and Web search. Social networking applications such as *Friendster* (www.frienster.com) or *Orkut* (www.orkut.com) allow users to create, maintain and participate in online communities, and provide a range of applications and services to help these communities socialise more effectively on-line and off-line. Inevitably, the members of a given community will all share certain characteristics and interests; for example, the members of a "caving and potholing" community will obviously all have an interest in caving and potholing activities, but

---

* The support of the Informatics Research Initiative of Enterprise Ireland is gratefully acknowledged.

W. Nejdl and P. De Bra (Eds.): AH 2004, LNCS 3137, pp. 95–103, 2004.

they are also likely to share a range of peripheral preferences too; a general interest in outdoor activities, they may be regular travelers, etc. The point is that these well-defined communities of like-minded individuals provide a backdrop for *social search* applications; search engines that are sensitive to the needs and preferences of a specific community of users, operating within a well-defined topical domain. Indeed social search is an increasingly important topic for the search industry and many commentators have predicted that it will become the "next big thing". In this paper we will describe our own model of social search, called I-SPY, but other similar services such as *Eurekster* (www.eurkster.com) are rapidly emerging to try and take advantage of this social dimension to search. Indeed it is worth speculating about the intentions of Google in this regard, especially since they have launched their own social networking service (www.orkut.com) but have yet to announce how they plan to integrate it with the Google search engine.

I-SPY operates as a post-processing engine for traditional search engines, or as a meta-search service over a number of underlying search engines. It allows groups of users to establish online search communities and *anonymously* records their interaction patterns as they search. These interaction patterns – the queries provided and the resulting selections – allow I-SPY to adaptively re-rank the result-lists of future queries in a way that is sensitive to the preferences of a given community of users. For example, over time I-SPY will learn that a community of AI researchers are more likely to be interested in the work of the Berkeley professor than the basketball star when they search under the vague query, "Micheal Jordan"; I-SPY actively promotes such relevant sites for this community of users. In the following sections we will describe the operation of I-SPY in detail (see Sect. 3) and present the results of a live-user study over a particular community of users (Sect. 4). First we will outline related work with a particular focus on research that has sought to exploit the interaction patterns of users to provide other types of adaptive, collaborative information services on the Web. We will look, in particular, at collaborative browsing services a their relationship to our own proposal for collaborative search.

2 Related Work

The research described in this paper – the I-SPY system and its collaborative-ranking features – touches on a number of areas of related research. One legitimate view of our work is that I-SPY is focused on disambiguating vague queries, that it provides a form of context-sensitive search. As such we could compare our work to other attempts at developing context-sensitive search techniques, differentiating between explicit [6] and implicit [7] forms of context or between external [8] or local [9] sources of context. Alternatively, one might view I-SPY's approach to search as a way of coping with disparities between the query-space and indexing-space and cite related work in which researchers have attempted to leverage knowledge about the query-space to solve this problem and improve search performance [10–12]. Indeed, these particular perspectives are considered in [13, 14]. However, as indicated in the introduction, we will take a different standpoint, one that looks at I-SPY from an interaction perspective, one that highlights the social and collaborative aspects of information seeking activities.

To begin with it is worth highlighting the work of Hill and Hollan [15] in which they introduced the concept of *computational wear* in the context of digital information.

Real world objects are history-rich – a well-read book naturally falls open on a popular page, important chapters become dog-eared with regular use, and paragraphs may be underlined or annotated with margin notes – and this history often helps us to make better use of these objects. In contrast, digital information is usually history-poor – Web pages do not change as surfers view them, for example – and this lack of history can limit the manner in which we can use and benefit from digital information. Hill and Hollan describe ways in which interaction histories can be incorporated into digital objects. Specifically they describe the *Edit Wear* and *Read Wear* applications which allow the user to leave *wear marks* on a document as they edit or read it. These wear marks are represented visually as part of the document's scroll-bar and help the user to quickly appreciate where the main focus of editing or reading activities has been.

The *Footprints* project [16], inspired by the work of Hill and Hollan, applied the idea of computational wear and interaction histories to the Web, building a number of tools to help users navigate through sites. For example, one tool graphically represented the traffic through a Web site, allowing surfers to appreciate the links that are being followed regularly by others. Another Footprints tool visualises the paths (sequences of links) followed by individual surfers. These tools represent the interaction histories of previous users, and they allow the current user to adapt their browsing pattern as appropriate. Rather than surfing blind, the current user can be guided by the actions of others. The Footprints tools facilitate a form of collaborative browsing, an idea that is closely related to the work of [17].

The I-SPY philosophy is related to the above. I-SPY also attempts to exploit inter-action history or computational wear, as we shall discuss in the next section, but rather than focusing on editing or reading documents, or browsing Web pages, I-SPY focuses on search. It records the interactions of searchers with result-lists and uses these inter-actions to improve result-ranking and helps the searcher to understand which results have been found relevant in the past. Thus search becomes a more social activity. New searchers benefit from the searches carried out by past users. They see the results that past users have liked, and they benefit from an ordering of results that is sensitive to the degree to which these past results have been preferred.

3   An Architecture for Social Search

The basic architecture for our model of social search, implemented by I-SPY (ispy.ucd. ie), is presented in Fig. 1. On the face of it, I-SPY is a meta-search engine, adapting a user query, q_T, for a series of underlying search engines, $S_1, ...S_n$, and merging each of their result-lists, $R_1, ..., R_n$, to produce a final result-list, R, that is returned to the user. The uniqueness of I-SPY stems from a combination of important features: (1) its capturing of interaction histories; (2) the use of these interaction histories to re-rank search results; and (3) its ability to separate the interaction histories of individual search communities (social groups) so that this re-ranking can take place in a community-sensitive manner.

3.1   Interaction Histories

Each time a user selects a page, p_j, from a result-list generated by I-SPY in response to a query, q_i, a record of this selection is noted by incrementing a counter in I-SPY's so-called *hit-matrix*, H; see Fig. 1. Thus, the value of H_{ij} represents the number of

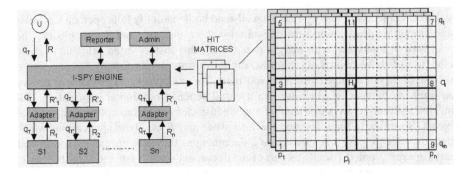

Fig. 1. The I-SPY system architecture for social, collaborative search.

times that p_j has been selected for query q_i. The hit-matrix represents the interaction history (in the sense of [16]) relative to a set of queries and their relevant results.

3.2   Collaborative Ranking

The hit-matrix is a record of what past searchers have viewed as relevant to their queries and I-SPY takes advantage of this information to re-rank some of the search results that are returned from the meta-search. If any of the meta-search results, for a query q_T, have non-zero hit-values in the hit-matrix row that corresponds to q_T, then this provides further evidence (the number of past selections) that these results are relevant to q_T. Furthermore the degree of relevance can be estimated as the percentage of selections that a given page has received for this query; see Equation 1. This relevance score can be used to rank these previously selected results ahead of the other results returned by the meta-search. So the first results presented to the user are those that have been previously selected for their query, ordered according to their past selection probability(see Fig. 2(a)). The remainder of the results are ordered according to their standard meta-search score. The hope is that the promoted results will turn out to be more relevant to the searchers, helping them to locate their target information more efficiently; we will test this hypothesis directly in Sect. 4.

$$Relevance(p_j, q_T) = \frac{H_{Tj}}{\sum_{\forall j} H_{Tj}} \qquad (1)$$

3.3   Search Communities

I-SPY is designed to support multiple hit-matrices, each for a different community of searchers. For example, consider one group of searchers interested in motoring information and another interested in wildlife. The query, *"jaguar"* has very different meanings for each of these communities: the former are looking for information about the high-performance car while the latter are interested in the big cat variety. Ordinarily a standard search engine or meta-search engine would respond to each community in the same way. However, with I-SPY, the likelihood is that the previous interactions

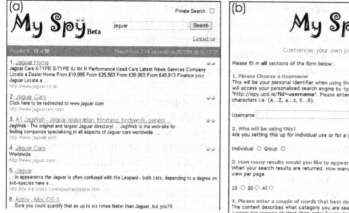

Fig. 2. (A) A result-list for a motoring community for the query "jaguar", the eyes denote promoted results; (B) I-SPY's on-line configuration form facilitates the creation of new community-specific search services.

of the motoring community will have produced a hit-matrix that prioritises car-related sites for the *"jaguar"* query, while the wildlife hit-matrix will prioritise wildlife-related sites; see Fig. 2(A).

Thus, I-SPY's collaborative ranking is designed to operate for well-defined communities of searchers. To facilitate this I-SPY allows individual users or user-groups to configure their own search service by filling out an online form; see Fig. 2(b). The result is a unique hit-matrix that is linked to a search community and a URL that contains a version of I-SPY whose queries are associated with this new hit-matrix. Alternatively, the searchers can add a piece of javascript to their site to include a search-box that is linked to their own hit-matrix.

4   Evaluation

Collaborative ranking on its own is unlikely to be successful in a general-purpose search context because the alternative meanings of vague queries are likely to be merged in the hit-matrix; for example, we would expect to find selections for car sites and wildlife sites recorded for the "jaguar" query in a general-purpose search engine. The secret of I-SPY is that this problem is largely eliminated once we allow for the separation of interaction histories for different communities of users. And we believe that this particular combination of collaborative ranking and community-based search will pay dividends when it comes to improving overall search performance. To test this hypothesis we report on a live trial of I-SPY that was carried out in late 2003 on a community of third-year computer science students.

4.1   Setup

A total of 92 students were asked to answer 25 general knowledge computer science questions. They were directed to use I-SPY (configured to use Google, HotBot, AllThe

Web, and Teoma) to source their answers and they were divided into two groups of 45 and 47 students, respectively. The first group served as a *training group*. They did not benefit from I-SPY's collaborative ranking technique – the results were ranked using the standard meta-search ranking function only – but their queries and selections were used to construct a hit-matrix for the second group of users (the *test group*) who did benefit from I-SPY's collaborative ranking.

Each user group was allotted 45 minutes to complete the questions. Overall more than 70% of the training group's queries were repeated by the test group, and these repeated queries were used by approximately 65% of the 97 students. This high repeat rate suggests a close correspondence between the query formation capabilities of each group of users. However, it is worth pointing out that the test users tended to use slightly shorter (fewer terms) queries than the training users; the average query length for the test group was 2.16, compared to 2.57 for the training group. All other things being equal this might suggest that the training group were better able to produce focused queries and that the training users might be at a slight advantage when it comes to their inherent search abilities.

4.2   Selection Behaviour

Our first question concerns the selection behaviour of the training and test users. If I-SPY's collaborative ranking technique is working to promote more relevant results to higher positions within result-lists then we should find that the test users are selecting results nearer to the top of result-lists, when compared to the selections of the training users.

Fig. 3(a) plots the position of result selections during each search session for the training and test users; for each search session we plot the median position of the selected results. Although the position of results vary considerably from search session to search session, as expected, there is a marked difference between the position of results for the training and test users and it is clear that the test users are selecting results that appear nearer to the top of result-lists (lower position values) when compared to the training users, due to the improved position of relevant results for the test users as a consequence of I-SPY's collaborative ranking technique. To provide a clearer picture of the benefits of I-SPY's collaborative ranking we can summarise the results of Fig. 3(a) by computing the mean position values of the selections of the training group and compare these to the mean positions of the selections of the test group; see Fig. 3(b). The test users selected results with an average position of 2.24 whereas the training users selected results with an average position of 4.26; a 47% reduction in the position of selected results for the test users compared to the training users, and a strong indicator of the benefit of I-SPY's collaborative ranking function.

These results indicate that the test users were more likely to select results from higher positions within the result-lists. We argue that this is because these users were able to benefit from the interaction histories of their peers within the training group because I-SPY's collaborative ranking technique was actively promoting the selections of these peers. The hope is that these community preferences will turn out to be useful results, when it comes to the students answering their questions, and we will consider this issue in the next section.

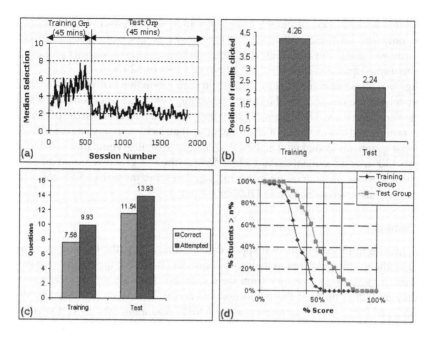

Fig. 3. (a) Median positions of selected results; (b) Mean positions of all result selections between training and test groups; (c) Mean number of questions attempted/correctly answered per student; (d) Percentage of students that achieve a given test-score.

4.3 Search Accuracy

Of course finding out that the test users selected results from higher positions in the result-lists, compared to the training users, does not really tell us anything about the usefulness of these results. It may be, for example, that the selections of the training users were not so relevant to the task at hand and that I-SPY's eagerness to promote these misleading results simply encouraged the test users to follow false-leads, and thus hampered their ability to answer the test questions. If this is the case then our experiment in social search will have failed. If, however, the promoted results were more likely to be relevant, then we should find that the test users were able to answer questions more efficiently. We should find that the test users attempt more questions than the training users and that they answer more of these attempted questions correctly. In short, we should find that the test students achieve higher overall test-scores.

Fig. 3(c) compare the training and test users in terms of the mean number of questions attempted per student/user and the mean number of correctly answered questions per student. The results indicate a clear advantage for the test users: they did in fact attempt more questions on average than the training group (9.93 versus 13.93, respectively) and they did answer more of these questions correctly (7.58 versus 11.54, respectively).It is worth noting that both these differences are significant at the 0.01 significance level. Indeed it is revealing to note that the test group of users answered more questions correctly (11.54) than the training group even managed to attempt (9.93). To look at this another way: of the 9.93 questions attempted, on average, by the training group, only 76% of these questions (7.58) are answered correctly. The test group not only managed to attempt 40% more questions but they answered a higher proportion of these attempted questions correctly (11.54 out of 13.93 or 82%).

Fig. 3(d) plots the percentage of students in each group that achieved different overall test-scores; the test score is the overall percentage of the 25 questions that a student has answered correctly. These scores clarify the gap that exists between the performance of the training and test groups. For example, more than twice as many test students (70% of the test group, or 33 students) achieved a pass grade of 40% compared to the training students (30%, or 13 students). And while 56% of the test group achieved an honours grade (55%), none of the training group managed to score more than 52% and 5 of the test students achieved a distinction (70% or greater).

4.4 Summary

To begin with in this experiment it appeared that, if anything, the training users might be at a slight advantage owing to their longer queries. However, the results clearly indicate superior search performance from the test group. They attempted more questions and they answered more of these questions correctly. This advantage must be due to the model of social search implemented by I-SPY. And although this is a small-scale experiment, 97 academically-related students on a limited search task, we believe that this positive outcome speaks to the potential of social search as a valuable approach to more focused search.

5   Conclusions

In this paper we have argued for the benefits of social search and we have described a particular approach that integrates ideas from social networking and adaptive information retrieval to provide a personalized search service to well-defined communities of like-minded individuals. The I-SPY system has delivered significant performance advantages in live search scenarios, with communities able to locate the right information faster and more reliably by leveraging the past search behaviour of their peers.

I-SPY delivers this level of personalization in an relatively anonymous fashion. Individual community members are not tracked, nor are they identified. Instead, personalization operates at the level of the community rather than the individual. We believe that this level of personalization strikes the right balance between accuracy and privacy: the community-based ranking of results is sufficiently accurate for the individual user to benefit from the social search, but at the same time they can be confident that their privacy and identity have been protected.

In recent work we have considered a number of issues arising out of this model of social search. We have proposed the use of various strategies to protect against fraudulent search activity. For example, we can frustrate users who attempt to drive the promotion of certain result pages, by making repeated selections, by discounting or filtering sequences of consecutive result selections. Similarly we have proposed the use of decay models to reduce hit-values over time in order to reduce the natural bias that operates in favour of older pages; older pages will have had more of an opportunity to attract hits and may therefore be promoted above newer but more relevant pages. Finally, we have recently explored the possibility of leveraging the interaction histories of *similar* queries to the target query – right now I-SPY operates on the basis of exact matches between the target query and the entries of the hit-matrix – and our initial results show that such an extension has the potential to improve the performance of I-SPY still further by increasing its precision and recall characteristics [18].

References

1. Selberg, E., Etzioni, O.: The Meta-Crawler Architecture for Resource Aggregation on the Web. IEEE Expert **Jan-Feb** (1997) 11–14
2. Dreilinger, D., Howe, A.: Experiences with Selecting Search Engines Using Meta Search. ACM Transactions on Information Systems **15(3)** (1997) 195–222
3. Brin, S., Page, L.: The Anatomy of A Large-Scale Web Search Engine. In: Proceedings of the Seventh International World-Wide Web Conference. (1998)
4. Kleinberg, J.M.: Authoritative sources in a hyperlinked environment. In: Proceedings of the Ninth Annual ACM-SIAM Symposium on Discrete Algorithms. (1998) 668–677
5. Lawrence, S.: Context in Web Search. IEEE Data Engineering Bulletin **23(3)** (2000) 25–32
6. Glover, E., Lawrence, S., Gordon, M.D., Birmingham, W.P., Giles, C.L.: Web Search - Your Way. Communications of the ACM (2000)
7. Rhodes, B.J., Starner, T.: Remembrance Agent: A Continuously Running Automated Information Retrieval System. In: Proceedings of the First International Conference on the Practical Applications of Intelligent Agents and Multi-Agent Technologies. (1996) 487–495
8. Budzik, J., Hammond, K.: User Interactions with Everyday Applications as Context for Just-In-Time Information Access. In: Proceedings International Conference on Intelligent User Interfaces., ACM Press (2000)
9. Bharat, K.: SearchPad: Explicit Capture of Search Context to Support Web Search. In: Proceedings of the Ninth International World-Wide Web Conference. (2000)
10. Raghavan, V.V., Sever, H.: On the reuse of past optimal queries. In: Proceedings of the 18th annual international ACM SIGIR conference on Research and development in information retrieval, ACM Press (1995) 344–350
11. Fitzpatrick, L., Dent, M.: Automatic feedback using past queries: social searching? In: Proceedings of the 20th annual international ACM SIGIR conference on Research and development in information retrieval, ACM Press (1997) 306–313
12. Glance, N.S.: Community search assistant. In: Proceedings of the 6th international conference on Intelligent user interfaces, ACM Press (2001) 91–96
13. Freyne, J., Smyth, B., Coyle, M., Briggs, P., Balfe, E.: Further experiments in collaborative ranking in community-based web search. AI Review: An international Science and Engineering Journal (In Press) (2004)
14. Freyne, J., Smyth, B.: Query based indexing in collaborative search. In: Submitted to the 2nd International Conference in Intelligent Information Processing. (2004)
15. Hill, W., Hollan, J., Wroblewzki, D., T.McCandless: Edit Wear and Read Wear. In: Proceedings of the SIGCHI Conference on Human Factors in Computing Systems, ACM Press (1992) 3–9
16. Wexelblat, A., Maes, P.: Footprints: History-Rich Web Browsing. In: Proceedings of the Third International Conference on Computer-Assisted Information Retrieval. (1997) Montreal, Quebec, Canada.
17. M.Twindale, D.N., Paice, C.: Browsing is a collaborative process. Information Processing and Management **33(6)** (1997) 761–83
18. Balfe, E., Smyth, B.: Case based collaborative web search. In: Proceedings of 7th European Conference on Cased Based Reasoning. (2004)

Recent Soft Computing Approaches to User Modeling in Adaptive Hypermedia

Enrique Frías-Martínez[1], George Magoulas[2], Sherry Chen[1], and Robert Macredie[1]

[1]Department of Information Systems & Computing
Brunel University
Uxbridge, Middlesex, UB8 3PH UK
{enrique.frias-martinez,sherry.chen,robert.macredie}@brunel.ac.uk
[2]School of Computer Science and Information Systems
Birkbeck College, University of London
Malet Street, London WC1E 7HX UK
gmagoulas@dcs.bbk.ac.uk

Abstract. The ability of an adaptive hypermedia system to create tailored environments depends mainly on the amount and accuracy of information stored in each user model. One of the difficulties that user modeling faces is the necessity of capturing the imprecise nature of human behavior. Soft Computing has the ability to handle and process uncertainty which makes it possible to model and simulate human decision-making. This paper surveys different soft computing techniques that can be used to efficiently and accurately capture user behavior. The paper also presents guidelines that show which techniques should be used according to the task implemented by the application.

1 Introduction

Adaptive hypermedia (AH) can be defined as the technology that allows personalization for each individual user of a hypermedia application, its content and its presentation according to user preferences and characteristics [29]. The process of personalization of a hypermedia application is implemented through a decision making and personalization engine which adapts the contents according to a user model. In this context it is clear that the key element of an adaptive hypermedia application is the user model. The more information a user model has, the better the content and presentation will be personalized. We consider a user model as a set of information structures designed to represent one or more of the following elements [18]: (1) representation of assumptions about the knowledge, goals, plans preferences, tasks and/or abilities about one or more types of users; (2) representation of relevant common characteristics of users pertaining to specific user subgroups (stereotypes); (3) the classification of a user in one or more of these subgroups; (4) the recording of user behaviour; (5) the formation of assumptions about the user based on the interaction history and/or (6) the generalization of the interaction histories of many users into stereotypes. Fig. 1 presents the architecture of a generic AH system.

W. Nejdl and P. De Bra (Eds.): AH 2004, LNCS 3137, pp. 104–114, 2004.
© Springer-Verlag Berlin Heidelberg 2004

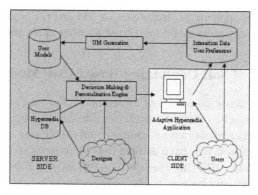

Fig. 1. Generic Architecture of an Adaptive Hypermedia Application.

The architecture of an adaptive hypermedia system is usually divided in two parts: the server side and the client side. The server side generates the user models from a data base containing the interactions of the users with the system and the personal data/preferences that each user has given to the system. These user models, in combination with a hypermedia database, are used by the "Decision Making and Personalization Engine" module to identify user needs, decide on the types of adaptation to be performed and communicate them to an adaptive interface. In this paper, we are going to focus on the "User Model (UM) Generation" module.

A typical user exhibits patterns when accessing a hypermedia system. Machine learning techniques can be applied to recognize regularities in user trails and to integrate them as part of the user model. The limitations of traditional machine learning techniques for modeling human behavior led to the introduction of Soft Computing (SC) for User Modeling (UM). SC technologies provide an approximate solution to an ill-defined problem and can create user models in an environment, such as a hypermedia application, in which users are not willing to give feedback on their actions and/or designers are not able to fully define all possible interactions. Human interaction is a key component of any hypermedia application, which implies that the data available will be usually imprecise, incomplete and heterogeneous. In this context SC seems to be the appropriate paradigm to handle the uncertainty and fuzziness of the information available to create user models [28]. The elements that a user model captures (goals, plans, preferences, common characteristics of users) can exploit the ability of SC of mixing different behaviors and capturing human decision processes in order to implement a system that is more flexible and sensible in relation to user interests. Different techniques provide different capabilities. For example, Fuzzy Logic provides a mechanism to mimic human decision-making that can be used to infer goals and plans; Neural Networks a flexible mechanism for the representation of common characteristics of a user and the definition of complex stereotypes; Fuzzy Clustering a mechanism in which a user can be part of more than one stereotype at the same time and Neuro-Fuzzy systems a mechanism to capture and tune expert knowledge which can be used to obtain assumptions about the user.

This paper presents a survey of different SC techniques available for modeling user behavior. The paper's intentions are (1) to give a perspective to the AH community about the potential of applying SC techniques to UM and (2) to give basic guidelines about which techniques can be useful for a given adaptive application.

2 A Taxonomy of Soft Computing-Based User Models

User models can be classified according to two main elements: (1) *the granularity of the model*, a model can be created for each individual user (content-based modeling) or for clusters of users (collaborative modeling); and (2) *the type of task* for which the model is going to be used. We have defined four basic types of tasks: (i) *Prediction* (P), (ii) *Recommendation* (R), (iii) *Classification* (C) and (iv) *Filtering* (F). Prediction is the capability of anticipating user needs using past user behavior. A basic assumption is made with this approach: a user's immediate future is very similar to his/her immediate past. In the literature this is traditionally presented as *content-based filtering*. Recommendation is the capability of suggesting interesting elements to a user based on some extra information; for example from the items to be recommended or from the behavior of other users. In this context, recommendation is what in the literature is known as *collaborative filtering*. Classification builds a model that maps or classifies data items into one of several predefined classes. Filtering is defined as the selection of a subset of items that are interesting to a user from the original set of items. In general, any of the previous tasks can be implemented using knowledge stored in the different user model elements described in Section 1. For example, a filtering task can be implemented using knowledge stored in user preferences, or by classifying the user in a stereotype (or in more than one stereotypes). A prediction task can be implemented using the knowledge captured by the user's goals but also by the classification of the user in a stereotype, etc. In the following subsections we present a number of SC techniques and give examples of AH applications that employ the particular technique, specifying the task implemented and the granularity of the model.

2.1 Fuzzy Logic

Fuzzy Logic (FL) defines a framework in which the inherent ambiguity of real information can be captured, modeled and used to reason with uncertainty. An introduction to FL can be found in [17] and [40]. FL is not a machine learning technique, nevertheless due to its ability to handle uncertainty it is used in combination with other machine learning techniques in order to produce behavior models that are able to capture and to manage the uncertainty of human behavior. A traditional fuzzy logic inference system is divided into three steps: (1) fuzzification; (2) fuzzy inference; and (3) defuzzification. FL in UM does not necessarily realize these three steps, but a subset of them. Typically FL has been used to implement applications that are based on a recommendation task. In these applications FL provides the ability of mixing different user preferences and profiles that are satisfied to a certain degree. FL has been used to implement recommendation tasks [27], where fuzzy inference is used for recommendation purposes using user profiles obtained with hierarchical unsupervised clustering. In [1] fuzzy logic was used to model user behavior and give recommendation using this fuzzy behavior model. Although there is not strictly a fuzzy inference process, the stereotypes that characterize users are modeled using membership functions, and the recommendation process is done using a fuzzy AND operator. [32] presents a system designed to recommend products in an e-commerce site, according to how well this product satisfies user preferences. The score of an item (according to how much that item matches user interests) is done using an OWA (Ordered Weighted Averaging) operator. This family of operators allows the representation of fuzzy logic connectives and the aggregation of different user preferences.

FL has been used for filtering [38]. In this case FL provides a soft filtering process based on the degree of concordance between user preferences and the elements being filtered.

Table 1 summarizes relevant studies and applications of FL for UM. The columns detail the application, the data, the results obtained, the type of task (T) for which the SC technique was used and (I/G) if the system created a model for each individual (I) or for groups of users (G).

Table 1. Characteristics of some Fuzzy Logic- based User Modeling applications.

	Application	Data	Outcome	T	I/G
[27] Nasraoui and Petenes (2003)	Web recommendation system based on a fuzzy inference engine that uses a rule-based representation of the user profile.	12 days access log data of the Web site of the Dep. Comp. Eng. at the University of Missouri.	Fuzzy recommendation achieves high coverage compared to other machine learning solutions.	R	G
[38] Vrettos and Stafylopati (2001)	Agent for information retrieval and filtering in the context of e-learning.	Cranfield data set (www.cs.utk.edu/lsi) which includes 1398 documents, 225 queries and an average of 8.2 relevant documents per query.	Re-ranking the search according to user's profile.	F	I
[1] Ardissono and Goy (1997)	Introduction of personalization techniques in a shell supporting the construction of adaptive web stores.	Not Presented.	FL can be applied in electronic sales to produce personalized environments.	R	I
[32] Schmitt et al. (2003)	Recommendation of items of an e-commerce site to its users using a structure-based system.	Preferences specified by the user.	On-line demo: www2.dfki.de:8080 /mautmachine/html	R	I

2.2 Neural Networks

A Neural Network (NN) is an information processing paradigm that is inspired by the way biological nervous systems, such as the brain, process information. Comprehensive introductions to Neural Networks can be found in [8] and [12]. Neural networks, with their remarkable ability to derive meaning from complicated or imprecise data, can be used to extract complex patterns. A trained neural network can be thought of as an expert in the category of information it has been given to analyse.

NNs is a powerful method to model human behaviour Traditionally, NNs have been used for classification and recommendation in order to group together users with the same characteristics and create profiles. Some examples are in [5], which uses NN to classify user navigation paths, and [11], which uses Self Organizing Maps (SOM), an unsupervised NN that transforms highly dimensional data into a two dimensional grid, to classify documents based on a subjectively predefined set of clusters in a specific domain. NNs have also been used for recommendation in [31], which predicts the next step for a given user trajectory in a virtual environment, and in [2, 3] which models student behavior for an intelligent tutoring system. NNs have also been used for filtering and prediction in [34] and [33] respectively. Table 2 summarizes some applications of Neural Networks for UM.

Table 2. Characteristics of some Neural Networks- based User Modeling applications.

	Application	Training Data	Outcome	T	I /G
[5] Bidel et al. (2003)	Classification and tracking of user navigation.	Data generated from an on-line encyclopedia.	A labelled approach to the problem produces better accuracy.	C	G
[31] Sas et al. (2003)	Prediction of user's next step in a virtual environment	30 users performed exploration and searching within the environment.	Very accurate predictions of the next step	R	G
[34] Shepperd (2002)	Adaptive filtering system for electronic news using stereotypes.	The Halifax Herald Ltd.	Very useful for readers with specific information needs.	F	I
[2, 3] Beck and Woolf. (1998)	Construction of a student model for an intelligent tutoring system.	Data collected by the tutoring system	NN-based recommendation to each individual.	R	G
[33] Shavlik and Eliassi (2001)	Adaptive agents that retrieve and extract information by accepting user preferences in the form of instructions.	Instructions given directly by the user and user rated web pages.	Faciliates creating intelligent agents combining user instructions with machine learning.	F / P	I

2.3 Genetic Algorithms

Genetic Algorithms (GAs) are search algorithms based on the mechanics of natural selection [10]. A GA begins with a set of solutions (chromosomes) called the population. Solutions from one population are taken and used to form a new population, which are closer to the optimum solution to the problem at hand. GAs are a search strategy that is tailored for vast, complex, multimodal search spaces.

In general GAs have been used for Recommendation in the form of rules, which can capture user goals and preferences, because they perform a global search and cope better with attribute interaction than algorithms used in data mining, where the search is more local. Examples of this approach are [30] for student modeling and [23] for profiling of e-commerce customers. Nevertheless, they have also been applied for filtering [7]. Table 3 summarizes relevant applications of GAs for UM.

2.4 Fuzzy Clustering

In non-fuzzy or hard clustering, data is divided into crisp clusters, where each data point belongs to exactly one cluster. In Fuzzy Clustering (FC), the data points can belong to more than one cluster and associated with each data point are membership grades which indicate the degree to which it belongs to the different clusters. One of the key elements of any FC system is the definition of the concept of distance used for the creation of the clusters. The most widely used fuzzy clustering algorithm is the Fuzzy C-Means (FCM) Algorithm [4]. There are other algorithms, which basically are variations of the original FCM, like the Fuzzy c-Medoids Algorithm (FCMdd) or the Fuzzy c-Trimered Medoids Algorithm (FCTMdd) [19].

Table 3. Characteristics of some Genetic- based User Modeling applications.

	Application	Input Data	Outcome	T	I/G
[23] Min et al. (2001)	Profiling behavior of e-commerce customers.	Set of questions regarding size of company, e-purchasing usage, etc.	GA are useful for the discovery of profiles of e-commerce customers.	R	G
[30] Romero et al. (2003)	Discovering prediction rules from student usage information to improve web courses.	Stored information of a Linux course developed with AHA!.	The rules produced are better that traditional rule extraction algorithms.	R	G
[7] Fan et al. (2000)	Personalization of search engines using automatic term weight-ing	Cranfield text Collection and Federal Register (FR) text collection.	GA Automatic weighting improves the retrieval performance quite dramatically.	F	G

Table 4. Characteristics of some Fuzzy Clustering- based User Modeling applications.

	Application	Input Data	Outcome	T	I/G
[20] Lampinen and Koivisto (2002)	Obtain application profiles from network traffic data to manage network resources.	274000 samples of different applications from an edge router of a LAN network.	FCM produced better results than SOM. A method for the comparison of both solutions is also introduced.	R	G
[25] Nasraoui et al. (1999)	A new algorithm (CARD) to mine user profiles from access logs is proposed.	12 day log data of the Dep. of Comp. Eng.. at Univ. of Missouri.	CARD is very effective for clustering many different profiles in user sessions.	R	G
[16] Joshi et al. (2000)	Two algorithms to mine user profiles: FCM dd and FCTMdd.	CSEE logs of Univ. of Maryland	Both algorithms extract interesting user profiles. FCM is not able to handle noise as effectively as FCTM.	C	G
[19] Krishnapura et al. (2001)	Web access log analy-sis for user profiling using RFCMdd (Ro-bust Fuzzy c-Medoids).	Five days of CSEE web server activity of Univ. of Maryland.	RFCMdd is very effective for clustering of relational data.	C	G

Typically, FC applied to UM has to use techniques that can handle relational data because the information used to create stereotypes (pages visited, characteristics of the user, etc.) cannot be represented by numerical vectors. In these systems the definition of distance is done using vectorial representations of user interactions with the adaptive hypermedia system. FC for UM, by its definition, is used for recommendation and classification tasks. [20], [25] and [26] are examples of applications that implement a recommendation task using FC. Examples of classification tasks are [16] and [19]. Table 4 summarizes some studies and applications of FC for UM.

2.5 Neuro-fuzzy Systems

Neuro-Fuzzy systems (NFS) use NNs to extract rules and/or membership functions from input-output data to be used in a Fuzzy Inference System. With this approach, the drawbacks of NNs and FL, the black box behavior of NNs and the problems of finding suitable membership values for FL, are avoided. NFS automate the process of transferring expert or domain knowledge into fuzzy rules. [14] and [15] describe with more detail the basic concepts of NFS. One of the most important NFS is ANFIS [13], which has been used in a wide range of applications [6]. NFS are especially suited for applications where user interaction in model design or interpretation is desired.

NFS are basically FL systems with an automatic learning process provided by NN. The combination of NN and fuzzy sets offers a powerful method to model human behavior which allows NFS to be used for a variety of tasks. [21] and [35] use a NFS for Recommendation in an e-commerce site and for an on-line course respectively. [22] uses NFS to implement multi-attribute decision making with the purpose of planning the contents of a web-course according to the knowledge level of the student. [9] use NFS for prediction of a simulated aircraft control. Table 5 summarizes some studies and applications of NFS for UM.

Table 5. Characteristics of some NeuroFuzzy- based User Modeling applications.

	Application	Test bed	Outcome	T	I/G
[21] Lee (2001)	Mobile web shopping agent that finds products that suit user needs using a NFS and FL.	A test is implemented using a product data-base with 200 items and 8 categories.	Provides a more efficient result when compared with other solutions; processing time is shorter.	R	I
[35] Stathacopoulou et al. (2003)	Student Modeling	A set of simulated students.	High accuracy in the diagnosis of student problems during learning.	C/P	G
[22] Magoulas et al. (2001)	Intelligent decision making for recommending educational content in a web-based course depending on knowledge level	"Introduction to Computer Science" course of the Univ. of Athens.	Successful handling of fuzziness associated with the evaluation of learner's knowledge.	C/R	G
[9] George and Cardullo (1999)	Modeling of human behavior.	10 subjects collected data for the one dimensional compensatory task.	Generate a model of human behavior.	P	G

3 Criteria for the Selection of Techniques

Maybe seen from the preceding discussion, no SC technique is ideal for all situations. Each one captures different relationships among the data available. In this section we present guidelines to help decide which technique to use when developing an AH application. Table 6 summarizes the characteristics of the techniques presented along seven dimensions. The first four dimensions capture the main problems that machine learning for user modeling faces according to [39]: Computational Complexity, i.e. off-line processing; Dynamic Modeling, which indicates the suitability of the technique to change a user model on-the-fly; Labeled/Unlabeled, which reflects the need of labeled data; and Size of training data, which reflects the amount of data needed to produce a reliable user model. The remaining dimensions present other relevant information: the ability of the techniques to handle uncertainty (Uncertainty), i.e. to produce user model that takes into account the inherent fuzziness of user modeling; the ability to handle noisy data (Noisy Data), i.e. how noisy training data will affect the user model produced; and the interpretability (Interpret.) of the results, i.e. how easy is for a human to understand the knowledge captured.

Table 6. Characteristics of different Soft Computing techniques applied to User Modeling.

	Complexity	Dynamic Modeling	Labeled / Unlabeled	Size of Training Data	Uncertainty	Noisy Data	Inter-pret.
Fuzzy Logic	Med	Yes	N/A	N/A	Yes	Yes	High
Neural Networks	High	Yes	Both	High	Yes	Yes	Low
Genetic Algorithms	High	No	N/A	N/A	No	Yes	Low
Fuzzy Clustering	High/Med	No	Both	Med/High	Yes	Yes	Low
Neuro-Fuzzy	High	Yes	Labelled	Med/High	Yes	Yes	Med/High

For example, NNs have a high training complexity, although they can have a real-time response time. NFS have a High/Medium interpretability, which depends on the architecture of the system, for example ANFIS produce systems with high interpretability. Traditional GAs are not able to cope with dynamic modeling problems, nevertheless some recent approaches present dynamic modeling using evolutionary computation for specific problems [36]. Two are the main criteria that determine the soft computing technique that is going to be used by a specific adaptive application: (1) the type of task and (2) the interpretability needed for the results. As was previously discussed the main types of task are: Prediction; Recommendation; Classification; and Filtering. There are two possible values for Interpretability, needed or not relevant. The first one expresses the necessity of having a human understandable output while the second one states that this factor is not important. Table 7 presents guidelines related to what soft computing techniques are useful considering the criteria previously introduced. The techniques are classified according to the set of references used in this study. This does not necessarily mean that the techniques cannot be used to implement other types of tasks. For example, NNs are basically used for task that need no interpretability. Nevertheless some recent approaches describe techniques to extract the knowledge embedded in NN [37]. The combination of Tables 6 and 7 can be used to guide a choice of which technique to use for user modeling in an AH system. First, Table 7 can be used to identify the set of techniques suitable for the adaptive application and, after that, Table 6 can be used to refine the search and take the final decision.

Table 7. Techniques recommended for each combination of the decision variables.

Task	Interpretability	
	Needed	**Not Needed**
Prediction	NeuroFuzzy	Neural Networks
Recommendation	NeuroFuzzy Fuzzy Logic	Neural networks Genetic Algorithms Fuzzy Clustering
Classification	Neuro Fuzzy	Neural Networks Fuzzy Clustering
Filtering	Fuzzy Logic	Neural Networks Genetic Algorithms

4 Conclusions

This paper has presented a brief review of the state of the art of SC techniques use within the area of adaptive hypermedia systems. The review demonstrates that one of the main problems that the development of AH faces is the lack of any kind of standardization for the design of user models. In order to improve this situation this paper has tried to give a set of guidelines that formalize the design of user models using a SC approach. It is our opinion that the future of User Modeling is in hybrid systems. As has been shown, each technique captures different elements of user behavior. The combination of these SC techniques among themselves and with other machine learning techniques, will provide a useful framework to efficiently capture the natural complexity of human behavior.

Acknowledgments

The work presented in this paper is funded by the UK Arts and Humanities Research Board (AHRB grant reference: MRG/AN9183/APN16300).

References

1. Ardissono, L., Goy, A.:Tailoring the Interaction with Users in Electronic Shops, Proceedings of the 7th International Conference on User Modeling, UM97, Banff, Canada, 1997
2. Beck, J., Jia, P., Sison, J., Mostow, J.: Predicting Student Help-Request Behavior in an Intelligent Tutor for Reading, Proc. of the 9th Int. Conf. on User Modeling, LNAI 2702, pp. 303-312, 2003
3. Beck, J.E., Woolf, B.P.: Using a Learning Agent with a Student Model, LNCS 1452, 1998
4. Bezdek, J.C.: Pattern Recognition with Fuzzy Objective Function Algorithms, Plenum Press, 1981
5. Bidel, S, Lemoine, L., Piat, F.: Statistical machine learning for tracking hypermedia user behavior, 2nd Workshop on Machine Learning, Information Retrieval and User Modeling, 9th Int. Conf. in UM, 2003

6. Bonissone,P., Badami, C., Chiang, X.: Industrial Applications of Fuzzy Logic at General Electric, Proceedings of the IEEE, 83(3), pp. 450-465, 1995

7. Fan, W., Gordon, M. D., Pathak, P.: Personalization of Search Engine Services for Effective Retrieval and Knowledge management. In Proc. Of the 21st Int. Conf. on Information Systems, pp. 20-34, 2000

8. Fausett L., Fundamentals of Neural Networks, Prentice-Hall, 1994

9. George G., Cardullo, F.: Application of Neuro-Fuzzy Systems to Behavioral Representation in Computer Generated Forces, Proc. 8th Conf. on Comp. Generated Forces, pp. 575-585, 1999

10. Goldberg, D.: Genetic Algorithms in Search, Optimization, and Machine Learning. Addison-Wesley, 1989

11. Goren-Bar, D., Kuflik, T., Lev, D., Shoval, P.: Automatic Personal Categorization Using Artificial Neural Networks, 8th International Conference on User Modeling 2001, LNAI 2109, pp. 188-198, 2001

12. Haykin S., Neural Networks, 2nd Edition, Prentice Hall, 1999

13. Jang, J.S.: ANFIS: Adaptive-Network-Based Fuzzy Inference Systems, IEEE Transactions on Systems, Man, and Cybernetics, Vol. 23(3), pp. 665-685, May 1993.

14. Jang, J.S.R., Sun, C.T.: Neurofuzzy modelling and control,in *Proceedings IEEE*, 1995

15. Jang, J.S.R., Sun, C.T:*Neurofuzzy and Soft Computing*, Prentice Hal, 1997

16. Joshi, A., Joshi, K., Krishnapuram, R., On mining Web Access Logs, in Proceedings of the ACM-SIGMOD Workshop on Research Issues in Data Mining and Knowledge Discovery, pp. 63-69, 2000

17. Klir, J., Yuan,B.: Fuzzy Sets and Fuzzy Logic. Theory and Applications, Prentice Hall, 1995

18. Kobsa, A.: Generic User Modeling Systems, User Modeling and User-Adapted Interaction 11, 49-63, 2001

19. Krishnapuram, R., Joshi, A., Nasraoui, O., Yi, L., Low-Complexity Fuzzy Relational Clustering Algorithms for Web Mining, in IEEE Transactions on Fuzzy Systems, Vol. 9 (4), pp. 595-608, 2001

20. Lampinen, T., Koivisto, H.: Profiling Network Applications with Fuzzy C-Means Clustering and Self-Organising Map, Int. Conf. on Fuzzy Systems and Knowledge Discovery, 2002

21. Lee, R.S.T.:iJADE IWShopper: A New Age of Intelligent Web Shopping System Based on Fuzzy-Neuro Agent Technology. In Web Intelligence: Research and Development, LNAI 2198, pp. 403-412, 2002

22. Magoulas, G.D., Papanikolau, K.A., Grigoriadou, M.: Neuro-fuzzy synergism for planning the content in a web-based course, Informatica Vol. 25(1), 2001

23. Min, H., Smolinski, T., Boratyn, G.: A GA-based Data Mining Approach to Profiling the Adopters of E-purchasing, Proc. of the 3rd Int. Conf. on Information Reuse and Integration, pp. 1-6, 2001

24. Nasraoui, O., Cardona, C., Rojas, C., Gonzalez, F.: Mining Evolving User Profiles in Noisy Web Clickstream Data with a Scalable Immune System Clustering Algorithm. In Workshop Notes of WEBKDD 2003: Web Mining as Premise to Effective&Intelligent Web Applications, pp. 71-81, 2003

25. Nasraoui, O., Frigui, H., Joshi, A., Krishnapuram, R.: Mining Web Access Logs Using Relational Competitive Fuzzy Clustering, 8th Intl. Fuzzy Systems Association World Congress - IFSA 99, 1999

26. Nasraoui, O., Krishnapuram, R.: Extracting Web User Profiles Using Relational Competitive Fuzzy Clustering. In International Journal on Artificial Intelligence Tools, Vol. 9(4), pp. 509-526, 2000

27. Nasraoui, O., Petenes, C.: Combining Web Usage Mining and Fuzzy Inference for Website Personalization. In WEBKDD 2003: Web Mining as Premise to Effective Web Applications, pp. 37-46, 2003

28. Pal, S.K., Talwar, V., Mitra, P.: Web Mining in Soft Computing Framework: Relevance, State of the Art and Future Directions, IEEE Transactions on Neural Networks, Vol. 13(5), pp.1163 - 1177, 2002

29. Perkowitz, M., Etzioni, O.: Adaptive Web Sites. Communications of the ACM, Vol. 43(8), 152-158, 2000

30. Romero, C., Ventura, S., de Bra, P.: Discovering Prediction Rules in AHA! Courses, Proceedings of the 9th International Conference on User Modeling, LNAI 2702, pp. 25-34, 2003

31. Sas, C., Reilly, R., O'Hare, G.: A Connectionist Model of Spatial Knowledge Acquisition in a Virtual Environment. In 2nd Workshop on Machine Learning, Information Retrieval and User Modeling, 2003

32. Schmitt, C., Dengler, D., Bauer, M.: Multivariate Preference Models and Decision Making with the MAUT Machine, in Proc. of the 9th Int. Conf. on User Modeling, LNAI 2702, pp. 297-302, 2003

33. Shavlik, J., Eliassi, T.: A System for building intelligent Agents that Learn to retrieve and Extract Information. In International Journal on User Modeling and User Adapted Interaction, 2001.

34. Sheperd, A., Watters, C., Marath, A.T.: Adaptive User Modeling for Filtering Electronic News. In Proc. of the 35th Annual Hawaii Intl. Conf. on System Sciences (HICSS-02), Vol. 4, 2002

35. Stathacopoulou, R., Grigoriadou, M., Magoulas, G.D.: A Neuro-fuzzy Approach in Student Modeling, Proceedings of the 9th Int. Conf. on User Modeling, UM2003, LNAI 2702, pp. 337-342, 2003

36. Sternberg, M., Reynolds, R.G.: Using cultural algorithms to support re-engineering of rule-based expert systems in dynamic performance environments: a case study in fraud detection Sternberg, IEEE Transactions on Evolutionary Computation ,Vol. 1(4), pp. 225-243, 1997

37. Ticlek, A.B., Andrews, R., Golea, M., Diederich, J.: The truth will come to light: directions and challenges in extracting the knowledge embedded within trained artificial neural networks
IEEE Trans. on Neural Networks, Vol. 9(6), pp. 1057-1068, 1998

38. Vrettos, S., Stafylopatis, A.: A Fuzzy Rule-Based Agent for Web Retrieval-Filtering. In Web Intelligence: Research and Development, LNAI 2198, pp. 448-453, 2002

39. Webb, G.I., Pazzani, M.J., Billsus, D.: Machine Learning for User Modeling. In User Modeling an User-Adapted Interaction, (11), pp. 19-29, 2001

40. Yan, J., Ryan, M., Power, J.: Using Fuzzy Logic, Prentice Hall, 1994

A Flexible Composition Engine for Adaptive Web Sites

Serge Garlatti[1] and Sébastien Iksal[2]

[1] IASC Dept. – GET – ENST Bretagne
Technopôle de Brest Iroise
CS 83818, 29238 Brest Cedex, France
serge.garlatti@enst-bretagne.fr

[2] LIUM – University of Maine – IUT de Laval
52 rue des Docteurs Calmette et Guérin
BP 2045 – 53020 Laval Cedex 09, France
sebastien.iksal@univ-lemans.fr

Abstract. Nowadays, adaptive web sites must have the ability to use distributed repositories. The variety of available data sources and user profiles quickly lead to a combinatorial explosion of web site versions. It is impossible to manage these web sites without some form of automation. We are interested in web sites for which users belong to a kind of community of practices: they share a common knowledge to work together. We claim that the explicit knowledge of communities is the key issue to automate the hypermedia generation and thus to ensure consistency and comprehension. We have designed a flexible adaptive composition engine. In our framework, hypermedia consistency is managed by an author through content, adaptation and sites structure at knowledge level and based on his know-how. Our major contribution consists of: (i) a semantic organization of resources, (ii) a declarative specification of adaptation and (iii) the flexibility of the composition engine.

Keywords: Adaptation, Virtual Document, Composition Engine, Semantic Web, Metadata, User Model.

1 Introduction

Adaptive web sites have the ability to provide different kinds of content, navigation tools and layouts according to user needs [1]. Nowadays, adaptive web sites must have the ability to use distributed repositories [2, 3] and/or web services [4]. The variety of available data sources and user profiles quickly lead to a combinatorial explosion of web site versions. As soon as a hypermedia is computed on the fly from distributed data sources, the consistency and the comprehension of the resulting hypermedia is closely related to the content, the site structure and the adaptation policies dedicated to users' tasks. We are interested in web sites for which users belong to a kind of community of practices[5]. We claim that the explicit knowledge of communities is the key issue to automate the hypermedia generation and thus to ensure consistency and comprehension. Indeed, the specification of the content, site structure and adaptation policies will be based on this explicit knowledge. Thus, the adaptive hypermedia design is an intensive knowledge-driven process.

W. Nejdl and P. De Bra (Eds.): AH 2004, LNCS 3137, pp. 115–125, 2004.

The dynamic generation and the reuse of resources can be considered as virtual documents. Virtual documents are web documents for which the content, the site structure and the layout are created as needed [6]. They have a **composition engine** which can **select** and **filter** resources, **organize** and **assemble** them. The composition engine needs to rely on a precise search engine through the internet to get the relevant content. Intelligent search engines, relying on the semantic web initiative [7], semantic metadata and corresponding ontologies, associated with resources overcome the limitations of keyword-based information access.

We have designed a flexible composition engine, called SCARCE - SemantiC and Adaptive Retrieval and Composition Engine - based on a semantic web approach. We don't manage timed multimedia presentation like in Geurts [8] and Megalou [9]. In our framework, hypermedia consistency is managed by an author in a generic document and based on his know-how. Filtering is viewed as an adaptive navigation method which can be specified by declarative properties. Our major contribution consists of: (i) a semantic organization of resources, (ii) a declarative specification of adaptation and (iii) the flexibility of the composition engine. The main benefit of this approach is: as the main virtual document mechanisms have declarative parameters, it is easier to maintain and to design adaptive hypermedia. Indeed, new hypermedia may be generated as soon as the declaration of selection, filtering or organization is modified. Of course, it is limited by the core principles underlying the composition engine. SCARCE is the core of ICCARS[1], the CANDLE[2] European project and KMP[3].

First of all, the design principles of our approach are presented. Secondly, we define the core principles underlying our adaptive composition engine. Finally, we conclude on flexibility and the current development.

2   Design Principles

New adaptive hypermedia systems use the Web as an information space where resources are distributed. So, ensuring resource interoperability takes place at three different levels: i) at address level, the URL/URI referring to resources whatever their location, ii) at syntactic level, where resources are described in XML and have a DTD to explicit their logical structure; they have to be layout independent iii) at semantic level, where resources have metadata defining contexts, conditions and rules for reuse and adaptation. Consequently, new adaptive hypermedia architectures have to separate resource management, organization, adaptation and layout to ensure interoperability. We consider an adaptive hypermedia as an adaptive ontology-driven virtual document, defined as follows: an adaptive virtual document consists of a set of resources, their metadata, different ontologies and an adaptive composition engine which is able to **select** and to **filter** the relevant resources, to **organize** and to **assemble** them accord-

---

[1] ICCARS : Integrated and Collaborative Computer Assisted Reporting System
     (http://iccars.enst-bretagne.fr)
[2] CANDLE : Collaborative And Network Distributed Learning Environment
     (http://www.candle.eu.org)
[3] KMP: Knowledge Management Portal, RNRT Project

ing to the user. The selection, filtering and organization are managed at semantic level and the assembly at logical and layout level. Thus, our adaptive composition engine consists of three composition engines: semantic, logical and layout.

Traditional adaptive hypermedia used to have a domain model, a user model and adaptation rules. The domain model is used to convey the resource semantic. The adaptation rules are based on the features of the user model and the resources to manage adaptation methods. The content is typically known to the author of the application and under his control [3].

With distributed resources, metadata schema is needed to retrieve and reuse them. Metadata schema enables designers to associate roles / functions with indexes. In our framework, the metadata schema is dedicated to a community of practice. Moreover, we use a document model to define the web site structure at knowledge level. These models are formalized in different ontologies as follows: **metadata ontology** at the information level which describes the indexing structure of resources, some index values are taken in the domain and document ontologies; **domain ontology** for representing contents; **document ontology** for defining narrative structures which represent the author's competences and know-how for creating adaptive document [10]. It defines the different categories of resources, the set of semantic relationships and the generic document properties and their categories; **a user ontology** which may define different stereotypes and individual features.

First, we present the principles underlying organization, selection and filtering.

- Organization is combined with selection and is based on a generic directed graph, having a single root, in which generic nodes have a content specification - selection - and generic arcs that are semantic relationships. The generic graph features are described in the document ontology. This graph represents user needs and it represents author or enterprise know-how.

- Selection is an information retrieval process on a set of resources indexed with a unique metadata schema. Metadata have to be used for information retrieval and filtering which is a selection refinement. A subset of the metadata schema is used for selection specification and another one for filtering specification.

- Filtering is based on adaptive navigation methods. The principle is as follows:

  - First, selected resources are evaluated: the evaluation aim is to put each resource in one equivalence class according to class membership rules. We have chosen to have up to five equivalence classes of resources for usability reasons, named Very Bad, Bad, To Consider, Good and Very Good. Indeed, it might be difficult for a user to deal with too many equivalence classes [1, 11].

  - Second, one adaptive technique is chosen for the current user, its preferences and the stereotypes associated with adaptive navigation techniques. Then this technique is applied to delete, annotate, hide, etc. some equivalence classes of resources. Whether all selected resources are deleted in a node, this node and all its sub-nodes are deleted and that leads to content adaptation.

At run time, a generic document can be viewed as a directed graph organizing a set of queries – one per node – associated with adaptive navigation techniques. The different flexibility aspects are: i) a composition engine has the ability to generate dynamically hypermedia according to its core principles. The reusability of our engine is limited by these principles. It is possible to maintain and to modify a web site easily by changing some specifications. ii) To design new web sites, it is possible be necessary to change one or more ontologies to deal with new communities or community evolutions. iii) As the adaptive composition engine is divided into three engines, it is possible to only change each level separately. Nevertheless, consistency between the three levels must be kept.

3 Adaptive Composition Engine

In a digital document, three different views may coexist: semantic, logical and layout [12]. Each view has a specific structure organizing it. The semantic structure of a document conveys the organization of the meaning of the document content. The semantic structure can play the role of a site map in a hypermedia document or the role of the "knowledge tree" in the approach of P. Brusilovsky [2]. The logical structure reflects the syntactic organization of a document. The layout view describes how the documents appear on a device. Our composition engine is divided into three engines: semantic composition, logical composition and layout composition (cf. Fig. 1) according to these three views. For us, these views are closely related to the semantic web architecture: i) semantic: logic, ontology, RDFS/RDF, ii) logical: syntactic level encoded in XML, iii) layout: XSL/XSLT. The four mechanisms of virtual documents are implemented as follows: selection, filtering and organization are achieved in the semantic composition; assembly is divided into logical and layout compositions.

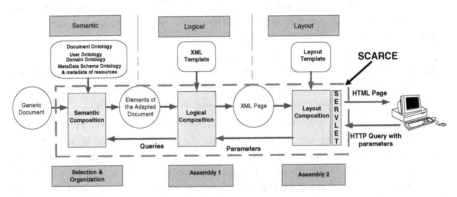

Fig. 1. The Composition Engine Architecture

The semantic composition engine computes on the fly a semantic graph from a generic document stage by stage. A generic document is composed of an information space – a set of fragments[4], a generic directed graph in which generic nodes have a

---

[4] In our framework, fragments are reusable resources with associated metadata. Atomic fragments are information units and cannot be decomposed. Abstract fragments are composed of other fragments (atomic and/or abstract) and one or several directed graphs organizing them.

content specification – for selection - and edges are semantic relationships, a set of equivalence classes and their membership rules, and one user stereotype per adaptive navigation technique (cf. Fig 2). A detailed description of the generic document can be found in [13]. The semantic graph represents a narrative structure adapted to the current user and linked to its corresponding content.

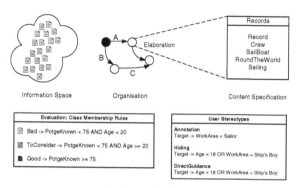

Fig. 2. A generic document

The aim of the logical and layout composition engines is to convert the semantic graph into an adapted hypermedia according to the nature of the document. The logical composition engine queries the semantic engine to build and to browse the semantic graph according to user interactions. It computes for each semantic graph node an XML web page with its content and navigation tools. An XML template is used to get an XML web page. The layout composition engine generates an HTML page from the XML web page in applying the layout rules given by the layout.

The semantic and logical composition engines rely on OntoBroker[5]. It is used to browse the different ontologies and to retrieve resources which match the content specifications by means of the resource metadata included in [14].

4 Adaptive Composition

A web page is mainly composed of three different dynamic components (local and global navigation guides and content) (cf. Fig. 3). A stage corresponds to the computation of the next web page according to the user interaction in the current web page. Then we describe the process from one stage to another one. In Fig. 3, the local navigation guide is composed of three different types of links: previous pages, current page and next pages. In this example, annotation is used for adaptive navigation technique. Thus, it is necessary to evaluate the corresponding resources and also to choose an adaptive technique. Consequently, the next web pages have to be computed in advance to be able to display and to annotate these links. The computation of the next web page is divided into two parts: the first one is the adaptive semantic composition and the second one is the logical and layout composition.

---

[5] The most advanced industrial environment at the beginning of the study which was compatible with the Web standards (RDF/RDFS, OWL).

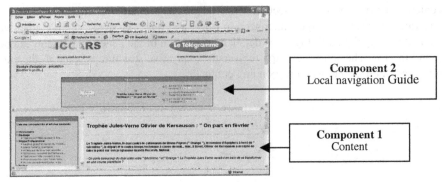

Fig. 3. Web Page layout

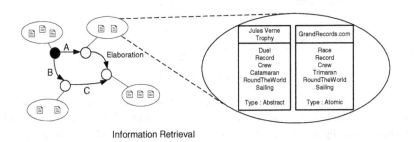

Information Retrieval

Fig. 4. Selection

4.1 Adaptive Semantic Composition

The semantic composition engine computes a semantic graph stage by stage. A web page is associated to a node of the semantic graph and generally, the node of the next page has already been computed. This one is associated to a node in the generic directed graph. Then, in a stage, all direct neighbors of this generic node are processed. During instantiation and for each neighbor, the generic directed graph is expanded as follows: a generic node and its content specification leads to several nodes in the corresponding semantic graph, one per selected resource, all generic arcs directly related to a generic node are replaced by several arcs one per selected resource.

For each neighbor, the semantic composition engine consists of three mechanisms: the first one selects the relevant resources for the current node, the second one evaluates the resources and classifies them in different equivalence classes and the third one determines the allowed adaptive navigation techniques and applies one.

- First of all, the content specification is used to query the search engine and selects the relevant resources from the information space associated with the generic document. The outcome of this process is a set of fragment variants in the current node. These fragments differ in a subset of the metadata schema, for instance, the knowledge level for some domain concepts, the technical properties, etc. From the content specification given previously (cf. Fig. 4), two fragment variants are retrieved. One is an atomic fragment and the other one an abstract fragment.

- Secondly, all fragment variants are evaluated. For each fragment, the metadata subset dedicated to variants and the user model are used to match all class membership rules. Each fragment variant belongs to one class and then a new semantic property is added. This property is called "class member" and its value can be one from "very good" to "very bad". This property will be used to manage adaptive techniques in the logical composition engine. In the Fig. 5, we can observe the outcome of several evaluations on different nodes and the different corresponding classification. The fragments of the Fig. 3 are evaluated to "Good" and "Bad". The user (cf. Fig. 6) has 19 years old, in this case he knows less than 75% of the concepts for one fragment and more than 75% for the second.

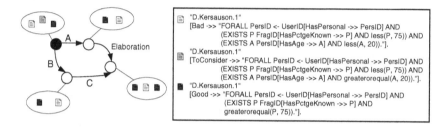

Fig. 5. Evaluation: apply class membership rules

- Thirdly, the user model is compared to all stereotypes associated with the different adaptive techniques. Those which fit the user model are allowed for the current user. In the Fig. 6, "hiding" and "direct guidance" are allowed for the user "S". According to user preferences, the first allowed technique in the total order given by the user is chosen. In this example, "hiding" is selected.

Fig. 6. Choice of an adaptive technique

- Finally, according to the enabled adaptive navigation technique, a fragment variant is kept or not in the current node. For instance, if a user is allowed to have annotation, hiding and direct guidance techniques, all fragment variants are kept whatever their class. Indeed, it is necessary to keep all fragments to be able to annotate them. On the contrary, if a user is only allowed to have hiding and direct guidance, the fragment variants evaluated as the most relevant are only kept. Such a case is described in the example of the Fig. 7. The others are deleted because the user is not allowed to use them. Consequently, this kind of deletion leads to content adaptation. Some adaptive navigation techniques, like hiding, partial hiding or direct guidance, allow the removal of the irrelevant fragment variants whether they are the only techniques available. They have direct consequences on the document content and structure and then on content adaptation. Whether some fragment variants are deleted, the document content and structure may be modified.

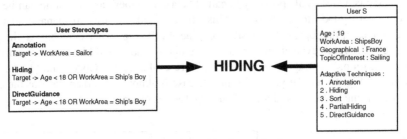

Fig. 7. Apply an adaptive method

5   Logical and Layout Composition

According to the user interaction, the servlet engine (cf. Fig. 1) receives the HTTP request with parameters and transmits them to the layout composition engine. The layout composition engine sends the parameters to the logical composition engine. For example, we assume that the user asks for the next web pages by means of the local navigation guide. A link looks like that:

```
"http://hoel.enst-bretagne.fr/iccars/parcours_dossier?type=report&frame=
MAIN&structureID=S.1.M.Kersauson.1&structureName=Kersauson et Jules
Verne&componentID=C.3.S.1.M.Kersauson.1-Iksal&fragmentID=
F.Kersauson.3-Iksal"
```

- This HTTP request is composed of six parameters:
    1. The URL of the current virtual document:
       `http://hoel.enst-bretagne.fr/iccars/parcours_dossier?`
    2. The XML template for the next web page: `type=report`,
    3. The part of the web page which will be changed: `frame=MAIN`
    4. Data (ID and Name) about the narrative structure chosen by the user[6]:
       `structureID=S.1.M.Kersauson.1&structureName=Kersauson et Jules Verne`
    5. The identifier of the next node: `componentID=C.3.S.1.M.Kersauson.1-Iksal`
    6. The identifier of the corresponding fragment: `fragmentID=F.Kersauson.3-Iksal`

By means of these parameters, the logical composition engine can choose the XML template for the current document (parameters 1 and 2). The XML template contains the logical structure and a set of queries to instantiate a new XML web page. This engine builds this XML page which is composed of the content, the description of the navigation guides and also some data about the adaptive technique and the evaluation state of each link. Parameters 4 and 5 are used to get the next node in the semantic graph and all the direct neighbors in the corresponding generic directed graph. Parameter 6 is used to get the web page content. These parameters – 4, 5 and 6 – are

---

[6] Virtual documents may have several narrative structures conveying different messages to the user.

used for querying the semantic composition engine and then to instantiate the XML template. From the new XML web page and a layout template, the layout composition engine is able to generate a web page. The layout engine is able to re-display the XML page with a new adaptive method, by re-parsing the XML page.

In navigation tools, links have properties for managing adaptation [15]. Fig. 8 shows the local navigation guide in an instantiated XML web page with link properties for adaptation. This guide is composed of the previous web pages, the current and the next ones. For each next link, there is a property giving the evaluation state given by the semantic composition engine which will be processed by the layout composition engine to transform each state into a particular clue on the web page (cf. Fig. 3).

```
<component_title>Navigation locale</component_title>
<local_navigation structureID="S.1.M.Kersauson.1" structureName="Kersauson et Jules Verne"
strategy="Annotation">
<previous>
<begin />
</previous>
<current type="CM_Molecule">Trophée Jules-Verne Olivier de Kersauson : '' On part en
févrie-r''</current>
<next>
<next_article_link componentID="C.3.S.1.M.Kersauson.1-Iksal" fragmentID="F.Kersauson.3-
Iksal">
[comp-1] A l'assaut de tous les records
<evaluation_state>3</evaluation_state>
</next_article_link>
<next_article_link componentID="C.2.S.1.M.Kersauson.1-Iksal" fragmentID="F.Kersauson.7-
Iksal">
[comp-0] Grandsrecords.com Toute Toile dehors
<evaluation_state>1</evaluation_state>
</next_article_link>
<next_report_link go_structureID="S.1.M.Kersauson.2"
from_componentID="C.4.S.1.M.Kersauson.1-Iksal" from_fragmentID="F.M.Kersauson.2-Iksal">
[comp-2] Le bateau de Kersauson
<evaluation_state>3</evaluation_state>
</next_report_link>
</next>
</local_navigation>
</component>
</panel>
</page>
```

Fig. 8. Local navigation guide as an XML component in a web page

6   Conclusion

In this paper, we have presented a flexible adaptive composition engine based on a semantic web approach. It ensures interoperability in separating resource management, organization, adaptation and layout. Content, organization and adaptation are specified by an author according to its explicit community knowledge. Thus, hypermedia consistency and comprehension are guaranteed.

Flexibility is due to the declarative parameters of the engines. The layout engine uses a XSLT template, and the logical composition engine uses an XML template as parameter. The semantic composition engine is based on a generic document and a ontology-based inference engine. It is possible to only change separately the parameters of each engine. Nevertheless, consistency between the three engines must be kept.

In the semantic composition engine, flexibility is also due to the filtering specification which is defined by semantic properties associated with a generic document. The management of adaptive techniques is made at an abstract level for the entire document. Consequently, it is easier to generate new hypermedia because it is sufficient to modify these semantic properties. Then, an author can deal with new adaptive documents and new user behaviors without changing the generic document a lot. Nevertheless, the management of adaptation at document level does not enable an author to change the adaptation mechanism at a very fine level of granularity. For instance, it is not possible to specify for each link or content how to manage adaptation like in AHA. In our framework, we could associate semantic properties for adaptation to semantic links types for having a finer level of granularity.

SCARCE engines are currently implemented in Java and linked to the servlet engine. In ICCARS and CANDLE, the ontology-based inference engine used is Ontobroker. In KMP, we are developing a new interface in the semantic composition engine for Corese [16], which is compatible with Web standards (RDF/RDFS, OWL).

References

1. Brusilovsky, P., *Methods and techniques of adaptive hypermedia.* User Modeling and User-Adapted Interaction, 1996. 6(2-3): p. 87-129.
2. Brusilovsky, P. and H. Su. *Adaptive Visualization Component of a distributed Web-base Adaptive Educational System.* in *ITS 2002.* 2002. Biarritz: Springer Verlag.
3. Aroyo, L., P. De Bra, and G.-J. Houben. *Embedding Information Retrieval in Adaptive Hypermedia: IR meets AHA!* in *AH 2003: Workshop on Adaptive Hypermedia And Adaptive Web-Based Systems.* 2003: Technische Universiteit Eindhoven.
4. Conlan, O., et al. *Applying Adaptive Hypermedia Techniques to Semantic Web Service Composition.* in *Workshop on Adaptive Hypermedia and Adaptive Web-Based Systems in The Twelth International World Wide Web Conference.* 2003. Budapest, Hungary.
5. Wenger, E., *Communities of Practice - Learning, Meaning and Identity.* Learning in Doing: Social, Cognitive and Computational Perspectives. 1998, Cambridge University Press.
6. Milosavljevic, M., F. Vitali, and C. Watters. *Introduction of the virtual document workshop.* in *Workshop on Virtual Document, Hypertext Funstionality and the Web.* 1999. Toronto.
7. Berners-lee, T., *Weaving the Web.* 1999, San Francisco: Harper.
8. Geurts, J.P., et al., *Towards ontology-driven discourse: from semantic graphs to multimedia presentations.* 2003, Centrum voor Wiskunde en Informatica.
9. Megalou, E. and T. Hadzilacos, *Semantic Abstractions in Multimedia Domain.* IEEE Transactions on Knowledge and Data Engineering, 2003. 15(1): p. 136-160.
10. Iksal, S., et al., *Semantic composition of special reports on the Web: A cognitive approach,* in *Hypertextes et Hypermédia H2PTM'01,* P. Balpe, et al., Eds. 2001, Hermès. p. 363-378.
11. De Bra, P. and L. Calvi, *AHA! An open Adaptive Hypermedia Architecture.* The New Review of Hypermedia and Multimedia, 1998. 4: p. 115-139.
12. Christophides, V., *Electronic Document Management Systems.* 1998, UCH/FORTH: http://www.ics.forth.gr/~christop/.
13. Garlatti, S., S. Iksal, and P. Tanguy, *SCARCE: an Adaptive Hypermedia Environment Based on Virtual Documents and the Semantic Web,* in *Adaptable and Adaptive Hypermedia Systems,* S.Y. Chen and G.D. Magoulas, Eds. 2004, Idea Group. p. To be appear.

14. Fensel, D., et al. *On2broker in a Nutshell*. in *the 8th World Wide Web Conference*. 1999. Toronto.

15. Brusilovsky, P., E. Schwarz, and G. Weber. *ELM-ART: An intelligent tutoring system on World Wide Web*. in *Third International Conference on Intelligent Tutoring Systems, ITS-96*. 1996. Montreal.

16. Corby, O. and C. Faron-Zucker. *Corese: A Corporate Semantic Web Engine*. in *Workshop on Real World RDF and Semantic Web Applications 11th International World Wide Web Conference*. 2002. Hawaii.

Intelligent Support to the Retrieval
of Information About Hydric Resources*

Cristina Gena and Liliana Ardissono

Dipartimento di Informatica, Università di Torino
Corso Svizzera 185, Torino, Italy
{cgena,liliana}@di.unito.it

Abstract. This paper presents the adaptive search features offered by ACQUA, a
Web-based system presenting information about the hydric resources of the Piedmont Italian Region. ACQUA enables the user to retrieve qualitative and quantitative data in different formats, supporting direct data manipulation. Moreover,
the system supports the user in the search for information by complementing her
explicit search queries with follow-up queries frequently occurring together in
navigation paths. In this way, the user may retrieve complete information in an
efficient way. The paper describes the results of an evaluation of the adaptivity
features carried out with real users.

1 Introduction

Public Web sites play a central role in the dissemination of information at low cost, but
they frequently fail to present the information in a satisfactory way. For example, most
data is presented in static Web pages hardly satisfying individual information needs;
see [7]. Moreover, qualitative and quantitative data is typically presented in a format that
cannot be directly exploited for processing purposes. Therefore, users cannot directly
exploit the retrieved data for interpretation (e. g., to generate histograms and charts, or
to compute aggregated data, such as maximum, minimum and mean values).

Indeed, advanced user modeling and content generation techniques have the potential to enhance the interaction capabilities of these Web sites. However, these techniques
cannot be easily adopted at the current stage, because of serious scalability and maintenance requirements. However, we believe that some minimalistic Adaptive Hypermedia
techniques could be applied to enhance the interaction with the user without overloading the Web sites too much. For example, lightweight techniques could be employed to
present data in different formats, so that it can be visualized and processed in heterogeneous software environments. Moreover, simple personalization rules could be applied
to speed up the user's search activity, at least in the most common types of search.

In this paper, we describe the content generation and personalization techniques applied in the ACQUA prototype information system, which presents data about hydric
resources of the Piedmont Region. The system provides the information requested by

* This work was funded by Regione Piemonte, Direzione Risorse Idriche. We thank G. Negro,
  G. Amadore, S. Grisello, A. Giannetta, M. Governa, E. Quinto, M. Demeo and V. Pellegrino,
  who assisted us during the system development and provided the domain specific knowledge.

W. Nejdl and P. De Bra (Eds.): AH 2004, LNCS 3137, pp. 126–135, 2004.

Fig. 1. Portion of the page describing the Torino observation point on Po river.

the user in pictorial and machine processable formats. Moreover, the system comple-
ments the search results with related data usually searched for, in order to speed up the
search task. In order to prove the usefulness of the adaptive features offered by our system, we evaluated them with real users. The rest of this paper is organized as follows:
Sect. 2 presents the project within which the ACQUA prototype was developed. Sect. 3
describes the information about hydric resources managed by the system. The search
features offered by the system are described in Sect. 4 and evaluated in Sect. 5. Sect. 6
compares our work to the related one and concludes the paper.

2   The Project

In 2003, the Hydric Resources Division of the Piedmont Region and the University
of Torino started a project for the development of ACQUA, an interactive Web site
presenting information about hydric resources derived from the monitoring activities
on the territory. The goal was to present up to date information thus reducing the need
to deliver data on a one-to-one basis via e-mail messages and paper publications. The
technicians of the Division guided us in the development of the Web site by providing
application requirements and a repository of e-mail messages which they exchanged
with users along the years. The messages provided us with evidence about the types of
users interested in hydric resources, the inspected information and the regularities in the
data search. Most questions came from other Public Administrations, technicians (e. g.,
companies building bridges, houses, etc.), attorneys (typically interested in data about
specific regions, e. g., as a consequence of environmental disasters), farmers (interested
in the bio-chemical state of their fields), students (university and PhD).

```
RIVERS: Qualitative data:
          Environmental State parameters:
             Environmental State (SECA): sufficient;
             Ecological State (SECA): class 3;
             IBE index: 7;
             ...
          Biological parameters:
             Acarus (A): 6;
             Biological quality: class 6;
          Chemical, physical and micro-biological parameters:
             Escherichia coli: 8300 UFC/100 ml;
             Total Azote: 9.63 mg/l;
             ...
       Quantitative data:
          Hydrometric level: 0.023 m;
          Average daily capacity: 47 mc/s;  ...
```

Fig. 2. Sample qualitative and quantitative parameters per resource type.

Following a user-centered approach, we developed the system by involving domain experts and final users starting from the first design phases. After a requirement analysis phase, we developed mock-ups which we discussed and redesigned after several focus group sessions with experts and users involved in the project. We exploited the feedback to develop our first prototype, which was first evaluated in a usability test by involving external users not cooperating at the project. After having solved the usability problems discovered in the test, the final prototype, described in this paper, was tested with real users representative of the users the Web site is devoted to; see Sect. 5.

As the system is devoted to the Public Administration, we had to satisfy usability and predictability requirements imposing the design of a simple user interface. Specifically, the system behavior should be highly predictable in order to support first-time visitors and to avoid frustrating professional users who would regularly use it for work purposes. Moreover, the user interface should be optimized for standard browsers.

3   Information About Hydric Resources

The information about hydric resources concerns rivers, lakes and underground waters and includes:

– Descriptive information about resources and observation points: e. g., maps of the points, charts representing environmental changes, pictures, documents, publications and descriptions of the monitoring stations. For instance, Fig. 1 ("Caratteristiche della stazione di monitoraggio TORINO" - Features of the Torino monitoring station) provides coordinates and other information about the observation point on Po river, located in Torino, Parco Michelotti.
– Measurement parameters concerning physical dimensions and other features characterizing the environmental state of the resources. These parameters are further distinguished in two main classes: *Qualitative parameters* are periodically measured by technicians who visit the observation points, collect data and take samples for laboratory tests. *Quantitative parameters* are monitored by automatic stations carrying out the measurements on a daily basis.

Resources may have more than one observation point. For instance, rivers are monitored in several points to check their status in the areas they flow through. Different sets of

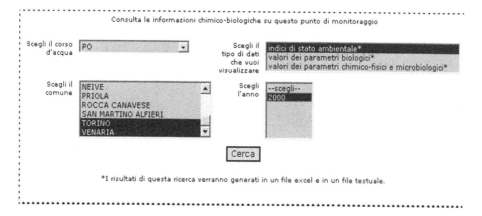

Fig. 3. Searching qualitative data (environmental state index) about Po river in the Torino and Venaria observation points.

qualitative and quantitative parameters describe the various resources. Fig. 2 shows some parameters concerning rivers; for each parameter, the name, an example value and the measurement unit are reported. The data about hydric resources is stored in a relational database updated in manual or automatic way. Qualitative and quantitative parameters are separately managed to reflect the fact that they are collected in different stations, following a different temporal scheduling.

4   The ACQUA Prototype System

4.1   Basic Interaction Features

The ACQUA system (demo available at http://acqua.di.unito.it) supports the search for information about hydric resources, including maps, descriptive information, raw and aggregated data. We present the system by focusing on information about rivers, which is sufficiently rich to give a flavor of the overall system. The ACQUA system should serve two main categories of users. The *novice users*, such as students and generic citizens, visit the Web site on an occasional basis and are not familiar with the presented content. The *expert users*, such as technicians, farmers and the personnel of other Public Administrations, frequently visit the site and are familiar with the domain specific information. In order to take these users' interaction requirements into account, the system offers two search facilities: the *simple search* facility, not described in this paper, supports a geographical search modality and guides the user step by step in the search for information. The *advanced search* facility, targeted to the expert users, supports a faster search for information by proposing forms where the user may compose the queries in a single step. Fig. 3 shows the main window of the advanced search: the user may select the river(s) to analyze (top-left menu), the type of information (top right menu) and the town(s) of the observation points (bottom-left menu). Moreover, the user can specify the temporal interval of search (year(s)).

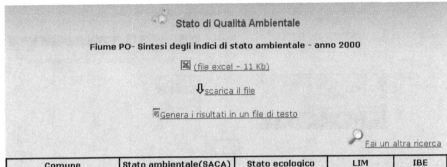

Fig. 4. Search results: environmental state index of Po river in the Torino and Venaria points.

Notice that the data archive stores partial information about hydric resources. For instance, the observation stations have been set up at different times; thus, not all the data series are complete. Moreover, critical data cannot be presented in the Web site until it is validated by human experts against measurement errors. In order to prevent the user from defining search queries that will not produce any results, the system constrains the time intervals for the search depending on the availability of data. For instance, as shown in Fig. 3, the environmental state indexes describing the Po river can be searched only as far as year 2000 is concerned. The user is allowed to retrieve data at different granularity levels, e. g., inspecting on one or more observation points, or retrieving data about more or less extended temporal intervals. In addition to this type of information, the database stores some data series for which the most interesting aggregated data (e. g., minimum, maximum and mean value) are already computed and can be directly downloaded by the user.

The results of the user's queries are displayed in Web pages showing different types of information. For instance, Fig. 4 ("Stato di Qualità Ambientale" - Quality of environmental state) shows the results of the query performed in Fig. 3, where the user asks for the environmental state of Po river, in the Torino and Venaria observation points. The top of the page summarizes the user's query ("Fiume PO - Sintesi degli Indici ..." - Po river, synthesis of environmental state indexes - 2000). The search results are available in different formats: by following the links below the title, they can be downloaded as a MS Excel® table suitable for data analysis or as a plain text file ("Genera i risultati in un file di testo"). Moreover, the results are shown in a table reporting: the town of the observation points ("Comune"), the values of the environmental state (SACA), the values of the ecological state (SECA), and so forth[1].

---

[1] Other formats, e. g., XML, could be generated to make data portable to other applications, but we did not add such formats in the current system because at the moment most users are only interested in the pictorial and in the Excel® tables.

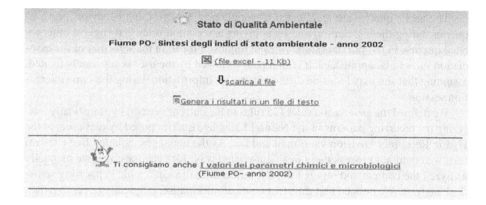

Fig. 5. Annotated search results: a link suggests follow-up queries.

4.2 Adaptive Features of the Prototype

The information provided by the ACQUA system concerns several aspects about hydric resources (see Sect. 3). In order to guarantee that the user can easily understand the search results, we imposed some restrictions on the queries that she can perform. For instance, as far as qualitative data about rivers is concerned, the user may request the environmental state indexes, or details about biological, microbiological and chemical parameters. However, she is not allowed to combine the queries because the results would be confusing. Therefore, if the user wants to retrieve different types of information, she has to execute more than one search query.

Although the separation of search paths enforces the clarity of the presented results, it makes the retrieval of different types of information a lengthy task. As a compromise between clarity and efficiency, we have extended the system with a personalized search feature that supports the retrieval of information strictly related to the user's explicit search goals. When possible, the system anticipates the user's information needs and proposes supplementary *follow-up queries* as links [8] that the user can follow to retrieve the the extended search results without starting the query specification from the beginning. For instance, see Fig. 5: the higher portion of the figure is similar to the previous one, but the system's recommendations are proposed in the lower portion of the page ("Ti consigliamo anche i valori dei parametri chimici e microbiologici" - We also suggest results about chemical and micro-biological parameters).

IF the user asks for (quantitative) historical data for more than one observation point
THEN suggest qualitative data
IF the user asks for chemical data for more than one observation point
THEN suggest biological data
IF the user asks for biological and chemical data and environmental state indexes
THEN suggest quantitative data

Fig. 6. Some association rules for the anticipation of the user's information needs.

The user's queries are anticipated by monitoring her browsing behavior (previous queries during the interaction) and by applying association rules that suggest other related queries. Fig. 6 presents some rules in linguistic form. In the selection of the association rules to be applied, each search path followed by the user is separately treated, assuming that she may focus on different types of information during the same interaction session.

We defined the association rules (25 rules in the current system) by statistically analyzing the recurring patterns in the Natural Language queries posed by real users to the Hydric Resources Division via e-mail and fax. As the messages included free (Italian) text, we could not process them in an automated way: for each message, we manually analyzed the content and inputed the relevant information in a table supporting statistical analysis. We noticed that different kinds of information frequently occur together, depending on the user's request (e. g., qualitative and quantitative data). Therefore, we defined association rules based on the observed frequency derived from these requests. The association rules are represented as *condition - action* rules:

- The *condition* part is a boolean condition on the user's search path in the Web site. For instance, which type of data she has asked about, how many observation points she has selected for the analysis, which temporal interval she has selected, and similar.
- The *action* part is the extended query to be proposed by the system; e. g., select another type of data on the same observation points and temporal interval.

At the current stage, the association rules are mutually exclusive and are managed by employing a simple inference mechanism. In future revisions of the rule set, we might introduce priorities to handle the possible conflicts.

5   Evaluation of the Adaptive Features Offered by ACQUA

Subjects. We evaluated 10 potential users of systems, 4 females and 6 males, 30-50 aged. All the subjects work in the hydric resource field and none of them was involved in the project.

Procedure. The subjects were split in two groups (5 subjects each) and randomly assigned to one of the two groups. The experimental group had to solve the tasks using the adaptive Web site, while the control group had to solve tasks without adaptation.

Experimental tasks. Each subject had to solve 7 tasks, each one representing a real task the user can perform in the Web site. The tasks were strictly correlated and could be grouped in three main search activities the user often performs together, as our correlation study suggests (see Sect. 4.2). The first activity conveyed the whole information useful to an environmental impact study. The second one supported constructions feasibility studies. The third activity supported lawyers studies and work. In the first activity (that includes tasks 1, 2 and 3), we asked the user to search for the complete sets of qualitative data - environmental, chemical, biological - concerning two observation points on the Po river. In the second activity (tasks 4 and 5), the user was requested to search for quantitative data about the Po river in Turin, and then to search for the related information about underground water. In the third activity (tasks 6 and 7), the user had to search for quantitative data about the Po river in Turin at a specific day, and then to retrieve detailed information about the related observation point.

In the control group, the users had to submit a new query for every task, in order to obtain the requested results. In the experimental group, the users could obtain the related information by clicking on the annotated link showing the follow-up query (see Fig. 5). The adaptive suggestion appeared in tasks 2, 3, 5 and 7 after an initial query generating the results to be correlated. In that way the user did not submit a new query by filling a form, but the related results were automatically generated by exploiting the association rules described in Sect. 4.2.

Experimental design. Single factor (the adaptivity) between-subjects design.

Measures. The subjects' performances were recorded by using Camtasia Studio®. We measured the task completion time and the subjects' satisfaction (by means of a post-task walkthrough).

Hypothesis. We hypothesized that the users working in the experimental group could obtain better performance results.

Results. The ANOVA showed that the subjects of the experimental group had better performance results. In addition, we calculated the effect size (treatment magnitude) and the power (sensitivity) as suggested in [2]. The effect size (ω^2) measures the strength, or the magnitude, of the treatment effects in an experiment. In behavioral sciences small, medium, large effects of ω^2 are $0,01/0,06/>0,15$ respectively. The power of an experiment (n') is the ability to recognize treatment effects. The power can be used for estimating the sample size. In social science the accepted value of the power is equal to $0,80$, which means that the 80% of repeated experiments will produce the same results.

- *task 2*. ANOVA: $F(1,8)= 12,45$ $p<0,01$; $\omega^2=0,53$; $n'=3,49$.
- *task 3*. ANOVA: $F(1,8)= 12,12$ $p<0,01$; $\omega^2=0,53$; $n'=3,60$.
- *task 5*. ANOVA: $F(1,8)= 14,16$ $p<0,01$; $\omega^2=0,57$; $n'=3,04$.
- *task 7*. ANOVA: $F(1,8)= 9,23$ $p<0,05$; $\omega^2=0,45$; $n'=4,86$.

Notice that the results are significative and we obtained a large estimate of the magnitude of the treatment effect. In addition, by exploiting a power of $0,80$ and the corresponding ω^2 for each task we could determine the requested sample size, which fits our sample size ($n=5$).

Post-task walkthrough. During a post-task walkthrough the subjects are asked to think about the event and comment to their actions. After each test we talked with the subjects in order to collect their impressions and to discuss about their performance and the problems they experienced during the text. In this session we wanted also to collect some feedback useful to produce a qualitative evaluation of the site. As a recent study pointed out [9], statistical analyses are often false, misleading and too narrow, while insights and qualititative studies do not suffer from these problems because they strictly rely to the users' observed behavior and reactions. Even if our experimental evaluation reported significant results supporting our hypothesis, the actual behavior of the users could be different. An ethnographic study was not feasible at that time, because the information needed to feed the databases was partial. Therefore, we opted for a post-task walkthrough to collect some deeper insights.

In most cases the interviewed users were satisfied about the site. Most of them encountered some difficulties in execution of the starting query of task 2, thus we modified the interface form. All the users of the experimental group exploited the suggested adaptive link, but they were not aware of its personalized features. When we explained the adaptations, they noticed the particularity of the suggestion ("We also recommend you..."). However, they were attracted from the suggestions and they really appreciated the possibility of skipping the execution of a new query. The adaptive suggestions were considered visible but not intrusive. Also the users of the control group reported similar considerations when the adaptive features of the site were explained. Even if they did not found the suggestions in their tasks, they explored the results page in order to find some shortcuts to proceed in the task execution. After having followed some links, they went back to the previous query page or to the home page by exploiting the browser's "Back" button. In both conditions, a common behavior pattern emerged: the users explored the results page before starting a new search. Nevertheless, their behavior could be influenced by the test condition, because tested users usually pay more attention to their own actions and to the page design. Even if they were satisfied about the adaptations features, only the real usage can demonstrate our hypothesis. However, both quantitative and qualitative test results are encouraging and we think that the adaptation results are shown in the right portion of the pages. After this test, we presented the adaptive version of the site to the expert users of the Hydric Resources Division collaborating to the project. They confirmed the correctness of the association rules we exploited for the adaptation and they decided to replace the non-adaptive version of the prototype with the adaptive one.

6   Discussion

We presented the interactive features offered by the ACQUA prototype system to support the search of qualitative and quantitative information about Piedmont hydric resources. The system has a simple user interface, designed to meet simplicity, usability and predictability requirements, but it offers advanced interactive features enabling the user to create her own view on the information space. Two search features, targeted to novice and expert users, are available, and the search results are presented in pictorial and machine readable formats, in order to support data manipulation at the user side. Moreover, the system analyzes the user's queries to identify her information needs, and it exploits personalized association rules to propose *follow-up queries* complementing the search results with strictly related information. The follow-up queries are performed on demand; thus, the user can ignore them if she is not interested in the additional data, and the system does not need to retrieve and pre-cache uninteresting information.

The advanced search features we presented differ from the related work in various respects. On the one hand, the inferences made in our system are simpler than the probabilistic ones applied in other automated assistants, such as Lumière [5], which exploit Bayesian Networks to capture the dependencies between the user actions. The point is that the user visiting our Web site is only searching data, and she is not carrying out a complex task requiring a problem solving activity. Therefore, lightweight rules associating contextually related search queries are sufficient to predict the implicit user interests and to complement the search for information accordingly. Our approach also differs from the *follow-up question answering* techniques proposed in [8]: our follow-up queries are pre-compiled in a set of association rules, instead of being generated by a planner, in order to efficiently manage the query identification process.

On the other hand, we apply query analysis techniques to identify regularities in search patterns. This is is different from the typical inferences carried out in recommender systems, which reason about regularities in the selection of individual items (e. g., see [4, 3]), or about the features of the selected items (e. g., see [1]) to identify the user's priorities. Other strategies for personalized Web search have been proposed in [6]. Different from our work, that system does not personalize the proposed results but supplies a small set of categories as context for each query. The system combines both the user's search history and a general user profile extracted automatically from a category hierarchy to offer a personalized context disambiguating the proposed query results. In our system, we did not manage long-term user preferences because we noticed that, during different interaction sections, the same users are interested in rather different types of information. We thus decided to base the system's recommendations only on the analysis of her search behavior.

Before concluding this presentation it is worth mentioning that, although the first set of adaptation rules supporting the user's search task has been manually defined, this was a lengthy work and could not be easily replicated to revise the rules along time. However, if the Hydric Resource Division adopts the ACQUA system as its official information system, the log files generated by the system will provide structured evidence about user behavior. Thus, datamining techniques could be exploited to automatically recognize usage patterns and revise the adaptation rules. In our future work, we will also exploit some ontology management techniques in order to design a domain ontology supporting the description of the user's navigation behavior at an abstraction level suitable for efficient automated analysis.

References

1. D. Billsus and M. Pazzani. A personal news agent that talks, learns and explains. In *Proc. 3rd Int. Conf. on Autonomous Agents (Agents '99)*, pages 268–275, Seattle, WA, 1999.
2. D.N. Chin. Empirical evaluation of user models and user-adapted systems. *User Modeling and User-Adapted Interaction*, 11(1-2):181–194, 2001.
3. P. Cotter and B. Smyth. WAPing the Web: content personalization for WAP-enabled devices. In *Proc. International Conference on Adaptive Hypermedia and Adaptive Web-based Systems (AH 2000)*, pages 98–108, Trento, Italy, 2000.
4. GroupLens. Grouplens research. http://www.ncs.umn.edu/Research/GroupLens, 2002.
5. E. Horvitz, J. Breese, D. Heckerman, D. Hovel, and K. Rommelse. The Lumière project: Bayesian user modeling for inferring the goals and needs of software users. In *Proc. 14th Conf. on Uncertainty in Artificial Intelligence (UAI '98)*, San Francisco, CA, 1998.
6. F. Liu, C. Yu, and W. Meng. Personalized web search by mapping user query to categories. In *Proc. CIKM'02*, McLean, Virginia, USA, 2002.
7. M. Maybury and P. Brusilovsky, editors. *The adaptive Web*, volume 45. Communications of the ACM, 2002.
8. J.D. Moore and V.O. Mittal. Dynamically generated follow-up questions. *IEEE Computer*, 29(7):75–86, 1996.
9. J. Nielsen. Risks of quantitative studies. In *Alertbox*, http://www.useit.com/alertbox/20040301.html, 2004.

CUMAPH: Cognitive User Modeling
for Adaptive Presentation of Hyper-documents.
An Experimental Study

Halima Habieb-Mammar[1] and Franck Tarpin-Bernard[1,2]

[1] Interaction Collaborative Télé-activités Téléenseignement (ICTT), INSA de Lyon
20 Avenue Jean Capelle, 69211 Villeurbanne Cedex, France
{halima.habieb,franck.tarpin-bernard}@insa-lyon.fr
http://ictt.insa-lyon.fr
[2] Scientific Brain Training (SBT)
Batiment CEI, 66 Bd Niels Bohr - BP 2132 - 69603 Villeurbanne cedex
http://www.sbt.fr

Abstract. In this paper we present the CUMAPH environment (Cognitive User Modeling for Adaptive Presentation of Hyper-document). The aim of this environment is to adapt hyper-document presentation to the cognitive user profile. The architecture of this environment is based on four main components: a cognitive user model, a hyper-document generation process, an adaptive process and a generic style sheet. These components and their combinations are described in detail. To validate our approach, an experimental study was conducted upon a population of 50 students. The experimental steps and the main results obtained are discussed in this paper.

1 Introduction

One of the main goals of Adaptive Hypermedia (AH) systems consists in decreasing the cognitive overload caused by the presence of information that is irrelevant to the goals and/or the abilities of Web users. In [3], Brusilovsky presented taxonomy of techniques and methods related to AH systems. Following this taxonomy, we can distinguish two types of adaptation techniques used to support this goal: adaptive-presentation techniques and link-adaptation techniques. Links adaptation provides navigational support to hyper-documents users. The adaptive presentation goal is to adapt the content of the pages according to the users' goals, abilities, knowledge, language or other user characteristics.

In this paper, we deal with the adaptive presentation of hyper-documents. We present an environment called CUMAPH for "Cognitive User Modeling for Adaptive Presentation of Hyper-documents". This environment is based on four components: a cognitive user model, a hyper-document generation process, an adaptive process and a generic style sheet to present the adapted hyper-documents. We view presentation adaptation as a process of selection of the most suitable combination of interactive elements. By combination, we mean an item or a collection of multimedia items (text,

W. Nejdl and P. De Bra (Eds.): AH 2004, LNCS 3137, pp. 136–145, 2004.

images, audio and video) that describe an element (a concept, an explanation, etc.). The best combination is the one that fits most the user abilities. Some degrees of freedom are left to the user to visualize the items he/she wants. Techniques dealing with user profile construction are drawn from work in cognitive psychology and human computer interface.

We focus our work on output media in the context of hypermedia. The first section deals with the description of main CUMAPH components. Then, we present and discuss the results of an experimental study. These results indicate that our approach is promising and they give valuable feedback about future work.

2 Description of the CUMAPH Environment

CUMAPH is an environment where the hyper-document presentation is adapted according to the cognitive user model. We stress the point that it is the combination of four main components that enable the hyper-document adaptivity. These components are shown in Fig. 1.

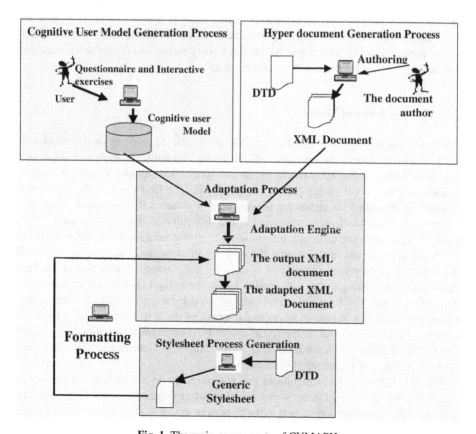

Fig. 1. The main components of CUMAPH

2.1   Generation Process of a Cognitive User Model

The process consists in executing a sequence of interactive exercises then computing the cognitive profile. The main components of the output profile are cognitive indicators dispatched into 5 sectors: *memory, attention, executive functions, language and visual & spatial capacities* [7]. In detail, 25 indicators have been determined. In our process, we are not using all the indicators. However, the most frequently used were: working memory (verbal, visual or auditory), memory (long term and short term), categorization, comprehension, inhibition, visual and spatial exploration, form recognition and glossary.

Using the cognitive indicators, we have modeled the cognitive sectors that are most called upon while performing an exercise. However, in practice, an exercise does not imply a unique sector. Every cognitive activity results from a parallel or hierarchical processing of many cognitive abilities. For each exercise, we have determined the indicators needed and chosen weight factors ($0 \leq p_i \leq 10$). After each exercise, the performance (P) of the user is computed using the average performance (M) and the standard deviation (σ) of this performance that are stored in our database. Our database is made up of results by other users with the same characteristics (age, gender and level of education). A user with an average performance will obtain a score of 50 (the default value) and someone with a very good performance of $M+2\sigma$ will obtain 90 (2.5% of the population) [7]. This cognitive profile is very stable and is calculated once and for all (it can be updated when the user gets older).

2.2   Hyper-document Model

The hyper-document is structured in an XML document [5] made up of several blocks. Each block can usually be presented into different elements. Each element is associated to different media. Each media has an attribute called **signature** which is a representation of the "level of complexity" ranged [0,5]. The first value of the attribute is defined by the author. It stands for the quantity of either verbal, or visual or musical information that the element contains i.e. the difficulty of the text (the term "difficulty" is related to the difficulty encountered to understand the text), the quantity of information contained in the image, the quantity of noise and the language in which the message is expressed. This level is used by the process of selection of the best combination according to the user profile. Later, the system changes each attribute by computing a material signature which will be used by the style sheet for the layout. For textual modality, this level refers to the length of the text. For the image, the level concerns its dimension. As for the sound modality, it concerns its duration. *T[x]* stands for Textual elements with the level x, *G[x]* for Graphical element and *S[x]* for Sound element (music, jingle, recorded voice etc.).

The DTD (Data Type Description) that structures the hyper-document is shown in Fig. 2 [5]. We have built an authoring tool for our environment and we have tried to provide further information related to the hyper-document in such a way that helps the author to incrementally edit his/her documents (Fig. 3).

```
Page [title, style]
    {bloc [name, group, position]
        {element [name, signature, state]
            {content [type="text" [{link}] : "sound" [duration, autostart] :
                           "image" [width, high link]
            }
        }
    rules
            {combi}
        exclude
            {combi}
    links
    {link [key_word, url, position] }
    }
```

Fig. 2. Data Type Description

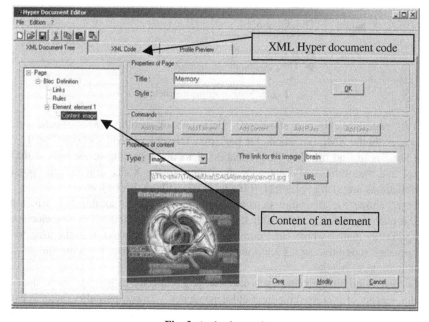

Fig. 3. Authoring tool

2.3 Adapting Hyper-documents on the Fly

There are several reasons why the dynamic generation of web pages is preferable to keeping static pages on disk. The first one is to tailor presentation to each user. Furthermore, if the information can be put together in many ways, the sheer number of possible variants can make static pages impractical [6]. In the CUMAPH environment, the user profile generation process yields a user profile which constitutes the input data for the adaptation process. This profile enables the selection of the most adapted output media.

Prior to any process, a generic style sheet, which contains the layout of a complete page to be presented, has to be defined. For a specific subject, the final layout of this page is brought through the adaptive process. This page is the most suitable one to the user profile. To illustrate the adaptation process, we hereafter give an example of a page dealing with the *Memory* item extracted from a course called "Brain Saga".

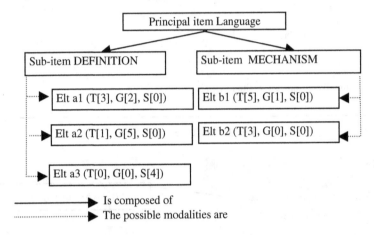

Fig. 4. XML document structure

This page presents two sub-items: "definition of memory" and "mechanism of memory". In the XML document, the page may fall under two blocks (see Fig. 4).
The issue is to find the "best" combination of media according to the will of the designer and the abilities of the reader. According to the XML structure, the possible combinations are: (Elt a1, Elt b2), (Elt a2, Elt b2), (Elt a3, Elt b1), etc.

Fig. 5 shows the algorithm steps to select the multimedia combination which best fit the user cognitive model. After the building of the combinations, we calculate a compatibility matrix whose lines correspond to criteria extracted from the user profile components (cognitive styles and interaction styles) and whose rows are the possible combinations of media.

For each combination and each criterion (e.g. capacity to manage more than one media, respect of preferred media, field-dependency...) a compatibility factor is calculated using arithmetic formula that combine the user profile and the characteristics of the combination. The combination of media that results in the biggest sum is considered as the most compatible one.

Then, the ASP program on the server side builds an enriched XML document that contains the whole page to be presented. Depending on the combination that has been selected, the ASP program values a *state* attribute into each tag (0 if hidden, 1 if visible, 2 if reduced).

On the other side, the user profile which contains the indicators to be explored is structured into a database and constitutes the second input for the presentation adaptation process. The last input of the process is the style sheet which transforms the final XML document and presents it as the final adapted page.

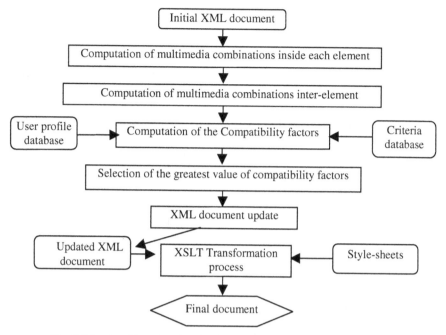

Fig. 5. The algorithm steps in selecting the "best" multimedia combination

Here are the two first criteria we used:

$$(Nb\_Vi*Sc\_Vi+Nb\_Ve*Sc\_Ve)/(Nb\_Vi+Nb\_Ve) \tag{1}$$

$$100*(Nb\_Vi+Nb\_Ve+Nb\_S)/Nb\_Max \tag{2}$$

The first criterion is used for computing the best combination that fits the profile. The second one is used to favour the selection of a multimedia combination. These criteria use the visual and the verbal scores: Sc_Vi / Sc_Ve that are calculated using the formula (3) / (4).

$$Sc\_Vi=(WM\_Vi+STM\_Vi+LTM\_Vi+Rec+Exp)/5 \tag{3}$$

$$Sc\_Ve=(STM\_Ve+STM\_Ve+LTM\_Ve+Glos+Cat+Comp)/6 \tag{4}$$

Where:
WM_Ve: Verbal Working Memory,
STM_Ve/ Vi: Verbal/ Visual Short Term Memory,
LTM_Ve/Vi : Verbal/Visual Long Term Memory
Rec: Form Recognition, *Exp*: Visual and spatial Exploration, *Glos*: Glossary
Cat: Category, *Comp:* Comprehension
Nb_Vi/Ve/S: respectively the number of Visual, Verbal and Sound media
Nb_Max = Max(Nb_Vi+Nb_Ve+Nb_S)

3 The Experiment

3.1 The Technique

The most common approach to evaluating an adaptive system is to compare it to its non adaptive version. This approach was adopted by the evaluations of both MetaDoc [1] and PUSH [6]. Although these evaluations showed that the adaptive versions of the systems improved the users' performance in several information tasks, the quality of the non-adapted version can often be discussed. Other approaches consist in splitting a population in two opposite groups A & B (e.g. visual vs verbal profile) and experiment the system using counter balanced situations. This kind of technique is very efficient if it is possible to split the population in opposite groups. In our situation, this technique is not applicable because cognitive profiles are very varied.

To avoid these drawbacks, here is what we do for each subject:

- perform a module (6 interactive exercises from the SBT company) that builds up the cognitive profile
- Generate a randomized cognitive profile
- Give them 20 minutes to navigate through a web-course that is adapted according to the randomized profile
- Evaluate their knowledge using a marked questionnaire
- Ask them qualitative information about the comfort of the experiment.

Then we analyze the result and try to show that coherent adaptation, that is when the randomized profile is close to the real profile, give better result than less coherent adaptation, whatever the real profile are.

50 subjects (third year industrial engineering students of INSA-LYON) took part in the experiment. Because of technical issues during the cognitive evaluation process (mainly sound devices issues), we have excluded 11 students whose audio profiles were aberrant. Hence, 39 students have been included in the analysis.

For the second step of the experiment we use a hyper-document called "*Saga du Cerveau*" Brain Story [5]. This course has been generated through the authoring tool described above. This course has been chosen because the initial knowledge of each subject was null on this topic. By this course we aimed to explain to users what cognitive abilities are.

3.2 The Results

First, trying to identify the different cognitive profiles of the users, using a clustering statistic method, we built 6 homogeneous groups (fig. 6). It is very interesting to see that we have a "natural" distribution according to each main score (visual, verbal and auditory) splitting high and low scores. A profile score which is the average of the three scores is calculated. Then, we have defined 6 groups using the average profile (M) and the standard deviation (S): [<M-2S] [M-2S ; M-S] [M-S ; M] [M; M+S] [M+S ; M+2S] [>M+2S]. For each user, we defined a cProfile value [1..6] depending on which group the user belongs to.

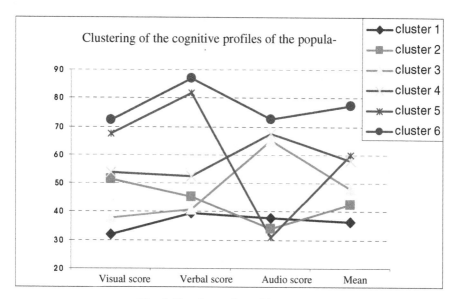

Fig. 6. The clustered cognitive profiles

We then split our population into 4 groups considering the "adaptation distance" which is calculated using an Euclidian distance between the real profile (defined by the three scores) and the randomized distance. The first two groups have a distance shorter than the average distance whereas the two others have a longer one.

Considering the mark obtained to the questionnaire, we defined 6 groups using the average mark (M) and the standard deviation (S): [<M-2S] [M-2S ; M-S] [M-S ; M] [M; M+S] [M+S ; M+2S] [>M+2S]. For each user, we defined a cMark value [1..6] depending on which group the user belongs to.

Finally, we consider the difference E=cMark-cProfile to measure the evolution of a user in the population. Indeed, if E is positive that means that the subject has a better position in the evaluation test than his/her cognitive profile suggests. On the opposite, a negative value shows a regression. This value is very interesting because it does not depend on the user level but shows if the adaptation process helps him/her to obtain better results.

Table 1. Evolution of users according to the adaptation distance

E=cMark-cProfile	-2	-1	0	1	2	3	Population	Average E
Very short distance	0	1	3	3	0	2	9	0.89
Short Distance	0	1	3	3	3	0	10	0.80
Long Distance	2	4	1	2	2	0	11	-0.18
Very long distance	2	3	3	0	1	0	9	-0.56

Thus positive effects are observed when the adaptation is done correctly and negative effects are observed when the randomized profile is too far than the real one. This confirms that adaptation is useful and efficient.

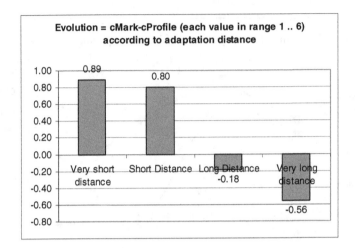

Fig. 7. Evolution of users according to the adaptation distance

Thanks to a deep analysis of the test mark, we noticed that the 3 members (the most brilliant users) all belong to the "Long Distance" and "Very long Distance" groups but still have quite good marks. This is not surprising as most brilliant people have the best abilities to adapt themselves to inadequate media. Obviously, they are less sensitive to the adaptation process than the others. In our next analysis, we chose to eliminate them.

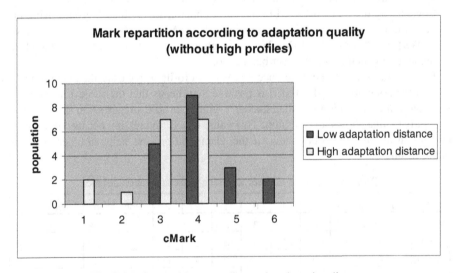

Fig. 8. Mark repartition according to the adaptation distance

In this new analysis, we have another proof of the efficiency of the adaptation as the high marks are only present for low adaptation distance whereas low marks are only met with high adaptation distance.

4 Conclusion

In this paper we presented CUMAPH, an environment for adaptive hyper-document presentation based on four components: a cognitive user model, a hyper-document generation process, an adaptive process and a generic style sheet to present the adapted hyper-documents. All these components have been implemented and the environment has been experimented in order to validate the approach, especially the efficiency of the cognitive adaptation.

The results of our experiment show that adaptive presentation of hyper-documents can contribute to the improvement of the performance of users during the hyper-document exploration. With very rich multimedia documents we may wonder if the user can achieve the same result. It will be interesting to compare our results with the results of the exploration of multimedia hyper-documents. The interest of our approach is to decrease the cognitive overloading as we only present necessary items.

References

1. Boyle, C. and Encarnacion, A. O. MetaDoc: An Adaptive Hypertext Reading System, User Modeling and User-Adapted Interaction, Vol.4, No.1, pp.1-19, 1994.
2. Brusilovsky, P. and Su, H.-D. Adaptive Visualization Component of a Distributed Web-based Adaptive Educational System. In: Intelligent Tutoring Systems. Vol. 2363, (Proceedings of 6th International Conference on Intelligent Tutoring Systems, ITS'2002, Biarritz, France, June 2-7, 2002) Berlin: Springer-Verlag, pp. 229-238.
3. Brusilovsky, P. Methods and Techniques of Adaptive Hypermedia. User Modeling and User-Adapted Interaction, 6, pp. 87-129. 1996 (Reprinted in Adaptive Hypertext and Hypermedia, Kluwer Academic Publishers, 1998, pp. 1-43).
4. De-Bra, P., Brusilovsky, P., Houben, G.J. Adaptive Hypermedia: From Systems to Framework. ACM Computing Surveys 31:4. (URL: http://www.cs.brown.edu/memex/ACM_HypertextTestbed/papers/25.html).
5. Habieb-Mammar, F. Tarpin-Bernard, P. Prévôt Adaptive presentation of multimedia interface Case study: "Brain Story" Course. User Modeling'03, Pittsburg USA. Mai 2003.
6. Hook, K. Evaluating the utility and usability of an adaptive hypermedia system. In: J.
7. Moore, E. Edmonds and A. Puerta (eds.) Proceedings of 1997 International Conference on Intelligent User Interfaces, Orlando, Florida, January 7-9, 1997, ACM, pp. 179-186, 1997.
8. Tarpin-Bernard, F. Habieb Mammar, H. Croisile, B. Noir, M. A supervised Program for Cognitive e-Training. WebNet'2001, World Orlando. October 2001.
9. Tsandilas, T. and schraefel, m. c. Adaptive Presentation Supporting Focus and Context. In De Bra, P., Eds. Proceedings of AH 2003: pp. 193-200, Nottingham, UK, 2003.
10. Vassileva, J A Practical Architecture for User Modeling in a Hypermedia-Based Information System. User Modeling'94, pages 115-120, Hyannis, MA, 1994.

Personalized Web Advertising Method

Przemysław Kazienko[1] and Michał Adamski[1,2]

[1] Wrocław University of Technology, Department of Information Systems,
Wybrzeże S. Wyspiańskiego 27, 50-370 Wrocław, Poland
kazienko@pwr.wroc.pl, http://www.pwr.wroc.pl/~kazienko
[2] Universidade Nova de Lisboa, Faculdade de Ciências e Tecnologia,
Monte de Caparica, 2829-516 Caparica, Portugal
michal.adamski@iol.pt

Abstract. Personalization of online advertising is a great challenge while the market is moving and adapting to the realities of the Internet. Many existing approaches to advertisement recommendation are based on demographic targeting or on information gained directly from the user. In this paper we introduce the AD ROSA system for automatic web banner personalization, which integrates web usage and content mining techniques to reduce user input and to respect the user's privacy. Furthermore, the advertising campaign policy, an important factor for both the publisher and advertiser, is taken into consideration. To enable online personalized advertising the integration of all relevant information is performed in one vector space.

1 Introduction

In the age of disappearing borders and mixed societies the current demographic targeting of freely available Web content seems to be insufficient. The market consists of human beings, not demographics, so web personalization should depend on an individual's behavior rather than on stereotypes created according to his or her geographical location or other demographic features (e.g. gender, age). Traditional advertising serving the same offers for everyone does not meet the current requirements of businesses. To increase the effectiveness, the right person should receive the right message at the right time and in the right context [1].

Web advertising is mainly done with banners – graphical elements on a web page, or with their 'mutations' – displayed in a new layer or new window of the browser. There are many other forms of online advertisements like sponsored links or articles, or mail-outs, but in this article we will only concentrate on banners and similar forms.

Users, showered with hundreds of advertisements, often pay less attention to banners appearing on a web page as bitmap images or animations, and this seems to be the main problem of web advertising. The solution is to increase the correspondence between user interests and the subject of the displayed advertisement [4].

Two significant research domains may be distinguished within Internet advertising: scheduling and personalization. The main goal of the former is to maximize the total click-through-rate for all advertisements by appropriately managing of exposition time and advertising space on the web page [3, 14].

The latter seems to be an important and difficult challenge for current advertisers. It aims to assign a suitable advertisement to the user, so it is necessary to have some

W. Nejdl and P. De Bra (Eds.): AH 2004, LNCS 3137, pp. 146–155, 2004.

information about the user. Many web portals create user profiles using the information gained during the registration process or ask the user to answer some questions about their preferences. However, this requires a lot of time and effort, and that can discourage many users. Besides, users tend to give incorrect data when being concerned for their privacy [13]. Even reliable data becomes out-of-date with the evolution of the online customer's interests. An alternative solution is to exploit information stored in the web server logs. This method is safe in regard to privacy fears and may also be useful for news portals or web sites where users do not need to log in to use the service [19]. Another approach to advertisement personalization is presented in [11]. Short-term and long-term interests of the user were identified. Short-term interests are derived from the keywords submitted by the user in searching services. However, such keywords may often have nothing in common with the user's regular preferences. Long-term interests are proposed to be taken from user profiles, which are completed by users and stored in the database of the system. However, advertising personalization was performed using only short-term information.

A system based on web usage mining and clustering of navigation paths to create usage patterns was presented in [19]. Pages from both the publisher's web site and the advertisements' target sites are manually classified into thematic categories by experts. The assignment of appropriate advertisements to each active user is accomplished according to pages (categories) visited by the given user during the current session. This matching is based on fuzzy rules stored in the system. The fuzzy approach was also used in target advertising based on user profiles [21].

Three main advertising models can be distinguished [5]: broker, portal and advertiser models. In the *broker model* there exists an advertising broker that connects publishers (web sites in which advertisements would be displayed) and advertisers (companies providing banners to be emitted). The broker often provides some targeting options. This model is applied i.e. by DoubleClick [15]. The *portal model* (used by large web portals) is the special case of the broker model: the publisher owns the advertisement management software and cooperates with many advertisers. The *advertiser model*, in which the advertiser manages the advertisements, allows big online store to display its banners on pages of particular portals.

2   Advertisement Features

Nowadays most online advertising systems use the principle of *the customer-based targeting*. Each user is identified and classified according to his or her geographical location (IP address) and browser settings sent with the HTTP request, navigation habits and user profiles (preferences) completed by the user during the registration process. This data is used to personalize the displayed banner advertisement [2, 11].

Analyzing advertising offers of the greatest Polish portals (*www.wp.pl, www.onet.pl*), we observed many target criteria available for advertisers. Apart from the demographic data of a user (age, gender, location, etc.), advertisements can be targeted towards the user's education, profession or interests. Furthermore, the publisher can choose the time of day of the emission, particular parts of the web page, and limit the number of emissions for a single user. An advertiser is usually charged on the basis of cost per month per one thousand emissions of advertisement (CPM). Another approach is the usage of click-though-rate (CTR) - the ratio of the number of clicks to the emission number [2]. It should be mentioned that the average CTR is currently decreasing as a consequence of the increasing number of total advertisements displayed [17].

The method presented below takes into consideration most of the contemporary applied aspects of advertising campaigns with respect to users' privacy rights.

3   AD ROSA System – Method Overview

The advertising method proposed in this paper solves the problem of automatic personalization of web banner advertisements with respect to user privacy (none of the user's personal details are stored in a database) and recent advertising campaign policy. It is based on knowledge extraction from the web pages' content and historical user sessions as well as the current behavior of the online user, using data mining techniques. The implementation of data mining to web content and web usage is usually called web content and web usage mining, respectively [12, 20]. There are also some integration methods of both these approaches [8, 9, 12].

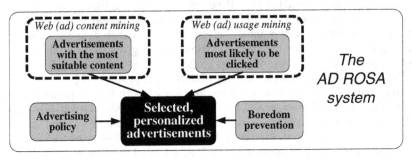

Fig. 1. Factors of advertisement selection in the AD ROSA system

The proposed method uses both web mining techniques and combines in one personalized framework several useful factors of advertising: the most suitable content (the content of the advertiser's web site), click probability, advertising policy i.e. arising from contracts and boredom prevention mechanisms (Fig. 1). The latest, are responsible for periodical rotation – the scheduling of advertisements for the user. The AD ROSA system is part of the ROSA project [6, 7, 8, 10].

Historical user sessions are stored in the database and clustered to obtain typical, aggregated user sessions (Fig. 2). The cluster's centroid corresponds to one *usage pattern* of the publisher's web site. Each user session is linked up to the set of advertisements visited (clicked) by the user during this session (*visited ad vector*). Having a cluster of sessions, the AD ROSA system can also extract information about related, visited advertisements, by counting the mean vector (*ad visiting pattern vector*) from all visited vectors related to sessions from the cluster. Thus, one web usage pattern (centroid) corresponds to exactly one ad visiting pattern (centroid).

The site content of the publisher's web pages is automatically processed in the similar way. Content thematic groups - *conceptual spaces* - are received using the clustering of term vectors extracted from the HTML content of web pages [8, 9].

In order to recommend a suitable advertisement for the user we have to know its general subject matter. This is achieved by text (HTML) content analysis of the advertisement target web site. The AD ROSA system automatically downloads advertiser's web pages and processes only the terms, which occur in the publisher's web pages. As a result we obtain *advertising conceptual spaces* corresponding to the appropriate *publisher's conceptual spaces*.

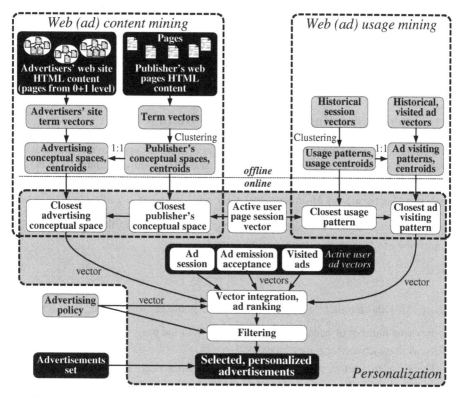

Fig. 2. The overview of the personalized advertising method in the AD ROSA system

A user requesting a web page is assigned to both the closest usage pattern and the closest conceptual space, based on the user's previous behavior during the session - the *active user page session vector*. Assuming that he or she will behave like others (usage pattern) and is interested in web pages similar to those recently visited (conceptual space), the AD ROSA system can recommend to the user the most suitable advertisements. Advertisements related to the closest conceptual space link to web sites with content appropriate for the current user, so they should be displayed to the user. The closest usage pattern and in consequence the closest ad visiting pattern enables the selection of advertisements that are most likely to be clicked by the user.

User behavior (*active user session vector*) as well as information about already displayed or visited banners (*active user ad session* and *active user ad visited vector*) are stored by the system separately for each user. They all prevent the too frequent emission of the same advertisement for one user and provide control over the number of emissions contracted in the advertising campaign. A new, personalized advertisement ranking is determined for the user after each user's request. This process exploits information mentioned above and the targeting parameters established by the advertiser (*advertising policy*), like limited emissions per user during a single session (*active user ad emission acceptance vector*). As a further advantage for the publisher, some additional priority features of each advertisement can be set up manually (*advertising policy*). This provides an opportunity to increase the ranking's value for more profitable advertisements.

Finally, the personalized ranking list is filtered using additional advertising policy features: limitation to certain web browsers, time of day of the emission, etc. In the end the AD ROSA system returns to the web server the list of *n* top ranked, filtered advertisements that are dynamically incorporated into the returned web page content.

4   Content Processing – Web Content Mining

The publisher's web content is processed using *crawler* - an agent that downloads and indexes the content of all pages from the web site [10]. Terms obtained from HTML content are filtered using several statistical features to extract best descriptors [9]. For each selected term t_i an M-dimensional *term page vector* $\boldsymbol{tp_j} = < w_{j1}^{tp}, w_{j2}^{tp}, ..., w_{jM}^{tp} >$ is created. The coordinate w_{ji}^{tp} denotes the weight of the term t_j in the document (page) d_i according to Information Retrieval theory [18]:

$$w_{ji}^{tp} = tf_{ji} * \log\left(\frac{M}{n^{t_j}}\right) \tag{1}$$

where: M – the number of pages in the whole publisher's web site, tf_{ji} - term frequency (the number of occurrences) of the term t_j in the page d_i, and n^{t_j} – the number of pages in which the term t_j occurs.

The set of $\boldsymbol{tp_j}$ vectors is clustered, using the group average link – a hierarchical agglomerative clustering method (HACM) - to discover groups of terms that are close to each other [16]. Applying this method to a selected web site with ca. 3100 pages and 500 filtered descriptors, 41 clusters were obtained [9].

Terms from one cluster describe the *publisher's conceptual spaces* (thematic groups) existing within the publisher's web site. Once we have clusters we can calculate essences of *conceptual spaces* – centroid (mean) vectors - as follows:

$$ctp_k = \frac{1}{max_k} \sum_{l=1}^{n_k} tp_{lk} \tag{2}$$

where ctp_k– the centroid of the k-th cluster; $\boldsymbol{tp_{lk}}$ – the l-th term vector belonging to the k-th cluster; n_k – the number of terms in the k-th cluster; max_k – the maximum value of the sum of component coordinates in the k-th cluster, used for normalization [8].

The content of the target web site of an advertisement is processed similarly. A typical banner links to the main page of the target service (level 0), which often includes just a menu or is the redirection page. For that reason the AD ROSA system also analyzes all pages from the next level (level 1) – pages from the same domain linked to the level 0 page. All pages from levels 0 and 1 are concatenated and treated by the system as the advertiser's content.

For each term extracted from target pages, which simultaneously exist in the set of term page vectors, *the advertiser term vector* $ta_j = < w_{j1}^{ta}, w_{j2}^{ta}, ..., w_{jN}^{ta} >$ is created; where N – the number of advertisements (web sites). The coordinate w_{ji}^{ta} denotes the weight of the term t_j in the advertiser's web site (a_i) and is calculated using (1). Please note that one advertiser term vector ta_j corresponds to exactly one publisher's term page vector tp_j. For that reason terms from publisher's web pages that do not occur in any advertiser's web site have the vector ta_j with all coordinates set to zero. This ensures a uniform term domain for both the publisher's and the advertiser's content.

Advertiser term vectors ta_j are not clustered because the equivalent publisher's term page vectors have already been clustered. Since one vector ta_j corresponds to one vector tp_j, one publisher's conceptual space is equivalent to one *advertising conceptual space*. Only one mean vector - centroid cta_k - for each k-th *advertising conceptual space* is calculated.

5 Session and Clicked Advertisement Processing – Usage Mining

The first step of usage mining is the acquisition of HTTP requests and the extraction of sessions. A user session is a series of pages requested by the user during one visit to the publisher's web site. Since web server logs do not provide any easy methods of grouping these requests into sessions, each request coming to the web server should be captured and assigned to a particular session using a unique identifier passed to a client's browser [8]. Each j-th user session stored by the system is represented by the M-dimensional *session vector* $s_j = < w_{j1}^s, w_{j2}^s, ..., w_{jM}^s >$; where $w_{ji}^s \in \{0,1\}$ denotes whether the i-th page was visited (1) or not (0) during the j-th session.

Historical session vectors s_j are clustered into K' separated usage clusters in the same way as term page vectors tp_j. The centroid cs_k of such a cluster (*usage pattern*) describes one typical user's behavior - the navigation path throughout the web site. For an example web site with over 7700 sessions (35000 requests) 19 clusters were created [9]. Please note that coordinates of the centroid cs_k belong to the range $[0,1]$.

Data about visited (clicked) advertisements during the j-th user session is stored in *the visited ad vectors* $v_j = < w_{j1}^v, w_{j2}^v, ..., w_{jN}^v >$; w_{j1}^v is the number of clicks of the i-th advertisement during the j-th session. For each user session s, there exists exactly one corresponding *visited ad vector* v. Thus, having the k'-th session cluster cs_k we also obtain the appropriate cluster of *visited ad vectors* without clustering procedure - similarly to *the publisher's* and *the advertising conceptual spaces*. For each k'-th cluster the centroid - *visiting pattern* $cv_{k'} = < w_{k'1}^{cv}, w_{k'2}^{cv}, ..., w_{k'N}^{cv} >$, $w_{k'i}^{cv} \in [0,1]$, is found:

$$cv_{k'} = \frac{1}{max_{k'}} \sum_{l=1}^{n_{k'}} v_{lk'}, \ max_{k'} > 0, \tag{3}$$

where $n_{k'}$ – the number of vectors in the k'-th cluster, $max_{k'}$ – the maximum, aggregated value of visits of a single advertisements in the k'-th cluster:

$max_{k'} = \max\limits_{i=1,2,...N} \left(\sum\limits_{l=1}^{n_{k'}} w_{li}^{v} \right)$. The assumption $max_{k'} > 0$ means there must be at least one visit to any advertisement in the cluster. Otherwise all coordinates of $cv_{k'}$ are set to 0. Note that for the most often visited advertisement in the cluster $w_{k'\bar{i}}^{cv} = 1$.

6 Active User Monitoring

The behavior of each active user visiting the publisher's web site is monitored until the end of the user's session. The AD ROSA system keeps the information about documents visited by all active users. For the j-th active user the *page session vector* $ps_j = < w_{j1}^{ps}, w_{j2}^{ps}, ..., w_{jM}^{ps} >$ is maintained; where $w_{ji}^{ps} \in [0,1]$ denotes the importance (timeliness) of the i-th page for j-th active user:

$$w_{ji}^{ps} \begin{cases} (\lambda)^{n_{ji}^{ps}}, & \text{when document } d_i \text{ was visited during the } j\text{-th active session} \\ 0, & \text{when document } d_i \text{ was not visited during the } j\text{-th active session} \end{cases} \tag{4}$$

where: λ – the constant parameter for the interval $[0,1]$, determined experimentally, in the implementation $\lambda=0.95$ was assumed; n_{ji}^{ps} – the consecutive index of the document d_i in the j-th active session in reverse order. For the just viewed document $n_{ji}^{ps} = 0$ ($w_{ji}^{ps} = 1$), for the previous document $n_{ji}^{ps} = 1$ ($w_{ji}^{ps} = \lambda \leq 1$), etc. If the document was visited more than once, the lowest value is assumed to n_{ji}^{ps} [9].

The active user ad session vector $as_j = < w_{j1}^{as}, w_{j2}^{as}, ..., w_{jN}^{as} >$ plays a similar role to the page session vector in relation to displayed advertisements. It prevents advertisements from being displayed too often and enables their periodical rotation. The coordinate $w_{ji}^{as} \in [0,1]$ denotes when the i-th advertisement was displayed to the j-th current user. Values in the vector are always updated after advertisements have been assigned to the user and displayed on the web page. The w_{ji}^{as} value is set to 1 for the just emitted i-th advertisement after the j-th user's request. At the same time all other w_{ji}^{as} values are decreased using factor $\alpha \in [0,1]$, as follows:

$$w_{ji}^{as} = \alpha^{*} w_{ji}^{as} . \tag{5}$$

It was assumed in the implementation that $\alpha=0.8$. *The active user ad session vector* as_j with value zero at all positions is created with the first request from the active user and is removed after the user's session has finished.

Information about the number of emissions of every advertisement is stored in *the ad emission vector* $e = < w_{j1}^{e}, w_{j2}^{e}, ..., w_{jN}^{e} >$; where value of w_{ji}^{e} is the number of emissions of the i-th advertisement for the j-th active user. Information kept in *the ad emission vector* is necessary in order not to display one advertisement too many times to one user, and is useful in controlling advertising policy.

7 Advertising Policy

A lot of publishers allow limiting emission of one advertisement to a user during a single user's session. The number of permitted emissions of the i-th advertisement is denoted by the coordinate w_i^{epu} of *the emission per user vector* $epu = <w_1^{epu}, w_2^{epu}, ..., w_N^{epu}>$. The information about the acceptance of the emission for the j-th active user the i-th advertisement is stored in *the active user ad emission acceptance vector* $uea_j = <w_{j1}^{uea}, w_{j2}^{uea}, ..., w_{jN}^{uea}>$. The values of its coordinates depend on the general limit of emissions (epu) and the current number of emissions of the i-th advertisement to the j-th active user (e), as follows:

$$w_{ji}^{uea} = \begin{cases} 1, & \text{if } w_i^{epu} - w_{ji}^e > 0 \quad \text{or} \quad \text{"emission is unlimited"} \\ 0, & \text{otherwise} \end{cases} \tag{6}$$

As mentioned above, the publisher has the ability to increase the importance of each advertisement. The adequate, manually set priorities are stored in *the ad priority vector* $p = <w_1^p, w_2^p, ..., w_N^p>$, where $w_i^p \in [0,1]$.

8 Vector Integration, Personalized Ranking, Filtering

At each HTTP request from the j-th user the AD ROSA system again assigns to this user, described by ps_j (see section 6), the closest *publisher's conceptual space* (ctp_k) and the closest *usage pattern* ($cs_{k'}$), searching for centroids with the minimum value of $cos(ps_j, ctp_k)$ and $cos(ps_j, cs_{k'})$, respectively. Each *publisher's conceptual space* ctp_k corresponds to one *advertising conceptual space* cta_k and each *usage pattern* $cs_{k'}$ is related to one *visiting pattern* $cv_{k'}$. In consequence, we obtain cta_k and $cv_{k'}$, suitable for the current behavior (ps_j) of the j-th active user.

Having obtained all the above-mentioned vectors, the personalized advertisement ranking is created for each user: the list of the most appropriate advertisements is obtained by sorting coordinates of the *rank vector* - $rank_j$. This vector integrates all the N-dimensional vectors engaged into the personalization process:

$$rank_j = (1-v_j) \otimes (1-as_j) \otimes uea_j \otimes p \otimes (cta_k + cv_{k'} + \beta), \tag{7}$$

Operator $\otimes$, used for two vectors, denotes the multiplication of individual coordinates of these vectors: the i-th coordinate of the first vector is multiplied by the i-th coordinate of the second vector, $i=1,2,...,N$. This produces the third vector with the same dimension.

The closest *advertising conceptual space* and *visited pattern* may have all coordinates equal to 0, when similar users have not visited any advertisements and the terms from the closest *publisher's conceptual space* do not occur in any advertiser's web sites. For that reason, the constant $\beta=0,5$ was introduced. It enables new advertisements to be recommended, even through they could have null values in cta_k and $cv_{k'}$.

Ranking vector includes all information useful for recommendation. Owing to $1-v_j$ banners clicked by the current user are omitted, while $1-as_j$ prevents individual advertisements from being exposed too often for one user. uea_j is responsible for monitoring whether the limit of advertisements per one user has been reached and p respects manually specified priorities. cv_k, is used in order to encourage the display of advertisements that have been clicked by users who visited similar web pages as the current user. Similarly, the use of cta_k promotes the display of advertisements linking to web sites that contain similar words to the pages previously visited by the current user.

Next, the ordered list of advertisements is filtered using additional advertising policy features stored in the database. In this way the requirements of certain web browsers or the time of day of the emission can be fulfilled. All advertisements are also filtered according to their shape, strictly determined by the page layout. As a result, the AD ROSA system delivers personalized, periodically changed advertisements meeting various advertising policy features.

9   Conclusions and Future Work

The method of advertising personalization presented in this paper integrates information coming from different sources: web usage mining, web content mining, advertising policy and boredom prevention. The large number of considered factors means that the same user on the same page may each time be recommended different advertisements. All processes in the method (Fig. 2) are performed automatically by the system, which decreases management costs. The idea of personalization based on "user-friendly" data acquisition (without the user's effort) makes the AD ROSA system applicable in almost any open-access, anonymous web portals and can widen demographic personalization systems used in many web sites. The integration of the AD ROSA system with the ROSA core systems, which recommends hyperlinks, results in the complex personalization system satisfying both users and advertisers.

Future work will concentrate on the optimization of online processes and the development of an advertisement scheduling system, which is an important issue when dealing with many advertisers. In e-commerce, the method can be extended to include purchases history and product ratings gathered by the system.

References

1. Adams R.: Intelligent advertising. AI & Society, Vol.18, No.1 (2004) 68 - 81.
2. Aggarwal C.C., Wolf J.L., Yu P.S.: A Framework for the Optimizing of WWW Advertising. Trends in Distributed Systems for Electronic Commerce, International IFIP/GI Working Conference, TREC'98, Hamburg, Germany, LNCS 1402, Springer Verlag (1998) 1-10.
3. Amiri A., Menon S.: Efficient Scheduling of Internet Banner Advertisements. ACM Transactions on Internet Technology, Vol. 3, No. 4 (2003) 334–346.
4. Baudisch P., Leopold D.: User-configurable advertising profiles applied to Web page banners. Proc. of the First Berlin Economics Workshop, Berlin, Germany (1997)
   http://patrickbaudisch.com/publications/1997-Baudisch-Berlin-UserConfigurableAdvertisingProfiles.pdf.
5. Bilhev G., Marston D.: Personalised advertising – exploiting the distributed user profile. BT Technology Journal, Vol. 21, Issue 1 (2003) 84-90.
6. Kazienko P.: Multi-agent Web Recommendation Method Based on Indirect Association Rules. KES'2004, 8th International Conference on Knowledge-Based Intelligent Information & Engineering Systems, Wellington, New Zealand, LNAI, Springer Verlag (2004).

7. Kazienko P., Kiewra M.: Integration of Relational Databases and Web Site Content for Product and Page Recommendation. 8th International Database Engineering & Applications Symposium. IDEAS '04, Coimbra, Portugal, IEEE Computer Society (2004).
8. Kazienko P., Kiewra M.: Link Recommendation Method Based on Web Content and Usage Mining. New Trends in Intelligent Information Processing and Web Mining Proc. of the International IIS: IIPWM '03 Conference, Advances in Soft Computing, Springer Verlag (2003) 529-534.
9. Kazienko P., Kiewra M.: Personalized Recommendation of Web Pages. Chapter 10 in: Nguyen T. (ed.) Intelligent Technologies for Inconsistent Knowledge Processing. Advanced Knowledge International, Adelaide, South Australia (2004) pp. 163-183.
10. Kazienko P., Kiewra M.: ROSA - Multi-agent System for Web Services Personalization. AWIC'03. First Atlantic Web Intelligence Conference Proceedings, LNAI 2663, Springer Verlag (2003) 297-306.
11. Langheinrich M., Nakamura A., Abe N., Kamba T., Koseki Y.: Unintrusive Customization Techniques for Web Advertising. Computer Networks, Vol. 31 (11-16) (1999) 1259-1272.
12. Mobasher B., Dai H., Luo T., Sun Y., Zhu J.: Integrating Web Usage and Content Mining for More Effective Personalization. EC-Web 2000, LNCS 1875, Springer (2000) 156-176.
13. Montaner M., López B., de la Rosa J. L.: A Taxonomy of Recommender Agents on the Internet, Artificial Intelligence Review, Kluwer Academic Pub. Vol. 19 (4) (2003) 285-330.
14. Nakamura A.: Improvements in Practical Aspects of Optimally Scheduling Web Advertising. Proceedings of the 11th Int. WWW Conference, WWW2002, ACM Press, (2002) 536-541 http://www2002.org/CDROM/refereed/295/.
15. Online Advertising. DoubleClick Inc. (2004) http://www.doubleclick.com/us/products/online_advertising/
16. Rasmussen E.: Clustering algorithms. In: Frakes W., Baeza-Yates R. (eds): Information retrieval: data, structures & algorithms. Chap. 16, Englewood Cliffs, NJ, Prentice Hall (1992) 419-442.
17. Rodgers Z.: Volume Up, Click-Throughs Down in Q4 '03 Serving Report. Jupitermedia Corporation, February 5 (2004) http://www.clickz.com/stats/markets/advertising/article.php/3309271.
18. Salton G.: Automatic Text Processing. The Transformation, Analysis, and Retrieval of Information by Computer. Addison-Wesley, Reading, MA (1989).
19. Sung Min Bae, Sang Chan Park, Sung Ho Ha: Fuzzy Web Ad Selector Based on Web Usage Mining. IEEE Intelligent Systems, Vol. 18, No. 6, November/December (2003) 62-69.
20. Yao Y.Y., Hamilton H.J., Wang X.: PagePrompter: An Intelligent Agent for Web Navigation Created Using Data Mining Techniques. RSCTC 2002, LNCS 2475 Springer Verlag (2002) 506-513.
21. Yager R.R.: Targeted E-commerce Marketing Using Fuzzy Intelligent Agents. IEEE Intelligent Systems, Vol. 15. No. 6, November/December (2000) 42-45.

Flexible Navigation Support
in the WINDS Learning Environment
for Architecture and Design

Milos Kravcik and Marcus Specht

Fraunhofer Institute for Applied Information Technology,
53754 Sankt Augustin, Germany
{Milos.Kravcik,Marcus.Specht}@fit.fraunhofer.de

Abstract. The paper presents the knowledge structure of the WINDS system and shows the implementation of its learning environment, which is adaptive and adaptable. It supports different learning approaches and gives the learner guidance by coaching. The content of the WINDS virtual university is structured in SCORM compliant learning objects and connected with a semantic layer of learning concepts. The usage of this structure in the ALE learning environment is described and results from a first evaluation study are reported.

1 Introduction

In the last 4 years the Fraunhofer Institute FIT worked together with 28 partners in the European project WINDS to create a highly flexible and innovative environment for authoring learning content, supporting teachers for course tutoring, and learners for expository and explorative learning. In the first phase of the project a rather heterogeneous list of requirements was elicited due to a variety of pedagogical models and didactical approaches applied in the different universities and by the different professors. This was the basis and need for the design of a system that allows supporting those different pedagogical models when learners work on learning materials. As one of the key ideas we identified the structuring of the domain knowledge in two different layers: the learning object layer and the index (semantic) layer. This is very similar to current approaches for connecting semantic web approaches and adaptive hypermedia for learning and knowledge management.

The WINDS project [1] is based on tight cooperation of end users and software developers to implement technology solutions for distance learning in the area of design and architecture. The result of this effort includes a sound and effective methodology for e-Learning in the area of design and architecture, a learning management system called Adaptive Learning Environment (ALE) and a couple of tens of teachers deeply involved in the course development and experiments. ALE integrates the functionality of web based e-Learning systems and adaptive educational hypermedia systems with special support for the design learning processes.

The WINDS authoring environment is described in [8]. In this paper, we want to present the learning environment that provides a flexible learning material and concept space and therefore supports the learner with different navigation and exploration strategies.

W. Nejdl and P. De Bra (Eds.): AH 2004, LNCS 3137, pp. 156–165, 2004.

2 Learning in WINDS

One of the key objectives in WINDS was to enable different learning approaches in ALE. *Meaningful learning* [2] is based on the belief that the best way to teach is to build on what the student already knows. *Concept maps* provide a technique to aid meaningful learning by representing knowledge in graphs. The explicitly represented conceptual framework that is behind each course enables active acquisition of knowledge. The framework can be also used as a network for navigation, allowing for *discovery learning* [3]. The explicit references to the course conceptual framework made by the tutor during homework design revision enable *learning by doing*, i.e. the acquisition of skills strongly referenced or related to knowledge.

In the design area *case-based reasoning* (CBR) is extremely important, as an approach to learning and problem solving based on previous experience [4, 5]. A past experience is stored in the form of solved problems ("cases") in a so-called case base. A new problem is solved based on adapting solutions of known similar problems to this new problem. This kind of inference is necessary for addressing ill-defined or complex problems. Our most natural and powerful learning strategies are the automatic ones that situate learning in real-world experience. Key to such reasoning is a memory that can access the right experiences (cases) at the times they are needed. ALE supports CBR by a coaching strategy, recommending cases related to the current content object through concepts.

3 Learning Environment

The ALE learning environment is both *adaptive* and *adaptable*. It means the system can automatically adapt to the user given a user model and the user can influence the adaptation by means of the preferences. The user can always enter a configuration dialogue to specify such parameters like the preferred language and learning style (access to the related questionnaires is provided). Based on this information the system selects a suitable way of navigation and presentation. The knowledge driving the adaptation process is represented in adaptive hypermedia systems both as a *domain model* and a *student (user) model*. *Adaptive annotation* techniques are employed to display the annotated course structure in ALE. The different states of learning objects are represented by adaptive link annotations using icons and alternative texts. The WINDS learning environment allows users to play and navigate course materials in an individualized way and get personalized recommendations by means of *adaptive navigation support*. The component for navigating course materials will be referenced in the following as *course player*. To allow the course player for individual navigation paths the environment was implemented in a modular way to be easily extended and adapted to the individual needs. During the discussion in the consortium a variety of needs for different navigation support in course materials became obvious and therefore different navigation metaphors where integrated in the course playing environment. On the one hand straightforward navigation patterns in more technical and knowledge driven course materials were preferred, on the other hand more explorative navigation had to be supported for open and complex courseware in more artistic approaches.

3.1 Domain Model

To model the domain in ALE the *network model* has been chosen. This is an advanced form of domain modelling by means of a semantic network. Each concept (index term) in this network is defined by its name, description, synonyms and relations with other concepts. In the semantic space concepts possess a single and unequivocal meaning. The system can automatically generate occurrences of the concept in the course – in learning elements and in related external documents as well.

The system ability to recognize the occurrence of a concept in the paragraphs enriches the semantic space by a second type of relation, the one that interconnects the concepts and the learning objects. At the semantic level, this knowledge structure allows a fine control of structure as well as quality of the contents and further supports learning procedures that support the *learner centered* meaning construction strategies. In other words, ALE activates the *meaningful learning* oriented pedagogy.

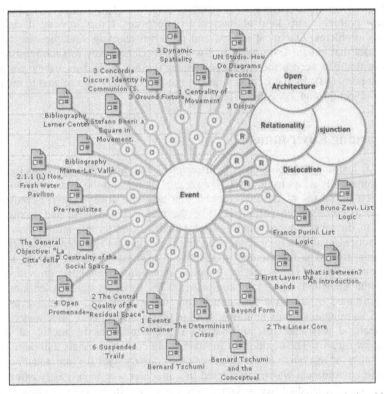

Fig. 1. Interactive concept map shows concepts, learning objects, and their relationships

To support context exploration enhanced *concept based navigation* is provided by ALE. Aside the currently displayed learning object or directly in its content all related concepts can be shown, and for each such concept all its occurrences (in learning elements) as well. Alternatively, one can observe relationships between concepts and learning elements or between related concepts also on an interactive concept map (Fig. 1). These facilities can help the student to comprehend the context relationships and to access the relevant concepts or learning elements in an easy way reducing the cognitive overhead of learners and supporting exploratory learning.

3.2 Learner Model

The ALE system can provide adaptation and coaching based on the user learning style. To find out his or her preferred learning styles the user can fill in the Felder-Silverman Questionnaire [6] with 44 questions. Then the learning style preferences are stored in the user model, but the user can change them directly in *Preferences*.

For student modeling the *historic model* is employed implementing an overlay model [7] for the learning objects enrolled by the learner. It stores all the events related to the student and the status of each learning object regarding the student. According to this status the hyperlinks to learning objects are annotated for the particular student. An *event* is a record in the database with the information that a particular user performed a certain action with a specific learning object, together with a timestamp when it happened. For instance:

- the user U logged in on 2003-10-22 at 10:33:20
- the user U enrolled the course C on 2003-10-22 at 10:43:20
- the user U requested the learning object O on 2003-10-22 at 10:53:20
- the user U mastered the test T on 2003-10-22 at 10:57:23

Such information can be relevant both for the student wanting to recall the history of her behavior and for the tutor controlling the student's progress. Additionally another record is created that reflects the *status* of the learning object for the user, for instance with the following meanings:

- learning object O has been requested by the user U
- test T has been mastered by the user U

The learner model includes the user *preferences* and the user *knowledge* that can be assumed (seen learning objects) and verified (by the system). The user model always reflects the current state of the user's progress. The information is available both for the tutor to control the student's study process and for the system to adapt the course presentation and navigation for the student. Recommendations are generated according to the user's learning style and knowledge. The states of the learning objects in ALE can be considered from several points of view or in several dimensions. The system distinguishes three of them that are relatively independent: *user's readiness, interaction history*, and *tested knowledge*.

Interaction History: Depending on the history of the user interaction with the system a *learning object* can be *seen, partially seen*, or *not seen*. A *learning object* is *not seen* if it has not been accessed yet. If the element has been accessed it is considered as *seen*. This is the most general information about the learning object that should be always applicable.

Tested Knowledge: Students can check their knowledge by means of special learning objects called *tests*. Each test checks the student's knowledge that can be related to one or more learning objects specified by the author of the test (each test item can be associated with one or no learning object – learning element or learning unit). This status of learning objects is applicable only if the author provides corresponding tests.

User's Readiness: If the author has specified the *learning object prerequisites* the system can distinguish the learning objects for which the student is *ready* from those for which the student is *not ready* according to the interaction history or alternatively tested knowledge.

3.3   Course Player Interface

The ALE course player interface is based on the visualization of the navigation structure that allows for the navigation of the course content and in parallel displays the index terms of the semantic layer occurring in the current learning context (Fig. 2). The system allows for the adaptation to personal needs by switching functional modules on and off by the user. On the left hand side the navigation visualizes course structure, participants, workspace, and search. On the right hand side dynamically computed and contextualized modules are shown. In detail, the following modules are applicable by the learner:

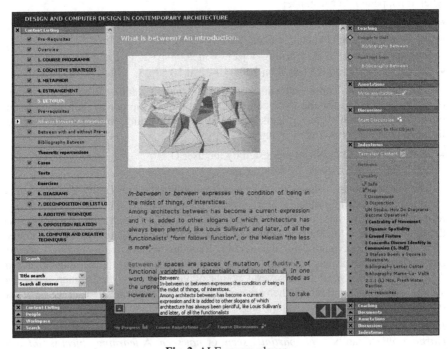

Fig. 2. ALE course player

- *Content Listing Module:* shows the current course structure with annotations about special status and the type of learning objects (e.g. hot topics for learning units that are currently emphasized by the tutor)
- *People Module:* shows links to the personal information of the course users and visualizes which tutors or co-learners are online (awareness)
- *Workspace Module:* provides the links to the workspace folders for collaboration, homework, and projects

- *Search Module:* allows for search in the current course or in all courses, this basically allows the student to instantly switch between courses she is subscribed to
- *Index Terms Module:* shows the index terms (and their occurrences) related to the currently selected learning object; the system allows switching to the term view to highlight the index term locations in the text
- *Documents Module:* shows the related external documents specified by the author
- *Coaching Module:* dynamically computes recommendation about next best learning objects for the student
- *Annotation Module:* with each learning object the learner can write her own annotations and see all the public annotations
- *Discussion Module:* each learning object has corresponding threaded discussions

Beside the modules a basic navigation is integrated that supports depth first browsing of the course structure. The content is always visualized in the middle pane and is rendered to be scrolled vertically. For viewing paragraphs another important aspect of the WINDS structure and pedagogical background was visualized. Content blocks have pedagogical roles that correspond with specific cascading style sheets. This gives a nice visual structure supporting comprehensive reading of the materials.

3.4 Navigation

The possibility of pursuing free navigation in a learning system is a characteristic of fundamental importance in terms of the active construction of meaning. We know, in fact, that in interactions with the learning system, the ability to construct the so-called active knowledge, strongly connected to the pre-existing structures, depends on the means' capacity to adapt to the learners' actual needs and interests. The artificial intelligence techniques applied to date to intelligent tutoring systems have addressed this problem at the guidance level, through the modulation of the guiding algorithms. ALE - although keeping the architecture that is typical of a LMS with guidance capacity - proposes a solution based on the structure of knowledge which indirectly guides possible navigation in the semantic space.

There can be two basic alternative structures specified for a course – one is the default hierarchical course structure (an analogy of the table of contents in a book) and the second is formed by the concepts (like the index in a book). Students can view the both structures in the course player, together with the current learning object. Should it cause too much cognitive overhead the student can close any of the additional modules.

To support context exploration enhanced *concept based navigation* is provided by ALE. Together with the currently displayed learning object all related concepts can be listed, and for each such concept all its occurrences (in learning elements) as well. The list allows selection of other paragraphs where the concept occurs. In this way the learner can easily access a wide spectrum of propositions involving the concept of interest. This fosters an inductive way of learning relationships among concepts. Alternatively one can observe relationships between concepts and learning elements or between related concepts also on an interactive concept map. These facilities can help the student to comprehend the context relationships and to access the relevant concepts or learning elements in an easy way supporting exploratory learning.

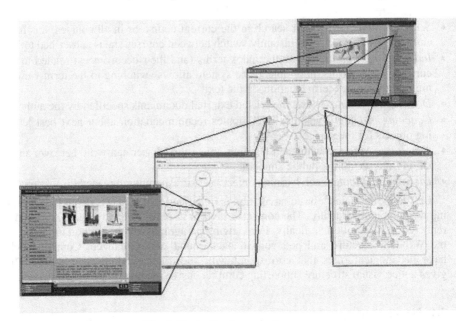

Fig. 3. Navigation in semantic space

Navigation in the semantic space (Fig. 3) can start from an occurrence of a concept, then the concept map is accessed which allows finding the paragraphs related to the concept, and therefore to define its meaning limit, or to navigate towards co-related concepts.

One of the aims in WINDS is the support of multidisciplinary learning, that is, the capacity to link knowledge coming from different disciplines. ALE supports the construction of multi-disciplinary knowledge through the possibility of linking meanings of concepts coming from different courses. In ALE each course has a semantic space, that is, a space for meaning. The terminological overlaying of concepts belonging to different courses having completely different meanings (e.g. simply consider the concept "Space") is common experience in WINDS. ALE allows the navigation of the courses through simple research. The WINDS system contains 21 courses. Courses share subsets of concept labels. Concepts usually have different meaning in different courses. Searching through courses allows the comparison of different concept meanings in different semantic spaces.

3.5 Coaching Strategies

ALE supports several different coaching strategies. The simplest but traditional strategy provides sequential navigation. Other, more advanced strategies take into account the user behaviour history (what the user has already seen) and preferences. The coaching strategies can be clustered in *history based navigation support, adaptive learning style guidance, cooperation support* (to find a suitable peer) and *case based navigation support* (cases are emphasized in concept occurrences). The system exploits the user tracking and modeling frameworks to realize a user model and an evaluated diagnostic inventory for learning styles and learning object metadata to create individualized navigation guidance. The coaching strategies are visualized to the learner in a switchable coaching module.

The implemented *history based coaching strategies* include the following ones:

- *Missing Prerequisite:* if the current learning object has missing (first level) prerequisites (specified in LOM based metadata), they are provided
- *Next Not Seen Learning Object:* the next learning object (using depth first search) that has not yet been visited by the learner is available
- *Complete Current Learning Unit:* in the current learning unit another learning object that has not been visited is provided

Learning style strategies follow the principle that each student will see content in a different way and has individual likes, dislikes and preferences for certain content. The ALE system has a diagnostic framework integrated that serves two purposes.

First, students can take the Felder-Silverman Test for finding out what their individual learning style is. The test consists of 44 questions; the results of these questions are condensed into the preferences of the student. If the student is not satisfied with the test outcome, these preferences can also be set manually in the *Preferences module.* Depending on the student preferences the system then scans through the content and looks for the best matching materials.

Second, it is theoretically possible not only to change the sequence of content but to change the appearance of a page of content as well. The system could replace an image with a textual explanation of the image content and vice versa. However, this works only partly in reality because of missing content. To make a course truly adaptive, the author would have to provide the same information in different forms like image or text. Even audio presentation would be possible, allowing students to listen to content being read by a speaker. The downside of this is the more amount of work for the author when he has to provide content in different forms.

The *Next Best Learning Object* is based on the results of the learning style questionnaire available from the ALE portal. The results are stored in the user model indicating whether the user has significant preferences in four dimensions: Sensitive – Intuitive, Verbal – Visual, Active – Reflective and Sequential – Global. Taking into account the types of learning objects and their metadata the system tries to find the best next learning object for the user. It uses a classification schema of the learning objects from the LOM Metadata for the educational metadata *Learning Object Type* and *Interactivity Type.*

3.6 Design Practice

Design teaching passes through daily practice and long revision processes. Protocol analysis studies of students' revision activities have demonstrated that these activities consist principally in the construction of reasons that have lead to solutions (design rational). Thus these are principal objectives of teaching in this area. ALE enables to control the homework workflow by means of the learning element *Exercise.* This learning element can be created by the author and consists of:

- Task(s) and a file (if needed) - created by the author
- Homework files - submitted by students
- Assessment files - submitted by tutors

The homework workflow process consists of the following steps:

1. The author creates an Exercise, specifies the task(s) and possibly uploads a file to be elaborated by the students as their homework.
2. The student downloads the homework file (if available), elaborates it or prepares a new file according to the task(s) and delivers the homework.
3. Tutors have an overview of all the homework submitted and their assessments. The tutor downloads available homework exercises delivered by students. Then the tutor can work off-line to assess the homework. The tutor uploads assessments, assigns the note for each exercise individually and emphasizes the works of particular didactic interest to demonstrate typical errors, good examples, exemplar solutions, interesting case studies, etc. Tutors can also assign one or more index terms to an individual homework.
4. The student receives the assessment and the note. Each student can see just his or her own homework and its assessment. Assessments of homework marked as special are available to all students. In the index term viewer a list of related homework assessments is displayed according to the assignment done by the tutor.

4   Usability Evaluation

In January – February 2004 we have performed a usability evaluation [9] of the ALE learning environment with 15 students. Every student was to solve 4 basis tasks:

- Find the specified learning unit
- Learn the learning unit
- Contact the tutor
- Enter a contribution (annotation or discussion)

The students were observed in a lab through video and after finishing the tasks they have filled prepared questionnaires. 13 students completed the tasks, 5 of them worked efficiently, 6 moderately and 2 students reported problems. Concerning the usability of the system 3 students considered the user interface as good, 4 found it also good, but preferred traditional media, 4 learners regarded the ALE interface not yet good and 2 persons were principally negative.

The evaluation has shown that most of the students were able to complete the given tasks without external support. In open ended questionnaires the students reported that the system was unobtrusive and inspiring for self exploration if no external introduction is available. Observations of the test sessions revealed that improvements in terms of self descriptiveness, conformity to user expectations and detectability (ISO 9241 standard) can increase the efficiency of the learning environment.

5   Conclusion

In this paper we have presented the adaptive learning environment created in the WINDS project to support individualized education in the area of design and architecture. The main objective was to enable various learning approaches providing alternative navigation and coaching facilities. The system can adapt to the student preferences and learning style. This feature can be further elaborated so that the system analyzes the user behaviour to adjust the user model accordingly. The performed evaluation has shown some opportunities for usability improvements and the potential to encourage meaningful learning by the ALE system.

Acknowledgements

WINDS (Web based intelligent design system) is EU funded project in the 5th framework of the IST programme # IST-1999-10253.

References

1. Specht, M., et al. Adaptive Learning Environment for Teaching and Learning in WINDS. In 2nd International conference on Adaptive Hypermedia and Adaptive Web-based Systems. 2002. Malaga.
2. Novak, J., Learning, Creating, and Using Knowledge - Concept Maps as Facilitative Tools in Schools and Corporations. 1998, Mahwah, NJ: Lawrence Erlbaum Associates, Inc.
3. Papert, S., Mindstorms: Children, computers, and powerful ideas. 1980, New York: Basic Books.
4. Riesbeck, C. K., Schank, R. C. (1989). Inside Case-Based Reasoning. Mahwah, NJ: Erlbaum.
5. Kolodner, J. L. (1993). Case-Based Reasoning. San Mateo, CA: Morgan Kaufmann.
6. Felder, R.M. and L.K. Silverman, Learning an teaching styles in engineering education. Engineering Education, 1988. 78 (7): p. 674-681.
7. Carr, B. and I. Goldstein, Overlays: A theory of modelling for computer aided instruction. 1977, Cambridge, MA: Massachusetts Institute of Technology, AI Laboratory.
8. Kravcik, M., Specht, M., Oppermann, R.: Evaluation of WINDS Authoring Environment. In: Proc. of the AH 2004 Conference (2004)
9. Oppermann, R., Reiterer, H.: Software Evaluation using the 9241 Evaluator. Behaviour & Information Technology, 4/5 (1997) 232 - 245

Evaluation of WINDS Authoring Environment

Milos Kravcik, Marcus Specht, and Reinhard Oppermann

Fraunhofer Institute for Applied Information Technology,
53754 Sankt Augustin, Germany
{Milos.Kravcik,Marcus.Specht,Reinhard.Oppermann}
@fit.fraunhofer.de

Abstract. Authoring tools for adaptive educational hypermedia are still rarely available for a wider public. In the WINDS project, we have developed the Adaptive Learning Environment (ALE) for various European universities active in the area of design and architecture. Teachers without programming skills have created 21 courses in the ALE authoring environment, which simplifies the process providing learning object templates and enabling reusability of materials. This paper describes the WINDS authoring approach and presents some evaluation results.

1 Introduction

Although education is a traditional field for deployment of adaptive hypermedia systems, there are still not many authoring tools for development of adaptive educational applications [1]. Most of these tools serve just for research and experimental purposes. Additionally the authoring process is usually not simple enough for teachers without special knowledge and skills.

The main aim of the WINDS project was to contribute to the reorganization of the pedagogical, cultural, and functional aspects of design education at the university level. The traditional approach to design teaching shows some frequent problems that increase learning time and reduce knowledge retention. The WINDS project offers specialized tools for teaching professional skills. The ALE system provides a new methodological approach to design education on the web. It is adaptive and adaptable, supporting individualized learning by personalization of study materials according to the learner model and history of actions performed. Course authors can reuse materials and create flexible learning objects. The system is compliant with several existing electronic learning standards and specifications (e.g. LOM, Cisco), what enables interoperability with other similar systems. To support this we develop SCORM export and import facilities, although currently the WINDS courses are available just for the project partners. The crucial idea was to keep the authoring process simple so that users without programming knowledge can create adaptive courses. Authors design the default structure for the course and choose from predefined templates when creating learning objects. Then they specify metadata and other attributes, like pedagogical roles, for the objects. Based on these attributes and the learner model the learning environment [2] provides adaptive link annotation and adaptive navigation support for the user.

W. Nejdl and P. De Bra (Eds.): AH 2004, LNCS 3137, pp. 166–175, 2004.
© Springer-Verlag Berlin Heidelberg 2004

2   Course Structure

The most important issues in current e-Learning include content exchange as well as reusability of learning objects in different contexts. The ALE system [3, 4, 5] supports authors in building independent learning objects and structuring them in a default course hierarchy. Nevertheless, the underlying knowledge representation and storage allows for reuse of learning objects and combining them in new dynamically generated courses later on. This assures that the system is able to produce individualized courseware for students depending on their current state of knowledge, their preferences and learning styles. Based on the current definition of learning objects the system allows for generating adaptive educational hypermedia courses with personalized curriculum sequences and personalized content selection on a level of units and pages.

The building blocks in ALE should provide the basis for consistent content generation with maximal flexibility for dynamic generation of online courses. This means the key feature required from these building blocks is their reusability. Following these aims, these basic learning object types are:

- *Course Units* - top-level elements that have only subunits but no super-units
- *Learning Units* - the means for course structuring
- *Learning Elements* - the basic chunks of information with templates for different pedagogical purposes
- *Index Terms* - the fundamental concepts of a common glossary for a course

All these learning objects can be associated with a subset of the Learning Object Metadata specification [6]. The course authors can also specify basic relations between learning objects. These will include prerequisite relations, *part_of*, and *related_to* relations between course units, learning units, and learning elements. Additionally all learning objects in a course unit are linked dynamically with the underlying index defined by the course authors. Each learning element has its own didactical goal.

Learning Units are containers that enable creation of a hierarchical structure in the course. In ALE, there are also special types of *Learning Units* that can be chosen from the list of *Categories*:

- *Learning Unit* - contains Paragraphs and Exercises
- *Quiz* - contains Tests (with correct and incorrect answers)
- *Questionnaire* - contains questions to get feedback from learners; the results of the questionnaires are presented to tutors

Learning elements represent the course content and they form three subgroups – (the first two types are available in the list of *Materials*):

- *Paragraphs* - the contents of the course
- *Exercises* - the practice tasks in a course
- *Tests* - the course assessment

Authors can reference external resources, called *Documents,* for further readings. Furthermore, each course contains an *Index*, where the author defines concepts and relations among them. The ALE system provides an opportunity to export courses for offline use into the standalone HTML format and the index into XML.

2.1 Paragraphs

Paragraphs are content elements that can be of different types reflecting their expected educational purpose and structure. The author can choose either a general paragraph type - *Basic Paragraph* (*Flexible Page*) with arbitrary number or types of content blocks - or one of the types according to the Cisco specification [7] - *Cover Story, Simple Statement, Simple Explanation, Picture Comparison, Procedure Description, Process Description, Guideline and Case.* Originally, the system offered all these types, later on we simplified the offer as authors used mostly the *Basic Paragraph.* According to a newer Cisco document [8], five learning object types are enough to classify any learning objective – *Concept, Fact, Procedure, Process* and *Principle.* All paragraph types consist of reusable assets called *content blocks* that can have different pedagogical functions [7]. Complex paragraphs combine several elements with different pedagogical functions to fulfill a pedagogical goal.

2.2 Assessment

Tests are assessment elements to measure the knowledge of the students. As a test typically contains just one question and alternative answers, the authors can group them into containers called *Quizzes.* To collect feedback on learning materials and the usage of the material by different student groups *Questionnaires* are available to authors. The results of the questionnaires are presented to tutors. The author can select from these types of tests - *Text Single Choice Test, Text Multiple Choice Test, Picture Single Choice Test, Picture Multiple Choice Test, Gap Filling Test, Matching Pair Test and Ordering Test.*

2.3 Exercise

To improve the control over the homework workflow ALE provides the *Exercise* learning element. This learning element consists of the following content blocks - *Task* and possible a file (created by Author), *Homework* files (original files edited by Students) and *Assessments* (homework files edited by Tutors). Tutors can emphasize the homework files of particular didactic interest to demonstrate typical errors, good examples, exemplar solutions, interesting case studies, etc. They can also assign index terms to a specific homework.

2.4 Index Terms

Index terms (concepts) provide means to interrelate heterogeneous course contents, to find individualised paths through the learning materials and to support concept based navigation. The ALE course index component allows the maintenance of index terms together with their respective definitions. Furthermore, the author can specify relations of different types (e.g. *is_a, part_of, related_to*) between terms, allowing for a graph like exploration of terms and their definitions. Educational materials are interconnected with the index by *multi concept indexing.* Each learning object can relate to many concepts. Automatic indexing of learning objects simplifies this process. The system finds for each concept (all the synonyms) its occurrences in all the learning objects of the course.

2.5 External Documents

External documents relevant to the course domain explain in more detail some specific issues or provide up-to-date information in a similar way like specialized portals do. Such external documents serve also as resources for homework and projects. These materials can go into more details than the course or give alternative views of the domain.

2.6 Cooperation Facilities

To support cooperative learning and asynchronous communication among authors as well as among students and tutors ALE provides the following facilities:

- *Annotations*: Users can create private and public annotations related to the whole course or to a particular learning object and edit them later on.
- *Discussions*: Users can start threaded discussions and contribute to the existing ones. A discussion can relate to the whole course or to a particular learning object.
- *Shared Space*: The course author can create a shared workspace for the course. This is established on a BSCW (Basic Support for Cooperative Work) server and enables the students with access to the server to use the space for cooperation and sharing purposes.

3 Authoring Environment

In the first stage, WINDS authors define the course prerequisites and the performance goals. They can do it informally in a special paragraph, however, it is recommended to do it also in the *Description* attribute, which is a part of the *General* category according to the LOM metadata standard, as students can view this information before they enroll the course. Then the authors can search for existing solutions (according to metadata and other attributes), structure them and develop the content.

WINDS authors can combine top-down and bottom-up design approach when building a course. They do not need any programming skills as they create their learning elements by composing reusable data components into a coherent document. At the beginning of the course authoring process, users typically create its structure formed by a hierarchy of units and subunits. Afterwards the units can be filled with study materials. The *review – modification* cycle is repeated before the publishing phase. The authors compose each learning element as a sequence of atomic units that are reusable basic data components, e.g. text, image, audio, video. Learning units at a higher level form a course hierarchy - they are built as sequences of learning elements and other learning units.

ALE has been considered as currently the most advanced form-based interface among adaptive educational hypermedia systems [1]. This kind of interface is more intuitive for authors than that one provided by markup based authoring tools. The main components of the authoring interface are the navigation tree on the left side and the content frame on the right side of the window (Fig. 1). The navigation tree gives an overview of all courses authored (*Course authoring*) and additionally all the learning elements created by the author can be listed (*Content Catalogue*).

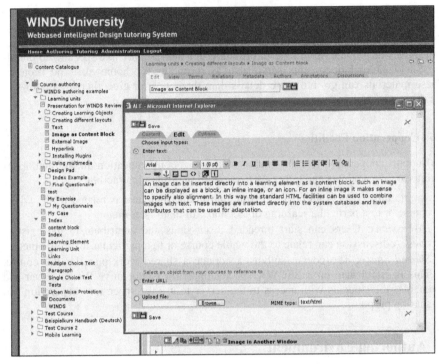

Fig. 1. Content Block Authoring in Learning Element

The *Content Catalogue* contains all the learning elements created by the author in the system. These materials can be reused. A course has three main folders presented on the left side of the page under *Courses to teach*:

- The *Learning units* folder includes all the learning units and learning elements forming the structure and content of the course.
- The *Index* is at the beginning a universal department index prepared in advance and chosen by the author who can enhance it.
- The *Documents* are supplementary sources of information relevant to the course. Specialised portals with up-to-date materials can be referenced here.

3.1 Learning Object Authoring

Authoring of learning objects in ALE is template based. When authors add a new learning unit, they can choose from different types of *Categories* – learning unit, quiz and questionnaire. Similarly, when they create a new paragraph they select from the list of *Materials* – paragraph types and exercise. The *Test* menu includes all the test types. For the author the following forms are provided and are accessible via different tabs (Fig. 1):

- *Edit* to change the structure and content of the course. The learning objects can be added, moved, copied, disconnected or deleted within the course structure. The author can publish the current learning unit and copy it to a buffer as well as edit the learning elements.

- *Terms* (just for learning elements, not for learning units) to show the content of learning elements or (external) documents with index term entries highlighted and displaying the corresponding term descriptions on demand.
- *View* to display the learning objects in the same way like students will see them.
- *Tests* (just for learning units) to show all the tests in the learning unit
- *Relations* to specify prerequisite units and alternative versions in other languages.
- *Metadata* to provide information related to Learning Object Metadata (general, life cycle, technical, educational, rights).
- *Authors* of the course are presented.
- *Annotations* related to the current learning object are listed.
- *Discussions* related to the current learning object are displayed.

In the learning element template, the author adds content blocks to compose new paragraphs. All paragraph types consist of reusable content blocks that can have different pedagogical functions. In the paragraph templates, all the content blocks can be provided as a text (ASCII or HTML) typed into the template, or an imported file, or a given URL that is just a link to a page not integrated into the course (Fig. 1). For each content block options related to its copyrights and presentation in the context of the other content blocks can be specified. The author can specify both prerequisite and language relations between learning objects. For the current learning object, the author selects the related ones from the lists provided by the system. For each prerequisite relation also its weight can be specified.

3.2 Metadata Authoring

Metadata is information about an object to enhance the opportunities of the object usage. In WINDS, this means that metadata can help people to discover, manage, evaluate, exchange, and reuse learning objects. In the educational sector, several important initiatives address this problem by defining a structure for interoperable descriptions of learning objects. In the ALE system, each *Learning Object* can have metadata and the authors can add metadata to the content blocks in their *Paragraphs* to specify their media types, copyrights and display parameters. Metadata in WINDS are compliant with the LOM standard (*Learning Object Metadata*). WINDS authors can set up the following types of metadata in the ALE system (Fig. 2) – General, Lifecycle, Technical, Educational, and Rights.

3.3 Test Authoring

The system has its own *Test Editor* providing test templates. The author specifies the question and alternative answers. An answer item consists of the following parts:

- *True?* - the indicator whether the answer is correct or not
- *Item text* - the text (and picture in the latter two cases) forming the answer itself
- *Follow up text* - the text obtained by the student after choosing this item
- *Charged object* - the learning object that is in charge for the item
- *Actions* - the button to remove the item

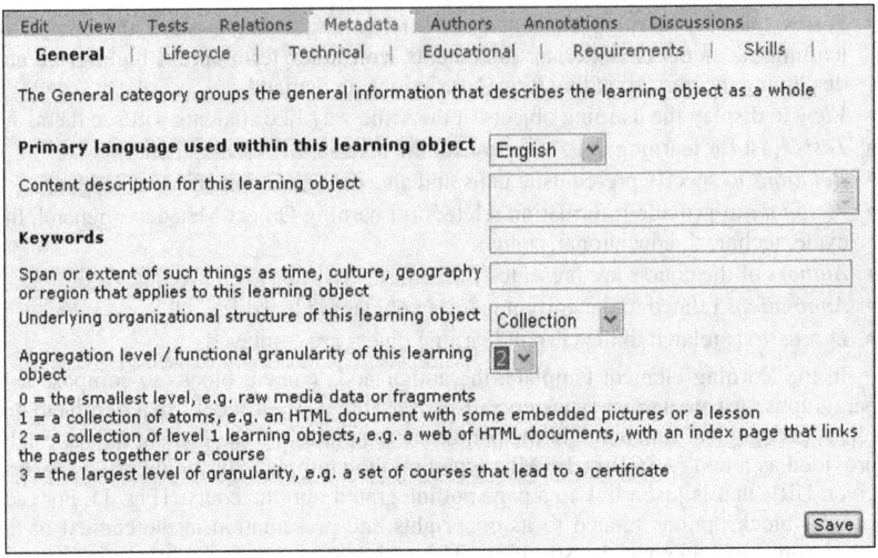

Fig. 2. Metadata Authoring

4 Quantitative Evaluations

The WINDS authors have created 21 courses. Each course is a part of the curriculum at the university where its authors come from. It enables evaluation of the value this type of education provides to the learners. Such experiments are currently going on. There have been 5519 learning objects created (262.8 learning objects per course in average). From them 3521 learning objects (63.8%) contain some kind of metadata; the average number per course is 167.7. The courses contain 889 categories (average 42.3), 3637 materials (average 173.2) and 993 tests (average 47.3). This gives in average 3.7 materials per test. Almost one third of the courses have no online tests (Table 1). There are relatively big differences between some courses. It suggests that authors consider rather different course structures for their courses what can also reflect the educational methodology employed, e.g. in blending learning the amount of online materials can vary according to the specific demands.

The overview of Categories shows one very interesting figure – the average number of learning objects per Category is exactly 7. This is the optimal value for this parameter taking into account the cognitive capacity of a human for processing information [8]. Additionally to this fact, almost all the courses have this value in the recommended interval, i.e. 7±2. The system can support authors in structuring the course in correspondence with this finding and notify them when there are too few or too many learning objects in a learning unit. WINDS authors did not often use the opportunity to group individual Tests into the Quiz aggregates and the Questionnaires have not been used virtually at all. This can be explained by the fact that these types were not available at the beginning though both have been introduced later on according to the authors' demands. The feedback from students is probably supposed to be received in a different way, e.g. face to face or by e-mail.

Table 1. Overview of Learning Objects (learning objects, learning objects with metadata, categories, materials, tests, content blocks, index terms)

	LO	MD	C	M	T	CB	IT
A	300	266	36	195	69	580	129
B	243	243	37	199	7	1629	288
C	204	49	28	160	16	368	97
D	491	472	84	407	0	543	56
E	974	267	134	281	559	617	117
F	78	59	18	54	6	162	22
G	806	703	148	614	44	1814	94
H	93	74	20	69	4	263	42
I	124	124	13	105	6	344	19
J	281	135	9	232	40	472	18
K	235	133	20	169	46	479	63
L	302	149	56	237	9	714	76
M	268	178	66	145	57	357	239
N	53	30	14	29	10	53	39
O	166	147	29	137	0	299	90
P	65	54	14	51	0	106	49
Q	241	14	27	149	65	249	34
R	265	210	63	147	55	683	75
S	139	83	33	106	0	310	45
T	97	39	16	81	0	187	73
U	94	92	24	70	0	313	79
Σ	5519	3521	889	3637	993	10542	1744
μ	262.8	167.7	42.3	173.2	47.3	502.1	83

The course content itself is stored in paragraphs offered to WINDS authors as Materials. ALE provides templates for specific types of paragraphs selected according to the CISCO specification. These templates can help to structure the materials properly, but we have learned that in the area of design and architecture authors prefer flexibility instead of predefined fixed structure. Materials with the flexible structure (Basic, Case, Exercise) represent 88.6% of all created paragraphs. The Case and Exercise types have been introduced in the last phase of the project what explains why they are not included in many courses. Another good value is the average depth of the Materials in the course. Having 186 Materials in an average course the average depth 3 suggest that the course structure is well balanced. The system can recommend structural changes of the course if the average and maximal depth of Materials does not correspond with the total number of materials included. Here the theory of well-balanced trees can be applied.

To assess the learner automatically by the system WINDS authors have created various types of tests. Although design and architecture depend on pictures the WINDS, authors have created mostly Multiple and Single Choice Tests where the alternative answers do not include pictures – they represent 91% of all Tests. Here again the development history could play a significant role as the less used types of tests have been introduced later on according to the requirements of authors. The figure showing approximately one test (exactly 0.9) per course or learning unit in average looks relatively low when we realize that a test is typically just one question with alternative answers. However, as has been already mentioned the WINDS courses are not intended to be used exclusively online – they complement the more traditional educational approaches at universities.

The WINDS courses include 10542 content blocks what means more than 500 atomic units per course. One third of them comes from two courses. The materials contain slightly more than 3 assets in average. Almost two thirds of content blocks are in text format, images represent more than one third of them. Java applets, Flash components and other applications occur occasionally, video very rarely and audio virtually absents. This distribution reflects the development effort necessary for individual media as well as their need in this domain. Reusability is not measurable in our system as it is based on the copy and paste method that can be applied on various levels – learning unit, material, content block and index.

WINDS courses contain 1744 index terms and 1121 relations between them. Per course there are approximately 90 synonyms and 850 occurrences in Materials, what makes almost 5 concept occurrences per Material. This is quite a rich interconnection between the two alternative structures that can provide a good base for concept based navigation and explorative learning. External documents are seldom referenced – just 3 courses have more than 2 such references, most of the courses ignore them at all. Then there are just 2.5 concept occurrences per external document.

5   Qualitative Evaluations

Usability experts found [9] that as formative evaluation is concerned a few users can help to find most of the significant weaknesses. In our case, an evaluation [10] with 4 lecturers has been performed in January and February 2004. Every lecturer was to solve 4 basis tasks, each of them within 30-40 minutes. These tasks include creation of the course structure (hierarchy), authoring of the course content, preparation of a test and processing the feedback from learners. The lecturers were observed in a lab through video and after finishing the tasks, they have filled prepared questionnaires. All the lecturers were able to create a basic course in the WINDS system without external support. In open-ended questionnaires, the lectures reported that the authoring environment was unobtrusive and inspiring for self-exploration if no external introduction is available. Observations of the test sessions revealed that some particular improvements could increase the efficiency of the authoring environment. It concerns dialogue criteria (ISO 9241, part 10) and information presentation (ISO 9241, part 12): self-descriptiveness (the meaning of icons was not always clear), conformity to user expectations, error tolerance, personalization (specification of colours, font type and size), novice learner support as well as simplicity, clarity, consistency, detectability and comprehensibility.

6   Conclusion

One of the main issues in development of advanced technology learning environments is a gap between pedagogues and technicians. The WINDS project has attempted to overcome this gap. Teachers of design and architecture specified their pedagogical requirements to be considered by software developers in the implementation of a unique adaptive learning environment. As the result, authors without programming skills could create adaptive educational hypermedia courses. The performed evaluation has shown specific usability improvements issues of the ALE authoring system. Compliancy of the learning materials with the current standards opens future possibilities to deliver the content in a flexible way.

Acknowledgements

WINDS (Web based intelligent design system) is EU funded project in the 5th framework of the IST programme # IST-1999-10253.

References

1. Brusilovsky, P.: Developing Adaptive Educational Hypermedia Systems: from Design Models to Authoring Tools. In: Authoring Tools for Advanced Technology Learning Environments. Kluwer (2003)
2. Kravcik, M., Specht, M.: Flexible Navigation Support in the WINDS Learning Environment for Architecture and Design. In: Proc. of the AH 2004 Conference (2004)
3. Specht, M., Kravcik, M., Pesin, L., Klemke, R.: Integrated Authoring Environment for Web Based Courses in WINDS. In: Proc. of the ICL 2001 Workshop (2001)
4. Specht, M., Kravcik, M., Pesin, L., Klemke, R.: Authoring Adaptive Educational Hypermedia in WINDS. In: Online-Proc. the ABIS 2001 Workshop (2001)
5. Kravcik, M., Specht, M.: Authoring Adaptive Courses – ALE Approach. In: Proc. of the IASTED International Conference on Web-Based Education (2004)
6. Draft Standard for Learning Object Metadata. IEEE (2002)
7. Reusable Learning Object Strategy, Version 3.1. Cisco Systems (2000)
8. Miller, G. A.: The Magical Number Seven, Plus or Minus Two: Some Limits on Our Capacity for Processing Information. The Psychological review, 63 (1956) 81-97
9. Nielsen, J.: Risks of Quantitative Studies. Jakob Nielsen's Alertbox (2004)
10. Oppermann, R., Reiterer, H.: Software Evaluation using the 9241 Evaluator. Behaviour & Information Technology, 4/5 (1997) 232 - 245

On the Dynamic Generation of Compound Critiques in Conversational Recommender Systems

Kevin McCarthy, James Reilly, Lorraine McGinty, and Barry Smyth

Adaptive Information Cluster*, Smart Media Institute,
Department of Computer Science, University College Dublin (UCD), Ireland
{kevin.mccarthy,james.d.reilly,lorraine.mcginty,barry.smyth}
@ucd.ie

Abstract. Conversational recommender systems help to guide users through a product-space towards a particular product that meets their specific requirements. During the course of a "conversation" with the user the recommender system will suggest certain products and use feedback from the user to refine future suggestions. Critiquing has proven to be a powerful and popular form of feedback. Critiques allow the user to express a preference over part of the feature-space; for example, in a vacation/travel recommender a user might indicate that they are looking for a *"less expensive"* vacation than the one suggested, thereby critiquing the *price* feature. Usually the set of critiques that the user can chose from is fixed as part of the basic recommender interface. In this paper we will propose a more dynamic critiquing approach where high-quality critiques are automatically generated during each recommendation cycle from the remaining product-cases. We show that these dynamic critiques can lead to more efficient recommendation performance by helping the user to more rapidly focus in on the right region of the product-space.

1 Introduction

Conversational recommender systems are designed to assist users to navigate through complex product spaces. The *navigation by proposing* strategy recommends one or more products to the user during each recommendation cycle, and the user can provide feedback to indicate their preference as a way of informing new recommendations during subsequent cycles until the desired product has been accepted [13]. Navigation by proposing can be guided by different forms of feedback. For example, [8] focuses on preference-based feedback where the user indicates a simple preference for one of k cases that are recommended during a given cycle. Preference-based feedback is perhaps the simplest form of feedback, offering only minimal guidance to the recommender system, and generally resulting in protracted recommendation sessions. However, it is particularly useful in domains where the users have minimal domain expertise, but where they are able to recognise good recommendations, and recent advances have demonstrated a variety of ways to improve its effectiveness [7, 9, 14].

---

* This material is based on works supported by Science Foundation Ireland under Grant No. 03/IN.3/I361.

W. Nejdl and P. De Bra (Eds.): AH 2004, LNCS 3137, pp. 176–184, 2004.

In this work, however, we are interested in a different form of feedback, *critiquing*, which affords the user an opportunity to provide more informative feedback; see [1–3]. By critiquing a product recommendation, a user can express a preference over a specific feature of a product. For example, in a vacation/travel recommender a user might indicate that they are looking for a vacation that is *"closer to home"*; *"closer to home"* is a critique over the *travel-time* feature of the vacation case. This is an example of a *unit critique*, a critique over a single feature. Sometimes, recommenders allow the user to select compound critiques; see [2]. For example, our holiday-maker may indicate that they are looking for a *"more luxurious"* vacation. In this case *"more luxurious"* is a compound critique that operates over multiple case features including *price* (greater price) and *accommodation* (higher standard).

In the past, critiquing-based recommender systems have generally adopted a fixed interaction style, in the sense that the same fixed set of critiques are presented to the user during each cycle [1–3]. In this paper we propose a more dynamic critiquing strategy that extends recent work reported in [6] and that focuses on the generation of compound critiques as a way of helping users to navigate more efficiently through a product-space. We describe how compound critiques can be *dynamically* generated on a cycle-by-cycle basis by data mining the feature patterns of the remaining product cases (see Sect. 2). These compound critiques are then filtered and a high-quality subset is presented to the user along with the standard (fixed) unit critiques; in this way the feedback offered by the recommender system interface can be adapted to the current recommendation session and cycle. In Sect. 3 we will evaluate different strategies for generating compound critiques to show that, in general, the availability of these dynamic compound critiques can lead to significant improvements in recommendation performance as well as offering the end-user a number of additional advantages.

2   Mining Dynamic Critiques

In this work we will assume a conversational recommender system in the image of the well-known *FindMe* recommender systems [3]. Each recommendation session is initiated by an initial user query and this results in the retrieval of the most similar case (*the recommended case*) and a set of critiques, both fixed and dynamic. The user will have the opportunity to accept this case, thereby ending the recommendation session, or to critique it. If they critique the case, the critique acts as a filter over the remaining cases, such that the case chosen for the next cycle is the one that is compatible with the critique and maximally similar to the previously recommended case. In this section we will describe how dynamic critiques can be discovered and selected for presentation as part of each recommendation cycle.

2.1   From Cases to Critique Patterns

The first step to discovering useful compound critiques is to generate a set of so-called *critique patterns* from the remaining cases. Each remaining case is compared to the current recommended case and the relative feature differences (a set of individual feature critiques) between the remaining case and the recommended case make up the critique

	Current Case	Case c from CB	Critique Pattern
HolidayType	Education	Language	!=
Price (Euro)	3738	2039	<
NumberOfPersons	2	1	<
Region	Egypt	Malta	!=
Transportation	Plane	Plane	=
Duration (Days)	14	21	>
Season (Month)	October	September	!=
Accommodation	4 Stars	2 Stars	<
Hotel	Anlage Arabia	Sprachkurs Malta	!=

Fig. 1. Illustrating how a critique pattern is generated.

pattern. Fig. 1 presents an example from the vacation/travel domain. It shows the recommended case (a 14-day educational trip for 2 to Egypt, staying in a 4-star hotel at a cost of 3738 Euro) that has been selected for recommendation to the user in the current cycle, and it shows a remaining case, c, from the case-base (a 21-day trip for 1 to Malta, staying in 2-star hotel). The resulting critique pattern reflects how case c differs from the current case in terms of individual feature critiques. For example, the critique pattern includes a "<" critique for *price* since case c is cheaper than the current case. Similarly, there is a ">" critique for *duration* because the remaining case refers to a longer vacation. These critique patterns make up the *pattern-base*. They are generated during each cycle, once a recommended case has been chosen, and they serve as the source of compound critiques.

2.2 Discovering Compound Critiques

We wish to discover compound critiques that operate over multiple features and that have the potential, if chosen by the user, to filter out a great many cases from further consideration. The objective is to look for sets of individual feature critiques that tend to recur within the pattern-base. For example, we might find that 30% of the remaining cases are for a longer vacation in a better hotel at a higher price, $\{[Duration >],$ $[Accommodation >], [Price >]\}$. This is a useful compound critique because it helps to inform the user about some important characteristics of the remaining cases and, if chosen, has the ability to eliminate 70% of the remaining cases.

Identifying suitable compound critiques means looking for these recurring patterns within the pattern-base. This is similar to so-called *market-basket analysis* methods, which aim to find regularities in the shopping behaviour of customers [5]: each critique pattern is equivalent to the shopping basket for a single customer, and the individual critiques correspond to the items in this basket. The combinatorics of a typical task domain – thousands of products and customers – make this a challenging problem, leading to an explosion in the number of possible groups of recurring items. However, it is not so acute in our critiquing scenario because there are only a limited number of possible critiques. For instance, each numeric feature can have a "<" or a ">" critique and each nominal feature can have a "=" or a "! =" critique, so there are only $2n$ possible critiques in a case-base where the cases are made up of n individual features.

The well-known Apriori algorithm[5, 12] can be used to efficiently locate compound critiques. It characterises recurring item subsets as association rules of the form $A \rightarrow B$: from the presence of a certain set of critiques (A) one can infer the presence of certain other critiques (B). For example, one might learn that from the presence of the critique, $[Price <]$, we can infer the presence of $[Duration <]$ with a high degree of probability; in other words the pattern $\{[Price <],[Duration <]\}$ is commonplace.

Apriori measures the importance of a rule in terms of its *support* and *confidence*. Support is the percentage of patterns for which the rule is correct; that is, the number of patterns that contain both A and B divided by the total number of patterns. Confidence, on the other hand, is a measure of the number of patterns in which the rule is correct relative to the number of patterns in which the rule is applicable; that is, the number of patterns that contain both A and B divided by the number of patterns containing A. For instance, we would find that the rule $[Accommodation >] \rightarrow [Price >]$ has a support of 0.2 if there are a total of 100 critique patterns but only 20 of them contain $[Accommodation >]$ and $[Price >]$. Likewise, the confidence of this rule would be 0.5 if 40 of the critique patterns contain only $[Accommodation >]$. Apriori is a multi-pass algorithm, where, in the kth pass, all large itemsets of cardinality k are computed. Initially *frequent itemsets* are determined. These are sets of items that have at least a predefined minimum support. Then, during each iteration those itemsets that exceed the minimum support threshold are extended. Apriori is efficient because it exploits the simple observation that no superset of an infrequent itemset can be frequent, to prune away candidate itemsets.

Our specific proposal is to use Apriori, during each recommendation cycle, to generate a collection of compound critiques (frequent itemsets over the pattern-base), and to then select a small subset of the *best* of these compound critiques for presentation to the user to complement the standard unit critiques.

2.3   Grading Compound Critiques

We can expect a large number of compound critiques, of different sizes, to be generated during a typical recommendation cycle. So we need some technique for selecting a small number to present to the user. On the one hand, we would like to present compound critiques that are likely to be applicable to the user, in the sense that they are likely to constrain the remaining cases in the direction of their target case. This way there is a good chance that these compound critiques will be selected over any of the unit critiques. However, this criterion is difficult to cater for since it is rarely clear what target case the user is seeking. On the other hand, we would like to present compound critiques that can filter out large numbers of cases so that there is a greater chance that the target case will be retrieved in the next cycle. This criterion is more straightforward to address. The support of a compound critique is a direct measure of its ability to filter out few or many cases. A low support value means the critique is present in a small proportion of critique patters, and thus it is only applicable to a few remaining cases. If applied the critique will therefore eliminate many cases from consideration.

The above suggests two alternative strategies for selecting the best critiques to present to the user. We might select those critiques with the highest support values to increase the chances that they will be chosen by the user, but then these critiques are unlikely to filter out many cases from consideration. Alternatively we may select the critiques with the lowest support values, because these critiques will eliminate many cases from consideration, but they are less likely to be chosen by the user because they are less likely to lead to the desired target case. In the next section we will evaluate these strategies relative to a standard benchmark.

3   Evaluation

In this evaluation we will use the well-known Travel dataset is used as a source of case and query data (available from *http://www.ai-cbr.org*). This dataset consists of over 1000 vacation cases, each described in terms of 9 features including *price, duration, region, hotel* etc. We will compare a standard FindMe-style recommender employing unit critiquing (STD) to three variations of our dynamic critiquing approach that differ in the way that a small subset of critiques are selected for presentation during each cycle: (1) LS - the top 5 critiques with the lowest support are presented to the user; (2) HS - the top 5 critiques with the highest support are presented; (3) RAND - A random set of 5 critiques are presented. Incidentally, during each recommendation cycle Apriori is set to generate itemsets with a minimum support threshold of 0.7, which means that compound critiques will have a minimum support of 0.7.

3.1   Methodology

We adopt a similar *leave-one-out* methodology to [7, 9, 10]. Each case (*base*) in the case-base is temporarily removed and used in two ways. First, it serves as the basis for a set of queries by taking random subsets of its features. We focus on subsets of 1, 3 and 5 features to allow us to distinguish between hard, moderate and easy queries, respectively. Second, we select the case that is most similar to each original base. These cases are the recommendation *targets* for the experiments. Thus, the base represents the ideal query for a 'user', the generated query is the initial query that the 'user' provides to the recommender, and the target is the best available case for the 'user'. Each generated query is a test problem for the recommender, and in each recommendation cycle the 'user' picks a critique that is compatible with the known target case; that is, a critique that, when applied to the remaining cases, results in the target case being left in the filtered set of cases. In a typical cycle there may be a number of critiques (unit and compound) that satisfy this condition and the actual one chosen by the 'user' depends on the system being used: LS picks the compound critique with the lowest support, HS picks the one with the highest support, and RAND picks a random critique. Each leave-one-out pass through the case-base is repeated 10 times and recommendation sessions terminate when the target case is returned. As mentioned above, we have set the support threshold for Apriori to be 0.7, so only critiques with this support level or higher are considered during the generation stage of each cycle.

3.2   Compound Critique Numbers and Sizes

Before discussing the impact that our compound critiques have on recommendation efficiency it is worth considering the number of critiques that are discovered during

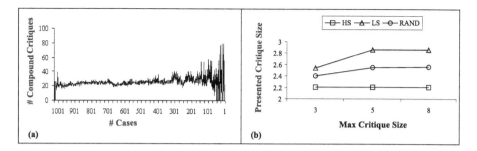

Fig. 2. (a) Number of generated compound critiques; (b) Size of presented compound critiques.

a typical cycle, and the sizes of the critiques that are selected and presented back to users. Fig. 2(a) is a graph of the numbers of compound critiques that are discovered for different numbers of remaining cases. It is interesting to note the degree of stability relative to the number of remaining cases here. For most case-base sizes about 20-25 compound critiques (with support > 0.7) are discovered, although the statistics are less reliable when there are fewer than 100 cases due to the smaller number of instances encountered. Fig. 2(b) graphs the average size of the critiques that are selected (by HS, LS and RAND) for presentation to the user for different itemset (critique) size-limits used by Apriori; by limiting the number of Apriori iterations we can limit the sizes of the discovered critiques. It is interesting to note how the sizes of the presented critiques remains fairly stable for different maximum critique sizes. The HS critiques tend to be small because smaller critiques (fewer constraints) are likely to be more commonplace within the pattern-base, and thus have higher support values. Here we find that the average size of the HS critiques presented to be about 2.2 features. In contrast the LS critiques will have a natural tendency to be larger (they will be less commonplace and so have lower support values). However, their size remains limited to between 2.5 and 3 features per critique; in other words, even when Apriori is permitted to seek out much larger critiques, it tends not to find them, at least relative to the underlying 0.7 support limit used. This is potentially good news as it means that the compound critiques returned to the user are a manageable size (2 - 3 features), but of course whether these critiques turn out to be useful remains to be seen.

3.3   Frequency of Application

When compound critiques are presented to the 'user', how often are they selected? We compute the probability that a compound critique will be selected in cycle k by calculating the proportion of times that a compound critique was selected in a kth cycle throughout our experiment. Fig. 3(a) plots these probabilities for each critiquing strategy for up to the 50th recommendation cycle. As expected compound critiques are more likely to be selected under HS (90%-100% application frequency) than LS (55% to 70% application frequency), because HS critiques will filter out fewer cases and these critiques are more likely to lead to the target case, on average. Under RAND, compound critiques are chosen only about 30% of the time.

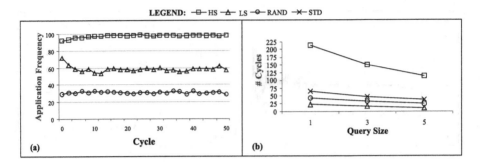

Fig. 3. (a) The application frequency of compound critiques; (b) The recommendation efficiency of different critiquing strategies.

3.4   Recommendation Efficiency

At the end of the day the success of our dynamic critique strategy depends on its ability to improve recommendation efficiency by reducing the average session length. To test this we we record the number of cycles required before the target case is retrieved for each recommendation technique, and we average these values for different sizes of initial queries.

The results are presented in Fig. 3(b) which shows a graph of average session length against initial query length. The results point to the significant benefits offered by LS, compared to standard critiquing, and the significant problems of using HS. The STD technique results in average session lengths of between 36 and 65 cycles, as initial queries increase in their level of detail (increases in size from 1 to 5). However, the LS strategy reduces cycle length by between 62% and 69%, presenting session lengths of between 12 and 24 cycles. The LS critiques are not only being chosen moderately frequently, they are having a significantly positive impact on recommendation efficiency. In contrast, the more regularly applied HS critiques reduce efficiency considerably, increasing session length by a factor of 3 across the various query sizes. In other words, although the HS critiques are usually compatible with the target case (they are regularly applied) they have limited ability to focus the search and filter out fewer cases. The result is that HS performs more poorly than the unit critiques applied by STD. Even in the case where users choose a random critique (RAND) significant benefits are still available. The session lengths for RAND are between 23 and 45 cycles offering a 31% to 36% reduction in cycles compared to STD.

4   Dynamic Critiquing and Explanation

In addition to the obvious performance advantages of dynamic critiquing it is also worth considering what we might term its *'explanatory benefits'*. The issue of explanation has recently become a hot topic in recommender research of late, with a number of researchers proposing the need for some form of explanation to the user by the recommender system in order to help them understand the reason behind recommendations [11, 4]. We believe that dynamic compound critiques have a important role to play in this regard. Unlike fixed or unit critiques, dynamic compound critiques help users to understand some of the common interactions that exist between groups of features among the remaining cases. For example, in the Travel domain, the compound critique [*Accommodation* >], [*Price* >] tells the user that better accommodation goes hand-in-hand with higher prices, not surprising perhaps. Other compound critiques might be more surprising though. For example, at some point in the recommendation process it might be the case that a critique such as [*Accommodation* >], [*Duration* <] becomes commonplace, indicating that better accommodation standards are only available for shorter durations than the current recommended case. Moreover, by tagging this critique with its support value we can inform the user about the proportion of remaining cases that are satisfied by the critique.

The point is that in many recommender domains, where the user is likely to have incomplete knowledge about the finer details of the feature-space, and perhaps little or no knowledge of detailed feature interactions, then compound critiques may help to clarify these interactions. This will help the user to better understand the options that are available beyond the current recommendation cycle. For this reason we believe that users will actually find it easier to work with compound critiques than unit critiques and this may, for example, help the user to make fewer critiquing errors. For instance, with standard critiquing in the Travel domain a user might naively select the [*Price* <] critique in the mistaken belief that this may deliver a cheaper vacation that satisfies all of their other requirements. However, reducing price in this way may lead to a reduction in duration or accommodation quality that the user might not find acceptable and, as a result, they will have to backtrack. This problem is less likely to occur if the compound critique [*Price* <], [*Duration* <], [*Accommodation* <] is presented because the user will come to understand the implications of a price-drop prior to selecting any critique. Of course all of these claims need to be validated in real-user trails, but this is something that we will leave as a hypothesis for now, one that we plan to validate in the near future.

5   Conclusions

Critiquing is an important form of feedback in conversational recommender systems, but usually users are presented with a set of fixed critiques, often only unit critiques that operate over just a single feature at a time. We have described a technique for automatically generating compound critiques during each cycle of a conversational recommendation session, and devised a strategy for selecting a small number of high-quality compound critiques for presentation to the user. Our experiments indicate that this critiquing strategy has the potential to offer significant performance improvements – reducing session length by up to nearly 70% – as well as offering some user-interaction benefits such as improved explanatory power.

It is worth commenting on the computational efficiency of our approach to dynamic critiquing. Although Apriori is usually used for off-line data-mining, we find it to be efficient enough to meet our real-time requirements. In our setup critique generation takes less than 200 msec per cycle (based on the a Pentium 4 2.8 GHz) and thus does not add a significant computational overhead. The scalability of using Apriori for generating compound critiques is a matter for further research.

In summary, we believe that dynamic critiquing is a powerful technique that it likely to be generally applicable across a wide range of recommendation tasks, and our experiments indicate that similar benefits are achievable in these other domains; see [6].

References

1. R. Burke. Interactive Critiquing for Catalog Navigation in E-Commerce. *Artificial Intelligence Review*, 18(3-4):245–267, 2002.
2. R. Burke, K. Hammond, and B. Young. Knowledge-based navigation of complex information spaces. In *Proceedings of the Thirteenth National Conference on Artificial Intelligence*, pages 462–468. AAAI Press/MIT Press, 1996. Portland, OR.
3. R. Burke, K. Hammond, and B.C. Young. The FindMe Approach to Assisted Browsing. *Journal of IEEE Expert*, 12(4):32–40, 1997.
4. P. Cunningham, D. Doyle, and J. Loughrey. An Evaluation of the Usefulness of Case-Based Explanation. . In K. Ashley and D. Bridge, editors, *Case-Based Reasoning Research and Development. LNAI, Vol. 2689.*, pages 191–199. Springer-Verlag, 2003. Berlin.
5. Z. Hu, W.N. Chin, and M. Takeichi. Calculating a New Data Mining Algorithm for Market Basket Analysis. *Lecture Notes in Computer Science*, 1753:169–175, 2000.
6. J. Reilly, K. McCarthy, L. McGinty, B. Smyth. Dynamic Critiquing. In P. A. Gonzalez Calero and P. Funk, editors, *Proceedings of the European Conference on Case-Based Reasoning (ECCBR-04)*. Springer, 2004. Madrid, Spain.
7. L. McGinty and B. Smyth. Comparison-Based Recommendation. In Susan Craw, editor, *Proceedings of the Sixth European Conference on Case-Based Reasoning (ECCBR-02)*, pages 575–589. Springer, 2002. Aberdeen, Scotland.
8. L. McGinty and B. Smyth. Evaluating Preference-Based Feedback in Recommender Systems. In R. Sutcliffe, editor, *Proceedings of the Thirteenth National Conference on Artificial Intelligence and Cognitive Science*. Springer, 2002. Limerick, Ireland.
9. L. McGinty and B. Smyth. On The Role of Diversity in Conversational Systems. In D. Bridge and K. Ashley, editors, *Proceedings of the Fifth International Conference on Case-Based Reasoning (ICCBR-03)*, pages 276–290. Springer, 2003. Troindheim, Norway.
10. L. McGinty and B. Smyth. Tweaking Critiquing. In *Proceedings of the Workshop on Personalization and Web Techniques at the International Joint Conference on Artificial Intelligence (IJCAI-03)*, pages 20–27. Morgan-Kaufmann, 2003. Acapulco, Mexico.
11. D. McSherry. Explanation of Retrieval Mismatches in Recommender System Dialogues. . In *Proceedings of the ICCBR-03 Workshop on Mixed-Initiative Case-Based Reasoning*, pages 191–199, 2003. Trondheim, Norway.
12. R. Srikant H. Toivonen R. Agrawal, H. Mannila and A. Inkeri Verkamo. Fast Discovery of Association Rules in Large Databases. *Advances in Knowledge Discovery and Data Mining*, pages 307–328, 1996.
13. H. Shimazu. ExpertClerk : Navigating Shoppers' Buying Process with the Combination of Asking and Proposing. In Bernhard Nebel, editor, *Proceedings of the Seventeenth International Joint Conference on Artificial Intelligence (IJCAI-01)*, pages 1443–1448. Morgan Kaufmann, 2001. Seattle, Washington, USA.
14. B. Smyth and L. McGinty. The Power of Suggestion. In *Proceedings of the International Joint Conference on Artificial Intelligence (IJCAI-03)*, pages 127–138. Morgan-Kaufmann, 2003. Acapulco, Mexico.

Evaluating Adaptive Problem Selection

Antonija Mitrovic and Brent Martin

Intelligent Computer Tutoring Group
Computer Science Department, University of Canterbury
Private Bag 4800, Christchurch, New Zealand
{tanja,brent}@cosc.canterbury.ac.nz

Abstract. This paper presents an evaluation study that compares two different problem selection strategies for an Intelligent Tutoring System (ITS). The first strategy uses static problem complexities specified by the teacher to select problems that are appropriate for a student based on his/her current level of ability. The other strategy is more adaptive: individual problem difficulties are calculated for each student based on the student's specific knowledge, and the appropriate problem is then selected based on these dynamic difficulty measures. The study was performed in the context of the SQL-Tutor system. The results show that adaptive problem selection based on dynamically generated problem difficulties can have a positive effect on student learning performance.

1 Introduction

One of the adaptive decisions that ITSs make is problem selection. An appropriate problem is one that is challenging for the student, but still not too hard: the student should be able to solve the problem with the system's support. Most ITSs select problems based on the state of the student model (i. e. based on the student's knowledge), thus providing adaptive problem selection.

In this paper, we compare two problem selection strategies, both of which use the student model to select problems adaptively. The difference between them is that one strategy uses static problem complexities assigned by the domain expert, while the other one dynamically computes the problem difficulty for the given student at a certain moment during learning. The motivation for these measures comes from Brusilovsky [2]. Within the ITEM/IP system, task sequencing was based on problem *complexity* (also referred to as structural complexity [3]) and problem *difficulty* (referred to as conceptual complexity [3]). In this system, the problem complexity was a static measure of how complex the problem was, in terms of the number of statements needed in the solution. On the other hand, problem difficulty was dynamically computed from the student model, and represented the number of concepts the students does not know.

In the next section we discuss the system we used in the study, and the two different versions of it that implement the two problem-selection strategies. In Sect. 3 we present our hypotheses and the design of the experiment. Sect. 4 presents the results, while the conclusions are given in Sect. 5.

W. Nejdl and P. De Bra (Eds.): AH 2004, LNCS 3137, pp. 185–194, 2004.

2 SQL-Tutor and the Versions Used in the Study

We performed an experiment in the context of SQL-Tutor, an ITS that teaches the SQL database language. For a detailed discussion of the system, see [5, 7]; here we present only some of its features. SQL-Tutor consists of an interface, a pedagogical module, which determines the timing and content of pedagogical actions, and a student modeller, which analyzes student answers. The system contains definitions of several databases and a set of problems and their ideal solutions. Each problem is assigned a static level of complexity by the domain expert based on the domain concepts that are necessary to solve the problem. SQL-Tutor contains no problem solver: to check the correctness of the student's solution, SQL-Tutor compares it to the correct solution, using domain knowledge represented in the form of more than 650 constraints. It uses Constraint-Based Modeling (CBM) [8, 9] for both domain and student models.

Student may select problems in SQL-Tutor in several ways: they may work their way through a series of problems for each database, ask the system to select a problem on the basis of his/her student model, select a problem from the list, or select a type of problem they want to work on such that the system selects a problem of that type on the basis of their student model. For this study we developed two versions of the system, differing from each other in the problem selection strategy. Both strategies use the student model to determine which problems are appropriate for the current level of student's knowledge.

In both versions of SQL-Tutor used in this study, when the student asks for a new problem, they will be presented with a page showing their student model and asking them to select the type of problem they would like to work on. This encourages the student to reflect on their knowledge in order to identify the type of problem they have difficulties with. To support this reflection, we open the student model to the users. The constraint base of SQL-Tutor is large, and therefore it is not possible to show the student's progress directly in terms of constraints. Instead, we collapse the student model into six parts, corresponding to the six clauses of an SQL query. A previous study [6] showed that such a visualization of the student model has a positive effect on learning, especially for less able students, and helps students select appropriate problems.

Fig. 1 presents the problem selection page. The student model is displayed in terms of the progress over the six clauses. To measure progress on a clause, we compute the percentage of constraints relevant to that clause that the student has used so far. The student model tracks how the student has used each constraint, and computes an estimate of the student's understanding of the constraint based on the last n uses of that constraint. We use these estimates to compute how well the student knows all the constraints relevant for the clause. The correctly known constraints are shown in green (the first part of the bars in Fig. 1), while the ones the student has problems with are shown in red (second segment of the bars). The total shows the coverage of a particular constraint.

SQL-Tutor suggests the type of problem the student should work on. In Fig. 1, the system suggests the WHERE clause. To suggest a clause, the system checks the student level, which ranges from 1 to 9 and is proportional to the number of constraints the student knows. If the student level is less than 3, the system selects one of the initial three clauses (SELECT, FROM and WHERE), for which the problems are easier. For

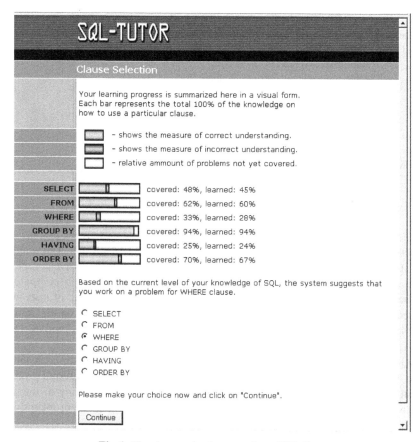

Fig. 1. The clause selection page from SQL-Tutor

students whose level exceeds this threshold, the system selects one of all six clauses. SQL-Tutor then chooses the candidate clause that the student has had most problems with. This is based on a simple measure: we find all constraints relevant for a clause and average the probabilities that the student knows these constraints.

Once the type of problem (i. e. the clause) has been selected, SQL-Tutor searches for problems of that type. Out of all relevant problems, the system selects ones that are at the appropriate level for the student. These are the problems whose levels equal or exceed the current student ability level.

The problem level differs in the two versions of the system used. The control version uses the static, pre-defined problem complexity. In contrast, the experimental version computes the problem difficulty dynamically based on the student model. The problem difficulty ranges from 1 to 9, and is computed as the (scaled) weighted sum of probability of the student having already learned each constraint relevant for the problem (Equation 1).

$$Diff(Prob) = \sum_i w_i p(c_i) \tag{1}$$

```
(p 68
    "Check the names of join attributes in FROM! You need to use qualified names."
    (and (match '(?*d1 ?t1 ??s1 "JOIN" ?t2 ??s2 "ON" ?a1 "=" ?a2 ?*d2)
            (from-clause SS) bindings)
        (valid-table (find-schema (current-database *student*)) ?t1)
        (equalp ?t1 ?t2)
        (not (null ?s1))
        (not (null ?s2)))
    (and (qualified-name ?a1)
        (qualified-name ?a2))
"FROM")
```

Fig. 2. An example constraint

The probability that the student has learned the constraint is simply the proportion of correct applications of the constraint for the last five times it was relevant. The weight of a constraint (w_i) is a number between 0 to 1, which represents the relative complexity of the constraint in relation to the whole constraint set. This weight is computed as the total number of tests the constraint contains divided by the number of tests in the most complex constraint the system possesses. For example, constraint 68 illustrated in Fig. 2 has a total of seven tests in its relevance and satisfaction condition, and its weight is 0.41.

SQL-Tutor shows all the relevant problems for the chosen clause, sorted according to the complexity/difficulty, and one of them is highlighted as the preferred problem. The student is free to either accept the suggested problem or select any of the other available problems, including previously solved ones. The order of the problems gives them help in making their selection.

3 Experiment Design

We hypothesized that problem selection based on the dynamically computed problem difficulty would be superior to that based on static problem complexities. To evaluate this hypothesis, we performed an experiment with the students enrolled in an introductory database course at the University of Canterbury. Participation in the experiment was voluntary. Prior to the study, students attended four lectures on SQL and had two laboratories on the Oracle RDBMS. There were two additional lectures and three labs during the experiment. SQL-Tutor was demonstrated to students in a lecture on 15 September 2003. The pre-test, consisting of four multi-choice questions, was administered online the first time students accessed SQL-Tutor. Two questions contained the text of a problem for which students were asked to select the correct SQL query. The other two questions asked about SQL constructs.

The students were randomly allocated to one of the two versions of the system. The course involved a lab test on SQL on 16 October 2003, which provided additional motivation for students to practise with SQL-Tutor. The post-test was administered online the first time a student logged on to the system on or after 15th October 2003. The maximum mark for the pre/post tests was 4.

4   Results

Of the 110 students enrolled in the course, 79 students logged on to SQL-Tutor at least once. The mean score for the pre-test for all students was 54.75% (sd=25.02%). The students were randomly allocated to one of the versions of the system. A t-test showed no significant differences between the pre-test scores for the two groups. However, some students looked at the system only briefly. We therefore excluded the logs of students who did not attempt any problems. Further, we noted that some students had logged on to SQL-Tutor on the last day of the study, and therefore some of them submitted the post-tests before solving any problems. Such students have not benefited by working on the system, so we removed them also. The logs of remaining 59 students (29 in the control, and 30 in the experimental group) were then analysed.

As the study was voluntary, not all students completed it, and we do not have post-test results for all the students. Table 1 gives the number of students in each group who sat both tests, and reports various statistics for only these students. The two subgroups are still comparable, as there is no significant difference on the pre-test performance. Both groups had lower scores on the post-tests, although not significantly. The maximal number of solved problems was 49 for the control, and 36 for the experimental group. There was a significant difference on the lab test-performance between all students who used SQL-Tutor before the last day of the study (mean=60.68%) and the rest of the class (mean=52.10%). However, this has to be taken with caution, as the study was voluntary.

Table 1. Some statistics about the groups

	Pre-test	Post-test	Lab test	Sessions	Solved	Time
Control (n=13)	57.69	55.77	53	3.08	15.87	182
	(34.43)	(34.09)	(20.77)	(2.45)	(13.29)	(166)
Exper. (n=9)	50	47.22	55.67	2.6	14.2	136
	(17.68)	(23.20)	(15.42)	(1.85)	(12.18)	(131)

We also compared the effect the two systems had on learning. Fig. 3 plots learning curves, indicating the proportion of times the constraints were violated for the *nth* problem for which the student encountered that particular constraint. Such curves give a measure of how well the learners improved their performance with respect to the constraint set over time. While the curve is slightly steeper for the control group, it must be remembered this group had a higher average pre-test score, and may therefore represent more able learners.

We then considered whether the two systems might affect the learning rate differently for students of different ability. We analyzed the logs of all 59 students, divided the two groups further according to pre-test scores and used those groups where there were a reasonable number of students with that score. Table 2 summarises the resulting groups.

Fig. 4 shows the learning curves for the two systems for each pre-test score. Note that the curves have been cut off at N=5 to counter the effects of having small sample sizes, because the number of participating constraints decreases with N. For the control

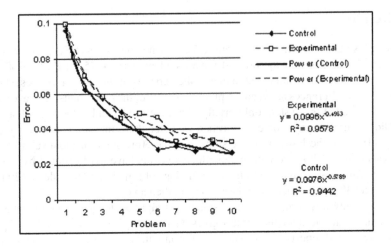

Fig. 3. Learning curves for the two groups

Table 2. Groups used for learning speed analysis

Pre-test score	N (control group)	N (experimental group)
1	9	9
2	11	17
3	9	4

group, the slope of the curve for a score of 2 is considerably greater than for scores of 1 and 3, suggesting that the static problem difficulty is more suited to intermediate learners than those with lower or higher initial ability, with lower ability learners faring very poorly. Conversely, the experimental group students with a score of 1 or 2 perform about the same, while the more advanced students demonstrate a much higher learning speed.

We tested the statistical significance of these results by plotting individual curves for each student and comparing the average power curve slopes. We also computed the average initial slope and power curve fit. The initial slope gives a measure of the absolute decrease in errors after encountering a constraint once: the higher this value, the more learning is taking place. The power curve fit is a further indicator of how much learning is being achieved, by showing how well the students' performance fits the expected model of learning [1]. Fig. 5 plots these values as a function of pre-test score for the two groups, while Table 3 summarises those comparisons that displayed statistical significance at p=0.05. We also performed one-way ANOVA tests on the parameters for each of the two main groups, which indicated that the curve fit varied significantly for the control group (p=0.003) while the slope did for the experiment group (p=0.027).

The analysis of the power curves across scores suggests that the two methods differ in how they fit students of different abilities. The static problem difficulty appears to suit medium students much better than either beginner or advanced students; both the curve slope and fit peaks for this score. Conversely, the dynamic difficulty appears to be

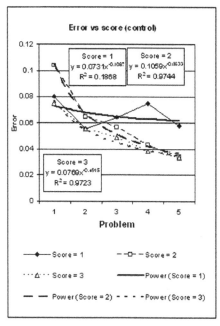
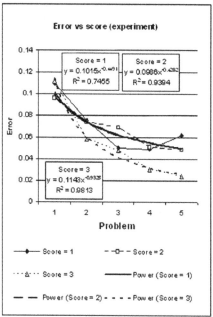

Fig. 4. Learning curves versus score for each group

Table 3. Significant differences between control and experiment

Comparison	Control Mean	Control SD	Exper. Mean	Exper. SD	Significance
Initial slope, score=1	0.024	0.015	0.063	0.039	p=0.04
Curve fit, score=1	0.20	0.14	0.56	0.31	p=0.03
Curve fit, score=3	0.44	0.36	0.93	0.03	p=0.04

best suited to advanced students, while serving medium students moderately well, and improving the performance of lower ability students with respect to the static system. For the experiment group, the learning rate (slope) trends upwards with ability, suggesting that the system may possibly be advancing each group at a rate proportional to their ability.

Finally, we compared the students' behaviour when selecting a new problem to work on. The experimental group selected a total of 396 problems (an average of 20.84 each), while the control group had 530 selections (23.04). Both groups typically adopted the problem suggested by SQL-Tutor or selected another problem on the same level (67.93/70.75% for experimental/control groups). However, the control group students asked for problems that were more difficult than what the system selected in preference to easier ones (19.24/12.1%), while those in the experimental group were twice as likely to ask for an easier problem (17.93% versus 8.68%). From this analysis it seems that dynamic problem difficulties may cause more complex problems to be selected, and hence

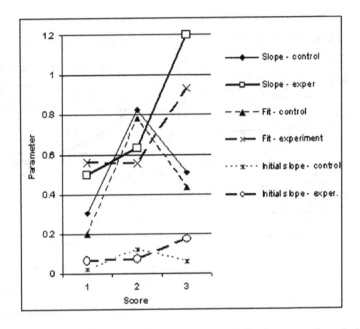

Fig. 5. Curve parameters versus score for each group

the students chose one at a lower level. Further, the success rate for a selected problem (Fig. 6) increases fairly slowly relative to the difficulty of the problem selected (easier, same as or harder than the system selection) for the experimental group, whereas for the control group the proportion of problems abandoned varies considerably, with more than half of the more difficult problems not being completed. This suggests that dynamic problem difficulties are better matched to the student's level, in that the problems just outside the suggested difficulty are only moderately easier/harder, whereas for the statically ordered problems the student may find them considerably less/more of a challenge.

5   Conclusions

This experiment aimed to determine whether adaptive problem selection could improve the learning experience of students using an Intelligent Tutoring System. SQL-Tutor was modified to calculate problem difficulty based on individual knowledge elements (constraints) in the student model, and this was used to adaptively select the next problem. The modified system was then evaluated against the standard SQL-Tutor using a class of University students.

There is a significant difference between the two problem selection strategies in the way they suit users of differing ability: dynamically computed problem difficulty performed well for a wide range of students, whereas static problem complexity performed well for students of intermediate ability, but fared badly for beginners and advanced stu-

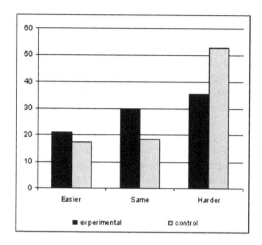

Fig. 6. Percentage of abandoned problems

dents. The results were statistically significant. This suggests problem selection benefits from being more adaptive.

The experimental system described included a moderate level of adaptation: problem choice was guided by how each problem was mapped onto the student model, and this mapping had a fairly large granularity (only 9 difficulty ratings). However, there are other ways the system could be made more adaptive. For example, the student's level is derived from their coverage of the domain model, which could be problematic if there is a mis-match between this value and the calculated problem difficulties: the system may repeatedly give the students problems that are too hard or too easy. In [4] we used an adaptive student level that increased each time the student answered a problem correctly the first time, and decreased when they got an answer wrong. Such an approach may further improve the match between student and problem.

To be effective, ITSs need to be well matched to their students. Adaptive problem selection is just one area where this match can be strengthened. The results of this study indicate that such an approach has merit.

References

1. Anderson, J. R., Lebiere, C.: The atomic components of thought. Mahwah, NJ: Erlbaum (1988)
2. Brusilovsky, P.: Intelligent Tutor, Environment and Manual for Introductory Programming. Educational and Training Technology International **29** (1) (1992) 26–34
3. Brusilovsky, P.: A Framework for Intelligent Knowledge Sequencing and Task Sequencing. In: C. Frasson, G. Gauthier and G. McCalla (eds) Proc. ITS 1992, Springer-Verlag, Berlin Heidelberg New York (1992) 499–506
4. Martin, B., Mitrovic, A.: Automatic Problem Generation in Constraint-Based Tutors. In: S. Cerri, G. Gouarderes and F. Paraguacu (eds.) Proc. 6th Int. Conf on Intelligent Tutoring Systems ITS 2002, Biarritz, France, LCNS 2363, Springer-Verlag, Berlin Heidelberg New York (2002) 388–398

5. Mitrovic, A.: An Intelligent SQL Tutor on the Web. Artificial Intelligence in Education, **13** (2-4) (2003) 173–197
6. Mitrovic, A., Martin, B.: Evaluating the Effects of Open Student Models on Learning. In: P. de Bra, P. Brusilovsky and R. Conejo (eds) Proc. AH 2002, LCNS 2347, Springer-Verlag, Berlin Heidelberg New York (2002) 296-305
7. Mitrovic, A., Martin, B., Mayo, M.: Using Evaluation to Shape ITS Design: Results and Experiences with SQL-Tutor. User Modeling and User-Adapted Interaction, **12** (2-3) (2002) 243–279
8. Mitrovic, A., Ohlsson, S.: Evaluation of a Constraint-based Tutor for a Database Language. Artificial Intelligence in Education, **10** (3-4) (1999) 238–256
9. Ohlsson, S.: Constraint-based Student Modeling. In: Greer, J.E., McCalla, G (eds): Student Modeling: the key to Individualized Knowledge-based Instruction (1994) 167–189

Adaptive Presentation and Navigation
for Geospatial Imagery Tasks

Dympna O'Sullivan[1], Eoin McLoughlin[1], Michela Bertolotto[1], and David C. Wilson[2]

[1] Smart Media Institute, Department of Computer Science, University College Dublin,
Belfield, Dublin 4, Ireland
{dymphna.osullivan,eoin.A.mcloughlin,michela.bertolotto}@ucd.ie
[2] Department of Software and Information Systems
University of North Carolina at Charlotte, USA
davils@uncc.edu

Abstract. Advances in technology for digital image capture have given rise to information overload problems in the geosciences and fields that rely on geospatial image retrieval. To help address such imagery information overload, our research is developing methods to extract and apply contextual knowledge relating user task goals to the images being used. As users analyze imagery retrieved to support specific tasks, multiple relevant images and salient image content can be captured together with task annotations to provide a basis for contextual knowledge management support. This paper describes how our environment for image interaction leverages captured task-based knowledge to support adaptive presentation and navigation in the space of available imagery.

1 Introduction

As the quantity of geospatial image data continually increases, intelligent support for relevant image retrieval is crucial to help manage large repositories of geospatial imagery, such as digital satellite and aerial photographs. This is especially true for organizations that rely on geospatial applications, such as for intelligence operations, recreational and professional mapping and industrial planning. Geospatial image applications, in particular, can benefit from enhanced retrieval support, as many standard content-based image retrieval approaches (e.g., low-level color analysis) are often not as effective for typical geospatial image content [1]. In our research, we are helping to address this problem by fusing information about underlying visual data with task-based contextual information, gathered from users as they engage in tasks involving selection and analysis of relevant imagery [2].

We have developed a task-based knowledge-management environment that can facilitate users in work that already involves selecting, composing, and summarizing aspects of digital imagery in support of current tasks. As users employ image interaction tools to highlight relevant image aspects and make notes, these expert human insights can be captured in a form that the system can use, along with behaviors, insights, results, and context development. In turn, available and previously captured knowledge context enables automatic retrieval of imagery related to the current context, as well as access to previous user task interactions.

As this repository of task-based contextual knowledge continues to grow, the system can make use of the relationships established among the underlying images to

W. Nejdl and P. De Bra (Eds.): AH 2004, LNCS 3137, pp. 195–204, 2004.
© Springer-Verlag Berlin Heidelberg 2004

facilitate different kinds of retrieval access, pathways for navigation, and modes of presentation. In particular, this paper describes how the captured knowledge can be leveraged to provide an intelligent user interface that adapts content presentation in response to changes in current user context and provides navigation through the space of available imagery based on captured relationships.

This research extends captured knowledge to influence not only the relevant imagery and associated knowledge that is presented to the user, but also the manner in which they are presented in order to maximize the effectiveness of the interaction. This involves capturing knowledge at the interface level, maintaining user context based on interactions with the interface, and adaptively presenting the most relevant results based on changing user context. The interface needs to account for user context changes in presenting (1) individual image results, (2) associated captured knowledge in the form of annotations, (3) encapsulated prior task experiences, and (4) the relative associations and relevance of the preceding points. By tracking user behavior and capturing task knowledge as compacted contextual knowledge parcels, we can provide new avenues for navigating through information along with captured associations (e.g., two images used in addressing a single task), as well as presentation (e.g., highlighting the previous annotations most relevant to the current user context). Because captured task knowledge can involve a lot of information, we are particularly interested in developing adaptive content presentation for smart interfacing that can provide the user with enough cues to judge the relevance of a previous task experience, but in a form compact enough to enable ease of viewing, comparison, and selection among multiple candidates.

This paper presents our environment for capturing and reusing experiences and rationale through image annotation. The paper begins with a brief discussion of related research in Sect. 2, and it continues with a description of the image library interaction that provides a baseline for contextual knowledge capture in Sect. 3. Sect. 4 describes the user tools available for image annotation. Sect. 5 introduces our methods for calculating annotation-based retrieval, and Sect. 6 presents our approaches for smart adaptive content presentation and navigation. An initial evaluation is described in Sect. 7, and we conclude with a brief description of future work.

2   Background and Related Research

In our research we are working with large collections of experience and case-based context, enabled by automatic capture of user context. We aim to shield our users from the burden of making explicit queries by using implicit analysis [3,4], and we observe how they proceed with their task, recording this as user context. By situating intelligent support within task environments, as for example in [5], we can monitor, interpret, and respond to user actions concerned with rich task domains based on a relatively constrained task environment model.

Our approach to knowledge capture is very much in the spirit of work for capturing rationale in aerospace design [6] and automotive design feasibility analysis [7]; however, the emphasis is on self-directed annotations provided by users as a means of task analysis support, rather than prompting users for particular kinds of choices. Our work draws on research in contextualizing user tasks (e.g., [8]) and anticipating user needs (e.g., [9]). Our approach to unobtrusive retrieval of relevant information based on local context is also related to techniques presented in [10].

3   System Overview

When a user logs into the image interaction environment, they are directed to an interface that enables them to search directly for imagery corresponding to their current task needs. A typical task-based query to our image repository is a straightforward request to a geospatial image database, and it may consist of any combination of specified metadata, semantic task information, and a sketched configuration of image-objects. As the user specifies their query this information is captured by the system and added to their current context. For example, urban planners interested in building a shopping center in Boston, USA, might wish to view recent images of possible building sites. They could outline a metadata query specifying the location in which they are interested. They could enhance their query by means of a sketch, outlining undeveloped areas of land bordered by residential developments. They can also provide a textual description of the kind of imagery they would like returned. For example, in this case they could specify that they are interested in retrieving images of undeveloped land of low elevation with a good infrastructure. The interfaces we have developed for outlining task queries are shown below in Fig. 1.

Fig. 1. Image Query Screens

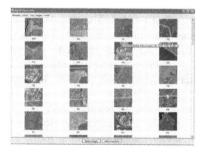

Fig. 2. Matching Images

Users may search for images in one of two ways. Firstly they may perform a basic image retrieval search whereby individual images that match their search criteria are returned. Secondly they may search a knowledge base of other users' tasks. We refer to the work of each of these individual similar users as "sessions". These user sessions are constructed by recording all of the contextual knowledge input by a user while addressing their own task goal. If the user chooses to perform an image retrieval search the resulting matching images are returned to them as shown in Fig. 2.

In order to allow multiple candidates to be displayed we present the matching images as a ranked list of thumbnails. A subset of the most relevant metadata for each image is available as tool tip text when mousing over the image. Once the images and their associated percentage matching score are returned the system personalizes the current task by adding the returned information to the current user context. The user can browse the images retrieved in the results screen and select any images that are relevant to the task at hand.

As the user interacts with the images the current user context is continuously and automatically assembled. The system records which images the user browses and if the user selects an image for further analysis that another user may have found helpful in a similar task context the score assigned to that image will increase. The scores of any other images that may have proved useful in that particular similar task or other associated tasks from the knowledge base are automatically updated in response. Conversely, matching image scores will decrease if the images have been employed to complete tasks the system deems unrelated to the current task. The matching image scores are recalculated automatically in response to user interaction and the interface is redrawn to reflect the current task context. All the selected images are then collected into the current user context and made available for annotation.

4   Capturing User Context and Task Knowledge

As part of our effort to capture task knowledge and also to assist the user in organizing information about relevant imagery, we have developed tools for direct image manipulation, including filters, transformations, highlighting, sketching, and post-it type media annotations. These allow the user to identify regions of interest that can be linked to clarifications and rationale. From a system perspective the tools provide us with a mechanism to capture fine- grained task context in an unobtrusive manner and to personalize users' tasks by constantly augmenting their task context. The resulting captured context provides a basis for computing similarity scores between the current session and the session of a previous user. We combine user queries resulting and selected imagery, user annotations and similarity scores to construct encapsulated user sessions. Once we have captured this relative knowledge we take advantage of it by converting it to a format that is usable and practical for system users. This is achieved through the construction of intelligent adaptive interfaces and associated navigation techniques that allow users to effortlessly browse and retrieve relevant contextual information.

To illustrate the annotation tools, we return briefly to our shopping center example. After retrieving and selecting imagery relevant to Boston, the user can annotate each image using a substantial set of image annotation tools. Fig. 3 illustrates our image manipulation interface. Buttons on the left margin of the screen represent sketching and transformation tools as well as some filters. The multimedia annotation tools are located along the bottom of the interface. Returning to our shopping center example, in Fig. 3, the user has made use of the transformation and annotation tools in carrying out their task. They have circled and highlighted some residential areas, indicating their awareness that the area would provide a large customer base. They have highlighted a large road running through the heart of the image showing interest in the infrastructure of the area. They have also added a textual comment to an undeveloped area peripheral to the residential area indicating the feasibility of development in this area. The user has also uploaded a video file to the same area of the image. The textual and media annotations are represented by icons, which are painted on the image.

If the user mouses over any of these icons the region associated with the annotation is emphasized by a rectangle drawn around the icon. This is shown by the dark rectangle around the comment icon in Fig. 3. The user can click on any of these icons to display a pop-up description. The system also supports annotation by cut, copy and paste between a given image and other images in the dataset, as well as images in any application that supports clipboard functionality for the given operating system. Once a user has finished interacting with the system all captured information is stored as an encapsulated session case in the case-base.

Fig. 3. Image Annotation to Capture Task Context

5 Calculating Similarity Using Annotations

Capturing task-based knowledge enables a powerful cycle of proactive support that facilitates knowledge sharing by retrieving potentially relevant information from other user experiences based on task context. Currently, we are focusing our annotation-based retrieval on textual annotations. We use information retrieval metrics as a basis for similarity. Given a textual representation of the task context, we can match previously annotated session images to the current context. The task descriptions and image query elements can be used to retrieve entire sessions as relevant to the current task. By calculating similarity using annotations we can calculate not only overall matching scores for the particular session but also scores for the individual query elements, annotations and images annotated in the course of a session. Based on these similarity metrics resulting from captured context we can create a detailed and informative interface displaying exactly which elements have contributed to a particular session or a particular images' position in the ranked list of returned similar sessions or matching imagery. The task-based retrieval employs indexes in three separate spaces - Annotation Index, Image Index and Session Index. For a full description of our similarity indices please refer to [2].

   Task-based image retrieval serves two purposes. First, task-based similarity can be used directly to access annotated images in the image library. Second, it can be integrated with similarities from the other types of query information, such as by image content, to provide a more refined overall metric for retrieval. By merging task-based knowledge from previous user experiences with the current task content we create a foundation for interface adaptation. As a user proceeds with their task the current context is captured and combined with the three indices from above and new similarity matching scores are calculated. Based on these new results content presentation is adapted accordingly.

6 Adaptive Content Presentation for Similar User Sessions

If when entering a query to the system, a user chooses to view information provided by similar users they are presented with the interface shown in Fig. 4. In designing this interface we endeavored to present an abstraction of all the contextual information we had recorded during the course of the similar user's task. One challenge here was how to present a condensed summary of a similar user's entire session in a limited space while retaining enough information so that our user can quickly discriminate potential relevancy.

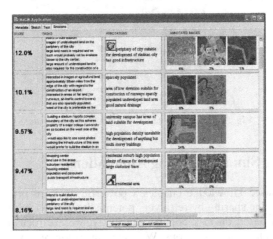

Fig. 4. Similar Sessions

Each row in the interface corresponds to one session result, ranked according to matching session score. Every session is summarised to include the same type of information for the purpose of consistent presentation. As all the contextual information for each session is encapsulated in one row of the interface the user can easily navigate relevant information in all its different formats. Below is a detailed description of the information displayed for each session.

Percent similarity score
This score represents how comparable this similar session is to the current session. This is an overall score calculated using all of the similarity indexes (annotation, image and session).

The most discriminating query information
This includes metadata and task descriptions entered by the similar user. Since we have captured which results were actually used, we know which queries were most fruitful. According to our similarity metrics these queries are similar to the queries entered by the current user. They may also have made annotations to the imagery that

the current user will find helpful. As there may be large volumes of text to be displayed in this column, a tool tip text is displayed when a user mouses over the space informing them that they may scroll down for all task descriptions.

The most important annotations

Annotations may be textual in nature or they can be multimedia based. These annotations have been judged by the system to be most likely to help our user in fulfilling their task. Multimedia annotations are represented in a succinct manner by media buttons. These media buttons, if clicked on, play any audio or video files uploaded during the session. All textual annotations may be displayed in web browser thereby giving the user the opportunity to read annotations uploaded from the World Wide Web and to link to any other relevant material from those documents. This type of navigation allows us to build context from web pages around the actual relevant images. By virtue of system interaction a link structure can be created between different types of knowledge. If a user clicks on a media button then the system deems that the user is interested in this work and that this annotation has a high similarity to the current context so the session scores are recalculated using the current context and the annotation just accessed as new parameters for similarity. Our adaptive similar sessions interface is redrawn to reflect the new task context.

Thumbnail versions of the most important images

These are images that have been annotated as part of the similar task. Beneath each image is an associated matching image score. These scores are calculated by comparing any textual annotations associated with these individual images to the current context. These scores therefore provide a measure of how relevant each individual image is to the current task. If the user wishes to view the annotations made to any of these images, they may do so by clicking on the thumbnail, which brings up the image and all its annotations (see Fig. 3). The icons representing the textual and media annotations adapt their levels of transparency depending on how similar each individual annotation is to the current context. This provides a direct interface interpretation of relevance in terms of visual cues, which can adapt with current user context. If the current user selects an image for closer examination, the similar session scores and the individual session images matching scores are updated in response to this interaction. For example if our user browses the annotations of another user or annotates images that another user has already found useful in the context of their task, the scores assigned to any similar sessions and any relevant images within that session will increase. The matching sessions and matching images are reordered according to their new context and the interface is then redrawn to reflect this.

The user may further annotate images from similar sessions if they wish and/or retain the previous users annotations by adding it to their current session context. Once the user saves the desired annotations, they are transferred to the current user's view of the image.

7 Evaluation

In evaluating our approach, we were interested in showing that the system is capable of capturing and deciphering fine-grained task specific knowledge and displaying it in a way that users find useful. We also wanted to investigate whether the retrieved information and proactive recommendations made by the system based on the acquired knowledge were valuable and could be used effectively to facilitate knowledge sharing. Thus the focus of the evaluation for this paper is on session-based retrieval. Our initial testing evaluates whether the system is presenting relevant sessions appropriately, and we expect to move on to more extensive user testing in future work. Our test dataset consists of 1600 annotated images from the astronomy domain that have been annotated by expert users.

In order to evaluate session retrieval we applied clustering techniques to our dataset. The library was clustered into five categories for evaluation. These categories were "Telescope", "Mars", "Nebula", "Comet" and "Manned Space Exploration". Once the dataset was portioned we automatically created fifteen user sessions (fifteen cases) in our case base. The user sessions were created by outlining three different task descriptions in each of the five clustered categories. An example of a task description in the Mars category was "Interested in retrieving imagery of Mars that shows that there may once have been or is now water on the planet".

The fifteen sessions were created by entering task descriptions such as the one above. Image searches were performed on the dataset using these fifteen task descriptions as queries. From the returned images the top five most relevant images were selected for annotation. These five images were then annotated with their original annotation from the annotated dataset. Each user session created was then saved to include the task query, the resulting images, the images selected for annotation and the annotations applied to each image as an encapsulated case in the knowledge base. When the fifteen user sessions had been added the annotations were indexed and therefore included for retrieval. Once the annotations had been indexed, we began to assess how effectively the system performs session retrieval. We referred once again to the five clusters in the dataset and created generic task descriptions relating to each of the five outlined categories. An example of a generic task description for the Nebula category was "Interested in the gaseous content of nebulae". The generic task descriptions were then entered as queries to the system and a search for similar sessions performed. The desired outcome was that the generic task description would best match the three more specific cases already assigned to that cluster. This evaluation was a relative comparison of returned sessions and the aim of this experiment was to demonstrate that in response to a particular query the scores of those sessions correctly classified was on should be much higher than the scores of those incorrectly classified.

For the returned sessions for each query we calculated the average percentage "Case in Cluster" score and the average percentage "Case not in Cluster" score. The average percentage "Case in Cluster" score was calculated by averaging the scores associated with each of the three sessions of more specific task description. The average percentage "Case not in Cluster" score was the average score associated with all other returned sessions. Even though the three generated sessions within each cluster were not always returned as the top three sessions, the average percentage "Case in Cluster" score was always higher than the average percentage "Case not in Cluster" score. For some of the different categories the "Case in Cluster" and "Case not in Cluster" scores are shown in the graphs in Fig. 5 below. The lighter circular dots represent the three sessions that are relevant to the particular category while the darker rectangular dots represent all other sessions returned. These results demonstrate that the system is effective at retrieving the most contextually relevant information available from the knowledge base and that combining this information with current context supplied by users as a basis for interface adaptation leads to increasingly refined and more task-specific results.

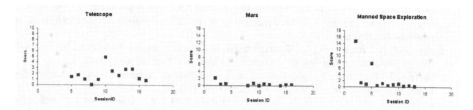

Fig. 5. Session Retrieval Results

We then repeated the session evaluation using a small group of human subjects to judge the relevancy of the results returned by the system for Session Retrieval. The subjects entered the generic task descriptions and were then asked to choose and place the top three most relevant sessions from the results. In 85% of cases the subjects agreed with the results returned by the system. These results reveal that collecting task-specific information supplied inherently by user interactions as encapsulated sessions allows users to quickly judge the relevance of previous task experiences by enabling natural navigation through large quantities of important and contextual information.

8 Conclusions

We have introduced our approach to developing a context aware adaptive system for managing and retrieving imagery and knowledge. The system makes use of knowledge acquisition techniques to capture human expertise and attempts to understand this task-specific context so it may adapt information displayed based on the current context. This enables adaptive presentation, such as of session content and iconography relevance, as well as opportunities for navigation, such as between images based on annotation or session grouping. We are investigating the possibility of implementing user profiling to improve adaptation techniques by capturing information specific to individual users. Our research will continue to investigate the possibilities for exposing aspects of captured knowledge in the interface, such as finer visual cues in iconography and maintaining user orientation as result presentation changes with user context.

Acknowledgements

The support of the Research Innovation Fund initiative of Enterprise Ireland is gratefully acknowledged.

References

1. Carswell, J.: Using Raster Sketches for Digital Image Retrieval, PhD Thesis, University of Maine, Orono, Maine, USA (2000)

2. O'Sullivan, D., McLoughlin, E., Wilson, D. C., and Bertolotto M.: Capturing Task Knowledge for GeoSpatial Imagery. In: Proceedings K-CAP 2003 (Second International Conference on Knowledge Capture), Florida, USA, ACM press (2003) 78-87
3. O'Sullivan, D., Smyth, B. and Wilson, D.: Explicit vs. implicit profiling - a case-study in electronic programme guides. In: Proceedings of the 18th International Joint Conference on Artificial Intelligence (2003)
4. Claypool, M., Brown, D., Le, P. and Wased, M.: Implicit interest indicators. In: Proceedings of International Conference on Intelligent User Interfaces (2001) 33–40
5. Budzik, J., Birnbaum, L., and Hammond, K.: Information access in context. Knowledge Based Systems. Elsevier Science 37-53 (2001) 14 (1-2)
6. Leake, D.B. and Wilson, D.C.: A case-based framework for interactive capture and reuse of design knowledge. Applied Intelligence. Kluwer. Boston (2001) 14(1) 77-94
7. Birnbaum, L., Hammond, K., Leake, D., Marlow, C., and Yang, H.: Integrating information resources: A case study of engineering design support. In: Proceedings of the Third International Conference on Case-Based Reasoning, Springer Verlag, Berlin, (1999) 482–496
8. Budzik, J. and Hammond, K.: Watson: Anticipating and Contextualizing Information Needs". 62nd Annual Meeting of American Society for Information Science (1999)
9. Lieberman, H.: Letizia: An agent that assists web browsing. In: Proceedings of the Thirteenth International Joint Conference on Artificial Intelligence, San Francisco, CA, Morgan Kaufmann (1995)
10. Maes P. and Rhodes, B.J.: Just-in-time information retrieval agents. In: IBM Systems Journal 39 (2000) 685-704

Myriad: An Architecture
for Contextualized Information Retrieval and Delivery

Cécile Paris[1], Mingfang Wu[1], Keith Vander Linden[2], Matthew Post[2], and Shijian Lu[1]

[1] CSIRO ICT Center,
NSW, Sydney, Australia
{Cecile.Paris,Mingfang.Wu,Shijian.Lu}@csiro.au
[2] Department of Computer Science, Calvin College,
Grand Rapids, MI USA
{kvlinden,mpost89}@calvin.edu

Abstract. Users' information needs are largely driven by the context in which they make their decisions. This context is dynamic. It includes the users' characteristics, their current domain of application, the tasks they commonly perform and the device they are currently using. This context is also evolving. When one information need is satisfied, another is likely to emerge. An information access system must, therefore, be able to track this dynamic and evolving context, and exploit it to retrieve actionable information from appropriate sources and deliver it in a form suitable for the current situation. This paper presents a generic architecture that supports the construction of information retrieval and delivery systems that make use of context. The architecture, called Myriad, includes an adaptive virtual document planner, and explicit, dynamic representations of the user's current context.

1 Introduction

Knowledge workers are increasingly dependent upon the availability of the right information in the right form for their daily work. Their information needs are largely driven by the context in which they make their decisions. This context is dynamic. It includes their characteristics, their current domain of application, the tasks they commonly perform and the device they are currently using. This context is also evolving. When one information need is satisfied, another is likely to emerge. An information access system must, therefore, be able to track this dynamic and evolving context, to exploit it to retrieve information from appropriate sources, and to deliver that information in a form that is appropriately tailored to the user's context.

Thus, the challenges for such an information access system come in both retrieval and delivery. First, the system must interact with heterogeneous databases and document collections, so a unified interface or integrated framework for accessing these systems is essential. Second, the system must deliver the information retrieved from these various sources in a manner that is adapted and reorganized to suit the user's needs at that time.

W. Nejdl and P. De Bra (Eds.): AH 2004, LNCS 3137, pp. 205–214, 2004.

This paper presents a generic architecture that supports the construction of an information access system for contextualized guided information retrieval and delivery. The architecture, called Myriad, includes an adaptive virtual document planner, and a set of models for explicit and dynamic representation of the user's current context. This architecture extends our previous work on tailored information delivery [17, 18] by adding support for adaptation based on the users' tasks and interaction history.

2 Related Work

Delivering appropriate information in an appropriate form and adapted to an individual user's need is a key theme in the adaptive hypermedia community [4]. The aim of adaptive hypermedia systems is to provide a personalized information space for users to browse. This personalized access is achieved through content level adaptation (or adaptive presentation) and link-level adaptation (or adaptive navigation support) [3]. The adaptive presentation selects and presents information according to users' goal and knowledge backgrounds, while the link level adaptation provides navigation support to help users orient themselves within the hypermedia space.

Adaptive hypermedia systems adapt information to a user's needs by building an explicit user model and exploiting it throughout the interaction with the user, e.g., [9, 10, 12]. A user model may include users' search goals, knowledge of the application domain, and some personal characteristics such as preference and background. Traditional adaptive hypermedia systems assume the existence of a closed set of documents that are authored by humans and manually linked in a hyper-information space. A user model is usually implemented as an overlay of an underlying concept model. Each concept is associated with a value that indicates a user's current state of knowledge with respect to that concept. An adaptive engine, therefore, can simply compare the value of a concept in its user model with the conditions of a concept in its conceptual model in order to filter out a sub-hypermedia space that suits a user's goal and knowledge level. One of the assumptions behind these adaptive hypermedia systems is that the system designers/authors know the documents in a collection and have a global map of how the hypermedia space is to be presented to the user [7]. This assumption makes it difficult for adaptive hypermedia systems to be scaled to large and open document collections. Adaptive hypermedia systems are hard, therefore, to deploy in the web environment because information access system designers cannot know in advance every document in the collection. The web and even some organizations' internal web sites are simply too large and too open. Although documents could, in principle, be annotated with meta-data, many are not.

In the Information Retrieval (IR) community, the user model tends to be implicit, represented simply as a query. The advantage of this model is that it is easy to implement and can be scaled to any open document collection; this model has been successful in retrieving documents from large document collections. However, this model has two major disadvantages. First, the resulting IR systems simply deliver the documents that are retrieved, without any contextual adaptation. Thus different users typing the same query will get the same set of responses. While this kind of delivery gives users

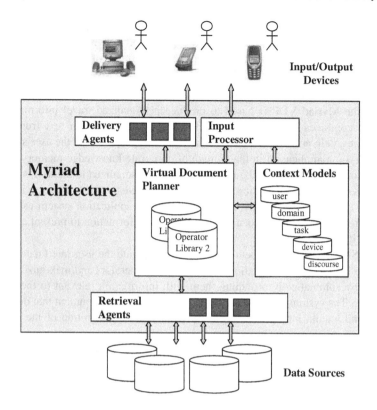

Fig. 1. The Myriad Architecture

access to information, it doesn't concern itself with user understanding. Second, this query based model does not consider the user's evolving search context; every query is treated as a one-off retrieval task that has no connection to the previous queries that result from the same information need. Consequently, the search result is discrete and not presented as a coherent whole.

The proposed Myriad architecture attempts to make the best use of the advantages of both the delivery-driven approach of adaptive hypermedia systems and the retrieval-driven approach of information retrieval systems. This enables Myriad to support both the retrieval of information from open heterogeneous databases and the delivery of that information within the users' information-seeking context.

3   An Adaptive Hypermedia Architecture

The Myriad architecture supports the construction of information access systems that provide information retrieval from heterogeneous databases and adaptive hypermedia delivery. Fig. 1 shows the basic components of this architecture. The core of this architecture is the Virtual Document Planner (VDP). This planner receives information requests from the users via the input processor and uses the contents of various context models to drive its operation. It deploys retrieval agents to select contents appropriate to the users' current information need and context, and delivery agents to present this content with appropriate links in a coherent way. A number of information application systems have been, and are currently being built using the Myriad architecture:

- **Tiddler** – a tailored information delivery system. It used the document planner on which the Myriad VDP is based to produce personalized travel information [18]. Tiddler combines structured information from databases with text from existing web pages, delivering this information in a form appropriate for the user's device.
- **PERCY** – an application in the domain of corporate knowledge memory. It generates a coherent e-brochure about a corporation, personalized to the user's query and user type [17]. This application exploits a user profile, a set of discourse roles and a set of web data resources. Given a user query, the application system uses the discourse roles and the user model to decide which information to present and how to present it in a coherent way.
- **DFDMSA** – a new system being developed to mediate the user interface in an aviation application. This application aims to support operators and maximize their efficiency by automatically providing them with information relevant to their tasks at the time. The system provides a task-based interaction environment that delivers tailored multimedia information from the analysis and recognition of the operator's activity [5, 6].
- **Skil** – a new system being developed to provide a computer assisted training environment in a medical domain. This application integrates recent advances in the area of haptic virtual environments and natural language generation. It aims to reduce the complexity of a three dimensional scene in order to allow reasoning about the user's actions and to deliver tailored information.
- **Tiger** – a new system being developed to provide actionable information in the context of an organization. Here, actionable information is information that has been retrieved, processed, analyzed, and synthesized in context for a person to consider and then act upon.

This section discusses the basic components of the Myriad architecture, using the current Tiger prototype system as an example. Fig. 2 shows a sample output of this system. Here, we see a web-based presentation of information requested by a professor about a student. The information includes data that are private to the professor and other data that are more publicly accessible.

3.1 Input Processor

The input processor is responsible for receiving input from the user, identifying the information need and posting it to the VDP as the communicative goal. It assumes that the user has been authenticated and their input device determined. Any input received from the user, whether it be through a typed or spoken query or a hyperlink, will be processed by the input processor and stored in the user's discourse history.

The Myriad architecture currently uses a finite state parser as the key technology in the input processor [13]. This parser uses an augmented transition language to trans-

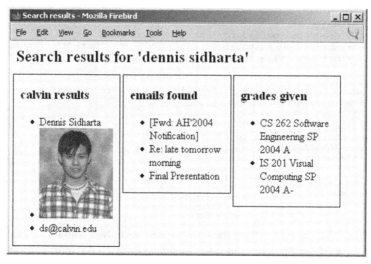

Fig. 2. Sample Tiger Output

late natural language queries from the user into goal statements appropriate as input to the VDP. Different information application systems can specify different input parsing grammars depending upon the sorts of questions they are likely to receive from users.

For the Tiger example in Fig. 2, the input processor received the query:

```
Tell me about Dennis Sidharta
```

and translated it into the instantiated communicative goal:

```
DESCRIBE <Dennis Sidharta> TO <current user>
```

This goal was then passed to the VDP to drive the information retrieval and delivery process.

3.2   Virtual Document Planner

The VDP is the central component of the Myriad architecture. Its implementation is based on Moore and Paris's [16] generic planning mechanism and the Tiddler document planner [18], both of which used plan operators to drive both the selection of appropriate content and the construction of an hierarchical plan that represents an appropriate presentation of that content. This sort of planner has frequently been used in the language engineering community to drive information presentation [16, 19]. Its resources are represented as libraries of declarative plan operators. Myriad supports the construction of multiple plan operator libraries for each information application.

For example, the Tiddler system included two plan operator libraries: discourse operators, which built a content plan (structured in terms of Rhetorical Structure Theory [15]), and presentation operators, which structured it in a manner appropriate for the user's current context. The Skil prototype adds a third library of interaction operators, which specifies interaction goals for training lessons.

In the Tiger example, the communicative goal passed to the VDP (see above) matches the following discourse plan operator (specified in XML):

```
<operator>
  …
  <effect>(describe ?person to ?user)</effect>
  <constraint>(set ?grading (retrieval:JDBCAgent ?person))</constraint>
  <constraint>(set ?file "results.html")</constraint>
  …
  <satellite>
    <type>optional</type><relation>elaboration</relation>
    <value>(CalvinPersonAgent ?file ?person)</value>
  </satellite>
  <satellite>
    <type>optional</type><relation>elaboration</relation>
    <value>(IMAPAgent ?file ?person)</value>
  </satellite>
  <nucleus>
    <value>(JDBCAgent ?file ?person)</value>
  </nucleus>
  …
</operator>
```

Here, we see that the effect of the operator can be unified with the communicative goal (i.e., if we bind ?person to <dennis sidharta> and ?user to <current user>). This operator is constrained to work only when the JDBC retrieval agent can find grades for the student in the user's database (see the first constraint). Otherwise, another plan operator must be found. The nucleus and two satellites insert the "calvin results", the "emails" and the "grades given", as shown in Fig. 2.

3.3 Context Models

Myriad's approach to adaptivity is to capture the user's context by monitoring their interactions with the system and reflecting them in the context models. The five basic context models are discussed here. All of the models are represented using a KL-ONE styled representation scheme [2] and can be configured for each new information application as appropriate:

- **User Model** – The user model represents the user's long-term (or stereotypical) profile and their short-term information goal. The long-term profile is application dependent, but could include a user's job description or the user's role in an organization. The short-term goal is a user's current information need, which is usually specified in the user's query. For example, Skil relies on the user model to dictate the varying levels of explanation of a particular concept that are required by novices and by experienced users, while PERCY and Tiddler rely on the user's profile and interests to direct the content of their presentations.
- **Domain Model** – The domain model consists of hierarchies of concepts, properties and relationships relevant within the application domain. Myriad does not attempt to develop a definitive ontological model, but rather allows application developers to specify the model that is relevant for them. The Tiger model, for example, distinguishes between people, companies, and other conscious entities.
  Unlike typical adaptive hypermedia systems, Myriad does not require its domain model concepts be related to documents in the knowledge base. The binding between documents and concept instances could happen just as well at retrieval time.

- **Task Model** – The task model is used to describe the tasks commonly performed by users of the application. For each user task, the model specifies the relevant sub-steps, conditions and effects. These tasks are specified using the Diane+ task modeling formalism [20]. For example, DFDMSA bases its retrieval and presentation on detailed models of its users' tasks.
- **Device Model** – The device model specifies the characteristics of a user's current input/output device. In Tiddler, for example, different user devices, such as cell phones or desktop machines, lead to the use of different VDP plan operators and thus to different output content, structure and presentation.
- **Discourse Model** – The discourse model keeps track of the user's information searching history. These histories may contain the questions that the user has posed to the system and the documents that the user opens for each question. This model can be used to predicate the user's future interest, as in [11, 13], and to generate a search summary toward the end of the user's search session.

Taken together, these five models represent the context of the user's information need. Generally, the relevant context elements from the domain, task, device and discourse models are linked from the user's instance in the user model. The domain model is primarily used to define a set of concepts (and their relationships) used by the other models and by the VDP. In the Tiger example, part of the user model entry for the professor requesting information is as follows (again, specified in XML):

```
<instance>
   ...
  <type>Professor</type>
  <link>
    <slot>name</slot>
    <value>Keith Vander Linden</value>
  </link>
  <link>
    <slot>email</slot>
    <value>kvlinden@calvin.edu</value>
  </link>
  <link>
    <slot>imapagent:hostname</slot>
    <value>mailhost.calvin.edu</value>
  </link>
  <link>
    <slot>imapagent:username</slot>
    <value>kvlinden</value>
  </link>
   ...
</instance>
```

Here, the user is a `professor`, as indicated by the `type` specification. The user's name is given, as is his email address and his IMAP mail hostname and username. Addition information (not shown) is specified for how to query his personal grading database and how to access his personal account on the Calvin information server. Myriad prompts the user at runtime for private values such as passwords.

3.4 Retrieval Agents and Information Access Tools

Retrieval agents receive a specification from the VDP and then use appropriate information access tools and information sources to find information according to the specification. For the Tiger application, we have implemented a number of retrieval agents within the Myriad architecture. They include:

- **GoogleAgent** – This agent queries the Google search engine for information specified by the VDP. It is able to take advantage of any of the features exposed by Google's search API and to return those results to the VDP.
- **IMAPAgent** – This agent provides a generalized mechanism for searching the current user's IMAP mail account. In the Tiger example, this agent retrieved the emails shown in Fig. 2.
- **JDBCAgent** – This agent provides a generalized mechanism for querying databases via JDBC. Users can customize this agent to query either personal or public database sources for any type of information to which they have access. In the Tiger example, this agent retrieved the student grades shown in Fig. 2.
- **LocalPersonAgent** – This agent accesses a web form to search a local database of students, faculty, and staff, and returns that person's picture, email address, position, department, and phone number. In the Tiger example, this agent retrieved the "Calvin Results" shown in Fig. 2.

Here, we can see that retrieval agents range in degree of scope, from the very general (e.g., the GoogleAgent) to the very localized (e.g., the LocalPersonAgent). This allows application developers to use Myriad to support tools that provide access to heterogeneous data sources, retrieving private data when available, and resorting to more public data when necessary. In the Tiger example, for instance, if the grading agent had failed to find grades for the given student, then the plan operator discussed above would have failed and another more general operator would have been run instead. The more general operator would have called the GoogleAgent.

3.5 Delivery Agents

Delivery agents take content from the retrieval agents and present that content in the various ways as directed by the VDP. For example, a delivery agent could organize the retrieved information and present it in a manner that suits a user's current interaction platform. Another delivery agent could take a set of retrieved documents and call a clustering function to group the documents into topic related clusters [22]. In the Tiger example, the output was delivered in HTML format for a web browser.

4 Discussion and Future Work

The Myriad architecture has been evolving from our earlier applications (Tiddler and PERCY) that supported user, domain and device models, to applications supporting task models (DFDMSA), and discourse models (Skil and Tiger). The adaptation is also evolving from adaptability, based on a profile including user preferences and device capabilities, to adaptivity, based on not only user profile but also the domain model, task model and discourse model.

Future work on the Myriad architecture primarily centers on further development of the current Myriad applications and on the features Myriad provides to support this development. In particular, a greater variety of retrieval and delivery agents are required as well as a more general set of VDP plan operator libraries that can more easily be adapted to new information application domains.

References

1. Aroyo, L., De Bra, P. and Houben, G. J.: Embedding Information Retrieval in Adaptive-Hypermedia: IR meets AHA! In Proceedings of the AH2003 Workshop, Budapest, Hungary, May (2003) 63-76
2. Brachman, R. J., & Schmolze, J.: An Overview of the KL-ONE Knowledge Representation System, Cognitive Science, 9, (1985) 171-216
3. Brusilovsky, P.: Methods and techniques of adaptive hypermedia. User Modelling and User-Adapted Interaction, 6 (2-3), (1996) 87-129
4. Brusilovsky, P.: Adaptive hypermedia. User Modelling and User Adapted Interaction, Ten Year Anniversary Issue (Alfred Kobsa, ed.) 11 (1/2), (2001) 87-110
5. Colineau, N., Lampert, A. and Paris, C.: Task-Sensitive User Interfaces: grouping information provision within the context of the user's activity. To appear in Proceedings of Advanced Visual Interfaces (AI 2004), Gallipoli, Italy, May 25-28, (2004)
6. Colineau, N. and Paris, C.: Task-Driven Information Presentation. In Proc. of the Annual Conference of the Computer-Human Interaction (OZCHI'03), Special Interest Group of the Ergonomics Society of Australia, Brisbane, Australia, Nov 25-28 (2003)
7. De Bra, P. and Calvi, L.: AHA! An Open Adaptive Hypermedia Architecture. The New Review of Hypermedia and Multimedia, vol. 4, Taylor Graham Publishers (1998) 115-139
8. De Bra, P.: Adaptive Hypermedia on the Web: Methods, techniques and applications, Proc. of the AACE WebNet'98 Conference, Orlando, Fl., (1998) 220-225
9. De Bra, P.: Houben, G. J., and Wu, H. AHAM: A Dexter-based Reference Model for Adaptive Hypermedia. In Proceedings of ACM Hypertext (1999) 115-139.
10. Frasincar, G., Houben, G. J., Vdovjak, R.: An RMM-Based Methodology for Hypermedia Presentation Design. In Proc. Advances in Databases and Information Systems, LNCS 2151, Springer (2001) 323-337
11. Gates, K. F., Lawhead, P. B. and Wilkins, D. E.: Toward an adaptive WWW: a case study in customized hypermedia. New Review of Multimedia and Hypermedia 4, (1998) 89-113
12. Halasz, F., and Schwartz, M. The Dexter Hypertext Reference Model. CACM, 37(2) (1994) 30-39
13. Joachims, T., Freitag, D. and Mitchell, T.: WebWatcher: A Tour Guide for the World Wide Web. Proceedings of 15th International Joint Conference on Artificial Intelligence, IJCAI;97 (1997) 770-775
14. Jurafsky, D. and Martin, J.: Speech and Language Processing, Prentice Hall (2000)
15. Mann, W. C. and Thompson, S. A.: Rhetorical Structure Theory: toward a Functional Theory of Text Organisation. In Text 8(3) (1998) 243-281
16. Moore, J. D. and Paris, C. L.: Planning Text for Advisory Dialogues: Capturing Intentional and Rhetorical Information. In Computational Linguistics, Cambridge, MA, Vol 19(4), (1993) 651-694

17. Paris, C., Wu, M., Vercoustre, A., Wan, S., Wilkins, P. and Wilkinson, R.: An Empirical Study of the Effect of Coherent and Tailored Document Delivery as an Interface to Organizational Websites. In The Proceedings of the Adaptive Hypermedia Workshop at the 2003 User Modelling Conference, Pittsburgh, USA, June 22, (2003) 133-144
18. Paris, C., Wan, S., Wilkinson, R. and Wu, M.: Generating Personal Travel Guides – and who wants them? In Proceedings of the International Conference on User Modelling (UM2001); M. Bauer, P. Gmytrasiewicz and J. Vassileva (eds). Sonthofen, Germany, July 13-18 (2001) 251-253
19. Reiter, E. and Dale, R.: Building Natural Language Generations Systems. Cambridge University Press (2000)
20. Tarby, J. C. and Barthet, M. F.: The Diane+ method. In Computer-Aided Design of User Interfaces, in Proceedings of the Second International Workshop on Computer-Aided Design of User Interfaces (CADUI'96). Namur, Belgium, 5-7 June (1996)
21. Terveen, L.: Overview of Human-Computer Collaboration. Knowledge-based Systems, 8 April-June (1995) 67-81
22. Wu, M., Fuller, M. and Wilkinson, R.: Using clustering and classification approaches in interactive retrieval. Information Processing and Management, vol. 37 (2001) 459-484

Cross-Media and Elastic Time Adaptive Presentations: The Integration of a Talking Head Tool into a Hypermedia Formatter*

Rogério Ferreira Rodrigues[1], Paula Salgado Lucena Rodrigues[1],
Bruno Feijó[1], Luiz Velho[2], and Luiz Fernando Gomes Soares[1]

[1] DI – PUC-Rio
Rua Marquês de São Vicente, 225, Rio de Janeiro, RJ, Brazil - 22453-900
{rogerio,pslucena,bruno,lfgs}@inf.puc-rio.br
[2] IMPA – Inst. de Mat. Pura e Aplicada
Estrada Dona Castorina, 110, Rio de Janeiro, RJ, Brazil - 22460-320
{lvelho}@impa.br

Abstract. This paper describes the integration of a facial animation tool (*Expressive Talking Heads - ETHs*) with an adaptive hypermedia formatter (*HyperProp formatter*). This formatter is able to adjust document presentations based on the document temporal constraints (e.g. synchronization relationships), the presentation platform parameters (e.g. available bandwidth and devices), and the user profile (e.g. language, accessibility, etc.). This work describes how ETHs augments the capability for creating adaptive hypermedia documents with HyperProp formatter. The paper also presents the adaptation facilities offered by the main hypermedia language (*Nested Context Language - NCL*) HyperProp system works with, and details the implementation extensions of Expressive Talking Heads that turned it an adaptive presentation tool.

1 Introduction

The expressiveness power of a hypermedia presentation system is closely related to its capacity of dealing with different media formats. On the other hand, the decoupling of the presentation management functions (e.g. synchronization control, presentation adaptation, prefetching control, etc.) from the media content exhibition tasks gives more flexibility and extensibility to the system [15]. Therefore, the proposal is to establish an architecture where media players (presentation tools) are modules that can be plugged to the presentation system core element, which is usually named *hypermedia formatter* (or *hypermedia engine*). To accomplish this goal, an opened interface should be specified by the formatter to allow not only the incorporation of external presentation tools, but also to enable these incorporated presentation tools to interact with each other.

---

* This work was granted by the Brazilian Telecommunications Technological Development Fund (FUNTTEL), through contract 0594/02, and by CNPq.

W. Nejdl and P. De Bra (Eds.): AH 2004, LNCS 3137, pp. 215–224, 2004.

Following this approach, this paper describes the integration of the HyperProp system formatter [15, 16] with a talking head presentation tool, named Expressive Talking Heads (ETHs) [12]. ETHs is a tool able to present a synthesized speech, synchronized with lip movements and facial expressions (mainly emotions), where the speech and face animation are dynamically generated from an input markup text.

The HyperProp formatter uses an event-driven model to control document presentations. The system can receive document specifications in higher-level authoring languages, like NCL [13] and SMIL [18]. In order to illustrate the adaptation capabilities of HyperProp formatter integrated with ETHs, the paper uses an NCL document example.

Cross-media adaptations [2] are supported by switch elements, allowing, for example, the same text content to be presented by a talking head tool or as a common formatted text. Switch elements can also allow the synthesized speech to be adapted to different language accents. Elastic-time adaptation [1, 9, 11], in the context of this work, permits the synthesized speech to be played with different speeds, aiming at maintaining the voice temporal relationships with other media objects, thus meeting the requirements of the document specifications. All adaptations are guided by context parameters, like user and platform characteristics, and can be static or dynamic. The NCL document example used in the paper illustrates these possible adaptations.

The paper is organized as follows. Sect. 2 describes ETHs and explains how the integration with HyperProp formatter was conducted. Sect. 3 illustrates with a document example the system facilities for developing adaptive hypermedia documents, discussing the adaptation issues in the integrated system. Sect. 4 compares the proposal with related work. Finally, Sect. 5 presents the paper conclusions.

2   Expressive Talking Heads Meets HyperProp

2.1   Expressive Talking Heads

The Expressive Talking Heads (ETHs) is a tool that is able to interactively receive markup texts and to generate the animation of a virtual character face speaking the texts [12]. The text markups can set speech idiom accents (e.g. American or British English), voice gender (e.g. male or female), character emotion (e.g. natural, frightened, annoyed, happy), eyes and head positioning, text anchors, among others. The anchor markup, in particular, is a very important feature, since it gives authors the possibility of defining relationships among arbitrary speech segments (spoken by ETHs) and other document media objects, which can eventually be other speech segments. Fig. 1 depicts the ETHs architecture.

ETHs contains a parser component that is responsible for separating the speech content itself (text without markups) from the speech and animation markups. The parser interacts with the tool synthesizer to build the facial animation and lip-sync data structures.

The ETHs parser sends each fragment of marked text to the synthesizer (Festival [17] and MBROLA [5] in the figure) that first creates the speech phonetic description (list of phoneme entries, each one containing the phoneme label, duration and pitch). From this phonetic structure, the parser can identify the phonemes corresponding to the beginning and end of the fragment and thus to assign the beginning and end phonemes for each anchor, emotion, eyes positioning, etc. All these information are stored in the animation data structure. When finishing handling all fragments of marked text, the parser concatenates the several phonetic structures and, together with the speech metadata (idiom, gender, etc.), sends these new data to the synthesizer to have the digitized speech audio generated. Note that it is possible to adapt the speech idiom and the voice gender to a user preference, since the MBROLA synthesizer offers a rich base of distinct voices.

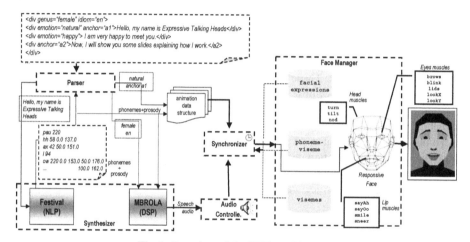

Fig. 1. Overview of the ETHs architecture.

During the synthesis process, the ETHs parser can modify the phonetic structure in order to produce a more realistic speech sound, for example, introducing a random pause-duration between sentences[1]. Moreover, the ETHs tool is designed to permit its user applications to interfere in the synthesis process. This can be used, as explained later, to adjust the duration of the synthesized speech, adapting the hypermedia presentation to context parameters.

The face manager module of ETHs links it to another external subsystem, named Responsive Face [14]. Actually, the ETHs face was inherited from this subsystem, which defines a three-dimensional polygonal mesh, as illustrated in Fig. 1. The face is animated by the application of relax and contract commands over the mesh edges (face muscles). ETHs improves the Responsive Face features adding speech and applying to its face the concept of visemes. Viseme is the name given to a mouth configuration for a specific phoneme. The ETHs face manager defines a table containing

---

[1]   As another example, when text markups appear inside a sentence, the created phonetic structure contains one pause phoneme at its beginning and another one at its end. If the phonemes were simply concatenated, the resultant speech sound would have uncomfortable gaps. Therefore, the ETHs parser suppresses these kinds of pause phonemes.

the phoneme-viseme mapping and also a base of 16 visemes for English phonemes [6], inheriting the 8 emotion facial expressions already defined by Responsive
Face. Each base entry stores the values for contracting/relaxing the face corresponding
muscles commanding the Responsive Face.

The ETHs synchronizer module is responsible for the fine synchronization between
the speech and the facial muscle movements. Parallel to the audio file reproduction,
the synchronizer polls the audio controller to check the effective playing instant. Using
the phoneme durations, the synchronizer discovers the current phoneme and the current character emotion. Then the synchronizer gets the associated viseme and facial
expression muscle contracting/relaxing values, and asks the face manager to apply
these values over the Responsive Face. Actually, instead of working just with the
current phoneme, the synchronizer uses diphones (two consecutive phonemes interpolated by their durations), since the lip positions for the same phoneme generally
changes according to the phoneme context (speech co-articulation aspect).

The synchronizer also monitors the text anchor list in order to find when a speech
anchor begins or finishes. These events are notified to components that had register
themselves as ETHs anchor observers [8]. The synchronization module also has components to control the head and eyes movements, in order to produce a more natural
output.

To facilitate the ETHs use, its services are available through a single facade [8] that
hides the internal organization described in this section. The Expressive Talking Heads
and the Responsive Face are currently implemented in Java. More details about Expressive Talking Heads project can be found at http://www.telemidia.puc-rio.br/~pslr/
eths/.

2.2   Presentation Tool Adapter for Integrating ETHs into HyperProp

To enable the incorporation of new presentation tools (or media players), the Hyper-
Prop formatter specifies an integration API. This interface defines the methods that the
presentation tools must implement and how they should notify the formatter about
presentation event occurrences (user interaction, start/end of content anchor presentation, etc.). Media players that do not implement the required methods, or do not know
how to control the HyperProp event state machine [15], should be plugged to the formatter through an adapter component [8]. This was the strategy used to integrate
ETHs with the HyperProp formatter.

When initialized, the ETHs adapter receives from the formatter the media object
that should be controlled and a descriptor; a set of parameters specifying how the
object should be played. Besides the content reference, the media object contains the
list of presentation events that should be monitored. These events have associated
anchors (fragments of text to be marked up).

Different from the embedded anchor model used by ETHs, the HyperProp formatter allows anchors to be externally defined. This separation aims to allow specifying
relationships among hypermedia nodes independent from their content. As a consequence of the different anchor paradigms, the ETHs adapter must analyze the formatter external anchors and then dynamically embed them into the text content, using the

ETHs markup definitions (Sect. 2.1). Afterwards the adapter asks the ETHs (through its facade) to perform the synthesis.

Among all its presentation parameters, the descriptor has an attribute specifying the expected duration of the media-object content presentation. The ETHs adapter compares this value with the sum of all phoneme durations and tries to make them equal by adjusting the phoneme durations. If the adapter does not succeed on this task, it reports the fact to the formatter. As mentioned in the previous section, the adapter can alter the phonetic structure since it is an ETHs user application. It does this, basically, modifying the pause phonemes. It is worth mentioning that the adapter may not only adjust the whole content duration, but also adapt each anchor-duration separately.

After all elastic time adaptations, the adapter asks the ETHs for concluding the synthesis. The adapter then registers itself as an ETHs anchor observer and waits for the presentation start command coming from the formatter. When the start command is triggered, the adapter passes the request to the ETHs, which initiates its synchronizer component. The adapter then stays monitoring anchor notifications to convert them into transitions in HyperProp event state machines [15].

3 Adaptive Document Presentation in HyperProp+ETHs

Fig. 2 presents an example of hypermedia document specification using NCL [13]. Due to the lack of space, some document parts were omitted, being replaced with ellipses[2]. The HyperProp formatter has a converter that translates the NCL specification into its execution model [16].

When preparing the document presentation, the HyperProp formatter first analyses the document switches (analogous to SMIL switches [18]) to select, for each of them, the best alternative given by the test rules. However, different from SMIL, the switch test attributes are defined in a presentation rule base (lines 5-18), enabling the same rule to be reused more than once. In the example, the defined rules allow testing the user knowledge level, and the user preference for synthesis and the speech accent. As it can be observed, some rules are grouped defining composite rules. The parameters used in the presentation rules are based on the formatter contextual information (user profile and platform characteristics). In the current implementation, the formatter locally maintains the contextual information, but it is possible to integrate the formatter with third-party context management systems [16]. The formatter also has a dialog interface that enables users editing context parameter values.

The document node switch defined in lines 46-51 specifies two alternatives of text nodes, whose selection depends on the user knowledge level. Besides content alternatives (node switches), NCL (and the HyperProp formatter) allows authors defining alternatives of presentation characteristics for the same content, denoted as descriptor switches (lines 26-39). This possibility makes the ETHs tool very useful. In the example, the same text explanation has three presentation alternatives: if the user does not enable the speech synthesis feature, the text will be presented in its original format

---

[2] The complete NCL document and a downloadable version of HyperProp formatter can be found at http://www.telemidia.puc-rio.br/products/formatter/.

using the *textDesc* descriptor; if the user agrees on having speech synthesis and the user speech accent preference is for American English, the text node will be presented using the *speechDescEn* descriptor. Otherwise, the text will be synthesized and presented with a British accent. As it is depicted in Fig. 2, node and descriptor switches can be combined, automatically generating a larger amount of alternatives. In the example, the node switch combined with the nested descriptor switches gives 6 different alternatives for presenting the explanation to the user.

```
01 <?xml version="1.0" encoding="UTF-8"?>
02 <ncl ...>
03 <head>
04 <layout>...</layout>
05 <presentationRuleBase>
06  <presentationRule id="rule01" var="userLevel" op="eq" value="beginner"/>
07  <presentationRule id="rule02" var="userLevel" op="eq" value="expert"/>
08  <presentationRule id="rule03" var="synthEnabled" op="eq" value="true"/>
09  <presentationRule id="rule04" var="synthEnabled" op="eq" value="false"/>
10  <compositePresentationRule id="rule05" op="and">
11   <presentationRule id="rule05a" idref="rule03"/>
12   <presentationRule id="rule05b" var="speechAccent" op="eq" value="en"/>
13  </compositePresentationRule>
14  <compositePresentationRule id="rule06" op="and">
15   <presentationRule id="rule06a" idref="rule03"/>
16   <presentationRule id="rule06b" var="speechAccent" op="eq" value="en-uk"/>
17  </compositePresentationRule>
18 </presentationRuleBase>
19 <costFunctionBase>
20  <costFunction id="speechCost" xsi:type="linear"
21    deltaShrink="15%"  deltaStretch="15%"  minDurCost="10"  maxDurCost="10"/>
22 </costFunctionBase>
23 <descriptorBase>
24  <descriptor id="videoDesc" dur="30" .../>
25  <descriptor id="subtDesc" nodeRule="rule03".../>
26  <descriptorSwitch id="explanationDesc">
27   <bindRule rule="rule04" component="textDesc"/>
28   <bindRule rule="rule05" component="speechDescEn"/>
29   <bindRule rule="rule06" component="speechDescUk"/>
30   <descriptor id="textDesc" .../>
31   <descriptor id="speechDescEn" costFunction="speechCost"
32     player="HF_ETHsAdapter">
33    <param name="idiom" value="en"/>
34   </descriptor>
35   <descriptor id="speechDescUk" costFunction="speechCost"
36     player="HF_ETHsAdapter">
37    <param name="idiom" value="en-uk"/>
38   </descriptor>
39  </descriptorSwitch>
40 </descriptorBase>
41 </head>
42 <body>
43  <port id="entryPoint" component="explanation">
44  <video id="video" descriptor="videoDesc" src="..."/>
45  <text id="subtitle" descriptor="subtDesc" src="..."/>
46  <switch id="explanation">
47   <bindRule rule="rule01" component="beginnerExplanation"/>
48   <bindRule rule="rule02" component="expertExplanation"/>
49   <text id="beginnerExplanation" src="..." descriptor="explanationDesc"/>
50   <text id="expertExplanation" src="..." descriptor="explanationDesc"/>
51  </switch>
52  <linkBase>...</linkBase>
53 </body>
54 </ncl>
```

Fig. 2. Adaptive NCL document.

Still in the switch adaptation phase, the formatter looks for rules directly associated with descriptors, as in the subtitle descriptor in line 25. In this example, since the subtitle text node (line 45) is associated with the *subtDesc* descriptor, the text node will be enabled during the presentation only if the user chooses to have the text synthesis (*rule03*), otherwise the explanation will appear as a text and the subtitle becomes unnecessary (disabled).

If the formatter encounters a rule that cannot be resolved at presentation compile time, the formatter maintains the switch information in its execution plan [16], and delays the selection to be done on-the-fly. Similarly, if a context parameter value changes after initiating the presentation, the formatter re-evaluates the rules and, therefore, the node and descriptor switches.

After this first adaptation phase, the HyperProp formatter runs the cross-media adaptation mechanisms. The formatter looks for nodes with presentation characteristics that specify a content transformation. In Fig. 2, the descriptor *player* attribute in lines 32 and 36 gives this content transformation information, specifying ETHs as the presentation tool for node contents that are associated with this descriptor. If this attribute was not defined, the formatter would instantiate the default presentation tool for showing the node content, as occurs when the *textDesc* descriptor is selected.

In the third adaptation phase, the HyperProp formatter runs its elastic time algorithm [1]. In NCL (and also in the HyperProp execution model), the spatio-temporal synchronization among media objects is specified through links, grouped into the document linkbases (line 52) [13]. The formatter uses object durations and link specifications to build the document time chains [16]. NCL and the HyperProp formatter also enable object durations to be flexibly specified. In the example, there is an element (lines 20-22) specifying that durations using the specified cost function can be 15% shrunk or 15% stretched. However, the deviation from the ideal value linearly increases the price paid with the change. The cost function in the example is used by the speech descriptor (either with American or British accent) to inform how much the speech audio may be adjusted. When combined with the document temporal constraints, cost functions give metrics for the formatter finding the optimum temporal configuration. HyperProp uses tension graph formalism and a solver utility (*solve tension*) to perform the optimized computation [1].

Although not shown in the example, document link relationships establish that the explanation node switch should begin in parallel with the video presentation, and they should finish together. Since the video should last for 30 seconds (line 24), the selected alternative in the node switch must be presented during the same time. If the text is selected this can be easily accomplished. On the other hand, if the synthesis is performed, the ETHs adaptation capability (Sect. 2.2) is used to accommodate the speech duration.

Once the document execution starts, the formatter stays observing the dynamic context information and monitoring the presentation event occurring instants (time instant that transitions in the event state machines occur), and compares them with the originally predicted values. In case of any mismatch, on-the-fly elastic time adjustments are called.

To minimize the chances of needing runtime adjustments, the HyperProp formatter builds a prefetching plan, and anticipates object preparation requests [16]. The time wasted in a presentation preparation is estimated based on statistics computed from previous navigation. Prefetching is very helpful when using the ETHs adapter since the synthesis process may require considerable time[3]. To diminish this limitation, a slightly modified ETHs adapter was developed to handle previously synthesized audios. This adapter is useful in scenarios that do not tolerate synthesis delays, or when the formatter cannot have access to the synthesizer. For this new presentation tool the preparation time became about 15 times faster. However, without a speech synthesizer available, the temporal adjustment through the phonetic structure manipulation cannot be done.

Although not used in the example, another version of ETHs was developed to exclusively deal with speech synthesis. This simpler presentation tool can be used in HyperProp documents to accommodate user accessibility constraints (blind users, driver users, etc). With or without face animation, presentation tools like ETHs dynamically create alternative contents (dynamic cross-media adaptation), simplifying authoring maintenance and removing the needs for storing multiple versions.

ETHs can also be an alternative for adapting documents to devices with communication and processing limitations. Sending just the phonetic structure together with the synthesized audio requires less bandwidth than sending a face video, without excluding the visual information. Moreover, the face animation probably will require less resource usage than decompressing video algorithms.

4   Related Work

Originally proposed by Netscape, the support to plug-in technology is very common in web browsers. An API allows external applications to be integrated into the WWW navigation environment, offering a means to incorporate content formats that are not recognized by web browsers. However, the API does not offer support for defining relationships among objects presented by different plug-ins, or even between plug-ins and HTML pages. As another drawback, the plug-in lifetime is tied up to the lifetime of the HTML page containing it.

Bouvin and Schade [3] propose an extension for plug-in API aiming to allow the creation of links among objects or object internal anchors presented by different plug-ins. However, in the described extension, links are always interactive; there is no support for defining temporal synchronization relationships, like those offered by the HyperProp formatter.

Regarding media-object duration adaptation, there is some work that deals with the elastic time computation problem in multimedia presentations [9, 11]. However, none of them comments about how to apply these adjustments in continuous-media contents. The duration adjustment implemented in the ETHs adapter is a step towards this goal. The mechanism is useful to satisfy constraints specified by document authors,

---

[3] For instance, experiments showed a mean of 15 seconds for the synthesis of 100 words.

whenever objects with durations that do not match the inter-media specified relationships are found [1, 16]. The ETHs adjustment mechanism may also be used to compensate jitters imposed by networks and operating systems.

SMIL formatters (also known as SMIL players) [18] and the Cardio-OP application [10] are able to adapt presentations from content switches and based on contextual information. In Cardio-OP, queries [2] also allow dynamic building of document fragment alternatives. However, neither SMIL nor Cardio-OP allows duration adjustments. Actually, we are now investigating how to extend SMIL to accommodate elastic time computation algorithms and how to make use of Expressive Talking Heads in SMIL presentations.

It is possible to find in the literature researches dealing with facial animation issues, lip-sync, facial emotions, etc. VideoRewrite [4] and MikeTalk [6] are two examples that produce a very good result in lip movements. However, they are not interactive, that is, they require a large amount of time in order to prepare the animation and generate a pre-compiled video containing the result, what makes very difficult the data edition for subsequent adjustments. Reference [7] describes an implementation of a tool for supporting talking head applications in the web, using MPEG-4 as the basis for animating the faces. Although offering the support, the authors lead the implementation of user applications to a future work.

5 Conclusions

This paper describes the integration of a talking head tool into an adaptive hypermedia formatter. The talking head adapter developed in the context of this work offers a simple solution for the complex task of adjusting continuous inter-related media object durations. As an example, in the MPEG system standard it is difficult to stretch or shrink an audio stream maintaining it synchronized with a video stream. In Expressive Talking Heads (ETHs), face movements (animation) are synchronized with synthesized speech. Integrated into the HyperProp formatter, ETHs content presentation can also be synchronized with other media objects (slides, figures, etc.). Since in ETHs the visual output is synthesized based on the audio information, and the later has a well-known phonetic structure, adjustments in the second structure naturally reflect on the other one.

The presence of a talking head tool cooperating with hypermedia presentation systems increases the expressiveness of document presentations and scene descriptions. We are now working on the migration of the HyperProp formatter to ITV set-top box platforms. Our first adaptation target is non-profit advertisements (for example, programming advertisements of the broadcaster itself), in a sequence of commercials, which can be elastic-time adjusted in order to satisfy the programming grade time constraints. A more careful analysis of the overhead imposed by the synthesis process is also left as a future work, besides investigating algorithms and heuristics that better accommodate prefetching and on-the-fly adaptation requirements.

References

1. Bachelet B., Mahey P., Rodrigues R.F., Soares L.F.G.: Elastic Time Computation for Hypermedia Documents. VI Brazilian Symposium on Multimedia and Hypermedia Systems - SBMídia'2000, Natal, Brazil, (2000) 47-62
2. Boll S., Klas W., Wandel J.: A Cross-Media Adaptation Strategy for Multimedia Presentation. ACM Multimedia, Orlando, USA, (1999)
3. Bouvin N.O., Schade R.: Integrating Temporal Media and Open Hypermedia on the World Wide Web. Eighth Int. World Wide Web Conference, (1999) 375-387
4. Bregler C., Covell M., Slaney M.: Video Rewrite: Driving visual speech with audio. SIGGRAPH'97, Los Angeles, USA, (1997)
5. Dutoit T. et al.: A Short Introduction to Text-to-Speech Synthesis. Technical Report, TTS Research Team, TCTS Lab, Faculté Polytechnique de Mons, Belgium, (1997)
6. Ezzat T., Poggio T.: Visual Speech Synthesis by Morphing Visemes. Technical Report 1658, Center for Biological & Computational Learning and the Artificial Intelligence Lab, Massachusetts Institute of Technology, USA, (1999)
7. Gachery S. Magnenat-Thalmann N.: Designing MPEG-4 Facial Animation Tables for Web Applications. Multimedia Modeling Conference, Amsterdam, Netherlands, (2001)
8. Gamma E. et al.: Design Patterns: Elements of Reusable Object-Oriented Software. Addison Wesley, (1995)
9. Kim M., Song J.: Multimedia Documents with Elastic Time. ACM International Conference on Multimedia, San Francisco, USA, (1995)
10. Klas W., Greiner C., Friedl R.: Cardio-OP – Gallery of Cardiac Surgery. IEEE International Conference on Multimedia Computing and Systems, Florence, Italy, 1999.
11. Layaïda N., Sabry-Ismail L., Roisin, C.: Dealing with uncertain durations in synchronized multimedia presentations. MM Tools and Applications Journal, 18(3), (2002) 213-231
12. Lucena P.S. "Expressive Talking Heads: uma Ferramenta com Fala e Expressão Facial Sincronizadas para o Desenvolvimento de Aplicações Interativas". *Master Dissertation*, Dep. Informática, PUC-Rio, Rio de Janeiro, Brazil, (2002). (*in portuguese*)
13. Muchaluat-Saade D.C, Silva H.V.O., Rodrigues R.F., Soares L.F.G.. "NCL 2.0: Exploiting and Integrating New Concepts to Hypermedia Declarative Languages". Technical Report, Lab. TeleMídia, PUC-Rio, Rio de Janeiro, Brazil, (2004). Available in ftp://ftp.telemidia.puc-rio.br/pub/docs/techreports/2004_02_muchaluat.pdf
14. Perlin K.: Responsive Face, Media Research Lab, New York University, USA, (1997), Available in http://mrl.nyu.edu/~perlin/ demox/Face.html.
15. Rodrigues R.F., Rodrigues L.M., Soares L.F.G.: A Framework for Event-Driven Hypermedia Presentation Systems, Multimedia Modeling Conference - MMM'2001, Amsterdam, Netherlands, (2001) 169-185.
16. Rodrigues R.F., Soares L.F.G.: Inter and Intra Media-Object QoS Provisioning in Adaptive Formatters, ACM Symposium on Document Engineering, Grenoble, (2003)
17. Watt A., Taylor P., Caley R.: The Festival Speech Synthesis System: System Documentation. Technical Report, University of Edinburgh, Scotland, (1999).
18. World-Wide Web Consortium.: Synchronized Multimedia Integration Language (SMIL 2.0) Specification. W3C Recommendation, (2001).

Assessing Cognitive Load
in Adaptive Hypermedia Systems:
Physiological and Behavioral Methods*

Holger Schultheis[1] and Anthony Jameson[2]

[1] Dept. of Computer Science, Saarland University, 66123 Saarbrücken, Germany
schulth@studcs.uni-sb.de
[2] DFKI, Stuhlsatzenhausweg 3, 66123 Saarbrücken, Germany
jameson@dfki.de

Abstract. It could be advantageous in many situations for an adaptive hypermedia system to have information about the cognitive load that the user is currently
experiencing. A literature review of the methods proposed to assess cognitive
load reveals: (1) that pupil size seems to be one of the most promising indicators of cognitive load in applied contexts and (2) that its suitability for use as an
on-line index in everyday situations has not yet been tested adequately. Therefore, the aim of the present study was to evaluate the usefulness of the pupil size
index in such situations. To this end, pupil diameter and event-related brain potentials were measured while subjects read texts of different levels of difficulty.
As had been hypothesized, more difficult texts led to lower reading speed, higher
subjective load ratings, and a reduced P300 amplitude. But text difficulty, surpris-
ingly, had no effect on pupil size. These results indicate that pupil size may not be
suitable as an index of cognitive load for adaptive hypermedia systems. Instead,
behavioral indicators such as reading speed may be more suitable.

1 Introduction

1.1 Assessing Cognitive Load for Adaptive Hypermedia Systems

There are many situations in which it would be useful for an adaptive hypermedia system to be able to assess the current cognitive load of the user. For example, suppose that
the system notices that the current user is experiencing high cognitive load while reading a particular page. The system might then (a) insert more explanations and examples,
(b) select as subsequent pages some pages that are inherently easier to read, or (c) eliminate unnecessary distractions (e. g., background music). Similarly, if the user's current
cognitive load is lower than an optimal level, the system might increase its density of
information presentation.

In some cases, prediction of cognitive load may be possible on basis of the page's
intrinsic difficulty and the user's level of knowledgeability with respect to the subject
matter; this type of estimation is commonly made in intelligent tutoring systems. But

---

* We thank Boris Brandherm for many fruitful discussions and the research group of Axel Meck-
linger for invaluable support in the EEG part of the study.

W. Nejdl and P. De Bra (Eds.): AH 2004, LNCS 3137, pp. 225–234, 2004.

since such predictions cannot be entirely precise and reliable, it might be useful to have a more direct way of assessing cognitive load. In particular, it is desirable to obtain load estimates which are fairly time-specific, so that the system can adapt quickly to a change in the users state.

But assessing the cognitive load of a given user is, unfortunately, in itself a difficult task. As a result, a range of different load assessment techniques has been proposed (see e. g., [1, 2]) over the years. The overall aim of the work presented here was to find the assessment method that seems best suited for building a user-adaptive system that utilizes information about the cognitive load of the user on-line while the user is reading text presented on a computer screen. In the rest of this section, the most important classes of assessment methods are discussed briefly with regard to their appropriateness as on-line measures of cognitive load. The remainder of the paper reports on and discusses an experiment in which an especially promising technique – measurement of pupil diameter – was evaluated.

1.2   Measures of Cognitive Load

Although there exist many methods for the assessment of cognitive load, each method can be assigned to one of four classes: 1. analytic measures, 2. subjective measures, 3. performance measures, and 4. psychophysiological measures.

1. As has already been mentioned, load estimation can be based on general (i. e. not interaction-specific) information about the system and the user(s). For example, information about the intrinsic difficulty of a hypertext page and about the expertise of the user working on this page can form a basis for the prediction of the user's load. But as this technique, which relies heavily on prior knowledge, does not take into account information about the current interaction, unforeseeable situations and individual peculiarities may lead to suboptimal system behavior.

2. Subjective measures involve questions which ask the user to rate the cognitive load that she has experienced or is experiencing. For example, a scale for a self-report of cognitive load could appear on each page of the hypertext system. But subjective reports are distorted by memory and consciousness effects. Moreover, administering the scale(s) after a certain page has been read would not enable the system to react to the user's needs while she is still reading that page. Asking the user for a report during the reading of a page, on the other hand, could be distracting.

3. With the third group of methods, the user's cognitive load is inferred from her overt behavior, or *performance*. A piece of evidence of this type might be, for instance, the speed with which the user reads the hypertext: This technique may not reflect all of the variations in cognitive load, and it is appropriate only if the activity yields a sufficiently high rate of observable behavior. These disadvantages can be avoided through the introduction of a *secondary task*. For example, the reader of the hypertext might be given the task of attending to a flashing light and pushing a button when a certain pattern of flashes occurs. Poor performance on the secondary task, for example, indicates that the primary task of reading induces high cognitive load. Although this approach in part avoids the disadvantages just mentioned, introducing a secondary task may itself be problematic, because it may disturb the user's main activity.

4. Finally, changes in various bodily processes and states are observed to covary with changes in cognitive load. Therefore, monitoring of these body functions sometimes allows load to be inferred. A major advantage of psychophysiological measures is the continuous availability of bodily data, which potentially allows load to be measured with a high rate and high degree of sensitivity. What is more, without the introduction of an extra task, information about cognitive load is available even in situations in which overt behavior is relatively rare. Consequently, compared with the other classes, psychophysiological methods seem to be especially promising for on-line assessment in adaptive hypermedia systems.

Unfortunately, with many of the existing psychophysiological measures on-line assessment in an applied context is not currently feasible. Most of them require electrodes to be attached to the body (e. g., electroencephalogram, electrocardiogram, muscle tension) or the use of equipment that entirely rules out deployment in everyday situations (e. g., functional Magnetic Resonance Imaging, Positron Emission Tomography, magnetoencephalogram). Others, again, seem to be too indirectly linked to cognitive load (e. g., blink rate, blink duration) or to be too slow for on-line measurement (e. g., hormone level). In contrast, the measurement of the varying size of a person's pupil has none of these disadvantages. Not only is it regarded as "one of the most sensitive workload measures available" [3], but it is also assumed to respond to changes in load within several hundred milliseconds [4, 5]. Moreover, it is not necessary to attach any electrodes or other equipment to the user: The measurement can be accomplished with a remote eye tracker, which can be placed near the computer monitor. In sum, in addition to the advantages typical of all psychophysiological indicators, the measurement of pupil size has a combination of properties that seem uniquely well suited for the assessment of cognitive load during the use of adaptive hypermedia systems.

Over the last 40 years, a lot of studies have demonstrated the sensitivity of a person's pupil size to their cognitive load in a wide variety of tasks (see, e. g., [4] for a review): The higher the load, the bigger the pupil. In general, in these experiments at least two tasks of different difficulty were employed; subjects had to perform the tasks while their pupil diameter was recorded. The actual tasks used in these studies include, to name only a few: memorizing 3 vs. 7 digits [4]; shadowing words vs. translating them [6]; reading syntactically simple vs. complex sentences [7]; and telling the truth vs. lying [8]. These studies consistently reported larger pupil diameters during more difficult tasks.

But since pupil size is also especially sensitive to a number of influences not related to cognitive load (e. g., ambient light), previous works utilizing pupil size as a cognitive load indicator all used at least three of the following five means to control those influences: (a) constant lighting; (b) avoidance of eye movements; (c) use of nonvisual (e. g., acoustic) stimuli; (d) use of many similar, short tasks; and (e) evaluating only mean values averaged across tasks and subjects.

Such strict control of the environment is not realistic in connection with an adaptive hypermedia system; and averaging over tasks and subjects is not suitable for diagnosing the current load of a single person. Thus, to be truly useful in the situations of interest to us, pupil size should be a good indicator even if some or all of the above constraints are relaxed. To find out whether this result can be obtained, we designed and conducted a new experiment, which is discussed in the rest of this paper.

1.3   Measures Used in the Experiment

The aim of the experiment was to evaluate the utility of pupil size as an on-line measure of cognitive load for an adaptive hypermedia system, not actually to employ it in such an environment. As a result, we drew on additional techniques – some of which are not appropriate for applied contexts (see 1.2) – to provide information about the load. More precisely, behavioral, subjective and ERP measures were used. Whereas the first two methods are fairly straightforward, the third one may require some explanation, which will be given in the following paragraphs.

Processing of stimuli is accompanied by changes in brain activity, that is, activation or inhibition of certain neuronal ensembles. This neural activity is mainly electric, and it therefore generates electrical fields. These fields extend to regions outside the skull and can be recorded around the head. In particular, certain environmental events (e. g., a sound or a flash of light) give rise to characteristic and consistent variations in the electrical field around the head. These variations recorded from the scalp via electrodes are termed *event-related brain potentials* (*ERPs*). With regard to cognitive load measurement, one particular ERP, the P300, is of special interest. In general, this potential is elicited when a low-probability task-relevant stimulus is encountered (i. e., a stimulus to which the subject is attending). Moreover, it has been shown (see, e. g., [9]) that the more attention (mental effort) is devoted to the task associated with the evoking stimulus, the higher is the P300 amplitude.

The most common procedure up to now for utilizing this property of the P300 in load assessment has been to introduce a secondary task containing stimuli that elicit the P300. The magnitude of the evoked P300 gives information about the cognitive load in the main task: The larger the amplitude, the smaller the load. But with this method the subject is required to perform a secondary task, which may cause the same problems as those associated with the secondary task measure (1.2). To circumvent these disadvantages, we applied a different, relatively new technique that relies on the *Novelty-P300* [10]. This special subtype of the P300 is elicited by highly unexpected, previously unexperienced (i. e., novel) stimuli even if these stimuli are not attended to. As a result, the evoking stimuli do not have to be embedded in a secondary task. Instead, the Novelty-P300 can be elicited by a sequence of stimuli which are (a) presented simultaneously with the task of the user but (b) not relevant to that task. Regarding cognitive load, the Novelty-P300 has the same properties as the original P300: As [11] have shown, the Novelty-P300 is smaller for higher load. As in the approach described in [11], in our experiment P300s were elicited by sequences of sounds (cf. Sect. 2).

2   Method

Material. As material to be read at the computer by each subject, we prepared 8 texts – 4 easy and 4 difficult – of approximately equal lengths. (Easy and difficult texts averaged 342 and 339 words, respectively, in length.) Difficulty was determined through subjective assessment and confirmed objectively in terms of the sources of the texts: Easy texts were taken from schoolbooks for the fifth grade and from children's books, while difficult texts were taken from schoolbooks for the 12th grade and from philosophical treatises. Text sequence was pseudopermuted via the Latin squares approach.

Given the fixed scheme ABBABAAB, where A and B denote difficulty classes, and a fixed order of texts within each class, different sequences were constructed via rotation of the texts of each class through the indicated positions.

Participants. Thirteen subjects, 8 female and 5 male, took part in the experiment. Their ages ranged from 20 to 41 years, with a mean age of 25.5 years. All were native speakers of German. They received either course credit or a monetary reward for their participation. In particular, to motivate careful reading, we paid subjects an extra reward of € 0.20 for each content question (see below) that they answered correctly.

Procedure. Subjects were seated facing a computer screen located at a distance of approximately 50 cm. For control of illumination, no external light was allowed to enter the room. The task of the participants was to read on the computer screen the texts described above. Presentation of each text comprised five phases: First, to produce a baseline value for pupil diameter, subjects were asked to fixate for 20 s a circle in the middle of a screen of Xs that had been arranged like the letters in normal text. Then, a real text was shown. Participants read the text at their own pace until they felt that they had understood it[1]. Then, four 7-alternative multiple-choice questions about the content of the text were to be answered. Finally, subjective ratings of text difficulty and the subject's own willingness to be interrupted were elicited as subjective load indicators.

Pupil size and point of gaze were measured throughout the whole experiment. In contrast, ERPs could be recorded only in the presence of eliciting tones, which were presented only during the actual reading of the texts. Besides, reading speed and number of correct responses were computed as behavioral measures of cognitive load.

Technology. Pupil diameter and point of gaze were recorded at 50 Hz with an ASL 504 remote eye tracking system that used pan/tilt optics.

In addition to vertical and horizontal electrooculograms, EEG was registered from 62 electrodes at a sampling rate of 500 Hz[2].

For checking the luminosity of each text as displayed on the computer screen, a Gossen Lunasix F light meter was employed. Measurements indicated that luminosity was equal for all texts and the baseline screen.

ERPs were elicited by different types of tones played in random sequences to the subjects through speakers positioned to the left and right of the computer screen. Every 550 ms, a *standard*, a *deviant*, or a *novel* tone was presented for 200 ms with probabilities of 0.8, 0.1, and 0.1, respectively. Standard tones were 600 Hz sinus tones, deviant tones were 660 Hz sinus tones and novel tones were unique, nonsinus sounds (e. g., a honking sound) that were expected to evoke the Novelty-P300. With respect to the five means of control mentioned in 1.2, our setup led to the following relaxations: (a) use of visual stimuli (the texts); (b) occurrence of eye movements; and (c) use of relatively few but long tasks.

---

[1] In fact, reading time for each text was limited to 5 minutes, but no subject exceeded this time.

[2] For those interested in the details of this method: The electrodes were arranged according to the 10–10 system. Measurements took place referenced to the left mastoid with the forehead serving as ground and electrode impedance below 10 $k\Omega$. Signals were filtered on-line with a 0–70 Hz bandpass and a 50 Hz notch.

3   Results

Except where otherwise stated, the analyses reported in the following paragraphs are repeated-measures analyses of variance. Where appropriate, statistical significance was determined after correction of the degrees of freedom using Huynh-Feldt epsilon. The level of significance for all reported analyses was set to $\alpha = 0.05$.

Behavioral Data. More difficult reading, as [7] have shown, leads not only to higher load as indexed by the pupil but also to a smaller number of correct responses and slower reading. Accordingly, a lower reading speed and a lower number of correct responses for difficult texts were hypothesized for the current study. With respect to reading speed, this hypothesis was confirmed statistically ($F_{(5,62)} = 30.08$, $p < 0.001$, see Fig. 1a). This was not the case for the number of correct responses. Although in our data the answers to questions about difficult texts were less often correct than answers referring to easy texts (see Fig. 1b), a statistical comparison using the McNemar test revealed no significant difference ($\chi^2 = 2.64$, $p > 0.1$).

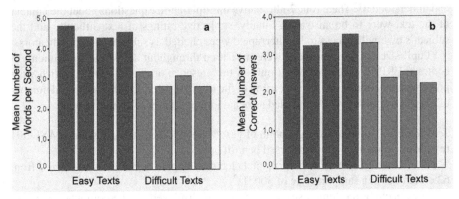

Fig. 1. (a) Mean reading speed in words per second and (b) mean number of correct answers for each of the eight texts.

Subjective Data. The subjective ratings of load consisted of judging on a 4-point scale both the experienced difficulty (1 = "easy" – 4 = "difficult") and how annoying an interruption during reading would have been (1 = "no problem" – 4 = "very annoying"). As expected, difficult texts were judged to be significantly more difficult ($F_{(7,84)} = 42.58$, $p < 0.001$, see Fig. 2a) and lower in terms of interruptibility ($F_{(7,84)} = 27.97$, $p < 0.001$, see Fig. 2b) than easy texts.

ERP Data. Since the Novelty-P300 is assumed to be especially pronounced over the upper forehead and the center of the scalp (see, e. g., [10]), examination was confined to two electrodes at these locations[3]. The first step of the analysis was to visually study the electrooculogram recordings so as to reject or correct trials that showed eye movement

---

[3] To be precise, these electrodes were FCz and Cz according to the 10–10-system.

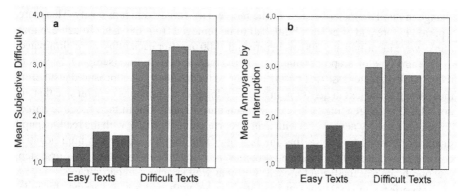

Fig. 2. Part (a): Mean subjective difficulty ratings, ranging from "easy" (= 1) to "difficult" (= 4) for all eight texts. Part (b): Mean annoyance-by-interruption ratings ranging from "no problem" (= 1) to "very annoying" (= 4) for each of the eight texts.

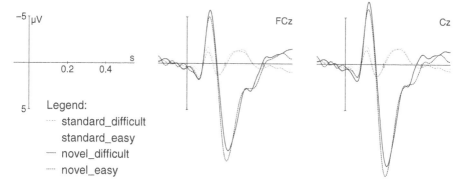

Fig. 3. Grand average ERPs elicited by standard and novel sounds while reading easy and difficult texts.

artifacts or blink artifacts. From the resulting trials, for each subject four average curves (curves evoked by standard and novel sounds while reading easy or difficult texts) were built, which, collapsed over participants, resulted in the grand average waves displayed in Fig. 3. P300 amplitude was then defined as the local maximum of the difference curve – obtained by subtracting easy/difficult standard curves from the corresponding novel curves – in the time from 164 to 274 ms after stimulus onset. In accordance with theory, the P300 amplitude at the two electrodes was significantly larger (one-tailed) during the reading of easy as opposed to difficult texts ($F_{(1,12)} = 3.5$, $p < 0.05$). In other words, the ERP method revealed a higher cognitive load while reading difficult vs. easy texts.

Pupil Data. As with the ERP data, prior to further analyses eye blinks had to be identified in and eliminated from the pupil measurements. With each blink, just before the eye is completely closed the pupil is partly obscured. In addition, eye closure gives rise to a change in pupil diameter because of the momentary variation in luminosity. Therefore, a period before and after each blink had to be removed from the data. To achieve this, blinks were identified and 200 ms before and 1000 ms after each blink were eliminated.

A third type of preprocessing already planned at design time (see Sect. 2) was to relate pupil diameter assessed during reading to the baseline value measured just before the reading of the text in question. In this way, long-term variations in pupil size that are not related to the reading tasks can be taken into account. But in fact, baseline values correlated strongly negatively (with a mean correlation of -0.72) with the reading pupil diameter obtained by subtracting the baseline from the raw data. Such high negative correlations indicate that baseline correction is not justified. Therefore, in a first step, raw pupil data was analyzed for each subject as well as across all participants.

Text effects on single subject level were tested with analyses of variance for independent measurements. Even though difficulty effects were significant for each subject, the difficult texts gave rise to larger pupil diameters for only 6 of them, whereas the opposite relation was observed for the remaining 7 (see Fig. 4 for an example). Accordingly, there were no significant difficulty effects across all subjects ($F_{(3,46)} = 1.14$, $p > 0.3$, see Fig. 5).

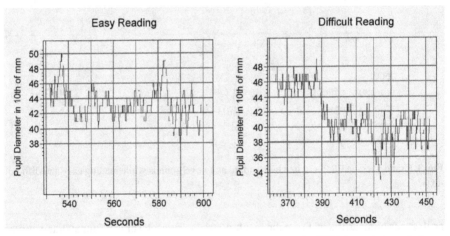

Fig. 4. Pupil diameter for one subject while reading an easy and a difficult text, respectively.

Because the lack of any difference in the pupil diameters was surprising, we conducted a number of additional tests, for example, considering only the first few seconds of the text reading; and correcting pupil diameter measurements to take into account differences in the measurements due to different points of gaze. In all analyses, there was no hint of a consistent difference in pupil diameters between the two conditions.

4   Discussion

Of the four measures of cognitive load used in this study, three – reading speed, subjective load and P300 amplitude – show a clear effect of text difficulty, indicating that

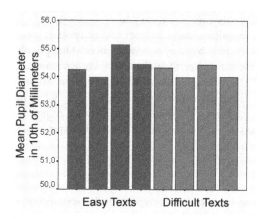

Fig. 5. Mean pupil diameter for all subjects during the reading of easy and difficult texts.

demanding texts indeed induced an increased cognitive load. But this difference in load was not observable in pupil diameter. This result is surprising in that many previous studies (see Sect. 1.2) had consistently reported the sensitivity of the pupil size measure. But they did so in rather strictly controlled settings, and the present study suggests that their results do not generalize to settings that are typical of adaptive hypermedia systems.

This unexpected result has recently been confirmed by independent research: Iqbal et al. [12] examined pupil-size sensitivity to load variations in four different tasks, one of which was a reading task similar to the one employed in this experiment. For two of these tasks (file management on a computer and the reading of texts), no overall pupil size difference between easy and difficult conditions could be found. On the other hand, an analysis of the file management task on the subtask level revealed pupil size differences corresponding to the level of cognitive load in the subtasks. So it seems that pupil size may differ between easy and difficult conditions only in certain periods of a task. Whereas identification of appropriate subtasks was possible for the file management task, it is not obvious how a reasonable decomposition could be achieved for reading. Moreover, such a decomposition would most likely be dependent on the particular text. Consequently, our results and those of Iqbal et al. [12] indicate that pupil-size – although it may be sensitive to load in general – is not a suitable measure of load for tasks that involve continuous reading.

Although this result is a negative result, we believe that it is worth drawing attention to. There have been many reports of relationships between pupil diameter and cognitive load; and more generally, there has been a lot of optimism about the prospects of using physiological methods for the assessment of computer users' cognitive or affective states. If only positive results along these lines are published, a seriously distorted impression of the potential of these methods is likely to arise. Our study illustrates that the utility of physiological assessment methods can depend strongly on the nature of the task and the situation of use.

For the type of setting considered here, using behavioral indicators instead of physiological measures may be more appropriate. As was mentioned above, (Sect. 3) reading speed was considerably higher for easy texts. Consequently, reading speed might be used to assess the cognitive load of a user currently studying a hypertext page. Of course, one has to find a suitable way to assess speed. One possibility is to utilize the eye tracker to record the time taken to read a text of known length. The advantage of this approach would be that – as long as the user is reading – an up-to-date estimate of load is available. This particular approach can be realized only when information about the placement of text on the screen is available. But in other situations, it may be possible to assess reading speed on the basis of actions like button presses and mouse clicks.

References

1. Wilson, G.F., Eggemeier, F.T.: Psychophysiological assessment of workload in multi-task environments. In Damos, D.L., ed.: Multiple-Task Performance. Taylor and Francis, London (1991) 329–360
2. Tsang, P., Wilson, G.F.: Mental workload. In Salvendy, G., ed.: Handbook of Human Factors and Ergonomics. Wiley, New York (1997) 417–449
3. O'Donnell, R.D., Eggemeier, F.T.: Workload assessment methodology. In Boff, K., Kauffmann, L., Thomas, J., eds.: Handbook of Perception and Human Performance. Wiley, New York (1986) 42–1–42–49
4. Beatty, J.: Task-evoked pupillary responses, processing load, and the structure of processing resources. Psychological Bulletin **91** (1982) 276–292
5. Kramer, A.F.: Physiological metrics of mental workload: A review of recent progress. In Damos, D.L., ed.: Multiple-Task Performance. Taylor and Francis, London (1991) 279–327
6. Hyönä, J., Tommola, J., Alaja, A.M.: Pupil dilation as a measure of processing load in simulaneous interprtation and other language tasks. The Quarterly Journal of Experimental Psychology **48A** (1995) 598–612
7. Just, M.A., Carpenter, P.A.: The intensity dimension of thought: Pupillometric indices of sentence processing. Canadian Journal of Experimental Psychology **47(2)** (1993) 310–339
8. Dionisio, D.P., Granholm, E., Hillix, W.A., Perrine, W.F.: Differentiation of deception using pupillary responses as an index of cognitive processing. Psychophysiology **38** (2001) 205–211
9. Sirevaag, E.J., Kramer, A.F., Coles, M.G., Donchin, E.: Resource reciprocity: An event-related brain potential analysis. Acta Psychologica **70** (1989) 77–97
10. Friedman, D., Cycowicz, Y.M., Gaeta, H.: The novelty P3: An event-related brain potential (ERP) sign of the brain's evaluation of novelty. Neuroscience and Biobehavioral Reviews **25(4)** (2001) 355–373
11. Ullsperger, P., Freude, G., Erdmann, U.: Auditory probe sensitivity to mental workload changes - an event-related potential study. International Journal of Psychophysiology **40** (2001) 201–209
12. Iqbal, S.T., Zheng, X.S., Bailey, B.P.: Task-evoked pupillary response to mental workload in human-computer interaction. In: Proceedings of the ACM Conference on Human Factors in Computing Systems, Vienna, Austria (2004) 1477–1480

Context-Aware Recommendations in the Mobile Tourist Application COMPASS

Mark van Setten, Stanislav Pokraev, and Johan Koolwaaij

Telematica Instituut, P.O. Box 589, 7500 AN, Enschede, The Netherlands
{Mark.vanSetten,Stanislav.Pokraev,Johan.Koolwaaij}@telin.nl

Abstract. This paper describes the context-aware mobile tourist application COMPASS that adapts its services to the user's needs based on both the user's interests and his current context. In order to provide context-aware recommendations, a recommender system has been integrated with a context-aware application platform. We describe how this integration has been accomplished and how users feel about such an adaptive tourist application.

1 Introduction

With several mobile technologies like mobile data networks (GPRS and UMTS), positioning systems (GPS), mobile phones and personal digital assistants (PDAs) getting more mature, it becomes possible to offer online services to people whenever and wherever they are. Such online services are especially useful for people in places they have never been to before. Apart from business travellers and truck drivers, a large group of such people consists of tourists. Often, tourists do not know their way, nor which restaurants, museums, shops, public services, etcetera are available to them. The number of potential places to visit can be quite overwhelming, especially in touristic regions. Adaptive systems can help a tourist to find places matching his interests and his current situation.

In this paper, we consider two such adaptive systems: recommender systems and context-aware systems. We describe their integration in a mobile tourist application and how users feel about adaptive systems providing context-aware recommendations. We start by introducing context-awareness and recommender systems and how these two types of adaptive systems enhance each other (Sect. 2). This is followed by an overview of our mobile tourist application COMPASS (Sect. 3). Sect. 4 describes the architecture of COMPASS and the underlying platform focussing on the integration of the recommender system and context-awareness system. Sect. 5 discusses the results of a survey on the usefulness of this combination according to possible users. Sect. 6 ends this paper with conclusions on context-aware recommendations.

2 Context-Aware Recommendations

Context is any information that can be used to characterize the situation of any person, place or object that is considered relevant to the interaction between a user and an application, including the user and application themselves [4]. Examples of contex-

W. Nejdl and P. De Bra (Eds.): AH 2004, LNCS 3137, pp. 235–244, 2004.

tual information are location, time, proximity, user status and network capabilities. A general definition of context-aware systems is given in [4]: "A system is context-aware if it uses context to provide relevant information and/or services to the user, where relevancy depends on the user's task."

The key goal of context-aware systems is to *provide a user with relevant information and/or services based on his current context*. This goal matches with the goal of recommender systems. Resnick and Varian [10] define recommender systems as systems that use opinions of a community of users to help individuals in that community more effectively identify content of interest from a potentially overwhelming set of choices. However, recommender systems do not only have to incorporate the opinions of other users, but may also use other methods, such as content-based reasoning. For this reason, we define recommender systems as systems capable of helping people to *quickly and easily find their way through large amounts of information by determining what is of interest to a user* [14]. Both context-aware systems and recommender systems are used *to provide users with relevant information and/or services*; the first based on the user's context; the second based on the user's interests. Therefore, the next logical step is to combine these two systems.

Context and interests can be used as hard or soft criteria in the selection of relevant services. Hard criteria limit the set of available services; those services that do not match a hard criterion are discarded from the set. Soft criteria are used to order the set of selected services or to present a relevance score to the user for each selected service. For example, location, by far the most exploited context factor, can be used to select only the services within a certain distance from the user (hard criterion); location can also be used to decrease the predicted relevance of a service the further away that service is located from the user (soft criterion). In recommender systems, the interests of a user are mostly used as soft criteria where the predicted level of interest is presented as a score, using for example a number of stars. However, interests can also be used as hard criteria by only selecting services that match the users' interests. In our application COMPASS, location is used as a hard criterion to select relevant services that are close to the user; the predicted interest of the user is used as a soft criterion, just like some other contextual factors (see Sect. 4.4).

3   The COMPASS Application

COMPASS is an acronym for COntext-aware Mobile Personal ASSistant and is an application that serves a tourist with information and services (ranging from buildings to buddies) needed in his specific context that are interesting to him given his goal for that moment. For example, a tourist expressing an interest in history and architecture is served with information about nearby monuments built before 1890. A tourist expressing the wish to find a place for the night gets a list of hotels and campsites in and around town that match his preferences for accommodations.

After start-up, COMPASS shows the user a map of his current location. The location is either obtained from the mobile network or from other devices such as GPS receivers. Depending on the user's profile and goal, a selection of nearby buildings, buddies and other objects is shown on the map and in a list. The map and the objects shown are updated when the user moves or his profile or goal changes. Other context changes might also force the map to change. For example, an increase in the user's speed by starting to drive in a car causes the map to zoom out automatically as the user's notion of nearness can be defined by what he can reach in a certain amount of time. Clicking on objects on the map usually means interacting with services provided by that object (see middle image of Fig. 1), e.g. calling a buddy, reserving a table at a restaurant, or booking tickets for a show.

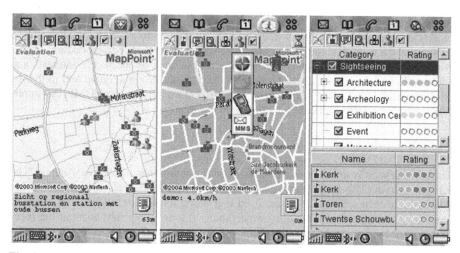

Fig. 1. Screenshots of the COMPASS application: objects near the user on the map, interacting with services offered by objects and a list of objects near the user with relevance scores.

The application is built upon the WASP platform (see Sect. 4.2) that provides generic supporting services such as a context manager and service registry. The platform and system are based on web services technology combined with semantic web technology. Web services are believed to help the integration of diverse applications while the semantic web promises to increase the "intelligence" of the web, enabling richer discovery, information integration, navigation and automation of tasks. However, the current web services technologies, based on WSDL and UDDI, do not provide a means for building semantic context-aware services. Therefore we extended existing web service standards with additional semantics to enable more intelligent, semantic retrieval of services while taking into account the contextual information associated with the user's request.

The platform is open, which means that third parties can easily integrate their information and services with the platform; these services can then transparently be found and used by the population of COMPASS users. For example, an organization that owns a collection of digitized old postcards wrapped its database with postcards as an internet-accessible web service, published the web service in the public service registry of the platform and related the web service's interface to the registry's ontology. The net effect is that all COMPASS users with an interest in such postcards are now able to view postcards depicting objects near their location instantaneously. Depending on the visualisation, they see a map of their environment with icons indicating the location depicted on the old postcards (see the left image in Fig. 1) or a thumbnail list of the postcards. Clicking on an icon displays the postcard, the date of the picture and a short description. This way, it is quite easy to recall the atmosphere of early times while walking through a street or neighbourhood.

The COMPASS application accomplishes this functionality by querying the service registry for search services that are bound to deliver objects related to the user's context. The underlying platform retrieves services matching the hard criteria of the user's context and goal. For example, for someone located in Enschede and looking for sightseeing attractions it delivers search services for museums, landmarks, architectural buildings, etc. Next, the relevant search services are queried to retrieve the objects matching the context's hard criteria, e.g. to be within a certain radius from the location of the user. The retrieved objects are then sent to the recommendation engine which scores each object based on the soft criteria, such as the user's interests and context. The retrieved objects and scores are then displayed on the map and in the list of objects (see Fig. 1). The openness of the platform underlying the COMPASS application makes it easily applicable in other domains as well.

3.1 Related Work

There are related research projects in the tourist domain using adaptive systems. The Intrigue system [2] is an interactive agenda offered by a tourist information server that assists the user in creating a personalised tour along tourist attractions. This research focuses on planning and scheduling a personalised tour taking into account the location of each tourist attraction and the interests' of the user. Console et al. [3] created a prototype system called MastroCARonte, which provides personalised services that adapt to the user and his context onboard cars. This research focuses on the effects of having such adaptive systems onboard cars.

The research focus of the COMPASS system is on the open platform, which allows easy creation of context-aware personalised applications and the services that are part of such a platform, including a service registry, a context manager and a recommendation engine. The next section discusses this open platform with a focus on the context manager and recommendation engine.

4 System Architecture

In the discussion of the architecture of the WASP platform underlying COMPASS and the architecture of the COMPASS application itself, we focus on the retrieval of services taking into account context and user's interests, as the topic of this paper the integration of context-awareness and recommendations. The overall architecture of the WASP platform and the COMPASS application is shown in Fig. 2.

Four main groups can be identified in the architecture: third party services, the WASP platform, the COMPASS application and the recommendation service.

4.1 Third Party Services

The *3G (GPRS, UMTS) network services* provide network access capabilities, such as user identification, call setup, messaging, charging, etc. These network capabilities are accessible via web services interfaces and offered by mobile network operators.

The *context services* provide information about the context of a user, e.g. the user status (free or busy), his location, etc. Some of this information is obtained from the 3G network via web services. This group includes both services that provide information about the user such as his shopping list or his schedule, as well as services that are independent from the user but which might be relevant when selecting services, e.g. weather or traffic information services.

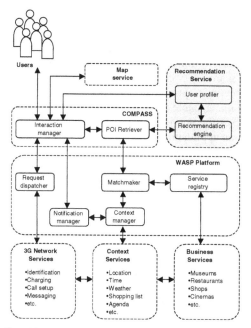

Fig. 2. The overall architecture of the WASP platform and the COMPASS application.

Business services are those services that offer information and services for an application build on the platform. In the COMPASS application these are businesses that offer so-called points of interest (POI): museums and their catalogues, monumental buildings and historical information associated with them, restaurants and their menus, shops and their current promotions, hotels with reservation services, digitized old postcards, etc.

4.2 WASP Platform Components

The *Request dispatcher* is a component responsible for forwarding user requests to the appropriate 3G-network platform. This way, users can switch transparently to different network operators or, for instance, use different messaging services.

The *Notification manager* provides functionality for applications to subscribe and receive notifications when the context of a particular user changes. For instance, when a user moves around in a city, his location changes. The notification manager notifies the application about this change and provides the new location of the user. The application can then adapt itself to this change in the user's location.

The *Context manager* retrieves information about the user's context by contacting the appropriate context services (see Sect. 4.1). It is also responsible for aggregating the context or deriving new context based on domain specific rules. For instance, the context manager can infer whether a user walks or drives given the speed of the user and the geographical properties of his location (city street, highway, sea or river, etc) or simply from the fact that his phone is attached to a car kit. The context manager is also responsible to update the notification manager on changes in the context.

The *Service registry* contains information about the services provided by third parties. To improve the semantic of service descriptions we use semantic web technology, notably OWL [8], to create additional annotations of service elements. This way, the platform enables service providers to formally describe their services in detail and to bring those service descriptions in correspondence with existing ontologies. On the other hand, it enables search services to perform a subtle search, by using constraints, relations between concepts, approximate matches and semantically rich queries [9], which delivers a more manageable result set.

The *Matchmaker* uses the service registry to discover the services that match the request received from an application (in this case the POI retriever of COMPASS, see Sect. 4.3). Once services are discovered, based on their types, capabilities and models, the matchmaker component filters out the services that do not match the hard criteria set by the application. To perform this action, the component uses the context ontology and domain-specific rules provided by the application.

4.3 The COMPASS Application

The *Interaction manager* is a server side component responsible for finding the most appropriate way to communicate a user's request and assist the interaction of the user and the client side application (on the mobile phone, PDA or other device). For example, if a user clicks on a POI representing a restaurant, the interaction manager can, for example, automatically retrieve the restaurant's menu and present it to the user or prompt to setup a phone call in order for the user to make a reservation.

The *POI retriever* receives a request from the interaction manager when the user context changes or from an action by the user. It creates a search request that is sent to the matchmaker component. After the matchmaker component returns the list of POIs matching the issued request and hard criteria of the user context, the POI retriever sends this list together with the user's identity and the context information to the recommendation service, which assigned scores to each POI indicating the predicted relevance of the POI for the user (see Sect. 4.4). The POI retriever than sends the list of POIs with scores to the client side application, which displays the POIs.

The COMPASS application also uses external *map service*, such as Microsoft Mappoint [7] for regular maps, a map service providing aerial photographs and a map service providing old cadastral maps. These web services are used to offer dynamic and interactive maps, providing navigation support, etc. COMPASS allows the user to switch between the various types of available maps, while keeping all other functionality, such as displaying POIs on the map and services associated with POIs.

4.4 The Recommendation Service

The *recommendation engine* uses multiple prediction strategies to predict how interesting each POI is for the user. A prediction strategy selects and/or combines multiple prediction techniques by deciding which prediction techniques are the most suitable to provide a prediction based on the most up-to-date knowledge about the current user, other users, the information for which a prediction is requested, other information items and the system itself [14]. Used prediction methods include social filtering [12], case-based reasoning (CBR) [11], item-item filtering [5] and category learning [13]. For different classes of POIs, different prediction strategies can be defined in the engine. As the semantics of POIs are described by an ontology, the recommendation engine is aware of the class hierarchy of each POI. For example, a Chinese restaurant is an Asian restaurant, which is a restaurant, which is a place to eat or drink, which is a POI. This means that the engine can select a prediction strategy appropriate for each class of POI. If a prediction strategy exists for the actual class of a POI that strategy is chosen, otherwise the engine moves up the class hierarchy until it finds a parent class that has a prediction strategy associated with it. In our hierarchy, POI is the root class, which has a default prediction strategy assigned to it.

For COMPASS, prediction techniques have also been developed that base their predictions on contextual factors; e.g. one technique predicts the relevance based on the time past since the last time the user visited a POI of that class. The more recent the user has been in such a POI, the lower the predicted relevance. This technique has been used in prediction strategies for POIs such as restaurants and museums. The time passed between the last visit and the current time is used as a sort of "linear decay time" for the predicted relevance. This is based on the idea of "Yesterday, I ate in a Greek restaurant, so today I will probably want to eat somewhere else." The rate in which the predicted interest returns to its full strength differs per user per type of POI.

The *user profiler* maintains the profiles of all users. It is used by the recommendation engine to retrieve and store knowledge about users, such as the interests of users and ratings provided by users. The interaction manager can also directly access the profile manager; this way, the interaction manager can also store user preferences or it can retrieve (parts of) the user profile and present it to the user.

The recommendation service is not part of the WASP platform as some prediction techniques are domain dependent or need to be tuned to specific domains, e.g. a similarity function had to be defined for the CBR-based prediction technique that compares two POIs with each other and returns a similarity score. However, the recommendation service is also not part of the COMPASS application; this allows other applications in the tourist domain to use the same recommendation service. However, the WASP platform contains the generic parts of the recommendation service: prediction techniques for which only the domain specific parts still have to be implemented and a mechanism for defining prediction strategies that combine the various prediction techniques. Each instance of a recommendation service now only needs to implement the domain specific parts, such as the similarity function for case-based reasoning, define the prediction strategies and associate these strategies to the different object classes for which predictions need to be generated.

5   User Experience

So far, this paper has shown the possibilities of the combination of context-awareness and recommender systems and a way to integrate the two. However, it did not address another important question: how useful do users perceive context-aware recommendations? We investigated the usefulness of context-aware recommendations by performing a survey amongst 57 people consisting of 23 females and 34 males. The participants ranged in age from 10 till 70 and had a wide variety of backgrounds and professions.

The survey was an unsupervised online survey. Participants were taken through the usage of context-aware recommendations in COMPASS. They were lead via a scenario and screenshots through the various aspects of recommendations: searching for a type of POI, seeing a list of found POIs near the user's location with relevance scores, providing feedback on the recommendations, seeing the effects of providing feedback, seeing the effects on the recommendations of trying to visit similar POIs after a few days, etc. The survey asked participants both about the perceived usefulness of the context-aware recommendations (quantitatively) and why they felt that it was useful or not (qualitatively). A survey was chosen over real usage in order to provide each user with the same adapted system; large variations in context could have influenced the opinions of users too much for results to be comparable.

To avoid biasing the results with generic interests of participants in certain POIs, we focused the survey on restaurants. We assumed that everybody visits a restaurant every now and then and that most people do not have a positive of negative interest towards restaurants in general; museums for example could have biased the results, as some people do not like to visit museums at all.

Two context factors were included in the survey, namely location and time. Location was implemented by showing only restaurants in the centre of the city in which the users was supposed to be. Hence location was used as a hard criterion. However, time was used as a soft criterion and combined with the predicted interests; time was used to determine the last time the user visited a restaurant of the same type and by temporarily decreasing the predictions based on this time period.

Table 1 shows the quantitative results of the perceived usefulness in using predictions and the added context-aware factor 'last time visited' in the COMPASS application.

Table 1. Usefulness of context-aware recommendations

| | Not useful at all | | | | Very useful | | |
	-2	-1	0	1	2	Average	St. Dev.
Predictions	8.8%	8.8%	19.3%	35.1%	28.1%	0.65	1.232
Time Decay	24.6%	19.3%	14%	31.6%	10.5%	-0.16	1.386

The results show that most people believe that using predictions based on the user's interests is useful. For about half of the participants (50.9%), the addition of 'last time visited' had a negative influence on the perceived usefulness; the difference between the perceived usefulness of only predictions and the perceived usefulness of predictions combined with 'last time visited' was negative (for 36.8% the perceived usefulness stayed the same, and for 12.3% perceived usefulness increased).

We believe there are two possible reasons for the decrease in perceived usefulness. The first is that 'last time visited' is not a good additional context factor; combining other context factors with the predicted interests may increase or not influence the perceived usefulness, such as average costs of eating in the restaurant. However, a lot of the comments made by participants indicated another reason: they were about "the application becomes too intelligent", "I can think and decide for myself" and "it makes the application too complex". This indicates that some people do not like an application like COMPASS to take too many contextual factors into account in recommendations; they want to be able to decide for themselves which factors are important when selecting a POI. This desire for being in control by users is similar to the findings of Alpert et al. [1] in adaptive e-commerce systems.

6 Conclusions

In this paper, we discussed the combination of context-awareness and recommender systems and how this has been applied in the mobile tourist application COMPASS. We discussed how the two fit together and how they have been integrated in the architecture of our platform and application. A user survey indicated how useful people perceive an adaptive tourist service that recommenders points of interests by taking into account the user's interests and contextual factors such as last time visited.

Context-awareness and recommender systems can enhance and complement each other; they both help users in finding relevant and interesting objects, ranging from information and services to points of interests, based on their interests and current context. However, one has to be careful with such adaptive services. Although most people like and see the benefits of recommendations and context-awareness, there are people who may object when systems start to include too many factors in their predictions; they prefer to be able to think and decide for themselves, instead of having systems thinking and deciding for them. A simple solution may be to allow users to specify themselves what type of knowledge about the user or contextual information should be taken into account in recommendations, make the adaptation more scrutable [6]; e.g. "do recommend items based on my interests, location and prices, but do not include last time visited."

Acknowledgements

This research is part of the Freeband project WASP (http://www.freeband.nl), the PhD project Duine (http://duine.telin.nl) and the PhD project Seine at the Telematica Instituut (http://www.telin.nl). The authors like to thank the participants of the survey and Mettina Veenstra, Rogier Brussee and Tom Broens for their helpful comments.

References

1. Alpert, S.R., Karat, J., Karat, C.M., Brodie, C., Vergo, J.G.: User Attitudes Regarding a User-Adaptive eCommerce Web Site. In: User Modeling and User Adaptive Interaction 13, 4 (2003) 373-396
2. Ardissono, L., Goy, A., Giovanna, P., Segnan, S., Torasso, P.: Ubiquitous User Assistance in a Tourist Information Server. In: De Bra, P., Brusilovsky, P., Conejo, R. (eds) Adaptive Hypermedia and Adaptive Web-Based Systems, Proceedings of the second International Conference, AH 2002, Málaga, Spain, May, Springer-Verlag, LNCS 2347 (2002) 14-23
3. Console, L., Gioria, S., Lombardi, I., Surano, V., Torre, I.: Adaptation and Personalization on Board Cars: A Framework and Its Application to Tourist Services. In: De Bra, P., Brusilovsky, P., Conejo, R. (eds) Adaptive Hypermedia and Adaptive Web-Based Systems, Proceedings of the second International Conference, AH 2002, Málaga, Spain, May, Springer-Verlag, LNCS 2347 (2002) 112-121
4. Dey, A. K.: Providing Architectural Support for Building Context-Aware Applications. Ph.D. thesis, College of Computing, Georgia Institute of Technology (2000) Online: http://www.cc.gatech.edu/fce/ctk/pubs/dey-thesis.pdf
5. Herlocker, J., Konstan, J. A.: Content-Independent Task-Focused Recommendation. In: IEEE Internet Computing, 5 (2001) 40-47

6. Kay, J.: A Scrutable User Modelling Shell for User-Adapted Interaction. Basser Department of Computer Science, University of Sydney, Australia (1999) Online: http://www.cs.usyd.edu.au/~judy/Homec/Pubs/thesis.pdf
7. Microsoft Mappoint, http://www.microsoft.com/mappoint
8. OWL, Ontology Web Language, http://www.w3.org/2001/sw/WebOnt
9. Pokraev, S., Koolwaaij, J., Wibbels, M.: Extending UDDI with context-aware features based on semantic service descriptions. The 2003 International Conference on Web Services (ICWS 2003) Las Vegas, USA (2003), 184-190
10. Resnick, P., Varian, H.R.: Recommender Systems. Communications of the ACM 40 (1997) 50-58
11. Riesbeck, C. K., Schank, R.: Inside CBR. Lawrence Erlbaum Associates, Northvale, NJ, USA (1989)
12. Shardanand, U., Maes, P.: Social information filtering: algorithms for automated "Word of Mouth". In: Proceedings of Human factors in computing systems 1995 (New York, USA). ACM (1995) 210-217
13. van Setten, M.: Experiments with a recommendation technique that learns category interests. In: Proceedings of IADIS WWW/Internet, Lisabon, Portugal (2002) 722-725
14. van Setten, M., Veenstra, M., Nijholt, A., van Dijk, B.: Case-Based Reasoning as a Prediction Strategy for Hybrid Recommender Systems. In: Proceedings of the Atlantic Web Intelligence Conference, Cancun, Mexico, Springer-Verlag, LNAI 3034 (2004) 13-22

Utilizing Artificial Learners
to Help Overcome the Cold-Start Problem in
a Pedagogically-Oriented Paper Recommendation System

Tiffany Tang[1,2] and Gordon McCalla[2]

[1] Department of Computing, Hong Kong Polytechnic University
Hung Hom, Kowloon, Hong Kong
cstiffany@comp.polyu.edu.hk
[2] Department of Computer Science, University of Saskatchewan
Saskatoon, Saskatchewan, Canada
mccalla@cs.usask.ca

Abstract. In this paper we discuss the cold-start problem in an evolvable paper recommendation e-learning system. We carried out an experiment using artificial and human learners at the same time. Artificial learners are used to solve the cold-start recommendation problem when no paper has been rated by the learners. Experimental results are encouraging, showing that using artificial learners achieves better performance in terms of learner subjective ratings; and more importantly, human learners are satisfied with the recommendations received.

1 Introduction

Recommender systems (**RS**) have been explored mostly in applications other than e-learning, such as e-commerce or news recommendation. In e-commerce, it is imperative to provide personalized experiences for consumers involved, which has proved to be effective for cross-selling, up-selling, and mass marketing [11]. In e-learning, however, we want to recommend items such as papers, web pages, and other articles where learners' (consumers') pedagogical characteristics should be considered. To maximize the utility of learning, the recommending mechanism should consider not only learners' interest towards the items as most other RSs do, but also their knowledge of domain concepts, for instance, not to recommend highly technical papers to a first-year-undergraduate student or popular-magazine articles to a senior-graduate student. In addition, items contained in a recommendation list might not have to be interesting to learners to be valuable. If the system continues to recommend something that cannot stimulate learners' interest in one way or another, however, it is also undesirable. Finally, for e-learning, customization should also be made not only of learning content, but also of the presentation style [5, 8].

To address these issues, in this paper we will discuss our work on recommending research papers for learners engaged in an evolving e-learning system [14]. Our system is designed to recommend research papers for students. This study extends our previous hybrid model-based/collaborative filtering recommendation approach [15], with a special focus on how to use simulated learners to solve the cold-start problem, the problem of making recommendations when there are not yet enough users for collaborative techniques to be effective.

W. Nejdl and P. De Bra (Eds.): AH 2004, LNCS 3137, pp. 245–254, 2004.

The rest of this paper is organized as follows. In the next section, we will argue the uniqueness of paper recommendation in e-learning systems, through the presentation of a motivational example and related work. In Sect. 3, we will present the technical aspects of our approach. In Sect. 4, we will discuss in detail the experiment we conducted as a way of assessing and comparing our proposed recommendation techniques. Finally, we conclude this paper by pointing out our future research plans.

2   What Is Special About Paper Recommendation for e-Learning System

2.1   Motivation

It is commonly recognized that the sources of data on which recommendation algorithms can perform include users' demographic data. In our paper, we will consider a special kind of user data different from the majority of recommender systems, i.e. pedagogically-oriented data. The pedagogically-oriented data is different in the sense that it can directly *affect* as well as *inform* recommendation process, thus enhancing the quality of recommendations in the context of the web-based learning environments. The main pedagogical features used are the learner's goal and background knowledge, although other factors such as learning preferences are also important. To illustrate, consider the three learners A, B, and C in Table 1.

Table 1. A comparison of learner model A, B and C

	Learner A	Learner B	Learner C
Knowledge in Statistics	Strong	Weak	Weak
Knowledge in Marketing and Management science	Strong	Weak	Weak
Knowledge in network security (e.g. SSL)	Strong	Weak	weak
Interest	Network security, social network	Network security, social network	Data mining & web mining application in e-commerce
Paper Preferences	Technical/theoretical	Application and magazine survey, technical/theoretical	Application and magazine survey

Suppose we have already made recommendations for the learners A, B and C. From Table 1, we can conclude that learner A and B have some overlapping interests, but since their knowledge background differs especially with respect to their technical background, the paper recommended to them would be different. But for learner B and C, although they have different application interests, their technical background is similar; therefore, they might receive similar technical papers.

2.2   Related Work

Paper Recommendations
There are several related works concerning tracking and recommending technical papers. Basu *et al.* [1] studied paper recommendation in the context of assigning con-

ference paper submissions to reviewing committee members. Bollacker *et al.* [2] refine CiteSeer through an automatic personalized paper-tracking module which retrieves each user's interests from well-maintained heterogeneous user profiles. Woodruff *et al.* [17] discuss an enhanced digital book with a spreading-activation-geared mechanism to make customized recommendations for readers with different type of background and knowledge. McNee *et al.* [9] investigate the adoption of collaborative filtering techniques to recommend papers for researchers; however, the paper did not address the issue of how to recommend a research paper, rather, how to recommend *additional* references for a target research paper. In the context of an e-learning system, additional readings cannot be recommended purely through an analysis of the citation matrix of a target paper.

These works are different from ours in that we not only recommend papers according to learners' interests, but also pick up those *not-so-interesting-yet-pedagogically-suitable* papers for them. In some cases pedagogically valuable papers might not be interesting and papers with significant influence on the research community might not be pedagogically suitable for learners. We argue that the main goal of recommending papers is to provide learners with necessary knowledge of a given topic and personalize the learning environment in order to motivate them to explore more.

Curriculum Sequencing and Adaptive Hypermedia

Adaptive hypermedia has been studied extensively recently. According to Brusilovsky [4], generally, there are two kinds of adaptation: adaptive navigation ("link level") and adaptive presentation ("content level"). Adaptive presentation is then subgrouped into text and multimedia adaptation; while adaptive navigation is mainly subgrouped into link ordering [7], link annotation [10], link hiding (including removal, hiding and disabling [6]). Early research in adaptive hypermedia has concentrated mostly on adaptive presentation technology [3], capable of adaptively presenting the content of a given page or collections of pages which have been viewed by a user. More recently, more aspects of learners are utilized in order to tailor the delivered content, e.g. [13]. It is obvious that the contents of the pages are used as clues to derive important learning features of students such as their interests, knowledge state etc. From another perspective, part of this branch of study can be viewed alternatively as content-based recommendations when users' past reading items/pages are recorded and analyzed. Over the past few years, link-oriented adaptation technologies are increasingly reported in the literature [5, 6, 16]. For instance, ELM-ART [16] is an adaptive on-line textbook supporting several key features such as adaptive navigation, curriculum sequencing, and personalized diagnosis of student solutions for learners with different prior knowledge.

Cold-Start Recommendations

One difficult, though common problem for a RS is the cold-start problem, one of which is the new-item problem [12] when there are no ratings at all for new items in the system. In this case, as proposed in [12], the content features of items can help bridge the gap between existing items to new items, through the 'match-making' of their similarities. Unfortunately, until now, this type of the cold-start problem has only been studied in domains other than e-learning. And to make things worse, in the e-learning domain, the fact that there are not many students enrolled in a class each year, and there are many new papers published and added into a system can greatly increase the difficulty to find neighbors for a target learner. To solve this problem, we propose to utilize artificial learners.

3 Pedagogically-Oriented Paper Recommendation

Specifically, our goal can be stated as follows:
Given a collection of papers and a learner's profile, recommend and deliver a set of materials in a pedagogically appropriate sequence, so as to meet both the learner's pedagogical needs and the learner's interests.

To be precise, *papers* include online reading materials which can help learners understand the topic being taught, such as conference papers, journal papers, magazine articles etc. Ideally, the system will enhance a learner's utility such that the learner gains a maximum amount of knowledge and is well motivated in the end. Fig.1 shows two different types of recommendation technique being analyzed. In our current experiment, the recommendation processes shown in Fig. 1 are as follow.

① A tutor manually assigns the properties of each paper (paper model).
② Elicit learner group A's learner model through active/passive assessment.
③ *Model-based RS* recommends a paper to the learner by comparing learner model and paper model.
④ Learner group A rates the paper.
⑤ Elicit learner group B's learner model.
⑥ *Hybrid-CF module* recommends a paper by comparing learner model A and B and searching for the paper with the highest rating.
⑦ Learner group B rates the paper.

3.1 Pedagogical Model-Based Recommendation Technique

The model-based recommendation is achieved through a careful assessment and comparison of both learner and paper characteristics. In other words, each individual learner models will first be analyzed, in terms of not only their interest, but their pedagogical features, such as their background knowledge in specific topics. Paper models will also be analyzed based on the topic, technical level, material covered and presentation. The recommendation is carried out by matching the learner interest with the paper topics where the technical level of the paper should not impede the learner in understanding it. Therefore, the suitability of a paper toward a learner is calculated as the summation of the fitness of learner interest toward the paper and the easy of understanding the paper.

3.2 Pedagogical Hybrid Collaborative Filtering Technique

However, this model-based recommendation is very costly due to the following reasons:
- when a new paper is added into the system, a detailed identification is required, which cannot be done automatically;
- when a learner gains some new knowledge after reading a paper, a new matching process is required in order to find the next suitable paper for him/her, resulting in the updating of his/her learner model;

– the matching between learner model and paper model may not be a one-to-one mapping, which increases the complexity of the computation.

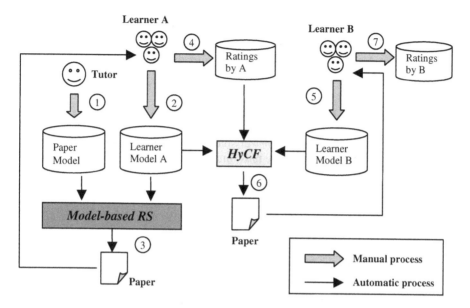

Fig. 1. Process of paper recommendation system

Alternatively, we can use a collaborative filtering technique (CF) to reduce the complexity of the recommendation process. The idea of CF is to let peer learners (nearest neighbors) filter out unsuitable papers, where the system does not need to know the detailed characteristics of them. Hence, the matching process is not performed from learner models to paper models, but from one learner model to other learner models, i.e. by comparing the closeness of both learners' interest and background knowledge in order to find nearest neighbors of a target learner.

3.3   The Cold-Start Problem and Artificial Learners

One of the disadvantages of CF is the "cold-start" problem [12], explained above. Unfortunately, the cold-start problem may appear frequently in paper recommendation, because there are many new papers published and often a relatively small number of students enrolled in a class each year, which increases the difficulty to find nearest neighbors of a target learner. Moreover, we cannot use random assignment for two reasons: it may degrade teaching quality, and learners do not have time to read too many irrelevant papers. Hence, we may use artificial learners (ArLs) as the solution. In this case, the recommendation process begins with generating ArLs with various learner models, and then assigning papers to them randomly. Then, we will use a program to generate 'fake' ratings according to learner characteristics. Thus, when a real human learner uses the system, we can use hybrid CF to recommend paper to them. And as more human learners use the system, eventually the 'fake' ratings will be replaced by real ratings. This technique may not as good as model-based RS, but it seems reasonable that it would be better than random assignment. The questions, therefore, are to discover the effectiveness of the hybrid-CF compared to the model-based RS and to determine whether or not the recommended papers by ArLs are use-ful for the human learner. To answer these questions, we have conducted two experi-ments: firstly, comparing the effectiveness of model-based recommendation and hy-brid-CF in situation with only ArLs, and secondly, to use ArLs to recommend papers to real human learners. A detailed description of the former can be found in [15], while the result of the latter will be described here.

4 Experimental Results and Discussions

In our experiments, we intend to answer some specific questions: when recommend-ing articles to learners. What are the most important criteria for recommendation? Are a student's interests more important than other aspects? Should we also recommend something which will aid their learning based on pedagogical characteristics? Can ArLs help solve the cold-start problem? Considering the evaluation methods, are artificial learner-based simulations (ArLSim) effective in providing insight, guide-lines, and affordable-means for future human-subject studies?

In our previous study, it has been shown that most learners are willing to read not-interesting-but-useful papers [14]. Therefore, we assume that learner interest may not the only factor in recommendation. In order to validate our proposed approach, we carried out both an artificial-learner-based simulation study and a human-subject study. For the ArLSim study [15], we found out that compared to the model-based recommendation, hybrid-CF can lower the computational cost, without compromising the quality of the recommendation, and therefore, is more desirable for e-learning system. In this paper, we will focus on our second experiment which is based on a human subject study.

4.1 Experiment Setup

The human subject study was conducted in a university in Hong Kong. The course is a senior level undergraduate course (literally the final year course) in software engi-neering, where the first author is the instructor of the course. There were altogether 48 students majoring in Internet Computing and Multimedia, and there were altogether 23 candidate papers in English related to software engineering and internet comput-ing. Those 23 papers were chosen from a pool of more than 40 papers originally se-lected for this course, as part of the required reading materials for the group project in the course. The length of the papers varies from 2 pages to 15 pages. However, most of them are popular articles that are suitable for those students.

For the purpose of testing, we first generated 50000 ArLs. Each ArL then rated the 23 papers according to their individual learner models (pure model-based). The rating mechanism was the same as we used in [15]. After that, we used human subjects as the target learners. Then, two cold-start recommendation techniques were applied for these target learners. The first technique used a hybrid CF approach, and the second used random assignment as the control.

We first distributed 48 surveys asking about students' interests, and their knowl-edge background (see Fig. 2). The background knowledge consists of knowledge items students have learned in other courses, items which are also needed to understand the papers. After we received 41 feedbacks, we used hybrid-CF to find the most suitable paper for each of them. Furthermore, we also selected another paper randomly. Thus, each student was assigned to read two papers within five days and was required to give a pair of feedback forms, one for each paper. The feedback form basically collected their subjective evaluation after reading the papers, mainly in multiple-choices format. One of the questions, for example, asked them to write a critical comment about the papers, and this became an indicator of their seriousness in reading the papers. None of the learners knew that one of the papers was selected randomly, but they did know that they were receiving personalized articles which could be used in their group project and adequately filling in their feedback form would give them a bonus mark for this course.

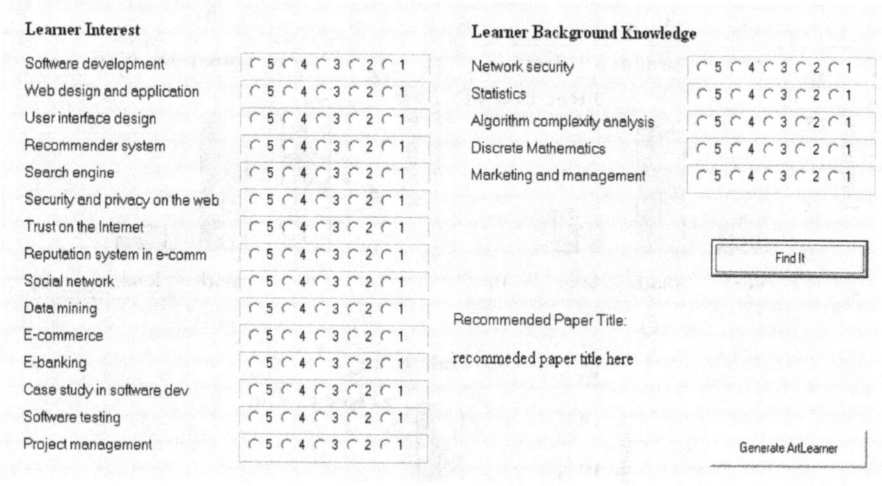

Learner Interest

Software development	5 4 3 2 1
Web design and application	5 4 3 2 1
User interface design	5 4 3 2 1
Recommender system	5 4 3 2 1
Search engine	5 4 3 2 1
Security and privacy on the web	5 4 3 2 1
Trust on the Internet	5 4 3 2 1
Reputation system in e-comm	5 4 3 2 1
Social network	5 4 3 2 1
Data mining	5 4 3 2 1
E-commerce	5 4 3 2 1
E-banking	5 4 3 2 1
Case study in software dev	5 4 3 2 1
Software testing	5 4 3 2 1
Project management	5 4 3 2 1

Learner Background Knowledge

Network security	5 4 3 2 1
Statistics	5 4 3 2 1
Algorithm complexity analysis	5 4 3 2 1
Discrete Mathematics	5 4 3 2 1
Marketing and management	5 4 3 2 1

[Find It]

Recommended Paper Title:

recommeded paper title here

[Generate ArtLearner]

Fig. 2. Survey questions for target learner

4.2   Experiment Results and Discussion

In all, 24 pairs of valid feedback forms were received on time, 6 pairs of feedback forms were received more than a week later, and 3 feedback forms were not valid, e.g. containing multiple answers, blanks, and combining information for both papers, and 8 students did   not return feedback forms. In this paper, we consider only the 24 pairs of valid feedbacks, displayed in Fig. 3. The vertical axis of the diagram denotes the number of subjects who answered the respective question. The horizontal axis denotes the criteria of the answer given by the subject on a 4-point scale, i.e. "very", "moderately", "less", and "not at all". Moreover, the left bar contains the results for the recommended paper, while the right bar is for the randomly assigned paper.

Fig. 3(a) shows that learners were more interested in the recommended paper (left bars) than a randomly selected paper (right bars). For example, 6 subjects felt that the recommended papers were very interesting, while only 1 subject felt that the random paper was very interesting. Fig. 3 (b) shows that learners felt that recommended papers were easier to understand than a randomly assigned one. This result conforms to our prediction, since the rating mechanism used by ArLs incorporates both learner interests and knowledge background in understanding a paper. Thus, a recommended paper generated by ArLs will also fit human interests and knowledge backgrounds.

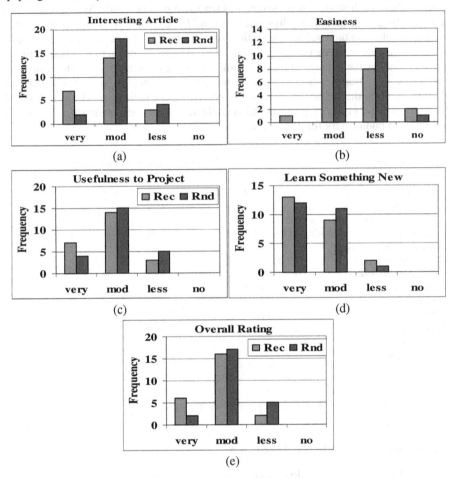

(a)   (b)

(c)   (d)

(e)

Fig. 3. Results of learner feedback

Fig. 3(c) shows the answer for the question whether the papers are useful to their class project or not. It can be seen from the result that most subjects felt that the recommended papers were more useful than random papers. However, when we asked them whether they learned something new or not after reading the paper, it is not clear whether or not a recommended paper really gave them more new knowledge, when compared to a randomly-assigned paper (see Fig. 3(d)). This result is not surprising; since all the candidate papers are actually well-selected for this course, where the value-added for learners is high (most subjects felt that they learned a lot after reading the papers). In future, we will expand the pool of papers to include less relevant ones in order to evaluate this effect.

Finally, Fig. 3(e) shows that recommended papers got higher ratings overall. The results justify our prediction that ArLs can be used to recommend papers to human learners, because it is better than randomly assigning paper to human learner. However, it is not clear if this result will be true for all kinds of learning material, because we only used well-selected papers in our experiment. From Fig. 3, it is ambiguous whether the overall ratings depend on learner interest or "easiness" of the paper. However, from the individual data we found that the correlation between "interesting article" and "overall rating" is 0.645, while the correlation between "easiness" and "overall rating" is 0.144. Thus, we conclude that "interesting article" is a more important factor in determining learner overall rating. Furthermore, the correlation between "usefulness to project" and "overall rating" is 0.652 and the correlation between "learn something new" and "overall rating" is 0.399, which tell us that learner give higher weight on the paper that can help their project (*contextual* learning goal).

In addition, we also studied the effect of 'peer-to-peer' recommendations made by each learner after he/she read the papers. Overall, the result is quite encouraging, showing that learners will tend to recommend those papers specially tailored for them to other similar learners. Detailed results will not be discussed here due to limited space.

Although a simulation program can only model part of the real environment where human learners involve and has been questioned on its effectiveness and validness, it remains to be an amicable and affordable tool to gain insights for paper recommendations in complex settings. Our experiment of using artificial learners to solve the cold-start paper recommendation problem is the first effort of this kind, and will shed lights on future simulation studies for web-based adaptive learning systems.

5 Concluding Remarks

In this paper, we pointed out differences in making recommendations in e-learning and other domains. In order to solve "cold-start" recommendation, we propose to use artificial learners to rate new papers. Then the system can make recommendations to human learners based on the ratings given by the artificial learners. Experimental results are encouraging, showing that using artificial learners achieve better performance in terms of learner subjective ratings; and more importantly, human learners are satisfied with the recommendations received, which demonstrate the effectiveness of artificial learners. Moreover, our experiment also shows that a learner's interest seems to be more important than their knowledge background, and a learner's goal is more important than their knowledge gain. In the future, we plan to carry on a more extensive study involving more students and papers.

References

1. Basu, C., Hirsh, H., Cohen, W. and Nevill-Manning, C. 2001. Technical paper recommendations: a study in combining multiple information sources. *JAIR*, 1, 231-252.
2. Bollacker, K., Lawrence, S. and C. Lee Giles, C. L. 1999. A system for automatic personalized tracking of scientific literature on the web. *ACM DL*, 105-113.
3. Boyle, C. and Encarnacion, A. O. 1994. MetaDoc: an adaptive hypertext reading system. *UMUAI*, 4, 1-19.
4. Brusilovsky, P. 2001. Adaptive hypermedia. *UMUAI*, 11(1/2), 87-110.

5. Brusilovsky, P. and Rizzo, R. 2002. Map-based horizontal navigation in educational hypertext. *Journal of Digital Information*, 3(1).
6. De Bra, P. and Calvi, L. 1998. AHA! An open adaptive hypermedia architecture. *The New Review of Hypermedia and Multimedia*, 4, 115-139.
7. Kaplan, C., Fenwick, J. and Chen, J. 1993. Adaptive hypertext navigation based on user goals and context. *UMUAI*, 3(3), 193-220.
8. Kobsa, A., Koenemann, J. and Pohl, W. 2001. Personalized hypermedia presentation techniques for improving online customer relationships.*The Knowledge Engineering Review* 16(2):111-155.
9. McNee, S, Albert, I., Cosley, D., Gopalkrishnan, P., Lam, S., Rashid, A., Konstan, J. and Riedl, J. 2002. On the Recommending of Citations for Research Papers. *ACM CSCW'02*. 116-125.
10. Pazzani, M., Muramatsu, J. and Billsus, D. 1996. Syskill and Webert: Identifying interesting web sites. *AAAI'96*, 54-61.
11. Schafer, J., Konstan, J. and Riedl, J. 2001. Electronic Commerce Recommender Applications. *Data Mining and Knowledge Discovery*, 5, (1/2, 2001), 115-152.
12. Schein, A., Popescul, A., Ungar, L.H. and Pennock, D. 2002, *SIGIR'02*. 253-260.
13. Stern, M. K. and Woolf, B.P. 2000. Adaptive content in an online lecture system. *AH*, 227-238.
14. Tang, T.Y and McCalla, G. 2003. Smart recommendations for an evolving e-learning system. In *Workshop on Technologies for Electronic Documents for Supporting Learning, AIED'2003*.
15. Tang, T.Y. and McCalla, G. 2004. Evaluating a Smart Recommender for an Evolving E-Learning System: A Simulation-Based Study. *Canadian AI Conference*, Canada.
16. Weber, G.,and Brusilovsky, P. 2001. ELM-ART: an adaptive versatile system for web-based instruction. *International Journal of AI in Education*. 12: 1-35.
17. Woodruff, A., Gossweiler, R., Pitkow, J., Chi, E. and Card, S. 2000. Enhancing a digital book with a reading recommender. In *ACM CHI 2000*.153-160.

Unison-CF: A Multiple-Component, Adaptive Collaborative Filtering System

Manolis Vozalis and Konstantinos G. Margaritis

University of Macedonia, Dept. of Applied Informatics
Parallel Distributed Processing Laboratory
Egnatia 156, P.O. 1591, 54006, Thessaloniki, Greece
{mans,kmarg}@uom.gr
http://macedonia.uom.gr/~{mans,kmarg}

Abstract. In this paper we present the Unison-CF algorithm, which provides an efficient way to combine multiple collaborative filtering approaches, drawing advantages from each one of them. Each collaborative filtering approach is treated as a separate component, allowing the Unison-CF algorithm to be easily extended. We evaluate the Unison-CF algorithm by applying it on three existing filtering approaches: User-based Filtering, Item-based Filtering and Hybrid-CF. Adaptation is utilized and evaluated as part of the filtering approaches combination. Our experiments show that the Unison-CF algorithm generates promising results in improving the accuracy and coverage of the existing filtering algorithms.

Keywords: collaborative filtering, memory-based filtering, adaptation, personalization, prediction, recommender systems

1 Introduction

Recommender Systems were introduced as a computer-based intelligent technique to assist with the problem of information and product overload. Their purpose is to provide efficient personalized solutions in e-business domains, benefiting both the customer and the merchant.

Two basic entities are featured in all Recommender Systems: the *user* and the *item*. A user utilizes the Recommender System, providing his opinion about items. The *goal* of the Recommender System is to generate suggestions about new items for that particular user. The process is based on the *input* provided, usually expressed in the form of ratings from that user, and the *filtering algorithm*, which is applied on that input. All the ratings provided by m users on n items are collected in a *$m \times n$ user-item matrix*.

Recommender algorithms can be roughly divided into two wide categories. *Memory-based* and *Model-based Systems*. Memory-based Systems are more efficient, in that they generate their recommendations without a need for any preprocessing. Nevertheless, they suffer from serious scalability problems. User-based Collaborative Filtering [1], and Content-based Filtering both belong to this category of filtering algorithms. A different approach is taken by Model-based Systems [2]. These algorithms, which often approach the problem from a probabilistic perspective [3], produce their predictions by first developing a model of user ratings. The construction of that model requires time but once created, the generation of the recommendations can be really fast.

W. Nejdl and P. De Bra (Eds.): AH 2004, LNCS 3137, pp. 255–264, 2004.
© Springer-Verlag Berlin Heidelberg 2004

Hybrid systems are based on the idea that an effective combination of different filtering techniques will improve the Recommender System's overall efficiency [4]. Among existing hybrids, such as Fab [5], Ripper [6], Filterbots [7], PTV [8], Condliff's two stage mixed-effects Bayesian Recommender [9], Content-Boosted Collaborative Filtering [10], and Hybrid-CF [11] we selected P-Tango as the basis for our filtering approach. Claypool et al. [12] proposed P-Tango as an approach which combines different filtering methods, by first relating each of them to a distinct component and then basing its predictions on the *weighted average* of the predictions generated by those components. Initially, they give equal weights to all ratings, but as more ratings are added, they adjust the weights so as to minimize past error. Still, they do not provide details about how this weight adjustment is achieved, while at the same time they limit their experiments to the combination of User-based and Content-based Filtering.

In this paper we present the Unison-CF algorithm, which refines and extends the work of Claypool et al [12]. Our approach in combining existing filtering algorithms is based on keeping them as separate components. Each algorithm is executed on its own, generating its predictions. The way that these predictions are combined, varies depending on the preferred implementation of the Unison-CF algorithm. By keeping the utilized filtering methods as separate components, we make sure that the Unison-CF Algorithm is extensible, since any new approach can be easily incorporated and contribute directly in the final prediction.

This paper can be outlined as follows. Sect. 2 provides information about the utilized data set and the evaluation metrics. Sect. 3 presents an overview of the three filtering algorithms involved in our Unison-CF experiments. Sect. 4 includes a detailed description of the general Unison-CF algorithm, while providing a formal discussion of two variations: The Basic and the Adaptive Unison-CF Algorithms. Sect. 5 presents a summary of experimental results and attempts an overall method comparison. The paper is concluded in Sect. 6.

2   Experimental Methodology

In order to execute the experiments described in the subsequent sections of this paper we utilized the data publicly available from the GroupLens movie recommender system. The MovieLens data set, used by several researchers [13] [14] [15], consists of 100.000 ratings, assigned by 943 users on 1682 movies. Users included have stated their opinions for at least 20 movies, while ratings follow the 1(bad)-5(excellent) numerical scale. That initial data set was used as the basis to generate five distinct splits into training and test data.

Many techniques have been proposed and used to evaluate Recommender Systems [15]. The choice among them should be based on the selected user tasks and the nature of the data sets. We wanted to derive a predicted score for already rated items rather than generate a top-N recommendation list. For that purpose we selected the two evaluation metrics to apply in our experiments. The first metric was *Mean Absolute Error (MAE)* [16]. It is a statistical accuracy metric which measures the deviation of predictions, generated by the Recommender System, from the true rating values, as they were specified by the user. The second metric utilized was *Coverage* [17]. It measures the percentage of items for which a filtering algorithm can generate predictions.

3 The Base Algorithms

In this section we discuss the three filtering algorithms which will be utilized by the proposed algorithm. More emphasis is put on the explanation of Hybrid-CF, a recently documented hybrid filtering approach, which combines elements from the two aforementioned filtering algorithms.

3.1 User-Based Collaborative Filtering

The inspiration for User-based Collaborative Filtering methods comes from the fact that people who agreed in their subjective evaluation of past items are likely to agree again in the future [1]. The execution steps of the algorithm are (a) *Data Representation* of the ratings provided by m users on n items, (b) *Neighborhood Formation*, where the application of the selected similarity metric leads to the construction of the active user's neighborhood, and (c) *Prediction Generation*, where, based on this neighborhood, predictions for items rated by the active user are produced.

3.2 Item-Based Collaborative Filtering

Item-based Filtering is based on the creation of neighborhoods. Yet, unlike the User-based Collaborative Filtering approach, those neighbors consist of similar items rather than similar users [18]. The execution steps of the algorithm are (a) *Data Representation* of the ratings provided by m users on n items, (b) *Neighborhood Formation*, where based on item similarities computed by the selected similarity metric, the active item's neighborhood is constructed, and (c) *Prediction Generation*, where predictions are calculated as a weighted sum of ratings given by a user on all items in the active item's neighborhood.

3.3 The Hybrid-CF Algorithm

Vozalis and Margaritis described a hybrid approach that combines elements from two basic recommendation algorithms - User and Item-based Collaborative Filtering [11]. The execution steps of the algorithm are (a) *Data Representation* of the ratings provided by m users on n items, (b) *Item Neighborhood Formation*, where a neighborhood of items most similar to the active item, that is the item for which we wish a prediction, is constructed, (c) *User Neighborhood Formation*, where we construct the active user's neighborhood based exclusively on items from the active item's neighborhood, and (d) Prediction Generation, where the users included in the active user's neighborhood are used to produce predictions of ratings by the active user. Steps (b) and (c) represent the respective contributions of User-based and Item-based Filtering in the recommendation procedure.

4 The Unison-CF Algorithm

The Unison-CF Algorithm *refines* past research work [12] by formally introducing the concept of "adaptation" in the recommendation process, which can be utilized in order

to achieve weight adjustments. The Unison-CF Algorithm *extends* past research work
(a) by increasing the number of filtering algorithms that participate in the experiments,
and then, by comparing how different combinations of these methods, as components of
the Unison-CF algorithm, contrast, and (b) by presenting an alternative implementation
of the Unison-CF algorithm with fixed weights, and contrasting its results with cases
where weight adjustments were implemented.

At this point, we will distinguish two alternative forms of the Unison-CF Algorithm: the Basic Unison Algorithm and the Adaptive Unison-CF Algorithm. In the Basic Unison-CF Algorithm, the participation of the filtering methods remains fixed and
known from the beginning. On the other hand, the Adaptive Unison-CF Algorithm allows the errors, calculated throughout the recommendation process, to define the final
participation of the filtering methods. The following sections discuss these two basic
variations of the Unison-CF Algorithm. Each of them is supported by a number of specific algorithmic implementations and their experimental results.

4.1   The Basic Unison-CF Algorithm

The Basic Unison-CF Algorithm allows the contributing filtering algorithms, which
from now on will be termed "base algorithms", to conclude with their prediction generation process. It, then, combines their generated predictions via a weighted sum of the
following form:

$$uni\_pred_{aj} = w_1 * base\_pred_{1,aj} + w_2 * base\_pred_{2,aj} + ... + w_n * base\_pred_{n,aj} \quad (1)$$

This formula calculates the unison prediction of active user, u_a, on item i_j, based on
the predictions generated by the n base algorithms, $base\_pred_{i,aj}$, with $i = 1, 2, ..., n$,
and the weights, w_i, assigned to them. The final prediction is determined by two basic
factors: a) the base algorithms that participate in the unison recommendation procedure,
and b) the role assigned to each of these algorithms, mainly expressed through their
weights.

In the implementations which will follow, we tested two distinct approaches regarding the role of the contributing filtering algorithms.

1. *Equal Contribution*: When more than one base algorithms can generate predictions
   for the same {*user-item*} pair, the unison algorithm is set to assign identical significance to them. As a result, their contribution in the final recommendation stays
   fixed throughout the algorithm's execution, having an equal weight of $\frac{1}{n}$, where n is
   the number of contributing filtering algorithms. Consequently, Equal Contribution
   alters the general prediction formula of Basic Unison-CF Algorithm as follows:

$$uni\_pred_{ec,aj} = \frac{1}{n} * base\_pred_{1,aj} + \frac{1}{n} * base\_pred_{2,aj} + ... + \frac{1}{n} * base\_pred_{n,aj} \quad (2)$$

2. *Absolute Priority*: When more than one base algorithms can generate predictions
   for the same {*user-item*} pair, the unison algorithm is set to always select the prediction by the *privileged* component, $base_{pr}$, and present it as the Recommender
   System's final prediction. Nevertheless, when the component given absolute priority cannot generate a prediction, the unison algorithm checks whether any other of

the remaining base algorithms is able to fill that void. In that case, these components are utilized instead, boosting up the coverage. Consequently, Absolute Priority transforms the general prediction formula of Basic Unison-CF Algorithm as follows:

$$uni\_pred_{ap,aj} = \begin{cases} base\_pred_{pr,aj}, \ if \ \exists base\_pred_{pr,aj} \\ w_2 * base\_pred_{2,aj} + ... + w_n * base\_pred_{n,aj}, \ otherwise \end{cases}$$
$$(3)$$

In the first case, when there exists a prediction from the privileged component, $\exists base\_pred_{pr,aj}$, we set $w_1 = 1$, while the contribution of all the other components is cancelled out by setting $w_i = 0$, for $i = 2, 3, ..., n$. In the second case, there is no prediction for the privileged component, $base\_pred_{pr,aj} = 0$, meaning that the overall unison prediction is defined by the rest of the contributing filtering algorithms by setting the values of their weights, w_i, for $i = 2, 3, ..., n$, according to the scheme we select. They can either be equal, which translates to Equal Contribution for all remaining components, or, if we stick with the Absolute Priority scheme, the next component generating a prediction, $base_k$, will be the only one utilized ($w_k = 1$), while all the subsequent components will be totally ignored ($w_i = 0$, for $i = k + 1, ..., n$).

4.2 The Adaptive Unison-CF Algorithm

The Basic Unison-CF Algorithm incorporated a pre-defined behavior, allowing the algorithm's execution steps to be fully anticipated from the beginning. The Adaptive Unison-CF Algorithm retains the general form of the prediction formula 1, which should be utilized to generate predictions for active user, u_a, on item i_j.

Still, the essence of the prediction formula is altered by the introduction of the concept of *adaptation*, which is reflected by the definition of the participating weights, w_i, for $i = 1, 2, ..., n$. The basic idea behind adaptation is that the algorithm's behavior will change, or more precisely *adapt*, during the recommendation process. At this point, we can distinguish two diverse approaches of applying adaptation in the unison algorithm:

1. *Adaptation on a single, preceding user:* According to the first approach, the recommender system's behavior adapts by basing its predictions for the *current* user solely on the prediction errors observed for the *previous* user. Specifically, before proceeding with predictions for user u_a, we collect the predictions that the base algorithms, $base_1, base_2, ..., base_n$, generated for user u_{a-1}, and calculate their cumulative accuracy errors, $E_{1,a-1}, E_{2,a-1}, ..., E_{n,a-1}$. Error $E_{c,a-1}$ with $c = 1, 2, ..., n$, corresponds to the sum of differences between the predictions, $pr_{c,a-1j}$, generated by component $base_c$ for all items, $j = 1, 2, ..., l$, rated by previous user u_{a-1}, and the user's actual ratings, r_{a-1j}, on those items:

$$E_{c,a-1} = \sum_{j=1}^{l} |pr_{c,a-1j} - r_{a-1j}| \qquad (4)$$

Still, a filtering component may not be able to generate predictions for all l items that have been rated by user u_{a-1}. Let's assume that the number of items rated by user u_{a-1} for which base algorithms $base_1, base_2, ..., base_n$ were able to generate predictions are $l_{1,a-1}, l_{2,a-1}, ..., l_{n,a-1}$, where obviously $l_{c,a-1} \leq l$, for $c = 1, 2, ..., n$. Bearing that in mind and starting from the cumulative accuracy errors, $E_{c,a-1}$, we can now proceed and calculate the accuracy errors per prediction, $E_{pr,c,a-1}$, as follows:

$$E_{pr,c,a-1} = \frac{E_{c,a-1}}{l_{c,a-1}} \quad for \ c = 1, 2, ..., n \tag{5}$$

Error $E_{pr,c,a-1}$ represents the error per prediction generated by filtering component $base_c$ for user u_{a-1}. Taking these errors into consideration, we assign different weights, w_c for $c = 1, 2, ..., n$, to the base filtering approaches. These weights, normalized so that they add up to unity, are defined to be proportionally inverse to the same component's recommendation error per prediction for the previous user, $E_{pr,c,a-1}$:

$$w_c = \frac{1}{E_{pr,c,a-1}} \tag{6}$$

Once specified, the weights can be utilized in the unison prediction formula 1. As a result, a method with low prediction error for the previous user will have a higher impact in the prediction for the succeeding user. At the same time, a component with increased prediction error for the preceding user will assume a diminished role in the same prediction generation.

2. *Adaptation on all preceding users*: According to the second approach, the contribution of the base algorithms in the final recommendation adapts not by taking into account the predictions generated for a single, preceding user, but by collecting the predictions produced by the participating components for *all* preceding users, that is for users u_1 to u_{a-1}. Based on these predictions we evaluate the cumulative accuracy errors, $E_{c,all}$, for each of the n components and, thus, their participation in the total accuracy error. Error $E_{c,all}$ with $c = 1, 2, ..., n$, is calculated as follows:

$$E_{c,all} = \sum_{u=1}^{a-1} \sum_{j=1}^{l} |pr_{i,uj} - r_{uj}| \tag{7}$$

According to the formula, we start by computing the sum of differences between the predictions, $pr_{c,uj}$, generated by component $base_c$ for all items, $j = 1, 2, ..., l$, rated by user u, and the user's actual ratings, r_{uj}, on those items. We proceed by adding these sums for all users from u_1 to u_{a-1}. We can now calculate error $E_{pr,c,all}$, that is the error per prediction generated by filtering component c for all preceding users, by executing the steps which were described in the previous paragraph. These errors, computed for each filtering component, are added up in order to obtain the overall components error. The weights assigned to each component are set to be inverse proportionally to the corresponding component's participation in the total accuracy error. The difference from the previous approach is that by taking into account the whole prediction history, and not just the last user, the weight adaptation becomes slower as the recommendation procedure proceeds and more users are considered.

5   Overall Comparison of Unison-CF Implementations with Base Cases

In this section we will report the results from our experiments with seven distinct implementations of the Unison-CF algorithm, where we varied the number and type of filtering algorithms involved, as well as the way those filtering algorithms were combined. The main attributes of the Unison-CF implementations are outlined in Table 1.

Table 1. Brief Description of Unison-CF Implementations tested

	components	adaptability	functionality
Unison1	ub, ib	no	priority to the ub component
Unison2	ub, ib	no	equal weights to both components
Unison3	ub, ib, hcf	no	equal weights to all 3 components
Unison4	ub, ib, hcf	yes	adaptation on single, preceding user
Unison5	ub, ib, hcf	yes	adaptation on all previous users
Unison6	ub, hcf	yes	adaptation on all previous users
Unison7	ub, hcf	yes	adaptation on single, preceding user

Fig. 1 compares the mean absolute error and coverage values for the Unison-CF implementations we tested. It also contrasts them with the corresponding MAE and coverage values from User-based (*user-b*), Item-based (*item-b*) Filtering and Hybrid-CF (*hyb-cf*), in order to see how the Unison-CF implementations relate with the filtering algorithms that they combine.

A careful review of the coverage and accuracy figures leads to the following conclusions.

- The combination of different filtering approaches in a single Unison-CF implementation cannot improve on the best MAE values achieved by any of the involved filtering approaches. Its accuracy will lie between the best and the worst case of the filtering approaches that it unites.
- Unison-CF implementations are followed by a considerable increase in the coverage, when compared to the coverage of the filtering algorithms that they unite. Any increase in the number of components of a Unison-CF implementation may lead to a further increase of the average coverage, as documented by the coverage values of Unison-CF implementations that unite 3 base algorithms, when compared to those uniting only 2.
- If we want to single out the filtering algorithm with the best results regarding *accuracy*, we have to select Hybrid-CF. Its average MAE of 0,7545 was the best, with Unison7 (average MAE=0,7649) representing the next best case.
- If we want to single out the filtering algorithm with the best results regarding *coverage*, we have to select Unison5. Its average coverage of 98,3413% was the same as the coverage values achieved by Unison3 and Unison4. Nevertheless, Unison5 displayed a slightly better behavior as far as accuracy was concerned, and as a result it represents the best choice.

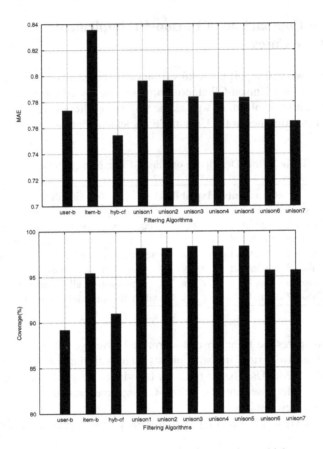

Fig. 1. Overall comparison of Unison-CF implementations with base cases

- If we want to single out the filtering algorithm with the best overall behavior, by taking into account both accuracy and coverage, we have to select Unison7. Its average MAE of 0,7649 was the second lowest, trailing only Hybrid-CF, when the rest of the Unison-CF implementations had MAE values ranging from 0,7963, as in the case of Unison2, to 0,7660, as in the case of Unison6. This significant advantage of Unison6 in accuracy did justify an average coverage of 95,6888%, which was slightly worse when compared to the average coverage values of the rest of the Unison-CF implementations, ranging around 98%.
- Adaptation on a single user fared extremely well against adaptation on all users. This result was unexpected and requires further investigation.

6   Conclusions

In this work we have presented the Unison-CF Algorithm, a hybrid filtering technique which can combine two or more collaborative filtering approaches with the help of a weighted sum. We also discussed two distinct variations of the Unison-CF Algorithm: The Basic Unison-CF Algorithm and the Adaptive Unison-CF Algorithm. The former incorporates a pre-defined behavior, expressed by the fixed values of its weights. The latter introduces the concept of adaptation, allowing the weights to adjust during the recommendation process. All discussions regarding the aforementioned algorithms did include a formal and detailed description of the execution steps required, therefore allowing them to be easily extended or applied on different base algorithms than those tested.

The descriptions of the proposed algorithms were supported by numerous experimental implementations, each of them incorporating distinct parameter settings. The settings were selected in order to contrast the utility of the Unison-CF Algorithm, in both of its variations, with the filtering approaches that it unites. The experimental results proved the promise held by the utilization of adaptation in the recommendation process. Furthermore, specific Unison-CF implementations displayed an overall behavior which improved on the base algorithms, according to the applied evaluation metrics.

For our future work we plan on experimenting with the concept of an "adaptation window", in order to test how a changing number of users participating in the Adaptive Unison-CF Algorithm will affect its efficiency.

References

1. Resnick, P., Iacovou, N., Sushak, M., Bergstrom, P., Riedl, J.: Grouplens: An open architecture for collaborative filtering of netnews. In: ACM 1994 Conference on Computer Supported Cooperative Work, New York, NY (1994) 175–186
2. Breese, J.S., Heckerman, D., Kadie, C.: Empirical analysis of predictive algorithms for collaborative filtering. In: Fourteenth Conference on Uncertainty in Artificial Intelligence, Madison, WI (1998)
3. Chen, Y.H., George, E.I.: A bayesian model for collaborative filtering. In: Proceedings of the Seventh International Workshop on Artificial Intelligence and Statistics. (1999)
4. Burke, R.: Hybrid recommender systems: Survey and experiments. User Modeling and User-Adapted Interaction **12** (2002) 331–370
5. Balabanovic, M., Shoham, Y.: Fab: Content-based, collaborative recommendation. Communications of the ACM **40** (1997)
6. Basu, C., Hirsh, H., Cohen, W.: Recommendation as classification: Using social and content-based information in recommendation. In: Proceedings of the 15th National Conference on Artificial Intelligence, Madison, WI (1998)
7. Sarwar, B.M., Konstan, J.A., Borchers, A., Herlocker, J., Miller, B., Riedl, J.T.: Using filtering agents to improve prediction quality in the grouplens research collaborative filtering system. In: Conference on Computer Supported Cooperative Work. (1998)
8. Smyth, B., Cotter, P.: Surfing the digital wave: Generation personalized tv listings using collaborative, case-based recommendation. In: Third International Conferece on Case-based Reasoning, Munich, Germany (1999)
9. Condliff, M.K., Lewis, D.D., Madigan, D., Posse, C.: Bayesian mixed-effects models for recommender systems. In: ACM SIGIR '99 Workshop on Recommender Systems: Algorithms and Evaluation, Berkeley, CA (1999)
10. Melville, P., Mooney, R.J., Nagarajan, R.: Content-boosted collaborative filtering. In: ACM SIGIR Workshop on Recommender Systems, New Orleans, LA (2001)

11. Vozalis, E., Margaritis, K.G.: On the combination of user-based and item-based collaborative filtering. Technical report, University of Macedonia, Greece (2003)
12. Claypool, M., Gokhale, A., Miranda, T., Murnikov, P., Netes, D., Sartin, M.: Combining content-based and collaborative filters in an online newspaper. In: ACM SIGIR Workshop on Recommender Systems-Implementation and Evaluation, Berkeley, CA (1999)
13. Schein, A.I., Popescul, A., Ungar, L.H., Pennock, D.M.: Methods and metrics for cold-start recommendations. In: ACM SIGIR-2002, Tampere, Finland (2002)
14. Ujjin, S., Bentley, P.J.: Particle swarm optimization recommender system. In: Proceedings of the IEEE Swarm Intelligence Sympoisum 2003, Indianapolis (2003)
15. Herlocker, J.L., Konstan, J.A., Terveen, L.G., Riedl, J.T.: Evaluating collaborative filtering recommender systems. ACM Transactions on Information Systems 22 (2004) 5–53
16. Shardanand, U., Maes, P.: Social information filtering: Algorithms for automating 'word of mouth'. In: Proceedings of Computer Human Interaction. (1995) 210–217
17. Herlocker, J.L.: Understanding and Improving Automated Collaborative Filtering Systems. PhD thesis, University of Minnesota (2000)
18. Sarwar, B.M., Karypis, G., Konstan, J.A., Riedl, J.T.: Item-based collaborative filtering recommendation algorithms. In: 10th International World Wide Web Conference (WWW10), Hong Kong (2001)

Using SiteRank for Decentralized Computation
of Web Document Ranking

Jie Wu and Karl Aberer

School of Computer and Communication Sciences
Swiss Federal Institute of Technology (EPF), Lausanne
1015 Lausanne, Switzerland
{jie.wu,karl.aberer}@epfl.ch

Abstract. The *PageRank* algorithm demonstrates the significance of the computation of document ranking of general importance or authority in Web information retrieval. However, doing a PageRank computation for the whole Web graph is both time-consuming and costly. State of the art Web crawler based search engines also suffer from the latency in retrieving a complete Web graph for the computation of PageRank. We look into the problem of computing PageRank in a decentralized and timely fashion by making use of *SiteRank* and aggregating rankings from multiple sites. A SiteRank is basically the ranking generated by applying the classical PageRank algorithm to the graph of Web sites, i.e., the Web graph at the granularity of Web sites instead of Web pages. Our empirical results show that SiteRank also follows a power-law distribution. Our experimental results demonstrate that the decomposition of global Web document ranking computation by making use of SiteRank is a very promising approach for computing global document rankings in a decentralized Web search system. In particular, by sharing SiteRank among member servers, such a search system also obtains a new means to fight link spamming.

Keywords: Web information retrieval, link structure analysis, search engine, ranking algorithm, decentralized framework

1 Introduction

Link-based rank computation is very important for Web information retrieval. Classical centralized algorithms like PageRank both time-consuming and costly for the whole Web graph. We look into the problem of rank computation in a decentralized and timely fashion by making use of SiteRank and aggregating rankings from multiple sites. We start from studying the Web graph at a higher abstraction level.

1.1 Different Abstractions for the Web Graph

Previous research work focused on the page granularity of the Web, i.e., a graph where the vertices are Web pages and the edges are links among pages. A typical result is the PageRank algorithm [8]. We propose to study the Web graph at the granularity of Web site. We call the graph at the document level the *DocGraph*, and the graph at the Web site level the *SiteGraph*. We also use the notion of *SiteLink* to designate hyperlinks among Web sites and *DocLink* for those among Web documents.

W. Nejdl and P. De Bra (Eds.): AH 2004, LNCS 3137, pp. 265–274, 2004.

Definition 1 *A SiteGraph $G_S(V_S, E_S)$ of (a part of) the Web is a graph consisting of:*

- *A set V_S of vertices, where each vertex $v_s \in V_S$ represents a Web site.*
- *A set E_S of edges, where each edge $e_s \in E_S$ is a directed SiteLink.*
- *Two mappings $o_s, t_s : E_S \rightarrow V_S$, where $o_s(e_s)$ is the originating Web site and $t_s(e_s)$ is the targeting Web site of the directed SiteLink e_s.*

Similarly, we use the notations $G_D(V_D, E_D), v_d, e_d$ for a DocGraph. We call the ranking of Web sites the SiteRank for the SiteGraph and the ranking of Web documents the *DocRank* for the DocGraph. PageRank is an example of DocRank, but DocRank can be computed in a way other than PageRank, for example, as in our approach in a decentralized fashion.

1.2   Contribution of the Work

Even though the Web site graph has been studied for applications such as identification of related hosts based on linkage and co-citation, it has not been considered in the context of ranking for search engines to the best of our knowledge. Our work explores the research possibilities in this direction, proposes insights on the potential of this approach and reports on initial results of it's implementation. More concretely, we study on how to make use of the SiteGraph and the derived SiteRank to support the derivation of rankings of Web sites and documents in the sense of general importance. Our main contributions can be summarized as follows:

1. Bringing up the idea of SiteRank to describe the general importance of Web sites in the Web. After verifying that the PageRank of our sample data set follows the well-known power-law, we find that the resulting SiteRank matches this distribution as well.
2. Evaluating the correlation between the importance of a Web site and the importance of the Web documents residing on the site. It turns out that Web documents of an important Web site tend to be more important than those of the less important sites.
3. Based on the previous observations, providing a decentralized approach for computing the global document ranking in decentralized architecture for Web and P2P search and reporting on a prototype implementation of it. As a consequence, the task of global ranking computation can be performed in a decentralized fashion and its cost is widely distributed.
4. Using a shared SiteRank is a very effective anti-rank-spamming approach for search engines that are built on our decentralized architecture. We assume all participating member servers agree on a universal SiteRank in the document rank computation which allows to exclude spamming sites more easily.

   In the next section we introduce our model and the algorithm to compute Site-Rank. We did several sets of experiments to evaluate the significance of this idea. We first verify that the PageRank distribution of the documents stored in our crawled data set follows a power-law. Then we try to uncover the relationship between documents' PageRank and SiteRank of the corresponding Web sites. Given the observations, we believe that making joint use of SiteRank and PageRank is an interesting direction to determine the global ranking of Web documents in a decentralized fashion. We show the influence of SiteRank on the computation of document rankings. Finally, after a short review on related work, we conclude our work and look into future research possibilities.

2 SiteRank and Its Distribution

A natural question of studying the Web graph at the granularity of Web sites is: are Web sites somehow comparable in the sense of general importance? We will further study the implications of it in the following sections.

2.1 Random Walks in SiteGraph

Intuitively, a random walk models a simple process of randomly navigating in the Web. In a SiteGraph, an Internet user would roam around the Web sites by following Web links. A surfer with no particular interests would choose a different site with a probability roughly specified by the ratio of links to that site and the total number of outgoing links of the current site. Based on this model similar to PageRank's random walks but at a higher abstraction level, we can derive the ranking of general importance for Web sites.

   Among other advantages using SiteRank opens a possibility to fight link spamming. Using information of the SiteGraph makes it difficult for PageRank spammers to spam rank of documents by creating huge number of pages pointing to a page to be spammed. Web pages are easy and inexpensive to create, thus spamming practices have become a frequent problem and nuisance in order to deceive Internet search engines. A Web site can easily, dynamically generate a large and unbounded number of dynamic Web pages by writing a simple server-side program. As a direct result the computed ranking results by algorithms like PageRank or HITS [7] are easily polluted and users have to find ways to fight rank spamming. In contrast, it is more difficult to create huge numbers of Web sites to apply such rank spamming techniques to boost the rank of a specific Web site. Other advantages of using SiteRank are discussed in [10].

2.2 The Algorithm and How to Compute

Taking the random surfing among the Web sites as a stochastic process, its transition probability matrix M_S is generated as follows:

$$M_S(i,j) = \begin{cases} \alpha_i * h_{ij} & h_i \neq 0, s_j \in ch(s_i) \\ 0 & h_i \neq 0, s_j \notin ch(s_i) \\ \frac{1}{N_S} & h_i = 0 \end{cases} \tag{1}$$

where N_S is the total number of Web sites, $s \in V_S$, simplified from v_s is a Web page, h_s is the number of SiteLinks originating from site s, $\alpha_s = \frac{1}{h_s}$ is the probability of a random surfer's following one particular SiteLink from site s, h_{ij} is the number of SiteLinks from site i to site j, $pa(s)$ is the set of parent sites of s, i.e. those sites pointing to s, $ch(s)$ is the set of child sites of s, i.e. those sites pointed to by s.

To ensure such a matrix may not have a non-trivial Eigenvector, we apply the technique of introducing a decay factor to the original SiteGraph, by the same means as that in the Page Rank algorithm:

$$M_S = p \times M_S + \frac{1-p}{N_S} \times I \qquad (2)$$

where the decay factor p is usually set to 0.85 and I is the matrix whose size is the same as that of M_S and all elements have the value of 1.

Theorem 1 *The Markov chain defined by M_S for the SiteGraph has a unique stationary probability distribution.*

Proof. Omitted. Please check [10].   □

Having this transition probability matrix for the SiteGraph, we can apply the standard Power Method for computing the principal eigenvector to obtain the ranking for the Web sites.

How to compute the SiteRank for individual member servers in the decentralized search system is another important problem since none of the servers could have the global information about the SiteGraph and the SiteLinks. The approach we adopt is similar to resource discovery in distributed networks [5]. The rudimentary idea is that member search servers exchange information of SiteGraph and SiteLinks among each other such that at a certain stage, the collected partial information about the SiteGraph can lead to a sufficiently good SiteRank result approximating the SiteRank generated by a centralized global SiteGraph. As every member server learns a non-local Web graph from arriving information from others, intentional spamming of SiteLink information by a Web site could be effectively detected when substantial mismatch is observed between information from different sources.

2.3   The Distribution of SiteRank on a Campus Web Graph

In this section we give a concrete example of the results that we obtain when computing the SiteRank values for all the Web sites of a Web graph. The evaluation presented here is made on a campus-wide Web graph, the EPFL domain which contains more than 600 independent Web sites identified by their hostnames or IP addresses. We used a Web crawler to retrieve more than 2.7 million Web documents by starting from the campus portal site and following the Web links to access all the other Web sites in this domain. Using this data set we extracted the information from the member Web sites and the SiteLinks among each other, we then applied the Power Method described above to the SiteGraph to obtain the SiteRank of them. When we generated the matrix representation of this graph, those links pointing from one local page to another local page on the same site are counted by the matrix element $M_S(i, i)$.

We draw a diagram in our technical report [10] where we display on the x axis the computed SiteRank values for the sites of the campus Web, and on the y axis we display the percentage of sites that has the particular SiteRank value. The diagram is drawn in a fashion similar to that of [9]. Both axes are displayed at a natural logarithmic scale. Suppose $Fraction(R)$ is the fraction of Web sites having SiteRank R, one of the interesting results of our work is that we found the SiteRank distribution is yet another property of the Web graph that also follows the power-law quite well:

$$Fraction(R) \propto 1/R^{0.95} \tag{3}$$

For comparison we also applied the standard PageRank algorithm to the link structure of the EPFL DocGraph to obtain the global ranking of all the Web documents in this campus Web graph. Suppose $fraction(r)$ is the fraction of pages having PageRank r, our data set shows typical power-law properties:

$$fraction(r) \propto 1/r^{1.69} \tag{4}$$

Both Log-Log figures, which can be found in [10], are not included here due to the space limit. This result is strikingly similar to that reported in a study on the Web structure [9]. Though the exponent here is a bit lower than the value found there which is around 2.1. Two reasons might account for this disparity, the difference in the nature of the different Web data sets we use and the incomplete crawling of our campus Web.

2.4 PageRank in Relation to SiteRank

Our next set of empirical experiments was conducted for elucidating the relationship between a document's PageRank and the SiteRank of the Web site the document resides on. We want to know if the intuitive assumption that importance of Web documents and Web sites is correlated, holds and in which form.

In another Fig. in [10], we display all (PageRank, SiteRank) order pairs. We find that almost all of the 1000 top ranked documents are located at the approximately top 90 sites. Furthermore, most of the top 100 documents are located at the top 30 Web sites. It appears as if there exists actually a correlation between a page's rank value and the SiteRank of its owner. Based on the experimental results and observations above, we believe our assumptions below are very reasonable:

1. v_s is important $\Rightarrow$ many important pages belong to v_s.
2. many important pages belonging to v_s $\Rightarrow$ v_s is an important Web site w.h.p. (with high probability).

Please note that these two statements are not tautological. If these statements hold true in a general sense or even if they are only true for most instead of all of the cases, we could safely distribute the weight of a Web site to its documents, proportional to their local weights, and use these distributed page weights to approximate the global ranking of documents. In the next section, we will present our preliminary results of such an attempt which shows that this approach is actually very promising for decentralized rank computation in a distributed search system.

3 SiteRank for Decentralized DocRank Computation

We want to distribute the task of computing page ranking to a set of distributed peers each of which crawls and stores a small fraction of the Web graph. Instead of setting up a centralized storage, indexing, link analysis system to compute the global PageRank of all documents based on the global Web graph and document link structure, we intend to have a decentralized system whose participating servers compute the global ranking of their locally crawled and stored subset of Web based on the local document link structure and the global SiteRank.

3.1   SiteRank for Computation of Global Document Ranking

To fulfill our aim, we propose a decentralized architecture for search systems. First, we need to define the *external pointing set* for each document $d \in V_D$ in the DocGraph $G_D(V_D, E_D)$ with SiteGraph $G_S(V_S, E_S)$.

Definition 2 *Assume $site(d_i)$ returns the Web site that d_i belongs to, the external pointing set for a Web document d_i is defined as a set of tuples:*

$$PS(d_i) = \{(v_{si}, n_{si}) : \exists d' \ st. \ (d', d_i) \in E_D, \ site(d') = v_{si} \ and \ not \ site(d_i) = v_{si}$$
$$n_{si} \ being \ the \ number \ of \ such \ d' \ of \ v_{si}\}$$

For every tuple, v_{si} is a Web site that has pages pointing to d_i and n_{si} is the number of such pages on v_{si}.

We decompose our computation of the global ranking for Web documents into three steps:

1. The computation of SiteRank. The algorithm is described above. Each Web site v_s has its SiteRank value $R_s(v_s) \in (0, 1)$.
2. The computation of the local ranking of Web documents, basically we compute the local PageRank vector r_I (I means internal links) based on the DocGraph local to the Web site. A vector of weight augmentation r_E (E means external links) is also computed for all local documents. The weight element r_E for document d_i is computed as:

$$r_E^i = \begin{cases} 0, & if \ PS(d_i) \ is \ empty \\ \sum_{(v_{si}, n_{si}) \in PS(d_i)} \frac{n_{si}}{N_{si}} R_s(v_{si}), & otherwise \end{cases}$$

where $N_{si} = \sum_{(v_{si}, n_{si}) \in PS(d_i)} n_{si}$ and $R_s(v_{si})$ is the SiteRank value of the Web site v_{si}. A local aggregation for document weight of d_i is then computed as follows:

$$r^i = w_I r_I^i + w_E r_E^i$$

We chose the values $(w_I, w_E) = (0.2, 0.8)$ for this local aggregation. This reflects a higher valuation of external links than internal links. One motivation for this choice is the relatively low number of links across Web sites as compared to the number of links within the same Web site.

3. The application of the ranking algebra [1] to combine both rankings to produce the final global ranking. Retraction to each document gives the final global DocRank value for the page:

$$r_G^i = r^i R_s(site(d_i))$$

3.2   Case Study

As we obtain the aggregate document ranking as described above, we evaluate the results both qualitatively and quantitatively. We performed the evaluations using the following approach: we chose two selected Web sites s_1 (sicwww.epfl.ch, the home of the computing center with 280 documents) and s_2 (the support site for SUN machines with 21685 documents), with substantially different characteristics, in particular the sizes. For those domains we computed the local internal and external rankings. We also put the EPFL portal Web server s_h (www.epfl.ch) in the collection, since this is a point where most of the other Web sites are connected to. We consider this subset of documents an excellent knowledge source for information of Web site importance.

The two ranking methods to be compared qualitatively are the global PageRank computed by using the global DocGraph for the link structure, and the aggregate DocRank computed by taking our SiteRank-based approach. We examined the top 25 of the documents belonging to s_1 or s_2 resulting from both ranking methods. In our aggregate ranking, more pages of greater importance are put in the top positions. In the global PageRank, two obviously important pages are ranked much lower than some software documentation pages in the global PageRank. We can assume that this is an effect due to the agglomerate structure of these document collections. This play a much less important role in our aggregate ranking due to the way of how the ranking is composed from local rankings using SiteRank. It demonstrates what a difference in quality we have made by using SiteRank in the computation.

For quantitative comparison of rankings we adopt the Spearman's Footrule with a weighting scheme:

$$F(r_{G0}, r_{G1}) = \sum_{i=1}^{n} w_0(i) w_1(i) |r_{G0}(i) - r_{G1}(i)| \tag{5}$$

In the formula, $r_{Gj}, j = 0, 1$ are the two ranking vectors to be compared. $r_{Gj}(i)$ is the rank of document i. Please note that the rank $r_{Gj}(i)$ is different from the computed rank weight r_{Gj}^i for a document d_i. The former is the order number of a document's place in the ranking list and can only be a positive integer, for example, if a document is the topmost one of the list, its rank is 1. The latter is the actual weight value computed by the algorithm which can only be a real number between 0 and 1.

We make this weighted customization since search engines return documents in ranking order and top ones receive generally much higher attention than documents listed later. As users mostly care about top listed documents we assign 90% of the weight to the T top-listed documents for $T < n$, i.e. $w_j(i) = \frac{0.9}{T}$ for $1 \le i \le T$ and $w_j(i) = \frac{0.1}{n-T}$ for $T+1 \le i \le n$. When $T = n$, $w_j(i) = \frac{1}{n}$ for $1 \le i \le n$.

We give now the results of the quantitative comparison in Fig. 1. The figure shows the ranking distances computed using the adapted Spearman's rule of different rankings with respect to the global ranking for varying values of T. Besides the aggregate ranking we include for comparison purposes other rankings that are computed for different contexts. The "subset" ranking is the ranking obtained by selecting exactly all documents that are involved in the computation of the aggregate ranking and applying the PageRank algorithm. This ranking thus uses exactly the same information that is available to

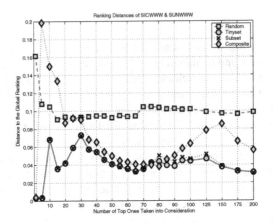

Fig. 1. Ranking Distances of SICWWW & SUNWWW

the computation of the aggregate ranking, i.e., the documents in the set $\{s_1, s_2, s_h\}$. The "tinyset" ranking is the ranking obtained by selecting exactly all documents in $\{s_1, s_2\}$ that are ranked by the aggregate ranking and applying PageRank to them. In addition, we included for calibration a randomly generated ranking. The results are shown in Fig. 1. One can observe that, interestingly, the result of the "composite" ranking appears to be much "worse" for low values of T than the global ranking. However, considering the qualitative analysis before, the result rather indicates that the global ranking seems to be poor, whereas the aggregate ranking is to be considered as the "good" ranking to be approximated. For larger values of T the aggregate ranking approximates then the rankings computed on the selected subsets. Also this is an interesting result, since the aggregate ranking is performed in a distributed manner, computing separate rankings for each of the three subdomains involved, whereas the "subset" and "tinyset" rankings can be considered as corresponding to a global ranking based on the union of the selected subdomains. This shows that by aggregation one can obtain at least as good results in a distributed manner as with global ranking using the same information.

3.3   Analysis of Reduction in Computation Cost

A member server can be a dedicated machine that crawls part of the Web. It can coexist in a Web server and compute the global document ranking for its own served Web documents. However, we need to assume that the SiteRank computation result of all Web sites in a Web graph, whose global document ranking is to be computed, is known to all member servers. This is reasonable as the number of Web sites even of whole Internet is estimated to be only at the magnitude of a dozen of million [3]. Thus the computation of the SiteRank of such a Web-scale SiteGraph is fully tractable in a low-end PC machine. Additionally, we assume that such a global SiteRank vector does not fluctuate very drastically such that it makes sense to perform such a global scale SiteRank computation infrequently and to share the result among all the member servers.

We provide a small comparison between the computation cost for the SiteRank and the PageRank. If we take the EPFL campus Web as an example, the reduction rate of the memory or disk space used to hold the matrix is:

$$\frac{Resource(SiteGraph)}{Resource(DocGraph)} = (591/2259102)^2 = 6.8 \times 10^{-6}\% \tag{6}$$

Moreover, we can use a 2-byte integer to represent every site, whereas we have to use at least a 4-byte or even 8-byte integer for pages, the rate becomes:

$$\text{reduction rate} = (25\% \sim 50\%) \times 6.8 \times 10^{-6}\% = (1.7 \sim 3.4) \times 10^{-6}\% \tag{7}$$

On the other hand, the rank computation of a matrix of size 591 can be easily performed in seconds, e.g. using a tool like Mathematica.

4 Conclusion

In many previous studies [4, 9], different snapshots of the Web have been investigated to find that not only the page in-degree, out-degree, but also the PageRank values follow the power law. We go one step further in our work to uncover that actually the SiteRank of Web sites in a Web graph also follows the power-law.

Many methods have been proposed for the rank computation of Web documents [2, 6]. However, none has been tried to decompose the computation to a two-step of first SiteRank then DocRank, which is our main contribution. One the other hand, most of existing approaches are logically centralized while ours is an inherently decentralized method. To the best of our knowledge, we are the first to use the study of the Web SiteGraph in the computation of Web document rankings for search engines in a decentralized fashion.

Based on observations on some useful correlation between the PageRank and SiteRank, we argue that decomposing the task of global Web document ranking computation to distributed participating member servers of a decentralized search system is a promising approach since we can make use of the SiteRank information to overcome the limit of a missing global view. At the same time, by doing the computation in such a complete decentralized fashion, the cost is largely reduced while we keep good quality of the ranking results. One interesting and important point is that PageRank spammers will find it difficult to spam SiteRank since they have to set up a large number of spamming Web sites to take advantage of the spamming SiteLinks.

References

1. Karl Aberer and Jie Wu. A framework for decentralized ranking in web information retrieval. In *Web Technologies and Applications: Proceedings of 5th Asia-Pacific Web Conference, APWeb 2003*, volume LNCS 2642, pages 213–226, Xi'an, China, September 2003. Springer-Verlag. September 27-29, 2003.
2. Serge Abiteboul, Mihai Preda, and Gregory Cobena. Adaptive on-line page importance computation. In *Proceedings of World Wide Wed Conference 2003 (WWW2003)*, Budapest, Hungary, May 2003. May 20-24, 2003.

3. Krishna Bharat, Bay-Wei Chang, Monika Henzinger, and Matthias Ruhl. Who links to whom: Mining linkage between web sites. In *Proceedings of the IEEE International Conference on Data Mining (ICDM '01)*, San Jose, USA, November 2001.
4. Michalis Faloutsos, Petros Faloutsos, and Christos Faloutsos. On power-law relationships of the internet topology. In *SIGCOMM*, pages 251–262, 1999.
5. Mor Harchol-Balter, Tom Leighton, and Daniel Lewin. Resource discovery in distributed networks. In *Proceedings of the eighteenth annual ACM symposium on Principles of distributed computing*, pages 229–237. ACM Press, 1999.
6. Sepandar D. Kamvar, Taher H. Haveliwala, Christopher D. Manning, and Gene H. Golub. Exploiting the block structure of theweb for computing pagerank. Technical report, Stanford University, March 2003. Submitted on 4th of March 2003.
7. Jon Kleinberg. Authoritative sources in a hyperlinked environment. In *Proceedings of the ACM-SIAM Symposium on Discrete Algorithms*, 1998.
8. Larry Page, Sergey Brin, Rajeev Motwani, and Terry Winograd. The pagerank citation ranking: Bringing order to the web. Technical report, Stanford University, January 1998.
9. Gopal Pandurangan, Prabhakara Raghavan, and Eli Upfal. Using pagerank to characterize web structure. In *8th Annual International Computing and Combinatorics Conference (CO-COON)*, 2002.
10. Jie Wu and Karl Aberer. Using siterank in p2p information retrieval. Technical Report IC/2004/31, Swiss Federal Institute of Technology, Lausanne, Switzerland, March 2004.

Web Information Retrieval Based on User Profile

Rachid Arezki[1], Pascal Poncelet[1], Gérard Dray[1], and David W. Pearson[2]

[1] Centre LGI2P EMA, Site EERIE Parc Scientifique Georges Besse
30035 Nimes Cedex 1, France
{rachid.arezki,pascal.poncelet,gerard.dray}@ema.fr
[2] EURISE, Jean Monnet University of Saint-Etienne 23, rue du Docteur Michelon
42023 Saint-Etienne, France
david.pearson@univ-st-etienne.fr

Abstract. With the growing popularity of the World Wide Web, the amount of available information is so great that finding the right and useful information becomes a very hard task for an end user. In this paper, we propose a new approach for personal Web information retrieval. The originality of our approach is a choice of indexing terms depending on the user request but also on his profile. The general idea is to consider that the need of a user depends on his request but also on his knowledge acquired through time on the thematic of his request.

1 Introduction

With the growing popularity of the World Wide Web, the amount of available information is so great that finding the right and useful information becomes a very difficult task. The end user, generally overloaded by information, can't efficiently perceive such information. In order to help the user in his task, the search engines available on the Web, propose through requests expressed by user in form of key words, a set of documents. Unfortunately, the quantity of returned results is also very large. Moreover, some relevant documents are often badly ranked and thus rarely consulted. *Blair&Maron* showed that the poor performance of IR systems is mainly due to the incapacity of users to formulate adequate requests [1]. Indeed, requests only formulated by key words express badly user information needs. In fact, these needs depend of course on the formulated request but also on the knowledge acquired by the user in his search domain: two users can formulate the same requests for different needs, and the same user for the same request may expect different answers in different periods of time [2]. For example, the results expected by an expert in java language who formulates the request "java course" are different from the results expected by a non expert which formulates the same request. A possible solution of this problem is to take into account the user profile in order to refine the ranks of the results returned by the Web search engines. In other words, the personalized Web information retrieval consists in finding a model able to consider efficiently user interests. In this article we present a new approach for information retrieval based on user profile. The originality of our approach is a choice of indexing terms depending on the user request but also on his profile. The general idea is to consider that the need of a user depends on his request but also on his knowledge acquired through time on the thematic of his request.

W. Nejdl and P. De Bra (Eds.): AH 2004, LNCS 3137, pp. 275–278, 2004.

We have developed *PAWebSearch*, a personal agent for Web information retrieval which supervises the user's actions and learns dynamically the user profile through the consulted documents (Web pages). For each information retrieval request carried out via a Web search engine (*Google, Yahoo,..*), *PAWebSearh* considers user request and results provided by the Web search engine for ranking these results according to the user profile.

The general principle of our approach is as follows. From a request q carried out by a user on a Web search engine, we recover all the results. Then, an analysis of user profile (user knowledge) allows us to obtain a set T of indexing terms. The construction of the indexing terms set T depends both on the user profile and on the user request q. We thus index all documents returned by search engine and request q according to the indexing term set T [1]. Then, to better adapt to the user's needs, the initial request vector q is transformed into q'. Proposing documents to the user is done by the calculation of similarities between the documents returned by the Web search engine and the request q'.

2   User Profile Representation

A user is defined by a tuple $p =< id, G >$, where id stands for a unique user identifier and G is a graph representing documents consulted by the user. The general idea is to analyze the content of the different documents and to store in the graph G co-occurrence frequency between various terms (words) of a document, as well as occurrence frequency of these terms. More precisely, $G= < V, E >$ is a labelled graph such as: (i) $V=\{(t_1, f_{t_1})..(t_n, f_{t_n})\}$ is a set of vertices of G, where each vertex (t_i, f_{t_i}) is represented by a term t_i and its frequency f_{t_i}. (ii) $E=\{(t_i, t_j, fco(t_i, t_j))/t_i, t_j \in V\}$ is a set of edges of G, where $fco(t_i, t_j)$ represents co-occurrence frequency between the terms t_i and t_j.

Algorithm 1: User Profile Learning
Input: consulted document d,
the user profile $p =< id, G >$
Output: updated user profile $p =< id, G >$
begin
    1. construction of the co-occurrence graph G_d
    2. **for** *each term t_i of G_d* **do**
        if $t_i \in G$ **then** $f_{t_i}^G = f_{t_i}^G + f_{t_i}^{G_d}$
        else
            create a new vertex (t_i, f_{t_i}) in the graph G such as
            $f_{t_i}^G = f_{t_i}^{G_d}$
    3. **for** *each edge $(t_i, t_j, fco(t_i, t_j))$ of G_d* **do**
        $fco_G(t_i, t_j) = fco_G(t_i, t_j) + fco_{G_d}(t_i, t_j)$
end
$fco_G(t_i, t_j)$ represents the frequency of co-occurrence
between terms (t_i, t_j) in the graph G.

The co-occurrence frequency (or co-frequency) between two words is defined as the frequency of both words occurring within a given textual unit. A textual unit can be k words window, a sentence, a paragraph, a section, or the whole of document. In the

---

[1] documents and requests are represented by vectors.

framework of our user profile, we consider that textual unit corresponds to a sentence, thus $fco(t_i, t_j)$ represents co-occurrence frequency between terms t_i and t_j in the set of sentences of the documents consulted by the user. As shown in algorithm 1, for each new consulted document d, a graph G_d is built, then G_d is added to the graph G representing the user profile.

3   Information Retrieval Model

We consider in this section that a request q was sent to a Web search engine, and that we have a set X of returned documents, and let p be a user profile. Our information retrieval model can be presented as a tuple $< X, Q, P, T, s, f >$, where X represents the set of documents (i.e. document collection), Q stands for the set of requests, P is the set of user's profiles, T represents the term set indexing, s is a similarity or distance function and f is the term set construction function. For a given request q and a profile p we have $T = f(p, q)$.

Our motivation is to integrate effectively the user interests in the information re-trieval process. Thus, the construction of the indexing term set T is done in a dynamic way and depends both on the user profile p and on the user request q (i.e. $T = f(p, q)$). For each new user request q, a new term set T is rebuilt. After the determination of the indexing term set T, the request q and each document of the collection X are rep-resented by vectors according to the indexing term set T. To better adapt to the user's needs, the initial request vector q is transformed into q'. The transformation of q to q' requires the construction of the profile-request matrix (Sect. 3.2).

3.1   Indexing Term Set Construction

The choice of the indexing terms takes into account user profile as well as information retrieval request. Our motivation is to choose indexing terms reflecting the knowledge of the user in the domain of his search. As shown by the algorithm 2, the indexing terms are selected among the terms of the user profile which are in co-occurrence with the terms of the initial request.

Algorithm 2: Indexing Term Set Construction
Input: user request q,
the user profile $p = < id, G >$
Output: indexing term set T
begin
    1. $T \leftarrow$ terms contained in the request q;
    2. **for** *each term t_i of q* **do**
        for *each term t_j of G such as $fco(t_i, t_j) > 0$* **do**
            if $\frac{(fco(t_i, t_j))^2}{ft_i \times ft_j} > \beta$ **then**
                $T = T \cup \{t_j\}$
end
β : constant representing the threshold of term selection.

3.2   Profile-Request Matrix

From the indexing terms obtained previously, we extract from the user profile p, the co-occurrence frequency matrix of the indexing term set T. This matrix represents se-mantic bonds between the various indexing terms. Let T_p be the set of terms contained in the user profile $p = <id, G>$. We call matrix *profile-request*, noted M_T, the square matrix of dimension $| T \times T |$ such that $T \subset T_p$, where each element m_{ij} of M_T is defined by:

$$m_{ij} = fco(t_i, t_j) \quad \text{where } (t_i, t_j) \in T^2$$

3.3 Request and Document Representation

From the profile-request matrix M_T, we can calculate the new request q' in order to adjust it according to the user profile. This request aims to reflect, as well as possible, the user interest in his search domain.

$$q' = (1 - \alpha) \times \frac{q}{|q|} + \alpha \times \frac{q \times M_T}{|q \times M_T|}$$

$|q|$ (repec. $|q \times M_T|$) is the Euclidean length of vector q (repec. $q \times M_T$), α: threshold such that $0 \leq \alpha \leq 1$, allowing hybridation between initial request $\frac{q}{|q|}$ and the enriched request $\frac{q \times M_T}{|q \times M_T|}$, the higher α is the more the user profile is considered.

4   Conclusion

We proposed in this paper a new approach for personalized information retrieval. The proposed model allows a better consideration of the user's interests in the information retrieval process by: (i) A choice of indexing terms which reflects as well as possible the user knowledge in his search domain. (ii) An enrichment of the user request by the matrix of profile-request.

In the models where the user is represented by vectors of terms, an iterative process of user profile re-indexing is necessary to take into account of new indexing terms. In our model none re-indexing of user profile is necessary, therefore it is very adapted to the Web, where information is very heterogeneous. The first experimental results carried out with *PAWebSearch* confirm the relevance of our approach. One of the prospects for research, is the application of the indexing term set construction method in the framework of a standard information retrieval model.

References

1. D.C. Blair and M.E. Maron. An evaluation of retrieval effectivness for a full-text document retrieval system. *Communication of the ACM*, 28(3):289–299, 1985.
2. C. Danilowicz and H.C. Nguyen. Using user profiles in intelligent information retrieval. In *Proceedings of the 13th International Symposium on Foundations of Intelligent Systems*, pages 223–231. Springer-Verlag, 2002.

Adaptive Support for Collaborative and Individual Learning (ASCIL): Integrating AHA! and CLAROLINE

Carlos Arteaga, Ramon Fabregat,
Jorge Eyzaguirre, and David Mérida

Institut de Informàtica i Aplicacions
Universitat de Girona
{carteaga,ramon,david}@eia.udg.es

Abstract. In this work we present a tool for Adaptive Support for Collaborative and Individual Learning (ASCIL). Taking as a base the fact that learning is not solely an individual nor collaborative process, we have come to the conclusion that it is an integrated activity which requires integral support. We have therefore applied two previously developed systems, AHA! and CLAROLINE, which we have integrated into ASCIL, a system which has the capacity to deliver adaptive support to individuals as well as collaborative learning. The interesting aspect of this present proposal is that the adaptive support for collaborative learning is integrated with the information contained in the User Model (student), which is kept in operation by AHA!. That is to say that the adaptive tasks are the result of individual learning in AHA! as a starting point.

1 Introduction

Learning is the result of individual cognitive processes through which information is assimilated. Knowledge is constructed in two ways. One is personal (individual learning) and the other is social (collaborative-cooperative learning). In the process of individual learning activities are specifically designed for the students to perform them by themselves. In the collaborative learning process, learning activities are designed for two or more people to participate.

Brusilovsky has defined an Adaptive Hypermedia System (AHS) [1]. According to formalizations based on [3], the AHS uses three basic components to achieve adaptability: the User Model, the Domain Model of the application and the Adaptation Model. The adaptive support for collaborative learning is newer than the individual learning adaptive support and its main objective is to encourage collaborative processes. Gaudioso explains the objectives of adaptation in adaptive support for collaborative learning in [5].

In this paper, we explain how collaborative and individual aspects can be combined in providing adaptive support to learning, and propose the tool ASCIL, which combines AHA! and CLAROLINE. The organization of this paper is as follows. In Sect. 2 we present the main characteristics of AHA! and CLAROLINE. In Sect. 3, the ASCIL system is explained. Finally, in Sect. 4 conclusions and a description of future tasks are presented.

W. Nejdl and P. De Bra (Eds.): AH 2004, LNCS 3137, pp. 279–282, 2004.

2 AHA! and CLAROLINE

AHA! (Adaptive Hypermedia Architecture) [4] is a system built with the aim of making it easy to generate adaptive courses for the Web. The adaptation in AHA! is carried out based on a series of rules included in the HTML pages. There are rules defined by the creator of the course that are used to determine what parts of the page are shown to the student. The conditions in the rules included in the pages are based on certain characteristics that the user supplies about themselves. These characteristics are kept in a very simple User Model (which says which concepts were learned by the user, or which interface preferences they have), which the designer can also create in the course using XML documents. AHA! uses note-taking techniques, discarding, hiding and adaptive link eliminations. The actual version of AHA! is 2.0 which includes authoring tools that facilitate the creation of courses. The incorporation of authoring tools makes AHA! an ideal candidate for creating Adaptive On-Line Courses. AHA! doesn't have support for collaborative learning, it is only for individual learning.

CLAROLINE [2] is an Open Source software based on PHP/MySQL. It is a collaborative learning environment allowing teachers or education institutions to create and administer courses through the web. CLAROLINE permits the teacher to structure courses, allocate material and administer activities. Giving them freedom to structure as well as set up study material. The process of individual learning, as seen in this tool, uses readings and/or documents in different formats. It also includes tools for interaction through the Internet. CLAROLINE has been developed to be a guide to a good teaching-learning process, not to substitute it. It seeks to be of use, guided by user requirements and open to integrating services and new tools to adapt to concrete scenarios contained in the course. Since it is open-code and also modular, it allows an administrator to, among other things, add and modify tools, change the appearance, and adapt databases. CLAROLINE doesn't have adaptive support for collaborative learning.

3 ASCIL: Integration of AHA! with CLAROLINE

In this paper we propose a tool for Adaptive Support for Collaborative and Individual Learning (ASCIL). It aims to encourage collaboration between students starting from: a) Their own progress in an individual learning environment (AHA!), b) Their disposition towards cooperation, and c) The maximum number of students which can be supported without having their own progress hindered in any way.

The learning model used is based in the idea that learning must be integral, that is, individual as well as collaborative. To implement the model, we chose AHA! and CLAROLINE given their specific characteristics and the fact that both have an open source nature. Another reason for this choice is that AHA! doesn't have support for collaborative learning, and CLAROLINE has no adaptive support mechanisms for individual learning and the support for collaborative learning is very limited. Our hypothesis is that an adaptive course created in AHA! can be used successfully as an information source to give adaptive support in adaptive activities of collaborative learning. Also, that the architecture allows other tools to develop activities for collaborative learning that increase the adaptive support towards collaboration.

In this paper we integrate CLAROLINE and AHA! to keep both individual learning and collaborative learning operational in one environment. Integrating both methods allows a more complete system from an individual point of view as well as from a collaborative learning one. This is how we arrived at adaptive learning from a collaborative learning perspective. As a result, we have an adaptive learning environment which allows students to become members of an adaptive course including adaptive support for individual learning as well as collaborative learning.

The Collaboration Model (see following table) seems simple but can easily be extended in order to carry out other adaptation tasks.

Attributes	Description
Student ID	Unique Identifier per student
Available {yes, no}.	If the user is available to cooperate with.
Conditions of learning	Extracted dynamically from the Student Model kept by AHA!. List of concepts and values of knowledge associated with each student.
Potential Collaborators (dynamic)	Set of students chosen by the adaptive engine. These comply with defined adaptation guidelines.
Number Of Students	Number of students who have this particular student in their team, from the Potential Collaborators team.

In the collaborative adaptive engine, the guideline for adaptation is represented simply and is implemented by a PHP procedure which is dynamically executed every time the student starts learning a new concept in AHA!. If the student **est** complies with the following condition, the procedure updates the set of Potential Collaborators of student E and updates the Amount Of Students. We assume that a student cannot give attention and support to more than a maximum number of students (MaxNumC).

```
est.concept     = E.concept &
est.knowledge (E.concept) =100 &
est.availability = yes &
est.AmountOfStudents <=MaxNumC
```

For this first prototype, the decision of cooperating or not is in the hands of every student, since the system only goes as far as building the team of Potential Collaborators.

In this version of the system, once there is a cluster of Potential Collaborators, cooperation is carried out using email and/or the chat services available in CLAROLINE. The information we have in CLAROLINE permits us to know in any given time if a user was or is connected. Therefore this makes email the exclusive tool for collaboration when disconnected. Students can choose the way they communicate. Given the modular structure of the system, new interaction mechanisms can be added that allow the development of other collaborative activities. In this case, the adaptive engine would need to be modified to include these new adaptation tasks.

4 Conclusions and Future Work

Two open source systems (AHA! and CLAROLINE) have been integrated in ASCIL and a practical system that can be applied in real educational environments has been obtained. It is important to emphasize that it is possible to amplify collaborative learning activities and include new objectives for adaptation. However, there are still many points left open, such as: What factors affect the construction of potential collaborators? How can we measure the effectiveness of the collaboration process? To what degree are students willing to cooperate with one another? These are not superficial problems and it is necessary to make specific examinations with students in order to reach valid conclusions.

The cooperation model needs to be extended in order to contain information on the interaction process itself. With this information the system will be able to make decisions, and in this way it will be possible to add more adaptive tasks such as those mentioned in [6].

References

1. P. Brusilovsky: Methods and techniques of adaptive hypermedia. User Modeling and User Adapted Interaction. v 6, n 2-3, pp 87- 129. (Special issue on adaptive hypertext and hypermedia). 1996
2. CLAROLINE. http://www.claroline.org
3. P. De Bra, G.J. Houben, H. Wu. AHAM: A Dexter-based Reference Model for Adaptive Hypermedia. .Proceedings of the ACM Conference on Hypertext and Hypermedia, pp. 147-156, Darmstadt, Germany, 1999.
4. P. De Bra. Design issues in adaptive hypermedia application development. In 2nd workshop on Adaptive systems and user modeling on the WWW.
5. E. Gaudioso and J.G. Boticario. User data management and usage model acquisition in an adaptive educational collaborative environment. In the Second International Conference on Adaptive Hypermedia and Adaptive Web-based Systems, n. 2347 in LNCS, pp. 143–152, Malaga, Spain, May 2002.
6. E. Gaudioso Contribuciones al Modelado del Usuario en Entornos Adaptativos de Aprendizaje y Colaboración a través del Internet mediante Técnicas de Aprendizaje Automático. PhD thesis , UNED. 2002

Specification of Adaptive Behavior
Using a General-Purpose Design Methodology
for Dynamic Web Applications

Peter Barna, Geert-Jan Houben, and Flavius Frasincar

Technische Universiteit Eindhoven
PO Box 513, NL-5600 MB Eindhoven, The Netherlands
{pbarna,houben,flaviusf}@win.tue.nl

Abstract. Methodologies for the design and engineering of web applications evolve to accommodate the increased dynamic nature of modern web applications. In this paper we show and demonstrate the similarity between the dynamics in web applications and adaptive hypermedia systems using a general purpose model-driven web design methodology (Hera). To do so we use a simple example. We also stress advantages of specifying adaptivity within models defined on the schema level.

1   Introduction

The dynamic nature and increasing complexity of modern web applications require rigorous design methodologies, e. g. WebML [4], OOHDM [10], Hera [11], and UWE [7], that need to evolve to accommodate the increasing demands. When we observe the recent advances in these methodologies, and we do so here in terms of Hera, we see the similarity between dynamic web applications and adaptive hypermedia systems (AHS) where a dynamically updated user model is used to affect the navigation and presentation structure. The goal of this paper is not to introduce yet another reference model for AHS (which is what Hera is not), but to stress and demonstrate with an implementation the fact that existing general-purpose web design methods can be successfully used for the design of adaptive web applications at model level.

2   Related Work

Next to systems originally developed for the purpose of adaptive hypermedia (e. g. AHA! [6], InterBook [3], or KBS HyperBook [8]) and next to reference models for such systems (e. g. AHAM [5], the Munich model [9]), there are general purpose web design methodologies taking into account adaptation and personalization aspects (at different levels). For instance, in WebML [4] the user model (in AHS terminology), there called the personalization sub-schema, is a part of its data model. The content management model specifies how this information is dynamically updated based on user actions. In OOHDM [10], most personalization and adaptation mechanisms are captured in the conceptual (class) model e. g. by means of the user and user group models.

W. Nejdl and P. De Bra (Eds.): AH 2004, LNCS 3137, pp. 283–286, 2004.

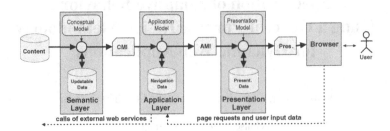

Fig. 1. Overall Hera architecture for dynamic applications

3   Design of Dynamic Web Applications in Hera

3.1   Methodology and Architecture

Hera is a model-driven methodology for web applications that distinguishes a number of design phases, where every phase results in the construction of a particular model describing a specific aspect of the web application:

- In the conceptual design phase the Conceptual Model (CM) defining the domain data is constructed.
- In the application design phase the Application Model (AM) defining the structure and behavior of the navigation view over the domain (conceptual) data is constructed.
- In the presentation design phase the Presentation Model (PM) defining the layout of generated hypermedia presentations is constructed.

Fig. 1 shows a view of a system hosting dynamic web applications based on the Hera architecture. Hypermedia presentations are dynamically generated page by page, by transforming data from the content subsequently through CM and AM instances to the final format (e. g. HTML) using Hera models. Updatable data (semantic layer), navigation data (application layer), and the presentation data (presentation layer) can be influenced by user inputs and store state information of appropriate layers. All models in Hera are defined in RDFS [1].

3.2   Implementation Example

The example is an excerpt of a virtual shopping basket used in an on-line book shop. Next to it, users' interests in particular authors are modelled and used.

Conceptual and Navigation Data Models. Fig. 2 (a) shows an excerpt of the shop's conceptual model (the *Book* and *Author* concepts) and a simple virtual shopping basket specified as a part of the navigation data model (the updatable *User* and *Interest* concepts and their properties). The *Interest* concept determines an interest of a user in particular author and is a part of the user model here.

Application Model. AM describes the navigation structure of the application and its dynamics in terms of slices (navigation nodes or their parts), their relationships, appearance conditions, and data manipulation operations associated with slice reference

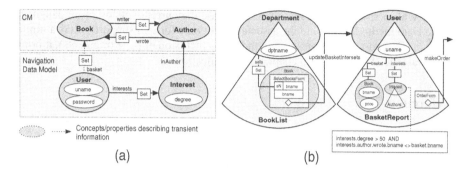

Fig. 2. Conceptual and Navigation Data Models (a), and Application Model (b)

relationships. AM is built on the top of CM, updatable data, and navigation data. Fig. 2 (b) shows the initial *Department.BookList* slice allowing the user to select a number of books from a list, and the *User.BasketReport* slice showing selected books (the content of the basket) and authors (via the *Interest.Authors* sub-slice) in which the user's interest exceeds a threshold value (50 in this case). The *updateBasketInterests* operation increases and decreases *Interest.degree* depending on the user's selections.

4   Adaptivity Specification with Hera

In our example we placed the user model into the navigation data model, because the perceived state of the user influences the navigation over the data content and typically this does not belong to the content. In most methodologies like WebML and OOHDM all the user-related data is put together with the content. Hera allows to make a strict separation of concerns regarding the modelling of domain content (CM), navigation view over the content (AM and its navigation data model), and presentation of the navigation (PM and its presentation data model, both out of the scope here).

All Hera models define a schema view on data. Hence, compared to the specification of models on instance level it does not limit the extent of the data content that can be conditionally included. In AHAM for example, the designer must specify which instances are included under what circumstances, whereas in Hera the designer specifies appearance conditions without referring to concrete instances, so the concrete data content doesn't have to be known to authors during the design of the system.

All models in Hera, including data models for updatable and navigation data, and the adaptivity conditions in AM, are specified in RDFS [1]. One of the reasons for choosing RDF(S) is that it is a flexible (supporting schema refinement and description enrichment) and extensible (allowing to define new resources) format that enables interoperability. Operations are expressed in SeRQL [2], one of the most advanced RDF(S) query languages.

5   Conclusions

Although the Hera methodology aims to support the design of general purpose web applications, we demonstrated how its support for dynamics in web applications is particularly fit to specify the design of AHS. While the current version of the languages of the Hera methodology (and the associated software for tool support) offers a limited range of adaptation techniques (e. g. conditional inclusion of page fragments), it brings the advantage of schema-level adaptation specification.

References

1. Brickley, D., Guha, R.V.: RDF Vocabulary Description Language 1.0: RDF Schema. W3C Recommandation (2004)
2. Broekstra, J., Kampman, A., van Harmelen, F.: Sesame: A Generic Architecture for Storing and Querying RDF and RDF Schema, The 1st International Semantic Web Conference, Springer Verlag (2002)
3. Brusilovsky, P., Eklund, J., and Schwarz, E.: Web-based education for all: A tool for developing adaptive courseware. The 7th World Wide Web Conference (1998)
4. Ceri, S., Fraternali, P., Bongio, A., Brambilla, M., Comai, S., Matera, M.: book Designing Data-Intensive Web Applications, Morgan Kaufmann Publishers (2003)
5. De Bra, P., Houben, G.J., Wu, H.: AHAM: A Dexter-based Reference Model for Adaptive Hypermedia. The 10th ACM Conference on Hypertext and Hypermedia, ACM Press (1999)
6. De Bra, P., Aerts, A., Houben, G.J., Wu, H.: Making General-Purpose Adaptive Hypermedia Work, The WebNet 2000 World Conference on the WWW and Internet, AACE (2000)
7. Koch, N., Kraus, A., Hennicker, R.: The Authoring Process of the UML-based Web Engineering Approach. The 1st International Workshop on Web-Oriented Software Technology (2001)
8. Nejdl, W., Wolpers, M.: KBS Hyperbook - A Data Driven Information System on the Web. The 8th World Wide Web Conference (1999)
9. Koch, N., Wirsing, M.: The Munich Reference Model for Adaptive Hypermedia Applications. The 2nd International Conference on Adaptive Hypermedia and Adaptive Web-based Systems, Springer Verlag (2002)
10. Schwabe, D., Rossi, G.: An Object Oriented Approach to Web-Based Application Design. Theory and Practice of Object Systems 4(4) (1998)
11. Vdovjak, R. Frasincar, F., Houben, G.J., Barna, P.: Engineering Semantic Web Information Systems in Hera, Journal of Web Engineering, 2(1&2) (2003)

Using the X3D Language for Adaptive Manipulation of 3D Web Content

Luca Chittaro and Roberto Ranon

HCI Lab, Dept. of Math and Computer Science, University of Udine,
via delle Scienze 206, 33100 Udine, Italy
{chittaro,ranon}@dimi.uniud.it

Abstract. Web sites that include 3D content, i.e. Web sites where users navigate and interact (at least partially) through a 3D graphical interface, are increasingly employed in different domains, such as tutoring and training, tourism, e-commerce and scientific visualization. However, while a substantial body of literature and software tools is available about making 2D Web sites adaptive, very little has been published on the problem of personalizing 3D Web content and interaction. In this paper, we describe how we are exploiting a recently proposed 3D Web technology, i.e. the X3D (eXtensible 3D) language, for adaptive manipulation of 3D Web content.

1 Introduction and Motivation

Recent advances in graphics computing power and network bandwidth have made it possible to increasingly employ 3D Web content in different domains, such as e-commerce, tutoring and training, tourism, scientific visualization, and entertainment. However, while a substantial body of literature and software tools is available about making 2D Web sites adaptive, very little has been published on the problem of personalizing 3D Web content, navigation and presentation.

As pointed out by [1], 2D Web sites are mainly a collection of connected information items that allows users to navigate from one item to another by simply selecting the desired one from a set of links. With 3D Web content, the situation is more complex. Content (3D models, images, text, audio, …) is organized in a 3D space, following a possibly complex spatial arrangement (e.g., the 3D model of a building or an entire city in tourism-related sites). The user navigates through 3D space by continuously controlling the position of her viewpoint (assuming, as in most cases, a first-person perspective) through mouse, or arrow-keys, or 3D pointing devices (when available). Moreover, users of 3D virtual environments do not only navigate and look at, but point, click or drag 3D objects (e.g., to activate some object behavior, such as opening a door). As a consequence, the space of possible adaptations in the case of 3D is more complex than in 2D Web sites, and largely unexplored. Consider, for example, the problem of adaptive content presentation: while in 2D Web sites one possibly prioritizes and then juxtaposes the (adapted) information fragments, with 3D Web content one would need also to properly arrange the content in 3D space (e.g., objects need not to overlap, must be adequately seen, free space must be enough for the user to navigate, …).

W. Nejdl and P. De Bra (Eds.): AH 2004, LNCS 3137, pp. 287–290, 2004.

One possible strategy to introduce adaptivity in the 3D context could be to re-formulate or extend adaptation techniques and tools developed in the AH field, as suggested by Brusilovsky [2]; for example, Hughes et al. [1] have developed methods for personalized navigation support in 3D virtual environments by re-formulating well-known AH adaptive navigation support techniques. However, using current AH techniques and tools for the 3D case is not straightforward. While some of the obstacles are related to the intrinsic features of 3D content (e.g., users' navigation and interaction is more complex), others arise from the fact that the languages for representing 3D content (the most common of which is currently VRML, the Virtual Reality Modeling Language) are very different from HTML.

These obstacles force one to develop 3D-specific methods and tools. For example, in [3, 4] we have proposed an architecture for delivering adaptive 3D Web content, called AWe3D (Adaptive Web3D), and applied it to an e-commerce context. The AWe3D architecture, while successful for experimenting with adaptivity of 3D Web content, suffers from two limitations: (i) it only deals with the personalization of 3D content written in the VRML language (and does not take into account other types of content); (ii) it is not easy to integrate existing AH technologies and tools.

Recently, a novel 3D Web technology, i.e. the X3D language [5] has been proposed (and submitted to ISO) by the Web3D Consortium as a replacement of the VRML language. One of the main differences between X3D and VRML is the definition of an XML encoding for the language. This feature opens the way for easier integration of 3D content with other Web content, technologies, and tools, including adaptive ones. As an example, in this paper we describe how we are exploiting the X3D language for implementing, in the context of 3D Web content, some well-known AH techniques, i.e., adaptive manipulation (insertion, removal, choice, alteration) of information fragments. Furthermore, the proposed method works with any XML-based language, making it suitable also for other media, e.g. text (XHTML), images (SVG) and multimedia (SMIL).

2 Exploiting the X3D Language for Adaptive Manipulation of 3D Web Content

Adaptive manipulation (e.g., insertion, removal, choice) of (textual) fragments is a well-known technique used in AH systems. For example, the AHA! architecture [6] implements it with *adaptive objects inclusion*, i.e., by using special XHTML <object> tags where adaptive content is to be inserted, and letting the adaptation engine select the proper content on the basis of the user model and adaptation rules. This solution has some nice properties: (i) it makes the enclosing file a regular XHTML file, which can be viewed without the adaptive engine, and (ii) if a fragment is needed in different places, it can be stored just once and conditionally included where and whenever needed.

However, this technique is not well suited to the case of X3D, since the language does not include the <object> tag (or a similar element): thus, using it would make a X3D file impossible to both validate and display/edit with visual authoring tools (note that authoring 3D content writing code is hard). Moreover, the adaptive object inclusion technique works at the level of entire XHTML files, and does not allow one to manipulate *only* specific elements or attribute values; note that many useful properties of X3D content (e.g., position, color and texture of 3D objects) can be altered by simply changing the values of some XML attributes. Furthermore, adaptive object inclusion does not allow removal of content.

To take into account these concerns, our solution to adaptive manipulation of X3D fragments is based on associating with a X3D file (whose content has to be adapted) a *Content Personalization Specification (CPS),* in the form of a separate XML document composed by a list of adaptiveContent elements. Each adaptiveContent element specifies that a specific fragment (element or attribute) in the corresponding X3D file will depend on the user model and adaptation rules.

We will explain the mechanism in detail by using the following example: consider an adaptive 3D store in which, according to the user's shopping interests: (i) the level of exposure of each product should vary (e.g. each product should become more/less visible by varying the size of its 3D model); (ii) some products should be removed, while other added (e.g., personalized special offers). A simplified version of the X3D file of the 3D store could be as follows:

```
<X3D>
  <head> ... </head>
  <Scene>
      <Transform DEF="prod_1" translation="…">
        <Shape>…</Shape>
      </Transform>
      <Transform DEF="prod_2" translation="…">
        <Shape>…</Shape>
      </Transform>
      …
  <Scene>
</X3D>
```

where each Transform element defines the position of a product in the 3D store, and the enclosed Shape element defines its 3D model. The following CPS defines the required adaptive manipulation of content:

```
<CPS>
<adaptiveContent DEF="prod_1" name="specialOffer_1"/>
<adaptiveContent DEF="prod_2" attribute="scale" name="prod_2.size"/>
…
</CPS>
```

The first adaptiveContent element specifies that the element in the X3D file whose DEF attribute is equal to prod_1 (DEF works in X3D as the id attribute in the XHTML language) must be substituted with content derived by the adaptation engine (including the possibility of no content, which enables adaptive removal of fragments, or content composed by multiple elements, which enables adaptive insertion of fragments); The second adaptiveContent element specifies that, in the element of the X3D file whose DEF attribute is equal to prod_2, the attribute scale (which controls the size of a 3D object) must take a value provided by the adaptation engine. The name attribute is a reference to a specific part of the user model.

When a X3D file is requested, by means of XSL transformations, we first translate the adaptiveContent elements into queries to adaptation engine, and then insert the returned fragments into the proper positions in the X3D file.

Since the proposed method does not rely on specific features of the X3D language, it may be also used with other XML-based languages (such as XHTML, SVG and SMIL).

3 Conclusions

The proposed method, besides extending our AWe3D architecture to the adaptation of non-3D content, allows one to integrate 3D content into existing AH architectures. As a proof of concept, we are currently developing an adaptive tutoring Web application (which uses 3D content) using the AHA! architecture. This will allow us also to more easily investigate the effectiveness of other AH methods and techniques in the context of 3D content.

Acknowledgements

Andrea Virgili played an important role in the implementation of the proposed method. This work is partially supported by the MIUR COFIN 2003 program.

References

1. Hughes, S., Brusilovsky, P., and Lewis, M.: Adaptive navigation support in 3D e-commerce activities. In: Proceedings of Workshop on Recommendation and Personalization in eCommerce at AH 2002 (2002) 132-139.
2. Brusilovsky, P., and Maybury M. T.: From Adaptive HyperMedia to the Adaptive Web. Communications of the ACM **45** 5 (2002) 31-33.
3. Chittaro L., Ranon R.: Adding Adaptive Features to Virtual Reality Interfaces for E-Commerce. In: Proceedings of AH-2000: International Conference on Adaptive Hypermedia and Adaptive Web-based Systems, Lecture Notes in Computer Science 1892, Springer-Verlag, (2000) 86-97.
4. Chittaro L., Ranon R.: Dynamic Generation of Personalized VRML Content: a General Approach and its Application to 3D E-Commerce. In: Proceedings of Web3D 2002: 7th International Conference on 3D Web Technology, ACM Press, New York (2002) 145-154.
5. Extensible 3D (X3D) International Draft Standards, ISO/IEC FDIS 19775:200x http://www.web3d.org/x3d/specifications/index.html
6. De Bra, P., Aerts, A., Berden, B., De Lange, B., Rousseau, B., Santic, T., Smits, D., Stash, N.: AHA! The Adaptive Hypermedia Architecture. In: Proceedings of the ACM Hypertext Conference, ACM Press, New York (2003) 81-84.

Evaluation of APeLS –
An Adaptive eLearning Service
Based on the Multi-model, Metadata-Driven Approach

Owen Conlan and Vincent P. Wade

Knowledge and Data Engineering Group
Trinity College, Dublin Ireland
{Owen.Conlan,Vincent.Wade}@cs.tcd.ie
http://kdeg.cs.tcd.ie

Abstract. The evaluation of learner and tutor feedback is essential in the production of high quality personalized eLearning services. There are few evaluations available in the Adaptive Hypermedia domain relative to the amount of research interest this domain is attracting. Many of the papers in this domain focus
on the technological design of systems without justifying the designs through
the lessons learned from evaluations. This paper evaluates the usability and effectiveness of using the multi-model, metadata-driven approach for producing
rich adaptive eLearning solutions that remain content and domain independent.
Through this independence, the eLearning services developed can utilize many
pedagogical approaches and a variety of models to produce a wide range of
highly flexible solutions. This paper identifies benefits to learners brought
through adopting the multi-model approach gathered over four years of student
evaluation. It briefly describes the evaluation of the Adaptive Personalized
eLearning Service (APeLS), a personalized eLearning service based on a generic adaptive engine.

1 Introduction

Adaptive content systems are generally either systems that provide high levels of
adaptivity on a specific content domain, such as ELM-ART II [4] or are generic adaptive systems that provide fundamental levels of adaptivity on non-specific domains
AHA! [2]. A general problem with the application of many Adaptive Hypermedia
systems to the area of eLearning is that the role of pedagogy is often undermined or
ignored. Twenty years of using ICT for learning has shown repeatedly that favoring
technological solutions over pedagogical soundness results in beautifully crafted systems that are unusable.

Traditionally adaptive eLearning systems are not independent from the content they
adapt. This is due to the fact that the deeper the pedagogical strategies and axes of
adaptivity are embedded the more tied to the specific con-tent and learning objects
they become. By intertwining the mechanisms that provide the adaptive effects with
the content that is being operated on many adaptive applications achieve high levels of

W. Nejdl and P. De Bra (Eds.): AH 2004, LNCS 3137, pp. 291–295, 2004.

adaptivity through manipulating the content. The sacrifice in this approach is that the content, which is often expensive and time-intensive to develop, is not easily reused. Similarly, it becomes difficult, if not impossible, to apply different pedagogical approaches in the personalization of the content. Conversely, many of the non-domain specific adaptive solutions sometimes facilitate the reuse of content. However, this reuse often comes at the cost of limiting the adaptive effects to light-weight approaches such as conditional fragments and link hiding.

Over the past four years the Adaptive Personalized eLearning Service (APeLS) [1] has been used as a personalized teaching tool as part of undergraduate degree level courses in Trinity College, Dublin. The development and improvement of this application has been based on the evolving Adaptive Engine (AE) at its core. The multi-model, metadata-driven approach, which aims to alleviate many the issues described above, is the methodology used in the design of the AE and APeLS. The use of this adaptive system has been evaluated over this period and some of the findings from the student evaluation are presented in this paper.

2 Trial and Evaluation

In Trinity College, Dublin (TCD) SQL is taught as part of seven degree programs across ten different courses. Each course differs based on the degree focus and ethos, objectives, student experience and complexity. Each of these courses have different subject emphasis and different lecturers responsible for teaching on the courses. Junior and Senior Sophister (3rd and 4th year) students in four degree courses degree courses at TCD utilize a personalized SQL (Structured Query Language) course as part of their studies on data storage and database design. A goal of the personalized SQL course is to facilitate the teaching of Structured Query Language as part of these diverse courses, supporting different objects, pedagogical styles, prior knowledge and academic scope. In 1998 and 1999 a non-adaptive SQL online resource, [3] also developed by TCD, was blended into the teaching of the database courses for the Computer Science and Computer Science Language and Linguistic students. This non-adaptive resource offered students a structured online course in SQL with supplementary features such as a live database that they could query via a web browser interface, a detailed case study that formed the basis of many of the examples found in the course and a project reference section.

Using the principles described in the multi-model, metadata driven approach [1] this non-adaptive SQL course was chosen as the basis of a personalized eLearning course in SQL. The multi-model approach describes the necessity for at least three separate and discrete models – learner, content and narrative. It is important to note that the curriculum of the course did not change with the introduction of the personalized eLearning service and that the content used in the personalized service is based directly on that of the original non-adaptive course. The personalized course on SQL is an adaptable, competencies-based course comprised of a didactic pedagogical narrative, over 330 fine-grained pagelets and a tutor-developed competency ontology of 92 terms that forms the domain model.

Table 1. Summary of Student Evaluation Questionnaires, 2000 – 2003

Question Response	None	Little	Some	Much
1) How much experience in SQL did you have before commencing the online SQL course?	29%	38%	27%	6%
2) How much experience did you have using online learning resources?	49%	19%	17%	15%

	Never	Rarely	Usually	Always
3) Did the course(s) generated reflect the answers you gave in the knowledge pre-test instrument?	2%	7%	58%	33%
4) Would you have liked more controls over the content included in the personalized courses?	23%	38%	28%	11%
5) Did the course(s) generated by the system reflect the course(s) you wanted?	3%	18%	63%	16%
6) Were the courses generated easy to navigate?	0%	10%	59%	31%
7) Was the quantity of content on each page satisfactory?	6%	25%	61%	8%
8) Would you have liked a greater level of control as to how the content was structured?	40%	47%	11%	2%

The evaluations have been carried out over the past four years (2000 – 2003, inclusive) and include two separate evaluations – student and tutor. The student evaluation, which is the focus of this paper, was carried out on over 500 students and attempts to determine the usability of the personalized SQL course, in particular focusing on learner satisfaction and the effectiveness of the service. Each of the students was presented with the same paper-based questionnaire giving them an opportunity to evaluate the personalized SQL course they had just completed. The questionnaire comprised thirty one mostly multiple choice questions (some of which are represented in Table 1, above) and an open comments section. Each question also had space for the student to elaborate on their answers.

Also as part of the evaluation of the personalized SQL course the effectiveness of the course was assessed by examining the students examination performance over the period of the evaluation (2000 – 2003) and for the previous two years when an online non-adaptive (based on the same content) version of the SQL was used (Fig. 1, above). The effectiveness of the personalized SQL course is examined by comparing it across to two different axes – how students performed using the non-adaptive online courses prior to the introduction of the personalized course and how students performed in examination questions related and not related to the material presented in the online SQL course. The former metric gives some historical perspective on the impact of the adaptive versus a non-adaptive course across different peer groups, while the latter metric shows how in the same peer groups the adaptive course affected their performance.

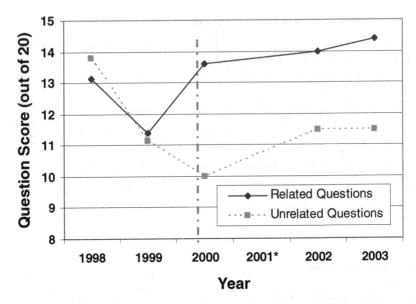

Fig. 1. Average Question Scores on Database Examinations, 1998 – 2003

Figure 1, above, summarizes the performance of six classes of final year students in two degree courses. Both of these courses receive a common lecture course, similar examinations and both use online tools to learn SQL. In 1998 and 1999 the online tools were non-adaptive. The personalized SQL course was first introduced in 2000 (signified by the vertical dotted line). The Question Score axis shows the average question score out of a possible twenty marks. The two lines shown on the graph represent the average question scores in questions related and unrelated to the material taught in the online SQL courses. The questions were not the same from year to year, but were similar and of comparable difficulty. * 2001 results are interpolated as statistics were.

3 Initial Findings and Conclusion

Initial findings from the student evaluation show that despite the majority of students having little or no experience of online learning or the subject matter (Table 1, Questions 1 & 2) the introduction of the personalized SQL course in 2000 had a beneficial effect on students' performance in the final examinations (Figure 1). As may be seen from the graph the students in 1998 scored well in both questions related and unrelated to SQL, yet in the following year their scores declined, possibly indicating a weaker class of students. From 2000, with the introduction of the personalized SQL course, the scores in questions related to SQL have risen steadily and the scores in these questions display an increase of 2-3 marks over the questions unrelated to SQL. In a question worth 20 marks this represents approximately a 10-15% increase in performance by the students. This difference may be attributed to the benefits of the personalized

SQL course, as the SQL content presented shared a common basis with that of the non-adaptive course.

Most students felt that the courses generated based on the prior knowledge pre-test instrument produced courses they expected and desired (Questions 3 & 5), however approximately 40% of students stated that they desired more control over the course content (Question 4). This was reflected in the comments of a number of students where they stated that they 'played' the pre-test instrument to create short personalized courses that could be tackled in short periods of time. They would re-personalize the course for each session with this aim. This finding highlights the innovation some learners can display in utilizing personalized eLearning.

This paper has briefly described the evaluation process of a personalized SQL course based on the Adaptive Personalized Learning Service (APeLS) and presented some initial findings from this evaluation.

References

1. Conlan, O., Wade, V., Bruen, C., Gargan, M. (2002) Multi-Model, Metadata Driven Approach to Adaptive Hypermedia Ser-vices for Personalized eLearning. In the Proceedings of Second International Conference on Adaptive Hypermedia and Adap-tive Web-Based Systems, AH 2002, 100-111.
2. De Bra, P., Aerts, A., Berden, B., De Lange, B., Rousseau, B., Santic, T., Smits, D., Stash, N., (2003) AHA! The Adaptive Hypermedia Architecture. In the Proceedings of the ACM Hypertext Conference, Nottingham, UK, August 2003.
3. Wade, V., Power, C. (1998) Evaluating the design and delivery of WWW based educational environments and courseware. In the Proceedings of the 6th annual conference on the teaching of computing and the 3rd annual conference on Integrating tech-nology into computer science education, 243 - 248 .
4. Weber, G. and Brusilovsky, P. (2001) ELM-ART: An adaptive versatile system for Web-based instruction. International Jour-nal of Artificial Intelligence in Education 12 (4), Special Issue on Adaptive and Intelligent Web-based Educational Systems, 351-384.

SearchGuide: Beyond the Results Page

Maurice Coyle and Barry Smyth*

Smart Media Institute, Department of Computer Science,
University College Dublin, Belfield, Dublin 4, Ireland
{Maurice.Coyle,Barry.Smyth}@ucd.ie

Abstract. Today's Web users are frequently frustrated at their inability to efficiently locate specific items of interest on the Internet. This is mainly due to the
sheer size and speed of growth of the Web; recent estimates suggest it contains
more than 10 billion pages and that it is growing by 60 terabytes per day [1]. Web
search engines are the primary way that users hunt for information but we argue
that in their present form they do not go far enough to help users locate relevant
information. We investigate ways of aiding the user past the initial results page
by leveraging information from previous search sessions.

1 Introduction

We argue that the current Web search paradigm falls short of providing users with a
comprehensive service. Upon selecting a result from the ranked list the user is, to all
intents and purposes, on their own. The search engine rarely provides any further assistance with regards to the selected page and how it is relevant and the interaction
between user and engine is effectively over.

Our work is motivated by the observation that many searches fail to be satisfied
by any of the results selected from the initial ranked list. We see these results as representing a *starting point* for search, not an *end point*. We envision a situation where
the search engine helps the user beyond the results page - in a sense the search engine
accompanies the user as they navigate from the results page, highlighting information
items that may help them in their search, information that has been used by other users
on related searches. This is related to the concepts of *computational wear* and *interaction histories*.

A number of systems use interaction histories to enhance applications involving
document use and Web browsing [2–4]. In the document use domain this involves highlighting areas of a document which have been heavily edited or read. As a browsing
aid, interaction histories are used to highlight links and paths that users have previously followed. We will introduce the use of interaction histories as a means of guiding
Web search, capturing search sessions in the form of queries entered and result URLs
selected by users from a ranked list.

The work presented in this paper builds on that of the I-SPY project [5, 6]. I-SPY
implements an approach to Web search called *collaborative search* because of the way
in which it takes advantage of the search histories of other users, ideally a community

---

* The support of the informatics initiative of Enterprise Ireland is gratefully acknowledged

W. Nejdl and P. De Bra (Eds.): AH 2004, LNCS 3137, pp. 296–299, 2004.

of like-minded users. Search sessions form the primary source of our knowledge for guiding the user past the initial results page. That is, we can identify related URLs (*paths*) based on the fact that previous users have clicked those links for the same or a similar query. We can also highlight the query terms in the document to focus the user's attention and provide hyperlinks to these occurrences, in essence creating *signposts* on a result page. These signposts should aid the user in rapidly navigating to areas of interest within the document.

We introduce the *SearchGuide* add-on to the I-SPY system, which follows a user past the initial results page and enhances their experience through the use of paths and signposts. The SearchGuide system is similar in some respects to the MIT-developed *Footprints* system in [3], in that it suggests possible paths that the user can follow, by adapting result page content based on previous users' actions. A similar system is Letizia [7], which is a browsing assistant. Letizia monitors browsing behaviour, attempting to guess which links from a document a user may be interested in using a set of heuristics (links the user has previously clicked, reading time, etc.) and also by searching for pages containing keywords that the user has explicitly entered or that have been in a page they have read.

2   The SearchGuide System

The SearchGuide system guides the user beyond the initial results page, pointing out areas of interest on selected pages and suggesting promising links within these pages. Both of these functions are driven by the current query terms and also the selections of past users who have viewed the current page.

Very briefly, in order to track users beyond the result page, SearchGuide is implemented as a proxy and results URLs are rewritten, with result selections being passed through SearchGuide. Selected result pages are rewritten so that their URLs are redirected through SearchGuide, transparently to the user.

2.1   Virtual Signposts

In many cases, it may be difficult to see why a result page is relevant for a given query. If a page is long, only a small section of it may be relevant and due to the page's length the user may have trouble finding that section. The SearchGuide analyses a result page's content and finds occurrences of the user-entered query's terms. These term occurrences are highlighted so the user can easily identify relevant sections of the document as they scroll through a page.

Using I-SPY's interaction histories we can highlight alternative query terms that have resulted in the selection of this page. Moreover, we can indicate the relevance of a query to the page: if the current page has been selected 50 times and query X has resulted in 20 of these selections, then query X has a relevance score of 40% for this page. Also, the relevance of the page to each query can be extracted from the I-SPY hit matrix and displayed as alt text for the query.

Finally, to help searchers navigate through a page of highlighted terms we use a query-sensitive navigation bar (see Fig. 1). This bar is calibrated to the length of the

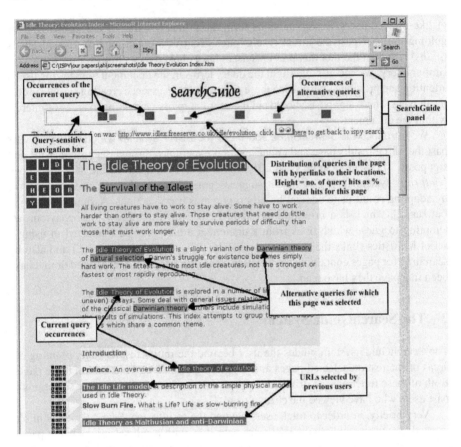

Fig. 1. Virtual signposts and paths highlighted by the SearchGuide for the query 'idle theory of evolution'

page and the positions of query terms within the page are highlighted. The height of a mark indicates the relevance of the page to the term and each mark is a hyperlink to the term. The current query is indicated by blue marks and alternative queries by grey marks. This navigation bar allows the user to form an immediate impression about the distribution of query terms in the page and helps them to quickly jump to specific query occurrences.

2.2   Suggesting Paths

A result page might not be directly relevant to a query but it may lead to a relevant page. SearchGuide helps users in 2 ways in this respect, by highlighting links which were selected from within this page by previous users who looked at the page and also links which were selected from the initial results page for the current or a similar query [8]. For both types of links, when they are highlighted the alt text is set to be the query which led to this page being selected.

In Fig. 1, the 'Idle Life model' and 'Idle Theory as Malthusian and anti-Darwinian' links have been highlighted since they have been previously selected by users who found this page interesting. Alt text can also be added to these links, indicating which queries led to the selection of the link. Other information such as how many times the URL has been selected and how many times the associated query was entered can also be included.

Thus, by using previous user clicks as a source of interaction histories, it is possible to present the user with a set of links in the current page which other users have found interesting for the same or a similar query, thereby focusing the user's attention to the more promising links on the page.

3   Conclusions

We have postulated that the current Web search paradigm could offer the user more help in finding the information they require. We argue that the single-shot style of interaction whereby the user is on their own once they select a result is insufficient. We have proposed a number of ways in which the user could be aided beyond the initial results page and implemented some of these features in the SearchGuide system. In future work we plan to explore this area further and provide an evaluation of the system demonstrating its potential as a search aid.

References

1. Roush, W.: Search Beyond Google. MIT Technology Review (2004) 34–45
2. Hill, W., Hollan, J., Wroblewzki, D., McCandless, T.: Edit Wear and Read Wear. In: Proceedings of the SIGCHI Conference on Human Factors in Computing Systems, ACM Press (1992) 3–9
3. Wexelblat, A., Maes, P.: Footprints: History-Rich Web Browsing. In: Proceedings of the Third International Conference on Computer-Assisted Information Retrieval. (1997) Montreal, Quebec, Canada.
4. Wexelblat, A.: History-Based Tools for Navigation. In: Proceedings of the Hawaii International Conference System Sciences, IEEE Press (1999)
5. Smyth, B., Balfe, E., Briggs, P., Coyle, M., Freyne, J.: Collaborative Web Search. In: Proceedings of the 18th International Joint Conference on Artificial Intelligence, IJCAI-03, Morgan Kaufmann (2003) 1417–1419 Acapulco, Mexico.
6. Freyne, J., Smyth, B., Coyle, M., Balfe, E., Briggs, P.: Further Experiments on Collaborative Ranking in Community-Based Web Search. AI Review: An International Science and Engineering Journal (In Press)
7. Lieberman, H.: Letizia: An Agent That Assists Web Browsing. In Mellish, C., ed.: Proceedings of the International Joint Conference on Artificial Intelligence, IJCAI'95, Morgan Kaufman (1995) 924–929 Montreal, Canada.
8. Balfe, E., Smyth, B.: Case-based Collaborative Web Search. In: Proceedings of the 7th European Conference on Case-Based Reasoning, Springer (2004) Madrid, Spain.

Modeling Learners as Individuals and as Groups

Roland Hübscher[1] and Sadhana Puntambekar[2]

[1] Department of Information Design and Corporate Communication, Bentley College,
175 Forest Street, Waltham, MA 02452-4705, USA
rhubscher@bentley.edu

[2] Department of Educational Psychology, University of Wisconsin,
1025 W Johnson St., Rm 880, Madison, WI 53706, USA
puntambekar@education.wisc.edu

Abstract. Adaptive navigation support normally attempts to make selecting a relevant hyperlink as easy as possible. However, in educational applications, this may have negative learning effects since selecting a link is sometimes an important educational problem for the student to solve. To provide appropriate scaffolding to students, it is necessary to understand how they navigate in hypermedia sites. By grouping students with similar conceptual (mis)understanding we were able to uncover a small set of characteristic navigation patterns, and to demonstrate that students with similar conceptual understanding have similar navigation patterns.

1 Introduction

One of the main application areas of adaptive hypermedia is educational technology. First, adaptive hypermedia can be used to individualize learning material for each student. Second, an adaptive hypermedia system can adapt itself to the evolving understanding of individual students. And third, it can help keep the student from getting lost in the vast hyperspace by implicitly or explicitly recommending certain well-selected links to follow.

In this paper, we focus on adaptive navigation support. Navigation support normally tries to simplify selecting a relevant link by reducing the complexity of deciding which page to visit next. This can be accomplished, for instance, by reducing the number of possible links to chose from. The most extreme case is the situation where only one "next" link is provided which is determined by the adaptive system to lead to the "best" page according to some internal pedagogical model and the user model of the learner.

However, as we have argued elsewhere [1], in an educational hypermedia system, quite often, selecting a link has to be considered an educationally important problem for the learner to solve. Thus, the learner ought to be scaffolded by the adaptive system to make the right choice, i. e., just making it as easy as possible for the learner to make the right choice is sometimes the wrong approach. Learning to select the appropriate link is a method that should be learned by the student while solving a specific problem leading not only to domain-specific understanding, but also to learning how to solve problems.

Thus, understanding how they navigate is just as important as knowing how they ought to do it. Only providing a normative model that drives the students towards the

W. Nejdl and P. De Bra (Eds.): AH 2004, LNCS 3137, pp. 300–303, 2004.

right pattern would be inconsistent with scaffolding since it is important for the scaffolder, the adaptive hypermedia system in this case, to assess the student's understanding and then providing the appropriate support. The incorrect behavior and its meaning needs to be recognized by the system to provide the proper guidance [2].

We studied the students' navigation patterns by developing group models based on the individual learners' user models. In the remainder of this paper, we will provide details of these models used to find (sub)groups of students with similar conceptual understanding.

2   Modeling Groups of Individuals

This work was based on earlier results that showed that learners' navigation patterns are characteristic of the learner's conceptual understanding of the domain described by the hypermedia system [3]. The hypermedia system used in this research is called CoMPASS, which displays each concept on a separate page and allows the user to navigate the concepts using textual hyperlinks as well as a clickable concept map.

We built simple models for the learners only based on their navigation behavior, i. e., which concepts the learners visited and in what order. It is clear that visiting a page does by no means imply that the user has studied the material or even understood. Nevertheless, the results of a classroom study showed that the navigation patterns of the students clearly indicates what the students have learned and at what depth [3].

The user model used in the mentioned study will be described next. Then, a group model will be introduced that was used to understand whether there are common patterns among students with similar conceptual understanding.

2.1   Modeling Individuals

The main goal of the user model is to capture the conceptual understanding of a student. To support our approach to group modeling described below, the user model needs to use a relatively simple representation so that the structural similarity between pairs of user models can be measured.

As mentioned earlier, the only data used to characterize a learner's navigation behavior is the order in which the concepts were visited in CoMPASS. This information is represented in a transition matrix D, where each entry D_{ij} represents how many times the user has traversed the link from page (or concept) i to page j. The transition matrix can be visualized by a directed graph where the nodes are the pages and the links are annotated by the number of traversals. Then, a modified Pathfinder Network Scaling (PFNet) procedure is applied to matrix D computing an approximate representation of the conceptual model of the user [4].

PFNets were developed to find relevant relations in data which described the proximity between concepts. Generally, all concepts are somehow related to all others, however, only the relevant relations should be retained. PFNet takes the transition matrix representing the navigation pattern of a user and removes redundant or even counterintuitive links resulting in a matrix W representing the student's conceptual model. A link from i to j is removed, if there is some indirect path from i to j via some other pages, if all the entries in D along this indirect path are at least as large as D_{ij}. Thus, the output matrix W of the Pathfinder procedure is exactly the same as the input D except for the removed links which are set to zero (no transition).

2.2 Similarity of Individual Learners

We are interested in groups of learners that have a similar conceptual understanding. Since PFNets capture the conceptual understanding of learners, students with similar PFNets are assigned to the same group. There are many graph similarity measures that can be applied to PFNets and often these measures are quite application-domain specific[1]. Since for our application, the relation between concepts is relevant, measures that capture the structural similarity of graphs are of interest. Several measures were considered, however, they all led to similar results so that a simple measure was chosen that has already been used to measure the similarity of PFNets [5].

Both graphs, i. e., PFNets, contain the same concepts. A concept is represented similarly in both graphs if it is connected to the same concepts in its respective graph. If they are connected to rather different concepts, they are structurally quite dissimilar.

More specifically, let C_X be the set of links going from some concept C in PFNet X to other concepts in X. C_Y is defined analogously for concept C in PFNet Y. Then the structural similarity of the X and Y with respect to C is the quotient of how many links the two networks have in common divided by the total number of links, i. e., $|C_X \cap C_Y|/|C_X \cup C_Y|$. Finally, the similarity of the two networks is computed as the average of the structural similarity of each concept in the networks.

2.3 Modeling Groups

A group of individuals is modeled almost the same way as individuals as follows. First, the transition matrices for all the group members are added and the PFNet procedure is applied to this new matrix. Thus, also group models are represented by PFNets.

Clustering algorithms are normally used to assign elements that are "close" to each other to the same group. In our case, the elements are the Pathfinder networks representing the students and the "distance" is measured by the similarity measure introduced above. Intuitively, the more similar two networks are, the closer they are. The K-Means clustering algorithm [6] was selected because of its simplicity and adequate results. Like many other greedy algorithms, k-means does not always find the optimal solution. However, the results we obtained were satisfactory.

After k-means has found a partition, the clusters can be analyzed by looking at each cluster member individually and by looking at the clusters' centroid, i. e., the group's conceptual model.

We applied the PFNet clustering method in a classroom study [3]. With the clustering algorithm we found that different students with similar understanding did indeed show similar navigation patterns. Most students showed one of three characteristic navigation patterns or some a combination thereof.

---

[1] See http://www.dbs.informatik.uni-muenchen.de/~seidl/graphs/ for an idea of the richness and complexity of this area.

3   Conclusions

The clustered PFNet representation was developed as a means to understand how (and whether) students' navigation behavior correlates with a certain conceptual understanding of the material.

Although the models for the individuals and for the groups are extremely simple, they have led to a better understanding of the close relationship between navigation and conceptual understanding. Although just visiting pages does in general not lead to learning, the fact that the learner has selected a certain link reflects his relational knowledge of the domain. We found that students with similar conceptual understanding of the material to be learned also showed similar navigation patterns. Furthermore, only a small set of characteristically different navigation patterns was found [3].

References

1. Hübscher, R., Puntambekar, S.: Adaptive navigation for learners in hypermedia is scaffolded navigation. In De Bra, P., Brusilovsky, P., eds.: Second International Conference on Adaptive Hypermedia and Adaptive Web-based Systems. Springer, Berlin (2002)
2. Puntambekar, S., Hübscher, R.: Tools for scaffolding students in a complex learning environment: What have we gained and what have we missed? Educational Psychologist (2004)
3. Puntambekar, S., Stylianou, A., Hübscher, R.: Improving navigation and learning in hypertext environments with navigable concept maps. Human-Computer Interaction **18** (2003) 395–428
4. Schvaneveldt, R.W., ed.: Pathfinder Associative Networks: Studies in Knowledge Organization. Ablex, Norwood (1990)
5. Goldsmith, T.E., Davenport, D.M.: Assessing structural similarity of graphs. In Schvaneveldt, R.W., ed.: Pathfinder Associative Networks: Studies in Knowledge Organization. Ablex, Norwood (1990) 75–87
6. Hansen, P., Mladenovic, N.: J-means: A new local search heuristic for minimum sum-of-squares clustering. Pattern Recognition **34** (2001) 405–413

Adaptive Help for Webbased Applications

Dorothea Iglezakis

Cath. University Eichstaett-Ingolstadt,
Department for Applied Computer Science,
Ostenstr. 14, 85072 Eichstaett, Germany
dorothea.iglezakis@ku-eichstaett.de

Abstract. This paper presents an approach that uses the techniques of plan recognition not only to infer short-term plans and goals, but also to infer the long-term procedural knowledge of a user in a non-binary way. The information about the procedural knowledge in terms of activation builds the user model of AdaptHelp, an adaptive help system for web-based systems. AdaptHelp is based onto established adaptive help systems, which are shortly presented and compared on the used mechanism and techniques.

1 Introduction

Although the first contents of the World-Wide-Web consist mainly of static HTML-based information sites, the number of dynamically generated and increasingly complex applications on the Web grows. With increasing complexity of these applications, the need to develop user-friendly support functions grows. The aim of adaptive help systems is to offer the right amount of information in the right moment by adapting the contents of the help system either to the knowledge or to the actual plans and goals of the individual user.

2 Adaptive Help Systems

Existing adaptive help systems use mainly two approaches to adapt the help information to the individual information requirements of different users. They either infer the knowledge of the user by observing the interaction of the user with the help system or consider the actual situation of a user by means of plan recognition. The following section presents the user models, input data, and adaptation mechanisms of the adaptive help systems KNOME [3], ORIMUHS [5], and EPIAIM [4], which infer the knowledge of the user, as well as the systems PUSH [6] and PLUS [2], which use plan recognition to infer the actual plan or information goal of the user.

KNOME is the user modeling component of the Unix Consultant, a natural language help system that generates explanations for UNIX-functions. KNOME uses the questions of the user as input data to calculate the probability that the user belongs to one of four global stereotypes. With the user model and the difficulty of a concept, the system infers the probability that the user knows about a knowledge item. The adaptation happens through output of the version of a help item corresponding to the most probable stereotype.

W. Nejdl and P. De Bra (Eds.): AH 2004, LNCS 3137, pp. 304–307, 2004.

ORIMUHS is an object-oriented multimedia-help component for graphical systems under a UNIX operating system. Like KNOME, ORIMUHS uses a global stereotype model. ORIMUHS infers the stereotype of the user by protocolling the activities into action graphs and comparing these individual action graphs with predefined action graphs for the stereotypes. The adaptation mechanism uses different versions for each help item to show the appropriate version of the help item.

EPIAIM is a knowledge-based system developed to support health care professionals in epidemiological data analysis. The user model consists in a set of predicates that specify the probability that a user knows about a concept or has practice in a subject area. EPIAIM builds the help contents according to production rules that specify which attributes of a concept are added dependent on the knowledge of the user. The selection of examples depends on the practice a user has in a certain area.

PUSH is a user sensitive hypermedia-help tool, which adapts to the information goal of the user. PUSH uses a short-term model for the current information goal of the user. The system infers this model through a combination of key hole plan recognition and intended plan recognition with the last actions of the user as input data. Each help item consists of different components that support the user in different ways. Dependent on the information goal, the content of a help item is adapted through showing or hiding specific components.

PLUS is a user support system that adapts to the actual plan of the user. The plan recognizer is based on a predefined hierarchically structured plan base. A plan consists of a set of actions with different parameters and an absolute or relative position. The plan recognition processes the low-level inputs (keystrokes, mouse-clicks) to identify the interaction style of the user for a simple user model and to build a dialog history. A spreading activation algorithm then builds hypotheses about the plan of the user. A plan completion component uses this information to generate action sequences for activated but not recognized plan hypotheses in a tutor help.

3   AdaptHelp – A Concept for an Adaptive Help Component for Web-Based Systems

AdaptHelp tries to combine the different approaches presented in the last section by using methods of plan recognition to infer the procedural knowledge of the user, while taking into account the specialties of the web environment.

In contrast to other adaptive web systems like learning environments or recommender systems, adaptive help systems cannot use additional input data like tests or questionnaires. The only possible input data that can be collected non-intrusively is therefore data that logs the activities of the user on the server.

3.1   Knowledge Modeling

All presented systems, which model the knowledge of a user, base on a binary concept of knowledge representation. A user either knows a concept or does not. From cognitive psychology we know that knowledge is not binary. The ACT-theory from Anderson and Lebière [1] delivers an empirically founded theory about learning and forgetting of memory contents. Each access of a memory item increases the activation of the corresponding memory trace. Without access, the activation fades over time. By logging the activities of the user, it is possible to measure the frequency of occupation with the concepts and tasks within the target application.

Knowledge items differ in the type of knowledge. Procedural knowledge covers knowledge about actions and activities, whereas declarative knowledge covers knowledge about facts. Especially for help systems, which have the goal of explaining and supporting the execution of tasks, the procedural knowledge of the user is central.

Therefore, a knowledge item in the context of AdaptHelp is the procedural knowledge about a single task of the target application. For example, if the target application is the configuration menu of an internet provider, one knowledge item could be the knowledge about adding a new e-mail address. Declarative knowledge items can function as prerequisites or as additional information to the procedural knowledge items.

3.2   User Model

Like the user models of the knowledge-modeling approaches presented in Sect. 2, the user model of AdaptHelp contains information about the individual knowledge of items in the target domain. In contrast to the binary concept of knowledge in the presented approaches, the approach of AdaptHelp models the knowledge in terms of current activation of an item.

The systems KNOME, and ORIMUHS infer the knowledge of a user with a general stereotype model. This kind of knowledge modeling works only in domains, where the concepts can be ordered by difficulty. Webbased applications offer mainly a set of services that are independent from each other. Therefore, a global stereotype model makes no sense for theses applications.

The user model of AdaptHelp is an overlay model that assigns an activation value to each knowledge item. The activation of an item is computed by the access time stamps of the corresponding tasks.

3.3   Activation of a Knowledge Item

The systems PLUS, PUSH, and ORIMUHS observe the activities of the user to recognize the plans, the information goal, or the stereotype of the user. This activation data also contains additional data, because it documents the experiences of the user and therefore allows to draw conclusions on the activation of the users' procedural knowledge.

Therefore, AdaptHelp uses extended logfiles of the WebServer as a data source to recognize the executed tasks of the user. The logfiles are in an XML-format and contain the name of the requested site with the used parameters and an identification of the requesting user for each request.

The actions in the logfiles are compared against predefined tasks. Each task consists of a sequence of actions. In the web context, each action corresponds to a web site with its parameters. A parameter represents additional data, which is sent to the site per GET, POST or SESSION variables. An action in a predefined task can set presence- and absence constraints over the parameters. The tasks are handled as regular expressions over the logged actions resulting in access timestamps for each task. On the basis of these timestamps, the base activation B_i of the knowledge item i is computed using the Base-Level Learning Equation from the ACT-theory ([1])

$$B_i = ln \left(\sum_{j=1}^{n} t_j^{-d} \right), \tag{1}$$

where t_j is the time since the jth practice of the corresponding task and $d \in]0; 1[$ is a domain dependent parameter, mainly set to 0.5.

3.4 Adaptation

As Höök [6] states, it is very difficult to write and to maintain different versions of the same help items for systems such as KNOME or ORIMUHS. The online assembling of the help items from standardized components like EPIAIM or PUSH is therefore a more promising approach.

The help items of AdaptHelp are written in an XML format that defines the structure of the items. Each item corresponds to one task in the target application and consists of different components. The adaptation happens through online assembling of the components to one help item, dependent of the actual activation of the target process.

3.5 Implementation and Further Work

At this moment, we implemented the process recognition part of AdaptHelp in C++. First performance tests show promising results. Tools to facilitate the writing process of the help items are in the planning phase. The implementation of the adaptation procedure will follow after experimental evaluations that test the helpfulness of different components of the help items for users with different levels of experience in the corresponding tasks.

References

1. John R. Anderson and Christian Lebiere. *The atomic Components of Thought.* Lawrence Erlbaum Associates, Mahwah, NJ, 1998.
2. Frank Berger, Thomas Fehrle, Kristof Klöckner, Volker Schölles, Markus A. Theis, and Wolfgang Wahlster. Plus, plan-based user support. Technical Report RR-93-15, DFKI, March 1993.
3. David N. Chin. *User Models in Dialog Systems*, chapter KNOME: Modeling What the User Knows in UC, pages 74–107. Springer, Berlin, 1989.
4. Fiorella de Rosis, Bernardina de Carolis, and Sebastiano Pizzutilo. User-tailored hypermedia explanations. In *Adaptive hypertext and hypermedia – Workshop held in conjunction with UM'94*, 1994.
5. Miguel Encarnação. Multi-level user support through adaptive hypermedia: A highly application-independent help component. In *Proceedings of the Conference on Intelligent User Interfaces IUI 97*, pages 187 – 194, Orlando Florida USA, 1997. ACM.
6. Kristina Höök. *A Glass Box Approach to Adaptive Hypermedia.* PhD thesis, Stockholm University, Swedish Institute of Computer Science, 1996.

Empirical Evaluation of an Adaptive Multiple Intelligence Based Tutoring System

Declan Kelly[1] and Brendan Tangney[2]

[1] National College of Ireland, Dublin, Ireland
dkelly@ncirl.ie
[2] University of Dublin, Trinity College, Ireland
tangney@tcd.ie

Abstract. EDUCE is an Intelligent Tutoring System for which a set of learning resources has been developed using the principles of Multiple Intelligences. It can dynamically identify learning characteristics and adaptively provide a customised learning material tailored to the learner. This paper describes a research study using EDUCE that examines the relationship between the adaptive presentation strategy, the level of choice available and the learning performance of science school students aged 12 to 14. The paper presents some preliminary results from a group of 18 students that have participated in the study so far. Results suggest that learning strategies that encourage the student to use as many resources as possible are the most effective. They suggest that learning gain can improve by presenting students initially with learning resources that are not usually used and subsequently providing a range of resources from which students may choose.

1 Introduction

Research on learning shows that students learn differently, that they process and represent knowledge in different ways, that it is possible to diagnose learning style and that some students lean more effectively when taught with appropriate strategies [5]. EDUCE [2, 3] is an Intelligent Tutoring System for which a set of learning resources has been developed using the principles of Multiple Intelligences [1]. It can dynamically identify user learning characteristics and adaptively provide a customised learning material tailored to the learner [4]. The multiple intelligence concept defines intelligence as the capacity to solve problems or fashion products that are of value and states that there are different ways to demonstrate this intelligence. It is a concept that offers a framework and a language for developing a broad range of content that supports creative, multi-modal teaching. In EDUCE four different intelligences are used to develop for categories of content: verbal/linguistic, visual/spatial, logical/mathematical and musical/rhythmic intelligences. Currently, science is the subject area for which content has been developed.

This paper describes an empirical study that examines the relationship between the adaptive presentation strategy, levels of choice and the learning performance of science school students aged 12 to 14 in a computer based adaptive learning environment

W. Nejdl and P. De Bra (Eds.): AH 2004, LNCS 3137, pp. 308–311, 2004.

using EDUCE. The goal of the research study is to address the following research questions:

- Does providing a range or learning resources improve learning gain and activity?
- Does increased personalisation of resources improve learning performance?
- What are the advantages in making adaptive presentation decisions in relation to giving the learner complete control?
- What is the difference between learning gain and activity when presenting resources that are preferred and resources that not preferred?

The results of this study may be significant for researchers and practitioners. For researchers, it will produce specific results that demonstrate the relationship between learning and the availability of different learning resources. For practitioners, it demonstrates how teaching in different ways can affect learning.

2 EDUCE

EDUCE holds a number of tutorials designed with help of subject matter experts. Each tutorial contains a set of content explaining a particular subject area. A tutorial consists of learning units that explain a particular concept. In each unit there are four different sets of learning resources, each based predominantly on one of the intelligences. The different resources explain a topic from a different angle or display the same information in a different way. Different instructional design strategies and techniques were used to create the content. For verbal/linguistic content it was the use of explanations, descriptions, highlighted keywords, term definitions and audio recordings. For logical/mathematical content it was the use of snumber, pattern recognition, relationships, questioning and exploration. For visual/spatial content it was the use of photographs, pictures, visual organisers and colour. For musical/rhythmic content it was the use of musical metaphors, raps and rhythms.

EDUCE holds a static MI profile of each student determined before the experiment using an MI inventory. EDUCE also builds a dynamic model of the student's MI profile by observing, analysing and recording the student's choice of MI differentiated material. Other information also stored in the student model includes the navigation history, the time spent on each learning unit, answers to interactive questions and feedback given by the student on navigation choices.

Content is presented using different presentation and instructional strategies that alternate between providing resources the student likes to use and does not like to use. In the static version of EDUCE, the most and least preferred resource is identified using the static MI profile. In the adaptive version of EDUCE, the dynamic student model is used to inform adaptive presentation decisions.

3 Research Design

The research purpose of this experiment is to explore the relationship between the independent variables: instructional strategy and level of choice, and the dependent variable: learning performance. Other variables such as MI profile, gender, previous computer experience and level of ability in school will also be examined.

There are four different levels of choice provided to different groups:

1. *Free* – student has the choice to view any resource in any order. No adaptive presentation decisions are made as the learner has complete control.
2. *Single* – student is only able to view one resource. This is determined by EDUCE based on an analysis of the MI inventory completed by the student.
3. *Multi* - student is first given one resource but has the option to go back and view alternative resources. The resource first given to the student is determined by EDUCE based on the analysis of the MI inventory completed by the student. The *Multi* choice level is the same as the *Single* choice level but with the option of going back and viewing alternative resources.
4. *Adaptive* – the student is first given one resource but has the option to go back and view alternative resources. The resource first given to the student is determined adaptively by EDUCE. The predictive engine within EDUCE [4] identifies the most preferred and least preferred resource from the online student computer interaction.

The instructional strategy or the presentation strategy for delivery instructional material encompasses two main strategies.

1. *Most preferred*: - showing resources the student prefers to use
2. *Least preferred*: - showing resources the student least prefers to use

For each learning unit, there are four MI based learning resources. Which of these resources are shown first is determined by the dynamic and static MI profile and the instructional strategy.

Learning performance is defined mainly by learning gain, learning activity and motivation. To calculate the learning gain each student before and after a tutorial will sit a pre-test and post test. The test for the pre-test and post-test is the same and consists of questions that appear during the tutorial. Learning activity is determined by the navigation profile. It is a measure of the different panels visited, the number of different resources used, the reuse of particular resources and the direction of navigation. Learning motivation or persistence is a measure of the student's progression within the tutorial and the attempts made to answer questions. The questions are multi-choice question with four options. Both learning activity and motivation are analysed to provide informed explanations on learning gain.

Content has been developed in the subject area of Science for the age group 12 to 14. Students have been randomly assigned to one of the four groups defined by the levels of choice. Each student sits through two tutorials. They will experience both instructional strategies of least preferred and most preferred. To ensure order effects are balanced out, students are randomly assigned to systematically varying sequence of conditions. The design of the experiment can be described as a mixed between/within subject design with counterbalance.

4 Preliminary Results and Future Work

One group of students consisting of 18 boys with an average of 13 have participated in the study so far. The group were divided into two groups, A and B. Group A use the Free choice version of EDUCE and had the choice to use resources in any order. Group B used the Adaptive choice version of EDUCE where the presentation decisions were made based on the dynamic student profile. Not withstanding the number of participants, the results were analysed to determine differences between the free choice version and the adaptive choice version. For the adaptive version, the results were analysed to determine any differences between the least preferred and most preferred strategy.

A one-way between groups analysis of variance on the learning gain both on the first day and on the second day was conducted to explore the impact of adaptivity and non-adaptivity. The three groups consisted of one group using the free choice version and two groups using the adaptive least/most preferred versions. There was no significant difference between the groups at the p<0.05 level. On inspecting the mean increase in learning gain for the different versions it interestingly reveals that the mean for the adaptive least preferred version was greater than the free choice version which was in turn greater than that of the adaptive most preferred version on both days.

To evaluate the impact of learning strategy on learning gain within subject, a paired-samples t-test was conducted There was a statistically significant increase in learning gain using the least preferred strategy (M=26.25, SD=13.024) and in using the most preferred strategy (M=10, SD=11.95), t(7)=2.489, p<0.042). The eta squared statistic (0.47) indicates a large effect size. This initial surprising result suggests that learning gain increases where students do not get their preferred learning resource. However on closer examination of the learning activity, it is found that students when given their least preferred learning resource increase their learning activity and are exposed to a wider range of resources. It suggests that strategies that increase learning activity and develop all faculties are effective in increasing learning gain.

Currently, the empirical study is underway and on completion more that 200 students will have participated in the research study.

References

1. Gardner H. (1983) Frames of Mind: The theory of multiple intelligences. New York. Basic Books.
2. Kelly, D. & Tangney, B. (2002): Incorporating Learning Characteristics into an Intelligent Tutor. In: Proceedings of the Sixth International Conference on ITSs, ITS2002.
3. Kelly, D. (2003). A Framework for using Multiple Intelligences in an ITS. Proceedings of EDMedia'03, World Conference on Educational Multimedia, Hypermedia & Telecommunications, Honolulu, HI.
4. Kelly, D. (2004). Predicting Learning Characteristics in a Multiple Intelligence based Tutoring System. In Proceedings of the Seventh International Conference on ITS's, ITS'04.
5. Riding, R. & Rayner. S, (1997): Cognitive Styles and learning strategies. David Fulton Publishers.

Evaluating Information Filtering Techniques in an Adaptive Recommender System

John O'Donovan and John Dunnion

Intelligent Information Retrieval Group,
Department of Computer Science,
University College Dublin,
Dublin, Ireland
{John.ODonovan,John.Dunnion}@ucd.ie

Abstract. With the huge increase in the volume of information available in digital form and the increasing diversity of Web applications, the need for efficient, reliable information filtering is critical. New algorithms that filter information for specific tastes are being developed to tackle the problem of information overload. This paper proposes that there is a substantial relative difference in the performances of various filtering algorithms as they are applied to different datasets, and that these performance differences can be leveraged to form the basis of an Adaptive Information Filtering System. We classify five different datasets based on a number of metrics, including sparsity, ratings distribution and user-item ratio, and develop a regression function over these metrics to predict the suitability of a particular recommendation algorithm for a previously unseen dataset. Our results show that the predicted best algorithm does perform best on the new dataset.

1 Introduction

In order to provide a more personalised and tailored service to their users, an increasing number of on-line services provide personalised recommendations, eg Amazon.com. There are two main techniques upon which recommendation algorithms are based: Collaborative and Content-Based Filtering [5]. In this paper, we focus on the collaborative approach, where users provide ratings for items in a particular domain, and the system exploits similarities and differences between users based on item ratings to compute its recommendations.

Collaborative Filtering (CF) is a broad term for the process of recommending items to users based on similarities in taste. The underlying principle of CF is as follows: if users A and B rate k items similarly, they are considered to share similar tastes and should rate other items similarly. CF techniques have the following advantages: they do not require items to be machine-analysable (as explained in [5]); they can arrive at serendipitous recommendations, that is, they can recommend relevant items that are completely different from those in a user's profile; and they require little knowledge engineering overhead. However, CF techniques are subject to two serious restrictions. With the Sparsity Problem, for any given case it is unlikely that two users have co-rated many of the items in the system. Accurate similarity measurements depend on high

W. Nejdl and P. De Bra (Eds.): AH 2004, LNCS 3137, pp. 312–315, 2004.

profile overlap, which can be costly to attain. The second, the Latency Problem, affects new or esoteric items, rendering them unrecommendable until they are included in a sufficient number of user profiles, as outlined in [9].

Different approaches to collaborative filtering and different implementations will be affected to varying degrees by these problems. Performance will also be dependent on the dataset to which CF is applied and the information used to compile a similarity model. For example, in a situation where the set of items to be recommended is relatively small and static and there is a large number of users, it would be better to employ an item-based approach [8][4] to CF, since the similarity model is built up over the large number of user profiles. In such a situation, a user-based filtering approach (as in [1]) would not perform as well since there would be insufficient items in each profile to provide the level of overlap required for a reliable similarity model. It is this type of observation that we endeavour to capture and exploit in this work. The architecture of our system, AdRec, is presented in Fig. 1.

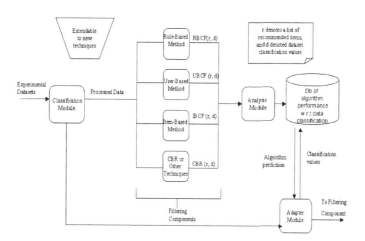

Fig. 1. AdRec System Architecture

2 Adaptive Information Filtering Using Regression

To achieve adaptability in our system, we make the assumption that our datasets can be adequately classified (for CF purposes) by a set of their salient features. These include user-item ratio, sparsity and data type. We tested our three collaborative recommendation algorithms, User-Based, Item-Based and Rule-Based CF, on four different experimental datasets, EachMovie, PTV, Jester and MovieLens, and noted the relative performance differences of each method with respect to the classification metrics. From this information it was possible to develop a regression function for algorithm prediction based on the classification metrics alone. We tested the performance of this function by introducing another dataset, SmartRadio, a music ratings set [3]. This set is classified according to the required metrics, and the resulting values are run through the regression function to attain an algorithm prediction. If we can successfully perform this algorithm prediction task, we can form the basis of a generic recommender system, which can employ cutting edge filtering techniques to a given system without having to manually tailor the recommendation engine for that system. The design of the system is completely modular, which has the advantage of allowing new techniques to be added as they develop.

A linear regression model [8] is built up using our evaluations in [6], this is based on a predictive function of several variables, as described in [7]:

$$E\{Y\} = \beta_0 + \beta_1 X_1 + \beta_2 X_2$$

Values for the β_is are obtained by taking all the classification metric values for each dataset and the best performing algorithm for that set, and solving the resulting system of simultaneous equations. The SmartRadio dataset was classified according to the same metrics and was found to be over 99% sparse and to have a user-item ratio of 1:9. This information was put through the regression function, which predicted the user-based algorithm for best performance.

3   Experimental Data and Evaluation

We aim to predict the best-performing algorithm using only the regression function learned from the classification metrics of the other datasets, and the values the new dataset has for these metrics. Having calculated our regression function from tests shown in [6], we run all of the algorithms again on the new dataset. Our predictive accuracy tests are simplified by keeping the neighbourhood size k and the test-train ratio constant at 30 and 80, respectively. These are optimal values found previously (see [6]).

For the initial training phase of the system, four experimental datasets are used: Jester[2], EachMovie, PTV[9] and MovieLens[1]. We selected subsets of 900 profiles from each of the above datasets comprised of the largest profiles (with the exception of PTV which only contains 622 profiles).

Table 1. Classification of Experimental Data

Dataset	User-Item Ratio	Sparsity	Type
PTV	1:6	94.25%	TV Programme Ratings
MovieLens	9:13	93.7%	Movie Ratings
Jester	9:1	54%	Joke Ratings
EachMovie	9:17	93%	Movie Ratings
SmartRadio	1:9 (approx)	99.98 %	Music Ratings

In this paper, we use predictive accuracy as the performance metric for the recommendation algorithms. For each dataset, We tailored a threshold value for each individual scale, based on distribution of ratings. We predict the "liked" items for the unseen test data and record accuracy on each dataset. User profiles are split into training and test data. The training data is fed to each filtering component individually and each generates its own predictions for the unseen test data. To build our regression model, we use our results from [6].

To validate our proposal, we need to show that the algorithm predicted by the regression function performs better than its competitors on our new dataset. We found that on the new dataset, the user-based algorithm performed 2% better than the other algorithms on a %-correct analysis. The user-based algorithm was also predicted to be the best performer by the regression function, thus showing, tentatively, that this approach does work. This data is based on a limited number of datasets, however, so gaussian smoothing was used in our regression model to interpolate over sparse data. Future work will include increasing the number of training datasets and hence the reliability of the results.

4   Conclusion and Future Work

The approach adopted by our system is based on a predictor for filtering techniques. More than simply developing specific filtering implementations, we produce an information filtering architecture, capable of incorporating new technologies as they arrive. One application of this adaptive recommender could be commercially deployed in cases where system developers do not have the time or expertise available to assess which information filtering technique best suits the particular requirements of their application. Future work will include the extension of the scope of test data to other domains, and a comparison of this approach to existing meta-learning systems. This should produce improvements, resulting in a more reliable test-bench and therefore a better regression function upon which to base our algorithm predictions.

References

1. Daniel Billsus and Michael J. Pazzani. Learning collaborative information filters. In *Proceedings of the 15th International Conference on Machine Learning*, pages 46–54. Morgan Kaufmann, San Francisco, CA, 1998.
2. Ken Goldberg, Theresa Roeder, Dhruv Gupta, and Chris Perkins. Eigentaste: A constant time collaborative filtering algorithm. *Information Retrieval*, 4(2):133–151, 2001.
3. C. Hayes, P. Cunningham, P. Clerkin, and M. Grimaldi. Programme-driven music radio, 2002.
4. George Karypis. Evaluation of item-based top-n recommendation algorithms. In *CIKM*, pages 247–254, 2001.
5. P. Melville, R. Mooney, and R. Nagarajan. Content-boosted collaborative filtering, 2001.
6. John O'Donovan and John Dunnion. A comparison of collaborative recommendation algorithms over diverse data. In *Proceedings of the National Conference on Artificial Intelligence and Cognitive Science (AICS), Ireland*, pages 101–104, September 17– September 19 2003.
7. Adrian E. Raftery, David Madigan, and Jennifer A. Hoeting. Bayesian model averaging for linear regression models. *Journal of the American Statistical Association*, 92(437):179–191, 1997.
8. Badrul M. Sarwar, George Karypis, Joseph A. Konstan, and John Reidl. Item-based collaborative filtering recommendation algorithms. In *World Wide Web*, pages 285–295, 2001.
9. B. Smyth, D. Wilson, and D. O'Sullivan. Improving the quality of the personalised electronic programme guide. In *Proceedings of TV'02, the 2nd Workshop on Personalisation in Future TV*, pages 42–55, May 2002.

Adaptive Educational Hypermedia Proposal Based on Learning Styles and Quality Evaluation

Marcela Prieto Ferraro[1], Helmut Leighton Álvarez[2], and Francisco García Peñalvo[3]

[1] University of Antofagasta, Educational Department, Chile
mprieto5@usuarios.retecal.es
[2] University of Salamanca, Institute of Educational Science, Spain
hleighton@usuarios.retecal.es
[3] University of Salamanca, Department of Computer Science, Spain
fgarcia@usal.es

Abstract. This is a proposal of how to determine quality attributes in the Adaptive Educational Hypermedia Systems based on Learning Styles for a later design of a quality evaluation methodology of these systems. Some specific learning styles and their relationships with the outlined instructional strategies are examined, in order to find in a further work a way of how to determine the quality attributes and standards for the elaboration of the quality evaluation methodology for this systems.

1 Introduction

The initial development of Adaptive Educational Hypermedia (AEH) systems based their adaptation on taking into account various characteristics of their potential users, represented in the supported user models [1]. Later on Adaptive Hypermedia Systems (AHS), designed for learning, take into account the students' learning styles. Is based on the assumptions that instruction need not to be identical for all learners, and also that adapting the instructional strategies could help the students to become more effective learners, causing an interesting improvement in the learning process [2].

There already exist some quality evaluation methodologies for both traditional software applications and web applications. But it is necessary to extend these methodologies or create new procedures of quality and standardization from the educational focus properly.

For this reason, the objective of this work is to describe and analyse some of the AEH based on Learning Styles and to carry out a proposal in order to obtain a methodology for determining standardization of their components and a methodology for quality measurement of these systems from the pedagogic point of view.

2 AEH Based on Learning Styles

The AEH systems, which based their adaptation capabilities on the potencial users' learning styles, have been sustained in different learning styles theories arguing, in some cases, criteria for such election.

W. Nejdl and P. De Bra (Eds.): AH 2004, LNCS 3137, pp. 316–319, 2004.

CS383 [3] adapts the form of representing the contents to different learning styles by means of different instructional strategies based on the use of different elements of textual character and hypermedia. ARTHUR [4] uses varied formats of information, for oneself content or concept, associating the format type to the learning styles, so students with different styles will receive the information in different formats. iWeaver system [5] also uses different forms to represent the same information with techniques of conditional text, so that different pages are composed for different students. Some systems not only adapt the content presentation, but also adapt the navigation options. In INSPIRE [6] the learning styles determine exclusively the adaptation of the presentation and it is reflected in different sequences of activities in function of them. MAS PLANG [7] adjusts the navigation tools to the learning styles, offering specific structural and also collaborative work tools. FEIJOO.NET [8] uses content and navigation adaptation techniques based both on learning styles.

In the systems that have been previously analyzed it has been proven that most of them do not use criteria for the selection of a certain theory of learning styles (or they did not make them explicit), except theoretical and empirical justification [3, 5, 8].

The criteria to select the learning style model are: the theoretical and empirical justification, if it possesses assessment instruments, if it describes the instructional strategies associated to each category, the cost and if it is appropriate for the learning context [9]. One way of adapting the instructional process is to adjust it to the individual student's preferences, in such a way of teaching the students using instructional methods that are related to their preferences [2]. If the modality of adaptation is adopted to the learning styles for instructional systems (live or technology based) it is necessary to select the appropriate instructional strategies with the learning goal of instruction and, secondary, on the base of these strategies, we can choose the most appropriate to each one of the learning styles [10].

3 Instructional Strategies

The educational theories present a continuous that goes from the lower to the top level of the learning objectives, this way they embrace from the more basic cognitive demands to those of the superior order. Although each educational theory is more favourable for certain kinds of learning, depending on the focus that is given to the instructive design, there exist certain instructional strategies which by varying its application, adapt themselves more to an existing theory than another, but without any doubt some of them would also allow the adaptation of the hypermedia systems in their interaction with the student. This way, [11] refers to the type of learning, control of learning, focus of learning, grouping for learning, support for learning and interactions for learning.

3.1 Instructional Strategies Based on Learning Styles

For example, if we use two of the learning styles defined in [12], activist and reflector, and we already cross this information with the presented instructional strategies, we will be able to analyse under this pedagogic approach the obtained achievements in an AEH based on Learning Styles (Table 1).

Table 1. Learning styles and instructional strategies

Style	Characteristics	Strategies
Activist	- To attempt things new, new experiences, new opportunities - To compete in team, to solve problems in team, to find people of similar mentality to dialogue, to direct debates and meetings - To generate ideas without formalisms nor structures, to change and to vary proposals, to take a risk, to attempt something different	- Control centred in the student - Interdisciplinary work - Work in even, teams and/or groups - Interaction with even
Reflector	- To observe, to investigate attentively, to gather information, to listen, to have possibilities to read or to get ready ahead of time, to listen to differents points of view, to exchange opinions with other previous agreement - To work without pressures or terms, to think before acting, to assimilate before commenting - To make detailed analysis, to carry out carefully pondered reports, to work conscientiously	- Control centred in the teacher - Work guided to the domain and topic - Work singular more than in team - Interaction with printed and audiovisual material

In Table 1 the main characteristics proposed by [12] and the instructional strategies described by [11] have been grouped for two learning styles. This way, we can visualize how to confront the process of learning in a practical way according to the student's style, and on the other hand, determine the characteristics of the AEHs based on Learning Styles in a clear way.

4   Conclusions and Further Work

We have suggested that an AEH system based on Learning Styles will be more effective for learners when the technology fits instructional designs principles. The application of pedagogic criteria is also necessary to choose the most appropriate learning style model for the AEH that will be designed.

To design quality AEH system based on Learning Styles imply to establish a set of attributes, depending on the specific educational theory applied. To establish the quality attributes requires a process where you can visualize all the factors involved in the system, from an educational point of view. This way, once the attributes and their characteristics have been established, we will be able to determine the metrics that allow us to measure how, and how much the system considers the different instructional strategies in its model of adaptation and how they are reflected in the interaction with the student. For it, we outline the necessity to settle down in the first place, a net that considers the different required learning types and the appropriate instructional strategies so that the objectives are achieved by the students. In second place, to carry out a net that classifies or establishes a taxonomy among the kind of learning type/instructional strategy with each learning style. This way, it will be possible to settle down standards of quality that allow us to measure the quality of an AEH based on Learning Styles.

Acknowledgements

Research supported by the Government of Castile and Lion Projects (ref. SA017/02, US09/05), and the European Union Project ODISEAME (ref. EUMEDIS B7-4100/2000/2165-79 P546)

References

1. Brusilovsky, P.: Adaptive Hypermedia. User Modeling and User-Adapted Interaction. Ten Year Anniversary Issue (Alfred Kobsa, ed.) Vol. 11 (1/2) (2001) 87-110
2. Jonassen, D. & Grabowski, B.: Handbook of individual differences. Lawrence Erlbaum Associates Hillsdale, N.J. (1993)
3. Carver,C. A., Howard, R. A., Lane, W.D.: Addressing Different Learning Styles Through Course Hypermedia. IEEE Transactions on Education. Vol. 42(1) (1999) 33-38
4. Gilbert, J. E. & Han, C. Y.: Adapting Instruction in Search of "A Significant Difference". Network and Computer Applications, Vol. 22, (1999) 149-160
5. Wolf, C.: iWeaver: Towards an Interactive Web-Based Adaptive Learning Environment to Address Individual Learning Styles. EURODL 2002. Available in: http://www.eurodl.org/materials/2002/2HTML/iWeaver.htm (2002)
6. Papanikolaou, K., Grigoriadou, M., Magoulas, G., Kornilakis, H.: Towards new forms of knowledge communication: the adaptive dimension of a web-based learning environment. Computers and Education, Vol. 39, (2002) 333-360
7. Peña, C., Marzo, J., de la Rosa, J., Fabregat, R.: Un sistema de tutoría inteligente adaptativo considerando estilos de aprendizaje. IE2002, Vigo (España), Noviembre 20-22 (2002)
8. Paule, M., Pérez, P., Pérez, J., González, M.: Feijoo.net: An Approach to Personalized E-learning Using Learning Styles. ICWE 2003: (2003) 112-115
9. Sampson, D. & Karagiannidis, C.: Accommodating Learning Styles in Adaptation Logics for Personalised Learning Systems. 14th World Conference of Educational Multimedia, Hypermedia and Telecommunications (ED-MEDIA 02). Denver, Colorado, USA, June 24-29 (2002)
10. Merrill, M.D.: Instructional Strategies and Learning Styles: Which takes Precedence?. In Robert Reiser and Jack Dempsey (Eds.) Trends and Issues in Instructional Technology. Merrill/Prentice Hall Englewood Cliffs, N.J. (2001)
11. Reigeluth, C. M. y Moore, J.: Cognitive Education and the Cognitive Domain. In Reigeluth, C. M. (Eds) A New Paradigm of Instructional Theory – Vol. II,.Lawrence Erlbaum Associates, Inc, Publishers (LEA) USA (1999) 51-68
12. Alonso, C., Gallego, D., Honey, P.: Los Estilos de Aprendizaje. Procedimientos de diagnóstico y mejora. Ediciones Mensajero Bilbao (1997)

Adaptive Course Player for Individual Learning Styles

Katja Reinhardt, Stefan Apelt, and Marcus Specht

Fraunhofer Institute for Applied Information Technology,
Schloß Birlinghoven, 53754 Sankt Augustin
{katja.reinhardt,stefan.apelt,marcus.specht}@fit.fraunhofer.de

Abstract. The paper describes the development and implementation of an adaptive course player that uses standardized learning materials, metadata, and a learning style model based on the Felder-Silverman learning style classification. The system implements adaptation of individual recommendations and content adaptation based on learning styles.

1 Introduction and Related Work

Current developments from the field of content standardization for learning objects and metadata (LOM, SCORM) open up new possibilities for adaptive educational hypermedia to work with masses of content and learning objects. For example in the context of the ProLearn[1] project a variety of learning object repositories will be used as the basis for personalized learning services. From our point of view the integration of educational brokerage approaches, content standardization and the effective design of adaptive methods for personalized learning services is one of the key issues for next generation e-learning. In adaptive educational systems adaptations to learning styles are not that often realized as adaptations to the knowledge of learners, but in some systems the learner model is extended by a component as a basis for adaptations to learning styles. INSPIRE [1] is an AEH-System, in which learning units are generated dynamically depending on current knowledge status, learning style and learning progress of a learner. The learning material can be retrieved via three function levels: Remember, Use and Find. The respective presentations of the educational material are mainly affected by the learning style of a learner. For differentiation of learning types INSPIRE uses the learning style model of Honey and Mumford [2]. Concepts are represented through instructional elements e.g. theory, examples, exercises, activities, questions. By combination of these instructional elements different variants of instructional strategies are defined for presentation of educational material depending on learning styles. TANGOW [3, 4] offers adaptive guidance on basis of learner profiles, learner activities and educational strategies. Learner profiles are created with the questionnaire of Felder and Soloman [6]. Educational elements are divided into exposition tasks (E) und exemplifications (e). For the learning styles, which are deduced from the dimensions sensitive - intuitive and global - sequential [5], adaptive sequencings of educational elements are generated. In the following paper we want to describe our approach for an Adaptive Course Player for individual learning styles. Based on an analysis of different learning style models, we want to describe the de-

---

[1] ProLearn is funded in the 6th framework programme by the European Commission for professional learning.

W. Nejdl and P. De Bra (Eds.): AH 2004, LNCS 3137, pp. 320–323, 2004.

sign and implementation of a learner model, of an adaptive coaching component and content adaptation algorithms based on learning styles and asset metadata.

2 Personalized Content Recommendation and Presentation

The base for our learning style model is determined with the Felder-Soloman instrument [6]. The learning style is a combination of the relevant learning preference of the four testable dimensions. Based on a standardized questionnaire 80 combinations of learning styles are possible. For the individual learning preferences Felder and Silverman [5] give recommendations for training measures in classical learning situations. These can be used as basis for interpretations regarding the adaptation design. In the adaptation component the strategies for learning element sequencing and content adaptation are represented. For the development of the adaptation strategies some techniques of adaptive navigation support and adaptive presentation [7] were consulted.

Learning Element Sequencing: The learning preferences of the dimensions *active - reflective* and *sensitive - intuitive* express, whether a learner has a preference for theoretical (intuitive) or for practical learning elements (sensitive) and whether a learner rather likes interactive (active) or less interactive learning elements (reflective). Therefore the sequencing of the learning elements *theory, example* and *exercise* mainly depend on these two dimensions. In order to be able to specify the sequencing of the learning elements they must be sorted according to suitable criteria for each individual learning preference. For the dimension *active - reflective* the sorting of the learning elements was made regarding their interactivity level. On this basis then the sequencing of in each case two learning preferences can be specified for all combinations. These combinations can be supplemented around the preferences of the dimension *sequential - global*. These preferences have no influence on the order of the learning elements, but on the number of navigation recommendations. Since a sequential learner rather goes in small steps through the learning units, also all learning elements of a learning unit are suggested to this learner for editing.

Content Adaptation: The learning preferences of the dimension *visual - verbal* expresses whether a learner rather learns with picture-based or with text-based contents. Therefore the dynamic generation of learning element contents mainly depends on these two learning preferences. The content elements, which are not relevant for a learning preference, can be hidden when presenting a page. However the problem is, that for a a visual learner not all texts can be hidden, but only those, for which equivalent explanations in form of picture-based content elements can be presented. But pictures mostly are visual additions to a text and therefore such pictures only can impart knowledge, when also text-based information is presented. The idea of hiding text-based content elements also can be used for adaptive multimedia presentation. The definition of appropriate strategies depends on the learning elements and the content elements of the learning materials available.

For the course materials described in this paper content adaptation strategies were defined for the learning elements *theory*, because this learning elements contain several text and picture-based content elements. For the learning elements *example* and *exercise* content adaptations are not applied because these exclusively contain exercise questions or instructional videos. In addition instructional videos (picture-based) with sound (spoken text) are suitable for visual and verbal learners. In the following the content elements for the theoretical learning elements are defined:

Text: text-based information to a concept

Additional text: additional text-based information to a concept **Statement:** important text-based information to a concept

Text of a picture: text-based information, which also is integrated in a picture or in a slideshow

Picture: picture-based supporting information to a concept **Slideshow:** multi-picture-based supporting information to a concept

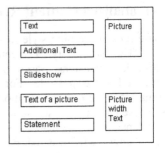

Fig. 1. Example of a learning element theory with all types of content elements

By hiding not relevant content elements depending on dimension *visual-verbal* different views of learning elements *theory* can be generated. Additionally by hiding the content element *additional text* the dimension *sequential - global* also can be considered. The sequential learner receives additional texts, because they prefer to work on learning material in detail and in small steps. Global learners do not get additional texts, because they rather go in larger steps through the learning materials.

3 Conclusion

In the presented paper we have described the implementation of adaptive methods for content sequencing and adaptive content presentations based on learning style preferences. We did not go into detail of the work we have done on metadata and the usage of learning style preferences with different content metadata. This would have extended the focus of this paper. Nevertheless the usage of learner model features in combination with different content metadata is implemented in the ALE system and we are currently in the phase of evaluating different approaches for their effectiveness and feasibility. From first evaluations of the system it has become clear that the application of adaptive content presentation has to be combined with user control in the GUI to allow users to adapt the content presentation. This is also consistent with previous findings on user control especially with more professional users and methods of adaptive hiding.

References

1. Papanikolaou, K., Grigoriadou, M., Kornilakis, H. und Magoulas, G. 2003. Personalizing the Interaction in a Web-based Educational Hypermedia System: the case of INSPIRE. Department of Informatics and Telecommunications, University of Athens. http://www.aegean.gr/culturaltec/c_karagiannidis/AEH/papanikolaou2003.pdf (2004-02-19)
2. Honey, P. und Mumford, A. 1992. The manual of Learning Styles, Peter Honey, Maidenhead.

3. Parades, P., Rodriguez, P. 2002. Considering Sensing-Intuitive Dimension to Exposition-Exemplification in Adaptive Sequencing. In: De Bra, P., Brusilovsky, P. und Conejo, R. (Hrsg.) *Lecture Notes In Computer Science* Proceedings of the Second International Conference on Adaptive Hypermedia and Adaptive Web-Based Systems, Springer-Verlag, Berlin Heidelberg, 556 -559.
4. Parades, P., Rodriguez, P. 2002. Considering Learning Styles in Adaptive Webbased Education. Proceedings of the 6th World Multiconference on Systemics, Cybernetics and Informatics en Orlando, Florida, 481-485.
   http://www.ii.uam.es/~pparedes/pubs/sci2002.pdf (2003-11-13)
5. Felder, R.M. und Silverman, L.K. 1988. Learning an teaching styles in engineering and education. In: Engineering Education, 78(7), 674-681.
   http://www.ncsu.edu/felder-public/Papers/LS-1988.pdf (2004-02-19)
6. Felder, R.M. und Soloman, B.A. 1999. Index of learning styles.
   http://www.ncsu.edu/felder-public/ILSpage.html (2004-02-19)
7. Brusilovsky, P. 1996. Methods and techniques of adaptive hypermedia. In: *User Modeling and User-Adapted Interaction* 6, 2-3, 87-129.
   http://www2.sis.pitt.edu/~peterb/papers/UMUAI96.pdf (2004-02-19)

Rhetorical Patterns for Adaptive Video Documentaries

Cesare Rocchi and Massimo Zancanaro

ITC-Irst,
via Sommarive 18
Povo Trento, Italy
{rocchi,zancana}@itc.it

Abstract. In this paper, we introduce an approach to the adaptive composition of video documentaries. The adaptation is based on templates that encode rules for the dynamic selection, sequencing and composition of video shots. We introduce a template language to define adaptation rules. Finally, we discuss *rhetorical patterns*, strategies that we abstracted out during the realization of a museum mobile guide.

1 Introduction

In a previous work [7], we introduced a model for adaptive video documentaries. The building blocks of our documentaries are not prerecorded and annotated movie clips, but shots that can be defined by means of a scripting language. A shot is made of camera movements, applied to 2D images, and a sequence of audio files. By means of this finer granularity, presentation designers can focus on both the structure of the final presentation and the content of single clips at the same time. This approach is a compromise between full-fledged generation like in [1] and juxtaposition of canned movie clips like in [5].

Adaptive hypermedia authors have often to deal with large and complex collections of media items (images, audio files and texts) [2, 3]. In implementing the content for a mobile guide in the context of the PEACH[1] project, we noted that designers had to face recurrent problems. It thus proved natural to abstract out patterns from the set of solutions that authors provided to such situations, as happens in the programming field and in hypermedia educational systems [4]. Since these patterns have to do with the discourse structure of the video documentaries, we call them *rhetorical patterns*.

2 XASCRIPT (Adaptive Template Language)

XASCRIPT is a language for the definition of templates, intensional descriptions of a set of *potential* documentaries, with multiple-choice points on user-dependent parameters. Adaptation rules are the tool that enables authors to state constraints and strategies to select shots and apply transition effects. An adaptation rule is a `<condition, action>` pair, where the condition tests the requirements and the action

---

[1] PEACH, Personal Experience with Active Cultural Heritage. See http://peach.itc.it

W. Nejdl and P. De Bra (Eds.): AH 2004, LNCS 3137, pp. 324–327, 2004.

composes the pieces of the documentary. Our framework allows defining many dimensions along which adaptivity can be realized. While designing templates, the author can always refer to two key variables: the *user* for which the documentary is going to be presented, and the *current documentary* under processing. In this way, the author explicitly inserts conditions related to user's features (e.g. preferences, previous seen presentations, device dimensions) and also conditions related to the current composition process (e.g. previous selected effect, list of already selected shots).

3 Rhetorical Patterns for Template Authoring

Although the implementation of templates for video documentaries can not be compared with a programming task, they have some commonalities. Presentation designers have to take into account many features like coherence of the selected content, cohesion of the presentation form, choice of transition effects, preferences of the user, etc. In the programming field, Design Patterns encode 'scheme of solutions' to recurrent problems. During the writing of templates for adaptive presentations, designers have to face recurrent problems. For example, they often have to address the following issues: **Deepening**: if the user has already been exposed to a topic *t*, how to select and present material related to *t* (e.g. highlight its features)? **Comparison**: Comparisons maximize the extent to which a visitor's understanding of an exhibit coheres with her other knowledge, and help to prevent the hearer from forming misconceptions. How to refer to previously mentioned material *m*, related to the current topic? **Suggestion**: suggestions are complementary to comparisons. If the user has not visited an exhibit *e* and the designer thinks that *e* - considering the current context - is worth a visit, how to lead the user to visit *e*? **Exemplification**: if the topic *t* is generic, say 'a painting techniques', how to provide visual and aural explanations, so that the user can more effectively understand *t*?

In analogy with the programming field, we define *Rhetorical Patterns* (RPs) the scheme of solutions to these problems. Each of the previous issues, in fact, relates to the structure of the discourse and how such a structure affects the message underlying the documentary. In our context RPs encode adaptation strategies, namely ways to find a solution given a context, a particular combination of user dependent features.

Each pattern has a name, a statement of the problem it is meant to solve, a list of applicability conditions, a list of motivations stating how and why the problem is solved by applying such a pattern, the solution, or a sketch of solution if the problem is generic and, finally, possible related patterns. In the examples presented below we show how a pattern can be mapped onto a schema or template in a straightforward way. Our approach is inspired by the Rhetorical Structure Theory (RST) presented by Mann and Thompson [6]. While the nature of RST is *descriptive*, in that rhetorical relations are meant to functionally relate pieces of text to one another, our approach is rather focused on the proposal of stereotypical solutions to recurrent problems in defining templates for video documentaries. The nature of rhetorical patterns proposed here is thus *prescriptive*, for they are a sort of recipes to prepare 'good' documentaries. We then foresee the possibility to couple recurrent problems to particular configurations of discourse structures that provide a solution to those problems. A *Suggestion* pattern, for instance, can be described as in table 1.

Table 1. *Suggestion* and *Composition* patterns

Name:	Suggestion	Comparison
Problem:	Lead the user to visit an exhibit.	Show similarities between two exhibits.
Conditions:	The current exhibit *e* is related to another one *o* (e.g. they share the same style, they depict the same scene). The user has not visited *o*.	The current exhibit *e* is related to another one *o*. The user has already visited *o*.
Motivation(s):	The user is explicitly told (via audio or video) to go and visit *o*. This helps her to understand similarities and/or differences between the two exhibits and contextualize her information absorption.	The comparison among two items can help the user to find the relation among them (e.g. slightly different painting style, same subject depicted by two different authors)
Solution:	At the end of the video presenting *e*, insert a shot which represents *e* and an audio file which points the user to *o*. If needed insert also spatial references to help the visitor finding *o* location.	Insert one or more shots which explicitly refer to the features of *o* and show their similarities. Screen can be split into two part to help the user recalling *o*.
Related Patterns:	Comparison. If condition 2 does not hold maybe a comparison applies.	Contrast. Besides similarities also differences can be presented.

The purpose of a suggestion is to persuade the visitor to see an exhibit. This is a suitable pattern if the currently presented exhibit or topic is related to another. This way the user is helped in contextualizing and relating information by means of similarities or even differences between two artworks.

```
...
<rule>
  <UM-expression>$user.hasVisited(<exhibit-id>)
  </UM-expression>
  <!--Insert here shots(s) presenting comparisons -->
  <!--Insert here a shot containing the suggestion -->
</rule>
</editing>
```

Fig. 1. A schema of template in which *Comparison* and *Suggestion* patterns find application

The solution is to insert a piece of video at the end of the presentation, which contains an explicit invitation to visit another exhibit and, if needed, the path to reach it.

Comparisons provide a framework in which the visitor can contextualize her knowledge. Besides preventing the visitor from misconceptions, comparisons allow also to relate items each others, thus enabling descriptions which are more effective, since they refer to things the visitors are familiar with. This pattern applies when there are two or more exhibits that share similarities. The solution is to insert media items that make explicit reference to concepts well known to the visitor, or pieces of art she has already visited.

Since they are related, Comparison and Suggestion patterns can be easily mapped onto the schema of template in Fig. 1.

We have also identified patterns for providing follow-ups, hiding media items, creating simple sequences (e.g. to enumerate similar items) and providing exemplifications. At the moment we are implementing a graphical user interface which allows authors to exploit our pattern approach during the writing of templates, by proposing schemata of templates like the one shown in Fig. 1.

4 Conclusions

In this paper, we presented an approach to facilitate the implementation of templates by discussing the notion of *Rhetorical Pattern*, schemata of solutions for recurrent problems that arise during the preparation of the templates. In our view these patterns help authors focusing on the interaction with the *information space* they organize and user's needs; and also to cope with the usually big amount of content to be organized during the authoring of a hypermedia system.

References

1. André E.: The Generation of Multimedia Documents. In: R. Dale, H. Moisl and H. Somers: A Handbook of Natural Language Processing: Techniques and Applications for the Processing of Language as Text, Marcel Dekker (2000) 305-327
2. Cristea A., deMooij A., Designer Adaptation in Adaptive Hypermedia Authoring. In: Proceedings of International Conference on Information Technology, Las Vegas (2003) 444-448
3. De Bra P., Aerts A., Smits D., Stash N.: AHA! Version 2.0, More Adaptation Flexibility for Authors. In: Proceedings of the AACE ELearn conference, Montreal, (2002) 240-246
4. Germán D. M., Cowan D. D.: Towards a Unified Catalog of Hypermedia Design Patterns. In: Proceedings of the 33rd Hawaii International Conference on System Sciences, Hawaii (2000)
5. Lindley C., Davis J., Nack F., Rutledge L.: The application of rhetorical structure theory to interactive news program generation from digital archives. Technical Report INS-R0101, CWI Centrum voor Wiskunde en Informatica, (2001)
6. Mann W. C., Thompson S.: Rhetorical Structure Theory: a Theory of Text Organization. In: The Structure of Discourse. Ablex Publishing Corporation (1987)
7. Rocchi, C., Zancanaro, M.: Adaptive Video Documentaries In: Proceedings of the HyperText Conference, Nottingham, (2003)

Location-Aware Adaptive Interfaces
for Information Access with Handheld Computers

Golha Sharifi[1], Ralph Deters[1], Julita Vassileva[1], Susan Bull[2], and Harald Röbig[2]

[1] Computer Science Department, University of Saskatchewan, Canada
[2] Electronic, Electrical and Computer Engineering, University of Birmingham, UK
jiv@cs.usask.ca, s.bull@bham.ac.uk

Abstract. Adpating to user context versus adapting to individual user features or behaviour patterns has been a topic of recent discussion. We believe both types of adaptation are valuable and the decision of which to apply, or how to combine the two, is domain or application specific. As an illustration, this paper presents two approaches to adapting the interface according to the type of user and the extent to which the user's task and location is predetermined.

1 Introduction

A challenge in ubiquitous computing is to design personalised interfaces and software enabling easy access to information while being sufficiently flexible to handle changes in a user's context and available resources [1]. Adapting to context, especially location and time, could help improve usability of small-screen interfaces [2]. Various issues are relevant in supporting adaptive mobile access to information: location, connectivity, task, schedule, user type and others. Which of these issues are most relevant depend on the domain and context of use of the application and device. While sharing the function of adapting interfaces for information access, different user modelling and adaptation techniques may be suitable in different contexts.

In this paper we focus on features for consideration in the development of adaptive interfaces for information access with handheld computers, in particular where the adaptivity is related to location and the activity to be performed. We use two examples to demonstrate different approaches according to whether activities are tied to location and class of user, or whether the coincidence of activity and location is based on user preference. Both are implemented for iPAQ Pocket PCs.

2 Mobi-Timar and My Chameleon

Mobi-Timar ('mobile caregiver' in Farsi) [3] supports access by homecare workers, to non-critical information such as scheduling and patient data, and supports communication between homecare workers. Each patient has a team of homecare workers, comprising nurses, physiotherapists, home health aides, social workers and dieticians. Tasks and duties are divided based on skills and availability. Providing homecare workers with small mobile devices and access to a wireless network allows them to retrieve information, receive and send notification of schedule changes, update the

W. Nejdl and P. De Bra (Eds.): AH 2004, LNCS 3137, pp. 328–331, 2004.

data/information system and communicate with others. However, there are two difficulties in implementing the handheld computer solution: (1) the non reliable connection due to uneven coverage of the area; (2) the benefits of a highly portable device bring problems of limited screen size, making it difficult to design a user interface providing the range of functionality needed to support users in their tasks. Mobi-Timar combines techniques from agent technologies, distributed database transaction management, user and task modeling [3]. One goal is to ensure seamless access to information despite frequent interruptions in connection caused by mobility of workers and unequal coverage of the area. The interface has to be designed for small wireless devices allowing workers to conveniently perform typical operations.

Health care and homecare workers have typical tasks, which have standard information needs. Therefore it is possible to: (1) predict the kind of information needed by the homecare worker using their schedule; (2) pre-fetch and/or adapt information appropriate for the task; (3) present it according to the user's preferences and limitations of the device. Fig. 1 illustrates the interface for different users.

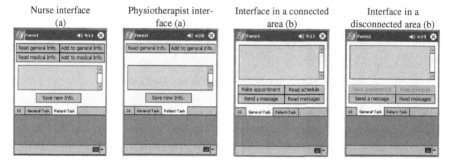

Fig. 1. Task (a) and location (b) - adapted interface for user types nurse and physiotherapist.

Agents are used to give the impression of seamless connection. They hide the changes in network bandwidth from users by pre-fetching information before the time it is required, by means of task, user and context modelling, and adaptation techniques related to these. When the context (time, location) and the current task of the user is known, the interface can provide those specific functionalities needed.

Chameleons are known for the fact that their appearance matches features of their local environment. 'My Chameleon' belongs to the mobile user - wherever the user is, his or her chameleon adapts its interface to suit the user's requirements at that place. It provides easy 'one click' access to applications, tasks, files, documents needed by the user, according to their current location. It is being used by university students. University students often work quite flexibly in a range of locations. They typically have individual usage patterns related to their locations of use [4] and could therefore benefit from an adaptive interface for their small-screen device.

Ensuring seamless connection is not so important, as many of the activities pursued by students on their handheld computer (as revealed in a logbook study [4]) do not require connectivity. The goal is to provide easy access to those tasks, files and applications that a student habitually uses on their handheld device, in their various locations of use. The responsibility remains with the student of ensuring that they have the particular documents that they will require. Although students tend to use different files in different locations, from the logbook data it was often more difficult to predict where they might be at any one time except for during their scheduled lecture and lab sessions. Consequently, the problem of pre-fetching anticipated useful information or documents before students leave a connected area is not considered. The interface of My Chameleon is illustrated in Fig. 2.

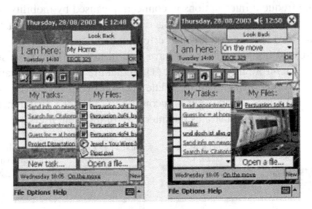

Fig. 2. Screens for a user at two locations

Within My Chameleon users only access files, tasks, applications and schedule. The techniques are therefore straightforward. As stated above, a typical user has specific, individual usage patterns. My Chameleon maintains a model of these patterns. Each time a user accesses a document or application in a particular location (e.g. home) or category (e.g. 'on the move'), the weighting for that item being required again in that location or category, increases.

Table 1 summarises issues relevant to location-aware adaptive interfaces for mobile devices, highlighting the important features in the two applications presented.

Table 1. Issues relevant to location-aware adaptive interfaces for mobile information access

	abstract category	loca-tion	schedule	specified task	connecti-vity	control of UM	user type	UM technique	dyna-mic
M-T		+	+	+	+		+	stereotype	
M C	+	+	+			+		individual	+

User Model: Homecare workers are classified by profession. Therefore, Mobi-Timar user models use stereotypes which do not change over time, as a homecare worker's duties remain the same. Individual user models extend stereotypes with personal information, preferences, rank and experience, and may occasionally change. For My Chameleon, the logbook study revealed no possibility for using stereotypes. Although users had identifiable usage patterns, these were *individual* patterns. Thus individual data forms the content of My Chameleon user models, which may remain similar, or may change if activities change over time.

Task Model: Each Mobi-Timar user has to perform standard tasks. Each task needs specific types of information, and the information needs of tasks typically do not vary over time. There are no pre-defined tasks in My Chameleon. Any user may perform any task, and these are defined by the user. The nature of a user's activities may remain similar over time, or may differ according to course requirements.

Schedule: The Mobi-Timar schedule predicts task and context (time, location), so information can be pre-fetched. In My Chameleon the calendar predicts where a user is likely to be, to allow easy confirmation of the current location. Unlike Mobi-Timar, where users will definitely be at the predicted location, students are less reliable and may need to select their location from a menu. A second difference is that rather than specifying a location, students may use a descriptor corresponding to an abstract category (e.g. 'user modelling course' or 'on the move'), which is useful for atypical activities in a location.

Connectivity Model: Mobi-Timar's connectivity model contains a map of network connectivity for each location. An important issue is how to deal with disconnection and weak connections using proxy agents, when to pre-fetch what information and how to ensure data consistency when a disconnected user enters data using mobile transaction management [3]. My Chameleon does not require a connectivity model as users have on their devices the files that they may need.

User Control of the User Model: Mobi-Timar users should not be able to change the stereotype model as it is pre-defined according to the required tasks for the user class. However, they can change some individual preferences, e.g. interface layout. In contrast, the My Chameleon user must be able to change their user model, as they may need to work with some documents for a restricted time. They must be able to 'expire' links if required.

3 Summary

This paper explored some relevant issues for user- and location-aware adaptive interfaces for mobile information access, contrasted in two systems: one with predetermined tasks and locations, using a predominately stereotype approach; and one that employs individual user models built from user preferences for location and activities.

References

1. Cheverst, K., de Carolis, N., Krueger, A.: Workshop: User Modeling in Ubiquitous Computing (Preface), 9th International Conference on User Modeling, Johnstown, PA (2003).
2. Brusilovsky, P.: Adaptive Hypermedia, User Modeling and User-Adapted Interaction 11(1-4), (2001) 87-110.
3. Sharifi, G., Vassileva, J., Deters, R. Seamless Communication and Access to Information for Mobile Users in a Wireless Environment. Proceedings ICEIS'2004 International Conference on Enterprise Information Systems, Porto (2004) 122-130.
4. Bull, S.: User Modelling and Mobile Learning, User Modeling 2003: 9th International Conference, Springer-Verlag, Berlin Heidelberg, (2003) 383-387.

PSO: A Language for Web Information Extraction and Web Page Clipping

Tetsuya Suzuki and Takehiro Tokuda

Department of Computer Science,
Tokyo Institute of Technology,
2-12-1-W8-71 Ohokayama, Meguro, Tokyo, Japan
{tetsuya,tokuda}@tt.cs.titech.ac.jp

Abstract. Web information extraction and Web page clipping are important technique in adaptive hypermedia which adapt or compose contents from real Web pages. A technical problem for them is robustness of specification of parts of Web pages against update of Web pages. In this paper we present a language called PSO for Web information extraction and Web page clipping. Thanks to operations called path set operations which the language provides for the problem, we can specify parts of Web pages with small differences in expected formats by structural similarity between Web pages. We also show application of the language to real Web pages.

1 Introduction

Web information extraction and Web page clipping are important technique in adaptive hypermedia which adapt or compose contents from real Web pages. Web information extraction is to extract essential information from Web pages. Web page clipping is to extract information from Web pages with their original layout.

A technical problem for them is how to specify parts of Web pages easily and safely because Web pages are often updated.

In this paper we present a language called PSO for Web information extraction and Web page clipping. The language provides operations called path set operations for the technical problem. We also show application of the language to real Web pages.

2 Path Set Operations

In this section we show an overview of path set operations we proposed in [8].

In path set operations, one Web page is viewed as one ordered tree whose nodes have attributes. The tree is an abstraction of the Document Object Model (DOM)[6] tree of the Web page. Fig.1(1) and (2) show an HTML document and its DOM tree respectively. Attributes of nodes of an ordered tree includes not only attributes of DOM nodes such as text="black" of a body element in Fig.1(1) but also types of DOM nodes and positions of DOM nodes among their siblings.

We define concepts over such ordered trees, and we represent an ordered tree as just a tree there. A *path* over a tree is a sequence of nodes over the tree from its root node to

W. Nejdl and P. De Bra (Eds.): AH 2004, LNCS 3137, pp. 332–335, 2004.

(1) An HTML document   (2) The DOM tree of the HTML document

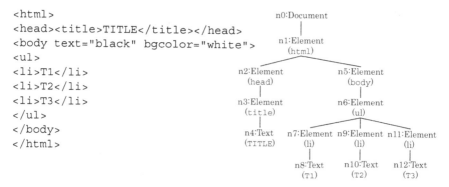

```
<html>
<head><title>TITLE</title></head>
<body text="black" bgcolor="white">
<ul>
<li>T1</li>
<li>T2</li>
<li>T3</li>
</ul>
</body>
</html>
```

Fig. 1. An HTML document and its DOM tree

an internal node or a leaf node. For example, a sequence of nodes (n0, n1, n5, n6, n7, n8) is a path of the tree of Fig.1(2). A *typed path set* is a pair of a tree and a set of paths over the tree. The tree is the *type* of the typed path set.

   Path set operations are mainly operations for typed path sets and include the following operations.

1. Path extraction operations based on similarity between paths.
2. Path extraction operations based on an order among paths.
3. Union, intersection and difference of typed path sets.
4. Operations to merge paths in a typed path set into a tree.
5. Operations to transform a tree to a node.

In the operations of the first group, we regard two paths with a smaller distance as more similar paths. A distance between two paths is computed by a DP matching method based on distances between nodes. A distance between two nodes is an editing cost to make them have same attributes. We can specify weight of attributes for the editing cost. The operations of the second group enable us to specify parts of Web pages before a path, those after a path, and those between two paths. The operations of the third group are applied to two typed path sets with a same type, and the resulting typed path set also has the same type. The operations of the fourth group are for Web page clipping. The operation of the fifth group are for information extraction: assembling of strings in a tree, extraction of attributes' values such as *href* attributes' values, and so on.

3   A Language PSO

In this section we explain a language PSO for Web information extraction and Web page clipping briefly.

   The language is a procedural language. A PSO program consists of procedures, and each procedure is written as one XML document.

Types of values the language provides are int for integers, string for strings, boolean for boolean values, pathset for typed path sets, tree for ordered attributed trees, array for arrays, and annotation for array annotations.

The language provides the following operations for typed path sets, ordered attributed trees, arrays, and array annotations.

1. Operations based on path set operations
2. Operations to specify parts of HTML/XML documents by XPath[5]
3. Operations to apply XSLT[7] programs to HTML/XML documents
4. Operations to download HTML/XML documents from the Internet
5. Operations to output HTML/XML documents as local files
6. Operations to transform arrays and typed path sets to XML documents

We give a supplementary explanation about operations in the sixth group. Programmers can construct a tree by arrays because an array can have not only other data types but also arrays as its elements. An array annotation is bound to an array, and it specifies tags and attributes in an XML document transformed from the array. Typed path sets can be exported as XML documents in Path Set Description Language(PSDL). Typed path sets in PSDL can be imported to PSO programs. PSDL is intended to preserve paths used for path extraction operations based on similarity between paths.

4   Application

We implemented a PSO interpreter in Java. The interpreter can accept even broken HTML documents thanks to CyberNeko HTML Parser[4]. The interpreter can be used from both shell command line and Java application programs.

We applied PSO programs to a small model of a typical news Web site and real Web sites. On a page of the small model, headlines are listed by categories of news. A PSO program successfully clips headlines of a category even if we change the order of categories on the page and the numbers of headlines of lists. The Web sites to which we applied PSO programs are 'Yahoo! News'[2], 'Yahoo! Weather'[3] and the Web site of the ministry of foreign affairs of Japan [1]. The PSO programs for the real Web sites successfully work if our assumptions about their formats hold. For example, news on the top page of the ministry of foreign affairs of Japan are categorized by dates. A PSO program extracts news from the top page and generates a RSS document as shown in Fig.2. As long as our assumption about a format of the top page holds, the program works well even if the number of dates on the top page and the number of headlines for each date change. It, however, recognizes two or more articles as one article when our assumption about the format does not hold under updated pages.

5   Conclusion and Future Work

We presented a procedural language PSO for Web information extraction and Web page clipping. The language provides a method to specify parts of Web pages by structural similarity between Web pages, and the similarity is computed by a DP matching method. Our future work would be to develop an environment which helps users to write PSO programs and to make more examples of PSO programs.

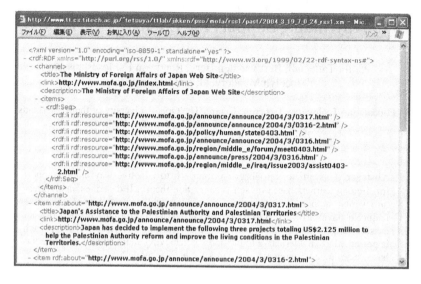

Fig. 2. A generated RSS document by a PSO program

References

1. The Ministry of Foreign Affairs of Japan. http://www.mofa.go.jp/index.html.
2. Yahoo! News. http://news.yahoo.com/.
3. Yahoo! Weather. http://weather.yahoo.com/.
4. Andy Clark. CyberNeko HTML Parser . http://www.apache.org/ andyc/neko/doc/html/.
5. Anders Berglund, Scott Boag, Don Chamberlin, Mary F. Fernandez, Michael Kay, Jonathan Robie, and Jerome Simeon. XML Path Language (XPath) 2.0. http://www.w3.org/TR/xpath20/, 2002.
6. Arnaud Le Hors, Philippe Le Hegaret, Lauren Wood, Gavin Nicol, Jonathan Robie, Mike Champion, and Steve Byrne. Document Object Model (DOM) Level 2 Core Specification Version 1.0. http://www.w3.org/TR/2000/REC-DOM-Level-2-Core-20001113/, 2000.
7. Michael Kay. XSL Transformations (XSLT) Version 2.0. http://www.w3.org/TR/xslt20/, 2002.
8. Tetsuya Suzuki and Takehiro Tokuda. Path set operations for clipping of parts of web pages and information extraction from web pages. In *Proceedings of the 15th International Conference on Software Engineering and Knowledge Engineering*, pages 547–554. Knowledge Systems Institute, 2003.

Swarm-Based Adaptation:
Wayfinding Support for Lifelong Learners

Colin Tattersall, Bert van den Berg, René van Es, José Janssen,
Jocelyn Manderveld, and Rob Koper*

Educational Technology Expertise Centre, The Open University of the Netherlands
Valkenburgerweg 177, 6419 AT Heerlen, The Netherlands
{cta,ebe,res,jja,jma,rkp}@ou.nl

Abstract. This article introduces an approach to adaptive wayfinding support
for lifelong learners based on self-organisation theory. It describes an architecture which supports the recording, processing and presentation of collective
learner behaviour designed to create a feedback loop informing learners of successful paths towards the attainment of their learning objectives. The approach
is presented as an alternative to methods of achieving adaptation in hypermedia-
based learning environments which involve learner modelling.

1 Introduction

Self-direction – the learner's assumption of "primary responsibility for and control
over decisions about planning, implementing and evaluating the learning experience"
[1] – lies at the heart of lifelong learning. However, self-directed learners are often
challenged to assume responsibilities, and the self-directed learner may be "confronted with the problem of how to find a way into and through a body of knowledge
that is unknown at the outset. Without the benefit of any explicit guidance, a self-
directed learner is obliged to map out a course of inquiry that seems appropriate, but
that may involve a certain amount of difficulty and disappointment that could have
been averted" [2]. This description calls to mind the image of the lifelong learner as
navigator, charting a course through educational waters. We follow Darken [3] in
using the term "wayfinding" to describe the cognitive, decision-making navigational
process carried out by self-directed learners as they assume responsibility for sequencing their learning interactions *en route* to the attainment of certain competen-
cies. Fixed curricula serve only to restrict the possibilities for self-direction – lifelong
learners need a flexible, adaptive approach to wayfinding support (termed adaptive
navigation support by Brusilovsky [4]), able to respond to their changing situations
and goals.

2 Wayfinding Support for Lifelong Learners

Flexibility in wayfinding support can be realised through so-called "learner support
services" [5]. However, individualised advice is costly. As a response to this financial

---

* The authors wish to thank Wim Waterink, Catherine Bolman and Pierre Höppener of The
Open University of The Netherlands for their contributions to this work.

W. Nejdl and P. De Bra (Eds.): AH 2004, LNCS 3137, pp. 336–339, 2004.

issue, research has explored the application of educational technologies to lifelong learning support. The authors of a recent CEDEFOP thematic workshop report [6] contend that Adaptive Hypermedia Systems (AHSs) are "particularly suited to implementing lifelong learning ... because they can tailor the learning environment and content to each individual learner's needs and aptitudes". AHS continues the Intelligent Tutoring Systems research line in seeking to "build a model of the goals, preferences and knowledge of the individual user and use this through the interaction for adaptation of the hypertext to the needs of the user" [7]. The reliance on accurate, detailed and up-to-date user models is both the theoretical strength of Adaptive Hypermedia and its practical Achilles heel. Without models, or with incorrect ones, adaptation falters, and Self [8] notes the absence of a theory of learning which might be used to maintain learner models. Is there, then, an alternative approach to wayfinding guidance for lifelong learners which might provide a cost-effective, flexible solution yet which does not rely upon learner modelling?

The ideal approach would avoid pre-planning of wayfinding guides so that courses, as it were, spontaneously acquire effective structures or organisations. Such self-organisation – "the acquiring of a spatial, temporal or functional structure without specific interference from the outside" [9] – can be seen in ant foraging trails [10]. Paths identified by ants are not pre-planned, but emerge as a result of indirect communication between members of an ant colony, a process known as stigmergy. In their overview article Theraulaz and Bonabeau [11] state, "The basic principle of stigmergy is extremely simple: Traces left and modifications made by individuals in their environment may feed back on them". Stigmergy can be considered as the basis for an approach to wayfinding support for lifelong learners. We can imagine learners' interactions with learning resources and activities being recorded automatically as they progress through a body of knowledge, then processed/aggregated and finally fed back to other learners. This would provide a new source of wayfinding guidance to lifelong learners giving clues as to efficient paths through a body of knowledge. Such an approach is cost-effective, since trail creation occurs unnoticed as a side effect of learner interaction with e-learning systems, it is flexible, able to emerge from and adapt to different circumstances, and it holds the prospect of being implementable, since its adaptivity does not depend upon learner modelling but rather on the behaviour of the "swarm" of learners.

3   An Architecture for Wayfinding Support in Lifelong Learning

Our work on wayfinding support is being carried out as part of the development of flexible lifelong learning facilities that meet the needs of learners at various levels of competence throughout their lives, which we term "Learning Networks" or LNs [12]. A Learning Network consists of learning events called Activity Nodes (ANs), such as courses, workshops, conferences, lessons, internet learning resources, etc.

In Learning Networks, the Learner's Position is defined as the set of ANs already completed in the LN. The Learner's Target is the set of ANs that is sufficient to reach a particular level of competence or expertise in the domain. These two concepts equate to "you are here" (position) and "there's where I want to be" (target), and the wayfinding guidance which is fed back concerns effective ways of getting from here to there, based on the behaviour of the swarm of previous learners.

Central to the approach are logs of learner information which indicate what a learner did and when. The use of internet technologies in e-learning has brought with it an increase in the level of standardisation of transmission protocols and data, and logging information is no exception. The World Wide Web Consortium has provided Common and Extended Log File Formats and a whole area of research is now dedicated to the processing and analysis of these files for various purposes, known as Web Usage Mining [13]. However, the events which are registered in these logs are extremely low level, especially when seen from the lifelong learning perspective. This complicates their analysis, making it difficult to know which users are interacting (since only IP addresses are logged) and what they are doing (since only cryptic Uniform Resource Locators (URLs) are logged). The characteristics of our domain suggest a different type of log is more appropriate, one which records not only which lifelong learner did what, but also whether or not this was successful (eg by including the results of an assessment).

Such a level of description is envisaged in the learner records data store described in the IEEE Draft Standard for Learning Technology – Learning Technology Systems Architecture [14]. This data store, specifically designed to cater for the nomadic nature of lifelong learners, is defined as a repository of "learner information, such as performance, preference, and other types of information".

With the notions of position, target and learner record in place, an architecture for self-organising wayfinding support can be introduced. Lifelong learners interact with the functionality available in a learning network. Learner-AN interaction is logged in a Learner Record Store along the lines envisaged by the IEEE draft architecture, including information on the learner, the AN, a timestamp and an indication of performance (for example, pass or fail). The lifelong learner is presented with feedback which reveals how other learners with the same target and from the same position, were successful in reaching the target. This information is derived from the collective log of learner interactions, following both filtering and processing. The filtering is used first to limit the feedback to involve only those learners with the same target, and then to limit it to relate to those learners who departed from the same position as the learner ("others with your target and position proceeded as follows"). The processing is used to rank the various next steps taken by other learners, favouring the next best step (eg the one taking the least time to complete or the one with the best chance of success). With this architecture in place, lifelong learners are given access to information hitherto unavailable to them, yet of importance to the wayfinding process. The learner is able to find answers to questions such as "How did other learners progress in this learning network from where am I now?", "Which path through the learning network offer the most chance of success?" and "What has been the most efficient (i.e. fastest) path taken by others through this Learning Network?".

4 Summary and Ongoing Research

This short paper has introduced the rationale behind our research into self-organising wayfinding support together with an outline of the architecture we have developed. Our approach is designed to adapt support for decisions on the sequencing of learning events not on the basis of a model of the individual learner but using information on the collective behaviour of other learners – a form of swarm intelligence.

We are currently analysing learner record information covering the many thousands of lifelong learners studying at our institution. Once our analysis is completed, we intend to simulate the introduction of an educational technology implementing the feedback loop to predict that impact of its introduction before carrying out experiments with lifelong learners to measure the actual value of the approach.

References

1. Brockett, R.G., Hiemstra, R: Self-direction in adult learning: Perspectives on theory, research, and practice, ed. P. Jarvis. 1991, London: Routledge.
2. Candy, P.C.: Self-Direction for Lifelong Learning. The Jossey-Bass Higher and Adult Education Series, ed. A.B.Knox. 1991, San Franciso: Jossey-Bass Inc.
3. Darken, R.P., Peterson, B.: Spatial Orientation, Wayfinding, and Representation, in Handbook of Virtual Environments: Design, Implementation, and Applications, K.M. Stanney, Editor. 2002, Lawrence Erlbaum Assoc: New Jersey.
4. Brusilovsky, P.: Adaptive Hypermedia. User Modeling and User-Adapted Interaction, 2001. 11: p. 87-110.
5. Simpson, O.: Supporting students in online, open and distance learning. Open and Distance Learning Series, ed. F. Lockwood. 2000, London: Kogan Page.
6. CEDEFOP: Adaptive Hypermedia - its role in lifelong learning. 2003, European Centre for the Development of Vocational Training.
7. De Bra, P., Brusilovsky, P., Houben, G.-J.: Adaptive Hypermedia: From Systems to Framework. ACM Computing Surveys, 1999. 31(4).
8. Self, J.: User Modelling in Open Learning Systems, in Tutoring and Monitoring Facilities for European Open Learning, J. Whiting and D.A. Bell, Editors. 1987, Elsevier: Amsterdam.
9. Hadeli, P. V., Zamfirescu, C.B., Van Brussel, H., Saint Germain, B., Holvoet, T., Steegmans, E.: Self-Organising in Multi-agent Coordination and Control Using Stigmergy, in The First Workshop on Self-Organising Engineering Applications (ESOA 2003). 2003. Melbourne, Australia.
10. Bonabeau, E., Dorigo, M., Theraulaz, G.: Introduction, in Swarm Intelligence, E. Bonabeau, Editor. 1999, Oxford University Press: Oxford.
11. Theraulaz, G., Bonabeau, E.: A Brief History of Stigmergy. Artificial Life, 1999. 5(2): p. 97-116.
12. Koper, E.J.R., Giesbers, B., Van Rosmalen, P., Sloep, P., Van Bruggen, J., Tattersall, C., Vogten, H., Brouns, F.: A Design Model for Lifelong Learning Networks. Interactive Learning Environments, 2004. (in press).
13. Punin, J.R., Krishnamoorthy, M.S., Zaki, M.J.: Web Usage Mining: Languages and Algorithms, in Studies in Classification, Data Analysis, and Knowledge Organization. 2001, Springer-Verlag.
14. IEEE: IEEE Draft Standard for Learning Technology - Learning Technology Systems Architecture, 2001, IEEE: New York.

Giving More Adaptation Flexibility to Authors of Adaptive Assessments

Aimilia Tzanavari[1], Symeon Retalis[2], and Panikos Pastellis[1]

[1] University of Cyprus, Department of Computer Science, 75 Kallipoleos St. P.O Box 20537
1678 - Nicosia, Cyprus
aimilia@ucy.ac.cy, pastelis@cytanet.com.cy
[2] University of Piraeus, Department of Technology Education and Digital Systems,
80 Karaoli & Dimitriou, 185 34 - Piraeus, Greece
retal@unipi.gr

Abstract. In this paper, we present AthenaQTI, a tool for authoring personal-ized assessments, which gives the author significant flexibility in terms of the adaptation that s/he can incorporate in the assessments s/he builds. We focus on presenting the functionality of the authoring environment and the tool's con-formance to the IMS-QTI specification, a fact that gives it the advantage of in-teroperability. Furthermore, we briefly describe the user model and the philoso-phy of its manipulation.

1 Introduction

Adding the adaptation capability to the assessment process in Educational Hyperme-dia Systems [1] has been proven advantageous, primarily for the reason that users are presented with personalized tests, tailored to their needs, preferences and current knowledge. Furthermore, with adaptive assessments the number of assessment items required can be adjusted, most of the times resulting in fewer items, which implies a shorter, less tedious assessment. There are two techniques used for adaptation within assessments: Adaptive Testing [7] and Adaptive Questions [2].

In Adaptive Testing, the criterion for selecting questions is to match the question's difficulty level with the user's estimated knowledge level. This is because it has been shown that these are the type of questions that are more "informative" in terms of conclusions one can draw on the user's knowledge. The goal is to accurately estimate the user's knowledge. In the Adaptive Questions technique a dynamic sequence of questions is generated depending on user's responses. In this case, several predefined rules, in conjunction with the user's responses, are those that lead to the selection of the question(s) to follow.

In this paper we present a web-based adaptive assessment authoring system, called AthenaQTI (Athena is a Learning Management System where the AthenaQTI tool is going to be integrated). We mainly focus on presenting the functionality of the au-thoring environment and the tool's conformance to the IMS QTI (Question and Test Interoperability) specification [5]. IMS QTI is a widely adopted and quite stable specification by the IMS Global Learning Consortium [4]. It proposes the representa-tion of tests in standard XML format, thus allowing interoperability between different assessment tools. Its structure contains elements such as assessments, sections (group-ings of questions) and items (formal name for questions).

W. Nejdl and P. De Bra (Eds.): AH 2004, LNCS 3137, pp. 340–343, 2004.

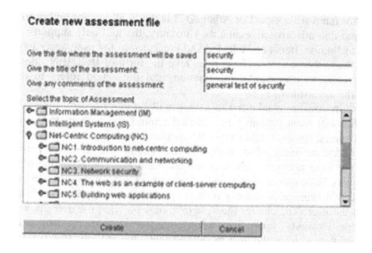

Fig. 1. 'Create new assessment' screen

2   The AthenaQTI Tool

AthenaQTI is a web-based adaptive assessment authoring system, with which authors/ educators are able to create: true/false, multiple choice (single, multiple or ordered response), fill-in the blanks, multiple image choice (single or ordered response) and image hot spot (multiple or ordered response) types of questions. The assessments are represented in XML [5] format, so that they can be easily exported and used by other applications that also conform to IMS QTI specification. Furthermore, authors can open and edit an existing assessment. The assessments are presented to users, who first have to log on, so that their user model is uploaded. Feedback is automatic and can be utilized in several ways. Multimedia objects can be embedded into assessments, so authors can create better interfaces and users can have a more attractive learning environment.

Assessments are structured exactly as QTI dictates, so that the AthenaQTI tool fully conforms to the specification. Moreover, we have innovated in a number of ways, starting from the use of the *qti-metadata* element, which is used for describing the subject domain that an assessment, section or item refers to. For experimental use, we have carefully analyzed the curriculum structure for studies in computer science provided by IEEE/ACM [3], in order to create a vocabulary that could be widely adopted. This vocabulary assisted us in the task of efficiently describing the topics that an assessment or a section refers to. Fig. 1 shows the screen for creating a new assessment, where the author can select the assessment's topic going down three levels if necessary. Based on the assessment's topic, all sections subsequently created will refer to a sub-topic. By allowing the author to select the appropriate topic for her/his assessment from a given hierarchically structured vocabulary, we alleviate several future difficulties. A brief discussion of these difficulties requires that we first visit the issue of adaptation in the system. It can be easily understood that in the case that the vocabulary needs to change (e.g. for a different subject domain), the tool's functionality remains the same.

The other innovative aspect of AthenaQTI is that it allows the author to create both adaptive and non-adaptive assessments. Currently, the tool only supports the adaptive questions technique. Items are selected and presented to the user, according to a set of rules that the author creates. These rules take the form of IF-THEN rules, where the condition refers to user model information, and the action refers to the resulting change in the assessment.

When users log on to take the test, they will be described by their personal user model. This will most probably be "carried around" throughout their navigation of other educational (or even other type of) applications as well. As the user model has to form an accurate image of the user, it needs to be updated frequently to include any changes. The core attribute, which is the one (and in some cases the only) used by most Adaptive Educational Hypermedia Systems for adaptation purposes, is the user's knowledge. Knowledge is directly related to educational applications, whose goal is to instruct the user. The clearer the system's view on what the user knows, the better it can adapt. However, apart from knowledge, we keep usage data and stereotype information, that is, from the user model elements that are monitored and changed by the system.

The user's knowledge is updated in our tool, based on the assessments'/sections' topics. The algorithm used to update the user's knowledge is again implicitly given by the author through the rules s/he creates. Examples may be "if the user's score in section C was over 80% then increase the knowledge of the section's topic by factor X". This leads to a user model whose "knowledge" element consists of topics (along with a degree of knowledge) that originate from a very specific vocabulary. In this way, if the user model is later used by a different educational application that is aware of this vocabulary, it will automatically be recognized without difficulty. Imagine if a user model includes "great knowledge" of "Artificial Intelligence" and the application that tries to use it and possibly examine the user's knowledge in "*AI*" assumes that it does not exist (since it is looking for a match with "AI")!

Usage data includes historical information about the user's performance in the assessment. It is very useful to be able to keep track of the user through a sequence of sections or items. This information is required in cases where the author wants to apply rules such as "if the user performed very well in section A and very poorly in section B, then give a new section with intermediate difficulty level".

Stereotypes are widely used in personalization, especially to overcome the "cold start" problem: how will the user model be initialized. In our tool, we allow the author to define the number of stereotypes s/he considers necessary for the particular assessment, as well as each one's characteristics. Following this, the author is able to employ stereotypes in the rules s/he builds, not only to be applied at the beginning of the assessment, but at any other point.

3   Conclusions

In this paper we presented AthenaQTI, a web-based adaptive assessment authoring tool that conforms to the IMS QTI specification. Up to our knowledge, SIETTE [6] is the most relevant tool to which AthenaQTI can be compared. In SIETTE, question selection is based on a function that estimates the probability of a correct answer to a particular question, ultimately leading to an estimation of the student's level of knowledge. The question (amongst the pool of the questions that have not been posed yet) with the highest probability will be posed. Our tool does not use functions to estimate any parameter; rather the author is given the flexibility to express his/her didactical philosophy and methods through the creation or appropriate rules. Furthermore, our tool supports a wider range of question types than SIETTE, which seems to handle mainly multiple-choice. The most important advancement of AthenaQTI lies in the fact that it fully conforms to the IMS QTI standard, making it very powerful since interoperability is currently a vital issue.

AthenaQTI is still in its infancy and we need to proceed to formal testing with real users, since we have only performed laboratory tests focusing on usability and software quality issues. Near future plans concern the evaluation of the adaptation features of the assessments created. This will involve testing with real users, observing and measuring a number of parameters, such as students' performance in non-adaptive and adaptive assessments.

References

1. Brusilovsky, P.: Adaptive and Intelligent Technologies for Web-based Education. In: Rollinger, C., Peylo, C. (eds.): Special Issue on Intelligent Systems and Teleteaching. Kunstliche Intelligenz, 4 (1999) 19-25
2. Chou, C.: Constructing a computer-assisted testing and evaluation system on the World Wide Web – the CATES experience. IEEE Transactions on Education 43(3) (2000) 266-272
3. IEEE/ACM Computing Curricula 2001 – CS Body of Knowledge, http://www.computer.org/education/cc2001/final/appa.htm
4. IMS Global Learning Consortium Inc., http://www.imsglobal.org/.
5. IMS Question and Test Interoperability Specification, http://www.imsglobal.org/question/
6. Ríos, A., Millán, E., Trella, M., Pérez-de-la-Cruz, J. L., Conejo, R.: Internet Based Evaluation System. In: Proceedings of the 9th World Conference of Artificial Intelligence and Education (1999) 387-394
7. Wainer, H., Dorans, N., Eignor, D., Flaugher, R., Green, B., Mislevy, R., Steinberg, L., Thissen, D. (eds.): Computerized Adaptive Testing: A primer. 2nd edn. Lawrence Erlbaum Associates, Hillsdate NJ (2000)

A Generic Adaptivity Model in Adaptive Hypermedia

Paul de Vrieze, Patrick van Bommel, and Theo van der Weide

University of Nijmegen
{pauldv,pvb,tvdw}@cs.kun.nl

Abstract. For adaptive hypermedia there is a strong model in form of the AHAM model and the AHA! system. This model, based on the Dexter Model, however is limited to application in hypermedia systems. In this paper we propose a new Generic Adaptivity Model. This state-machine based model can be used as the basis for adaptation in all kinds of applications.

1 Introduction

The AHAM model [1, 2] forms an important model in the area of adaptive hypermedia. This model, based on the Dexter Model, however is limited to application in hypermedia systems. In an aim to provide such a model for generic user modelling we have developed the Generic Adaptivity Model (GAM). This model provides a general model for an adaptation engine that can be used in a modular way to provide adaptivity in a variety of applications.

The Generic Adaptivity Model is based on our two-dimensional classification framework as defined in [3] and [4]. It includes push and pull modelling in the shape of rules and questions. This allows designers of adaptive systems to make better decisions on what to store in the User Model. This allows for more flexible adaptation systems.

A prototypical engine has been developed based on the model. Rules and questions are implemented using a simple but full featured imperative scripting language.

2 Generic Adaptivity Model

Aiming at a theory for providing adaptation to applications in general we have developed the Generic Adaptivity Model (GAM). The GAM model is based on a state-machine view on applications. In this state-machine based view we see an application as a state-machine. At each interaction an event gets generated. This event in someway induces an action that results into a state change in the system. Such a state change can be paramaterised by external values. A user model can be used as the source of such values. For this the events also get fed into the adaptation engine. (see Fig. 1)

Adaptation Description. The two main components of the GAM are formed by the Adaptation Description and the User Model. An *Adaptation Engine* (AE) requires a description of the adaptation it should perform. This description consists of several parts that together form a logical union. This logical union is the *Adaptation Description* (AD).

W. Nejdl and P. De Bra (Eds.): AH 2004, LNCS 3137, pp. 344–347, 2004.

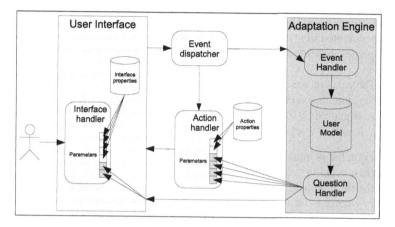

Fig. 1. An interactive system with user modeling

Interface Model. As our AE is general and does not limit itself to hypermedia there are many events that it might need to react on. Similarly there are many questions that a program might want to ask to the AE about the user.

To allow the programs that are clients of the AE to change the actual adaptation logic without needing a change itself, we have the *Interface Model* (IM). The Interface Model describes exactly which events and which questions are available to clients of the AE. It also describes their parameters. The IM does however not contain any logic and as such can be equal for two different adaptation models.

Domain Model. Like the AHAM model the GAM also provides a *Domain Model* (DM). In GAM however there is no notion of "concept" as used in the AHAM model. As the GAM model is a general model we cannot use abstractions like the Dexter Model [5]. The GAM model is a model on a higher level of abstraction in which the designer of the DM determines the meaning of the DM elements.

The Domain Model is a source from which the User Model is determined. Every element of the Domain Model has its reflection on the User Model.

The DM consists of definitions of attributes. These attributes have a type: string, integer, boolean, floating point value or an array of such attributes. Further the attributes have a name and a default value. This default value is the value that gets used for this attribute when no value is specified for the attribute in the user model.

Adaptation Model. The *Adaptation Model* (AM) specifies the actual dynamic behaviour of the AE with respect to this AD. The AM splits the dynamic behaviour into two phases. These phases correspond to the framework as we have described in [3] and [4]. Basically the two phases represent updating of the user model in response to events and the querying of the user model.

Handling of events happens with a system based on ECA rules [6] similar to AHAM. For querying we have, however, also added a question (or function) based system. This question system allows to store intermediate values at the right level in the User Model. We have evaluated in [4] that there are several advantages and disadvantages of storing user properties instead of calculating them from more basic properties.

Rules. The rules in the adaptation model correspond to push adaptation as described in [4]. They are also very similar to the rules as provided by AHAM. The rules in our model are triggered by the events posted to the AE.

Event handling works as follows:

1. An event list is initialised with the posted event.
2. The first event in the list is removed and taken for evaluation.
3. All the rules whose condition is true are evaluated, not only the first one!
4. Every change to an attribute in the user model generates a change event that has the name of the attribute as argument. All those events are added to the event list
5. If there is at least one event in the event list, go back to step 2.

Questions. Besides rules the Adaptation Model also provides questions. Questions are basically functions as seen from a programming context. Questions correspond to pull adaptation as described in [4]. As questions are used for querying the user model they are not allowed to update any values in it.

Question evaluation is fairly straightforward. The questions are specified as a program. In these programs it is possible to use other questions as functions for intermediate values. User Model attributes are also accessible as variables.

User Model. Besides the Adaptation Description, the GAM defines the existence of a User Model (UM) for each user. Each UM is tied to a specific AD and describes the properties of the user as specified by the DM.

Like the UM in AHAM our User Model is an *overlay User Model* that contains only the changed values. This allows for efficient storage and flexibility towards changes of the adaptation description.

3   Conclusion

Comparing the AHAM model to the GAM model we can find the following differences:

– The GAM aims to provide a generic adaptivity model. As such the GAM is more low-level than the AHAM model and does not provide high-level constructs by itself. The GAM however does allow the specification of more high-level models on top of the GAM model.
– The GAM provides an explicit interface model. In effect the AHAM model can be seen as having an implicit interface model. This is sufficient for AHAM as the set of events available within a web constant is fixed and limited to access to concepts/pages and AHAM does not offer questions.
– The biggest difference between AHAM and the GAM is that in the GAM the concepts of push and pull adaptation have been added. Thus allowing the adaptation to be more flexible in it's storage.

From the above we can conclude that the GAM model is more suited as a description for generic adaptivity than the AHAM model is. In the area of adaptive hypermedia we are currently still missing a model that on top of GAM can provide specific hypermedia concepts. However we believe that, once such a model has been developed, the GAM model is able to provide functionality that extends the AHAM model's functionality.

In further research we plan to create such a hypermedia model on top of GAM. We plan to use this model to create an adaptive hypermedia engine based on the generic engine we have already implemented. To compare the functionality of this engine we plan to write a translator that can translate AHA! documents into a form that can be understood by our engine.

Additionally we also plan to research how artificial intelligence techniques such as agent based learning and Bayesian or neural networks can be integrated into our model.

References

1. De Bra, P., Houben, G.J., Wu, H.: Aham: A dexter-based reference model for adaptive hyper-media. In: Proceedings of the ACM Conference on Hypertext and Hypermedia, Darmstadt, Germany (1999) 147–156
2. Wu, H.: A reference Architecture for Adaptive Hypermedia Applications. PhD thesis, Technical University of Eindhoven (2002) isbn: 90-386-0572-2.
3. de Vrieze, P., van Bommel, P., Klok, J., van der Weide, T.: Towards a two-dimensional frame-work for user models. In: Proceedings of the MAWIS03 workshop attached to the OOIS03 conference, Geneva (2003)
4. de Vrieze, P., van Bommel, P., Klok, J., van der Weide, T.: Adaptation in multimedia systems. Multimedia Tools and Applications (2004) to appear.
5. Halasz, F., Schwartz, M.: The dexter hypertext reference model. In: Proceedings of the NIST Hypertext Standardization Workshop, Gaithersburg, MD, USA (1990) 95–133
6. Aiken, A., Hellerstein, J., Widom, J.: Static analysis techniques for predicting behavior of active database rules. ACM Transactions on Database systems **20** (1995) 3–41

Extreme Adaptivity

Mário Amado Alves, Alípio Jorge, and José Paulo Leal

LIACC, University of Porto
823 Campo Alegre, 4150-180 Porto, Portugal
maa@liacc.up.pt, amjorge@liacc.up.pt, zp@ncc.up.pt

Abstract. This Doctoral Consortium paper focuses on Extreme Adaptivity, a set of top level requirements for adaptive hypertext systems, which has resulted from one year of examining the adaptive hypertext landscape. The complete specification of a system, KnowledgeAtoms, is also given, mainly as an example of Extreme Adaptivity. Additional methodological elements are discussed.

1 Overview and Some Background

On this paper I expose a number of results from the first year of my ongoing Ph. D. research on adaptive hypertext.

My overall objective is to design adaptive hypertext systems of pristine simplicity, and yet not less effective than the convoluted architectures that populate the landscape. Trying to define the principal elements required to achieve this goal, I have identified a set of high level requirements and design guidelines which I collectively called Extreme Adaptivity, and fully describe in Sect. 2.

Extreme Adaptivity draws on my experience as a creator as well as a user of web systems since the mid 1990's. This experience is one of continuing *insatisfaction*. Traditional websites are indeed "fossils cast in HTML" [7].

At the same time, I wanted better *knowledge bases*. Better as in more usable, flexible, expandable, searchable. Increasingly it become clear to me that *hypertext* was a necessary element to achieve this. Surely I was thinking of much of what is now called *content management*.

My first attempt was the CASBaH, a *Collective Authoring System Based on Hypertext*. More or less at the same time, *wikis* were invented, which are essentially the same thing. (See Sect. 4.1 for references.) Wikis live on to this day and in my opinion they still represent the best collective authoring system around.

But the spectre of fossilization is still lurking. All these systems require an explicit and continuing effort from the part of their users for organizing the contained information. What we really want is not content management, but content management *automation*.

And to solve this problem, I believe Extreme Adaptivity is required.

To practice what I preach, I'm developing KnowledgeAtoms, an extremely adaptive hypertext system targeted at knowledge bases. Sect. 3 is entirely devoted to this item.

Sect. 4 briefly discusses a number of related issues, including the selection of *spreading activation* as a method to explore knowledge bases.

On this paper the singular pronoun denotes the first author. The two co-authors are my supervisors. They are great supporters of all my work, but I choose to be the only

W. Nejdl and P. De Bra (Eds.): AH 2004, LNCS 3137, pp. 348–352, 2004.
© Springer-Verlag Berlin Heidelberg 2004

entity accountable for the positions expressed here. My work is also supported by Fundação para a Ciência e Tecnologia of Portugal financially with burse number SFRH / BD / 11109 / 2002.

2 Extreme Adaptivity

Extreme Adaptivity is a set of top level requirements and design guidelines for adaptive hypertext systems: No Documents, No Scroll, No Intrusion, Total User Control, Clear Labels, Full Incrementality, 50 ms.

No Documents. Users look for information, not documents. Documents are the pre-digital medium of recording and communicating information. The document metaphor on the digital world is unadjusted [3].

The system must give the sought information right there on the screen, formatted for the screen. The online 'page' is the screen, or the window. "The world of the screen could be anything at all, not just the imitation of paper" [5]. See also No Scroll.

Also, documents are for reading. Online users don't read – they scan [6].

No Scroll. A page that requires scrolling is not a page, it is a document – and as such it is banned (see No Documents). Online pages should fit the user's screen, or the window. Scrollable windows limit the view.

A document requiring scrolling is actually an even more ancient information medium than the modern document, or codex: it is a scroll. So scrolling in the online world is a regression of more than 2000 years, to pre-codex age.

No Intrusion. The user should not be imposed any work other than his normal behaviour. For example, usability questionnaires are banned. Adaptive input should be restricted to the user normal activity.

This also applies to authors. Regarding them, the baseline effort shall be that of the normal writing of texts including placement of non-text objects.

The general baseline effort is that of non-adaptive systems. The user shall not be imposed any extra effort with respect to this baseline.

Exception: Total User Control may require extra effort for user levels above normal users and authors, e.g. configurators.

Total User Control. The user must be able to control every aspect of the adaptive behaviour of the system. In particular, he must be able to turn adaptivity on and off, to escape artificial stupidity.

Clear Labels. A link must be, at the source, clear about its target. That is, the system must be so that users can have a clear idea of the effect of activating the link – before activating it.

Full Incrementality. Any operation on the system must be doable at any time, without requiring any kind of restart of the system, or stopping any functionality.

50 ms. This should be the maximum response time of the system to any user action. According to Auber [1] (who refers to [8] for details), 50 ms is the maximum delay between an action of the user and the displayed result on the screen for the user to believe in a causal link. Heer [4] (who refer to [2]) indicate that this time can be relaxed to 100 ms.

3   KnowledgeAtoms, an Extremely Adaptive Hypertext System

KnowledgeAtoms is an adaptive hypertext system targeted at knowledge bases, and designed to meet the requirements of Extreme Adaptivity. The development of a prototype web system is under way at the time of writing. Fig. 1 on the next page shows a fabricated screen.

3.1   Overview of Operation

Users interact with KnowledgeAtoms through pages. Each page shows a subset of the contained knowledge centred on one of the items. Users look for information by re-centring on another item.

Users can also enter a new item, and connect it to existing ones. The system features tools to automatically connect a new item to the most related ones. The new item can be a search query.

3.2   Overview of Adaptation

Adaptation is towards the collective mind. Recentring is construed as travelling between items. Each recentring step increments the corresponding travel count. The items shown on each page are the most related to the central one, according to a computation based on the travel counts.

The assumption here is that travel counts quantify relatedness. This assumption is reasonable because KnowledgeAtoms – as an extremely adaptive system – features Clear Labels.

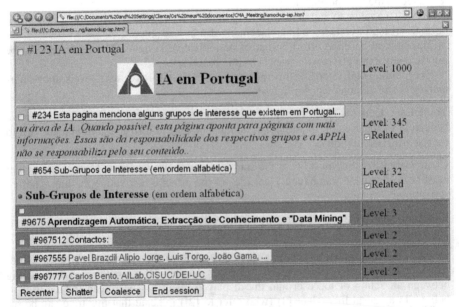

Fig. 1. Simulation of KnowledgeAtoms applied to the legacy data set "IA em Portugal."

3.3 Complete Top Level Specification

1. A page is an assembly of views of knowledge atoms and controls.
2. Each view represents an atom.
3. One of the atoms on a page is central, and is usually viewed at the top of the page.
4. The central view is expanded (see 7).
5. The others atoms on a page are the most related (see 17) to the central one.
6. Any expanded atom is more related (to the central one) than any contracted one.
7. A knowledge atom is a piece of information whose expanded view does not exceed the page size, and is usually substantially smaller than that, say 1/10.
8. The contracted view of a knowledge atom does not exceed its expanded view, and is usually smaller than that, say 1/5.
9. The user operates the system by executing controls on the page.
10. A control exists to recentre on a chosen atom.
11. This operation has the effect of replacing the current page with a newly assembled one (where the chosen atom is central).
12. This constitutes a travel from the previous to the chosen central atoms.
13. The system has the concepts of user and session.
14. Controls exist to terminate a session.
15. Sessions are owned by users.
16. A session is a set of travels.
17. Relatedness between atoms is based on travel information.
18. Controls exist to adjust the relatedness function, including restricting the set of available atoms, based on time and ownership of the atoms and of the travels.
19. Upon recentring or session termination, the expanded atoms are also considered travelled to, if evidence exists that the user has read them.
20. This evidence usually comes from the time spent on a page.
21. This evidence can also come from eye tracking technology.
22. A control exists to insert a new atom in the system.
23. Tools (perhaps controls) exist to automatically connect the new atom to others, i.e. to generate travels between them.
24. Controls exist to shatter an atom in two or more atoms, and to coalesce two or more items into one.

4 Additional Methodological Elements

I'm inclined to use spreading activation as a method for exploring the knowledge base. This follows an increasingly connectionist way of looking at the problem. This connectionism should be apparent in the specification of KnowledgeAtoms (Sect. 3).

Curiously enough, this connectionism is *not* of biological inspiration. I reached it by thinking about the best ways of structuring information using computers. It seems I have independently invented the brain.

My work has also a substantial software engineering part. Currently I'm developing Mneson, a software library for persistent graphs of basic values (integer, string, float). In other words, a network database system. I am using Mneson as a basis for KnowledgeAtoms. Incidentally, I am also using AWS, the Ada Web Server, for the web component. Reasons for utilizing these Ada libraries, and the Ada language, include:

- Independence from the buggy and difficult to configure alternative bases available (MySQL, Postgres, Apache).
- Ada's built-in real-time and concurrency features facilitate the implementation of certain spreading activation algorithms.
- And of course, the legendary rigour and reliability of the Ada language, the language of excellence for software engineering. 100% Ada, 0% bugs.

4.1 Related Sites (Alphabetically)

Ada. www.adaic.org, www.ada-auth.org, www.adapower.com, www.adaworld.com

AWS. http://libre.act-europe.fr/aws/

CASBaH. Linked on http://www.liacc.up.pt/~maa

Content Management Automation. A project under construction at LIACC. http://www.liacc.up.pt/~amjorge/Projectos/content-mgm/

IA em Portugal. Legacy website at http://www.appia.pt

LIACC. http://www.liacc.up.pt

Mneson. http://www.liacc.up.pt/~maa/mneson

Wikis. There are many. http://en.wikipedia.org has circa 500,000 articles. http://c2.com/cgi/wiki was probably the first wiki and at one time included a record of the CASBaH as an independent invention of the concept.

References

1. D. Auber, Using Strahler numbers for real time visual exploration of huge graphs. – 12 p. – Internet, March 8, 2003.
2. S. K. Card, T. P. Moran, A. Newell. The Psychology of Human-Computer Interaction. – Lawrence Erlbaum, 1983. – (Description apud Citeseer.)
3. J. H. Coombs, A. H. Renear, S. J. DeRose. Markup Systems and the Future of Scholarly Text Processing – pp. 933 – 947 In: Communications of the ACM, Volume 30, Issue 11 (November 1987). – ISSN 0001-0782.
4. J. Heer et al., AVID : Supporting the creation of scalable, responsive visualizations – Working paper, www.parc.com, 2003.
5. T. Nelson. Way Out of the Box – 99.10.08 – http://ted.hyperland.com, 1999.
6. J. Nielsen., Jakob Nielsen's Alertbox for October 1, 1997 : How Users Read on the Web. – http://www.useit.com/alertbox/9710a.html
7. M. Perkowitz, O. Etzioni. Adaptive Web Sites : Conceptual Cluster Mining. In: Proceedings of the 2nd Workshop on Adaptive Systems and User Modeling on the WWW. Edited by Peter Brusilovsky and Paul De Bra. (http://wwwis.win.tue.nl/asum99/perkowitz.html), 1999.
8. C. Ware., Information Visualization: Perception for design. – Morgan Kaufmann, 2000. – (Description apud Auber 2003.)

A Learner Model in a Distributed Environment

Cristina Carmona and Ricardo Conejo

Departamento de Lenguajes y Ciencias de la Computación
Universidad de Málaga
{cristina,conejo}@lcc.uma.es

Abstract. A learner model must store all the relevant information about a student, including knowledge and attitude. This paper proposes a domain independent learner model based in the classical overlay approach that can be used in a distributed environment. The model has two sub-models: the learner attitude model, where the static information about the user is stored (user's personal and technical characteristics, user's preferences, etc.) and the learner knowledge model, where the user's knowledge and performance is stored. The knowledge model has four layers: estimated, assessed, inferred by prerequisite and inferred by granularity. The learner model is used as a part of the MEDEA system, so the first and second layers are updated directly by the components of MEDEA and the third and fourth are updated by Bayesian inference.

1 Introduction

In an educational environment, a good learner model must include all features of the learner's knowledge and preferences that concern to his learning and performance [1]. This information is used to adapt the system to the user. However, to build this model is a very difficult task. In practice, a partial model is used. It is necessary to take into account (1) what information is included in the model; (2) how to obtain it; (3) how the model will represent the information; and finally, (4) how the model will process and update the information.

Actually, there are two kind of information stored in a learner model: the first one includes information that does not change over the learning process, like user's particular characteristics (name, age, gender...), learner's capabilities (degree, background knowledge...), learner's technical characteristics (computer expertise, connection speed...), learner's preferences (learning style, screen options...), etc. This information is usually collected at the beginning of the learning process using forms and tests. The second includes those that change over the learning process, like the learner's knowledge level for each knowledge unit, skills, goals, etc. This information can be obtained directly from the learner (goals), from tests (tests marks shows how much the user knows about the subject) or from the learner interaction with the system (number of pages visited, links selected, time spent on each page...).

One method widely used to represent the learner knowledge model is the overlay model where the learner knowledge is represented like a subset of expert knowledge [4-7]. A strict overlay model contains only a subset of the expert knowledge. It is called a perturbation model if it also includes information about incorrect knowledge. Another popular method is the use of stereotypes. Each stereotype represents some

W. Nejdl and P. De Bra (Eds.): AH 2004, LNCS 3137, pp. 353–359, 2004.

common characteristics in learning style, knowledge, etc. and the instruction is adapted to those features. Then the learner is classified in one or more stereotypes and inherits those features and also the adapted instruction [2, 3]. Stereotypes are often used in combination with other methods.

This paper proposes a learner model to be used in MEDEA [8]. MEDEA is an open system to develop Intelligent Tutorial Systems (ITS). It is composed of independent educative modules coordinated by a core that controls the instruction of the learner. MEDEA can decide which is the best module to explain a concept in each moment. The model has two sub-models: *the learner attitude model*, where the static information about the user is stored (user's personal and technical characteristics, user's preferences, etc.) and *the learner knowledge model*, where the user's knowledge and performance is stored. The knowledge model is based on the classical overlay approach with four layers: *estimated, assessed, inferred by prerequisite* and *inferred by granularity*.

This paper explains briefly the architecture of MEDEA and then it centers in the learner model proposed.

2   MEDEA

The elements that compose MEDEA architecture can be classified in three main groups: those that contain knowledge (*knowledge modules*), those that use this knowledge for making decisions along the instruction (*functional modules*) and those that serve to access and configure the system (*tools*). The base of MEDEA architecture is a core that plans the instruction based on a set of external tutorial components that are connected to the system. The domain and pedagogical knowledge is distributed between the core of MEDEA that serves as a master index, and these components. Fig. 1 shows the structure of MEDEA modules:

Knowledge Modules:

- *Domain Model.* This module contains knowledge about the subject to be taught. Domain concepts and relationships among them are represented.
- *Learner model.* This is the goal of this paper and will be described in next section.

Functional Modules:

- *Instructional planner.* This module will provide students with the necessary guidance during the learning process. It will design and compose the tutorial sessions, that is, it will decide in each moment the correct task to be performed by the student.
- *Learner Model Manager.* The function of this module is to create and update the learner model. The learner model is updated every time the learner interacts with the system.
- *The library of tutorial components.* A tutorial component is an external educational tool that is able to complete a tutorial task as make tests, present theory contents in hypertext, play a game, etc. MEDEA classifies tutorial components as *assessment components* [10] or *information components* [9]. The difference is that components of the first type are able to assess the student knowledge level about a concept.

Tools:

- *Configuration and definition tools.* Domain experts, teachers and designers will use this module, they will be able to introduce the contents, define and configure the data and knowledge modules using specific interfaces.
- *Administration tools.* Teachers will use this module to monitor the evolution of their students. It will show the progress of each student, the statistics about the course use, and average student performances, and other secretariat and administrative tasks.
- *Navigation tools.* Student uses this module to support their navigation and interaction with the whole system; it can be conceptualized as an advisor during the learning process.

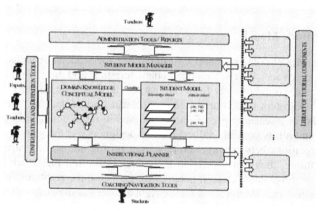

Fig. 1. MEDEA architecture

3 The Learner Model in MEDEA

The learner model in MEDEA is divided in two main sub-models: the *Attitude Model,* which contains those features that describe the student profile but are not related to his current state of knowledge and the *Knowledge Model,* which contains information about the learner's state of knowledge.

The *Knowledge Model* proposed is implemented by a multi-layer overlay model. The main characteristic of the overlay model is that for each domain concept an estimation of the user knowledge level on this concept is stored. If the model has multiple layers, it can have information from different sources. This information can be updated independently and without overwriting. The proposed model has four layers: (1) *estimated layer* that collects the indirect information and inferences of the student knowledge level based on the student behavior during the instruction. This value is given by the *informative components*; (2) *assessed layer*, it contains the marks obtained by a student using the systems *assessment components*; (3) *inferred by prerequisite layer,* this layer contains the values inferred for each concept via a Bayesian network that represents the *prerequisite* relationship between concepts; and (4) *inferred by granularity layer,* that contains the values inferred for each concept via a Bayesian network that represents the *belongs-to* relationship between concepts. Notice that the data of the first two layers are updated directly by the components, (they are considered as rough data) while the two later are updated by the learner model manager, as described in the next section.

The *instructional planner* can use all these layers to select the best concept to show in each moment. It is up to the planner strategy to decide what information to use. The role of the learner model manager is just to provide this information. For instance, a learning strategy that can be implemented by the planner would be to trigger an assessment component whenever there is a significance difference between values in the estimated layer and assessed layer. Another strategy can be to fully complete the study of a concept before entering a new one. Then the planner will look into the *inferred by granularity layer* to select the concept that is not completely known from a group of concepts already known, etc.

3.1 The Attitude Model

The Attitude Model contains static information of the student. It includes user's particular characteristics, user's technical characteristics and user's preferences. This information is obtained directly from the learner the first time he uses the system and each time he registers in a course. These data can be updated by user demand. The main features for a learning process are explained in more detail in Fig. 2 that shows the features and all its possible values. Course designers use the learner attitude model to establish relations between a concrete learner profile and some instruction parameters. For example, they can specify in the course definition that when a learner with low motivation level does a test, it is better to show him the right answer each time he makes a question, rather than show all the right answers at the end.

FEATURE	VALUES
Level: Cognitive development (formalization and abstract concepts understanding skills)	Beginner, Medium, Advanced
Motivation	High, Medium, Low
Learning style	Practice, Theory
Progress: The student learning speed	Poor, Regular, Good
Computer expertise: The student experience with computers	High, Medium, Low
Connection speed: Internet connection speed	High, Medium, Low

Fig. 2. Main features and values of the student attitude model

3.2 The Knowledge Model

Each layer of the Knowledge model is a list of elements that mainly contains the concept and the mark obtained by the student for that concept.

During the execution of MEDEA tutoring session, the learner is conducted through different informative and assessment components. The result of the interaction with each component is returned to MEDEA that calls the *learner model manager* to update the estimated and assessed layer respectively. This call also triggers the inference process over the prerequisite layer and granularity layer. The assessed values are used as initial values of certain nodes of a Bayesian networks that is explained in more detail in the next section.

3.2.1 Bayesian Networks for the Prerequisite and Granularity Layers

Domain model in MEDEA is structured by a set of nodes (concepts) and different relationships between them. Currently this learner model is just interested in *belongs-to* and *prerequisite* relationships. This approach is similar to the classical domain representation in ITS. For instance Fig. 3 shows an example of the domain model of a course divided in topics, subtopics and atomic concepts [11]. Each node in this graph is considered a concept in MEDEA. The light arrows represents the *belongs-to* relationship, (*granularity layer*), while the bold arrows represents the *prerequisite* relationship. (*prerequisite layer*). A Bayesian network is obtained from each type of relationship. This graph is divided in two, to assure that the Bayesian conditional probabilities comply with the independence conditional hypotheses. Each node of the network C_i can take a value x_{ik} among a finite number of possible values, representing the knowledge level of the learner for the corresponding concept i (i.e.: C_i can take values {low, medium, high}).

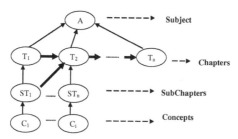

Fig. 3. Concepts' network

In order to initialize each network, the conditional probabilities must be estimated. Theoretically these probabilities can be obtained from real data of system usage (calibration), but if the course is constructed from scratch, they have to be empirically estimated. The problem of estimating these conditional probabilities is that they are meaningless for the course designer. This proposal includes a way of estimating these conditional probabilities from other data that are directly requested to the course designer.

The course designer is asked to provide the following information:

- A difficulty d_i of each concept.
- A weight of each relation (w^b_{ij} , w^p_{ij}), that is, the strength of each relation between the two concepts i and j . In the case of *belongs-to*, this weight w^b_{ij} shows how important the sub-concept i is inside the concept j. The sum of all w^b_{ij} of all the sub-concepts i of a concept j must be 1. In the case of *prerequisite*, this weight w^p_{ij} shows how strong the prerequisite is. The course designer may say if a concepts i is a strong (w^p_{ij} =1) or weak ($0 \le w^p_{ij}$ <1) prerequisite of another concept j. If a concept A is a strong prerequisite of B, then if the learner does not know A, then he neither knows B; but if A is a weak prerequisite of B, and the learner does not know A, he might have some knowledge of B.

From the information provided by the course designer, an estimation of the conditional probabilities of each layer network is done using an empirical formula.

In the case of the *prerequisite network*, the conditional probabilities of having a certain knowledge level y for a concept C_i, given the knowledge level $x_1 \ldots x_k$ of its prerequisite concepts $C_1 \ldots C_k$ is obtained by the formula (1):

$$P(C_i = y / C_1 = x_1, \ldots, C_k = x_k) = \begin{cases} \dfrac{W}{\min(x_1, \ldots, x_k)} + \dfrac{1-W}{N} & \text{if } y \leq \min(x_1, \ldots, x_k) \\[4mm] \dfrac{1-W}{N} & \text{if } y > \min(x_1, \ldots, x_k) \end{cases} \tag{1}$$

where:

- $W = max\ (w^p_{1i} \ldots w^p_{ki})$ is the maximum of all the weights of the relations between $C_1 \ldots C_k$ and C_i
- N is the number of all the possible values a concept can have.

Example: Let C be a concept with two prerequisites C_1, C_2; $w^p_1 = 0.8$ and $w^p_2 = 0.5$ the weights of the relations, so $W = max(0.5, 0.8) = 0.8$; and $N = 3$ (1=low, 2=medium, 3=high), then the probability distribution is:

C_1, C_2	$P(C=low/ C_1, C_2)$	$P(C=medium/C_1, C_2)$	$P(C=high/ C_1, C_2)$
C_1=low, C_2=low	0.86	0.07	0.07
C_1=low, C_2=medium	0.86	0.07	0.07
C_1=low, C_2=high	0.86	0.07	0.07
C_1=medium, C_2=low	0.86	0.07	0.07
C_1=medium, C_2=medium	0.46	0.46	0.07
C_1=medium, C_2=high	0.46	0.46	0.07
C_1=high, C_2=low	0.86	0.07	0.07
C_1=high, C_2=medium	0.46	0.46	0.07
C_1=high, C_2=high	0.33	0.33	0.33

This formula is based on the assumption that there is a low probability to know a concept better than its prerequisites. If a learner knows a prerequisite with level x, the probability to know the concept with level less than x will be high and homogeneous for all the levels but the probability to know it with a level higher than x will be low.

In the case of the *granularity network*, the conditional probabilities of having a certain knowledge level y for a concept C_i, given the knowledge level $x_1 \ldots x_k$ of its sub-concepts $C_1 \ldots C_k$ is obtained by the formula (2):

$$P(C_i = y / C_1 = x_1, \ldots, C_k = x_k) = \begin{cases} 1 & \text{if } y = round(w^b_{1i} x_1 + \ldots + w^b_{ki} x_k) \\ 0 & \text{in other case} \end{cases} \tag{2}$$

where:

- $w^b_{1i} \ldots w^b_{ki}$ are all the weights of the relations between C_i and $C_1 \ldots C_k$, respectively
- N is the number of all the possible values a concept can have.
- $round(x)$ is the function takes the integer value of x.

Example: Let C be a concept with two sub-concepts C_1, C_2; $w^b_1=0.8$ and $w^b_2=0.2$ the weights of the relations (C_1 is a very important sub-concept of C, but C_2 is less important); and $N=3$ (1=low, 2=medium, 3=high), then the probability distribution is:

C_1, C_2	$P(C=low/ C_1, C_2)$	$P(C=medium/ C_1, C_2)$	$P(C=high/ C_1, C_2)$
C_1=low, C_2=low	1	0	0
C_1=low, C_2=medium	1	0	0
C_1=low, C_2=high	1	0	0
C_1=medium, C_2=low	1	0	0
C_1=medium, C_2=medium	0	1	0
C_1=medium, C_2=high	0	1	0
C_1=high, C_2=low	0	1	0
C_1=high, C_2=medium	0	1	0
C_1=high, C_2=high	0	0	1

This empirical function has been obtained following the reasoning that the knowledge level of a concept depends of the weighted knowledge of its sub-concepts.

References

1. A.Kavcic: The Role of User Models in Adaptive Hypermedia Systems, *Proceedings of the 10th Mediterranean Electrotechnical Conference MEleCon 2000*, Lemesos, Cyprus (2000).
2. D.N.Chin: KNOME: Modeling what the user knows in UC, *User Models in Dialog Systems* (1989) 74-107.
3. J.Kay: Stereotypes, Student Models and Scrutability, *Proceedings of the 5th International Conference on Intelligent Tutoring Systems ITS2000*, Montreal, Canada (2000) 19-30.
4. P.De Bra, J.P.Ruiter: AHA! Adaptive Hypermedia for a All, *Proceedings of the World Conference of the WWW and Internet WebNet2001*, Orlando, Florida, USA (2001) 207-213.
5. M.Grigoriadou, K.Papanikolaou, H.Kornilakis, G.Magoulas: INSPIRE: An Intelligent System for Personalized Instruction in a Remote Environment, *Proceedings of Third workshop on Adaptive Hypertext and Hypermedia UM2001*, Sonthofen, Germany (2001) 13-24.
6. N.Henze, W.Nejdl: Student Modeling for the KBS Hyperbook System using Bayesian Networks, Technical Report, University of Hannover, available online at http://www.kbs.uni-hannover.de/paper/99/adaptivity.html (1999).
7. G.Weber, P.Brusilovsky: ELM-ART: An adaptive Versatile System for Web-based Instruction, *International Journal of Artificial Intelligence in Education 12 (4), Special Issue on Adaptive and Intelligent Web-based Educational Systems*, (2001) 351-384.
8. M.Trella, R.Conejo, D.Bueno, E.Guzman: An autonomous component architecture to develop WWW-ITS, *Workshop Adaptive Systems for Web-Based Education of the 2nd International Conference on Adaptive Hypermedia and Adaptive Web-Based Systems AH2002*, Malaga, Spain (2002) 69-80.
9. C.Carmona, D.Bueno, E.Guzman, R.Conejo: SIGUE: Making Web Courses Adaptive, *Proceedings of the 2nd International Conference on Adaptive Hypermedia and Adaptive Web-Based Systems AH2002*, Malaga, Spain (2002) 376-379.
10. E.Guzman, R.Conejo: An adaptive assessment tool integrable into Internet based learning systems, *International Conference on ICT in Education*, Badajoz, Spain (2002) 139-143.
11. E.Millán: Sistema Bayesiano para modelado del alumno. Phd Thesis (2000).

A Semantic Meta-model
for Adaptive Hypermedia Systems

Patricia Seefelder de Assis[1,2] and Daniel Schwabe[1]

[1] Departamento de Informática–Pontifícia Universidade Católica do Rio de Janeiro (PUC-Rio),
Caixa Postal 38.097, 22.453-900 – Rio de Janeiro – RJ – Brazil
patricia@iprj.uerj.br, dschwabe@inf.puc-rio.br
[2] 2Instituto Politécnico, Campus Regional de Nova Friburgo –
Membro do Grupo de Pesquisa Rede Operativa de Conhecimento e Aprendizagem - ROCA –
Universidade Estadual do Rio de Janeiro (UERJ)

Abstract. In this work we show a general meta-model for Adaptive Hypermedia Systems (AHSs) and discuss which research issues are necessary in order to improve this model. We argue that this meta-model shall then be described using ontologies from the Semantic Web and argument that a Semantic Meta-Model for AHSs may improve adaptation and serve as a basis for meta-adaptation.

1 Topic

Our aim is to use the fundamentals of the Semantic Web developing a Meta-Model for Adaptive Hypermedia Systems (AHSs) that allows direct implementation of the specified applications, including adaptation ontologies and rules based on them. This model may also serve as a basis for meta-adaptation.

2 Progress

We've already designed a general meta-model for Adaptive Hypermedia Systems (Fig. 1) using the UML class diagram notation [11][1]. The proposed meta-model is consistent with the Munich Model [7] and AHAM proposals [6], which states that an effective adaptation depends upon three main models [13]: Domain Model to describe how the content is structured, by specifying its concepts and relationships between them; User Model to represent user's knowledge, user's goals and user's preferences and Adaptation Model, which uses the DM and the UM to perform the adaptation. There must be a clear separation between these models. This meta-model proposes the definition of a Navigation Model and of a Presentation Model following the principles of OOHDM [10] which postulates the decoupling of conceptual, navigational and presentation aspects. Other models were identified, viz. Integration Model and User Context Model. Each model is enclosed in a UML package (grayed box in Fig. 1).

It should be noted that this meta-model represents the core functionality (with respect to adaptation) of AHSs, incorporating their essential features. In other words, it

---

[1] The UML notation was extended with a relation between class and package to represent that there is a relationship between this class and either class from the related package.

W. Nejdl and P. De Bra (Eds.): AH 2004, LNCS 3137, pp. 360–365, 2004.
© Springer-Verlag Berlin Heidelberg 2004

is safe to state that AHSs possess at least the main components, although in many cases extensions to the meta-model are necessary to accommodate specific features of particular systems.

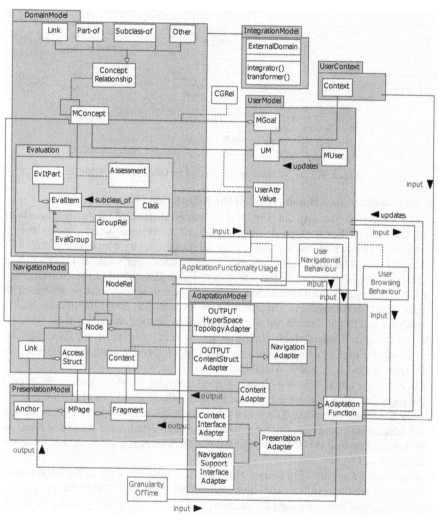

Fig. 1. A General Meta-Model for Adaptive Hypermedia Systems

This meta-model supports answers to the main questions related to adaptivity: what is being adapted (outputs), what is the adaptation based on (inputs) and how the adaptation is achieved (Adaptation Function). Fig. 1 shows an overview of the meta-model with inputs and outputs of the Adaptation Function in a different shade for legibility reasons. For reasons of space, it is not possible to describe the system (see [1] for details). We next exemplify Adaptation Functionality which can be better visualized in Fig. 2.

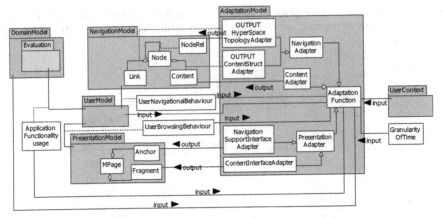

Fig. 2. Functional view of the general meta-model for AHSs

Inputs to Adaptation (Based on What the Adaptation Occurs)

- *Domain Model*: The way the content is structured in the DM may affect the adaptation. Example: For a given domain, a (hierarchically) composed concept may be considered known by the user only when all its elementary concepts are known;
- *User Profile*: The user profile, i.e. user's preferences, user's role and user's characteristics, typically influence the adaptation. Examples: whether the user is experienced or novice; whether the user prefers to access whole texts or abstracts; the user's preferred language. The information the user has about the domain and his goals related to the domain are also considered to be user characteristics;
- *User Context*: Under which condition the system is being used. Examples are: whether the user is using a personal computer or a cell phone; the physical location; the access bandwidth available.
- *User Navigational Behavior*: Most systems consider the navigation path, such as the pages previously accessed, as a factor that influences adaptation;
- *User Browsing Behavior:* The actions the user takes while browsing. For example, the adaptation could benefit from observing which articles the user only read, and which ones he also printed; how many times the user saw a video; which images he enlarged and so on;
- *Application Functionality Usage*: How the functionality of the application is used. Examples are the results of tests and considering previously bought items.
- *Granularity of Time*: It could be interesting to observe in which granularity of time the adaptation is made. Some possible examples are: adaptation made at login time; adaptation made after a user configuration action and system revision and adaptation after each navigation step. In addition, as noted in [4], it may be desirable to "freeze" the presentation adaptation of certain pages once the user has seen them, so they see exactly the same contents when revisiting the page. This also necessitates adjusting the granularity of time for adaptation.

What Is Adapted. The actual aspect that is adapted can be one of the following:

- *Content Adaptation.* Refers to the actual content. Example – colloquial text for non-experts vs. technical text for experts; simple text for beginners vs. detailed text for advanced users;

- *Navigation Adaptation.* We consider two kinds of navigation adaptation:
  - *Adaptation of the content structure* that occurs at node-level, adapting the particular way in which concepts are put together for navigation purposes. Example - including introduction for beginners vs. skipping introduction for advanced users; including "safety warning" the first time a critical content is browsed vs. not including it in subsequent visits;
  - *Adaptation of the hyperspace topology*, at link-level (anchor changes and index changes modify the navigation path). Example - including a link to "solution" in a problem used as an example vs. not including the link in a problem used as a test;
- *Presentation Adapter.* Two kinds are considered:
  - *Adaptation of navigation support interface* (anchor level). Example: Using drop-down menu vs. using explicit lists of anchors; using textual anchors vs. iconic anchors;
  - *Adaptation of Content Interface* (fragment level). Example: using fonts of different size according to users' age or highlighting certain types of information for emphasis.

How Is the Adaptation Achieved. A usual mechanism used to implement adaptation is the "condition-action rules".

2.1 Evaluation

By using this meta-model, we are able to compare AHSs identifying its features and weaknesses. The decoupling of the various aspects also enables to define what kind of adaptation should be provided based on the adaptation goals. To better illustrate this applicability of the meta-model, showing how it can be used to analyze actual systems, we have instantiated it for the major AHSs – AHAM [6], AHA! [5], InterBook [3], NetCoach [9,12] and KBS Hyperbook [8]. For reasons of space, it is not possible to present all instantiations here. Instead, we only give a brief analysis of the evaluation, illustrating the kinds of observations that emerge. Readers interested in full details are referred to [1].

The systems were modeled as instances of the reference meta-model. Albeit AHA! does not separate DM from AM, it was possible to identify both aspects. None of the systems distinguishes explicitly the navigational view and the presentation view. There is always a relationship between the UM and the concepts, usually representing the system's belief about the user's knowledge with respect to each concept.

KBS is the only system evaluated that doesn't consider the User Navigational Behavior in order to update the UM. Only feedback obtained from problems and project resolution is used to evaluate users' knowledge.

All systems analyzed provide Presentation Adaptation, adapting the navigation support interface by using link annotation. All of them provide adaptation of the hyperspace topology (navigation adaptation). AHAM and AHA! implement this by hiding undesirable links; Interbook and NetCoach offer direct guidance. Interbook also generates links on-the-fly. KBS assigns projects and goals, and generates trails adaptively. These features are also classified as adaptation of content structure (another kind of navigation adaptation). Other example of such adaptation is the conditional inclusion of fragments that occurs in AHAM and AHA!.

By characterizing the AHSs, the general meta-model can also serve as a basis for modeling meta-adaptive hypermedia systems. To exemplify, we refer to [2] and assume that novice users prefer adaptive guidance whereas experienced users benefit more from link annotation. A meta-adaptive function would have a rule that triggers the Hyperspace Topology Adapter for the first ones and the Navigation Support Interface Adapter for the others.

3 Forthcoming Work

The general meta-model was proposed using the UML notation, which has limited expressiveness, and is not directly processable. Our next goal is to describe this meta-model using ontologies, which will allow integration with the Semantic Web technologies, that are more suitable for the type of meta-reasoning we envision, and allow direct manipulation. Besides ontology specification techniques, we are also investigating different alternatives for specifying and implementing the adaptation function in this meta-model. The meta-model should also be extended to allow for the communication between different AHSs. The inclusion of the cognitive style as an input to the Adaptation Function is an additional topic of research.

4 Validation

In order to validate our work, we will develop a small educational application and test it with a group of users to prove the advantages of using the proposed semantic meta-model for AHSs. We will try to demonstrate that - besides systemizing the development of AHSs by clearly defining conceptual, navigational, presentation and implementation aspects - our model will allow a wider range of types of adaptation, partly due to meta-adaptation rules.

5 Conclusion

According to [2], there is an evidence that different known techniques work most efficiently in different context. So the selection of the most relevant adaptation technologies is a critical point in the development of AHSs. The object of our work is to propose a Semantic Meta-Model for Adaptive Hypermedia Systems that systemizes the development of such systems, while addressing the effectiveness of adaptation and providing a basis for meta-adaptation, i.e., for systems that are able to adapt the very adaptation technology to the given user and context.

It is not part of the scope of our work to show what kind of adaptation is adequate for which contexts, but we want to offer the mechanisms for this evaluation.

References

1. Assis, P.A.; Schwabe, D.; Barbosa, S.D.J.; "Meta Modeling of Adaptive Hypermedia Applications", Technical Report, Department of Informatics, PUC-Rio, 2004. (In Portuguese, forthcoming).

2. Brusilovsky, P. "Adaptive navigation support in educational hypermedia: The role of student knowledge level and the case for meta-adaptation". British Journal of Educational Technology, 34 (4), 487-497, 2003.
3. Brusilovsky, P., Eklund, J., and Schwarz, E. "Web-Based Education For All: A Tool For Developing Adaptive Courseware", In: Computer Networks and ISDN Systems. Proceedings of Seventh International World Wide Web Conference, 30 (1-7), p.291-300, 1998.
4. De Bra, P., Aerts, A., Berden, B., De Lange, B. Escape from the Tyranny of the Textbook: Adaptive Object Inclusion in AHA!. Proceedings of the AACE ELearn 2003 Conference, Phoenix, Arizona, pp. 65-71. 2003.
5. De Bra, P., Aerts, A., Smits, D., Stash, N. AHA! Version 2.0, More Adaptation Flexibility for Authors. Proceedings of the AACE ELearn'2002 conference, pp. 240-246. 2002.
6. De Bra, P., Houben, G.J., Wu, H. AHAM: A Dexter-based Reference Model for Adaptive Hypermedia, Proceedings of the ACM Conference on Hypertext and Hypermedia, pp. 147-156, Darmstadt, Germany, 1999. (Editors K. Tochtermann, J. Westbomke, U.K. Wiil, J. Leggett).
7. Koch, N.P. "Software Engineering for Adaptive Hypermedia Systems: Reference Model, Modeling Techniques and Development Process" PhD thesis - Institut für Informatik, Ludwig-Maximilians-Universität München, 2000.
8. Nejdl, W. and Wolpers, M. "KBS Hyperbook - a Data-Driven Information System on the Web". In: WWW8 CONFERENCE, Toronto, 1999.
9. NetCoach Manual. http://art.ph-freiburg.de/NetCoach-Manual last accessed March 2003
10. Rossi, G.; Schwabe, D.; Lyardet, F; "Web application models are more than conceptual models", Lecture Notes in Computer Science 1727, pp. 239-252, ISBN 3-540-66653-2, Proceedings of the World Wild Web and Conceptual Modeling'99 Workshop, ER'99 Conference, Springer, Paris, 1999
11. UML Resource Page. http://www.omg.org/uml/, last accessed December 2002.
12. Weber, G. and Brusilovsky, P. "ELM-ART: an adaptive versatile system for web-based instruction". In: International Journal of Artificial Intelligence in Education, 2001.
13. Wu, H., De Kort, E., De Bra, P. Design Issues for General-Purpose Adaptive Hypermedia Systems. Proceedings of the ACM Conference on Hypertext and Hypermedia, pp. 141-150, Aarhus, Denmark, 2001.

Adaptive Navigation for Self-assessment Quizzes

Sergey Sosnovsky[*]

University of Pittsburgh, School of Information Sciences,
135, North Bellefield Avenue, Pittsburgh, PA, 15260, USA
sas15@pitt.edu

Abstract. Web-based parameterized quizzes provide teachers and students with several advantages as the technology for self-assessment. However, the effect of these advantages is strongly reduced, if a student does not receive enough support and cannot see her/his progress during the course. We have developed the system QuizGuide, which attempts to solve this problem by navigating students through the quiz material of the course in adaptive way. Architecture, interface and plans of future system development are described here. The paper also presents first results of system evaluation.

1 Web-Based Quizzes as the Technology for Self-assessment

Starting from the development of first Web-based educational systems, several successful technologies for online knowledge evaluation have been proposed [1, 2]. However, web-based quizzes have always played the leading role because of two main reasons. First, it is relatively easy to organize all three main stages of the question "life cycle" [2]: authorization, delivery/presentation, and assessment/feedback generation, in comparison to such classes of web-based systems as online simulation, collaboration support system or web-based ITS. Second, this technology inherits from traditional in-class quizzes; it is natural for both teacher and students to use it for knowledge assessment in the new conditions of web-based and web-enhanced education.

With the transfer of question material to the web such context of using quizzes as the self-assessment of student knowledge took on a special significance. Two trends in modern education increasing the teacher burden have appeared: the courses become more intensive, and the number of students grows (especially due to the distance and continuous education). This leads to the lack of traditional formative feedback that student can get in class. Web-based technologies for self-assessment, such as web-based quizzes, can help to solve this problem by providing students with meaningful information about their progress through the course and potential weaknesses [3].

Another strength of self-assessment technology is the self-motivation of students [4]. In our evaluation study [5] performed on QuizPACK we analyzed the subjective students evaluation of the systems. It was based on the questionnaires, filled by students after the term period of using system. More then 80% of students using QuizPACK reported positive attitude to it and high interest in taking online self-assessment quizzes.

---

[*] This work is done by the author as a part of his graduate study (The authors' research adviser is Peter Brusilovsky).

W. Nejdl and P. De Bra (Eds.): AH 2004, LNCS 3137, pp. 366–371, 2004.
© Springer-Verlag Berlin Heidelberg 2004

The pedagogical value of self-assessment quizzes has been confirmed by the number of papers. Regression analysis performed in [5] showed positive dependency between student performance in class and both the amount of students' work with self-assessment quizzes and their success (percentage of positive answers). Study reported in [6] showed statistically significant evidence of improvement in learning course material when students were using online self-assessment quizzes.

2   QuizPACK – Parameterized Quizzes

However, to possess all mentioned advantages in full degree, a system for self-assessment needs fairly large number of quizzes. Otherwise, students will hardly benefit from it, since familiar static question-answer pairs cannot reflect the real student's progress as well as initiate additional motivation.

The alternative to the large library of static question is the parameterized questions. This way has been used in our QuizPACK system (see Fig. 1). The architecture and interface of QuizPACK are described in details in [7]; the evaluation of the system is given in [5]. Below we provide the brief overview of the main features of QuizPACK.

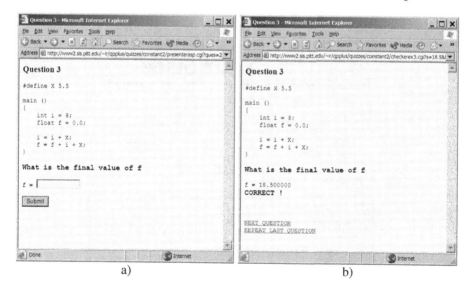

Fig. 1. Student interface of QuizPACK.

QuizPACK is the system for parameterized web-based quizzes authorization and delivery in the context of programming courses using C language. Each question in QuizPACK is actually a template containing a simple C program, one of the constants where is the generative parameter. When the question is delivered to a student parameter is instantiated with a randomly chosen value. Fig. 1 demonstrates the student interface of QuizPACK (the question sample – 1a, and the feedback on correct answer – 1b). After getting feedback students can proceed to the next question or go back and try previous question (with another value of the parameter) once again.

3   QuizGuide – Adaptive Quiz Navigation

QuizPACK evaluation study [5] and individual feedback, though positive, showed that students suffer from the lack of guidance. Indeed, as a self-assessment tool Quiz-PACK is supposed to help them in understanding their progress and finding knowledge gaps. However students could hardly estimate where their weakest topics are, and where they should feel confident without any support; they simply get lost. Even with the option of parameterizes quizzes and fairly large topics combining quizzes, we still needed to develop 46 quizzes to cover the whole course material. To assist students in getting valuable feedback that can help them to locate themselves in the course knowledge space we could apply the intelligent sequencing approach, which is used traditionally for the quiz adaptation. Instead we have developed the system QuizGuide, providing students with the adaptive navigation support by the means of such AH technique as adaptive link annotation (see for example [8]).

The student interface of QuizGuide (Fig. 2.) consists of two main parts: annotated list of hyperlinks to topics and quizzes and the frame for a question load and feedback generation.

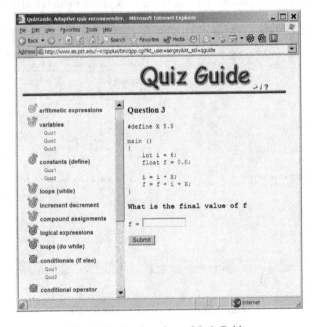

Fig. 2. Student interface of QuizGuide.

Adaptation in QuizGuide is performed on the basis of two traditional features of the user model: the knowledge level and the learning goal. Hyperlink to each topic is annotated with an icon reflecting the relevance of this topic in the terms of the current learning goal of the class and the level of knowledge that the individual student has for the specific topic. The annotation mechanism uses the "target-arrow" abstraction. Number of arrows in the target reflects the level of knowledge the student possesses for this topic: the more arrows the target has, the higher the level is. The target color shows the relevance of the topic concerning the current learning goal: the more intensive color means that the topic is close to the current goal. Topics, which are not ready to be studied because of a non-reached learning goal, are annotated with the crossed target. Hence we have four levels of knowledge (from zero to three arrows) and four levels of topic actuality (not-ready, current, previous and non-important).

When a student clicks on the topic name, the list of quizzes available for this topic drops out. One more click on the topic name rolls this list back. Since the student works only with one quiz at one time links to other quizzes are not necessary and could be reduced. It does not mean however, that the student cannon drop out several topics (see Fig. 2). A click on the quiz link opens first question of this quiz. To navigate through the quiz students can use the links Next Question or Repeat Previous Question. As it is seen from the figures 1 and 2 quizzes for QuizPACK and QuizGuide are the same. These systems use the common question material; and the work of students with any of this system is reflected in the common user model.

As you can see from Fig. 2, QuizGuide does not forbid students to work with any of topics; it only recommends them by annotation. Students still can take any quiz belonging to "non-ready" learning goal, and when the time comes for this topic to become the current learning goal, previous students' work with it will be taken into account. The list of topics is fixed for students could not get lost in the material.

Brief help can be loaded in the main screen by clicking on the question mark icon. Also the icon for refreshing the application is available. Each time the student clicks it the new request is sent to the user model and the values for all topics are recalculated.

23 topics are determined in the course. They are connected to each other with prerequisite relations. These topics form 15 learning goals. Actually, learning goals acts as the lectures in the class, forming the flat sequence. Different topics have from 1 to 3 quizzes with 3 to 5 questions in these quizzes. Total number of quizzes is 46. Total number of questions is more then 150. Quizzes have assigned complexity value (from 1 to 3); quizzes with different complexity have different influence on the knowledge level calculation.

4 Preliminary Evaluation

Currently QuizGuide has been used for a half of the term in the context of real class environment for the undergraduate course *Introduction to Programming* taught in the School of Information Science at the University of Pittsburgh. For more then a month before working with QuizGuide students had been taking traditional QuizPACK quizzes without adaptive navigation support. However, the quizzes they took were the same that are used by QuizGuide. All data, obtained during the non-adaptive stage of taking quizzes have been stored in the user model and then used by QuizGuide. During the last month both adaptive and non-adaptive interfaces for quizzes have been available for students, i.e. data got from non-adaptive quizzes and the one from QuizGuide are equally considered for the user model updating.

Statistics that we got so far demonstrates the strong evidence that adaptive navigation support for self-assessment quizzes provides additional motivation for students to take quizzes. The average session length for non-adaptive quizzes is about 10 questions, when the average length of QuizGuide session is 26 questions, which means after starting work with self-assessment quizzes students take about 2.5 times more quizzes when adaptive navigation support exists. Only tierce of sessions for non-adaptive quizzes has a length more then 10 questions, while for QuizGuide this ration is more then twice bigger.

The analysis of students' paths through the questions showed that with adaptive interface they have got an additional motivation to use the parametric nature of Quiz-PACK questions. If in the past they often tried to solve the same question with different parameter values until they solve it correctly, now they also have new educational goal – to reach the maximum knowledge level, to get three arrows on the target. . It results in more then 10% higher performance of work with a tool. The percentage of correct answers for the students who mainly used QuizPACK is only 32%, when the students, who had switched to QuizGuide and used it regularly, have this ratio on the level of 43%.

At the same time we observe, that students are not persistent in using QuizGuide. Some of them switch to QuizPACK and back. Some students use primarily non-adaptive self-assessment quizzes. The numbers of active students for QuizGuide and traditional QuizPACK quizzes are approximately the same, when the total number of students using a tool is greater for non-adaptive quizzes. We are going to collect more consistent statistics in the next month, which is the last before the final exam, and traditionally is characterized by the increased students' activity.

5 Future Work

The system is currently developing in several directions. In the next versions of adaptation mechanism we are is going to compare different formulas for knowledge level calculation. We plan to recommend to the students the "best quiz" on every step. Better-grained concepts structure is going to be designed. For this purpose we plan to use the developed parsing component for automatic indexing of C programs, which have been applied already for domain description in NavEx system [9].

The current architecture of QuizGuide/QuizPACK, allows adaptive and non-adaptive components to use the same set of quizzes. This opens the exceptional opportunities for adaptive navigation mechanism evaluation. In the future we are going to perform more exhaustive comparative analysis of QuizPACK and QuizGuide to estimate the pedagogical value of using adaptive annotation technology in this class of systems.

Finally, web-based author interface is developing, which can provide us with new users: teachers and students; new questions; and new statistics and feedback.

6 Summary

We have developed QuizGuide, the adaptive navigation system for web-based self-assessment quizzes. This paper described the architecture and interface of QuizGuide as well as the initial motivation for its creation. QuizGuide is strongly interconnected with our old non-adaptive system QuizPACK and uses the same question material as QuizPACK does. Preliminary evaluation of the system showed that students spend much more time with adaptive self-assessment quizzes then with non-adaptive ones; additional motivation leads to more extensive usage of parameterized nature of Quiz-PACK questions. Future plans include further interface and architecture development as well as system evaluation studies.

Acknowledgement

The work reported in this paper is supported by NSF grant # 7525 *Individualized Exercises for Assessment and Self-Assessment of Programming Knowledge.*

References

1. Hooper, M.: Assessment in WWW-Based Learning Systems: Opportunities and Challenges. Journal of Universal Computer Science, vol. 4 no. 4 (1998), 330-348.
2. Brusilovsky, P., Miller, P.: Course Delivery Systems for the Virtual University, In: T. Tschang and T. Della Senta (eds.): Access to Knowledge: New Information Technologies and the Emergence of the Virtual University. Amsterdam: Elsevier Science, 167-206.
3. Peat, M.: Online assessment: The use of web based self assessment materials to support self directed learning. In A. Herrmann and M.M. Kulski (eds.), Flexible Futures in Tertiary Teaching. Proceedings of the 9th Annual Teaching Learning Forum, 2-4 February 2000. Perth: Curtin University of Technology. http://lsn.curtin.edu.au/tlf/tlf2000/peat.html
4. AIMS website. Strategies for Assessing Student Knowledge and Performance. http://www.med.unc.edu/oed/testassess/assessment_strategies.htm
5. Sosnovsky S., Shcherbinina O., Brusilovsky P.: Web-based Parameterized Questions as a Tool for Learning. In: Allison Rossett (ed.), Proceedings of E-Learn'2003, Phoenix, Arizona, USA: AACE, 309-316.
6. Gayo-Avello, D., Fernández-Cuervo, H.: Online Self-Assessment as a Learning Method. In: Vladan Devedzic, J. Michael Spector, Demetrios G Sampson, Kinshuk (eds.), Proceedings of ICALT 2003, Athens, Greece: IEEE Computer Society, 254-255.
7. Pathak, S., Brusilovsky, P.: Assessing Student Programming Knowledge with Web-based Dynamic Parameterized Quizzes. In Proceedings of ED-MEDIA'2002 - World Conference on Educational Multimedia, Hypermedia and Telecommunications, Denver, Colorado, USA: AACE, 1548-1553.
8. De Bra, P.: Pros and Cons of Adaptive Hypermedia in Web-Based Education. Journal on CyberPsychology and Behavior, vol. 3, no. 1, (2000), Mary Ann Lievert Inc., 71-77.
9. Sosnovsky, S., Brusilovsky, P., Yudelson, M.: Supporting Adaptive Hypermedia Authors with Automated Content Indexing. In Proceedings of Workshop on Authoring Adaptive and Adaptable Educational Hypermedia at the AH-2004 Conference, Eindhoven, The Netherlands, August 23-26, 2004 (in Press).

Towards Adaptive Learning Designs[*]

Adriana Berlanga and Francisco J. García

University of Salamanca
37008, Salamanca, Spain
{solis13,fgarcia}@usal.es

Abstract. This paper outlines an ongoing research. Its objective is to propose an open model to define adaptive learning designs in such way that novice designers or teachers could configure them. Further, all elements are annotated with standardized metadata to facilitate their exchangeability and reusability.

1 Introduction

Adaptive Educational Hypermedia Systems (AEHS) provide the most suitable learning content, in the shape of paths for each student according to her/his knowledge and characteristics. However, from our perspective, they could be more successful if learning design strategies are used. A learning design considers the learning topic, the goals of instruction, the prerequisites, and the students' characteristics.

Additionally, in the era of the Adaptive Web [2], learners and teachers can improve the learning experience if students are able to reach resources adapted to their needs, and teachers integrate into their learning designs materials created by others.

This paper outlines an ongoing research project which goal is to propose a model to design adaptive learning designs for any field of knowledge, educational level, instructional design or learning style. In addition, the model will give authors the possibility to define the adaptive rules that will be executed. Nevertheless, these rules would be checked for inconstancies, and their efficiency would be audited.

Furthermore, the learning components will be interoperable, reusable and exchangeable, since the model will employ standardized metadata to annotate them.

The remainder of this paper is structured as follows. Sect. 2 outlines the proposed model, and explains its components. Sect. 3 exposes conclusions and further work.

2 The Open Model

The model is based on the following principles (see Fig. 1):

1. The learning domain is modularized in several components (learning style, test, rules, and learning design) that could be (re)used in other learning domains.
2. The structure of the learning domain is based on learning activities.

---

[*] Adriana Berlanga thanks the Mexican Council of Science and Technology (CONACyT) for its support. Research supported by the Government of Castile and Lion Projects (ref. SA017/02, US09/05).

W. Nejdl and P. De Bra (Eds.): AH 2004, LNCS 3137, pp. 372–375, 2004.

3. Adaptability is based on: (i) the learning style and the initial, current and final knowledge of the students; (ii) learning style of the learning activities.
4. Neither learning designs nor learning style approaches are prescribed.
5. Students and learning activities have/promote a mix of learning styles.
6. Learning designs are semantically defined following IMS specifications.
7. The efficiency of the adaptive rules created by authors is evaluated.

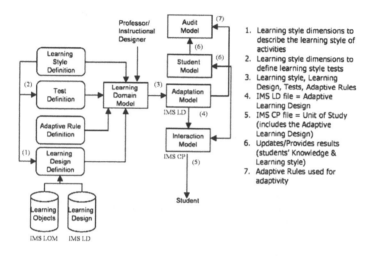

Fig. 1. Initial architecture of the Open Model

2.1 The Learning Domain Model

2.1.1 The Learning Style Definition. We claim that different learning style approaches should be used for different fields of knowledge and different types of students. Therefore, the open model does not set down any learning style.

In the learning style definition authors specify the learning style approach they judge is the best for their content and context. This definition will be used to define the learning style of activities and learners, as well as learning style tests.

2.1.2 The Learning Design Definition. Its objective is to describe the prerequisites, objectives, and activities that will be integrated into the instructional design. It defines the learning experience based on learning activities related to learning goals and prerequisites.

The IMS LD [6] specification is used to describe the learning design. However, the element learning style –used to perform the adaptivity– is not part of IMS LD. Consequently, it will be added to the definition of learning activities to annotate which learning styles they endorse and in what proportion.

2.1.3 The Test Definition. It depicts the assessments that will be used in the learning design. There are four types of tests: learning style, initial knowledge, current knowledge, and final knowledge. The results of these tests will be stored in the student model and will be used to describe and perform adaptive rules.

The learning style test identifies the learning style of the student. This type of test should be linked to a learning style definition created before, which will provide the dimensions of the learning style that will be measured. The knowledge tests (initial, current and final) measure the students' knowledge.

2.1.4 The Adaptive Rule Definition. Its aim is to provide the authors with a formalism to specify the rules that will be used to adequate the learning design to the students' characteristics. The definition of adaptive rules can be done by describing adaptive statements, adaptive techniques, or students' stereotypes.

Adaptive statements depict the conditions to execute an adaptive action. Authors define them by using different sets [1]. These sets are based on IMS LD, in such way that adaptive statements could be (re)used in other learning designs.

The definitions of techniques and stereotypes use the same sets as the adaptive statements. The former gives the author the possibility of storing adaptive techniques (later, s/he can evaluate if they have been successful using the Audit Model). In the latter, authors define adaptive statements for students with the same characteristics.

2.2 The Student Model

The student model contains information on the student, such as her/his learning styles, knowledge (initial, current, final), and interactions with the learning design.

To describe the students' learning style, we claim that each learner has a combination of the different dimensions defined by a learning style approach, not just one. Therefore, the learning styles of each student are stored in a vector defined as (BNF notation):

$$\textbf{<student-learning-style>} ::= \text{``[''} \{<\text{learning-style-approach-id}> \{\text{``,''} <\text{di-} \quad (1)$$
$$\text{mension-id}> \text{``,''} <\text{percentage-value}>\} [\text{``;''}]\} \text{``]''}$$

2.3 The Adaptive Model

The adaptive model integrates all the definitions of the learning domain model (learning design, test, learning style, adaptive rules), and automatically generates the IMS LD file that contains the deliverable learning design. The integration of the adaptive rule definitions uses the element <method> of IMS LD that prescribes the order of the activities, the learner properties and the conditions to personalize learning.

2.4 The Interaction Model

The interaction model has two functions. Firstly, it delivers an adaptive unit of learning for each student (i.e. an IMS CP [5] file). Secondly, it tracks the behaviour of the students. This includes data about which learning activities the student visited, and the results of the four types of tests. This information will update the student model.

2.5 The Audit Model

The aim of the audit model is twofold: to verify that the definition of the adaptive rules is coherent, well constructed and does not interfere with other definitions, and to determine if those rules are succeeding in providing an effective learning. To do so, it will consider the time the student spent to complete the learning activity, and her/his grades on the different tests. In addition, this model will help us to verify whether the proposed ideas are effective.

3 Conclusions

With the aim to improve the possibilities and services provided by AEHS, we consider it significant to study, on one hand, how different instructional designs can be adapted to the diversity of students, an on the other, which is the process to evaluate the efficiency of adaptivity.

We are extending the functionality of Hypermedia Composer (HyCo [3]) to convert it to an AEHS defined in line with the open model [4]. Currently, we are designing the authoring tool to describe learning designs in accordance with IMS LD. The next step is to delineate the tests and adaptive rules. Afterwards, we will integrate the other components of the model into HyCo.

References

1. Berlanga, A., Garcia, F.: An Open Model to define Adaptive Educational Hypermedia Systems based on Learning Technology Specifications. In Int. Workshop on Web Semantics (WebS 2004), in conjunction with 14th International Conference on Database and Expert Systems Applications (DEXA 2004) (Zaragoza, Spain, 2004). IEEE (to appear).
2. Brusilovsky, P., Nejdl, W.: Adaptive Hypermedia and Adaptive Web. In: Munindar P. Singh (ed.): Practical Handbook of Internet Computing. Crc Press. (2003).
3. García, F. and García, J.: Educational Hypermedia Resources Facilitator. Computers & Education. In press (2004).
4. Garcia, F., Berlanga, A., Moreno, M., Garcia, J., Carabias, J.: HyCo – An Authoring Tool to Create Semantic Learning Objects for Web-based E-Learning Systems. In International Conference on Web Engineering (ICWE 2004) (Munich, Germany, 2004). LNCS Springer-Verlag (to appear).
5. IMS CP. Content Packaging version 1.1.3. (2003).
6. IMS LD. Learning Design Specification version 1.1. (2003).

Time-Based Extensions to Adaptation Techniques*

Mária Bieliková and Rastislav Habala

Institute of Informatics and Software Engineering
Faculty of Informatics and Information Technologies
Slovak University of Technology
Ilkovičova 3, 842 16 Bratislava, Slovakia
http://www.fiit.stuba.sk/~bielik

Abstract. In this paper we present an approach to time-based adaptation in adaptive hypermedia systems. Time is used as a part of the context (or environment) model. We have proposed extensions of known adaptation techniques by means of the notion of time. We experimented with proposed extensions and implemented a software system called TIM, which adapts presentation of educational module administrative information according user characteristics and a context represented by time of information presentation.

1 Introduction

An important feature of effective delivery of information is adaptivity based on the presentation context. The presentation context is defined as a collection of data which depend on the current state of the presentation. It is often described using technology or user platform adaptation dimension (hardware, software, network bandwidth) or external environment adaptation dimension (user location, language, socio-political issues) [3]. We emphasize one of important characteristics to the context — time. Time is fundamental characteristic since the context and user characteristics are unstable and changing.

Our approach is based on the fact that some information is not valid forever. Presented information has defined an initial time of validity and/or end time of validity [2]. Moreover, during the validity time, relevance of this information can evolve. The task of the adaptive hypermedia (AH) system is to observe current time of information presentation besides other characteristics (user knowledge, preferences, etc.). Time constrained adaptation based on a time of the day is used in tourist guide adaptive systems ([4, 7]). The opening times of attractions represent important characteristic used in adaptation of the city guide.

We also support the domain model changes. Often the domain model evolves in time (e.g., new information is added or existing information is corrected). It is important to be able to observe this evolution. The AH system in this case serves a user the presentation of evolving information (e.g., changes of the content which occurred from the last user access to the AH system are highlighted).

---

* This work has been partially supported by the Grant Agency of Slovak Republic grant No. VG1/ 0162/03.

W. Nejdl and P. De Bra (Eds.): AH 2004, LNCS 3137, pp. 376–379, 2004.

Other options to exploiting time in adaptive hypermedia include targeting limited capacity of the human memory [1] or to provide models of versioning related to time (also known in software engineering as revisions [5]).

In this paper we concern time-based adaptive presentation and drawing user attention to domain model changes. We describe the most interesting extensions to known adaptation techniques with considering the time dimension. Proposed extensions are based on the model of time, which maps a real time to a symbolic time and provides necessary operations for working with both of them. Two basic structures form the basis of the time model: intervals and scopes.

Model of time is advantageous especially in cases when the domain model is going to be reused in various time periods, i.e. similar content is presented within various time intervals. Typical example of such functionality is a web-based whiteboard of university courses, presentation of scientific conferences or other professional repetitive activities. The domain model reuse in next execution of the event (be it university course or scientific conference) requires only setting-up the intervals' initial and end times of validity in the model of time.

2   Time-Based Adaptive Presentation

Inserting/removing fragments. Presentation of a fragment is determined according time (along other characteristics represented in user or context models). Obvious technique is to define meta-data related to the fragment, which serve for adaptation. Adaptation rules define adaptive fragment inserting or removing in dependence of time.

Simplest implementation uses attributes *from* and *to*, which represent simple time dependent rule: the fragment is presented only if current time is in the interval defined by *from* and *to* values. If the value of these attributes (real time or symbolic time) is not defined, we consider infinity instead.

Sorting fragments. Sort criteria are extended by time (real or symbolic). This technique is especially useful for application domain of adaptive electronic whiteboards. Typical fragments that should be sorted by time are organized as a list of announcements or messages to the users.

Sorting fragments technique is used in our AH system TIM along with the *collects* relation. The *collects* relation enables effective wrapping of evolving list of fragments. Adding a new element into the list does not require any modification of the concept representing the list.

Change emphasizing. For effective comprehension of evolving information it is important to have a mechanism for adaptive presentation according changes, which occurred from the last user visit and to which the user should pay attention. We proposed the technique as follows. The adaptation engine compares the content of presented fragment that has been valid in time of the last presentation of the fragment and its current content. The distinctions are determined and emphasized to the user. Moreover, changes can be propagated to the parents of the changed fragment (i.e., the change is presented also in fragments, which occur on a path from the starting fragment to the changed fragment). The changes are indicated by annotating links leading to the changed fragment.

Meaningful change discovery is not an easy task. The problem is automatic recognition of the change significance. Often the change presents spell correction. Some other time the content is renewed but it is not necessary to read it again. We implemented this technique with explicit tagging in the changed content. The changed region is enclosed to the block with assigned time of change. For enabling described feature we proposed technique for time versioning of models (used here for domain model). This technique enables us to determine the state and the content of each concept in arbitrary time in the history. It is a base for accomplishing a comparison of the content of two snapshots of the concept.

Change emphasizing was recognized as extremely useful feature of our AH system for students who periodically visited the course information during term. For visual change highlighting we use a change of the background color. It is possible to use this technique in combination with known adaptation techniques. For example, links inside the changed content can be annotated (colored). We use a change of the background color for emphasizing unlike the approach of Hothi et al. [6] where the background color change serves for dimming fragments.

3   Adaptive Navigation

Adaptive link sorting and hiding. Both techniques are extended and implemented alike sorting and inserting/removing fragments. Links are sorted also considering the time criterion. For example, fresh concepts are presented first. Sorting can be based on concept creation time or concept validity time. Adaptive link hiding regards also time while decision about the link presentation is performed (along other characteristics represented in user or context models).

Adaptive link annotation. Time-based adaptive link annotation supports increasing of attention to a change, which occurred in the concept representing a target of the link. We distinguish two types of changes. Providing the concept content has changed or a new fragment has been added to the concept content it is denoted as "change". Other case is adding a new fragment using the *collects* relation. This fact is visualized by annotating by "new" icon (it reflects semantics of the *collects* relation and its intended use for e-whiteboard systems).

Adaptive link annotation by denoting changes or news is propagated. We have proposed also a mechanism for controlling propagation. Sometimes it is necessary to stop the change propagation because as a result we will see the change indication in many places, which can confuse the user.

4   Conclusions

In this paper we presented time constrained adaptation techniques. Our approach enables adaptive presentation of time dependent information, tracking evolution of application domain model in time together with support of drawing the user's attention to the content changes and time-based content versioning. Important characteristic of proposed approach is the support of a domain model reuse in various time periods.

We developed a time-based AH web-based system called TIM (TIMe-Aware Adaptive Hypermedia System). TIM has been first time applied in summer term 2002/03 to the Principles of Software Engineering (PSE) course with about 130 students enrolled. TIM serves the students in two ways: it features as a leading familiarization with a course and it serves as a presentation of the course running (and evolving) information.

We evaluated the TIM from several points of view. First, the system demonstrated as an appropriate tool for presenting evolving information. Invaluable feature for the content developer is the domain model reuse (in subsequent years of the course offering). As the most frequent problem indicated by students was known problem with adaptive web-based systems – the *back button*. The user expects specific behavior when pressing "back" in a browser menu. However, in adaptive systems (in time-aware system especially) there is no *conventional back* because the state of presentation already changed. Even though the system has provides own back and forward buttons with expected semantics, the students used these buttons infrequently.

The most valuable feature designated by students was change propagation. The emphasizing based on highlighting background was proved effective similarly to dimming adaptation technique based on shading background [6].

Our future work concerns the research of time-based adaptation in different application domains together with improving mechanisms for debugging defined models by simulation of time pass.

References

1. Peter Ágh and Mária Bieliková. Improving learning using cognitive characteristics of human memory, 2002. Tech. report. Slovak University of Technology in Bratislava.
2. Mária Bieliková. Adaptive presentation of evolving information using XML. In T. Okamoto et al., editors, *Proc. of IEEE Int. Conf. of Advanced Learning Technologies - ICALT'2001*, pages 193–196, Madison, USA, 2001. IEEE Press.
3. Mario Cannataro, Alfredo Cuzzocrea, and Andrea Pugliese. XAHM: an adaptive hypermedia model based on XML. In *Proc. SEKE'02*, pages 627–634, Ischia, Italy, July 2002. ACM Press.
4. Keith Cheverst, Keith Mitchell, and Nige Daies. The role of adaptive hypermedia in a context-aware tourist GUIDE. *Communications of the ACM*, 45(5):47–51, 2002.
5. Reidar Conradi and Bernhard Westfechtel. Version models for software configuration management. *ACM Computing Surveys*, 30(2):232–282, June 1998.
6. Jatinder Hothi, Wendy Hall, and Tim Sly. A study comparing the use of shaded text and adaptive navigational support in adaptive hypermedia. In C. Strapparava P. Brusilovsky, O. Stock, editors, *Proc. of Int. Conf. on Adaptive Hypermedia and Adaptive Web-Based Systems*, pages 335–342, Italy, 2000. Springer LNCS 1892.
7. Daniela Petrelli et al. Modelling and adapting to context. *Personal and Ubiquitous Computing*, 5:20–24, 2001.

On the Use of Collaborative Filtering Techniques for the Prediction of Web Search Result Rank

Peter Briggs and Barry Smyth*

Smart Media Institute,
Department of Computer Science, University College Dublin (UCD), Ireland
{Peter.Briggs,Barry.Smyth}@ucd.ie

Abstract. In this paper we describe an experiment that applies collaborative filtering techniques to a Web search task, namely the prediction of the rank of relevant results for a given query. We compare the performance of two different collaborative filtering algorithms and argue that these approaches have the potential to generate accurate predictions, which in turn may help to improve existing Web search techniques.

1 Introduction

The sheer scale and rate of growth of the Web [6] are making it increasingly difficult for users to find relevant, high-quality information. As a result, Web search engines have become invaluable tools for sifting through the dizzying amount of information that users are confronted with on a daily basis. These search engines are *content-based* - that is, they focus on retrieving the documents whose contents most closely match the query-terms supplied by the user. Content-based techniques have been effective in the traditional information retrieval (IR) arena, where retrieval experts construct well-formed, specific queries to search for relevant documents within a relatively small, static, and largely homogenous collection of documents.

Despite proving useful in traditional IR environments, content-based retrieval methods are often inadequate in meeting the information needs of Web searchers. In contrast to the relatively manageable document collections that these techniques were originally designed for, the Web is a dynamic, unmoderated mass of heterogenous documents and files. And typical Web users are not experts when it comes to searching for documents - they routinely provide ambiguous queries [3], making it difficult for search engines to predict their needs. In such an environment, query and document terms are not always a good indication of relevance and so content-based approaches often fail.

In contrast to content-based IR systems, recommender systems have proven to be very effective when applied to content-poor domains. For example, *collaborative filtering* (CF) techniques have been successfully applied to a variety of domains including music [2], TV programs [8], news [4], and Web browsing/meta-search [5]. By employing CF techniques, users can be recommended items even though there may be no information available on the content of those items. Unlike content-based approaches, CF does not compare the requirements of a user to the content of an item. Instead,

---

* The support of the informatics initiative of Enterprise Ireland is gratefully acknowledged.

W. Nejdl and P. De Bra (Eds.): AH 2004, LNCS 3137, pp. 380–383, 2004.

the system maintains profiles that contain information relating to items that users have liked/disliked in the past. These user profiles can then be compared in terms of item likes/dislikes, and recommendations can be made to a particular user based on the items that similar users have previously preferred.

In Sect. 2, we describe an experiment on the application of CF to the field of Web search - specifically, the prediction of the rank of results returned by a search engine in response to a query. We believe that CF could compliment traditional content-based approaches, and allow relevant documents to be recommended to a user even when they do not contain the same terms as the user's query.

2   An Experiment in Web Search Rank Prediction

The basis of our experiment is a data-set generated using 250 queries consisting of the names of mammals. Each query had two forms - *vague* and *contextualised*. The former corresponds to the typical Web queries (e.g. "seal"), whereas the latter included additional terms to indicate its context (e.g. "mammal seal"). We submitted both forms of each query to the HotBot search engine and collected the first 1000 results. Next, we computed the intersection between the result-lists produced for each form of the query. Each vague query was then associated with a set of pairs, each pair consisting of an intersecting result (a result common to both result-lists) and the rank of that result in the contextualised result list. For example, if the result *www.wildlife.net* occured in both result lists for the queries *"seal"* and *"mammals seal"* then the pair {*www.wildlife.net,15*} would be associated with the query *"seal"*; assuming that the page was at rank 15 in the result-list for the contextualised query.

In our experiment, we followed a *leave-one-out* strategy to try to predict the rank for each result stored against each query by using all remaining results and queries. This produced a predicted rank score for each query/result pair that we could compare to the actual rank score in order to compute an overall prediction error. The idea was to use CF techniques so that each query served as a type of user profile. The results and ranks stored against this query corresponded to a set of ratings over items. In the style of [7], two basic prediction techniques were used and are outlined below.

The first prediction algorithm that we implemented was based on the *mean squared differences (MSD)* method used by [7]. Very briefly, query similarity (the similarity between the result sets for two queries) is based on the mean squared difference of their common result ranks. The predicted rank of the target page is based on the weighted (by query similarity) average of the ranks of the target for similar queries. In addition we developed a number of variations of this MSD algorithm by limiting predictions to queries whose mean-squared difference values did not exceed set thresholds. In this way, it was possible to ensure that only highly similar queries were used as the basis for predictions in order to test if this improved the overall prediction quality.

The second prediction algorithm, *Resnick*, is proposed by [4] in GroupLens. This approach also generates predictions based on a weighted average of the target page's rank for related queries, but instead of relying on MSD as the basis for similarity and weighting, Pearson's correlation coefficient is used. Once again a thresholding technique was used to produce different variations that limited the set of queries that could be used in a prediction. In contrast to the MSD thresholds, in this case the higher the threshold, the stricter the criteria.

3   Results

In this preliminary analysis of our experimental results, we examine the quality of the result rank predictions generated by each of our implemented algorithms (see [1] for a more detailed analysis). One measure of prediction accuracy is to look at the correlation between predicted and actual ranks. This is presented in Fig. 1 as a graph of correlation vs. prediction coverage for each of the MSD and Resnick thresholds. As the various thresholds become more strict, prediction coverage tends to fall; fewer queries are considered similar enough to participate in prediction, and so some result ranks may not be predictable at all.

Significant increases in prediction correlation are available to MSD, especially at the low coverage levels. For example, MSD achieves a correlation of .9 at 45% coverage compared to a correlation of .72 for Resnick. Moreover we find that as coverage falls and thresholds become more strict, MSD benefits from increasing correlation scores - a useful trade-off that is less prominent in the case of Resnick. In this prediction task, accuracy is likely to be more important than coverage and hence the benefits due to MSD become more important still.

As another measure of prediction accuracy, we examined the number of predictions that the algorithms could make that were within 5 positions of their actual rank, and within 10 positions of their actual rank. At its strictest threshold, MSD performs best with 11.1% and 21.2% of its predictions falling within 5 and 10 positions of their actual places respectively. Resnick, again at its strictest threshold, does not do so well with 6.3% of its predictions having a positional error of 5 or less, and 12.7% having an error of 10 or less.

4   Conclusions

We have described the results of an experiment in applying CF techniques to the Web search task of predicting the rank of relevant results for a given query. In general we have found the predictions from the MSD algorithm to be superior to those produced by Resnick, but further research is required. Although this experiment merely scratches the

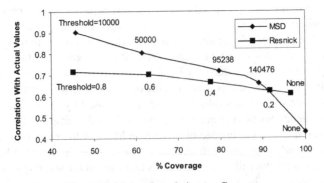

Fig. 1. Prediction Correlation vs. Coverage

surface when it comes to this prediction task, the results that we obtained are positive and indicate that CF techniques can predict the rank of relevant search results with a reasonable degree of accuracy.

In a Web search environment, historical query/document selection figures could be used to predict result ranks, and so relevant results could be recommended for queries based on the results that were selected for other similar queries. These pages might be missed by traditional search engines whose content-based techniques measure relevance solely by term matching, and so fail to recognise less obvious relationships between documents and queries. A CF approach could compliment existing content-based Web search technology, and help to bridge the gap caused by query/document vocabulary mismatches.

References

1. P. Briggs and B. Smyth. Predicting the Relevance of Web Search Results: A Collaborative Filtering Approach. In *Proceedings of the 2nd STarting AI Researchers Symposium, (STAIRS 2004) held in conjuction with ECAI 2004*. IOS Press, 2004. Valencia, Spain.
2. C. Hayes, P. Cunningham, P. Clerkin, and M. Grimaldi. Programme-driven music radio. In *Proceedings of the 15th European Conference on Artificial Intelligence*, 2002.
3. S. Lawrence and C. Lee Giles. Context and Page Analysis for Improved Web Search. *IEEE Internet Computing*, 2(4):38–46, 1998.
4. P. Resnick, N. Iacovou, M. Suchak, P. Bergstrom, and J. Riedl. GroupLens: An open architecture for collaborative filtering of netnews. In *Proceedings of the 1994 Conference on Computer Supported Collaborative Work*, pages 175–186, 1994.
5. G. Rodriguez-Mula, H. Garcia-Molina, and A. Paepcke. Collaborative value filtering on the web. *Computer Networks and ISDN Systems*, 30:736–8, 2000.
6. Wade Roush. Search Beyond Google. *MIT Technology Review*, pages 34–45, 2004.
7. U. Shardanand and P. Maes. Social information filtering: Algorithms for automating "word of mouth". In *Proceedings of the Conference on Human Factors in Computing Systems (CHI '95)*, pages 210–217. ACM Press, 1995. New York, USA.
8. B. Smyth and P. Cotter. PTV: Intelligent Personalised TV Guides. In *Proceedings of the 12th Conference on Innovative Applications of Artificial Intelligence. (IAAI-2000)*. AAAI Press, 2000.

A Thematic Guided Tour Model
for Contextualized Concept Presentations

Benjamin Buffereau and Philippe Picouet

Department of Artificial Intelligence and Cognitive Sciences
ENST Bretagne - Technopôle de Brest Iroise
B.P. 832, 29285 Brest Cedex, France
{benjamin.buffereau,philippe.picouet}@enst-bretagne.fr

Abstract. Since adaptive hypermedia systems generally confront with the difficulty to combine concept-based hyperspace generation with multi-concept indexing, we propose in this article an adaptive hypermedia model that achieves a
fruitful separation of the resource space and the user space. On the one hand,
the resource space benefits a powerful indexing model. On the other hand, the
user space is generated from the knowledge space as thematic guided tours
specified at a schema level. These guided tours take advantage of the indexing
model to contextualize concept presentations and ensure global and local coherence. The model fulfills the requirements of an open, time-evolving, multi-
author AHS and can be applied to a community web context.

1 Introduction

Most of Adaptive Hypermedia Systems (AHSs) distinguish between the knowledge
space and the hyperspace. The knowledge space usually models the knowledge domain as a graph where nodes are concepts and arcs represent relations between concepts, whereas the hyperspace organizes the textual or multimedia material as sets of
pages and hyperlinks. Pages are linked to concepts through indexing relations. The
relationship between the knowledge space and the hyperspace divide AHs into two
main categories. On the one hand, concept-based hyperspaces are built from the concept graph, propose one concept presentation per page, and rely on single concept
indexing. On the other hand, manually designed hyperspaces are created by hand and
use multi-concept indexing [1].

The concept-based hyperspace approach allows to build user-adapted views of the
hyperspace, by selecting and computing sub-graphs of the domain model. For example, user-adapted tables of contents can dynamically be derived from the concept
graph using rules representing specific learning strategies [3]. However, a major
drawback of this approach is the lack of independence between the hyperspace and
the knowledge space: as each page must be indexed by exactly one concept, each
addition or reorganization of the educational material implies restructuring the domain model. Single-concept indexing, though sufficient for simple AHS systems,
does not fulfill the requirements of the semantic/community web context [2] where
multiple authors produce information resources or gather it from the Web, index it,
and organize it in complex presentations.

In order to combine the concept-based hyperspace approach with multi-concept indexing, we propose to divide the hyperspace into two distinct subspaces, namely the

W. Nejdl and P. De Bra (Eds.): AH 2004, LNCS 3137, pp. 384–388, 2004.
© Springer-Verlag Berlin Heidelberg 2004

resource space and the user space. The resource space is connected to the knowledge space through many-to-many indexing relations. The user navigates in its own space of tailored views on the concept graph, where each page corresponds to a concept presentation dynamically composed by resource selection and assembling. To guaranty the coherence of user navigation, we pay particular attention to the cognitive factors of user orientation and user understanding [4] and propose to structure the user space around dynamically generated, user-adapted thematic guided tours taking the shape of rooted, oriented trees of concept presentations. The guided tour theme, structure and content are declared as a high-level view over the knowledge space.

2 The Indexing Model

Though it is quite easy for an indexer to locate concept occurrences in information resources, a trickier question is to determine the precise signification of those occurrences. The knowledge space can be used to describe the information brought by the resources about the concepts, by transforming the concept graph into a knowledge unit graph, thus allowing the indexer to build knowledge unit indexes from concept occurrence indexes.

We consider a knowledge space modeled in RDF [5] as a graph where nodes represent concepts or literals, and arcs represent concept attributes and relations. Each concept has a unique type, while each relation or attribute has a label. An equivalent representation of this concept graph is obtained by reifying each RDF statement as described in [5]. It results in a new graph where nodes represent concepts, statements or literals, and arcs are labeled subject, predicate and object. We call this graph the *knowledge unit graph*, as its nodes can be seen as knowledge units, i.e. small pieces of domain knowledge. In the following, we will talk about the *knowledge units associated to a concept* to refer to the nodes of the knowledge unit graph representing the concept itself, or any statement having the concept as subject or object. This includes statements representing concept attributes, and statements representing relations with other concepts.

The knowledge unit graph allows the indexer to produce an accurate, fine-grained description of the resource subject, by enumerating the knowledge units presented in the resource. The description of the resource subject in terms of knowledge units is called its *knowledge unit index*.

3 The Content Unit Model

The content unit model aims at recursively assembling resources in larger units, until it results in a coherent and complete concept presentation. A content unit is authored by a content producer who selects and organizes the resources related to a given concept (i.e. the resources indexed by associated knowledge units). It summarizes all the possible versions of the concept presentation, adapted to different contexts. It is based on two composition principles, one to represent alternative versions of the content, and one to represent logical transitions. The recursive nature of content units composition facilitates content reuse and update.

There are three types of content units (CU), namely *atomic CUs*, *sequence CUs* and *alternative CUs*. An atomic CU contains a single resource, while the two others contain a list of content units. An alternative CU represents a possible choice between its sub-elements[1]. A sequence CU represents an ordered aggregation of its sub-elements.

A content unit has different possible realizations. The *realization* of a content unit is the sequence of resources obtained by choosing one sub-element for each alternative content unit. The knowledge unit index of a realization is calculated automatically as the union of the indexes of the resources composing the realization. This index serves as a description of the realization subject.

Each concept of the knowledge space is associated a content unit. The different realizations of the same content unit differ by their indexes, i.e. the knowledge units they present about the concept. The choice of a realization to present a concept depends on the context, expressed in terms of knowledge units to be presented. The next section explains how concept presentations are contextualized in a guided tour to reflect the guided tour theme, ensure local coherence and avoid redundancies.

4   The Thematic Guided Tour Model

Thematic guided tours are generated dynamically from a specification, following a two-step process. First, the guided tour structure is constructed by querying the knowledge unit graph. Second, a content unit realization is chosen for each concept presentation, taking into account the presentation context.

4.1   Guided Tour Specification

A thematic guided tour specification can be described[2] as a rooted tree where a node represents a set of concepts of the domain, and an arc represent a transition from one set of concepts to the other. The set of concepts described by a node is defined by a concept type, and optionally by restrictions on concept attribute values. Moreover, the set may be ordered following values of an attribute. Arcs of the specification are used to connect concepts of two sets whenever they are connected in the domain model.

Fig. 1 shows an example of guided tour specification. The theme of the guided tour could informally be expressed as "the painters of the 20th century ordered by birthdates, the painters who influenced them, their paintings ordered by style and the museum where they are exhibited if the museum is located in France".

4.2   Guided Tour Structure

The guided tour structure is generated by applying the specification to the domain model. Incomplete paths are allowed in structure generation. The resulting guided tour structure is a rooted tree of concepts, organized in layers of concepts of the same type. If specified, concepts of a same layer are ordered according to the specification.

---

[1] Optional content is represented as an alternative between a content unit and an empty atomic content unit.

[2] The guided tour specification format and the guided tour generation process are not fully described due to a lack of space.

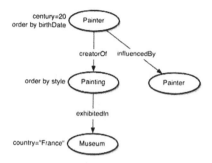

Fig. 1. Guided tour specification

Figure 2 presents a possible guided tour obtained from the specification of Fig. 1. As each concept is presented only once in the guided tour, it has a unique position in the guided tour structure. Thus, hyperlinks are used to represent internal references when necessary. They are represented in Fig. 2 as dotted arrows.

The guided tour structure is presented to the user as a hierarchical table of contents where each entry is a concept presentation. The table of contents acts both as a navigation tool, and as an overview of the global coherence of the guided tour, thus improving user orientation and understanding [4].

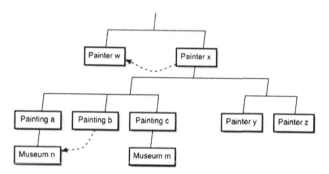

Fig. 2. Guided tour structure

4.3   Guided Tour Content

In addition to constructing the guided tour structure, the guided tour generation process also selects the knowledge units to be included in the guided tour. Those units are the selected concepts, the concept attributes used to restrict and order the concepts, and the relations used to link concept presentations. The *presentation context* of a concept is the set of knowledge units associated to the concept, selected by the guided tour generation process, and not yet presented. To present a concept, the system dynamically chooses the realization of the corresponding content unit whose subject best fits the presentation context. The "ideal" realization, if available, presents exactly the knowledge units defined in the presentation context.

For example, the knowledge units associated to MuseumN of Fig. 2 and selected during guided tour generation are 1: MuseumN, 2: (MuseumN, country,

"France"), 3: (PaintingA, exhibitedIn, MuseumN), and 4: (PaintingB, exhibitedIn, MuseumN). As knowledge units 3 and 4 are also associated to PaintingA and PaintingB respectively, they may also be used to present
those concepts. So the presentation context of MuseumN is composed of knowledge
units 1 and 2, and possibly 3 and 4, depending on user navigation and on the content
unit realizations available to present PaintingA and PaintingB.

To summarize it, the content generation process takes into account four factors to
contextualize a concept presentation: the theme of the guided tour (through the specification), the formal knowledge about the concept (through domain model querying),
the resources available to present it (through the choice of a realization), and user
knowledge/navigation. Contextualizing a presentation is useful to stick to the guided
tour theme, but also to improve local coherence [4], as it helps the user understand the
relationships between a concept and its neighbors in the structure. Finally, previous
presentations are taken into account to avoid presenting twice the same knowledge
unit.

5 Conclusion

The models presented above (indexing model, content unit model and guided tour
model) constitute three of the four main building bricks of an open, time-evolving,
multi-author AHS that can easily be coupled to a community web portal. The last
brick, namely the profile model, is quite orthogonal to the others, and was omitted for
the sake of concision. Another issue not explored here and subject of future work is
how to choose a guided tour from user goals expressed in terms of target knowledge
units.

The benefits of the approach are two fold. From the author point of view, the distinction between resources, content units and itineraries offer good opportunities of
content reuse and collaborative work. From the user point of view, guided tours are a
source of tailored and well-structured information to discover a knowledge domain.

References

1. Brusilovsky P., 'Developing Adaptive Educational Hypermedia Systems: From Design
   Models to Authoring Tools', in "Authoring Tools for Advanced Technology Learning Environments", Tom Murray, Stephen Blessing, Shaaron Ainsworth Ed., Kluwer, November
   2003.
2. Constantopoulos P., Christophides V., Plexousakis D.: Semantic Web Workshop: Models,
   Architectures and Management. SIGMOD Record 30(3): 96-100 (2001)
3. Steinacker, A. et al., 'Dynamically generated tables of contents as guided tours in adaptive
   hypermedia systems'. Educationnal Multimedia/Hypermedia and Telecommunications,
   1998, Proceedings of ED-MEDIA/ED-TELECOM'99, 1999.
4. Thüring, M. et al., 'Hypermedia and cognition: Designing for comprehension', in
   'Communication of the ACM', Vol. 38, No. 8, pp. 57-66, 1995.
5. Resource Description Framework model and syntax, W3C recommandation,
   http://www.w3.org/TR/REC-rdf-syntax.

A Fuzzy Set Based Tutoring System
for Adaptive Learning

Sook-young Choi[1] and Hyung-jung Yang[2]

[1] Dept. of Computer Education of Woosuk University
490 Hujong-ri Samrae-up Wanju-kun Chonbuk 565-701, Korea
sychoi@core.woosuk.ac.kr
[2] K-Tech Multimedia DB Research Institute
Hjyang0225@yahoo.co.kr

Abstract. This paper proposes a web-based adaptive tutoring system based on fuzzy set that provides learning materials and questions dynamically according to students' knowledge state and gives advices for the learning after an evaluation. For this, we construct a fuzzy level set considering the importance degree of learning goals, the difficulty degree of learning materials, and the relation degree between learning goals and learning materials. Using the fuzzy level set, our system offers learning materials and questions adapted to individual students. Moreover, a result of the test is evaluated with fuzzy linguistic variable.

1 Introduction

The adaptive instruction system is capable of adapting to the individual, which could provide learners with adaptable learning methods and learning materials considering the learning characteristics of each learner such as learning environment, learning goal and degree of previous learning.

To develop an adaptive instruction system, we integrate intelligent instruction technique based on fuzzy set and adaptive technique based on hypermedia.

Since fuzzy concept could effectively deal with uncertain, uncompleted and ambiguous information and support rational decision and inference through it, many studies using fuzzy concept have been performed in the various fields like decision and information classification [2, 3]. Especially, it is very difficult to evaluate students' knowledge in the education field. That is, the investigated data to evaluate learners' ability may not precise and include ambiguous data, thus it may be a hard work to evaluate it. To solve these problems, some work to use fuzzy concept have been developed [4-6].

In this paper, we propose an adaptive instruction system that provides individual learning materials and questions adapted to the learning characteristics of each student using fuzzy set, and gives advices for learning after fuzzy evaluation.

2 Fuzzy-Based Adaptive System

Our system is comprised of five different modules (see Fig. 1). The Learning-information-collection module monitors and handles learner's responses during learn-

W. Nejdl and P. De Bra (Eds.): AH 2004, LNCS 3137, pp. 389–392, 2004.
© Springer-Verlag Berlin Heidelberg 2004

ing process. Learning-achievement-evaluation module evaluates the learners' learning achievement using learning information and test results. Fuzzy-based-learning -management module constructs and manages fuzzy sets by level of each item to provide learning materials adapted to the learning level of each learner. Learning-materials-generation module provides learning materials and test items according to learners' learning state and level.

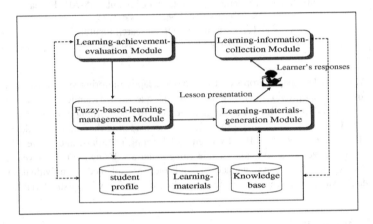

Fig. 1. Architecture of our system

To provide learning materials adapted to the knowledge level of each learner, we classified the knowledge level of each learner as follows.

Definition 1. Level set of learners' knowledge, L_s is defined into five steps as follows

$L_s = \{ \text{poor, basic, moderate, high, excellent} \}$

The lowest step *poor* in the level set means that the learning level is very low thus the system advises a student to learn prerequisite learning materials than current learning materials. *Excellent* means the highest level.

Table 1. Classification criterion of learning materials by learners' knowledge level

Factor Level	LT_I_{deg}	$LT\_F\_R_{deg}$	F_I_{deg}
basic	*most important*	*Most related*	*Easy*
moderate	from *most important* to *more important*	from *most related* to *more related*	from *easy* to *medium*
high	from *most important* to *more or less important*	from *most elated* to *more or less related*	from *medium* to *difficult*
excellent	from *most important* to *less important*	From *most elated* to *less related*	*Difficult*

It is necessary to design the domain knowledge structurally for learner-adaptive tutoring system. In order to support learning by level, our system importance degree of learning goals(LT_I_{deg}), the relation degree between learning goals and frames(LT_

F_R$_{deg}$), and difficulty degree of frames(F_D$_{deg}$) thus provides differently according to the learner's level. Table 1 shows the classification criterion of learning materials by level. However, they are fuzzy sets of which boundary is uncertain and are defined by each membership function. The following is a definition of fuzzy set by membership function

Definition 2. A Fuzzy set F in a classical universe of discourse U is characterized by the following membership function

$$\mu_F: U \rightarrow [0,1]$$

Where, $\mu_F(u)$ for each $u \in U$ denotes the grade of membership of u in the fuzzy set F.

Based on the above definition, we can write

$$F = \{ \mu_F(u_1)/u_1, \ \mu_F(u_2)/u_2, \ \ldots, \ \mu_F(u_n)/u_n \} \ for \ all \ u_i \in U, \ 1 \leq i \leq n$$

This membership function is used to define level sets of each item for learning materials adapted to learner' level as described in Table 1.

Definition 3. Let $L_c = \{$ *excellent, high, moderate, basic*$\} \subset L_s$ be level set, lt be learning goal, lt_i_{deg} be importance degree of learning goal. Then fuzzy level set by the importance degree with threshold value, α is defined as follows.

$$LT(l)_\alpha = \{ \ lt \ | \ \mu_l \ (lt\_i_{deg}) \geq \alpha, \ l \in L_C \ \}$$

Definition 4. Let f be frame, $lt\_f\_r_{deg}$ be relation degree of learning goal and frames. Then fuzzy level set of ordered tuple consisting of learning goal and frame by the relation degree with threshold value, α is defined as follows.

$$LT\_F(l)_\alpha = \{ \ (lt, f) \ | \ \mu_l(lt\_f\_r_{deg}) \geq \alpha, \ l \in LC \ \}$$

Definition 5. Let f_d_{deg} be the difficulty degree. Then fuzzy level set by the difficulty degree with threshold value, α is defined as follows.

$$F(l)_\alpha = \{ f \ | \ \mu_l(f\_d_{deg}) \geq \alpha, \ l \in LC \ \}$$

The final frame set provided according to the level of learner is composed as follows.

Definition 6. Let $l \ \square \ L_c$, for each $i\_\alpha, r\_\alpha, d\_\alpha$ be threshold value of the importance degree, relation degree, and difficulty degree respectively. Then final frame set $C(l)_{\alpha'}$ provided according to learner's level is composed as follows.

$$C(l)_{\alpha'} = \{ f \ | \ lt \in LT(l)_{i\_\alpha}, \ (lt,f) \in LT\_F(l)_{r\_\alpha}, \ f \in F(l)_{d\_\alpha} \}$$
$$Where \ \alpha' = (\ i\_\alpha, \ r\_\alpha, \ d\_\alpha)$$

For example, if a learner's level is high and the threshold value is 0.7, learning goals whose membership value of importance degree to learner's level set is over 0.7 are first selected. It means that the learning goals are ranged from *most important* to *more or less important*. Then frames are selected when the membership value of relation degree between the learning goals and frames is over the threshold value(from *most elated* to *more or less related)*. Finally, the frames whose membership value of difficulty to learner's level is the over threshold(from *medium* to *difficult)* are provided to the learner. That is, in case that learner's level is high, the system provides various and deep learning materials to include nearly all learning goals and in case that learner's level is low, the system provides only very important and easy learning materials.

The achievement degree of learning materials for each learner can be estimated on the basis of evaluation result of a test, and are obtained by the membership degree that questions belong to each level and whether the answers of questions are correct or not.

The knowledge level of each learner is determined depending on the level of question for test and the result of its evaluation. We defined rules to determine the level of each learner.

3 Conclusion

In this paper, we presented a web-based adaptive tutoring system based on fuzzy set. According to the evaluation of the level of learner's knowledge by fuzzy evaluation, our system provides learners with the learning materials and questions by fuzzy set. Using fuzzy concept for adaptive tutoring system makes effectively deal with the vague factors appeared in the learning and instruction process. However, most other systems have not considered providing learning materials depending on the evaluation of learner's level on the basis of fuzzy concept.

Experiments have been conducted to evaluate the behavior of the proposed model in adapting the lesson of a course. The result has been obtained using educational materials developed for a chapter of mathematic of middle school. The performance of the proposed approach has been evaluated by students and teachers in middle school and has been characterized as reliable.

References

1. Brusilovsky, P.: Adaptive Educational System on the World Web: A Review of Available Technologies, www-aml.cs.umassedu/stern/websits/itsworkshop/brusilovsky.html
2. Bellman, R. E and Zadeh, L.A.: "Decision-making in a fuzzy environment," Management Science, Vol. 17, No. 4, (1970) 141-146
3. Ebert, C.:Fuzzy Classification for Software Criticality Analysis, Expert System with Application, 11(3), (1996) 323-342
4. Weon, S., Kim, J.: Learning Achievement Evaluation Strategy using Fuzzy membership Function, 31th ASEE/IEEE Frontiers in Education Conference, (2001) 19-24
5. C. K.:Using Fuzzy Numbers in Educational Grading System, Fuzzy Set and Systems, 83(3), (1996) 311-324.
6. Panagiotou, M and Grigoriadou, M.: An Application of Fuzzy Logic to Student Modeling, Proc. of the IFIP World Conference on Computers in Education, Birmigham, (1995)

Offering Collaborative-Like Recommendations When Data Is Sparse: The Case of Attraction-Weighted Information Filtering

Arnaud De Bruyn[1], C. Lee Giles[2], and David M. Pennock[3]

[1] ESSEC Business School, Avenue Bernard Hirsch B.P. 105,
95021 Cergy-Pontoise Cedex, France
debruyn@essec.fr
[2] School of Information Sciences and Technology, Penn State University,
001 Thomas Building, University Park, PA 16802
giles@ist.psu.edu
[3] Yahoo! Labs, 74 N. Pasadena Ave., 3rd floor, Pasadena, CA 91103
david.pennock@overture.com

Abstract. We propose a low-dimensional weighting scheme to map information filtering recommendations into more relevant, collaborative filtering-like recommendations. Similarly to content-based systems, the closest (most similar) items are recommended, but distances between items are weighted by attraction indexes representing existing customers' preferences. Hence, the most preferred items are closer to all the other points in the space, and consequently more likely to be recommended. The approach is especially suitable when data is sparse, since attraction weights need only be computed across items, rather than for all user-item pairs. A first study conducted with consumers within an online bookseller context, indicates that our approach has merits: recommendations made by our attraction-weighted information filtering recommender system significantly outperform pure information filtering recommendations, and favorably compare to data-hungry collaborative filtering systems.

1 Introduction

Today, the ability to offer relevant recommendations to online visitors is a critical feature for most commercial websites, and many efforts have been dedicated to develop recommender systems suitable for this task.

Among those methods, *collaborative filtering* draws on an extensive database of consumers' ratings, preferences or past purchases to predict a visitor's affinity for items, based on comparisons to other consumers with similar tastes [1]. Another approach, *information filtering*, relies on item similarities and distance metrics across items to make recommendations.

The literature usually acknowledges the superiority of collaborative filtering over information filtering, while recognizing its vulnerability to information scarcity. Several algorithms have been proposed to combine the two [2-4], or to balance recom-

W. Nejdl and P. De Bra (Eds.): AH 2004, LNCS 3137, pp. 393–396, 2004.

mendations made by both systems using statistical inference [5] or by measuring the relative data availability and effectiveness of the two methods [6]. Rarely, however, has the literature reported how collaborative and information filtering algorithms might yield fundamentally similar recommendations, and how this interdependency might be leveraged to improve the quality of the recommendations made when data is sparse.

Our goals in this paper are (a) to integrate information filtering and collaborative filtering into a unique, conceptual framework of spatial preferences, and (b) to draw on this framework to propose and test with real users a mapping procedure that is able to provide collaborative-like recommendations using an adapted version of an information filtering algorithm.

2   Information and Collaborative Recommendation Spaces

When one browses books at Amazon.com, for instance, recommendations appear to be closely related in terms of content to the current item; although the underlying recommender system is built on a collaborative filtering algorithm, it is more likely to recommend similar than dissimilar items, even though the algorithm does not draw on similarity metrics to make recommendations. However, anecdotal evidence also suggests that, regardless of items' similarities, collaborative filtering recommends certain items (i.e., bestsellers) more often.

Let's note Ω the space of information filtering recommendations and Ω' the space of collaborative recommendations. Each point in the space represents an item. Items' coordinates are similar in Ω and Ω', and similarly to Ω, closer items in Ω' are more likely to be recommended. However, we represent distance metrics in Ω' (noted d') as follows:

$$d'(X_i, X_j) = \frac{d(X_i, X_j)}{a_j}, a_j > 0 : \forall j ,$$ (1)

where d represents the *distance* in Ω, and a_j represents an *attraction* index, an abstract measure of marketplace's preferences for X_j.

The measure d is not a proper distance metric anymore; if $a_i > a_j$, then $d'(X_i, X_j) > d'(X_j, X_i)$, and those items that have high attraction indexes are closer to all other items in the space, hence are more likely to be recommended.

If this model were an appropriate approximation of the truth, it would be possible to map an information filtering recommendation space into a collaborative recommendation space by choosing adequate measures of $a_i : \forall i$, while being less sensitive to information scarcity.

3   Empirical Investigation

We built a list of 6,000 business-related bestseller books, downloaded collaborative filtering recommendations made by Amazon.com, and built our own information filtering recommender system, based on the *TFIDF* scheme [7]. We used the popular *cosine* distances to compute similarities among items.

For the purpose of this work, we computed the *attraction* indexes a_i as follows:

$$a_i = 1 + \ln\left(\frac{1+\frac{c_i}{\bar{c}}}{1+\frac{s_i}{\bar{s}}}\right), \tag{2}$$

where c_i is the number of times X_i was recommended by collaborative filtering; s_i is the number of items that are very similar to X_i, i.e., that pass a certain similarity threshold (≥ 0.6); and $\bar{c}$ and $\bar{s}$ are the average values of c_i and s_i in the database.

It follows that, everything being equal, the more an item is recommended by collaborative filtering, the higher its attraction index. The denominator is a correction for uniqueness.

We offered book recommendations to 28 undergraduate business students, based on an initial book selection, and asked them to rate each recommendation on a seven-point scale.

Recommendations included collaborative filtering, information filtering, attraction-weighted information filtering, and random recommendations (included as a control group), representing a total of 737 book recommendations. Fig. 1 shows the average ratings obtained for each recommender systems as a function of respondents' self-reported expertise.

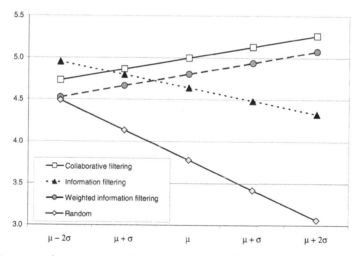

Fig. 1. Average ratings (regression lines) obtained by different recommender systems, as a function of respondents' expertise. μ=average expertise; σ=standard deviation

Respondents with very low expertise (i.e., μ-2σ, average expertise minus two standard deviations) give similar ratings to all methods: they cannot discriminate between thoughtful and random recommendations. Respondents with very high expertise (μ+2σ), on the other hand, strongly prefer collaborative and weighted information filtering recommendations, value pure information filtering recommendations significantly less, and give very low ratings to random recommendations. The fact that attraction-weighted information filtering is appreciated by expert respondents and achieves only marginally-lower ratings than collaborative filtering, is a very promising result, and seems to underline the added value of the mapping procedure we developed.

4 Discussion and Conclusions

We proposed a mapping procedure to conceptually link information filtering and collaborative filtering within a spatial model of preferences. Our assumption was that, by taking a spatial representation of similarity-based preferences (where the closest points represent the best recommendations), and by weighting each item by an appropriate *attraction* index to make the most preferred items 'closer' to all the others items in the recommendation space, it would be possible to improve information filtering recommendations. The results of a study conducted with real users showed promising results.

References

1. Resnick, Paul and Hal R. Varian (1997), "Recommender systems," Communications of the ACM, 40(3): 56–58.
2. Balabanovic, Marko and Yoav Shoham (1997), "Fab: Content-Based and Collaborative Recommendations," Communications of the ACM, 40 (3), 66-72.
3. Basu, Chumki, Haym Hirsh, and William Cohen (1998), "Recommendation as Classification: Combining Social and Content-Based Information in Recommendation," in Proceedings of the Fifteenth National Conference on Artificial Intelligence: AAAI.
4. Good, Nathaniel, J. Ben Schafer, Joseph A. Konstan, Al Borchers, Badrul Sarwar, Jon Herlocker, and John Riedl (1999), "Combining Collaborative Filtering with Personal Agents for Better Recommendations,".
5. Popescul, Alexandrin, Lyle H. Ungar, David M. Pennock, and Steve Lawrence (2001), "Probabilistic Models for Unified Collaborative and Content-Based Recommendation in Sparse-Data Environments," in Proceedings of the Seventeenth Conference on Uncertainty in Artificial Intelligence, Morgan Kaufmann (Ed.). San Francisco.
6. Claypool, Mark, Anuja Gokhale, Tim Miranda, Pavel Murnikov, Dmitry Netes, and Mathew Sartin (1999), "Combining Content-Based and Collaborative Filters in an Online Newspaper," in Proceedings of ACM SIGIR Workshop on Recommender.
7. Salton, G. (1991), "Developments in Automatic Text Retrieval," Science, 253, 974-79.

Using Concept Maps for Enhancing Adaptation Processes in Declarative Knowledge Learning

Fabien Delorme, Nicolas Delestre, and Jean-Pierre Pécuchet

Laboratoire PSI – INSA de Rouen
Place Emile Blondel - BP 08
F-76131 Mont-Saint-Aignan Cedex
{fabien.delorme,nicolas.delestre,jean-pierre.pecuchet}
@insa-rouen.fr

Abstract. This article deals with adaptation techniques in the field of declarative knowledge learning. After explaining how concepts can be represented, it introduces a learner evaluation technique based on a concept maps analysis. The way an epistemic learner model can be made from this evaluation is then proposed. Finally, adaptation techniques based on this model are presented. With this method, different adaptation schemes can be applied to the document depending on the learner's errors.

1 Introduction

The educational field is an interesting area for Adaptive Hypermedia. Despite their pedagogical limitations, static hyper-documents are often used as learning resources. Proposing learners documents adapted to their prior knowledge and to difficulties they meet in learning new concepts would be better. Several tools based on adaptive hypermedia for declarative knowledge learning already exist [1]. However, these tools are often based on a very simple learner model, thus limiting the adaptation capabilities. After explaining why we chose to promote conceptual learning as opposed to rote learning, this article explains how concepts can be represented and how the learner evaluation can take place. Then, adaptation techniques based on the learner model are proposed. Several techniques belonging to different categories are proposed, each one corresponding to a class of situation that can be met during the evaluation process.

2 Adaptive Hypermedia Based on Conceptual Learning

Our teaching strategy is based on conceptual learning, not on rote learning [2]: the learner's goal is to build knowledge, not to acquire static information. Thus, a classical Overlay representation [3] may not be satisfying: stating whether the learner masters or not a given unit of knowledge does not bring enough information for the adaptation. Knowing *why* the learner does not master a concept's definition would be better than just knowing he does not master it.

Thus, the way the document is adapted depends on the category of the learner's error, as presented in Sect. 3.2.

W. Nejdl and P. De Bra (Eds.): AH 2004, LNCS 3137, pp. 397–400, 2004.

2.1 Barth's Definition of Concepts

In [4], Barth proposes a framework for defining concepts in a learning context, based on Bruner's works. A concept can be decomposed in three related parts : a label, essential attributes (i. e. conditions that must be checked for a phenomenon to be an instance of the concept), and concrete instances. For example, the square concept would have the label "square", its essential attributes would be "is a geometric figure", "has four edges", "edges have the same length", and "at least two edges are perpendicular". Finally, its examples would be a set of concrete squares.

Thus, knowing what a concept is means being able to give its definition, i. e. associating the right attributes with a given label. We must insist on the fact that *nothing but all* the essential attributes should appear in the definition the learner gives. Any other definition should be considered partially wrong. For example, not mentioning the attribute "edges have the same length" would imply any rectangle to be considered as a square. In the same way, adding the attribute "edges are parallel with one of the axes" would imply some squares not to be recognized.

Pedagogical justifications for this approach can be found in [4].

2.2 Defining Concepts Using Concept Maps

A concept can be defined in plain text, or alternatively by the way of concept maps [5], each attribute linking the defined concept with one or more other concepts. For example, the attribute "a square is a geometric shape" can be represented as a link labeled "is a" between the concepts "square" and "geometric shape".

The learner is thus proposed to define concepts by the way of concept maps. Asking him to draw concept maps instead of writing plain text enables an easiest automated analysis. To do so we developed a concept map drawing software called *DIOGEn*. With this software, the learner is led during the concept mapping process. In *DIOGEn*, concepts and links the learner can use are based on a conceptual graph (CG) support [6]: concepts and links to use are previously fixed, they are hierarchically organized. In the same way, links are typed: some link types cannot be used for linking any kind of concepts, but only a given subset of them. Constraining the learner freedom in adding his own concepts and linking the way he wants can be seen as a limitation. However, experimentations we led shown that, when they are given enough concept and link types to draw maps, learners do not often use features letting them add new ones.

Software other than *DIOGEn* can be used as concept mapping tools, but none of them leads the learner in drawing concept maps the way we want.

3 Learner Modeling and Document Adaptation

When analyzing concept maps, different prototypical situations can be observed :

1. the learner did not make any map,
2. he made a correct map,
3. the map he made gives the definition from another concept: he mismatched these concepts,

4. the map he made misses a few essential attributes,
5. the map he made contains attributes that do not belong to the definition.

Each of these situations should be detected during the evaluation process and then imply a specific treatment during the adaptation process. The way an epistemic learner model can take these situations into consideration is described in Sect. 3.1, while the adaptation techniques are presented in Sect. 3.2.

3.1 Concept Maps Analysis

As we said in Sect. 2.2, concept maps are very close from CG. It is then very easy to represent them with CG.

Thus, what we want is to compare the CG the learner drew with the one the teacher made as a reference: the learner's graph is intended to be as close from the reference graph as possible. Since we also want to check the learner does not mismatch the concept he is defining with another one, we will also compare his graph with the reference graphs of other concepts. To do so, we need a comparison method to find, in a set of CG, which one is the closest from a given graph – in our situation, the learner's graph. Two methods are currently under development, the one adapted from Genest's works [7] and the other one based on Bayesian networks. Because of their lack of maturity, they will not be discussed in this paper.

Knowing which of the reference graphs is the closest from the learner's one then lets the system determine the epistemic learner model: if the closest graph is another concept's one, then we are in situation 3. If the closest graph is the empty one (a graph containing no concept and no link), then the situation is the first one. If the closest graph is the right one, then checking which attributes appear on the learner's graph lets the system determine whether the situation is the number 2., the number 4. or the number 5.

Now we made the epistemic model, we are able to make pertinent adaptations to the document.

3.2 Possible Adaptation Techniques

As we said, each of the situation we introduced above should imply a specific treatment, except if the map drawn by the learner is considered as correct. For each of these situations, at least one specific adaptation technique can be applied. However, each situation could bring many different adaptation mechanisms.

No Map Was Made. If no map was made by the learner, he obviously did not understand the lesson at all. The content of the document should then be remodeled: new didactic items should be applied, and more precisely new examples should be proposed. If possible, a new presentation of the definition should be proposed.

Mismatch Between Label and Definition. If the learner mismatched two concepts, i. e. if he defined one concept with the attributes of another one, it is important to show him the differences between these two concepts. Thus, he will be presented the name and examples of the concept he actually defined. The differences between this concept and the one the learner was supposed to define will also be emphasized in the definition.

Essential Attributes Were Forgotten. If the learner forgot essential attributes, it is possible to show him examples of other concepts checking all of the attributes he gave, proving him that the attributes he gave are not sufficient to define the concept. For example, if the learner did not mention a square's edges have the same length, showing him rectangles will prove him that an attribute is missing.

Non-essential Attributes Were Added. On the contrary, if the learner added undesired attributes, showing him examples of the concept that do *not* check these non-essential attributes will prove him that they are not essential. For example, if the learner states that a square's sides are always parallel with the axes, the system should show him squares oriented differently and tell him these are *actually* squares, thus making the wrong attribute obsolete for the learner.

4 Conclusion and Future Work

Some experimentations of *DIOGEn* already took place in the frame of computer science lessons in an engineer school. The epistemic model generation and the adaptation techniques are currently under development and cannot be discussed further yet.

References

1. Delestre, N.: METADYNE: un Hypermédia Adaptatif et Dynamique pour l'Enseignement. PhD thesis, Universite de Rouen (2000)
2. Ausubel, D.P.: The Psychology of Meaningful Verbal Learning. Grune & Stratton, New York (1963)
3. Carbonell, J.: Ai in cai: Artificial intelligence in computer-assisted instruction. IEEE Transactions on Man-Machine Systems **11-4** (1970) 190–202
4. Barth, B.M.: L'apprentissage de l'abstraction. Retz, Paris (1987)
5. Novak, J.D., Gowin, D.B.: Learning how to learn. Cambridge University Press (1984)
6. Sowa, J.: Conceptual Structures: Information Processing in Mind and Machine. Addison-Wesley (1984)
7. Genest, D.: Extension du modèle des graphes conceptuels pour la recherche d'informations. PhD thesis, Université Montpellier II (2000)

An Adaptive Tutoring System
Based on Hierarchical Graphs*

Sergio Gutiérrez, Abelardo Pardo, and Carlos Delgado Kloos

Department of Telematic Engineering, Carlos III University of Madrid, Spain
{sergut,abel,cdk}@it.uc3m.es
www.it.uc3m.es

Abstract. An adaptive tutoring system is presented based on hierarchical graphs that capture the sequencing of a set of learning objects depending on how students interact with them. The use of hierarchy allows the definition of complex transition structures over arbitrarily large sets of objects. Using this approach a tutoring tool has been designed and tested in the context of an introductory course in Computer Architecture. Experimental results clearly show the positive impact of the proposed content adaptation over how students learn concepts.

1 Introduction

One of the main advantages of Web Based Education is its ability to provide a large number of different resources to the user. There is the risk, however, of becoming *lost in cyberspace* [1]. Adaptive Educational Hypermedia is one possible technique to solve this problem by customizing the learning material to the specific needs of the user. Instead of the showing each user an identical set of documents, this material can be customized and a personal environment created for each learner [2].

Every learning experience benefits from tutoring. Tutoring maximizes the effectiveness of the learning process. There is significant research activity on the issue of tutoring applied to Web based education. Approaches range from simple content design methodologies to more sophisticated intelligent tutoring systems in which the task is performed by a program (see [3] for a survey). The usual trade off in this area is between generality and effectiveness. The more generic a tutoring system, the more difficult is to automate. Conversely, if tutoring is reduced to a specific context, automation is much more feasible while achieving an effective learning process (e.g. flight simulators).

Content sequencing is tightly coupled with the notion of content adaptation. Selecting different material is indeed a crucial aspect to adapt the learning experience to each student and make it more effective [4, 5].

The main motivation for the work presented in this document appears when these two aspects are combined: content sequencing and content adaptation. The goal is to provide a methodology that allows the sequencing of learning content to be adapted to each student individually. But an undesirable aspect appears when trying to obtain a

---

* Work partially funded by Programa Nacional de Tecnologías de la Información y de las Comunicaciones, project TIC2002-03635.

W. Nejdl and P. De Bra (Eds.): AH 2004, LNCS 3137, pp. 401–404, 2004.

highly personalized content sequencing. Courses tend to have a high number of learning objects, and designing a personalized sequencing strategy for each student quickly becomes unmanageable.

A solution for this problem has been proposed, based on *hierarchical graphs* [6]. The proposed scheme relies on a hierarchical approach.

In order to quantify the impact of such techniques in the learning experience, an experimental setting is required. For such purpose, a tool has been developed and a course module presented to the students. Experimental results in the context of an introductory course on computer architecture show the usefulness of this type of tutoring.

2   System Architecture

The concepts described in [6] have been implemented in a platform called *SIT* (System for Intelligent Tutoring). This platform provides a web based interface between the student and a set of learning objects hierarchically organized and with a transition structure defined based on conditions previously observed in the student's behavior.

In a preliminary stage, either a tutor or a content designer creates a hierarchical transition graph with respect to a set of learning objects. A set of students is then allowed to *navigate* this transition structure. The transitions are created based on a previously defined set of attributes. These attributes are updated by the platform based on the observations obtained from the interaction of the students with the different learning objects. The architecture of the system is illustrated in Fig. 1.

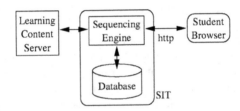

Fig. 1. System architecture

Students interact with the platform through a conventional web browser. Access to the tutor is done through a user name and password. Once a student is connected, a session is started and a learning object is selected and sent to the student. Once the student has finished working with the object, the *next step* button is pushed and a new object is sent to the student. This new object is computed based on the stored transition structure and a set of previously computed attributes. Students may disconnect at any time from the system and their working object is stored to be retrieved when a new session is started. Once the end of the hierarchical transition structure is reached, a message is shown to the student, and the session terminates.

The learning content server is depicted outside of the platform because the learning objects sent to the students do not necessarily need to be developed as part of the sequencing mechanism.

3   Experimental Setting

In order to verify if the use of the described framework is effective in a real life environment, a sample module was designed and tested in a real course and a set of experimental results were recorded. A first year course in Computer Architecture was selected for this purpose.

The module used for the experiment consisted of a total of nine *parametric exercises* [7] containing each of them a brief explanation of a concept as well as a set of related questions. Topics included integer encoding, symbolic encoding, different base conversions, numerical operations in base 2, etc. The exercises provide some feedback to the students depending on their answers.

The hierarchical graph used all nine parametric exercises each of them instantiated more than once for a total of 46 nodes. At several points of the graph, an exercise is instantiated with a given level of difficulty. Edges in the graph lead to easier or more difficult exercises depending on the number of correct answers given by the student in previous exercises.

The experiment had to be carefully designed as to capture an accurate measure of the effects of the proposed paradigm. To that end, the student group (a sample of 89 students) was randomly divided into two equally sized subgroups named *test* and *control*. Students in the test group traversed the graph previously described containing a non trivial sequencing strategy. That is, a set of learning objects were instantiated with different levels of difficulty depending on the answers previously obtained. The control group traversed a graph which contained a linear sequence of the nine exercises (no customization of objects, same sequence for each student). Finally, a pretest and a postest were inserted at the beginning and end of both graphs. The experimental results are shown in Table 1.

Table 1. Pretest and postest results for test and control groups

Exercise	Control Group			Test Group			Difference
	Pretest	Postest	Improv.	Pretest	Postest	Improv.	
1	78 %	68 %	-10 %	76 %	89 %	+16 %	26%
2	56 %	58 %	+2 %	46 %	100%	+54 %	52%
3	43 %	68 %	+25 %	59 %	89 %	+30 %	5%
4	70 %	79 %	+9 %	72 %	82 %	+10 %	1%
5	64 %	49 %	-15 %	54 %	65 %	+11 %	26%
6	60 %	30 %	-30 %	58 %	32 %	-26 %	4%
7	6 %	26 %	+20 %	3 %	54 %	+51 %	31%
8	51 %	52 %	+1 %	63 %	73 %	+10 %	9%
9	23 %	39 %	+13 %	16 %	36 %	+20 %	7%
Average	50.11 %	52.11 %	1.67 %	49.67 %	68.89 %	19.56 %	17.89 %

For each of the two groups, three columns are shown: results in the pretest, results in the postest and difference between the two tests. In all these columns the percentage of students that correctly solved the exercise is shown. The rightmost column shows the difference between the improvement detected in both groups.

The data in this table reflect several interesting aspects about the experiment. As it can be seen, comparing the second and fifth columns both groups have similar level of understanding of the concepts, an average of 50.11% (control) and 49.67% (test). As expected, solving the nine exercises and receiving certain amount of feedback in the control group produced an increase in the scores. Postest scores for the control group averaged 52.11% for an increase of 1.67%. However, for the test group, starting from a slightly lower score average in the pretest, the improvement in the postest is quite significant, going from 49.67 % to 68.89% for an increase of 19.56%.

The last column summarizes the difference *between the increases in both groups*. As it can be seen, scores in the test group improved 17.89% more than in the control group. This evidence allows to conclude that indeed the proposed framework used to adapt content to the students and sequence such content with the help of hierarchical graphs has a significant positive effect on the learning experience.

4   Conclusions and Future Work

An adaptive tutoring system based on hierarchical graphs has been presented and a platform to test this approach on a real environment has also been described. Given a set of learning objects and a hierarchical graph, each student interacts with the platform through a conventional browser. A personalized sequence is created based on how the student interacts with the learning objects. Experimental results showed a higher improvement in the results of students using a personalized sequence through this platform than in students following a linear sequence.

There are several open issues that are currently being explored. The experiment showed that producing a graph is a non trivial task that may benefit from tools specifically designed to help in such process. Also, the tool would benefit from the introduction of a student model. The conditions in the edges of the graph could be evaluated not only with respect to the environment but also based on the estimation obtained from such model.

References

1. Brusilovsky, P.: Adaptive educational hypermedia. In: International PEG Conference. (2001) 8–12
2. Cristea, A.: Authoring of adaptive and adaptable educational hypermedia: Where are we now and where are we going? In: IASTED International Conference in Web-Based Education. (2004)
3. Murray, T.: Authoring intelligent tutoring systems: An analysis fo the state of the art. Int. J. of Artificial Intelligence in Education **10** (1999) 98–129
4. Bra, P.D., Brusilovsky, P., Houben, G.: Adaptive hypermedia: From systems to framework. ACM Computing Surveys **31** (1999)
5. Bra, P.D., Brusilovsky, P., Eklund, J., Hall, W., Kobsa, A.: Adaptive hypermedia: purpose, methods, and techniques. In: Proc. of the ACM Conference on Hypertext and hypermedia. (1999)
6. Rioja, R.M.G., Santos, S.G., Pardo, A., Kloos, C.D.: A parametric exercise based tutoring system. In: Frontiers in Education Conference. (2003)
7. Brusilovsky, P., Miller, P.: Course delivery systems for the virtual university. In Tschang, F.T., Santa, T.D., eds.: Access to Knowledge: New Information Technologies and the Emergence of the Virtual University. Elsevier Science (2001) 167–206

A Brief Introduction to the New Architecture of SIETTE

Eduardo Guzmán and Ricardo Conejo

Departamento de Lenguajes y Ciencias de la Computación,
E.T.S.I. Informática, Bulevar Louis Pasteur, 35, 29071, Málaga, Spain
{guzman,conejo}@lcc.uma.es

Abstract. SIETTE is a web-based adaptive testing system released some years ago. It implements Computerized Adaptive Tests. In these tests the selection of the questions posed to students, the decision to finalize the test is accomplished adaptively. In this paper, we present the new architecture of SIETTE and some new features recently implemented.

1 Introduction

Systems that implement test-based assessment usually use heuristic-based techniques. However, there is another kind of tests, the *Computerized Adaptive Tests* (CAT) [7], which are based on a theory with underlying theoretical basis. This theory defines which questions (called *items*) must be posed to students, when the tests must finish, and how the student knowledge can be inferred from students' performance during the test. To this end, CATs use an underlying psychometric theory called *Item Response Theory* (IRT) [3]. In contrast to other testing assessment mechanisms, IRT ensures that obtained student knowledge estimations do not depend on the items used in the estimation process.

SIETTE is a web-based adaptive system for CAT generation and elicitation. In 1998, the first version of this system was developed [6]. However, from 2000 until these days, the second version of SIETTE has been re-implemented from scratch. A fully working version is available at http://www.lcc.uma.es/siette. A subject called "Demo" has been defined to show the new features of SIETTE.

It keeps the virtues of the preceding version, improves most of its drawbacks, and has added some other new features. The new implementation has been carried out because the previous architecture hindered the introduction of the new features.

In this paper, we provide a global snapshot of the new architecture of SIETTE, and some of the improvements introduced in the *student classroom* module.

2 The Architecture of SIETTE

SIETTE allows CAT construction and delivering through web interfaces. It can work as a standalone assessment tool or inside other web-based adaptive systems, as a student knowledge diagnosis tool. It is a multilingual system, currently translated to Spanish and English, but open to include other languages. Tests managed by SIETTE can be adaptive, but heuristic-based conventional tests can be also constructed. Fig. 1 collects the new architecture of the system. It comprises two main parts: the student workspace and the authoring environment.

W. Nejdl and P. De Bra (Eds.): AH 2004, LNCS 3137, pp. 405–408, 2004.
© Springer-Verlag Berlin Heidelberg 2004

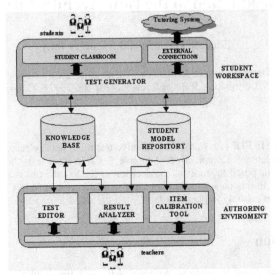

Fig. 1. Architecture of SIETTE

The *knowledge base*: It is where items, tests and topics are stored. All these contents are structured in subjects. Each subject comprises a set of topics. In turn, each topic can be decomposed into a set of subtopics following aggregation relations. Accordingly, all topics of a subject can be seen as a granularity hierarchy [5]. Items are associated to topics in such a way that if an item is related to a topic, it means it can be used to assess the topic and any parent of that topic. Tests are defined on the topics they assess, the rules for selecting items and the finalization criterion.

The *student model repository*: It stores the learner models of those that have taken a test. Learner models are probabilistic estimations of the students' knowledge is the topics of tests taken. Additionally, the students answers are also stored for statistical analysis and item calibration.

The *student workspace*: This is where students take tests. The main component of this module is the *test generator*. It delivers CATs that are suited to students' needs. Two interfaces can be used to access to generated tests:

- *Student classroom*: Here, students can take tests for self-assessment, and teachers can administer tests for grading.
- *Interface for external connections*: This interface permits SIETTE to work as a diagnosis tool in other web-based adaptive hypermedia educational systems. An propietary simple protocol [4] has been defined to this purpose.

The *authoring environment*: It is composed by a set of tools used by teachers. They allow content creation and update, as well as analyzing the performances of students that have taken tests, and the behavior of items used. It comprises:

- The *test editor*: Through this tool, teachers can define topics and subtopics, and introduce items of different kinds related to each topic or subtopic. They can also define different tests by given the rules to be used.
- The *result analyzer*: This tool presents graphically the data collected from the students' performance, like the number of students that have given a certain answer, etc.

- The *item calibration tool*: In CATs, items are characterized by means of probabilistic functions, the *Item Characteristic Curves* (ICCs). Each one of these functions predicts the behavior of students that answer the corresponding item, and are determined by a set of parameters. These parameters are inferred by calibration techniques [1]. Currently, this module is an under development.

3 The *Student Classroom*

In adaptive testing, when a student takes a test, he will be administered items one by one in terms of his knowledge level current estimation. The item selected to be administered is the one which will make the student's knowledge estimation more accurate. After the student answers the item, his knowledge level is estimated taking the response into account. This process is carried out until his knowledge estimation is accurate enough.

In SIETTE, student must provide a username and a password to access the tests. Although there are tests restricted to predefined sets of students, others can be freely accessed by simply supplying some optional personal information (e.g. name, surname, email, etc.). Students can be organized in groups defined by teachers. When the student has been authenticated, his personalized list of subjects is displayed. Three types of users profiles [4] are managed in SIETTE: teachers, learners and examinees. In terms of the student profile, the test generator adapts the test as follows:

- *Teachers*: They are responsible of test creation. Through this profile, they can have a look at their tests before any student takes them. Consequently, when a teacher accesses to the test generator tool, all the tests of his subjects (or the subjects on which he has privileges) are available.
- *Learners*: They are students that take tests for self-assessment. In this kind of tests, item correction is shown immediately after the student answers. These tests are administered with item hints and feedbacks.
- *Examinees*: They are students that take tests for academic grading. Item correction might be shown at the end or the test (or never). No item hints or feedbacks are provided.

4 Conclusions

A new version of SIETTE has been released. It is base upon a well-founded theory and generates CATs for grading or self-assessment. New features modify the adaptive behavior of Siette for the item selection, student assessment and the test finalization criteria. These criteria are based on the performance of the students while taking the tests. Furthermore SIETTE incorporates some adaptable features to the user profile, and can presents the test differently to teachers; to students that take the test for self-assessment (providing item correction, feedbacks and hints), and to those that take the test for grading.

Acknowledgement and Disclaimer

SIETTE is going to be used as a part of the project LeActiveMath, funded under FP6 (Contract. N° 507826). The content of any publication of any kind produced by the

LeActiveMath consortium is the sole responsibility of its authors and in no way represents the views of the EC and its services who cannot be held responsible for any use that might be made of data appearing therein..

References

1. Glas, C.A.W. Item calibration and parameter drift. In Van der Linden, W.J. and Glas, C.A.W. (eds.) Computerized Adaptive Testing: Theory and Practice. Kluwer Academic Publisher,(2000).
2. Guzmán, E. and Conejo, R. An adaptive assessment tool integrable into Internet-based learning systems. Méndez Vilas, A., Mesa González, J. A., and Solo de Zaldívar, I. Educational Technology: International Conference on TIC's in Education. I, pp. 139-143. 2002. Sociedad de la Información.
3. Hambleton, R.K., Swaminathan, J., and Rogers, H.J. Fundamentals of Item Response Theory. Sage publications, California, USA.
4. Kay, J. Stereotypes, Student Models and Scrutability.Proceedings of the International Conference on Intelligent Tutoring Systems (ITS 2000). (2000).
5. McCalla, G. I. and Greer, J. E. Granularity-Based Reasoning and Belief Revision in Student Models. Greer, J. E. and McCalla, G. Student Modeling: The Key to Individualized Knowledge-Based Instruction. 125, 39-62. 94. Berlin Heidelberg, Springer Verlag. NATO ASI Series.
6. Ríos, A., Millán, E., Trella, M., Pérez-de-la-Cruz, J. L., and Conejo, R. Internet Based Evaluation System. Lajoie, S. and Vivet, M. Open Learning Environments: New Computational Technologies to Support Learning, Exploration and Collaboration. Proceedings of the 9th World Conference of Artificial Intelligence and Education AIED'99. 387-394. 99. Amsterdam, IOS Press. (1999)
7. van der Linden, W.J. and Glas, C.A.W. Computerized Adaptive Testing: Theory and Practice. Kluwer Academic Publishers, Netherlands (2000).

A Reinforcement Learning Approach to Achieve Unobtrusive and Interactive Recommendation Systems for Web-Based Communities

Felix Hernandez, Elena Gaudioso, and Jesús G. Boticario

Dpto. de Inteligencia Artificial
Universidad Nacional de Educacion a Distancia
C/ Juan del Rosal 16, 28040 Madrid, Spain
{felixh,elena,jgb}@dia.uned.es

Abstract. Adaptive recommendation systems build a list of suggested links to nodes that usually cannot be reached directly from current web page. These *recommendations* are given by means of user models, where some parts of those models may be mined/learned from user's interactions with a web site.

However, user's interactions with the web site do not usually include user's interaction with the recommendation system. In other words, most of current systems adapt recommendations to users just by "looking over her shoulder". That occurs, in spite of the fact that taking into account user's behavior upon recommendation should be a main part of the adaptation mechanism, because recommendation is not transparent to a user.

Other recommendation systems interact with the user, but in an obtrusive way, making explicit requests to the user (prompting the user for rating) that are usually not followed.

In this paper we present a recommendation system "in front of the user", a system that looks directly at the user and interacts with her softly. Its key features are (i) it adapts to users by taking into account their interactions with a Web-based Communities Platform, and (ii) it adapts its own recommendations by unobtrusively taking into account the user behavior upon recommendations.

1 Introduction

Use of Web-based communities has been increasing in the last years. That may be caused because their use empowers collaborative work between their, perhaps very distant, users.

Users collaboration may be coordinated by means of, at least (could be more than one), an special user (so called expert) into each community, we call her *administrator*. However, coordination may become very difficult in large communities. There, an adaptive recommendation system would really improve collaborative and management tasks (i.e. helping some user to reach another user's comment or message).

Usually, *recommendations* are given by means of user models. In order to build those models, machine learning techniques are sometimes applied using user's interactions with the web site (see Sect. 2). Nevertheless, user's interactions with the web site do not usually include user's interaction with the recommendation system. However, user's behavior upon recommendation is needed, because recommendations are not transparent to users.

W. Nejdl and P. De Bra (Eds.): AH 2004, LNCS 3137, pp. 409–412, 2004.

Taking into account user's *real* interaction with the recommendation system is usually done by prompting users (see Sect. 2). This is often cause of unreliable responses, in the best of cases, where those responses exist.

Trying to solve those problems, we present in this paper an interactive, but unobtrusive machine learning recommendation system.

2   Previous Work

Adaptive recommendation systems attempt to infer the user's goal and interest from their browsing activity. In the last decade, several systems have applied machine learning techniques in order to identify user's goal and interest in user models [7]. They make use of those user models to generate personalized recommendations. In fact, user model is the unique source of adaptivity in most recommendation systems.

Some problems appear when trying to apply supervised machine learning to recommendation systems by means of user modeling [7]. One of the identified problems is the need for labeled data.

Labels are a kind of feedback obtained from user's interaction. For example, a current recommendation system suggests a link to a user, usually in regard to her interests. Then, and as an exemplification, if the user follows that link, the recommendation will be labeled as *positive*, hence *interesting*. Of course, this occurs by considering each recommendation as a different training example.

Therefore, feedback from labels for supervised machine learning is sometimes called *instructive* feedback [6]. Although other kind of feedback may be obtained from user's interactions, as will be showed later, most of current recommendation systems get only *instructive* feedback. Nevertheless, the correct labels may not be easily obtained from user's interaction. In this sense, looking at the way of getting labels from user's interaction, current machine learning adaptive recommendation systems can be viewed as *interactive* and *non interactive*. Current *non interactive* adaptive recommendation systems infer labels indirectly from user's browsing behavior, *interactive* ones take them by prompting user.

Letizia [2] is a *non-interactive* recommendation system that infers positive or negative evidence about user's interest by looking at her web browsing behavior. For example, following a link is a good indicator of interest in a page, but returning immediately indicates non interest. WebWatcher [3] infers the label of a recommended link as positive when it is followed from another page and negative when the link is non-visited.

It has to be stated that in non interactive systems, feedback from user is always taken indirectly, and therefore it could lead the recommendation system to wrong assumptions. As in the above example, following a recommended link could lead to label it as interesting incorrectly. Even worse, not following one could lead to label it as non interesting.

A non interactive recommendation system called ELFI [5] applies some innovative techniques in order to avoid classifying non visited documents as negative examples, considering in the learning process only positive examples of interesting documents.

Syskill&Webert [4] is an *interactive* recommendation system. To this end, labels are taken explicitly from requests of rating documents, as "hot" or "cold", to the user.

To sum up, currently, there are two main issues when developing recommendation systems. If they get information without interacting with the user they can make erroneous/bad assumptions. If they get information interacting with the user, they will not get useful information most of the time, because users hardly ever give explicit feedback [5].

Moreover, all above techniques adapt to the user only by modifying the user model that recommendation system has. However, this has to be neither the best nor the only way of adapting recommendations. In fact, following the example explained above, it might occur that a really interesting link could not be followed just because last recommendation was not successful enough. Therefore, updating user model may not be desirable in this case.

In our work, we have a mixure of two techniques: user's feedback obtained from interactions with web site, usual in current *non-interactive* recommendation systems, plus a different way of getting *unobtrusive* user's feedback from *interactions* with our recommendation system. To this end, we have a two adaptive layers recommendation system: a user modeling adaptive layer, called *user modeling subsystem* [1], and an adaptive recommendation layer formed by *recommendation agents*. These agents need to make use of the *user modeling subsystem* layer. This paper will show briefly this recommendation agents layer.

3   Interactive and Unobtrusive Recommendation Agents

Interactive recommendation agents are needed because, as started in section 1, taking into account user behavior upon recommendation should be a main part of the adaptation mechanism. In fact, a recommendation is not transparent to a user. Each recommendation has unlocated and undefined consequences. For example, making too many previous recommendations could prevent users from following the next recommendation, even to a predisposed one.

Nevertheless, forcing the user to interact after an agent recommendation has some troubles which have to do with obtrusive ways of getting user's interaction with recommendation systems.

The basic mechanism used by us in order to solve direct interaction with users is *reinforcement learning* [6]: "The reinforcement learning problem is meant to be a straightforward framing of the problem of learning from *interaction* to achieve a *goal*. The learner and decision-maker is called the *agent*. What it interacts with is called *environment*". Here, our agent's *environment* consists of the set of users who belong to the virtual community.

In reinforcement learning, every agent has a semantic meaningless objective: maximizing a numerical *sum* of rewards in time. In fact, the configuring job of administrator consists of giving sense to this reward for the adaptive task. This reward will be a non obtrusive way of getting feedback from user's recommendation system interactions.

So as to clarify, a frequent configuration is as follows: each time a recommendation agent makes an action different from do nothing, the agent receives a negative reinforcement. As a result of this, the administrator tells the recommendation agent that each useless recommendation has a cost for the user. However, each time a user follows a recommended link, the agent receives a positive reinforcement. Moreover, the more the user visits the recommended link the more reinforcement the agent may get, perhaps, distinguishing between having just a look at recommendation and a real interest in it. Consequently, reward does not give the agent a meaning of interest or disinterest in a recommendation, what is more, the lack of reward doesn't mean lack of interest either: reward is just the way of telling the agent when it is doing a good or a bad job.

Moreover, reward is never assigned to a concrete recommendation, but to the whole *policy* of recommendations. In other words, and recalling second paragraph: recommendation agent looks for maximizing a numerical *sum* of rewards in time. Therefore, when administrator assigns a positive reinforcement in a user's visit to a recommended link, she is telling the agent *what* the agent has to do globally: recommend links in order to be followed, but *not how* it should be executed.

Finally, as a kind of conclusion, it should be noticed that recommendation agent's adaptation does not proceed from updating user model.

References

1. F. Hernandez, E. Gaudioso, and J.G. Boticario. A multiagent approach to obtain open and flexible user models in adaptive learning communities. In *User Modeling*, volume 2702 of *LNAI*, pages 203–207, Johnstown, PA, USA, 2003. Springer.
2. H. Lieberman. Letizia: An agent that assists web browsing. In *Proceedings of the Fourteenth International Joint Conference on Artificial Intelligence (IJCAI-95)*, pages 924–929, Montreal, Quebec, Canada, 1995. Morgan Kaufmann publishers Inc.: San Mateo, CA, USA.
3. D. Mladenic. Personal webwatcher: Implementation and design. Technical Report IJS-DP-7472, Department of Intelligent Systems, J.Stefan Institute, Slovenia, 1996.
4. J. Pazzani, J. Muramatsu, and D. Billsus. Syskill & webert: Identifying interesting web sites. In *Proceedings of the National Conference on Artificial Intelligence, Vol. 1*, pages 54–61, 1996.
5. I. Schwab and A. Kobsa. Adaptivity through unobstrusive learning. *KI*, 3(5-9), 2002.
6. Richard S. Sutton and Andrew G. Barto. *Reinforcement Learning: An Introduction*. MIT Press, 1998.
7. G. I. Webb, M. J. Pazzani, and D. Billsus. Machine learning for user modeling. *User Modeling and User-Adapted Interaction*, 11:19–29, 2001.

GEAHS: A Generic Educational Adaptive Hypermedia System Based on Situation Calculus

Cédric Jacquiot[1], Yolaine Bourda[1], and Fabrice Popineau[2]

[1] Supélec, Plateau de Moulon, 3 rue Joliot-Curie, 91192 Gif/Yvette CEDEX, France
{cedric.jacquiot,yolaine.bourda}@supelec.fr
[2] Supélec, 2 r Edouard Belin, 57070 Metz, France
fabrice.popineau@supelec.fr
http://www.supelec.fr

Abstract. GEAHS is a platform designed to ease the development of Adaptive Educational Hypermedia, using standard formalisms. In this document, we explain the underlying principles of this platform. Genericity is achieved thanks to an adaptation engine based on situation calculus and RDF. This paper describes the main aspects of our system, as well as the use we make of situation calculus to create a simpler, more reusable adaptive hypermedia system.

1 Introduction

Many Adaptive Hypermedia Systems (AHSs) have been developed for educational purpose in the past few years. Most of them have been created for a precise purpose, and are not reusable. In other words, these systems have to be build from scratch any time one wants to develop a new teaching platform. P. Brusilowsky [1] described a methodology for creating an adaptive hypermedia. P. de Bra [2] studied the theoretic and generic ground that should be used for the creation of Adaptive Hypermedia Systems. Our goal has been threefold. First, we wanted to create an engine, based on principles close to those of AHAM [2], using standard or recommended formalisms, in order to make it as reusable as possible. Second, we wanted to provide a model both simple and powerful. We wish that as many people as possible are able to reuse our system. In order to achieve this, we also provide an extensible set of reusable adaptation rules. This way, it is possible to avoid the creation from scratch of new adaptation rules. The adaptation is provided with generic built-in rules and metadata that can be reused (and modified if necessary) by the AHS creators. Third, we wished to prove that situation calculus, introduced in [3] for adapting the semantic web, can be applied to the problem of generic adaptive hypermedia. We also wish to show that it is a satisfactory solution for the second goal we want to achieve.

Our architecture is composed of three interacting components : the learner model, designed to represent metadata about the learner (in RDF); the domain model, designed to represent metadata about the learning resources (in RDF); and the adaptation engine, composed of a set of rules as well as a situation calculus-based infering engine, which provides the adaptation (currently, we only provide link adaptation).

In Sect. 2, we will show how we use situation calculus for creating an adaptive hypermedia. In Sect. 3, we will see how we use logic to create our architecture. In Sect. 4, we will compare our situation calculus approach to the condition/action approach developed in [4].

W. Nejdl and P. De Bra (Eds.): AH 2004, LNCS 3137, pp. 413–416, 2004.
© Springer-Verlag Berlin Heidelberg 2004

2   Using Situation Calculus

Situation Calculus was first introduced in order to manage robotics problems. Nevertheless, the idea has emerged in [3] that Situation Calculus could be used for driving web applications. This way, situation calculus could help program agents that are often very complex.

Situation calculus [5] is based exclusively on FOL, i.e. deductions can be done using nothing but FOL. It is a subset of FOL to which has been added the notions of situations and actions. A situation is a group of static facts that can be evaluated at a given instant. Actions are more or less complex procedures that apply to a situation. An action can be possible or not. A set of primitive action can be given, and complex actions are built from the primitive actions (sequence, test, nondeterministic choice . . .).

An action a is made on a situation s leading to a situation s' if a is possible in situation s and if s' is the consequence of action a in situation s. Accomplishing a complex action results in accomplishing choices and sequences of primitive actions.

The predicates $poss$, do and $primitive\_action$ are predefined in situation calculus. $poss(action, situation)$ is true iff $action$ is possible in $situation$. $Primitive\_action(action)$ is true iff $action$ is a primitive action. $Do(action, situation1, situation2)$ is true iff $poss(action, situation1)$ and $action$ applied to $situation1$ leads to $situation2$.

In order to calculate the situation changes, the primitive action must be calculable, i.e. primitive actions must be defined. The fluents - the data describing a situation - must also be described. It is even the most important part, since calculating the next situation is achieved by calculating the next value of the fluents. The fluents' description gives us their new value from the action and previous situation. The way to calculate possibilities has to be given, since an action cannot be done if it is not possible.

On top of the basic situation calculus, we have added the notion of desirability. This notion is related to what a learner really needs to know to reach his objective. For example, if several documents have the current document as a common pre-requisite, they can all be possible documents to read next. But only those who are pre-requisites of the objective are really desirable.

We have worked on adapting situation calculus to our specific problem, and we found the following solution. First, we have split the possible actions into two kinds. The first kind is dedicated to the user's actions. The second kind is dedicated to the engine's actions. In a given situation, the system knows the up-to-date learner profile, the domain, and the position of the learner in the document space. This is considered to be the current situation. The system uses one type of action: displaying the links. This action does not trigger any rule. Once the possible links are displayed, the user can do actions. He/she can read the document, take a test, click on a link and so on.

3   Logic in GEAHS

Rules in GEAHS are described in FOL. First, FOL has a defined semantics. Then, in some cases, translating rules from natural language to FOL is not a difficult task. Our purpose has been to allow as many people as possible to create their own rules if they are not satisfied with the set of pre-defined rules we provide.

Rules can be written with classic FOL operators, even though it is not naturally provided in Prolog, the language we used to implement our system. In a future developpement, we intend to provide a simple interface to enter and modify the rules.

For an AHS creator, using such FOL rules can be simpler than using proprietary rules. First, if she happens to know FOL, her learning of our AH creation system will be much shorter. Then, if she already has rules written in FOL (which seems to be a natural way to express "logic" rules), she will be able to reuse them easily. Comparing these rules to other kinds of rules found in many adaptive systems, it does not seem more difficult to write FOL rules than to write rules in other formalisms. And at least these rules have a commonly-understood meaning.

We shall soon work on the problems of consistency and completion (including their tractability) of the rule sets.

As we implement the whole system in Prolog, we need all forms to be boiled down to Horn clauses in the end. Situation calculus was already implemented. We implemented the notion of desirability in the Golog program. We also created a module to allow people to write logic in its standard form. This module makes standard logic understandable by Prolog. The clauses are not transcribed into Horn clauses, but dynamically analysed. The analyse is mostly instantaneous, as the main logic operators are already parts of Prolog possibilities.

The main program is in charge of reading, writing and displaying data. It launches the Golog mechanism. This mechanism uses rules written in standard logic, which are analysed through our logic module.

In the end, all forms of logic are easily interfaced, working together in a simple way. We do have a homogeneous system, and this system's semantics are clearly defined.

4   Situation Calculus and Condition/Action

In Wu's condition/action system, the AHS creator defines a set of pairs of conditions and actions. Each time the user makes a physical action, or each time the user representation evolves, the rules' conditions are checked. If the condition is true, the corresponding action is triggered. As long as rules are triggered (possibly by other rules' consequences), their actions are applied. Rule triggering can loop. In order to be sure to achieve termination in a condition/action model, Wu and De Bra introduced restrictions to the rules that can be described using this formalism. In the end, the model they use is a transformed version of condition/action, and thus, non-standard.

In GEAHS, each time the user makes an action, the finite set of (ordered) rules is triggered. When a rule is applied, it can have consequences on other rules that come after it in the defined order, but it cannot trigger other rules. Thus, the risk for an AH creator to make up rules with no termination is reduced by the intrinsic functioning of our system. On the other hand, we did not prove yet that situation calculus is as expressive or efficient as condition/action.

5   Conclusion

GEAHS is a powerful system which allows all kinds of people - especially those who are not expert in computer science or software engineering - to create an AHS for education. All formalisms and techniques used for GEAHS are either standards/recommendations, or well-defined calculus based on FOL. This allows our system to import, export and reuse data from or to other systems and formalisms. This is a fundamental aspect in today's semantic web, if we want to be able to have fully distributed documents (coming from different sources).

Our future work will consist in several points. We wish to provide simple techniques for content and style adaptation. We also want to study the use of OWL, the Web Ontology Language for representing our data and metadata, since it provides pre-defined and useful relations. We also wish GEAHS to be able to determinate the consistency and completion of the set of rules on may create.

References

1. Brusilowsky, P.: Methods and Techniques of Adaptive Hypermedia. Adaptive Hypertext and Hypermedia. ED. Kluwer Publishing (1995) 1–43
2. De Bra, P., Houben, G-J, Wu, H.: AHAM: A Dexter-Based Reference Model for Adaptive Hypermedia. Conference on Hypertext (1999) 147–156
3. McIlraith, S.: Adapting Golog for Programming the Semantic Web. Conference on Knowledge Representation and Reasoning (2002)
4. Wu, H.: A Reference Architecture for Adaptive Hypermedia Applications. PhD Thesis, Eindhoven University of Technology, The Netherlands
5. Levesque, H., Reiter, R., Lesperance, Y., Lin F., Scherl, R.: GOLOG: A logic programming language for dynamic domains. Journal of Logic Programming **31** (1997) 59–84

Problem Solving with Adaptive Feedback

Rainer Lütticke

FernUniversität Hagen, Department of Computer Science,
Intelligent Information and Communication Systems, 58084 Hagen, Germany
Rainer.Luetticke@fernuni-hagen.de
http://pi7.fernuni-hagen.de/luetticke/

Abstract. The virtual laboratory (VILAB) supports interactive problem solving in computer science with access to complex software-tools. During the problem solving processes the learners get fast feedback by a tutoring component. This feedback based in the first version of VILAB only on intelligent error analyses of learners' solutions. Animated by the very positive results of the evaluation of this tutoring component we additionally implemented an user model. Thereby the feedback for a learner consists not only of adaptive information about his errors and performance, but also of adaptive hints for the improvement of his solution. Furthermore, the tutoring component can individually motivate the learners.

1 Introduction

We have developed an Internet-based virtual laboratory (VILAB[1]) for computer science instructing practical courses in online education at the largest German open and distance university (FernUniversität Hagen) [4]. Since summer 2002 this learning environment is in use for regular teaching.

VILAB is realised in a client-server architecture in which the Linux-based server is operated at the FernUniversität. The access to the server is managed by decentral user clients which must be connected with the Internet. Via remote-login to the server the users are directly routed to a navigation tool which is one of two user interfaces. The second user interface is a common browser opened on a client with an individual URL for every user. Via navigation tool local hypertext (e. g. problems) as well as documents out of the WWW can be selected and displayed in the browser. Complex graphical software-tools (e. g. SNNS[2] or MWR[3]) installed on the server can also be activated via navigation tool.

While the most adaptive learning environments are focused on the optimal presentation and sequencing of content VILAB is focused on problem solving like Andes, an intelligent tutoring system for physics [3]. The problems in VILAB are divided in different domains of computer science (e. g. relational data bases, neural networks, automatical natural language processing). The solutions are automatically analysed by the system and a tutoring component gives feedback for immediate improvements [3, 6]. After this the learner modifies his solution and a further analysis starts. This interaction lasts until the solution is correct.[4]

---

[1] http://pi7.fernuni-hagen.de/vilab/
[2] Stuttgart Neural Network Simulator
[3] tool for knowledge representation of multilayered extended semantic networks [4]
[4] Guided Tour: http://ki219.fernuni-hagen.de/tour_en/

W. Nejdl and P. De Bra (Eds.): AH 2004, LNCS 3137, pp. 417–420, 2004.

2 Analyses of Solutions and the Resulting Feedback

There exist different modes for the creation of the solution of a problem. For the standard tests (e. g. multiple choice test, asking for numbers, correlations, etc.) we use the WebAssign-System[5] [4]. Text areas in hypertext documents or in software-tools are used for free text (e. g. SQL queries or reformulation of semantic networks respectively). The most complex input mode of a solution is a graphic (e. g. building of neural or semantic networks) which can be created with the software-tools.

The tutoring component has a passive and an active error mode for two different kinds of problem solving support [1]. In the active mode ("interactive problem solving support") the tutoring component does not wait for the learner's final solution. If an error is interactively detected (e. g. action in a software-tool or "click" in a hypertext document leading to a wrong solution), it immediately sends information about the errors either in a newly displayed window or by graphical reactions. These reactions of the tutoring component are short, often technical, and hardly possess variants.

In the passive mode ("intelligent analysis of student solutions") the tutoring component has to identify errors from the learner's final result after he has requested for a correction or support [6]. The analysis of the learner's solution is realised by correction modules using different methods. Depending on the problem they can test the learner's solution and confront him with the consequences of his errors [6] (e. g. test of results of SQL-queries) or compare the solution with sample solution(s) by term or pattern analysis (similar to [5], but not so elaborated) or inferences. Additionally, the modules use a table with deductions from certain errors and a table with hints for understanding certain concepts and for prevention of certain errors based on experiences of teachers. Thereby the feedback of an analysis is adaptive to the individual errors.

The elements of the feedback (s. references in [4] consist of a statement about the degree of correctness of the solution, an error list, a description and explanation of errors, hints for improvement of the solution and the avoidance of errors, a listing of useful literature or lectures to derive lacking knowledge, a link to an easier problem which is connected with the actual problem, examples of similar exercises, an assessment of the learner's performance, and a motivation.

The output of an analysis is an error code with accompanying parameters. The content of these parameters is not a fixed number of possibilities, but based on the content of the learner's solution and its intelligent analysis. The error code is connected with a hypertext template including Javascript variables filled out by the parameters. The final hypertext document is copied to the individual URL of the user. This result in an automatical reload in the browser of the user managed by PHP scripts and the display of the feedback [4].

3 User Model

In winter term 2003/04 we added to the system an user model based on information collected in a data base. The elements of the model are: 1. learning type, 2. knowledge

---

[5] http://niobe.fernuni-hagen.de/WebAssign/

level, 3. solved problems in VILAB, 4. number of attempts to solve a problem, 5. distance of a learner's solution to a correct solution, and 6. the changing of this distance between two attempts. The last two elements are used for the monitoring of the learner while he is solving a problem [7]. The user model can combine information about the current state of the problem solving process (elements 4, 5, and 6) with long-term assessment of the learner's knowledge of computer science (elements 2 and 3) similar to the system Andes [3].

The learning type is determined by a multiple choice test before the learner begins to work in VILAB. The types (text oriented, examples oriented, and interaction oriented) are defined by the demands of learners on an e-learning system [2]. The knowledge level is determined by previously successful courses and result in locking problems and domains of VILAB. The distance is computed from the learner's solution to the sample solution(s) by individual measurements for every problem (e. g. number of wrong nodes and relations between nodes in semantic networks).

4   Adaptive Features Based on the User Model

Due to the "knowledge level" of a learner the system can automatically unlock problems of VILAB depending on the individual progress of problem solving. In this way, every learner gets access to problems adaptively fitting to his experience and practical background knowledge.

Including PHP code in the hypertext templates and filling PHP variables by data from the user model the feedback becomes adaptive for the learner. Depending on the values of the user model the parameters of the analysis of the learner's solution are displayed or masked, or they are modified. The input for these "display-functions" are the values of the elements of the user model. Three constraints are exemplary listed. A constraint for the display-functions is the dependency between learning type and the instruction method to improve solutions. Another constraint exists between the number of unsuccessful attempts to solve a problem, the distance of a solution to the correct solution, and the changing of this distance between two attempts on the one side and the extent and description of the error list on the other side. The content of the motivation is determined by nearly all values of the user model.

Using the models in this way the feedback is adaptive to the individual errors as well to the user's knowledge, preferences in support, and progress in solving the problem.

5   Evaluation and Perspective

Results of evaluations of VILAB without user models (40 questionnaires and informal interviews) show that the students like the kind of learning with the interactive tutoring component because the fast feedback gives the possibility to learn in "trial and error"-mode which ∼90% have used. The support of the tutoring component during the finding of the correct solution is important for ∼80% of the students. Although the component was helpful ∼40% wish a more adaptive feedback. Its motivation to find the right solution is helpful to prevent to give up the search for the right solution (∼30%). Comparing courses using VILAB and similar courses in former times without this learning environment the rate of successful finishers increases to ~50%. Additionally, from the view of the teacher learning with VILAB is connected with better results in examinations and better seminar talks. The tutoring component is so effective that newsgroups or emails to the teacher in courses with VILAB were ~50% less used.

With the implementation of the user model in VILAB and with its use in courses beginning in summer 2004 we think that we can further improve the learning success of the students. The more adaptive feedback will strengthen the positive effects of the tutoring component.

References

1. Brusilovsky, P.: Adaptive and Intelligent Technologies for Web-based Education. Künstliche Intelligenz **13(4)** (1999) 19–25
2. Ehlers, U.-D.: Quality in e-learning from a learner's perspective. In: Benrath, U. and Szücs, A. (eds.), Supporting the Learner in Distance Education and E-Learning, Proceedings of the 3rd EDEN Research Workshop, Bibliotheks- und Informationssystem der Universität Oldenburg (BIS) (2004) 130–137
3. Gertner, A.S., VanLehn, K.: Andes: A Coached Problem Solving Environment for Physics. In: Gauthier G., Frasson C., and VanLehn K. (eds.), Intelligent Tutoring Systems 2000, LNCS 1839, Springer (2000) 133–142
4. Lütticke, R., Helbig, H.: Practical courses in distance education supported by an interactive tutoring component. In: Benrath, U. and Szücs, A. (eds.), Supporting the Learner in Distance Education and E-Learning, Proceedings of the 3rd EDEN Research Workshop, Bibliotheks- und Informationssystem der Universität Oldenburg (BIS) (2004) 441–447
5. Martin, B., Mitrovic, A.: Tailoring Feedback by Correcting Student Answers. In: Gauthier G., Frasson C., and VanLehn K. (eds.), Intelligent Tutoring Systems 2000, LNCS 1839, Springer (2000) 383–392
6. Mathan, S., Koedinger K.R.: Recasting the Feedback Debate: Benefits of Tutoring Error Detection and Correction Skills. In: Hoppe, U., Verdejo, F., and Kay, J. (eds.), Artificial Intelligence in Education, Frontiers in Artificial Intelligence and Applications Vol. 97, IOS Press (2003) 13–20
7. Verdejo, M.F.: A Framework for Instructional Planning and Discourse Modeling in Intelligent Tutoring Systems. In: Costa, E. (ed.), New Directions for Intelligent Tutoring Systems, Springer (1992) 147–170

Machine Learning Methods for One-Session Ahead Prediction of Accesses to Page Categories [*]

José D. Martín-Guerrero[1], Emili Balaguer-Ballester[2],
Gustavo Camps-Valls[1], Alberto Palomares[2], Antonio J. Serrano-López[1],
Juan Gómez-Sanchís[1], and Emilio Soria-Olivas[1]

[1] Digital Signal Processing Group, University of Valencia, Spain
jose.d.martin@uv.es
[2] R & D Department, TISSAT S.A., Spain

Abstract. This paper presents a comparison among several well-known machine learning techniques when they are used to carry out a one-session ahead prediction of page categories. We use records belonging to 18 different categories accessed by users on the citizen web portal *Infoville XXI*. Our first approach is focused on predicting the frequency of accesses (normalized to the unity) corresponding to the user's next session. We have utilized Associative Memories (AMs), Classification and Regression Trees (CARTs), Multilayer Perceptrons (MLPs), and Support Vector Machines (SVMs). The Success Ratio (SR) averaged over all services is higher than 80% using any of these techniques. Nevertheless, given the numerous quantity of services taken into account, and the variability of SR among them, a balanced performance is desirable. When this issue is analysed, SVMs yielded the best overall performance. This study suggests that a prediction engine can be useful in order to customize user's interface.

1 Introduction

Prediction of users' web browsing can help to better understand end-user's behaviour on a certain web site. It may involve many further advantages for users and also for the company which develops the portal. The aim of this work is to develop and evaluate machine learning methods to predict users' web browsing. We are particularly interested in the applications of these models to a citizen portal. As a first approach, we focus on next session prediction. State-of-the-art models are benchmarked as predictive tools of page category accesses. The models used in this work are the following: Associative Memories (AMs), Multilayer Perceptrons (MLPs), Classification and Regression Trees (CARTs), and Support Vector Machines (SVMs). The data used to develop and validate the models come from records of the web portal *Infoville XXI* (http://www.infoville.es/). This web portal provides citizens with different kinds of services, related to bureaucracy, shopping or entertainment, for instance.

The rest of the paper is organized as follows. In Sect. 2, the predictive models used in this work are described briefly. Data processing is shown in Sect. 3. In Sect. 4, the

---

[*] This work has been partially supported by the research project CTIAUT2/A/03/112. The authors want to express their thanks to *Fundació OVSI (Oficina Valenciana per a la Societat de la Informació – Valencian Office for Information Society)* for providing the data used in this work.

W. Nejdl and P. De Bra (Eds.): AH 2004, LNCS 3137, pp. 421–424, 2004.

results achieved by different models are compared and analysed. We finish with the extracted conclusions and the future work in Sect. 5.

2 Predictive Models

The function of an AM is to recognize previously learned vectors, even in the case where some noise has been added. AMs only take into account local information stream. The response of each unit is determined exclusively by the information flowing through its own weight. AMs can be implemented with a single layer of computing units and *Hebbian learning*, derived from biological neurons [1], can be used.

CART is a binary decision tree algorithm [1], which has two branches in each internal node. Methodology is characterized by a pruning strategy, a binary-split search approach, automatic self-validation procedures, and a splitting criterion, which provides stable and good results. Their capabilities of knowledge discovery are also very important, since qualitative information about the structure of data can be obtained by analysing the surrogate and main splits of the tree.

The MLP is the most widely used neural network. It is composed of a layered arrangement of artificial neurons in which each neuron of a given layer feeds all the neurons of the next layer. This model forms a complex mapping from the input to the output [1]. The model is usually trained with the backpropagation (BP) learning algorithm. However, we used the Expanded Range Approximation (ERA) algorithm in order to alleviate the problem of falling into local minima [2].

An SVM is an approximate implementation of the method of structural risk minimization [1]. Basically, an SVM is trained to construct a hyperplane for which the margin of separation is maximized. SVMs have many attractive features. For instance, the solution of the quadratic programming (QP) problem [3] is globally optimized. In addition, SVMs can handle large feature spaces, can effectively avoid overfitting by controlling the margin, and can automatically identify a small subset made up of informative points, namely *support vectors* (SVs).

3 Data Processing

We used data recording accesses to the citizen web portal *Infoville XXI*. This web portal, which is supported by the Regional Government of Valencia (Spain), provides citizens with different services, from administrative services related to paperwork and payment of taxes, to leisure services, such as, entertainment for children, tourism, etc. In this work, we used records from June 2002 to February 2003.

A first preprocessing stage removed those users who presented an anomalous behaviour. Basically, they presented a great number of accesses in a short time, since they were fictitious users generated by the administrators of the portal for test purposes. Users with just one session were also removed since it was not possible to validate the predictions for them. Finally, the processed data set was formed by 5,129 users who logged in between 2 and 413 different sessions.

The second preprocessing stage was devoted to encode the data to the prediction tools. A preliminary study of the data set showed that 4,884 users ($\simeq 95\%$) accessed less than 30 times to the portal, and that only 4% of the sessions consisted of more than four accesses. This fact led us to consider only the first five accesses of each session, which would make the prediction task much more easier, and it only implied a loss of 0.7% from the overall set of accesses. Moreover, we were interested in reducing the dimensionality of the space defined by services, because a prediction in such a high dimensional space might constitute a very difficult task [4]. Therefore, we built 18 different page categories to represent 370 accessed services, as follows: fifteen categories labelled from #1 to #15 for each one of the 15 services registering the highest number of accesses (76.9% of the overall set); category #16 was formed by 12 services whose percentage of access was between 0.5% and 1% (7.5%); category #17 was formed by 33 services whose percentage of access was between 0.1% and 0.5% (8.1%); category #18 was formed by the 310 services remaining whose percentage of access was under 0.1% (7.5%).

4   Results

4.1   Prediction Setup

We developed models by using data from the current session s and the two previous sessions ($s - 2$ and $s - 1$) to carry out a one step ahead prediction (session $s + 1$). We did not take into account the clickstream sequence but only the frequency of each category to be accessed during the next session. This frequency was normalized to the unity for each session in order to adapt data to models' characteristics.

The data was transformed to patterns in order to be used for training and validating the models. The total number of patterns was 11,617. All the models used in this work were developed to avoid overfitting, hence, the data were split into three sets. A training set formed by 1,743 patterns was used to develop the models; a cross-validation set formed by other 1,743 patterns was also taken into account; and a test set formed by 8,131 patterns was used to assess the robustness capabilities of the prediction models.

4.2   Model Comparison

In order to carry out a model comparison, we transformed the frequency-based prediction in a measure of Success Rate (SR) by considering a correct prediction of a service when the error was lower than 0.1. It should be pointed out that this criterion may be overoptimistic in terms of the percentages achieved. This is because of the high number of non-accessed categories which are easily learned by the models. Therefore, it should be considered as a preliminary criterion of model comparison. High Average SRs (ASRs) are obtained for all the models, although the highest values correspond to SVMs. The values are similar for the three considered sets.

The ASRs using AMs were near 92%; it meant that the problem could be solved with high accuracy. In Fig. 1, CARTs, MLP, and SVMs are benchmarked. SRs are slightly higher for SVMs than for MLP, which are, in turn, much better than those obtained by CART. There are some categories whose prediction becomes considerably more difficult for all the algorithms (#1 and #17, for instance). The latter is particularly dramatic in the case of CARTs, since they show low SRs (around 60%) for some categories. MLP and SVMs also show this drawback but to a lesser extent.

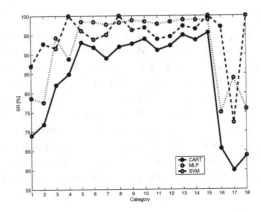

Fig. 1. Success Rates (SRs) [%] obtained by CARTs (solid line), MLP (dotted line) and SVMs (dashed line) are represented in y-axis, whereas the 18 different categories are represented in x-axis.

5 Conclusions and Future Work

This work presented a preliminary study about the feasibility of predicting users' accesses on a citizen web portal. Our preliminary study is focused on one-session ahead prediction. Achieved results show that SVMs performed best, although MLPs showed similar results. The high ASRs achieved in the prediction involve an important significance since they suggest that these tools can grasp the underlying behaviour of user's web browsing.

Our ongoing research focuses on choosing a more appropriate criterion to benchmark the model, since the one used in this work seems overoptimistic in terms of the percentages achieved. In particular, we are working in measures related to *immediate benefits*, which present the advantage that they can also be applied to other web portals; for instance, they are usual measures in e-commerce portals. Future work will be dedicated to find models capable to predict appropriately with less information than accesses from three sessions, and to predict beyond one-session ahead, as well. Results already obtained suggest that the most suitable tools for these tasks are MLP and SVMs. The final stage of this work will involve the application of these algorithms to customize user's interface in commercial software developed by Tissat, S.A.®.

References

1. Duda, R., Hart, P., Stork, D.: Pattern Classification. 2nd edn. John Wiley & Sons, NY (2000)
2. Gorse, D., Sheperd, A., Taylor, J.: The new ERA in supervised learning. Neural Networks **10** (1997) 343–352
3. Fletcher, R.: Practical Methods of Optimization. John Wiley & Sons, Inc. 2nd Edition (1987)
4. Cadez, I., D., H., Meek, C., Smyth, P., White, S.: Model-based clustering and visualization and navigation patterns on a Web site. Technical Report MSR–TR–0018, Microsoft Research, Microsoft Corporation, (2001)

Gender-Biased Adaptations
in Educational Adaptive Hypermedia*

Erica Melis and Carsten Ullrich

German Research Center for Artificial Intelligence, DFKI GmbH

1 Introduction

Studies (for instance, [1, 2]) show that there is a statistically relevant gender difference in computer usage. In this paper we address the question of what are the causes of this problem and how it can be relieved by adaptive means.

In trying to design systems that are sensitive to individual differences there is a dilemma – how can you make the system behave in a way appropriate for each individual without forcing people into stereotypes? We propose that the group characteristics can be taken as weak defaults and coupled with an adaptive mechanism to quickly take account of individual differences.

This paper starts with a summary of a study which derives a model of the mental factors that influence computer usage. Then, we refine that model and make it the basis of a Bayesian Net student model. The main section describes suggestions for Adaptive Hypermedia targeting the relevant mental factors and how adaptivity can help to avoid clichés and thus discrimination.

2 Gender Differences in Computer Usage

In [2], Dickhäuser and Stiensmeier-Pelster describe a study in which they investigate the causes of gender differences in computer usage. They derive a model which describes the internal factors and variables that influence the choice of an individual whether to use a computer.

In the model, the *attribution index* (the causes people attribute their (un)successful experiences to, e. g. personal incapability vs. computer failure) influences the *self-concept of ability* (judgment of the ability to work with a computer). The self-concept of ability determines the frequency of their *computer use*, the *value* (individual perception of value of working with a computer in a specific situation) and the *expectation* of using a computer successfully (additionally influenced by value). Value and expectation determine a person's *choice of using a computer* in a specific situation.

The values of some of the variables differ significantly between average male and female students. Generally speaking, female students have a significantly lower self-esteem with respect to their abilities in handling computers than males do (see also [3, 4]); they expect less success from an interaction with a computer, and are more likely to blame themselves in case something goes wrong. As a result, women considerably less often use a computer as a tool than men do.

---

* This publication was generated in the LeActiveMath project, funded under FP6, Cntr. 507826. The authors are solely responsible for its content.

W. Nejdl and P. De Bra (Eds.): AH 2004, LNCS 3137, pp. 425–428, 2004.

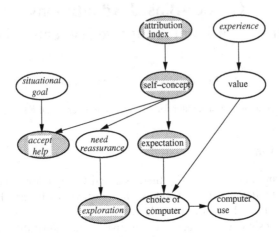

Fig. 1. Bayesian Net Student Model

3   Extended Student Model

The model provides the basis for a not yet implemented Bayesian Net student model (Fig. 1) whose nodes represent probability variables and whose arrows represent conditional dependencies of variables. The extended model contains additional variables (in italic font) because it represents mental factors relevant for educational adaptive hypermedia. Note that some new variables are behavioral rather than mental characteristics, e. g., *accept help*. The value of those non-mental probabilities can be diagnosed from behavioral symptoms when working with a learning system as opposed to mental characteristics that are diagnosed from questionnaires.

4   Consequences for Educational Adaptive Hypermedia

Using the extended model, several adaptations can take place which target those variables (marked by a dark background) that can be directly influenced.

Influencing the Failure Attribution Bias. In case of a system error it should clearly be specified that it is not the user who is to blame. This has to be announced as soon as possible, before a system failure can possibly occur.

   In e-learning, a user may have unsuccessful experiences due to her/his lack of own capability or own misconception. In particular, the problem solving process needs to be supported by offering guidance on how to solve the problem successfully and to prevent a mis-interpretation of an individual mistake as the system's fault. This is especially important, if interactive tools are used for exercises. In this case, the feedback should prevent a student to think that he/she is not able to solve a problem because of bugs in the tool. Therefore, in addition to stating that a solution step is not applicable in the current situation, feedback can provide a link to a list of applicable commands.

Preventing an Inadequate Judgment of Computer-Specific Capabilites. One of the consequences of a low judgment of computer-specific capabilites is a reluctance vis-à-vis exploring and using all features of a system. This is why a system should support and encourage a user's curiosity. Special emphasis should be put on first-time users of a system. A user should not be be overloaded by the features of a system but still know about the possible interactions that the systems offers on top of those from non adaptive hypermedia, i. e. by adaptively adding features to menus. Additionally, after some sessions the system should provide a list of the features not yet used, accompanied by an explanation why they are useful and an invitation to use them. When a feature is used, the system may immediately provide positive feedback together with an explanatory link to similar features that were not yet used. The links can be annotated using techniques of adaptive navigation support.

Raising the Expectation of Success Adaptively. A low expectation of success is a severe hindrance for using a tool or a software and in addition, negative experiences will be perceived more highly. One way to raise the expectation of a successful interaction consists in making these interactions explicit. For instance, exploring a hitherto unused feature can count as an successful experience on which the system provides feedback at the end of a session, e. g., by presenting a list of features used for the first time. With respect to the user's performance in a session, on logout time the system should provide a list of accomplishments achieved during the session, e. g., a list of solved exercises, read topics, etc.

How to Scaffold Help-Seeking Adaptively. Users need to be supported in using help correctly. Some users request too much help, other users are not much inclined to use help at all although it would improve learning. Therefore, a system needs to specially support users to notice the help opportunity and to use it the way they benefit most of it. Gräsel's experiments show that offering help is not enough but a special visual focus has to be put on the help as well [5]. In case a learner ignores highlighting of help and help-seeking has a low value, a help menu can open automatically. This will be interpreted as obtrusive by most users, therefore the help messages has to make explicit the reason why the menu was offered, i. e., by listing the actions of the user used for diagnosing the need for help.

Influencing the Situational Goal of a Session. Certain instructional items (such as worked-out examples with a request to self-explain) can focus the learner on understanding and reasoning, and stimulate such goals different from pure performance goals. Such items can be introduced adaptively into hypermedia generated by such systems as ACTIVEMATH [6].

5   The Escape Route from Cliché

A simplistic implementation of the described features would ask the user for his sex and adapt the system correspondingly. The problem with this one-time-adaptation approach is that users are faced with a system that incorporates a cliché and therefore, possibly scares off all users not exactly matching a stereotype. Using the sex of a user as a basis for adaptation has one definite advantage: it is easy to collect the information. However imprecise a differentiation on this basis may be, statistics show that this single information can provide information about an individual user that holds with a certain degree of probability. Over time and ideally, an e-learning system identifies the user's aptitudes, cognitive style, capabilities, and other individual characteristics and adapts accordingly.

Therefore, the sex of a user can initialize certain values in the user model, for instance, in the model of Fig. 1, the initial empirically average values. But then, user modeling continues rather than stopping at the level of averages and stereotypes. Individual differences of some characteristics can be assessed by monitoring the actions of a user. This information can be used to further refine the user model and to make the transition from the stereotype to the individual.

On way of assessing the individual attitudes consists in interactive choice of features on an individual basis. Each adaption should be accompanied by a possibility to confirm or disallows further application. This enables the user to influence the adaptations in the first place. Additionally, all settings should be accessible in a configuration panel. The decision of the user which feature to employ updates the user model as well.

References

1. Tollefsen, K.: Gender differences in information and communication technology based Norwegian higher education. In: Electronic Proceedings of the 24th Information Systems Research Seminar in Scandinavia (IRIS 24). (2001)
2. Dickhäuser, O., Stiensmeier-Pelster, J.: Gender differences in computer work: Evidence for the model of achievement-related choices. Contemporary Educational Psychology 27 (2002) 486–496
3. Canada, K., Brusca, F.: The technological gender gap: Evidence and recommendations for educators and computer-based instruction designers. Educational Technology Research & Development 39 (1992)
4. Rajagopal, I., Bojin, N.: A gendered world: Students and instructional technologies. First Monday 8 (2003)
5. Gräsel, C., Fischer, F., Mandl, H.: The use of additional information in problem-oriented learning environments. Learning Environments Research 3 (2001) 287–305
6. Melis, E., Andrès, E., Büdenbender, J., Frischauf, A., Goguadze, G., Libbrecht, P., Pollet, M., Ullrich, C.: Activemath: A generic and adaptive web-based learning environment. International Journal of Artificial Intelligence in Education 12 (2001) 385–407

An Overview of aLFanet:
An Adaptive iLMS Based on Standards

Olga C. Santos, Carmen Barrera, and Jesús G. Boticario

aDeNu Research Group, Artificial Intelligence Department, Computer Science School,
UNED, c/Juan del Rosal. 16. 28040 Madrid, Spain
ocsantos@dia.uned.es, cbarrera@invi.uned.es, jgb@dia.uned.es

Abstract. aLFanet (IST-2001-33288) aims to build an adaptive iLMS (intelligent Learning Management System) that provides personalised eLearning based on the combination of different types of adaptation (e.g. learning routes, interactions in services, peer-to-peer collaboration, presentation). It integrates new principles and tools in the fields of Learning Design and Artificial Intelligence, following existing standards in the educational field (IMS-LD, IMS-CP, IEEE-LOM, IMS-LIP, IMS-QTI) and multi-agents systems (FIPA). In this paper we present an overview of the project ongoing research and developments.

1 Introduction

Active Learning For Adaptive interNET (aLFanet) is an IST Project funded by the European Commission under the 5th Framework Program (IST-2001-33288) that addresses the problem of effective adaptive learning. The project is the result of the joint effort of four developer partners (Software AG España - SAGE, Universidad Nacional de Educación a Distancia - UNED, Open Universiteit Nederland – OUNL and ACE-Case) and two user partners (Ernst Klett Verlag GmbH and Electricidade de Portugal Mudança e Recursos Humanos S.A.).

The key features of aLFanet have been introduced in [4] and [3]. The first reference focuses its attention on the different actors that are involved in the system (i.e. authors, learners, tutors), and how each of them can benefit from it. In this paper, we describe how aLFanet can address self-learning. Thus, we assume that the course is already produced by the author and has been published in aLFanet. aLFanet includes an Authoring Tool developed by ACE-Case that allows authors to generate courses IMS – Learning Design (IMS-LD) compliant. Since we are focusing on self-learning, the tutor is not mandatory. It is undeniable that the figure of the human tutor enriches the performance of the course and can provide valuable feedback for the performance of the adaptation mechanisms used in aLFanet. However, many real learning scenarios do not include the figure of the tutor. In these cases, aLFanet drives users' interactions based on the combination of different learning routes defined at design-time (IMS-LD) and recommendations based on previous users' interactions. On the other hand, when a tutor is available, aLFanet reduces the tutor workload by automating tutoring tasks, e.g., automatic subgrouping of learners based on their interaction profile and by

W. Nejdl and P. De Bra (Eds.): AH 2004, LNCS 3137, pp. 429–432, 2004.

providing meaningful reports based on learners' interactions. As for the tutor, [5] describes how the tutor can be helped by the system in managing a collaborative task in a web based learning environment like aLFanet.

In this paper we focus on how learners can benefit from this adaptive learning environment. As stated in [4], learners in aLFanet are: 1) provided with a learning design based on advanced pedagogical models, which is adapted to the current context and the learners' particular needs, interests and goals; and 2) supported during the learning process by continuous monitoring the learning behaviour and providing intelligent personalized guidance in the way of adapted recommendations.

In [3] we identified three dimensions in which aLFanet can adapt to the user's preferences, interests and needs. The purpose of the following sections is to describe the adaptation basis of aLFanet and the ongoing progress of the project.

2   Adaptation in aLFanet

This section briefly describes aLFanet adaptation basis and focuses on the adaptation dimension worked at aDeNu Research Group [2].

2.1   Adaptation Basis

We have worked on the four dimensions of adaptation addressed by aLFanet [3]: 1) Adaptation specified in Learning Design, 2) Adaptation of Presentation (user interface), 3) Adaptation based on users' Interactions, and 4) Feedback to the author.

There are three fundamental sources to provide adaptation in an iLMS (intelligent Learning Management System): 1) learner's individual differences, 2) specification of learning resources, and 3) the course context. Regarding the first source, the learner's individual differences are obtained by directly collecting data from the learner about his/her learning styles, preferences, interest level on the course objectives and knowledge level (background and achieved) of the course objectives and stored using an extension of IMS – Learning Information Package (IMS-LIP). To specify the learning resources, the standard IEEE Learning Object Metadata (IEEE-LOM) is used. Finally, the context of the course is built from the analysis of the interactions done by learners in aLFanet.

2.2   Adaptation Based on Users' Interactions

Adaptation based on users' interactions focuses on user modeling and collaborative filtering techniques and deals with supporting learners in the optional contents and activities specified by the learning design to work with, the additional material to read, the services available in the LMS to use, the learning experience to share with other fellows, the contributions of fellows to access and/or assess, which fellows of the course to contact to, etc. This implies that it supports user's interactions with recommendations derived from other related users by recommending something that have been useful to other learners with similar learned profiles and in closely related learning situations. In [1] we describe in detail how to recommend some learning material to a learner based on implicit collaborative interactions.

To acquire the attributes to build the models needed for the adaptation tasks a machine learning multi-agent approach that combines knowledge-based methods and machine learning algorithms in a multi-agent architecture is used [1].

3 aLFanet Architecture

aLFanet integrates new principles and tools in the fields of Learning Design and Artificial Intelligence, following and extending, to cope with the adaptivity requirements, existing standards in the educational field[1] (IMS-LD, IMS-CP, IEEE-LOM, IMS-LIP, IMS-QTI) and multi-agent systems (FIPA). It has been implemented by a flexible and modular approach that facilitates its development, extensibility and integration of third parties developments that follow the supported standards.

In particular, it integrates an IMS Learning Design Engine (CopperCore[2]) developed as open source by OUNL, a web application for supporting course management, online communities and collaboration (.LRN[3]) originally developed at the Massachusetts Institute of Technology (MIT) but currently part of an open source project and, thus, extended by UNED to be integrated in aLFanet, an IMS QTI interpreter developed by SAGE and an infrastructure based on a multi-agent architecture where different types of agents interact to provide adapted recommendations to learners, developed by UNED.

4 Results and Future Work

As a result of the work performed on the-one-and-a-half year already spent in the project, a first version of aLFanet was delivered in February 2004. This version allows users to access the basic functionality of the running system. Currently the system provides the authoring tool (IMS-LD compliant) and the interactive space that integrates the personal and course working spaces. The latter includes the learning route of learning objects and activities, which are provided to the learner according to the IMS-LD specified by the author and what services of the LMS are to be used in the activities of the course (file storage area, fora, etc.).

aLFanet is course oriented. When the learner enters aLFanet, he/she is provided with an integrated view of the contributions of other users to the services belonging to the courses the learner is enrolled. He/she can access the different courses directly or via accessing the contributions done in the services. Once in the course, the activity tree defined by the learning design is given to the learner, as well as the learning objects and services to perform the activities. The activity tree depicts the different learning paths which drive user's interactions according to the learning design. The rest of

---

[1] http://www.imsglobal.org/specifications.cfm
[2] http://coppercore.org/
[3] http://dotlrn.org

services, resources and recommendations are provided according to the user's ongoing progress with the course activities.

The recommendations provided so far are explicitly defined. The reason for this is that in the first running version, the goal was to integrate both the learning design and the services available at the interactive space. Thus we can track and relate the interactions taking part in both and use the machine learning multi-agent approach. Right now, we are working on collecting the data that feed the machine learning algorithms and the inference rules of our approach and defining how different types of adaptation tasks are provided based on the models obtained from these data [1]. In these sense we are defining adaptation scenarios to be used by the author when designing courses for aLFanet. This work is going to be integrated in the second version of aLFanet to be delivered by July 2004.

An evaluation is being done on the first prototype regarding technical verification and usability. However, once the second version of aLFanet is delivered, an empirical evaluation of the system focusing on validating the effectiveness of the adaptive features by measuring whether they facilitate the learning process is to be started.

References

1. Barrera, C., Santos, O.C., Rodriguez, A. and Boticario, J.G.: Support to Learners based on Implicit Collaborative interactions. To appear in: Proceedings of the Workshop Artificial Intelligence in Computer Supported Collaborative Learning. 16th European Conference on Artificial Intelligence (2004)
2. Hernández, F., Gaudioso, E. and Boticario, J.G. A multiagent approach to obtain open and flexible user models in adaptive learning communities. In Proceedings of the 9th International Conference on User Modelling. Springer Verlag (2003)
3. Santos, O.C., Barrera, C., Gaudioso, E., Boticario, J.G. 'ALFANET: an adaptive e-learning platform'. In Méndez, A, Mesa, J.A., Mesa, J. (eds): Advances in Technology-Based Education: Toward a Knowledge-Based Society (2003) 1938-1942
4. Santos, O.C., Boticario, J.G., Koper, E.J.R. 'aLFanet'. In Méndez, A, Mesa, J.A., Mesa, J. (eds): Advances in Technology-Based Education: Toward a Knowledge-Based Society (2003) 2014
5. Santos, O.C., Rodríguez, A., Gaudioso E., Boticario, J.G. 'Helping the tutor to manage a collaborative task in a web-based learning environment'. In Calvo, R. and M. Grand-bastein, M. (eds): AIED2003 Supplementary Proceedings - Volume IV: Intelligent Management Systems. University of Sydney. (2003) 153-162

A General Meta-model
for Adaptive Hypermedia Systems

Patricia Seefelder de Assis[1,2] and Daniel Schwabe[1]

[1] Departamento de Informática–Pontifícia Universidade Católica do Rio de Janeiro (PUC-Rio) -
Caixa Postal 38.097 – 22.453-900 – Rio de Janeiro – RJ – Brazil
patricia@iprj.uerj.br, dschwabe@inf.puc-rio.br
[2] Instituto Politécnico, Campus Regional de Nova Friburgo – Membro do Grupo de Pesquisa
Rede Operativa de Conhecimento e Aprendizagem - ROCA – (UERJ)

Abstract. The emergence of meta-adaptive systems seems to be a natural evolution process in adaptive systems. Meta-adaptive systems are able to vary the adaptation technique based on various factors. This work analyzes the main aspects related to adaptivity by using a general meta-model of Adaptive Hypermedia Systems, intended to serve as a basis for a meta-adaptive system.

1 A General Meta-model for Adaptive Hypermedia Systems

The focus of recent research in adaptive hypermedia has been on adaptation technologies, but this is currently evolving towards the vision that the selection of the type of adaptation, and its corresponding mechanisms, should itself be adapted. This leads to meta-adaptive hypermedia systems, i.e., systems whose type of adaptation is also adaptable [3]. We propose a general meta-model for Adaptive Hypermedia Systems (AHSs) that withdraws their basic structure and identifies their features with respect to the supported adaptations. This characterization is worth as a first step to structure a meta-adaptive system.

The general meta-model represents the core functionality (with respect to adaptation) of AHSs, incorporating their essential features. In other words, it is safe to state that AHSs possess at least the main components, although in many cases extensions to the meta-model are necessary to accommodate specific features in particular systems. The proposal is based on the AHAM model [10] and on the Munich Reference Model [5], and is specified using the UML class diagram notation[1] [8]. Basically, an AHS should have an Adaptation Model (AM) able to perform the adaptation based on the Domain Model (DM) and on the User Model (UM) [10]. Following insights gained from the OOHDM design method [7], we provide a clear separation between content, navigation and interface by adding a Navigation Model and a Presentation Model. The Integration Model represents the possibility systems have to integrate external sources of data within DM, whereas User Context models under which condition the system is being used.

---

[1] The UML notation was extended to allow a relationship between packages and classes, denoting that every component of the package may be related to the class.

W. Nejdl and P. De Bra (Eds.): AH 2004, LNCS 3137, pp. 433–436, 2004.

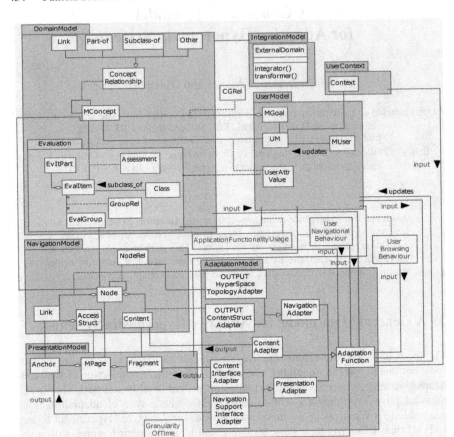

Fig. 1. A General Meta-Model for Adaptive Hypermedia Systems

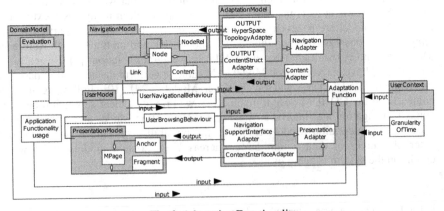

Fig. 2. Adaptation Functionality

The AM concerns the mechanisms used to represent the implementation aspects for the adaptation. The Adaptation Function (AF) is represented on Fig. 1 in a different shade for legibility reasons and can be better visualized in Fig. 2.

Inputs to the function represent what the adaptation is based on: Domain Model; User Model; User Navigational Behavior (navigation path); User Browsing Behavior (example: articles read); Application Functionality Usage (example: results of tests); User Context (example: the access bandwidth available) and in which "granularity of time" the adaptation is made (example: at login time vs. after each navigation step).

The AF has three sub-functions, according to what is adapted (outputs of the function). The actual aspect that is adapted can be one of the following: *Content Adaptation*, which refers to the actual content (example: colloquial text for non-experts vs. technical text for experts); *Navigation Adaptation*, that may be of two kinds - *Adaptation of the content structure* (node-level), adapting the particular way in which concepts are put together for navigation purposes (example: including introduction for beginners vs. skipping introduction for advanced users) and *Adaptation of the hyperspace topology* (link-level) where anchor changes and index changes modify the navigation path (example: including a link to "solution" in a problem used as an example vs. omitting the link in a problem used as a test) – and *Presentation Adaptation*, also of two kinds - *Adaptation of navigation support interface* (example: using drop-down menu vs. using explicit lists of anchors) and *Adaptation of Content interface* (example: highlighting certain types of information for emphasis).

2 Analysis of Adaptive Hypermedia Systems

To better illustrate the applicability of the meta-model, showing how it can be used to analyze actual systems, we have instantiated it for the major AHSs: AHAM [10], AHA! [4], InterBook [2], NetCoach [9] and KBS Hyperbook [6]. For reasons of space, we only give a brief analysis of NetCoach and AHAM, illustrating the kinds of observations that emerge. Readers interested in full details are referred to [1].

NetCoach (earlier known as ART-Web) is an authoring system for web-based distance learning courses. It considers concepts as internal representation of pages. The domain is a Knowledge Base composed of concepts and their semantic relationships. Well-defined relations are necessary for an effective adaptation (based on the way the domain is structured). The system's belief about the user knowledge of domain concepts is stored in the UM as information about whether the tests were worked on or solved (knowledge level), and about page state (which pages were visited, learned, inferred or known). The user may mark pages as known. The adaptation core in Net-Coach is the evaluation mechanism. The user may ask the system for direct guidance about the best (adapted) navigation path and the system uses information about the UM state and the general learning goal to dynamically compute the best next page to visit.

AHAM is the model underlying many Adaptive Hypermedia Systems. Besides users' knowledge about domain concepts, the UM may store domain-independent concepts. AHAM uses adaptation rules to describe the mechanism used to decide how to perform adaptation and how to update the UM based on the user's actions. The user may also update the UM. AHAM considers concepts and their relations as links and nodes. There is no separation between conceptual and navigational models and there is also a mix-up between conceptual and presentation models.

3 Future Work

The general meta-model must be improved by incorporating users' cognitive style as a possible input to the Adaptation Function and modeling a communication function enabling AHSs to communicate with each other [4].

As the UML notation has limited expressiveness and may not be directly processed, our next goal is to describe this meta-model using ontologies, which will allow integration with the Semantic Web technologies, that are more suitable for the type of meta-reasoning we envision, and allow direct manipulation. We are also investigating different alternatives for specifying and implementing the adaptation function in this meta-model.

References

1. Assis, P.A.; Schwabe, D.; Barbosa, S.D.J.; "Meta Modeling of Adaptive Hypermedia Applications", Technical Report, Department of Informatics, PUC-Rio, 2004. (In Portuguese, forthcoming).
2. Brusilovsky, P., Eklund, J., and Schwarz, E. "Web-Based Education For All: A Tool For Developing Adaptive Courseware".: Computer Networks and ISDN Systems. (Proceedings of WWW7), 30 (1-7), p.291-300, 1998.
3. Brusilovsky, P. "Adaptive navigation support in educational hypermedia: The role of student knowledge level and the case for meta-adaptation". British Journal of Educational Technology, 34 (4), 487-497, 2003.
4. De Bra, P., Aerts, A., Berden, B., De Lange, B., Rousseau, B., Santic, T., Smits, D., Stash, N.,AHA! The Adaptive Hypermedia Architecture. Proceedings of the ACM Hypertext Conference, Nottingham, UK, pp. 81-84, 2003.
5. Koch, N.P. "Software Engineering for Adaptive Hypermedia Systems: Reference Model, Modeling Techniques and Development Process" PhD thesis - Institut für Informatik, Ludwig-Maximilians-Universität München, 2000.
6. Nejdl, W. and Wolpers, M. "KBS Hyperbook - a Data-Driven Information System on the Web". In: WWW8 CONFERENCE, Toronto, 1999.
7. Rossi, G.; Schwabe, D.; Lyardet, F. (1999). Web application models are more than conceptual models. Lecture Notes in Computer Science 1727, pp. 239-252, Springer Verlag, ISBN 3-540-66653-2, (Proc. WWWCM'99 Workshop, ER'99), Paris.
8. UML Resource Page. http://www.omg.org/uml/, last accessed December 2002.
9. Weber, G., Kuhl H.-C. and Weibelzahl, S. "Developing adaptive internet based courses with the authoring system NetCoach". In: Reich, S., Tzagarakis, M.M. & De Bra, P.M.E., (Eds.) Hypermedia: Openness, Structural Awareness, and Adaptivity (pp. 226-238). Berlin: Springer-Verlag, 2001.
10. Wu, H., De Kort, E., De Bra, P. Design Issues for General-Purpose Adaptive Hypermedia Systems. Proceedings of the ACM Conference on Hypertext and Hypermedia, pp. 141-150, Aarhus, Denmark, 2001.

Adaptive Services for Customised Knowledge Delivery

Alexander Smirnov, Mikhail Pashkin, Nikolai Chilov,
Tatiana Levashova, and Andrew Krizhanovsky

St.Petersburg Institute for Informatics and Automation of
the Russian Academy of Sciences
39, 14th Line, St.Petersburg, 199178, Russia
smir@iias.spb.su

Abstract. The more information is available in the Internet the more difficult to find the right information. The idea of adaptive hypermedia systems is to provide users with personalised information that depends on the users' needs and requirements. The paper presents an approach to knowledge logistics that applies such principles to the process of knowledge delivery from distributed heterogeneous sources. More attention is paid to description of an adaptive service that can modify itself based on the user tasks and implemented within the framework of the approach.

1 Introduction

Rapid development of the Internet has made a huge amount of information about different problem areas available for users. Besides, nowadays, knowledge is becoming an important resource causing a need for systems working with knowledge, i.e. dealing with knowledge creation, classification, synthesis, analysis, storage, search and mapping. An efficient approach is needed in order to provide mechanisms which would allow a decision maker to have required knowledge "at hand" in an appropriate form for making correct and timely decisions. The approach has to provide for the dynamic and flexible knowledge management systems to keep up-to-date resource value assessment data, to support rapid conducting of complex operations, and to deliver results to users/knowledge customers in a personalised way.

Personalisation is one of the main principles for services and adaptive hypermedia systems [1]. As a possible approach dealing with this problem, knowledge logistics (KL) can be proposed [2]. This is a new direction in the knowledge management aimed at acquisition of the right knowledge from distributed sources, its integration and transfer to the right person within the right context, at the right time, for the right business purpose. It is based on individual user requirements, available knowledge sources, and current situation analysis. While current adaptive hypermedia systems mainly deal with text pages (e.g., [3]), KL might successfully complement them applying the principles, hypermedia systems are based on, to knowledge-based services. Similar cross-disciplinary efforts of using adaptive hypermedia techniques for other service-based applications have already been undertaken, e.g. in [4] they are used for semantic Web-service composition.

W. Nejdl and P. De Bra (Eds.): AH 2004, LNCS 3137, pp. 437–440, 2004.

This paper presents an approach to KL described in detail in [2] and illustrates how adaptive and customer-oriented services can be used within it. The approach considers the KL problem as a problem of a Knowledge Source Network (KSNet) configuration, and in this regard it has been referred to as KSNet-approach. KSNet-approach is based on application of such technologies as ontology & context management and open services.

2 Adaptive Services of the System "KSNet"

The KSNet-approach represents an integrated framework for a customer-oriented KL system. It addresses both knowledge management and knowledge fusion (KF), with KF being based on constraint satisfaction methodology. Ontology & context management is used to provide for knowledge consistency and relevance, and interoperability. KSNet-approach applies the mass customisation idea to the KL system serving the users (decision makers) who can be considered as knowledge customers. The main principles of the mass customisation idea used in the KSNet-approach are: (i) deliver personalised results to users/knowledge customers, (ii) modularisation and customisation around standardised products and services, and (iii) Just-in-Time (JIT) or even Just-before-Time (JBT) delivery. For this purpose the following two major stages of request processing were developed: (i) preparation when an application ontology (AO) for the request is built, and (ii) request processing based on the built AO. For subsequent requests related to the same problem the built AO is reused.

The open service oriented model applied to the system "KSNet" implementing the approach consists of service owners, service consumers, and "a third party" [5]. The system acts as a service provider for knowledge customer services and at the same time as a service requestor for knowledge suppliers – OKBC (Open Knowledge Base Connectivity) compatible knowledge representation systems. The main specific is that the service passes the request to the system where it goes through all the stages of the request processing scenario. When an answer for the request is found it goes to the service and then it is passed to the requestor.

KF service performs knowledge fusion based on AO describing the problem, user request ontology describing the user request and knowledge acquired from knowledge sources, and utilises such technologies as constraint satisfaction/propagation. In the prototype of the system "KSNet" the features of ILOG Configurator, Solver and Dispatcher [6] are used for this purpose. The service's behaviour is defined by the content of input messages.

The user request defines both the problem statement and what data has to be retrieved from ontology library and from knowledge sources. Thereby the problem statement is changed from one request to another while AO remains unchanged. The novel "on-the-fly" compilation mechanism in combination with ILOG is proposed to solve these varying problems. Generally speaking this mechanism is based on the following concepts (Fig. 1):

- a pre-processed user request defines (1) what ontologies are to be extracted from ontology library, and (2) what knowledge sources are to be used;

- C++ code is generated on the basis of information extracted from (1) the user request (goal, goal objects, etc.), (2) appropriate ontologies (classes, attributes, and constraints), and (3) suitable knowledge sources;
- the compilation is performed in an environment of the prepared in advance C++ project;
- failed compilations/executions do not interrupt the system work on the whole; an appropriate message for the user is generated.

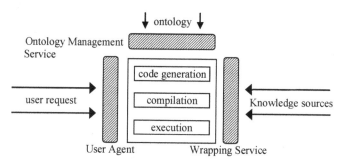

Fig. 1. Solver "on-the-fly" compilation mechanism

The implementation of the KF agent uses such fundamental ideas of programming languages as object-oriented approach and constraint programming and thereby the KF service is directly coupled with a solver. ILOG provides a library of reusable and maintainable C++ classes. These classes define objects in the application domain in a natural and intuitive way so that it is possible to clearly distinguish the problem representation from the problem solving. Therefore, if a problem statement changes then it is not necessary to rewrite the entire code as in case of "pure" C++. In the given case the problem statement is defined by ontology elements retrieved from the ontology library, therefore the problem of minimal code modification, fast and error-free is the important task here.

The essence of the proposed on-the-fly compilation mechanism is to put the AO elements (classes, attributes, constraints) to a C++ file directly. The KF service creates a C++ file based on these data and inserts program source code to a program (Microsoft Visual Studio project) prepared in advance. The program is compiled in order to create an executable file in the form of dynamic-link library (DLL). After that the KF service calls a function from DLL to solve the task. The call is performed via the XML-RPC [7] protocol (remote procedure calling via HTTP as a transport protocol and XML as an encoding language). XML-RPC is designed to be as simple as possible, while allowing complex data structures to be transmitted, processed and returned.

The KF service uses the mentioned technique of dynamic code generation (with ILOG Configurator commands embedded) to produce a solution set satisfying requirements of the user request and AO elements (classes, attributes, constraints, etc.).

The generated code (C++ file) consists of several parts:

- the ontology management agent passes a part of the program based on data from the ontology library;

- the wrapper passes a part of the program using local/remote knowledge sources;
- the KF service generates a part of the program based on user request processing as well as user requirements;
- the predefined part of code (unchangeable): an algorithm and strategy definition and an automatic answer generation.

Thus the C++ file is created on the basis of a special template. This template allows researchers and developers to comprehend and realise in more explicit and well-defined form (i) what information is needed to solve task, (ii) what knowledge sources are required, and (iii) what wrapper/wrapping service is responsible for delivering particular specified information block.

The approach was tested in a number of application domains, from such areas as supply chain management, logistics and healthcare services.

Acknowledgements

Some parts of the research were supported by ISTC partner project # 1993P funded by Air Force Research Laboratory at Rome, NY, project # 16.2.44 of the research program "Mathematical Modelling and Intelligent Systems", project # 1.9 of the research program "Fundamental Basics of Information Technologies and Computer Systems" of the Russian Academy of Sciences, grant # 02-01-00284 of the Russian Foundation for Basic Research, and the contract with Ford Motor Company. Some prototypes were developed using software granted by ILOG Inc.

References

1. Garlatti, S., Iksla, S.: A Semantic Web Approach for Adaptive Hypermedia. Proc. of AH2003: Workshop on Adaptive Hypermedia and Adaptive Web-Based Systems (2003). URL: http://wwwis.win.tue.nl/ah2003/proceedings.
2. Smirnov, A., Pashkin, M., Chilov, N., Levashova, T., Haritatos, F.: Knowledge Source Network Configuration Approach to Knowledge Logistics. Int. J. of General Systems, Vol. 32, No. 3. Taylor & Francis Group (2003) 251-269.
3. Brusilovsky, P., De Bra, P., Santic, T.: A Flexible Layout Model for a Web-Based Adaptive Hypermedia Architecture. Proc. of AH2003: Workshop on Adaptive Hypermedia and Adaptive Web-Based Systems. URL: http://wwwis.win.tue.nl/ah2003/proceedings.
4. Conlan, O., Lewis, D., Higel, S., o'Sullivan, D., Wade, V.: Applying Adaptive Hypermedia Techniques to Semantic Web Service Composition. Proc. of AH2003: Workshop on Adaptive Hypermedia and Adaptive Web-Based Systems (2003). URL: http://wwwis.win.tue.nl/ah2003/proceedings.
5. Smirnov, A., Pashkin, M., Chilov, N., Levashova, T.: Knowledge Logistics in Information Grid Environment. Zhuge, H. (ed.): The special issue "Semantic Grid and Knowledge Grid: The Next-Generation Web" of Int. J. on Future Generation Computer Systems, Vol. 20, No. 1. Elsevier Science (2003) 61-79.
6. ILOG corporate Web-site (2004) URL: http://www.ilog.com.
7. XML-RPC Web-site (2003) URL: http://www.xmlrpc.org.

Author Index

Aarts, Emile   1
Aberer, Karl   265
Adamski, Michał   146
Álvarez, Helmut Leighton   316
Alves, Mário Amado   348
Apelt, Stefan   320
Apted, Trent   4
Ardissono, Liliana   14, 126
Arezki, Rachid   275
Arteaga, Carlos   279

Balaguer-Ballester, Emili   421
Barna, Peter   283
Barrera, Carmen   429
Berlanga, Adriana   372
Bertolotto, Michela   195
Bieliková, Mária   376
Boticario, Jesús G.   409, 429
Bourda, Yolaine   413
Briggs, Peter   380
Brusilovsky, Peter   24
Buffereau, Benjamin   384
Bull, Susan   328

Camps-Valls, Gustavo   421
Carmona, Cristina   353
Chavan, Girish   24
Chen, Sherry   104
Chilov, Nikolai   437
Chirita, Paul-Alexandru   34
Chittaro, Luca   287
Choi, Sook-young   389
Conejo, Ricardo   353, 405
Conlan, Owen   55, 291
Cordasco, Gennaro   44
Coyle, Maurice   296

Dagger, Declan   55
De Bruyn, Arnaud   393
de Vrieze, Paul   344
Delestre, Nicolas   397
Delgado Kloos, Carlos   401
Delorme, Fabien   397
Deters, Ralph   328
Díaz, Alberto   65

Díaz, Oscar   75
Dolog, Peter   85
Dray, Gérard   275
Dunnion, John   312

Eyzaguirre, Jorge   279

Fabregat, Ramon   279
Farzan, Rosta   24
Feijó, Bruno   215
Ferreira Rodrigues, Rogério   215
Frías-Martínez, Enrique   104
Frasincar, Flavius   283
Freyne, Jill   95

García, Francisco J.   372
García Peñalvo, Francisco   316
Garlatti, Serge   115
Gaudioso, Elena   409
Gena, Cristina   126
Gervás, Pablo   65
Giles, C. Lee   393
Gomes Soares, Luiz Fernando   215
Goy, Anna   14
Gutiérrez, Sergio   401
Guzmán, Eduardo   405
Gómez-Sanchís, Juan   421

Habala, Rastislav   376
Habieb-Mammar, Halima   136
Henze, Nicola   85
Hernandez, Felix   409
Horvitz, Eric   3
Houben, Geert-Jan   283
Hübscher, Roland   300

Iglezakis, Dorothea   304
Iksal, Sébastien   115

Jacquiot, Cédric   413
Jameson, Anthony   225
Janssen, José   336
Jorge, Alípio   348

Kay, Judy   4
Kazienko, Przemysław   146
Kelly, Declan   308

Koolwaaij, Johan   235
Koper, Rob   336
Kravcik, Milos   156, 166
Krizhanovsky, Andrew   437

Leal, José Paulo   348
Levashova, Tatiana   437
Linden, Keith Vander   205
Lu, Shijian   205
Lum, Andrew   4
Lütticke, Rainer   417

Macredie, Robert   104
Magoulas, George   104
Manderveld, Jocelyn   336
Margaritis, Konstantinos G.   255
Martin, Brent   185
Martín-Guerrero, José D.   421
McCalla, Gordon   245
McCarthy, Kevin   176
McGinty, Lorraine   176
McLoughlin, Eoin   195
Melis, Erica   425
Mérida, David   279
Mitrovic, Antonija   185

Nejdl, Wolfgang   34, 85

O'Donovan, John   312
O'Sullivan, Dympna   195
Olmedilla, Daniel   34
Oppermann, Reinhard   166

Palomares, Alberto   421
Pardo, Abelardo   401
Paris, Cécile   205
Pashkin, Mikhail   437
Pastellis, Panikos   340
Paz, Iñaki   75
Pearson, David W.   275
Pécuchet, Jean-Pierre   397
Pennock, David M.   393
Petrone, Giovanna   14
Picouet, Philippe   384
Pokraev, Stanislav   235
Poncelet, Pascal   275
Popineau, Fabrice   413
Post, Matthew   205
Prieto Ferraro, Marcela   316
Puntambekar, Sadhana   300

Ranon, Roberto   287

Reilly, James   176
Reinhardt, Katja   320
Retalis, Symeon   340
Rocchi, Cesare   324
Röbig, Harald   328

Santos, Olga C.   429
Salgado Lucena Rodrigues, Paula   215
Scarano, Vittorio   44
Schultheis, Holger   225
Schwabe, Daniel   360, 433
Seefelder de Assis, Patricia   360, 433
Segnan, Marino   14
Serrano-López, Antonio J.   421
Sharifi, Golha   328
Sidner, Candace L.   2
Sintek, Michael   85
Smirnov, Alexander   437
Smyth, Barry   95, 176, 296, 380
Soria-Olivas, Emilio   421
Sosnovsky, Sergey   366
Specht, Marcus   156, 166, 320
Suzuki, Tetsuya   332

Tang, Tiffany   245
Tangney, Brendan   308
Tarpin-Bernard, Franck   136
Tattersall, Colin   336
Tokuda, Takehiro   332
Tzanavari, Aimilia   340

Ullrich, Carsten   425

Vassileva, Julita   328
van Bommel, Patrick   344
van den Berg, Bert   336
van der Weide, Theo   344
van Es, René   336
van Setten, Mark   235
Velho, Luiz   215
Vitolo, Cristiano   44
Vozalis, Manolis   255

Wade, Vincent P.   55, 291
Wilson, David C.   195
Wu, Jie   265
Wu, Mingfang   205

Yang, Hyung-jung   389

Zancanaro, Massimo   324

Lecture Notes in Computer Science

For information about Vols. 1–3063

please contact your bookseller or Springer

Vol. 3194: R. Camacho, R. King, A. Srinivasan (Eds.), Inductive Logic Programming. XI, 361 pages. 2004. (Subseries LNAI).

Vol. 3177: Z.R. Yang, H. Yin, R. Everson (Eds.), Intelligent Data Engineering and Automated Learning – IDEAL 2004. VXIII, 852 pages. 2004.

Vol. 3174: F. Yin, J. Wang, C. Guo (Eds.), Advances in Neural Networks - ISNN 2004. XXXV, 1021 pages. 2004.

Vol. 3172: M. Dorigo, M. Birattari, C. Blum, L. M.Gambardella, F. Mondada, T. Stützle (Eds.), Ant Colony, Optimization and Swarm Intelligence. XII, 434 pages. 2004.

Vol. 3158: I. Nikolaidis, M. Barbeau, E. Kranakis (Eds.), Ad-Hoc, Mobile, and Wireless Networks. IX, 344 pages. 2004.

Vol. 3157: C. Zhang, H. W. Guesgen, W.K. Yeap (Eds.), PRICAI 2004: Trends in Artificial Intelligence. XX, 1023 pages. 2004. (Subseries LNAI).

Vol. 3156: M. Joye, J.-J. Quisquater (Eds.), Cryptographic Hardware and Embedded Systems - CHES 2004. XIII, 455 pages. 2004.

Vol. 3155: P. Funk, P.A. González Calero (Eds.), Advanced in Case-Based Reasoning. XIII, 822 pages. 2004. (Subseries LNAI).

Vol. 3153: J. Fiala, V. Koubek, J. Kratochvíl (Eds.), Mathematical Foundations of Computer Science 2004. XIV, 902 pages. 2004.

Vol. 3152: M. Franklin (Ed.), Advances in Cryptology – CRYPTO 2004. XI, 579 pages. 2004.

Vol. 3150: G.-Z. Yang, T. Jiang (Eds.), Medical Imaging and Augmented Reality. XII, 378 pages. 2004.

Vol. 3148: R. Giacobazzi (Ed.), Static Analysis. XI, 393 pages. 2004.

Vol. 3146: P. Érdi, A. Esposito, M. Marinaro, S. Scarpetta (Eds.), Computational Neuroscience: Cortical Dynamics. XI, 161 pages. 2004.

Vol. 3144: M. Papatriantafilou, P. Hunel (Eds.), Principles of Distributed Systems. XI, 246 pages. 2004.

Vol. 3143: W. Liu, Y. Shi, Q. Li (Eds.), Advances in Web-Based Learning – ICWL 2004. XIV, 459 pages. 2004.

Vol. 3142: J. Diaz, J. Karhumäki, A. Lepistö, D. Sannella (Eds.), Automata, Languages and Programming. XIX, 1253 pages. 2004.

Vol. 3140: N. Koch, P. Fraternali, M. Wirsing (Eds.), Web Engineering. XXI, 623 pages. 2004.

Vol. 3139: F. Iida, R. Pfeifer, L. Steels, Y. Kuniyoshi (Eds.), Embodied Artificial Intelligence. IX, 331 pages. 2004. (Subseries LNAI).

Vol. 3138: A. Fred, T. Caelli, R.P.W. Duin, A. Campilho, D.d. Ridder (Eds.), Structural, Syntactic, and Statistical Pattern Recognition. XXII, 1168 pages. 2004.

Vol. 3137: P. De Bra, W. Nejdl (Eds.), Adaptive Hypermedia and Adaptive Web-Based Systems. XIV, 442 pages. 2004.

Vol. 3136: F. Meziane, E. Métais (Eds.), Natural Language Processing and Information Systems. XII, 436 pages. 2004.

Vol. 3134: C. Zannier, H. Erdogmus, L. Lindstrom (Eds.), Extreme Programming and Agile Methods - XP/Agile Universe 2004. XIV, 233 pages. 2004.

Vol. 3133: A.D. Pimentel, S. Vassiliadis (Eds.), Computer Systems: Architectures, Modeling, and Simulation. XIII, 562 pages. 2004.

Vol. 3131: V. Torra, Y. Narukawa (Eds.), Modeling Decisions for Artificial Intelligence. XI, 327 pages. 2004. (Subseries LNAI).

Vol. 3130: A. Syropoulos, K. Berry, Y. Haralambous, B. Hughes, S. Peter, J. Plaice (Eds.), TeX, XML, and Digital Typography. VIII, 265 pages. 2004.

Vol. 3129: Q. Li, G. Wang, L. Feng (Eds.), Advances in Web-Age Information Management. XVII, 753 pages. 2004.

Vol. 3128: D. Asonov (Ed.), Querying Databases Privately. IX, 115 pages. 2004.

Vol. 3127: K.E. Wolff, H.D. Pfeiffer, H.S. Delugach (Eds.), Conceptual Structures at Work. XI, 403 pages. 2004. (Subseries LNAI).

Vol. 3126: P. Dini, P. Lorenz, J.N.d. Souza (Eds.), Service Assurance with Partial and Intermittent Resources. XI, 312 pages. 2004.

Vol. 3125: D. Kozen (Ed.), Mathematics of Program Construction. X, 401 pages. 2004.

Vol. 3124: J.N. de Souza, P. Dini, P. Lorenz (Eds.), Telecommunications and Networking - ICT 2004. XXVI, 1390 pages. 2004.

Vol. 3123: A. Belz, R. Evans, P. Piwek (Eds.), Natural Language Generation. X, 219 pages. 2004. (Subseries LNAI).

Vol. 3122: K. Jansen, S. Khanna, J.D.P. Rolim, D. Ron (Eds.), Approximation, Randomization, and Combinatorial Optimization. IX, 428 pages. 2004.

Vol. 3121: S. Nikoletseas, J.D.P. Rolim (Eds.), Algorithmic Aspects of Wireless Sensor Networks. X, 201 pages. 2004.

Vol. 3120: J. Shawe-Taylor, Y. Singer (Eds.), Learning Theory. X, 648 pages. 2004. (Subseries LNAI).

Vol. 3118: K. Miesenberger, J. Klaus, W. Zagler, D. Burger (Eds.), Computer Helping People with Special Needs. XXIII, 1191 pages. 2004.

Vol. 3116: C. Rattray, S. Maharaj, C. Shankland (Eds.), Algebraic Methodology and Software Technology. XI, 569 pages. 2004.

Vol. 3114: R. Alur, D.A. Peled (Eds.), Computer Aided Verification. XII, 536 pages. 2004.

Vol. 3113: J. Karhumäki, H. Maurer, G. Paun, G. Rozenberg (Eds.), Theory Is Forever. X, 283 pages. 2004.

Vol. 3112: H. Williams, L. MacKinnon (Eds.), Key Technologies for Data Management. XII, 265 pages. 2004.

Vol. 3111: T. Hagerup, J. Katajainen (Eds.), Algorithm Theory - SWAT 2004. XI, 506 pages. 2004.

Vol. 3110: A. Juels (Ed.), Financial Cryptography. XI, 281 pages. 2004.

Vol. 3109: S.C. Sahinalp, S. Muthukrishnan, U. Dogrusoz (Eds.), Combinatorial Pattern Matching. XII, 486 pages. 2004.

Vol. 3108: H. Wang, J. Pieprzyk, V. Varadharajan (Eds.), Information Security and Privacy. XII, 494 pages. 2004.

Vol. 3107: J. Bosch, C. Krueger (Eds.), Software Reuse: Methods, Techniques and Tools. XI, 339 pages. 2004.

Vol. 3106: K.-Y. Chwa, J.I. Munro (Eds.), Computing and Combinatorics. XIII, 474 pages. 2004.

Vol. 3105: S. Göbel, U. Spierling, A. Hoffmann, I. Iurgel, O. Schneider, J. Dechau, A. Feix (Eds.), Technologies for Interactive Digital Storytelling and Entertainment. XVI, 304 pages. 2004.

Vol. 3104: R. Kralovic, O. Sykora (Eds.), Structural Information and Communication Complexity. X, 303 pages. 2004.

Vol. 3103: K. Deb, e. al. (Eds.), Genetic and Evolutionary Computation – GECCO 2004. XLIX, 1439 pages. 2004.

Vol. 3102: K. Deb, e. al. (Eds.), Genetic and Evolutionary Computation – GECCO 2004. L, 1445 pages. 2004.

Vol. 3101: M. Masoodian, S. Jones, B. Rogers (Eds.), Computer Human Interaction. XIV, 694 pages. 2004.

Vol. 3100: J.F. Peters, A. Skowron, J.W. Grzymała-Busse, B. Kostek, R.W. Świniarski, M.S. Szczuka (Eds.), Transactions on Rough Sets I. X, 405 pages. 2004.

Vol. 3099: J. Cortadella, W. Reisig (Eds.), Applications and Theory of Petri Nets 2004. XI, 505 pages. 2004.

Vol. 3098: J. Desel, W. Reisig, G. Rozenberg (Eds.), Lectures on Concurrency and Petri Nets. VIII, 849 pages. 2004.

Vol. 3097: D. Basin, M. Rusinowitch (Eds.), Automated Reasoning. XII, 493 pages. 2004. (Subseries LNAI).

Vol. 3096: G. Melnik, H. Holz (Eds.), Advances in Learning Software Organizations. X, 173 pages. 2004.

Vol. 3095: C. Bussler, D. Fensel, M.E. Orlowska, J. Yang (Eds.), Web Services, E-Business, and the Semantic Web. X, 147 pages. 2004.

Vol. 3094: A. Nürnberger, M. Detyniecki (Eds.), Adaptive Multimedia Retrieval. VIII, 229 pages. 2004.

Vol. 3093: S.K. Katsikas, S. Gritzalis, J. Lopez (Eds.), Public Key Infrastructure. XIII, 380 pages. 2004.

Vol. 3092: J. Eckstein, H. Baumeister (Eds.), Extreme Programming and Agile Processes in Software Engineering. XVI, 358 pages. 2004.

Vol. 3091: V. van Oostrom (Ed.), Rewriting Techniques and Applications. X, 313 pages. 2004.

Vol. 3089: M. Jakobsson, M. Yung, J. Zhou (Eds.), Applied Cryptography and Network Security. XIV, 510 pages. 2004.

Vol. 3087: D. Maltoni, A.K. Jain (Eds.), Biometric Authentication. XIII, 343 pages. 2004.

Vol. 3086: M. Odersky (Ed.), ECOOP 2004 – Object-Oriented Programming. XIII, 611 pages. 2004.

Vol. 3085: S. Berardi, M. Coppo, F. Damiani (Eds.), Types for Proofs and Programs. X, 409 pages. 2004.

Vol. 3084: A. Persson, J. Stirna (Eds.), Advanced Information Systems Engineering. XIV, 596 pages. 2004.

Vol. 3083: W. Emmerich, A.L. Wolf (Eds.), Component Deployment. X, 249 pages. 2004.

Vol. 3080: J. Desel, B. Pernici, M. Weske (Eds.), Business Process Management. X, 307 pages. 2004.

Vol. 3079: Z. Mammeri, P. Lorenz (Eds.), High Speed Networks and Multimedia Communications. XVIII, 1103 pages. 2004.

Vol. 3078: S. Cotin, D.N. Metaxas (Eds.), Medical Simulation. XVI, 296 pages. 2004.

Vol. 3077: F. Roli, J. Kittler, T. Windeatt (Eds.), Multiple Classifier Systems. XII, 386 pages. 2004.

Vol. 3076: D. Buell (Ed.), Algorithmic Number Theory. XI, 451 pages. 2004.

Vol. 3075: W. Lenski (Ed.), Logic versus Approximation. IX, 205 pages. 2004.

Vol. 3074: B. Kuijpers, P. Revesz (Eds.), Constraint Databases and Applications. XII, 181 pages. 2004.

Vol. 3073: H. Chen, R. Moore, D.D. Zeng, J. Leavitt (Eds.), Intelligence and Security Informatics. XV, 536 pages. 2004.

Vol. 3072: D. Zhang, A.K. Jain (Eds.), Biometric Authentication. XVII, 800 pages. 2004.

Vol. 3071: A. Omicini, P. Petta, J. Pitt (Eds.), Engineering Societies in the Agents World. XIII, 409 pages. 2004. (Subseries LNAI).

Vol. 3070: L. Rutkowski, J. Siekmann, R. Tadeusiewicz, L.A. Zadeh (Eds.), Artificial Intelligence and Soft Computing - ICAISC 2004. XXV, 1208 pages. 2004. (Subseries LNAI).

Vol. 3068: E. André, L. Dybkjær, W. Minker, P. Heisterkamp (Eds.), Affective Dialogue Systems. XII, 324 pages. 2004. (Subseries LNAI).

Vol. 3067: M. Dastani, J. Dix, A. El Fallah-Seghrouchni (Eds.), Programming Multi-Agent Systems. X, 221 pages. 2004. (Subseries LNAI).

Vol. 3066: S. Tsumoto, R. Słowiński, J. Komorowski, J.W. Grzymała-Busse (Eds.), Rough Sets and Current Trends in Computing. XX, 853 pages. 2004. (Subseries LNAI).

Vol. 3065: A. Lomuscio, D. Nute (Eds.), Deontic Logic in Computer Science. X, 275 pages. 2004. (Subseries LNAI).

Vol. 3064: D. Bienstock, G. Nemhauser (Eds.), Integer Programming and Combinatorial Optimization. XI, 445 pages. 2004.